Issues and Innovative Trends in Sustainable Growth – Strategy Challenges for Economic and Social Policies

Luminita Chivu / Constantin Ciutacu / Valeriu Ioan-Franc /
Jean-Vasile Andrei (eds.)

Issues and Innovative Trends in Sustainable Growth – Strategy Challenges for Economic and Social Policies

Proceedings ESPERA 2016
Part 2

PETER LANG

Bibliographic Information published by the Deutsche Nationalbibliothek
The Deutsche Nationalbibliothek lists this publication in the Deutsche Nationalbibliografie; detailed bibliographic data is available in the internet at http://dnb.d-nb.de.

Library of Congress Cataloging-in-Publication Data
A CIP catalog record for this book has been applied for at the Library of Congress.

Printed by CPI books GmbH, Leck.

ISBN 978-3-631-76223-3 (Print)
E-ISBN 978-3-653-06572-5 (E-PDF)
E-ISBN 978-3-653-70797-5 (EPUB)
E-ISBN 978-3-653-70798-2 (MOBI)
DOI 10.3726/978-3-653-06572-5

Peter Lang – Berlin · Bern · Bruxelles · New York · Oxford · Warszawa · Wien

This publication has been peer reviewed.

www.peterlang.com

Contents

Elena ZAMFIR

Senior researcher, Research Institute for Quality of Life, Romanian Academy, Calea 13 Septembrie, nr. 13, sector 5, 050711, Bucharest, Romania, e-mail: ezamfir1@gmail.com

The Quality of Life in Romania and Ethics of Social Action

Abstract: The paper is centered on the quality of life as a core objective of political programs, of development strategies for the country and of European projects. After the seventies, by its practical orientation, quality of life expanded rapidly from the sphere of theoretical research and analysis to the social action of changing/improving living conditions. Quality of life is not merely a simple academic topic or a nice phrase. It is increasingly present in the area of public debates, stimulating concerns/interest of political decision makers and of social stakeholders.

The first part of the present paper focuses on the main factors increasing quality of life, starting from its dimensions/components. The quality of life, due to its evaluating structure, implies the value a human being gives to his/her life: how good or bad is the life one is living, as a whole, and by particular components (family, profession, work, civic, social, cultural, political life, free time, interpersonal relationships, etc.). The quality of life is estimated by a plurality of social and economic indicators, distributed by distinct life components. At the same time, a population's degree of satisfaction or dissatisfaction with life, based on specific subjective indicators, measures the impact of the outcome of social development on human condition.

The second part of my paper points out the significance of quality of life as part of a strategy for maximizing the degree of individual satisfaction with his/her life. Thus, the quality of life is directly associated with a policy of change, of responsible action based on active and efficient interventions. The human significance of the direction of the development, of the targets, of the way of developing individual and collective action are integral parts of a strategy for a future country project. To this end, the orientations/options, the objectives and directions of development of a model/country project directly influence the satisfaction or dissatisfaction of the individual with his/her life. Validating the ethic norms for social action shall be supported in this context by: objective indicators for timely evaluation of the outcomes of changing the social and natural environment, subjective indicators of measuring the impact of these changes on the general satisfaction with life, comparative European statistics regarding welfare and quality of life, academic research analyses, public opinion surveys, official reports regarding social development. All of them represent measurement units/instruments and milestones for evaluating the social and human efficiency of actions based on moral regulations.

In the current context of globalization, expanding the moral knowledge by assumed accountability for social actions turns into a necessity, but also into a guarantee for a sustainable development process. In this context, my paper concludes that widening the moral conscience by assumed responsibility for social action turns into an integral part of an actual process of sustainable development.

Keywords: Quality of life, social indicators: subjective and objectives, ethics of social action, general satisfaction with life, wellbeing, welfare, country project

1. A short theoretical scheme for explaining quality of life

Quality of life emerges as a core objective of political programs, of country development strategies, and of European projects.

After the sixties and the seventies, the topic of the quality of life expanded quickly from the area of practical concern to sciences, of political programmes and also drew the attention of mass media. Romania is one of the few European countries that has massively taken over from sociological research the complex issue of the quality of life, from the time of its emergence. By ample theoretical analyses, and empirical research about the quality of life, the tie with the significance of the human dimension became more marked in the context of economic development (Zamfir, C., 1982, 1984, 1995; Zamfir, E., 1989, 1995, 1997, 2013, 2014; Marginean, I. and Balasa, A., 2005; Marginean, I. and Precupetu, I., 2008; Baltatescu, S., 2014).

Quality of life by its practical orientation turns into a milestone of social action for changing/improving living conditions. Quality of life represents the global, synthetic quality of all conditions and spheres of life.

Fig. 1: Life Structure

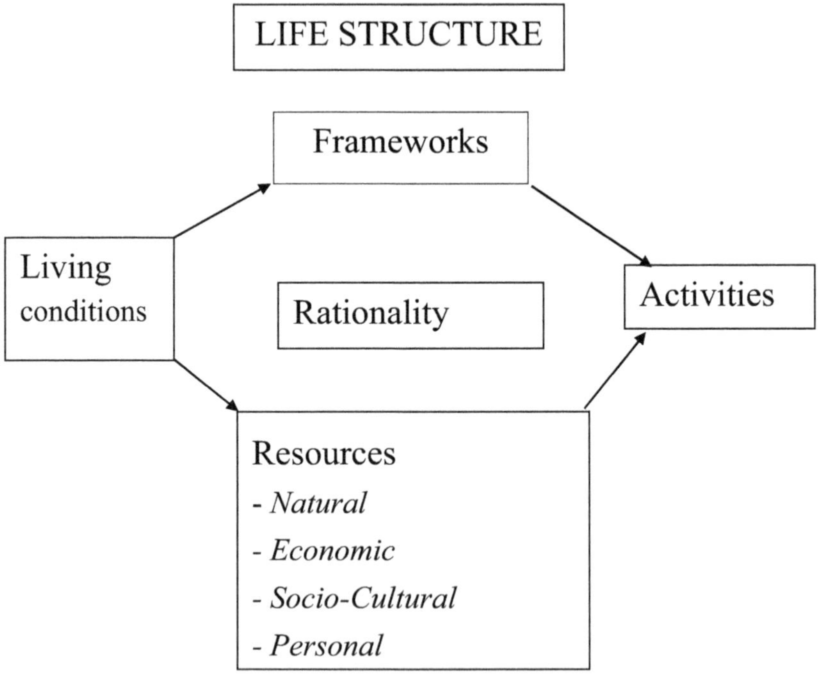

Source: Zamfir, C. (coord.), 1984.

Therefore, to evaluate quality of life, we should compulsorily take into account all dimensions of our life: frameworks; resources; activities' quality and living conditions. Is important to use specific analysis perspectives, with a focus on significance of all dimensions for each individual and on each sphere viewed from the multiple perspectives, taking into account the rationality of social actions based on moral responsibility.

Quality of life turned into a practical direction of action of the collective, diffusely connected to all activities in the social fields by specific development programs/country projects. Assuming quality of life as the ultimate direction of action and social development is a process in full development. Over time, and with growing capacity for identifying directions, objective, concrete specific targets of the quality of life were created within development strategies and evolution scenarios that would outline a possible future country model. This, as a desirable state, must lead to economic welfare and high quality of life. Attaining this end necessarily implies a clear setting of directions of actions, objectives/targets, milestones/progress indicators. The direction of action as a desirable state of society includes the will of the collective to act towards its achievement. From this viewpoint, quality of life emerges as an open projection of the collective and individual action in identifying opportunities and resources for substantiating some efficient measures and pragmatic solutions.

The current definitions of quality of life attempt to clarify the relational peculiarities of the concept by emphasizing the significance represented by the human being and the human condition. Most definitions included both perspectives of analysis: the objective one, the real state of the living environment, and the subjective one, expressing the state of life perceived by the human/subject by establishing the relationship to own needs (Diener, E. 1994; Land, K., 1975; Crosby, 1076, 1979). I have often underlined that quality of life is a concept with marked subjective specific features and strongly individualized. By virtue of subjectivity, the quality of life may have as many varied significances as possible, depending on cultural life norms and on the socio-economic and geographic context in which the individual lives. In this case, the quality of life envisages the 'subjective welfare/wellbeing' as outcome of the personal perception of the dimensions of life. Often, the general satisfaction with life is associated with happiness, pleasure or personal achievement (Zamfir, E. and Maggino, F., eds., 2013).

2. Quality of life in national social strategies. The role of responsibility for social actions

Unfortunately, during the last years, in Romania the confidence of Romanians in the direction of the development of the country is very low. The moral state of the population worsened swiftly. We are witness to marked demoralization and pessimism, even among the young generation.

Already in 2011, Eurostat (Euro barometer) indicated that the Romanian's evaluations regarding the direction of Romania are worrying: an important majority, around 70%, considered Romania headed in a wrong direction, and this majority percentage is markedly above the European average. The dynamics show that in 2013, Romanians considered the direction of Romanian society to be wrong (69%), against 14%, who considered the country heading in the right direction. In 2014, an election year, for the first time, the share of those believing that Romania is heading in a wrong direction decreased to less than 50%. This perception was short-lived. In 2016 an IRES survey on "The Welfare of Romanians" asked the question, "Do you believe that in Romania the evolutions are headed into the right or wrong direction?". A very high share (72%) considered the chosen direction was wrong, while only 24% considered the direction right.

Fig. 2: Romanians' perceptions about the direction in which Romania goes

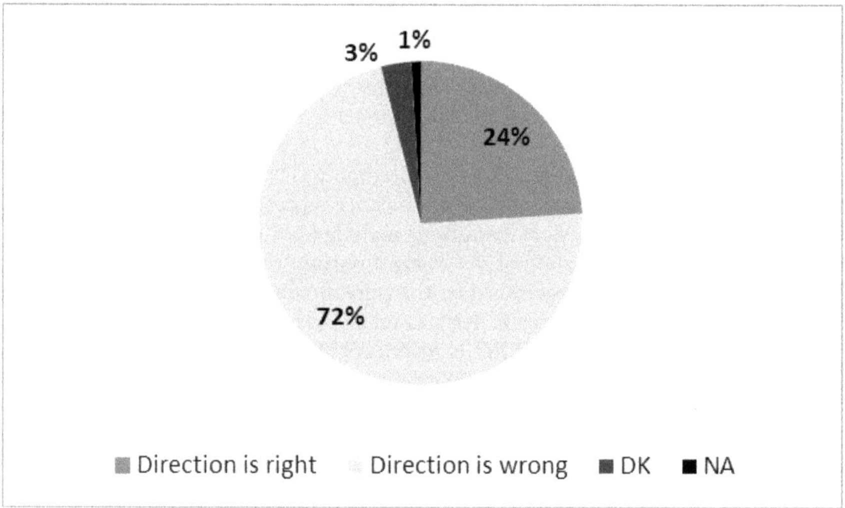

Source: IRES: The Welfare of Romanians, 2016.

If in 2013 only 69% believed that the direction of Romania was wrong, in 2016 their share was 62%. 2016 saw an increase by 3% compared to 2013, but also a spectacular one of 10% compared to the year 2015.

Fig. 3: Dynamics of perceptions about the direction of Romania over three years (% of respondents, 2013, 2015, 2016)

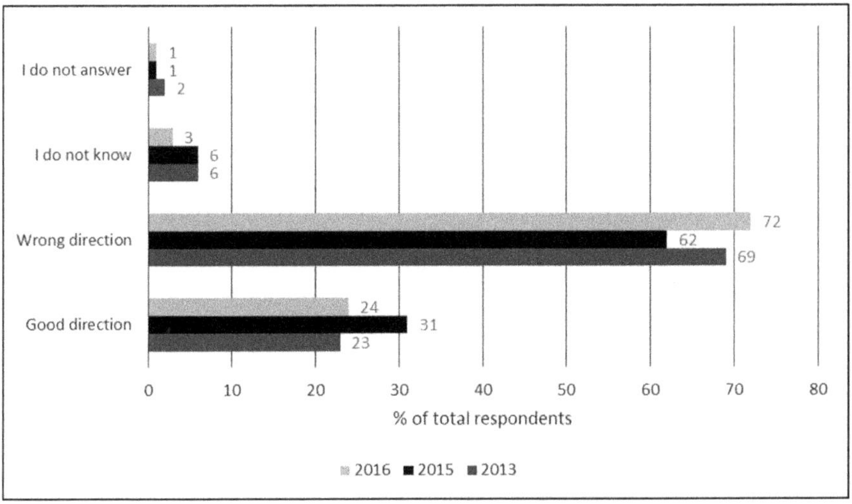

Source: IRES, The Welfare of Romanians, 2016.

Why this constant negative perception of the Romanians about the direction of the future development of Romania? What is the reason and source of dissatisfaction with the direction of Romania?

In 2016, in the same IRES survey, the answers of the Romanians to questions focused on their confidence in public institutions with a decisive role in determining the country's strategies (presidency, government, parliament, justice, the Romanian Intelligence Service (RIS), police, army) might provide explanations in this context. They are positively correlated with the negative perception of Romanians regarding the chosen direction of development. The lack of confidence showed by the Romanians regarding government is positively correlated with the previous question about the direction of the development of Romania.

According to the selection made by the Romanians, the highest degree of confidence (very much and much) places the army in the top position (24% very much, 47% much) followed by the police (14% very much, 37% much), the RIS (12% very much, 33% much), justice (8% very much and 27% much), and the president of the country (5% very much and 19% much). In this context, it is significant that the last positions, with the lowest degree of confidence, are held by the government and parliament. Thus, government, the decisive forum of change, has a confidence share of only 2% very much, and only 14% much.

Fig. 4: Annual dynamics (2013, 2015, and 2016)

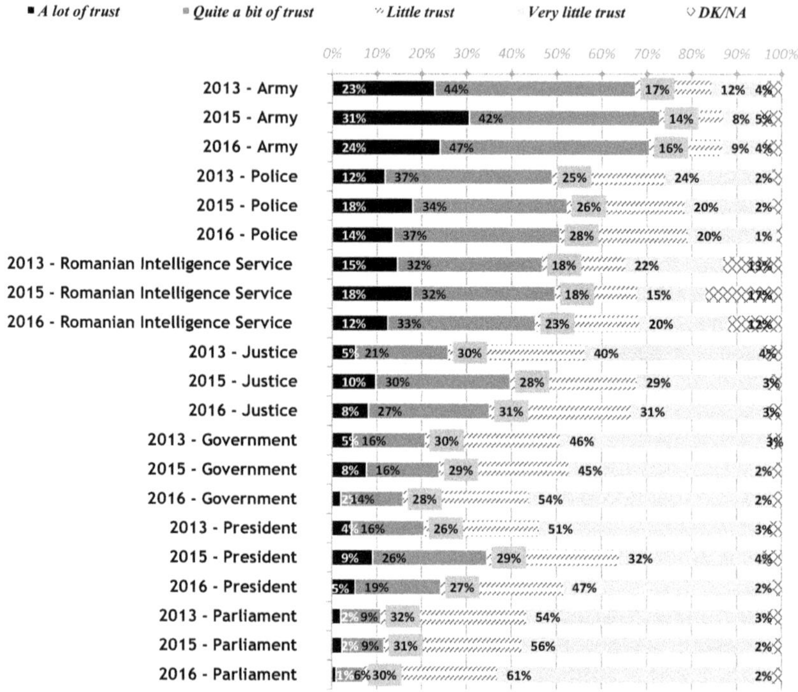

Source: IRES 2016, Welfare of Romanians.

Often, the estimation by Romanians that the country goes in a wrong direction is attributed to strategic errors and irresponsible decisions of the government. Taking into account the sluggishness and incoherence of legislative changes and the inarticulate character of democratic reform, parliament is ranked last with respect to Romanians' confidence, the lowest share of 1% having "very much" confidence and 6% "much" confidence in this body. In the last years, there has been a systematic discrediting of parliament. The toughest criticism against parliament was, as a rule, of a political kind.

Even though there are currently no objective/institutional performance indicators available regarding the quality/efficiency of the government's functioning, the global evaluations of the Romanians as compared to other EU countries indicate very low confidence in public institutions, especially in political ones.

In the last three years, the disappointment of the population with key institutions with a decisive role in selecting the country's strategies has been on constant increase. The general dissatisfaction of the population with the selected country development model should also be regarded in the wider context of defiance against the democratic culture inside the structures of public institutions. The lack of transparency of political and institutional decisions, the lack of responsibility of the decision-makers for their actions, the incompetence and disinterest regarding public money, the increasing corruption at top levels, uncivilized communication in the public dialogue, etc. are but few arguments to justify the dissatisfaction of Romanians with the political class. The low public control of the functioning of the public system gradually lead to a loss of interest in democracy culture at the institutional level. Abusive practices of the subjective authoritarian-type became more marked in this context.

In reality, strategic errors during the transition to market economy are responsible for the worrying degradation of the social and human fabric (Zamfir, E. et al., eds., 2015). Interpersonal and cooperation relations lost some of their human traditional consistency and significance. In time, estrangement and careful distancing from other individuals increased. The lack of a coherent, integrating vision regarding public policies during the transition, the unfair political competition of parties to access power had a negative impact on opting for a future country project (see the Strategy of the Academy, vol. 1, 2, 3, 4; 2015–2017 and the IQLR Social Report 2017). With all these unpredictable effects on individual and collective behavior, pessimism became demotivating, hindering social actions of the community-type.

It is interesting that while confidence in the political system is among the lowest in Europe, the Romanian community, despite the difficulties it faces, continues to trust "other people". In 2012, a year of deep social crisis, confidence in others was around the European average, representing one of the few positive aspects in Romania: 5.0 against 5.1 on a scale from 1 to 10. The countries with the highest levels of confidence in others are Finland and Denmark (7.1 and 7.0, respectively), followed by Sweden, the Netherlands and Iceland (6.4 and 6.3). The lowest levels of confidence are recorded in Cyprus (1.9), followed by Macedonia (3.6). The data of EUROSTAT – Quality of Life 2016 and info-graphics also place Romania above the EU average regarding "confidence in others" on which the Romanians might rely.

Academic researches and statistical institutions have worked toward developing indicators of quality of life status and for evaluating the operation of society. But these must be linked to moral rules of professional deontology, and thereafter spread out widely in public awareness and in individual behavior.

Already in 1946, the Romanian politician Mihail Manoilescu drew attention to some firm moral requirements in the political practice. He stipulated that "idealism, goodwill, good intentions are the foundations of political ethics" (Morar, V., 2011, p. 179). Unfortunately, in Romania, during the entire transition period, public policies lacked explicit concerns for moral regulations (rules, principles, values) required by responsible social actions. As mentioned by the ethics expert Vasile Morar, "within the Romanian public there is distrust regarding morale, in morale as moral, that is, in essence, distrust in the moral grounds of the original democratic values". All the while, liberty, life, dignity, happiness, justice, welfare assume positive moral values, called "virtues" in way of thinking, or called "impartial rules of moral rectitude" in another ethic tradition (Morar, V., 2011, p. 15). Ethics of social action was the absent topic in the area of the post-December public debates. Actually, a performance management of overseeing and controlling social risks under the conditions of a hard-to-control environment presupposes a moral of collective and/or individual action.

Social responsibility in the context of modern management is not consisting of simple sequential ethics: what happens here and now. Nor does it appear as a simple wish. On the contrary, it highlights future implications of social actions for new generations from a rather more general perspective, in the wide process of globalization. Thereby, social responsibility turns into a component part of rational decisions, and also of the permanent process of evaluating and monitoring the projects of social development. Severe social issues, by their consequences (waves of immigrants, multiplication of terrorist actions, increasing conflicts and tensions of the social, political, economic, ethnic, religious kind, the destruction of some traditional cultural life models, growing corruption, crime and delinquency, in particular juvenile delinquency), are just a few of the new warning signs for political decision-makers and social actors. To these, the issues gathered during the transition, which require immediate punctual mitigation are also added: extended poverty, social exclusion, marginalization, inefficient economy, under-employment, inequity, administrative incompetence, etc.

Ralf Dahrendorf underpinned in 1995, in his preface to the Romanian translation of "The Modern Social Conflict. An Essay on the Politics of Liberty", the necessity of social accountability for the political decision-makers in the process of social changes: "In the real world, people and groups struggle for power and welfare. Such struggle is the source of change. If, however, we would invent institutions for channelling the struggle, then we might control even the processes of change. This the more so as incontrollable change – revolution – destroys more than it achieves" (Ralf Dahrendorf, 1995, p. 5). Starting with the assumption that open modern societies face changes that might also take on the form of conflict, the decision-makers are accountable for how these are managed at an institutional level.

Knowledge about and the timely solving of conflicts by mediation and negotiation presupposes a modern administrative-institutional framework for its institutionalization (Zamfir, E., 2003). Therefore, the public social policies must establish clear targets regarding conflict management and control. Even if several of the conflicts of modern society cannot be solved by eliminating the causes, they might be maintained under control by institutionalizing the conflict or by diminishing its destructive effects. Giddens pointed out that "the patterns of inequality are different today from those of two or three decades ago, a phenomenon with significant political consequences. The contemporary societies have less disorderly fluidness than one believed. Changes during the lifetime are less predictable than before for good or bad reasons". In our opinion, the policy innovations must meet these evolutions () Giddens, A., 2007, p. 97).

How will the society and environment of the future look like? How friendly will our earth be in time? Which will be the effects of globalization on the human condition and identity? These are but few of the multiple questions to which quality of life may answer only by resorting to morals.

In the current context of globalization, expanding the moral knowledge by assumed accountability for social actions turns into a necessity, but also into a guarantee for sustainable development. In the scenarios proposed for a future development model of the world, the Club of Rome pointed out in the seventies the key significance of social accountability, as the core of the balance in sustainable development (see the reports of the Club of Rome: "The Limits to Growth", Meadows, D. H.; Meadows, D. L; Randers, Jorgen (eds.), 1972; "Mankind at crossroads: Second report to the Club of Rome", Mesarovics, M. and Pestel, E., 1975; Tinbergen, Jan: "Restructuring international order: Report to the Club of Rome", 1978; Gabor, D.; Colombo, U.; King, A.; Galli, R.: "Beyond the Age of Waste", 1983).

A balanced social and political development was proposed, accountable for the direct or indirect risks of uncontrolled economic growth. An organic economic growth customized to mankind was requested against an aberrant cancer-type growth. Sociologists, researchers, analysts emphasized then that individuals' social accountability in relation to environment (society, nature, geographic environment) is one condition for the quality of future life.

The clear determination of an order of moral priorities in future social development does not represent just a moral of good intentions or simple nice words. Actually, this requires precise ethical stipulations for the development of social action, controlled, however, by its effects in time. In this context, quality of life must resort to fundamental moral and political values. Thus, quality of life turns, on one hand, into an incentive for assuming social and/or individual accountability, and, on the other hand, into a measure of social progress for the current economic growth. Widening moral consciousness in controlling and determining the objectives or targets of growth for the quality of life becomes a compulsory requirement for the balance of the natural and social sphere in the process of development. This process may be recorded and measured empirically by precise impact studies that are conducted more and more in recent times. The impact studies might catch the implicit and/or perverse effects of new technologies and the indirect economic costs for the human condition and environment, the effects of launching new products in the market competition, the effects of new modern digital acquisitions, etc. (Zamfir, E., 1997, p. 293).

In post-December Romania, the social development programs, in particular those related to re-establishing social balance and social justice, ignored the moral implications of the actions of social decision-makers. Moral judgments did not accompany the evaluation of reform processes. Unfortunately, the deep moral crisis rendered acute by transition was an aggravating factor in triggering and maintaining the crisis in all other fields: economy, politics, education, culture, public administration, health, etc.

The unsuccessful outcomes of some social changes up to date have also highlighted a defective mechanism of determining the current social priorities within the country's strategies (Zamfir, E. and Zamfir, C., eds, 1995). The negative effects of economic-scientific-technical development on the human condition and the general satisfaction of the individual with his/her own life were systematically underestimated. Impact analyses that might have assisted in avoiding high risks of irrational social decisions were lacking, the risks were either of the populist kind or in an own personal gain. In epistemology, a fundamental rule of professional deontology prohibits any type of experiments on the human being or on the collective for the sake of knowledge. In this context, I would add the experiment of social changes for the sake of change. Socio-human sciences as instruments for building the life of the individual and the social life sphere make available true and precise "social and human engineering" tools that help us avoid the effects of the costly method of "trial and error". They involve rigorous analysis, diagnosis and forecast techniques of life in accordance with consolidated scientific theories pertaining to the social and human field. Only knowledge about these scientific mechanisms in the process of reform and social construction might ensure the accountability of social actions. In this case, social action under the umbrella of accountability emerges as a precondition for social sustainable development.

Anthony Giddens in "Europe in the Global Age" noticed that the Lisbon Strategy with its emphasis on "social justice and protection in the EU member-states pursues to modernise the European social model by improving the collective capacity to act and to offer new opportunities for everyone" by the asserted intention to promote "decent work as global objective at all levels" for increasing the adaptability of workers and to "enforce inclusion measures in the labour market" (Giddens, 2007, p. 96). Continuing in the same vein of ideas, I would mention that many developed European countries, within their social inclusion programs, focus on identifying/designing some solutions to support labor motivation and shaping some habits, and work out cultural rules for the assisted population by means of integrated services of social assistance (centered punctually on the profile of needs). However, in Romania, the good intention of attracting and maintaining individuals in the labor market was hindered by some damaging practices in the field of occupational policies.

Unjustified/inefficient layoffs from the budgetary system focused, to a large extent, only on the process by which unemployment emerged, and less on monitoring the final efficiency of this process. Thus, the integration of those trained by means of labor market inclusion programs remained partially solved. Seeking a job was one of the issues without any chances of being solved. Therefore, perhaps, the governmental programs regarding social support for families and children during periods of crisis and in conditions of austerity were subjected to severe criticism by sociologists, by the academic research environment, and by political analysts. They faced extremely hard public attacks due to the poor chances of feasibility and sustainability (Zamfir, E., 2012–1). There is an almost generalized opinion among experts that the assistance programs for families suffer from a lack of clarity regarding the direction of future actions, but also show obvious confusion regarding the reform strategy in the field of social assistance and social justice (Schraad-Tischler, D. and Schiller, C., 2016; "Social Report", IQLR, 2017). Very often, based on excessively unjustified ambitions to save money at the cost of the poor and with major risks of social exclusion, the governmental decision-makers drastically reduced the financing of specialized assistance services and concomitantly diminished the social functions of the state. This fact was completely inexplicable in the Romanian social context, especially when European countries provide numerous examples of active policies for maintaining or even expanding the social functions of the state, in particular during periods of crisis and austerity (Zamfir, E., 2012–2).

For maximizing the practical results of the strategy for the welfare state, quality of life was and is associated essentially with a plan of action, based on active, responsible interventions. Improving the social environment by collective actions is a permanent goal for increasing quality of life. It should be found in any strategy for a country project. The latter must answer major questions: What type of future development is considered (what model is selected)? In what direction do we plan to act? What is, finally, the significance of social changes for a human being's quality of life?

3. Conclusion

There has been much disappointment in the last years, and hence a lot of questions regarding the social and human efficiency of economic and technological growth. More specifically, the question "Might we consider that economic efficiency at the same time also implies social and human efficiency?" took a more consistent shape. Is economic growth and efficiency found automatically in a "better society"? In reality, the idea according to which economic growth in itself, directed according to its own internal logic, would be a better way of human growth, proved to be just a myth, just a simple illusion. Neglecting the negative impact of uncontrolled development, with destructive effects on the individual and the living environment, led to a fourfold crisis in the seventies: an ecologic crisis, a social crisis, a human crisis and even, paradoxically, an economic crisis. Irresponsible actions in using natural and social resources in economic development and modern technologies generated very high indirect economic costs with dramatic effects on man and the human condition. The effects are revealed by the devastating consequences on some communities affected by natural disasters (floods, droughts, earthquakes) but also by obvious, severe social injustices. The need to eliminate or diminish the risks of uncontrolled economic and technological growth remains an urgent issue for developing social programs for sustainable development.

In order to increase quality of life, starting from the Kantian imperative, it is necessary, possibly, to extend the sphere of moral accountability of public policies. Adjusted to quality of life, the new moral imperative might be as follows: Act so as to be accountable for the developing actions both in selecting the means of intervention, and the employed means themselves, while also being responsible for their future consequences, as well (Zamfir, E., 1989). In this case, the authority of the moral law extends both to the actual instruments/means chosen in the process of social change and to their future consequences.

It is compulsory that the moral law should govern not only the present area of developing social actions, but also the actual means, the instruments chosen for implementation. From this viewpoint, the severe consequences of costly social changes cannot be justified for the transition period by means of unfounded excuses such as: emergency mitigation, unfavorable context, internal or external pressures, not being clear regarding effects over time, etc. All these types of excuses are of the 'end justifies means' type. Therefore, the irresponsibility of political decision-makers during the transition period regarding the high and unjustified social and human costs of the pretended social reforms cannot be eliminated. These are actions with moral effects that cannot be prescribed in time. In fact, moral values and rules must accompany all stages of developing the change/reform processes. Continuing evaluation and monitoring of their effects over time are compulsory and necessary for ensuring the increase in quality of life.

Therefore, the moral imperative of the quality of life provides direction, a safe guidance for sustainable social changes, but also a way of achieving them through responsible rational actions. Currently, we no longer discuss harmonious development and social balance without a macro-social, global vision of the general objectives to be attained and of the ways by which these might be attained. But the global vision is achieved and improved permanently by the initiative/contribution of the parties: individuals, groups, institutions, and communities that creatively and responsibly assume their specific function within the process. Therefore, any good strategy of the integrative type will assume a democratic path for society's and communities' development (Zamfir, E., 2000).

Unfortunately, in post-December Romania, the social reform strategies completely ignored the necessity for an explicit system of moral values in the construction of the new social-democratic model. Also, the concern for building up a democratic culture was absent from the country programs and strategies as a distinct and time-defined achievable objective. The quality of the social, political and human environment related to democratic values, principles, rules and regulations of living was not found as a distinct objective within public policies or in official reports/documents related to the development of the country. Morals remained but a peripheral topic in the interest of the social actors. The studies of ethics, the cultural models of life and moral behavior emerged as a privilege of academic research. Their dissemination and influence in the public area was just marginal. They were not found at all, or toned down considerably in the curricula of schools and universities. In turn, the success of a strategic project for country development cannot ignore the rules of morals as an integral part of modern democracy and civilization. Perhaps, in the beginning, it was believed that this is given automatically, added supplementarily to the new post-communist country model. In fact, in a democratic regime, the selection of a country project presupposes a firm option for ethics of collective action. Unfortunately, the concern for building-up a democratic culture was also often absent from the country programs and strategies as a distinct and time-defined achievable objective. Actually, the current configuration of the social, economic and political state of Romania shows considerable voids in covering the real needs of the population and, moreover, in the sphere of expectations, options and life projects. This is also due to the fact that in determining the development's objectives, the choice regarding the reference framework, clarifying aims and the means of achieving the objectives represent just an intention or a unilateral act of political will of only the government, of the political-decision makers, as it often happened. In a democratic regime, the selection of a country project presupposes a firm option for an ethics of collective action. All social actors involved in social actions must be consulted both for the decision making, but also for evaluating and monitoring the programs. The modern society, characterized by its pragmatic orientation towards profit, has a severe deficit in the area of mechanisms for creating, and operating within a culture of social solidarity and of learning "how to build together."

This deficit becomes an important factor in limiting the mobility of those resources oriented potentially towards the collective. Actually, in any community, there is a wide range of professional capacities that may be used for programs in the interest of the community. However, this finality also implies a personal strategy for self-development and self-improvement according to a valuable model of development.

References

1. Bălţătescu, S., Fericirea în contextul social al tranziţiei postcomuniste din România (Happiness in the social context of post-communist transition in Romania), Cluj-Napoca: Ed. EIKON, 2014, p. 361.
2. Bauman, Z., Comunitatea. Căutarea siguranţei într-o lume nesigură (Community: Seeking Safety in an Insecure World), Ed. Antet, 2001, p. 117.
3. Crosby, Ph. B., Quality is Free. Mc.Graw Hill, New York, 1979, p. 309.
4. Dahrendorf, R., Conflictul social modern. Eseu despre politica libertăţii (The modern social conflict: the politics of liberty), Ed. Humanitas, Bucureşti, 1996, p. 287.
5. Diener, Ed., Assessing Subjective Well-Being: Progress and Opportunities, in: Assessing well-being: the collected works of Ed Diener, Springer, Dordrecht, Heidelberg, London, 2009, p. 274.
6. Gabor, D, Colombo, U; King, A; Galli, R. Să ieşim din epoca risipei: raport către Clubul de la Roma (Beyond the Age of Waste: A Report to the Club of Rome), Ed. Politică, Bucureşti, 1983, p. 335.
7. Giddens, A., Europa în epoca globală (Europe in the Global Age) Ed. Ziua, Bucureşti, 2007, p. 323.
8. Juran, J. M., The Quality trilogy. A Universal Approach to managing for Quality. In: Quality Progress, Vol. 19, No. 8, 1986, pp. 19–24.
9. Land, K. C., Spilerman, S. (eds.). Social Indicator Models. Russel Sage Foundation, New York, 1975, p. 424.
10. Mărginean, I.; Bălaşa, A. (coord.), Calitatea vieţii în România (Quality of life in Romania) Ed. Expert, 2005, p. 407.
11. Mărginean, I.; Precupeţu, I. (coord.), Calitatea vieţii şi dezvoltare durabilă: politici de întărire a coeziunii sociale (Quality of life and sustainable development: policies to strengthen social cohesion), Ed. Expert, Bucureşti, 2008, p. 311.

12. Meadows, D. H.; Meadows, D. L.; Randers, Jorgen (eds.), The Limits to Growth: A report for the Club of Rome's project on the predicament of mankind. New American Library, New York, 1972, p. 206.
13. Mesarovic, M.; Pestel, E., Omenirea la răspântie: Al doilea raport către Clubul de la Roma (Mankind at crossroads: second report to the Club of Rome) Ed. Politică, Bucureşti, 1975, p. 219.
14. Morar, V., Morala elementară: stări, praguri, virtuţi (Moral Elemental states, thresholds, virtues), Ed. Paideia, Bucureşti, 2011, p. 475.
15. Tinbergen, J., Restructurarea ordinii internaţionale: raport către Clubul de la Roma (Restructuring international order: report to the Club of Rome), Ed. Politică, Bucureşti, 1978, p. 575.
16. Vlad, I. V. (coord.), Strategia de dezvoltare a României în următorii 20 de ani (Romania's development strategy for the next 20 year), Ed. Academiei, Bucureşti, vol. 1, 2015, p. 480; vol. 2, 2016, p. 462; vol. 3a, 2016, p. 531; vol. 3b, 2016, p. 907.
17. Zamfir, C.; Rebedeu, I. (coord.), Modul de viaţă şi calitatea vieţii (Lifestyle and quality of life) Ed. Politică, Bucureşti, 1982, p. 351.
18. Zamfir, C. (coord.), Indicatori şi surse de variaţie a calităţii vieţii (Indicators and sources of variation in quality of life) Ed. Academiei RSR, Bucureşti, 1984, p. 188.
19. Zamfir, E., Incursiune în universul uman: noi ipostaze şi dimensiuni ale fericirii (Insights into the human world: new aspects and dimensions of happiness), Ed. Albatros, Bucureşti, 1989, p. 280.
20. Zamfir, E., Zamfir, C. (coord.), Politici sociale. România în context European. (Social policies. Romania in the European context), Ed. Alternative, Bucureşti, 1995, p. 280.
21. Zamfir, E., Psihologie socială: texte alese (Social Psychology: selected papers). Ed. Ankarom, Iaşi, 1997, p. 479.
22. Zamfir, E., Strategii antisărăcie şi dezvoltare comunitară (Antipoverty strategies and community development), Ed. Expert, Bucureşti, 2000, p. 560.
23. Zamfir E., Conflictul şi modalităţi de soluţionare (The conflict and how to solve it). Ed. Cartea Românească, Bucureşti, 2003, p. 252.
24. Zamfir, E., Legea asistenţei sociale şi riscurile dependenţei populaţiei de sistemul de ajutor social (Law on Social Assistance and risks of dependency population) in: Revista de Sociologie nr. 1/2012. Polirom, Iaşi, 2012, p. 115–130, p. 16.
25. Zamfir, E., Asistenţa socială faţă în faţă cu societatea riscurilor din perspectiva politicilor sociale europene (Social assistance face to face with risksociety from the perspective of European social policies) in: Revista Calitatea Vieţii 2/2012, Institutul de cercetare a Calităţii Vieţii, Bucureşti, p. 37, p. 123–160.
26. Zamfir, E., Magino, F. (editors), The European Culture of Human Rights: The Right to Happiness. The Cambridge Scholars Publishing, 2013, p. 487.
27. Zamfir, E.; Stănescu, S., Arpinte, D. (coord.). Asistenţa socială în România după 25 de ani: răspuns la problemele tranziţiei (Social assistance in Romania after 25 years: In response to the problems of transition), Ed. Eikon, Bucureşti; Şcoala Ardeleană, Cluj-Napoca. 2015, p. 645.

28. Schraad-Tischler, D.; Schiller, C. Social Justice in the EU. Index Report 2016. Social inclusion Monitor Europe. Bertelsman Stiftung, p. 196.
29. Institutul de Cercetare a Calităţii Vieţii, Academia Română. Raport social al ICCV 2017: Starea Socială a României. Calitatea vieţii: situaţia actuală şi perspective pentru 2038 (Social Report 2017 IQLR: Social Status of Romania. Quality of life: current situation and prospects for 2038), Bucureşti, 2017, p. 46.
30. Constanza, R. et al., An Integrative Approach to Quality of Life Measurement, Research, and Policy. In: S.A.P.I.EN.S., Vol. I, No. 1, 2008, https://sapiens.revues.org/58.

Ioan MĂRGINEAN

The Research Institute for Quality of Life, National Institute for Economic Research, Romanian Academy, imargin@iccv.ro

Recent Developments in the Process of Consolidating Democracy in Romania

Abstract: My intention in this paper is furthering the previous approaches to analyzing democracy and its consolidation in Romania after the collapse of the communist regime by the Revolution of December 1989. Those events were accompanied by the loss of human lives to open the way toward a new political path for Romania, with multiple effects on the lives of individuals. Actions for institutional building have been undertaken for more than a third of the century; a new constitution was adopted (1991) which stipulated the democratic regime, republican governance, fundamental rights and freedoms, as well as the duties of citizens, public authorities, etc. Local, parliamentary and presidential elections were held, extending to the European Parliament (after Romania's accession to the European Union in 2007) as well. At the same time, several national referenda were held.

Approaching such a topic is justified by the fact that the progress recorded at any given time is not set in stone; the situation develops, and deviations might occur, so that it is important to acknowledge all changes and their effects within the society. For the entire mentioned time interval, it might be appreciated that, as shown in the SWOT analysis, the democratic political regime was maintained and upheld, despite some failures along the way. The Romanian political scene was dominated by two directions, i.e. the social-democratic one (the Social-Democrat Party), and the liberal one (the Democrat-Liberal Party and the National Liberal Party, currently unified under the name of the latter), without any of these parties having absolute majority, save for the elections of May 1990. Therefore, government coalitions were built with consistent majorities, based on the temporary collaboration of the two major orientations.

As an EU and NATO member, the potential for the development of the country increases considerably, along with the opportunities for strengthening democracy, but this needs to be valued adequately, promoting actions designed to counteract all domestic dysfunctions related to public institutions, the efficient and high use of resources, eradication of corruption, etc. At the same time, it is necessary to pay more attention to improving the living conditions of the population, this being also a favorable factor for the functioning of the democracy, if it is accompanied by the support of the citizens and adequate government.

Keywords: politics, political parties, democracy, democracy consolidation

Introduction

Democracy is a social construct regarding the political regime and having as a backbone the citizens' rights and freedoms. My considerations are about representative democracy with its institutions, which turned into a topic of major scientific interest especially after the Second World War, when the first wave of democratization occurred in countries that in previous decades were ruled by dictatorial-fascist regimes and after their defeat entered into the influence sphere of western democracies (liberal democracies) such as Federal Germany and Italy (Almond and Verba, 1963; Barnes and Kaase, eds., 1979; Almond and Verba, eds., 1980).

However, this process didn't occur in Eastern Europe as well, the countries of the region entering into the influence sphere of the Soviets and turning toward the communist political regime.

The second wave of democracy comprised countries with dictatorial regimes that were under the influence of western democracies: Spain, Portugal, Greece, as well as some countries in Latin America (McDonough, Barnes, Lopez-Pina, 1986; Munck, 2009). By the end of the ninth decade, these changes also occured – more or less successfully – in countries with communist regimes (Dahl, 1991; Barnes and Simon, eds., 1998; Pollack et al., eds., 2003; Morlino, 2012).

Our interest is focused on analyzing the situation in Romania, as the country also entered into this third wave of democratization, opened by the Revolution of December 1989. Actually, some prior analysis approaches will continue in relation to building up democratic institutions and political participation; to the fulfilment of criteria so as to be able to discuss a democratic political regime and its strengthening (Marginean, 1991; 1994 in collaboration with Heath and Evans; 1997; 2000, 2004; 2004 in collaboration with Precupetu and Precupetu).

However, first, some general remarks will be made about the post-communist transition. This time the situation is completely different, compared to the other two waves of democratization at a global level, as mentioned above, because the involved countries did not face just a regime change, but also a change in the way their economy is organized, from the socialist state economy toward the market economy based on private ownership. At the same time, we notice that despite the authoritarian, repressive regime with a manipulative, populist propaganda system based on the personality cult of the leader, the term "democracy" was used frequently in phrases such as "people's democracy," "socialist democracy," including here the names of some countries as "the People's Republic of …." It results that the type of democracy to be built should be stipulated, i.e. one of the liberal type, based on the citizens' rights and freedoms.

1. Approaches to the post-communist democratization

There is no overstatement in considering the collapse of the communist political regimes as one of the most significant social-political, economic, cultural and spiritual processes of the 20th century, when many of the hopes of individuals and experts aimed for a "human-faced communism." The old scaffolding collapsed nevertheless under the pressure of the population's demands for freedom and welfare, in a specific international context.

For reference, I take into account predominantly the countries of Central and Eastern Europe which became members of the EU and the NATO.

An interesting approach to democratization and its consolidation was made by Robert Dahl in a scientific paper in March 1990 and included in a volume from the year 1991 dealing with the post-communist transition. The author, having significant experience in the field, enumerates five criteria of democratization:

"The highest officials of government come to depend, directly or indirectly, on popular elections; these elections were on the whole free and fair; freedom of expression was well protected; the right to form independent parties was protected; citizens had access to alternative sources of information not under the control of the government or otherwise monopolised" (Dahl, 1991, p. 10).

Of course, controlling the way how these requirements are fulfilled requires both an analysis of the content of the respective regulations, but also of their enforcement practices. For some of them, the checks are particularly complex, and some hidden aspects might remain that way. This is the case with elections. Because we deal with a competition in gaining political power, the stakes are very high, and, beyond the quality of legislation in the field and the proper organization, the behavior of participants also matters, from the candidates to the campaign teams, to various supporters and, obviously, voters with an interest in voting and exercizing knowledgeably their respective right. Actions of misleading by manipulation, unrealistic promises, slander against opponents, bribes, rigging the vote counting (including here computerized means) are, all in all, not excluded.

At the same time, Dahl mentions that the success of a democratic transition in the short term is influenced by the way it is achieved: "peacefulness or by violent revolution" (p. 13). The success is swifter in the case of peaceful transition, because in this way the "decline or disappearance of alternatives to democracy" occurs (ibid.), irrespective of their nature. The fact that transition is more difficult if accompanied by violence was confirmed in the case of Romania. Even though the institutions of the old regime were abolished and replaced by provisory bodies, violent conflicts in attaining power continued, with tragic episodes during the first months (Stănescu, 2014).

As also specified in the introduction to the work "Democracy and Political Culture in Eastern Europe" (Klingemann et al., eds., 2006), in several countries, among which Romania is included "...violence has been used as a means of democracy-building and this is obviously quite controversial."

Moreover, the authors emphasize, in accordance with the directions developed by Almond and Verba, that political culture "is usually not enough to enjoy favorable internal and external structural conditions. Nor it is enough to skilfully engineer institutions. It has become evident that it is difficult to understand the trajectories of the democracy-building without considering political culture" (ibid.).

In the paper by Pollak et al. (2003), the role of political culture for democracy is investigated and the hindrances against it are identified: "economic crises; increasing economic inequality; insufficient and ineffective political institutions; cultural heritage" (p. XIV). In its turn, political culture is constituted by a series of elements which are distributed on a scale "from attitudes (thin) to identities (thick)" (p. XVII).

In other approaches, in searching for the factors of influence on the democratic path, emphasis is placed on the role of social capital, in reality also insufficiently built in the former socialist countries: "What distinguishes East and West is the experience people had in communism and thereafter, personalized ties were not replaced with wider participation in voluntary organisations" (Badescu and Uslaner, 2003, p. 230).

The approach of Harald Widra (2007, after Michels, 1987; Przeworki, 1991) is also remarkable. He considers that the evolution to democracy was rather "by accident" than "on purpose". Based on these considerations, in analyzing the transition, it is important to have in view also "different points of departure, not only common destination and the imperative of convergence" (p. 1). Also: "The collapse of communism demonstrates inconsistency of deterministic accounts" (p. 3). On the other hand, "the threat of contagion with the totalitarian enemy reinforced a universal appeal to the values of liberal democracy" (p. 292).

Another interesting approach to the consolidation of democracy is that of Morlino (2012); the author refers to the quality of democracy (after Finer, 1970), and considers this indicated by accountability and mitigating the demands of citizens: "a higher implementation of freedom and equality for citizens and civil society should be linked to accountability and responsiveness" (p. 223).

In a 2010 paper, Przeworki enumerates the challenges that must be faced by democratic regimes, because they generate discontent, e.g. "equality in the economic field, the feeling of the population that their political participation is efficient; the government should undertake what it is expected to perform; the balance between order and non-intervention" (pp. 1–2).

2. Post-communist transition to democracy and its consolidation in Romania

We intend to bring to attention the process of building democracy in Romania, without going into details, and thereafter to develop a SWOT analysis (Strengths, Weaknesses, Opportunities, Threats) for the current situation.

As is already known, in Romania, the collapse of the communist regime was caused by a revolution with massive street protests which were brutally repressed, and with the loss of human lives. However, violence causing deaths (even more numerous) also continued after the liquidation of the institutions of the former regime (by bringing to justice and then executing the supreme commander and his wife, herself a high-ranking dignitary). The post-communist transition begins on 22 December 1989, as the provisory revolutionary bodies are constituted: the National Front of Salvation (FSN) and the Council of National Salvation (CSN), which later turns into the Provisory Council of National Union (CPUN). Many other changes follow, by setting up political parties and the reconstruction of the historical democratic parties, the preparation and development of the first parliamentary and presidential elections (20 May 1990), which were won by the FSN, turned into a political party. During the entire period, street conflicts were manifest with displays of conquering/maintaining power, which culminated in violent actions between 13 and 15 June 1990, a fact that drew criticism from Western democracies. In this way, the political life in the first months of transition to democracy based on violence extended the necessary period of changes, confirming the estimation of Dahl, mentioned above. However, the massive participation in voting, the wide diversity of electoral offers, and the gapbetween the score gained by each political party, support the statement regarding the significance of the respective elections. Actually, the voter turnout was 86% of the electoral body, and the presidential elections were won with 85% of the valid votes, i.e. 66% for each of the two parliamentary chambers (Datculescu, Liepelt, 1991). Indeed, if we take also into account the criteria stipulated by Robert Dahl in the cited work regarding the transition to democracy, the advance achieved at the level of the political life is preserved, because in May 1990 the provisory ruling of the country was concluded, and the shift to a legitimized ruling based on the popular vote was made. The government remained in power only until the fall of 1991, when it was removed as result of violent street protests, this time against the deterioration of living conditions.

It might be said that during the respective period, the main political options in Romania were crystallized. On one hand, the NSF, which split up in 1992, and one of the parties resulted from the split, continuing the initial NSF program, merged with other leftist forces, and in 2000 changed its name into Social-Democrat Party (SDP). On the other hand, the liberal orientation, mainly the historical parties, the National Liberal Party (NLP), and the National Christian-Democratic Peasant Party (NCDPP). From these two, only the former (which also underwent split-ups and mergers) still plays an important role. In the meantime, the other half of the NSF, which preserved the name, underwent several changes as well, adopted a center-right view and was renamed the Democrat Party, subsequently the Liberal-Democratic Party, and finally merged with NLP.

Otherwise, from the 1992 elections on, only a social-liberal coalition (PSD + PNL) continued to obtain parliamentary majority, until the time of the 2012 elections. As a result, during the other electoral cycles, post-electoral coalitions were built for ensuring the government, including the year 2016. It should be mentioned that, so far, these coalitions have not lasted for an entire electoral cycle, as they dissolved over time, like the one in 2012, a fact which had as an outcome the appointment of a technocratic government.

As result of the elections of 2016, the parliament is now constituted of the following political parties: SDP; NLP; URS (the Union for Romania's Salvation), DUHR (the Democratic Union of Hungarians in Romania); ALDR (the Alliance of Liberals and Democrats in Romania), PMP (Popular Movement Party), and 17 representatives of national minorities, with SDP and ALDR constituting the governmental alliance.

In a paper coordinated by Barnes and Simon (1998), based on research during the years 1990–1991 (in 10 countries of Central and Eastern Europe and one region from Russia) – although there are differences among countries – the general conclusion is that "support for democratic rules reached a sufficient level and prevented the quiet resistance to the ups and downs about actual development" (p. 17).

Important events related to the transition to democracy continued with the adoption of a democratic constitution and the organization of new elections in 1992. The winner was the ruling party, but this time without the majority of votes, and the liberal opposition registered significant advances. The constituted government was an alliance of left parties for a full mandate. Moreover, over the entire subsequent period, there has been only one other full mandate, also represented by the left orientation (2000–2004).

The 1996 polls generated the first change in government alternation, the power being gained by the historical parties. Alternations also take place in the case of all the other polls: after the 2000 one, which had a left orientation, in 2004 the center-right alliance followed (NLP + DP); in 2008 the center-left alliance (DLP + SDP); in 2012 a left-right alliance (SDP + NLP); and in 2016, SDP + ALDR.

However, as of 2004, in all the next electoral cycles, changes occurred in the governmental alliances, and in 2015, a technocratic government was appointed.

Returning to the analyses of the democratic process during the first years of transition, the approach of the work coordinated by Klingemann, Fuchs and Zielenka (2006, with data of World Values Survey, 1995) is revealing: the research highlights a differentiation between West and East, regarding the support of democracy of the former socialist countries. Thus, the theory of Huntington (1993) about the "clash of civilizations", in the opinion of the author, is not confirmed. Regarding Romania, the country ranks in the first half of this hierarchy (fifth position out of 13 countries) as a "strong democracy" with 28% (p. 4).

Similar analysis were performed by Romanian researchers (Marginean, I. 2000; Marginean, I.; Precupetu, M.; Precupetu, I. 2004; Precupetu, M; Precupetu, I. 2004; Precupetu, I. 2006; Voicu, M.; Voicu, B.; Constantin, A., 2010; Tufis, C. 2012).

A more advanced state of democracy is approached through a particular index by Munck (2009, pp. 62–63, after Schneider and Schneider, 2004). The implied indicators are those regarding compliance with the constitution and the outcomes of free and correct elections; the diminution in electoral volatility; the first and second political alternation; formal and informal agreements on governing rules; independent mass-media access. From this viewpoint, we may consider that after 2000, when the second alternation in power occurred, Romania meets the respective requirements.

Moreover, a comparative analysis of countries regarding "Institutional accountability" (Morlino, 2012) ranks Romania well in the middle of a scale from 1–5, i.e. value 3 (Poland 5, Hungary 4). For Romania, the considerations are that the country has "strengthened relatively autonomous courts, including the Constitutional Court of Romania (CCR); existence of decentralised units," but the relationship between the executive and legislative is also highlighted: "the executive plays a determinant role, strong personalisation of power" (p. 226).

An overregulation excess is noticed, so that in the period of May 1990–2014, 120,487 regulations were issued (Constantinescu, 2016, p. 68, after the Legislative Repertory of the Deputies' Chamber), with a peak in the year 2009 (8,785 normative acts, and an average of over 30 regulations per working day).

The faulty process of economic transition, with fraudulent ownership reversion, led to high social costs and the deterioration of the standard of living for a large part of the population (Zamfir, 2004). The economic restructuring was also more difficult because of the extensive industrialization and low competitiveness, with massive presence in the steel and chemical industry.

3. SWOT-analysis regarding the consolidation of democracy in Romania

Strengths of democracy in Romania

- Constitution and inclusion of the principles and institutions of liberal democracy;
- Adequate legislation for setting-up of political parties, the organization of elections and the employment in positions of public institutions;
- Significant social support for democracy as a political regime;
- Diversified political offers, while the options of the population are massively focused on center-orientation powers (center-left, center-right);
- Compliance with the terms for local, parliamentary and presidential elections;
- Favorable treatment of national minorities by ensuring a seat for each of them in parliament. The Hungarian minority, as the most numerous minority in censuses, always obtained an important number of seats in parliament and participated in government for several terms;
- A high entry rate of women into political parties, and into electoral competitions, in a sufficient number of eligible seats;
- Improved outcomes in the quality of democracy, through accountability and meeting the demands of the citizens;
- Diversified mass-media with high impact on public debates, the political ones included.

Weaknesses of the Romanian democracy

- Electoral volatility: parties failing to obtain seats in parliament during the second or third electoral cycle (below 5%, and thus not reaching the mandatory threshold);
- Political alliances which did not last for an entire electoral cycle (2004–2008; 2008–2012; 2012–2016);
- Significantly higher instability within the parties with break-ups and setting-up of new parties. The phenomenon might create confusion among the electorate;
- The lack of balance between the attributions of the public authorities, with the dominance of the executive;
- Relatively low interest of the population in participation by voting.

Opportunities for strengthening democracy in Romania

- Continuing to increase the accountability and responsiveness of elected officials and of all those serving public functions;

- Improving the cooperation between public powers and institutions;
- Consistent actions for combating corruption at the macro- and micro-level, without abuses. In general, it is necessary to strengthen the credibility of the legal system;
- Equal opportunities for social and political access without discrimination based on wealth, gender, age, ethnic group, etc.;
- More consistent civic and political involvement of the population;
- Improving the regulations that would ensure the balance of powers in the state, including regulations with respect to forming the government under the conditions in which no single party has a parliamentary majority;
- Enforcing the outcomes of the referendum regarding the number of parliamentary members (300 members; at present 465 members are included in the two chambers, but the previous legislature had 588 members in the two chambers);
- It is recommendable to organize presidential and parliamentary elections at the same time to avoid the division of the executive (president – government) under the existing conditions of differing political options;
- Placing a higher value on the country's connection to western democracies and on the benefits of being an EU and NATO member.

Threats for democracy in Romania

- Low confidence of the population in political parties and in many public institutions;
- Instituting privileges for higher dignitaries (for instance, special pensions for members of parliament, who, for 4 years of holding a mandate, receive a pension equivalent to 30 years of service of a person insured at the maximum contribution level. In order to be justified, the special pension for one mandate must not exceed currently 600 Lei, according to the pensions' law);
- A certain political instability results from decoupling the presidential from the parliamentary elections (the president has a 5-year mandate, the parliament a 4-year one) if the two powers of the state (executive and legislative) have different political options (only in 2024 are the two elections going to coincide);
- The excessive use of ordinances by the government (these ordinances have immediate effects, even if they are afterwards rescinded by the parliament);
- Foreign material and/or propaganda support for groups acting against the national interest;
- Threats that might emerge as a result of a tense international environment.

Conclusion

Leaving aside the failures and criticism of the state of democracy in Romania today, a positive trend is noticeable compared to the first period of transition. Nevertheless, we cannot say currently that in Romania, the desirable and best possible state of democracy is attained and nothing more should be done than preserving the present achievements. As is known, deviations can occur anytime which might endanger the democratic regime. Actually, no democracy is free from threats that might lead to regression or even to the adoption of authoritarian regimes (the most eloquent example is the situation of Europe in the fourth decade of the 20th century).

Doubtless, as for the present approach, there are several aspects of democracy in Romania which might be improved, from the ways in which citizens exercise control on the functioning of public institutions, to increasing the accountability and responsiveness of those with the power of decision regarding the needs and demands of the citizens, because a strong democracy marked by poverty and discontent of its population has low chances of putting to good use the opportunities and, as much as possible, preventating and reacting to threats. It is absolutely decisive that Romania protects its interests at the European and international level to a higher extent.

Democracy is strengthened in the context of power and governmental alternation by furthering competition between the parties for winning elections and increasing accountability in fulfilling their promises. Even if tensions are present during the days of electoral campaigns, collaborative relationships afterwards should prevail in attaining national objectives.

References

1. Almond, G., Verba, S.: The Civic Culture. Political Attitudes and Democracy. Five Nations. Princeton University Press, 1993.
2. Almond, G., Verba, S.y (eds.): The Civic Culture Revisited. Sage, Newbury Park, 1980.
3. Barnes, H. S., Kaase, M. (eds.): Political Action. Mass Participation in Five Western Democracies. Sage Beverly Hills, 1979.
4. Barnes, H. S., Simon, J. (eds.): The Post-Communist Citizen. Erasmus Foundation, Budapest, 1998.
5. Bădescu, G., Uslaner, E. M.: Social Capital and the Transition to Democracy. Abington, Routledge, 2003.
6. Constantinescu, C.: Leadership şi Turbulenţă. Editura Universităţii din Bucureşti, 2016.
7. Dahl, R. A.: "Transition to Democracy". In Gyorgy Szoboszlay (ed). Democracy and Political Transformation. Theories and East-Central European Realities. Hungarian Political Science Association, Budapest, 1991.
8. Datculescu, P.. Liepelt, K. (eds.): Renaşterea unei democraţii. Alegerile din România de la 20 mai 1990. IRSOP, Bucureşti, 1991.
9. Heath, A., Evans, G., Mărginean, I.: Politici şi clase sociale în Europa de Est. Cercetări Sociale, vol. 1, 1994, nr. 2, pp. 59–67.
10. Klingemann, H.-D., Fuchs, D., Zielenka, J. (eds.): Democracy and Political Culture in Eastern Europe. Routledge, Abingdon, 2006.
11. Mărginean, I.: Dimensiuni ale participării politice. Calitatea Vieţii, vol. 1, nr. 1–2, 1991, pp. 67–74.

12. Mărginean, I.: Indicators of Democratisation in Romania. Social Indicators Research. vol. 42, no. 3, 1997, pp. 353–366.
13. Mărginean, I.: Social Suport for Democracy. Central European Political Science Review, vol. 1, no. 2, 2000, pp. 186–206.
14. Mărginean I.: Economic Condition and Satisfaction with Democracy in Central Europe and Romania. Central European Political Science, vol. 5, no. 18, 2004, pp. 105–125.
15. Mărginean, I., Precupeţu, I., Precupeţu, M.: Consolidating Democracy in Romania: Political Atitudes and Values. In Pollack, Detlef et al. (eds.). Democratic Values in Central and Eastern Europe. Frankfurt Institute for Transformation Studies, 2004.
16. Mărginean, I., Precupeţu, I., Precupeţu, M.: Surse ale suportului politic pentru democraţie în ţările postcomuniste. Sociologie Românească, vol. 2, nr. 1, 2004, pp. 41–59.
17. McDonough, P., Barnes, H. S., Lopez-Pina, A.: The Growth of Democratic Legitimacy in Spain. American Political Science Review, vol. 80, no. 3, 1986, pp. 735–760.
18. Morlino, L.: Changes of Democracy Actors, Structure and Processes. Oxford University Press, 2012.
19. Munck, L. G.: Measuring Democracy. A Bridge Between Scholarship and Politics. The Johns Hopkins University Press, 2009.
20. Pollack, D. et al. (eds.): Political Culture in Post-Communist Europe. Attitudes in New Democracies. Ashgate, Aldershot, 2003.
21. Precupeţu, I., Precupeţu, M.: Mechanisms of Democratic Consolidation in Romania. Central European Political Science, vol. 5, no. 18, 2004, pp. 81–104.
22. Precupeţu, M.: Democratizare postcomunistă şi integrare europeană. Editura Academiei Române, Bucureşti, 2006.
23. Przeworki, A.: Democracy and the Market. Cambridge University Press, 1991.
24. Przeworki, A.: Democracy and the Limits of Self Government. Cambridge University Press, 2010.
25. Stănescu, I.: Puterea politică în România. De la communism la noul capitalism. Ed. Pro Universitaria, Bucureşti, 2014.
26. Tufiş, C.: Learning Democracy and the Market Economy in Post-Communist Romania. Institutul European, Iaşi, 2012.
27. Voicu, M., Voicu, B., Constantin, A.: Valori sociale ale tranziţiei postcomuniste. Ed. Lumen, Iaşi, 2010.
28. Widra, H.: Communism and the Emergence of Democracy. Cambridge University Press, 2007.
29. Zamfir, C.: O analiza critică a tranziţiei. Ce va fi "după". Ed. Polirom, Iaşi, 2004.

Maria Livia ŞTEFĂNESCU

Research Institute for Quality of Life – Romania,
email: livia.stefanescu@gmail.com

Ştefan ŞTEFĂNESCU

Research Institute for Quality of Life – Romania,
email: stefanst@fmi.unibuc.ro

What is Important in Life for Men and Women from Romania – A Comparative Study

Abstract: In this paper we analyze the opinions of the Romanian people regarding the importance in life of several variables such as: family, friends, leisure time, politics, work or religion. The responses of Romanians in 2012 about the common worth in their life are self-assessed data (SAH data). We established a hierarchy of the mentioned variables by the stochastic order relation applied to categorial ordinal variables. Since the stochastic order is not a total order relation, we suggested in addition a "progress" indicator (PSA) which is compatible with this relation. A minimal set of axioms are compulsorily imposed to design a concrete PSA coefficient for measuring the evolution aspects. By means of the PSA index it is possible to compare the structures of the males' and females' responses concerning the priorities of the Romanians in their life.

Keywords: SAH data, stochastic order, progress index, life priorities, World Values Survey

Introduction

The present paper refers partially to an ambitious project named SEO. The SEO project regards the comparative analysis of the opinions of different populations all over the globe about certain social and economic aspects. A general common questionnaire (GQ) was already applied to the majority of European countries, as well as to several world states. Within the SEO project, based on the GQ questionnaire, we obtained a lot of longitudinal information regarding the evolution, in the last 35 years, of the opinions of populations from over 50 countries, situated on different continents, with different social regimes and economic and social development stages.

Taking into consideration the limited space of our current presentation with regard to the vast SEO project we intend to promote, we will mention the following aspects:

From GQ general questionnaire, we have selected for statistical analysis only question Q1, that is: "For each of the following, indicate how important it is in your life: Family (F), Friends (M – mates), Leisure time (T), Politics (P), Work (W), Religion (R)."

- We are not referring to other types of questions of the GQ questionnaire which have a strong link with question Q1.
- We are not using complementary data to the question Q1, as they are present in many international data bases.
- From all the countries of the world, we use Romania as reference. We mention the fact that the data about Romania are the latest available at a governmental and European level. Taking into account this restrained environment, we will not be able to create hierarchies by following different classification criteria between the groups of states which include Romania.
- Regarding question Q1, we avoid any type of longitudinal analysis which entails the modification in time of Romanians' opinions.
- In the case of the variables F, M, T, P, W, R which define question Q1 we evaluate comparatively just the opinions of Romanian males and females. Although the questionnaire GQ refers to many characteristics of the interviewed persons, we will not compare the groups of individuals created by: age, education, income, size of the city of residence, political and religious orientation of the respondents, ethnicity, information level, type of community, etc.
- The data analysis is based on a statistical model. The statistical analysis follows a ranking of the variables F, M, T, P, W, R using the classical relation "$<_{st}$" of stochastic order. We also propose the PSA indicator intended to measure "the progress" made by a distribution of the answering options with regard to another distribution of the answers. The PSA index will detail quantitatively the qualitative results obtained by applying the order relation "$<_{st}$". At the same time, the PSA coefficient will solve the cases in which the distributions of the answers given by the two groups of persons cannot be compared from the point of view of the order relation "$<_{st}$".
- Besides the progress indicator PSA, we will not use other indexes for measuring various aspects of the answer distribution mode such as: polarization, diversity, inequality, segregation, dispersion, dependency.
- We will not use statistical tests to verify a possible homogeneity of the variables F, M, T, P, W, R. At the same time, we will not use other types of statistical tests which confirm or invalidate the dependence between variables that characterize question Q1.

Referring to the data that will be analyzed, we will mention the following:

- The answers to question Q1 are of the SAH type (self-assessed data). Therefore, the obtained data in this case are categorial, and there is an order relation between the categories (ordinal variables; Agresti 2002, 2007).
- The promoted statistical model operates with ordinal random variables and creates hierarchy based on the stochastic order "$<_{st}$" and the PSA "progress" index which was proposed.

In the vast SEO project which stands partially at the basis of the present paper, the following aims are to be explored:

- The exposure to certain current problems that regard all the world countries or just several groups of states.
- The proposal of appropriate social and economic policies designed to remedy the differences between the states. Also, this entails the measuring of the efficacy in time of the socio-economic policies which were adopted.
- Establishing, by certain criteria, Romania's position in a European and world context, as well as the analysis of the longitudinal evolution of the classifications obtained with regard to the policies existing at a given time.
- The evaluation of a possible development tendency both at regional and at world levels correlated with stressing out the utility of certain global policies.

The methodology will be partially presented below and will be extended and promoted within the vast SEO project. In this general context, we will disregard the particular approaches that refer to the present paper.

Some extra information will be presented in the subsequent sections.

1. Literature review

At the international level, several data bases were created which contain longitudinal economic and social information from several countries that are analyzed periodically. We will mention two such main databases used frequently by researchers: World Values Survey (WVS), and European Values Survey (EVS). The WVS and EVS databases contain data collected periodically over 35 years, the update interval being between 5 and 9 years. Over 40 countries are taken into account in the WVS, and over 20 European countries are in the EVS database. The number of countries included in the databases WVS and EVS increases continuously with new sampling activity. Therefore, in the case of the WVS database it is estimated that in 2017–2018, the collection of new data to be contained in wave 7 will comprise over 60 countries.

Each new data collection is based on the same GQ questionnaire, which allows for a longitudinal statistical analysis of the evolution of certain opinions of the population involved.

In general, the questions from the GQ questionnaire based on the WVS and EVS databases propose that the respondents choose one and only one answering option. Statistically we will work with categorial type data, which will impose specific methods for analyzing such data (Agresti 2002, 2007; Cliff and Keats 2003).

Romania contributed to socio-economic data for the WVS database starting from wave 3 (1997–1998). In this presentation, we will use the latest available data from the WVS database (Romania, wave 6, year 2012).

During 2010–2014, the Institute for Comparative Survey Research Vienna gathered the opinions of 86,000 persons from 60 countries regarding question Q1 from the questionnaire GQ (wave 6; https://knoema.com). The aim is to establish the relative importance of the set of values: family (F), friends (M), leisure time (T), politics (P), work (W) and religion (R).

Establishing the importance of these variables is frequently done through a direct percentage interpretation, also using frequency graphics (Voicu 2008). We will focus on the promotion of appropriate statistical models of classification.

Obviously, in order to rank the variables F, M, T, P, W, R it is necessary to have the definition of an order relation between the distributions of these variables. In literature, we find a lot of such order relations. In general, these relations refer to cardinal random variables. Naturally we should adapt the order relations from literature to ordinal categorial variables.

We will mention in the following the most widely known order relations that are used to differentiate among the distributions of ordinal type cardinal random variables. In this way, Shaked and Shanthikumar (2007) discuss the usual stochastic order "$<_{st}$" (p. 3), the hazard rate order "$<_{hr}$" (p. 16), the likelihood ratio order, "$<_{lr}$" (p. 42), the convolution order "$<_{conv}$" (p. 70) or the increasing/decreasing – convex/concave orders, "$<_{icx}$", "$<_{dcx}$", "$<_{icv}$", "$<_{dcv}$" (p. 181). Moreover, Shaked and Shanthikumar (2007) point out a multitude of properties of all these order relations, also suggesting possible applications. In this context, see also Belzunce (2010), Li and Li (2013) or Belzunce et al. (2016).

In the last period, new order relations have been proposed, along with their characteristic properties. In this way, Davidov and Peddada (2013) define linear stochastic order for multidimensional distributions. Bouhadjar et al. (2016) analyze in which way linear combinations of random variables influence different order relations.

Moreover, Bouhadjar et al. (2016) define "the stop-loss order" relation which has multiple applications for reinsurance contracts or for individual and collective risk models.

Finally, we propose using the classic order relation "$<_{st}$" in order to establish the relations between the six ordinal variables referred to in question Q1.

Revealing a relation $X <_{st} Y$ between the variables X and Y is frequently insufficient in practice, because this order relation is partial, specifying that X is "inferior" to Y without mentioning the size of the difference between Y and X. Taking this into account, we will introduce the PSA "progress" indicator intended to measure quantitatively the difference between the distributions of the variables Y and X.

Due to an extremely large number of dimensions which define the notion of progress, designing a progress indicator raises complex methodological problems, as well as many difficulties in the necessary data collection. Natoli and Zuhair (2011) choose an aggregate indicator, while the component coefficients are necessarily standardized (normalized). In this moment, at world level, there is no need to rapidly find a perfect index that measures the degree of "progress" recorded in the evolution of phenomena. The current research aimed at finding new coefficients, evidently imperfect, that should possess "better global qualities" compared to the old ones (Natoli and Zuhair, 2011). A methodology regarding the projection of a progress indicator is also suggested by Stern et al. (2014).

We have not identified in literature a progress indicator that will be directly applied to ordinal type category variables. Within several presentations of 2015, finalized by a preprint, we suggested a set of 9 conditions that must be mandatorily satisfied by a progress index applied to ordinal variables. The most important of these axioms requires that the progress index be compatible with the classic relation "$<_{st}$" of stochastic order. The PSA index that we proposed checks all the 9 proposed axioms. The concrete form of the PSA indicator for four ordinal classes will be presented in the subsequent section.

The recorded progress in the evolution of different phenomena can be observed indirectly if we refer to certain processes complimentary to the studied phenomenon. Concretely, in the case of socio-economic phenomena, we cannot consider a real progress if there are aspects of polarization, inequality, segregation, deprivation, absence of a diversity in manifestation, etc.

For all these processes, we find in literature a variety of indicators which are applicable to ordinal type categorial variables. This way, in the case of the process of bi-polarization, we notice in particular indicators used in the works of Berry and Mielke (1992), Blair and Lacy (1996), Apouey (2007), Permanyer and D'Ambrosio (2013). In the last years, new coefficients were suggested for measuring the inequality phenomenon for ordinal variables (Giudici and Raffinetti, 2011; Cowell and Flachaire, 2014).

The polarization and inequality indexes were also used in Romanian research in order to rank some categorial variables (Ştefănescu, 2015, 2016).

2. Some methodological details

In the case of the variables $X \in \{F, M, T, P, W, R\}$ which define question Q1 from the questionnaire GQ, the interviewed persons may choose between four answering options. Concretely, we have the following answering options: "not at all important" (code 1), "not very important" (code 2), "rather important" (code 3), "very important" (code 4). Therefore, all X type variables are categorial, each being characterized by four classes C_1, C_2, C_3, C_4. For the variable X, the class C_k comprises the individuals who opted for code k of the answers, $1 \leq k \leq 4$. We notice the fact that X is an ordinal categorial variable, because there is an increasing order between the classes C_k, that is: $C_1 < C_2 < C_3 < C_4$.

If p_k represents the probability that the random variable X takes the value k, $1 \leq k \leq 4$, then the distribution of X is completely defined by the vector $\underline{p} = (p_1, p_2, p_3, p_4)$.

Definition 1.1. Two distributions $\underline{p}$, $\underline{q}$ respect the stochastic order relation $\underline{p} <_{st} \underline{q}$ if the following three inequalities are verified:

$$p_1 \geq q_1,\ p_1 + p_2 \geq q_1 + q_2,\ p_4 \leq q_4$$

and, moreover, at least one of these inequalities is strict.

Remark 1.2. The classic definition of the stochastic order relation mentioned by Shaked and Shanthikumar (2007, p. 3) is equivalent to definition 1.1.

The relation $\underline{p} <_{st} \underline{q}$ has an obvious significance. Therefore, if $\underline{p} <_{st} \underline{q}$, then the distribution $\underline{p}$ compared with the distribution $\underline{q}$ is higher (percentage) in the first two unfavorable answering options ("not at all important" and "not very important", classes C_1, C_2) and also smaller (percentage) in the most favorable answering option ("very important", class C_4).

With regard to the stochastic order $\underline{p} <_{st} \underline{q}$, we propose the PSA coefficient to measure the level of "progress" of a distribution $\underline{p}$ that defines a categorial variable with four ordinal classes. We will not present here the set of axioms that lead us to the definition of the PSA index.

Definition 1.3. The progress indicator PSA ($\underline{p}$) is shown by the expression:

$$\text{PSA}(\underline{p}) = (1 - p_1 + p_3 + 2p_4) / 3$$

We can prove that the PSA ($\underline{p}$) progress indicator is compatible with the relation "$<_{st}$" of stochastic order. More precisely:

Proposition 1.4. For any two distributions $\underline{p}$, $\underline{q}$, if $\underline{p} <_{st} \underline{q}$ then PSA ($\underline{p}$) < PSA ($\underline{q}$).

Remark 1.5. Proposition 1.4 is very important, because it can establish a hierarchy between two distributions $\underline{p}$, $\underline{q}$ also in the case when the two are not comparable from the point of view of the stochastic order "$<_{st}$". Moreover, if we relate the distributions $\underline{p}$, $\underline{q}$, the stochastic order relation $\underline{p} <_{st} \underline{q}$ has a qualitative characteristic, $\underline{p}$ being smaller than $\underline{q}$. By comparison, the order relation based on the values of the coefficient PSA is quantitative, and the difference PSA ($\underline{q}$) – PSA ($\underline{p}$) measure the gap between $\underline{q}$ and $\underline{p}$.

3. Partial results

Table 3.1 presents the frequency of the answers of men and women from Romania regarding question Q1, variables F, M, T, P, W, R. From the brief analysis of these data we notice the special role given by the population to the family, and also the respondents' disinterest in politics. The hierarchy of values Q1 (variables F, M, T, P, W, R) and the comparison of these classifications for men and women do not seem to be an easy task if we use only the direct interpretation of data from table 3.1.

Table 3.1: Frequencies of the variables F, M, T, P, W, R (Romania 2012)

Var.	Not at all important (code 1)		Not very important (code 2)		Rather important (code 3)		Very important (code 4)	
	men	women	men	women	men	women	men	women
F	0	3	4	13	42	37	595	806
M	12	40	120	223	342	434	168	162
T	29	31	97	164	287	385	225	276
P	211	363	245	316	132	125	49	43
W	21	22	38	63	215	298	365	472
R	32	11	99	85	243	251	265	512

Source: File: F00003091-WV6_Romania2012_spss_v_2016_01_01.zip, Word Values Survey Database, wave 6 (2010–2014), Romania, http: www.worldvaluessurvey.org

By the stochastic order relation "$<_{st}$", we obtain, with regard to gender, a classification of the variables for question Q1 (Figures 3.2–3.3). In the graphics 3.2–3.3 the order relation $X<_{st}Y$ between two variables X and Y is represented by X→Y. In order to ease the interpretation of the structural relations between the variables of the system Q1, we avoided the supplementary plotting in figures 3.2–3.3 of the links between the variables F, M, T, P, W, R which result indirectly from the transitivity of the order relation "$<_{st}$".

Fig. 3.2: The order relations between the variables F, M, T, P, W, R (male)

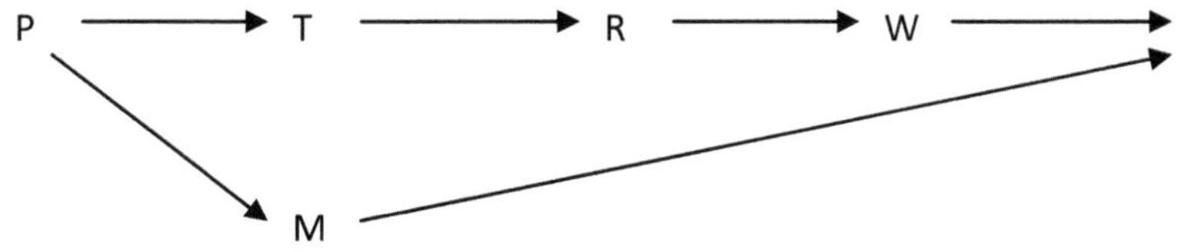

The stochastic order relation "$<_{st}$" is partial, because not any two variables X, Y can be comparable. This way, in figure 3.2 variable M cannot be compared with any of the variables T, R or W. In the same way, in figure 3.3, we do not have $W <_{st} R$, nor $R <_{st} W$. By using the progress index PSA, we avoided this major inconvenience (table 3.4). Moreover, the PSA indicator is compatible with the order relation "$<_{st}$" (proposition 1.4). The difference PSA (Y)–PSA (X) estimates quantitatively the gap between the distributions of variables Y and X when $X <_{st} Y$.

Fig. 3.3: The order relations between the variables F, M, T, P, W, R (female)

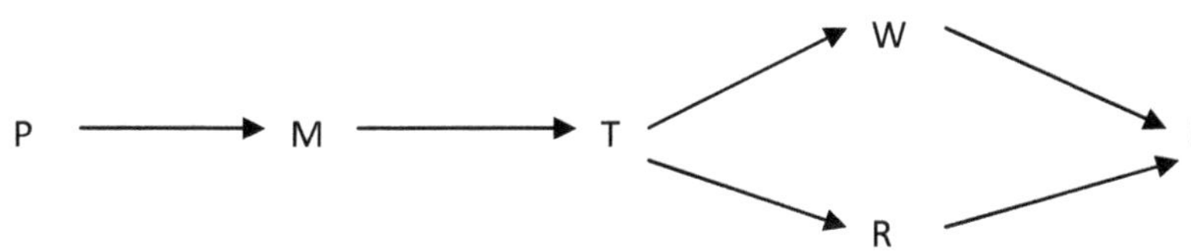

Table 3.4: PSA values for the variables F, M, T, P, W, R

Variable	F	M	T	P	W	R
male	0.974	0.679	0.703	0.343	0.815	0.720
female	0.972	0.612	0.686	0.274	0.809	0.824

4. Conclusions

Taking into consideration the Romanians' opinions in 2012, we have attempted to hierarchize the values system Q1: family (F), friends (M), leisure time (T), politics (P), work (W), religion (R).

Research regarding the subject Q1 has been taking place for several decades in numerous countries. In general, establishing the populations' priorities regarding the mentioned Q1 values has often been limited to the direct comparison of frequencies and their graphical representations. Our approach is different and is based on a statistical model that uses the stochastic order relation "$<_{st}$" (definition 1.1). In order to increase the accuracy of the comparisons between different variables of the values system Q1, we have introduced the PSA "progress" indicator. We will remind of the fact that the PSA index is compatible with the order relation "$<_{st}$" (proposition 1.4).

The opinions of men and women in Romania regarding the values Q1 are quite similar (figures 3.2–3.3, table 3.4). Therefore, by sorting the PSA coefficients in decreasing order, we have obtained two little different hierarchies, which are the following: F>W>R>T>M>P for men, and F>R>W>T>M>P for women (table 3.4). Religion is estimated by women before work, which is appreciated inversely by men (table 3.4).

Men as well as women mentioned in the first three places family, work and religion. On the last places, in decreasing order, there are the following: leisure time, friends and politics (table 3.4). For the entire Romanian population, "family" takes first place before any other Q1 values (table 3.4). In contrast, in last place, at a considerable difference from the rest of the Q1 values, we find "politics" (table 3.4).

Compared to men, women tend to be more interested in religion, opting less for politics and friends (table 3.4). The other Q1 variables have PSA values that are similar for men and women (table 3.4).

For the complex SEO project, including the current research, we intend to use other statistical approaches which have partially been mentioned in the introductory chapter.

References

1. Apouey, B.: "Measuring health polarization with self-assessed health data," Health Economics, 16 (9), 2007, pp. 875–894.
2. Agresti, A.: Categorical Data Analysis. Wiley Interscience: New Jersey, 2002, second edition.
3. Agresti, A.: An Introduction to Categorical Data Analysis. Wiley Interscience: New Jersey, 2007, second edition.
4. Belzunce, F.: "An introduction to the theory of stochastic orders." Boletín de Estadística e Investigaciíón Operativa, 26 (1), 2010, pp. 4–18.
5. Belzunce, F./Martínez-Riquelme, C./Mulero, J.: An Introduction to Stochastic Orders. Elsevier – Academic Press: Amsterdam, 2016.
6. Berry, K. J. / Mielke, P. W.: "Indices of ordinal variation", Perceptual and Motor Skills, 74, 1992, pp. 576–578.
7. Blair, J. / Lacy, M. G.: "Measures of variation for ordinal data as functions of the cumulative distribution," Perceptual & Motor Skills, 82 (2), 1996, pp. 411–418.

8. Bouhadjar, M./Zeghdoudi, H./Remita, M. R.: "On stochastic orders and their applications: Policy limits and deductibles." Appl. Math. Inf. Sci., 10 (4), 2016, pp. 1–8.
9. Cowell, F. A., Flachaire, E.: "Inequality with ordinal data," STICERD London School of Economics, Aix-Marseille University, Working paper, pp. 1–50, October 2014.
10. Norman, C./Keats, J. A.: Ordinal Measurement in the Behavioral Sciences. Lawrence Erlbaum: New Jersey, 2003.
11. Davidov, O./Peddada, S.: "The linear stochastic order and directed inference for multivariate ordered distributions." The Annals of Statistics, 41 (1), 2013, pp. 1–40.
12. Giudici, P., Raffinetti, E.: "A Gini concentration quality measure for ordinal variables," Quaderni del Dipartimento di Economia, Statistica e Diritto, Università di Pavia, Serie Statistica, no. 1/2011, pp. 1–18.
13. Li, H./Li, X.u (eds): Stochastic Orders in Reliability and Risk. Springer: New York, 2013.
14. Natoli, R./Zuhair, S.: "Measuring progress: A comparison of the GDP, HDI, GS and the RIE." Soc. Indic. Res. 103, 2011, pp. 33–56.
15. Permanyer, I./D'Ambrosio, C.: "Measuring social polarization with ordinal and categorical data." Journal of Public Economic Theory, 2013, 11 pages.
16. Shaked, M./Shanthikumar, G. J.: Stochastic Orders. Springer Science + Business Media: New York, 2007.
17. Stern, S./Wares, A./Orzell, S.: The Social Progress Index Methodology – 2014. Social Progress Imperative: Washington, 2014. www.socialprogressimperative.org.
18. Stefănescu, M. L.: "Analyzing the health status of the population using ordinal data," Computational Methods in Social Sciences, 3 (1), 2015, pp. 18–24.
19. Stefănescu, M. L.: "Establishing the health status of Romanians in an European context," Computational Methods in Social Sciences, 4 (1), 2016, pp. 58–66.
20. Voicu, B.: "Valorile Românilor." Newsletter, no. 2, December 2008, 4 pages, http://www.iccv.ro/valori, grant CNCSIS ID56/2007.

Dan CONSTANTINESCU

Ecological University of Bucharest,
email: dan.constantinescu@ueb.ro

Contributions to the Development of A Hierarchical Model of Human Resources Management

Abstract: The history of management thinking and practice highlights the existence of a consistent package of hierarchical marks that justify the effort of patterning a human resources' management. The analysis of the subordination relation regarded as a connection that generates the hierarchy, reveals its functional character, the pyramidal ordering principle of elements in the field of economic structures, being not only a result of methodological demands of scientific order, but also a demand of accomplishment of the administration of these systems.

Practically, the hierarchy defines exactly the system's structure, the relatively invariant aspect of it, through which all the other attributes of managerial architecture are externalized: integrality, homeostasis, self-structuring, hierarchy, self-generation and development.

Without denying the natural variability of managerial hierarchies, imposed by the complexity of the economic-social domain where it is manifest, we will demonstrate that the three elements that support this model stability, namely convergence, functionality and adaptability, offer it a quasi-general applicability.

Keywords: hierarchy, management, model, subordination

Introduction

The proposal of a managerial model based on the hierarchy principles, in a time in which the topic of the day is the institutional democratization bears with it the risk of being regarded with reservation. We assumed this risk, noticing that almost all negative connotations related to the notion of hierarchy do not refer to the key elements of the model, but to all the collateral aspects, as the implications for the social area of some excesses of the military and ecclesiastic practice.

Instead, we will observe the various favorable opinions to a hierarchical approach to the managerial structures, even when the model itself is missing. Therefore, the hierarchy is regarded as one of the main structure types met most of the times in control systems (Fedorenko 1979, p. 235), and the contemporary economy is built as a system with more than two levels, among which – in spite of the fact that they are not generally wide-spread – there are actually relations of subordination and supraordination with a guiding character (Kornai 1974, p. 6).

Clearer opinions, influenced probably by the thesis of the well-known Austrian biologist Bertalanffy (1973, p. 37), are situated in the area of the general systems theory or in macroeconomics' point of view. "The material organizational structures are formed preponderantly on the hierarchical levels, through the embodiment of the sub adjacent structures, the last ones being subdued to new restrictions, in favour of the structures that sinergycally enclose them" (Constantinescu 1986, p. 23).

Similar assertions which, through a double relation of equivalence, bring together from the conceptual point of view the notions of system, structure and hierarchy, lead, simply, to the idea that the last expression could represent a focused and precise enough image of the first ones. In other words, the hierarchy could be a model of the structured systems in general and of economic systems in particular. A question, and at the same time an interesting hypothesis, to which the present study is trying to offer an answer.

1. Historical coordinates

It can be claimed, without any exaggeration, that the benchmarks of hierarchy have accompanied the managerial practice from the oldest times. Thus, the Bible mentions the configuration on the hierarchical principles of the public management accomplished by Moses at his father-in-law's advice: "And Moses chose able men out of all Israel, and made them heads over the people, rulers of thousands, rulers of hundreds, rulers of fifties, and rulers of tens" (Exodus 18:25).

In the modern era, the mark of the hierarchical model is obvious from the first approaches of the classical scholars, Frederick Taylor defining a series of parameters of this model, the 4 basic principles of management stated by him representing an equal number of coordinates of a functional hierarchy.

Henry Fayol extends the study of the analysis of the topic of management to the company level, which allows him to offer the first image of the global hierarchical model through the 14 principles of leadership. The single administration, the centralization, the control unit, the subordination of individual interests to the general ones and the corporate spirit are thus the hierarchical benchmarks of organizational convergence. The fragmentation of work, the authority-responsibility binomial, the discipline and the scalar chain ensure the functional character of the managerial hierarchy. Finally, the initiative, the equity, the remuneration and the stability of the working force support the adaptation potential of the hierarchical structures, their flexibility in the natural dynamics of the socio-economic space.

Even if the precise translation of the concept introduced by Max Weber is "bureaucratic organization," this can be called "functional organization" or, simply, "hierarchy." The six characteristics of the "ideal bureaucracy" proposed by him are related to the same managerial triplet: convergence–functionality–adaptability. Actually, as the very idea of impartiality of the analysis, he proposes the impersonal system of leadership, based on rational authority, functional fraction and continuity, in other words, the first theoretical synthesis of the hierarchical model.

The representatives of the behaviorist school balance the two positions of the manager (subject and object of the hierarchy) just as significant, placing the human agent in the forefront of the organizational domain. Thus, in his work "How to Win

Friends and Influence People" (Carnegie 2007), the author insists on the functional office of the subordination relation, embodied in the managerial style and behavior. Abraham Maslow, well-known founder of the motivational theory (Maslow 1970), singularizes the hierarchical model in his well-known "pyramid of needs." Even if he does not relate it to the organizational hierarchical pyramid, the suggestion is relevant.

The contributions of the behaviorist approach to the evolution of the hierarchical model are not limited only to the role of human behavior in ensuring the functional character of the hierarchy, comprising valuable elements in the adaptability of the managerial structures such as the avoidance of overspecializing of services and employees, decentralization of the decisional process, accommodation of the official authority to the real one, the importance and the role of formal or informal groups.

Through the representatives of the quantity school, the basic benchmarks of the hierarchy benefit from in-depth knowledge of the formal aspects, in theory, mainly within the analysis of graphs and of decision factors, and the systemic management enriched managerial thinking with the concept of prioritization of the systems, thus underlining the vertical interdependence of the component entities.

The contingentional, situational approach includes in the hierarchical model the subordination to the force variables of the internal and external environment, especially those that generate relational effects (multiplying, exomorphic and endomorphic). From the identified contingent variables, which are over one hundred, the most frequent are connected to the size of the organization, operational technology, environmental uncertainty and individual differentiation (Robbins 1991, p. 38).

The Japanese management is, without any doubt, impregnated by cultural and religious features, influenced by a specific tradition and mentality, which differentiate it from the management hierarchy of the Western area. We will highlight the contribution of the American professor of Japanese origin, William Ouchi, embodied in the hybrid motivational model called "Z theory", by which the most productive hierarchical dominants of the two managerial cultures (X and Y) are combined for achieving the convergence of the outlet flows on the competition markets.

Excellence in business management is another evolution coordinate of the behaviorist's approach, embodied by its representatives through the eight attributes used by managers for gaining success in the companies they lead (Peters and Waterman 1984). It is important to note how the hierarchical benchmark models perfectly match the commune characteristics of the "elite" companies. For example, "the propensity for action" is equivalent to the functional character of the hierarchy, contrary to the "bureaucratic" one; "propensity for client" reveals the importance of supplier-type subordinations; "autonomy and entrepreneurship" are forms of delegation, individual or collective, on the hierarchical ladder of the managerial responsibilities.

The contribution of Henry Mintzberg to the development of a hierarchical model is difficult to subordinate to a distinct scientific trend, and it is accomplished through the formulation of ten manager roles (Mintzberg 1973, pp. 92–93). As a matter of fact, he does not do anything different than broadening the study of hierarchical structure functionality, by relating the roles to the functions formulated by Fayol. It is important to remember the finding that the roles are involved differently at different levels of the management hierarchy, the role of the leader being mostly requested at the lowest levels of the hierarchical pyramid, and the other roles – of representation, coordinator, monitor, disseminator, etc. – having a wider weight at the superior levels.

In the succession of different schools and trends there were disputes, confrontations and dogmatic positions. It is interesting that none of these approaches question either the existence of management itself or its basis of hierarchical nature. Even the authors who refer to a so-called "managerial crisis" rather regard the socio-cultural model and its implications for the work and organization than the hierarchical basis of the managerial systems.

2. Subordination – the connection generating the hierarchical model

As early as its definition, the notion of relation suggests the idea of an arrangement of the constituent subsystems within a structural and functional entity. Also, the relation represents, in fact, one of the main modalities to order concepts.

The arrangement of the managerial systems results from the specific features of the systems which they govern, characterized by the distribution or the time and spatial-territorial arrangement of the component elements (Iancu 1986, p. 39). The enhancement of the acting and decisional elements of an organization, in order to integrate the functions associated to the positions and divisions for the objectives of the entities which embedded them, it is practically accomplished through a connection which, below, we will call the subordination relation and will denote by δ.

The existence of this type of relations is caused by an assembly of factors, with objective and subjective determination, among which we can mention the propriety, the competence and the specialization. The same elements are at the basis of the subordination criteria and the dynamics of the mentioned factors is reflected in the whole relational assembly that defines the structural pattern of the organization.

Among the subordination relations we can distinguish (Kornai 1974, p. 62) decisional subordination – based on the directive reports, materialized in the prerogative to order, with the opportunity to apply sanctions and informational subordination – consisting in the (relative) monopolization at the management system of some information necessary to other systems. In practice, the information-decision symbiosis leads, for the most part, to the conjugation of the two aspects, so the managerial system elements are found, as a rule, in the complete informational-decisional subordination reports.

Without ignoring the necessity for and the elaboration criteria of diverse subject typologies, one could reveal the fact that the main relation categories in literature are linked, in fact, to the relations of subordination (Constantinescu 2003, pp. 16–17). The extension of the study to the informal relations allows us to observe the fact that the main categories, highlighted by Keith Davis, respect the general conditions of existing subordination relation: the integrating character, the information concentrated on the leader's level, the direct or mediated subordination to the authority center.

The subordination relation operates even at the external links level, with both the corporatist theories and the organizational aggregation based on the capital concentration principle leading to the subsystems arranged in a pyramidal space, specific to the supra- or subordination relations, from the profits centers to the transnational companies.

In the following table, we tried to structure a relations typology within the managerial systems, assuming that these relations do not represent anything else than specific forms and ways of subordination.

Table 1: The typology of subordination relations

Classification criteria	Alternatives	Subordination types
generator element of subordination	• the authority • informational monopoly	• decisional • informational
the essential factor of subordination	• property • competence • specialization	• by benefit • assumed • functional
ways of relation manifestation	• direct • delegation of competencies • through agents	• direct • through agent • "subordination chain"
regulation mode	• preset • institutional • undetermined	• formal • informal
individualization of joint elements	• total • for the authority center only • undetermined	• individual • group • between groups
subordination length	• formally unlimited • limited	• permanent • temporary
position of the authority center	• inside the analyzed system • outside, on the same hierarchical level • outside, on a superior hierarchical level	• inner • "producer" type • regulatory type
relational effects	• without structural implications • generation of new components • changing of another system • related elements' improvement	• structurally passive • multiplicative • exomorphic • endomorphic

Source: A synthesis of the author's research.

From the formal point of view, the subordination relation can be regarded as an order relation, more exactly, a relation of partial order as the existence of such a connection between the managerial structure components has optional character. The relation between the elements which are not in the direct subordination reports is accomplished through the nearest common authority center.

The reflexivity axiom [$x \delta x, \forall x \in N$, where N is the number of positions] can be treated from two different points of view. In a limited sense, we have the subordination of the acting components to the management ones, in the same administrative subdivision area; in a broader sense, the axiom reflects the fact that the managerial attributions are exercised not only in relation to subordinated components, but to their own activity. The reflexivity of the subordination relation is the basis for defining the concepts of functional autonomy, self-adjustment, self-control, etc.

According to the antisymmetric axiom [$x \delta y$ and $y \delta x \Rightarrow x = y$] two subsystems cannot be subordinate to one another, at the same time and from the same point of view. The two determinations (time and criterion) are strictly demanded because in practice, there can be a mutual temporary subordination, according to different subordination criteria. In these situations, we face different subordination relations.

The transitivity of the subordination relation [$x \delta y$ and $y \delta z \Rightarrow x \delta z$] reveals the significant elements in the analysis of this type of relation. The extension of the notion content, from the direct subordination to an element belonging to the immediate superior hierarchical level, to the mediated/indirect subordination, based on the complete responsibility principle, when the elements in relation are found in a subordination chain, also called "vertical chain" or "hierarchical line."

3. The formal model of hierarchy – conceptual limits

The hierarchy forms a basic concept in the general theory of systems and the pyramidal elements ordering principles in economic structures is not only a result of the methodological requirements, of a scientific origin, but a requirement of the management accomplishment for these systems.

A simple hierarchical structure (briefly, a hierarchy) can be revealed inside an entity of disjunctive elements if, excepting the unique maximal element – x_0, $\forall x_{k,i} \Rightarrow \exists x_{j,k-1}$ so that $x_{k,i} \delta x_{j,k-1}$, where x represents the post, k represents the hierarchical level and i and j fluctuate depending on the positions authority area to which x_i and x_j are subordinates.

The hierarchy definition can be accomplished iteratively or recursively, starting from the maximal element – x_0, in conditions of concomitant verification of the following hypothesis: there is a finite and a non-void set of elements $\{x_{1,i} / i = 1,2, \dots\}$; $x_{1,i} \Rightarrow x_{1,i} \delta x_0$ and $x_{1,i}$ are either minimal elements (of the hierarchy discussed), or maximal elements of other hierarchies.

If it is clear that the maximal element x_0 represents the top-manager or the supreme organizational authority, the minimal elements, no matter on what hierarchical level they are placed, belong to the executive positions area, with the exception of unipersonal compartments, or they belong to some management positions for other hierarchies. In the organizational hierarchy, the elements $x_{k-1,j}$ subordinated to the same $x_{k,i}$ form the compartment, but they do not necessarily belong to only one function.

Starting from the geometrical progression $N = 1 + a + a^2 + a^3 + ... + a^{n-1}$, by which the connection between the firm dimension, expressed in number of employees – N, the median authority area – a and number of hierarchical levels – n, we obtain $n = \frac{\log N}{\log a}$.

A derivative dimensional characteristic of the hierarchy can be calculated also, namely the firm's covering degree with management personnel – K, determined as relation between the number of managers and number of employees: $K = \frac{a^{n-1} - 1}{a^n - 1}$.

While some authors (Maliţa and Zidăroiu 1975, pp. 284–285) estimate that, in most organization forms known from practice, there are five hierarchical levels, also called control levels, the other studies (Daft, 1989) reveal a wide range of dissipation of the hierarchy characteristic, depending on the production types practiced.

Table 2: The variation of the hierarchy characteristics depending on the production type

Structure parameters	**Firms, by the production types**		
	Single and small series	**Large-scale series**	**Continual processes**
Hierarchical levels of authority: median (n) amplitude	 3 2–4	 4 3–8	 6 2–17
The authority area (*a*)	24–49	14–18	7–8
Staffing (K)	0.02–0.04	0.055–0.07	0.125–0.143

Source: Nica, 1994, p. 247.

In the optimal rating of basic parameters of the hierarchy, one can take into account some influence factors, such as: the activity diversity, type and complexity, the firm's dimension, the managers' competence and, last but not least, the mutual interconnections.

An optimization model, which takes the authority area – *a* as an independent variable, can be accomplished by means of an objective function – F(*a*), representing the firm's spending, which would sum up the wage costs for the firm's managers – $C_1(a)$ and the expenditures/losses caused by the increase in the authority area or by de decreasing of the coordonability of the managed system – $C_2(a)$.

Along with the alterations in costs having a significant impact, it is important to mention the alterations produced on the communicational plane, more exactly, on the response speed or on the response time of the system to the internal and external stimuli. The minimizing function, in this case, becomes the communicational complexity – L(*a*) that quantifies the potential number of associations in conditions of the fluctuation of the authority area and which includes the internal links – L_1, the intercompartimental relations – L_2 and the relations with the external environment – L_3.

In order to obtain an optimal area of authority – a^* and a^{**}, the objective functions mentioned would be minimized through graphical processors on the basis of mathematical programming, respecting the non-negativity conditions of variables *a* and n, as well as some restrictions that result from the economic and commercial experience of the firm.

On the basis of the research carried out by Graicunas (Nica 1994, p. 247) showing that for an arithmetic increase in of the authority area, the number of connections between manager and subordinates – C rises geometrically, according to the relation $C = a\frac{2^a + a - 1}{2}$, some authors estimate that the authority area for the groups where the manager uses all possible relations between him/her and the subordinates for coordinating their activity cannot be greater than 5, considering the maximum number of events a person can control simultaneously. This is the case of very interactive groups, specific to the top management.

A proper investigation, carried out in 2001, reveals that the number of the people directly subordinated to the general manager show quite large variations, even if the average – 6.42 is situated around this value (Constantinescu 2003, p. 26).

4. The hierarchical coordinates of the human resources management

In order to avoid the divagations caused by the use of overly analytical definitions, we estimate that the systemic approach offers the necessary frame to understand the managerial process, regarded as a specific activity, performed by a team/group of people, taking advantage by the tools offered by science, which they use with abilities related to the art of leadership. We will discuss the managerial system, or the managerial structure, as integrating notions of different aspects that finally refer to the same concept.

Studying from this perspective the different authors' opinions, one can identify the main traits of managerial systems, regarded as subsystems of the economic-social area, namely integrality, homeostasis, self-organization, hierarchy, self-generation, development (Iancu 1986, p. 21). In the previous list, the hierarchy defines the exact structure of the system, the relatively invariable aspect, through which all the other attributes of the managerial architecture are materialized.

So, the integrality of the systems we are looking at results from the definition of hierarchy definition, according to which every managerial component is an object of a subordinate relation. All the elements articulated through generative connections of the hierarchical pattern can be assimilated, without question, to the concept of a "black box". The homeostasis derives from the formal character of the relations of subordination, designed to provide the system, by compensation of the external fluctuations, with exactly the stable configuration designed by the rules and regulations, to which Max Weber refers as the so-called "ideal bureaucratic structure." The self-organization, the creation of new stable conditions intended to insure the system's survival through environmental changes and pressure, has to do with the quality of the managers as hierarchy subjects. We cannot omit the fact that the hierarchical model includes the external connections, among which we count regulatory subordinations and "supplier"-type ones. The self-generation of the elements in the managerial system is a consequence of the existence of relations which cause structural mutations. They manifest themselves concretely in the creation of new managerial components as a consequence of multiplicative subordinations of endomorphic nature, through the transformation of some exomorphic systems, and even through the modification of elements which are grouped together.

Moreover, complex fluctuations of informational-decisional type provide the management structures with the quality of self-formative mechanisms. The conscious development, as a materialization of the desired evolution, is based on the dependence of "industrial logic" – the managerial requirements associated with the technological-productive features of the work by "human logic" – the corresponding requirements specific to the human action, or of the social actors (Hoffman 1999, p. 97), when hierarchy essentially involves man in his double quality of object and subject of the management structure. As a result of this process, the managerial system is oriented towards reaching the established objectives, the command unity and action accomplished within the hierarchy through the subordination chains which have an essential role.

Beyond the natural variability of managerial hierarchies, imposed by the complexity of the economic-social space within which it manifests itself, three elements back up the permanence of this model and ensure a quasi-general applicability: convergence, functionality and adaptability. The convergence of the hierarchical structures is based on the accomplishment of the objective function of the governed systems, to which it preserves the attributes of integrality and homeostasis. According to the nature of the objectives, the ranking of the levels of management presents an integratory configuration, from the execution components to the strategic management and from the objectives regarding the accomplishment of the current activities to those of anticipation of the volume of demand and resources.

The functionality of managerial hierarchies is based on the division of management work, both vertically and horizontally. While the various approaches to the functions of the organizations and of the management offer a well-grounded explanation for the division of managerial attributions horizontally, the greatest difficulty of the vertical segmentation of the hierarchical system, called also the dilemma of management (Stăncioiu and Militaru 1999, pp. 117–119), consisting in the concomitant optimization of the time horizon and of the volume of resources assigned to each specific activity, under conditions in which the two challenges are antagonistic. The solution to this dilemma implies the selection for each hierarchical level of the most adequate problems for the qualification and the authority level of the involved managers, simultaneauosly with the assignment of the partial resolution of some problems to more or even all levels of the organizational pyramid.

Fig. 1: The model-phenomenon relation viewed by the hierarchy and management system characteristics

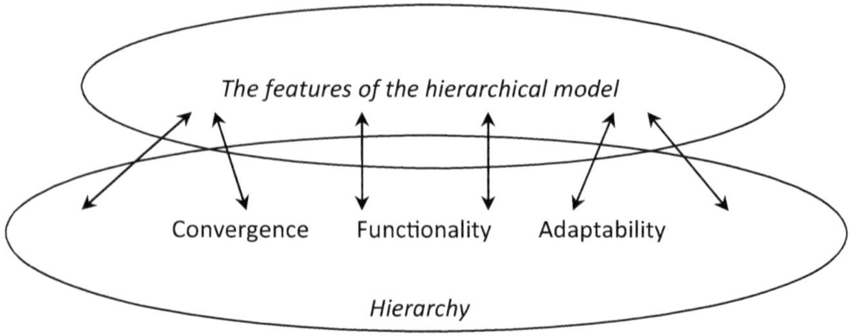

Source: A synthesis of the author's research.

The adaptability of the hierarchical model starts from the idea that there is no single and general valid recipe for an operational and efficient hierarchy. In literature, the most used term is "adequacy" of the structures to the features of the firm, starting from a number of reference variables (strategy, background, technology, human resources and age of the company), through the materialization of the principles of organizational design, along an iterative way that aims at optimizing some relations of the results/costs type or utility/costs type.

References

1. Bertalanffy, Ludwig von (1973), Théorie générale des systèmes, Dunod: Paris, p. 37.
2. Carnegie, Dale (2007), How to Win Friends and Influence People, Ebury Press, London.
3. Constantinescu, Paul (1986), Sisteme ierarhizate. Rolul informaţiei în geneză şi dezvoltare. Editura Academiei R. S. R., Bucureşti, p. 23.
4. Constantinescu, Dan (2003), Ierarhia în managementul sistemelor economice, Editura Economică, Bucureşti, pp. 16–17, 26.
5. Daft, Richard L. (1989), Management. The Dryden Press, New York.
6. Fedorenko, N. P. et al. (1979), Dicţionar de matematică şi cibernetică în economie. Editura Ştiinţifică şi Enciclopedică, Bucureşti, p. 235.
7. Hoffman, Oscar (1999), Management – fundamente socioumane. Editura Victor, Bucureşti, p. 97.

8. Iancu, Aurel et al. (1986), Structura economiei şi sistemul industrial, Editura Politică, Bucureşti, pp. 21, 39.
9. Kornai, Janos (1974), Anti-equilibrium, Editura Ştiinţifică, Bucureşti, pp. 6, 62.
10. Maliţa, Mircea/Zidăroiu, Corneliu – (1975), Matematica organizării, Editura Tehnică: Bucureşti, pp. 284–285.
11. Maslow, Abraham H. (1970), Motivation and personality, Harper and Row, New York.
12. Mintzberg, Henry (1973), The Nature of Managerial Work, Harper & Row, New York, pp. 92–93.
13. Panaite Nica et al. (1994), Managementul firmei. Editura Logos: Chişinău, p. 247.
14. Peters, Thomas J./Waterman, Robert H, Jr. (1984) In Search of Excellence: Lessons from America's Best-Run Companies, Harper & Row: New York.
15. Robbins, Stephen P. (1991), Management, Prentice-Hall New York, p. 38.
16. Stăncioiu, Ion/Militaru, Gheorghe – (1999), Management – elemente fundamentale, Editura Teora, Bucureşti, pp. 117–119.

Mariana STANCIU

Phd, Research Institute for Quality of Life,
e-mail: mariana3stanciu@gmail.com

Adina MIHĂILESCU

Phd, Research Institute for Quality of Life,
e-mail: adina.mihailescu@yahoo.com

Socio-Economic Support Granted to Elderly People from Romania at Present and in the Future

Abstract: The fact that the current public policy regarding the pension system does not compensate for the lack of vision in tackling demographic problems and lack of willingness to financially support the public system, the problem of anti-advertising among young generations, although 60–80% of their pension will come from the public system, is the main issue of this paper. Patterns of consumption and saving are in rapid change. Jobs in the economic field which produce wealth are highly fluctuating. Romania is a small economy, heavily exposed to international changes. As a consequence, pillar I still faces the unpredictability of policies in the decades to come. It's difficult to professionally consider longer term developments (4–5 years), due to the high speed of change in economic, social and political fields. Building a political will for maintaining the public pension system is essential for massively increasing the quality of life for both the elderly and the young generations through the extended families.

Keywords: elderly people, public pension system, security system, social policies

Introduction

Currently, the share of the elderly in the total population does not rank Romania among top 10 countries facing acute problems in this respect. Beyond the rhetoric of the current difficulties concerning the public pension system, Romania will face, however, extensive social effects of aging by the year 2035. If on 1 July 2012, the share of people aged 65+ in the total population of the country was 15% (3.2 million persons), according to the forecast of the National Institute of Statistics (NIS) [1], [2] (INS 2012; INS 2013), this percentage will reach 19.8% (3.6 million persons) by 2030, and 26.8% (3.7 million persons) by 2060.

Table 1: Evolution of the population in the age group 65+ and variations in design, 2012–2060

1 July 2012		2030			2060	
Thousand persons	**Share in percent/%**	**Variant**	**Thousand persons**	**Share in percent/%**	**Thousand persons**	**Share in percent/%**
65+ 3,206.3	15	Constant	3,550.3	19.7	3,457.0	26.7
		Optimistic	3,621.8	19.8	3,743.7	26.8
		Pessimistic	3,465.8	19.5	3,184.2	26.7
15–64 years 14,918.0	70	Constant	12,099.2	67.0	7,921.9	61.2
		Optimistic	12,158.1	67.6	8,333.1	62.6
		Pessimistic	12,021.4	66.6	7,464.7	59.7

Sources: 2012, Romania's population aging, INS; 2013 Romania's population prognosis for 2060 (2030, 2060), INS, pp. 29–44.

Therefore, the need to ensure minimum decent living conditions for older people will continue to concern us. Among the basic services that meet the needs of socio-economic security of the elderly, we find, of course, the public pension system and the social security system. As a result, these types of services should enjoy greater attention from the state, as has been the case already, at least for 2–3 decades, in the EU. For Europeans too, the great concerns are, considering the aging population, financial sustainability of the public pension systems.

By the year 2030, the share of able-to-work population will drop from 70% to 67.6% (optimistic version) and then to 62.6% (by 2060), and this will put pressure on funding the public pension system (INS 2013).

The fall of the salary system in the last 25 years, in the medium run, will cause an increase in the share of elderly people without pensions, which will put pressure on the financing of the social security system, since many of the elderly people will not be entitled to a pension, or, in the best case, will receive very small pensions as a result of lower or fluctuating contributions.

An additional factor of vulnerability of Romania's public pension system is the strong and somehow hidden pressure from the political decision-makers on the privatization of the system, as the collected funds are especially tempting for investors. The more or less veiled attack against the public system of collective insurance in old age (Pillar I) could be a social drama that will affect millions of elderly people, many of whom will be deprived of any support from their family, and also because of major shortages of community support services for the elderly. The acute need for community services for home care of the elderly is strongly felt even in present days, especially by those elderly deprived of family support. The difficulties of this vulnerable population group will be even bigger in the future.

The European social model is of particular importance to the development of the pension systems and social security.

Financing of the public pensions system in Romania – present and future

All public pension systems in the EU have made long-term efforts to ensure financing. In 2013, the European median allocation of the funds to pension systems slightly exceeded 12.5% of the GDP (2016, Eurostat). Some states allocated a higher percentage to the pension sector in GDP, such as Greece (17.5%) and Italy (16%). In this respect, Romania is still far from the European average allocation of pensions, with its only 8.1% of the GDP (*2013, Ageing Working Group, the Economic Policy Committee, EU). The number of elderly will increase from 3.2 million to 3.6 million persons during the period of 2012–2030, and life expectancy of older persons is expected to rise from 18.1 years for women and 9.1 years for men in 2016 to 21.3 years for women and 17.9 years for men (average at European level).

Moreover, according to an European Commission report (EC, DGECFIN 2015), public expenditure with pensions from Romania is expected to decline slightly from 8.2% (2013) to 8.1% of the GDP (2060), a demographic factor with the most powerful effect on this type of expenditure. According to the same sources, the older population's dependence ratio (population 65+ vs population 20–64) in Romania will increase from 26.2% (2013, EU 28–30.4%) to 56% (2053, EU 28–54.9%). The share of the Romanian population aged 20–65 (62.6% in 2013) will decrease by 11.4% until 2053, reaching 51.2% of the population. Therefore, the only chance for increasing the welfare of pensioners would be that the Romanian GDP grows substantially, thereby maintaining the share of current expenditure in GDP on public pensions. In addition to this, by 2030, it is probable that about 1,775,100 people will not have the right to a pension, i.e. to request social assistance from the state budget.

In fact, the financial sustainability of the Romanian pension system is threatened in several ways: by some structural imbalances of the national economy (which causes poor coverage through contributions following a territorial and demographic profiling), by the relatively low level of wages in Romania, by relatively extensive poverty among some of the potential categories of taxpayers (farmers, for example), by high rates of inactivity of the age groups of both 20–29 and 55–59 years.

The amount of pension

During the interval of 1990–2010, the number of pensioners in the public system of pensions grew from 3.58 million to 5.66 million (58%), while the number of taxpayers dropped from 7.997 million to 4.238 million (47%) (CNPV 2016). The amount of pension paid by Romania's public system is particularly low (the lowest in the EU, except for Bulgaria).

Table 2: Monthly level of pensions in some EU countries (€), 2011–2013

Country	**Pension rate/month**	**Country**	**Pension rate/month**
France	1,032	Slovakia	408
Spain	1,021	Poland	504
Greece	882	Lithuania	242
Portugal	833	Bulgaria	133
Germany	760	**Romania**	**180**

Source: Chrysopoulos Philip, 2015, Eurostat: Greek Pensions Average, €882, http://greece.greek reporter.com/2015/06/26/eurostat-greek-pensions-average-e882.

About 24% of pensioners from Romania, i.e. over 1.2 million people, receive below 500 lei per month. In 2016, the average pension in Romania was 893 lei, which means €200, representing 46% of the average net salary (1918 lei).

Social Situation of the Romanian elderly

In March 2010, the number of pensioners with severe material deprivation is high, respectively 554,018 (10% of total). The main reason, especially for persons aged 75+, is the very low level of pensions received in the last two decades.

The public system ranked the pensioners with sever material deprivation, by their level of income, below the absolute poverty line (MDL 247), 1,147,599 (20.8%) pensioners were ranked below the minimum subsistence threshold (364 lei), 1,933,619 (35%) were ranked below the relative poverty line (459 lei), and 2,119,610 (38.4%) were below the minimum threshold for decent living (489 lei). In 2008, pensioners already represent a significant percentage of the total population (27.9%), and poor pensioners accounted for 21.4% among poor people (CNPV 2010)

A large part of the elderly in Romania faces high risk of poverty and social exclusion (35% of the total population aged 65+: 28.8% men and 39.1% women (EC 2015).

Table 3: Poverty, social exclusion and severe material deprivation among elderly in Romania in 2013 (in percent/%)

Indicator	**2013**		
	Total	**Men**	**Women**
Risk of poverty and social exclusion 65+	35.0	28.8	39.1
Poverty rate 65+	15.0	9.7	18.6
Severe material deprivation 65+	27.5	23.8	29.9
Risk of poverty and social exclusion 75+	39.5	31.5	44.3
Poverty rate 75+	18.0	10.8	22.3
Severe material deprivation 75+	30.8	25.7	33.8

Source: 'The 2015, Pension Adequacy Report: current and future income adequacy in old age in the EU', European Commission, Directorate-General for Employment, Social Affairs and Inclusion, the Social Protection Committee, vol. II].

The low performance of the public pension system and social protection in Romania explains this social situation (Eurostat2016). The Romanian social protection institution has the lowest social efficacy in Europe. Its impact, as assessed by the distance between the pre- and post-transfer rates, is much lower than half the EU average.

The major problems of the public pension system

here are two main kinds of problems: current and future problems:

- The current ones stem from ignoring the effects of the economic and social impact of the reform. The most persistent problem is caused by the system of employment – labor code deficiency, inequities transferred from the wage level to the amount of retirement benefits, excessive bureaucratization of the retirement procedures, staff shortage, low performance of financing policies, management problems, etc.
- The prospective problems might come from the difficulties of forecasting expenditure on pensions, the probability of facing higher expectation of spending than the entries in the financial system as a result of the increase in the number of pensioners and in the number of unemployed persons entitled to at least a minimum pension. This will occur because of a certain reduction in the number of taxpayers. Among the prospective problems, we need to mention a significant increase in pension expenditures by the year 2035. According to "The 2015 Ageing Report" (EC, EPC 2015), public expenditure on pensions will fall (European average is 12.5% of GDP) from 8.2% (2013) to 8.1% of GDP (2060); this demographic factor generates the most powerful effect on this type of expenditure.

Social policies and directions for action

1. Increasing the number of contributors to the public pension system by increasing the employment rate (the goal of the Europe 2020 strategy) to 70%, that means the creation of about 1.7 million new jobs, at the present average wage, keeping unchanged all other conditions, knowing that around 3.4 million jobs already exist in the underground economy. Or, keeping the trend of the current employees and increasing the average wage in the economy by about 750 lei, while other variables should remain unchanged.

Additional policies

- Encouraging fertility through demographic policies along with a redefinition of the immigration policy.
- Encouraging the elderly to remain in employment after retirement age.
- The expansion of the contributory system for agricultural pensions.
- Eliminating privileges from the public pension system (special pensions).
- Taking measures to improve the pension contribution collection.
- Reorganizing the legislation concerning the funding of Pillar II of Pensions.
- The right to a pension for employees, the most important form of social protection of older persons.

The demographic perspective is not a reason to ignore financial sustainability of the public pension system in the long term, as it happens at present.

The reform of the public system of pensions is based on a giant deficit

The social security budget was financially independent until 1995, when early deficits were covered from the state budget – 10.954 million lei in 2010, more than 2.1% of the GDP. In 2011, the deficit was over 2.9% of the GDP. Only about 41% of the deficit was initiated by FASS (real public needs) in 2008. The rest of the deficit was caused by administrative decisions which introduced non-contributory benefits and other financial burdens on the system.

Social policies and directions of action

1. In order to increase long-term financial sustainability, the pension system needs structural changes which exceed its management tools, such as: (1) increasing the level of FASS financial empowerment so that dependence on transfers from state budget becomes small; (2) introducing a principle of saving resources within the FASS, by collecting present surpluses of this fund and recovering those from the past, which had been directed to other purposes.

2. The transfer of the minimum guaranteed pension (social benefit) responsible for 5% of the public pension system's deficit (does not question the necessity of such benefits) from the social security system to the social assistance system.
3. The diminishing of FASS resources because of errors, corruption and fraud. Average rates of fraud, errors and corruption (2010–2011 checks) in Romania are higher than those in the developed countries.
   The firm recovery of damages found in the system, which produced major financial losses, of approximately 5% of expenditures on pensions, i.e. approximately 2.1 billion lei (2012, when expenses on pensions were about 48 billion lei).
   The target for 2018 should be the creation of an institutional mechanism of recovering losses from the financial system.
4. A substantial decline in the quality of life of older populations (especially those without pension or with a very small pension). The average current pension does not offer, even now, after 27 years of economic changes, the necessary resources for a decent standard of living for the vast majority of pensioners. In 2013, the average amount of annual pension costs per recipient at normal age limit in the EU 28 (in Purchasing Power Standars, PPS) was 12,500 (PPS) per year; in the former socialist countries (excluding Romania and Bulgaria) it was between 5,000 and 8,000 (PPS) per year, while in Romania, it was 5,000 (PPS) per year (i.e. €2,160) (2016, Eurostat).

Relevant resources

There are 3 major alternatives for financing the monthly fund of social assurances (ASS) deficits:

1. Since the fund is supporting a system of intergenerational public solidarity, a transfer of resources from the state budget, as an item of public expenditure, should be included in the budget priorities as a social law based on the contributory principles.
2. But the increase in the contribution share in the fund of public pension system may put additional pressures on the cost of labor (very recommended).
3. Choosing an optimal mix between alternatives 1 and 2, balancing the contributions and the cost of labor in order to discourage tax evasion and encourage new entries into the public system of pensions.

Conclusions

The current problems of the public pension system do not come mainly from the lack of vision in demography, but mainly from the lack of willingness to financially support the public system, from anti-advertisement regarding the public system of pensions among the younger generations, although 60–80% of their pension will come from the public system. Patterns of consumption and saving are in rapid change. The jobs in businesses which produce wealth are highly fluctuating. Romania is a small economy heavily exposed to international changes. As a consequence, Pillar I of Romanian public pension policies still face unpredictability in the decades to come. The difficulty of professionally shaping longer-term developments (4–5 years), due to the high speed of change in economic, social and political fields, increases the predictibility for the next decades. In spite of it, building a political will for maintaining the public pension system is essential for massively increasing the quality of life for the elderly and the young generations through the extended families.

References

1. Philip C. 2015, Eurostat: Greek Pensions Average, http://greece.greekreporter.com/2015/06/26/eurostat-greek-pensions-average-e882.
2. The 2015 Ageing Report: Underlying Assumptions and Projection Methodologies, The European Commission (DG ECFIN) and the Economic Policy Committee (AWG).
3. 2016, The evolution in the number of pensioners and pensions from the State social insurance system in the first quarter of 2016, CNPV.
4. 1991–2015, Statistical Yearbook of Romania, 1991–2015. INS.
5. 2010, Poverty and standard of living of the elderly from Romania, CNPV.
6. 2011, Social Europe, Eurostat.
7. 2012, The ageing of the population of Romania, INS.
8. 2013, The prognosis of the Romanian population in the year 2060, INS.
9. 2015, The 2015 Pension Adequacy TSE Report: current and future income adequacy TSE in old age in the EU, European Commission, Directorate-General for Employment, Social Affairs and Inclusion, the Social Protection Committee, vol. II.
10. 2016, Changes in number of pensioners and the pensions from public system in the first quarter 2016, CNPV.
11. 2016, Elderly Infographs, Eurostat, http://ec.europa.eu/eurostat/cache/info graphs/elderly/index.html.
12. 2016, Expenditure on pensions, 2013 (% of GDP), Eurostat.
13. 2016, People at risk of poverty after social transfers, by country, 2008 and 2014 (% of population), Eurostat.
14. 2016, Total annual pension expenditure per beneficiary for old-age pensions, I-28, 2013 (in EUR and PPS, http://ec.europa.eu/eurostat/statistics-explained/index.php?title=File:Total_annual_pension_expenditure_per_beneficiary_for_old-age_pensions,_EU-28,_2013_(in_EUR_and_PPS).png&oldid=305786.

Delia COSTACHE

Faculty of Medicine – Transilvania University of Brasov,
e-mail: deliacostache68@gmail.com

Cristea COSTACHE

Faculty of Medicine – Transilvania University of Brasov,
e-mail: cristea_costache@yahoo.com

Iudith IPATE

Center for Study and Research on Biodiversity from Animal Genetic Resources Academy David Davidescu Romanian Academy,
e-mail: ipate.iudith@gmail.com

Economic Analysis of Hospitalization Costs in Trichinosis – Epidemiological Statistical Issues to Manage the Zoonoses

Abstract: The accomplished economic survey was intended to follow the effects of cost decrease, targeting clinical, biological and immunological trichinosis diagnoses, hospitalization expenses of patients infected with Trichinella spiralis, costs that are currently generating significant economic damage through negative externalities caused by sick leaves, removal of people active from production, social absenteeism, seizure and removal of infested meat consumption, financial losses being found both in households, household budget and overall economy. The health of a community has become more vulnerable and dependent on the health of other communities due to open borders and rapid transport opportunities to every corner of the world. The transport of people and goods as well as enhanced migration pose a risk that can be partially controlled by health authorities, despite the effectiveness of national policies adopted in this field. Thus, development and health problems of less developed societies may indirectly also affect developed societies. These types of problems must generate common strategies for regional cooperation, between countries, with the support of global organizations, with the objective of finding solutions to global problems or improving community health and living standards.

Keywords: costs, zoonoses, health, innovative solutions

Introduction

The economic study deals with the influence of the diminution in the cost for the clinical, biological and immunological diagnosis of trichinosis, hospitalization expenses on patients infected with Trichinella spiralis, costs that currently generate significant economic damages due to negative externalities, consisting in medical leaves, removal of active individuals from the work environment, social absenteeism, confiscation and removal of infested meat from consumption, significant financial losses both to people's own households and family budgets, and also in the country's economy as a whole (Costache et al. 2011).

The health of a community has become much more vulnerable and dependent on the health of other communities because of the opening of borders and the possibilities of rapid transportation to any corner of the world. The transport/movement of people and goods, as well as the increase of migration, pose a risk that can be only partially controlled by health authorities, despite the effectiveness of national policies adopted in this field. Thus, development and health problems of less developed societies may also indirectly affect/touch developed societies as well. This kind of problems should generate common strategies for regional cooperation between countries, benefiting from the support of world organizations to find solutions to global or community health problems and improve living standards (Brown, 2011; Costache et al. 2011).

Literature review

Trichinosis has re-emerged as a significant salmonella infection in different parts of the world, reminding us that the control of this disease depends primarily on vigilance (Brown, 2011).

The biological diversity of these parasites suggests that scientists and managers need to work together in revising the methods of measurement and evaluation of the biological diversity (Costache et al. 2011; Ipate at all, 2009).

It is necessary to widely expand modern diagnostic techniques of molecular genetics to recognize parasitic antigens in biological products and to expand these technologies to zoonoses with aggressive evolution, especially in the zoonotic geographical areas of origin. It is also important to develop parasitic vaccines, specific to different zoonoses, by creating a prophylaxis medium with potentially reduced morbidity (Brown, 2011; Costache et al. 2011).

Therefore, mastering the risk management in food safety in case of massive infestations and the danger to which the people may be exposed is very important (ECDPC, 2011;Murell, Pozio, 2011).

Thus, according to the European Union (EU) and the World Health Organization (WHO) – food safety is everybody's responsibility, from its origin up to the table; that is why the implementation of new legislation covering all aspects of food, from farm to fork, is essential. Harmonization of national control systems with the European ones on food safety and improvement of communication between consumers and stakeholders are also necessary (Dupouy, Murell, 2007, ECDPC 2011; INSP, 2011).

Material and method

Food safety encompasses a range of rules and laws related to the handling, preparation and storage of food products, so that food poisoning produced by bacteria, viruses, parasites, and prions be prevented. The consumer is at the end of the food chain. Food safety cannot be realized unless responsibility is assumed by all those involved in the food sector, from professionals to consumers. Various procedures and control mechanisms are used along the food chain to ensure that the food reaching the consumers' tables are edible and that the contamination risk is reduced as much as possible. As a result of the benefits of safe and sanogen food, the population is healthier.

Our research falls within the general objectives of the postdoctoral research project, helping to secure the food resources of mankind, observing the principles of bioeconomics and eco-economics for the correct management of food-transmitted parasitosis, developing targeted projects or programs about livestock biodiversity and food biotechnology based on the economic and bioeconomic issues necessary in ecosanogenesis. In the near future, these will increase the visibility of Romanian research internationally.

Aspects of the epidemio-economic situation of trichinosis at European level compared to Romania

Direct and indirect costs generated by detecting Trichinella in animals during veterinary health inspection at slaughterhouses are estimated at about €570 million per year. This parasitic zoonosis is one of the most expensive in the European Union.

According to an investigation of the International Commission for Trichinosis carried out in 2004, 1,100 trichinosis cases were recorded in Europe, out of which 984 came from Bulgaria, Croatia, Romania and Serbia (Dupouy, Murell, 2007; ECDPC, 2011).

The war in Yugoslavia resulted in a complete disruption of veterinary services and an increase of trichinosis in the silvatic and domestic fauna.

Traveling and immigration represent another way of importing infestations with Trichinella from highly endemic areas (Argentina, China, Laos, Romania, former Yugoslavia). Infestation occurs either through consumption in the countries of origin of some seriously risky products (raw sausage meat of wild boar or other venison), or by importing them. Such epidemics were reported in Germany, Denmark, France, Spain, Italy and the United Kingdom (Murell, Pozio, 2011).

Economically speaking, the diminishing costs to establish the clinical, biological and immunological diagnosis of trichinosis, unfortunately, ranks Romania first in Europe regarding an endemic epidemics of human trichinosis spread unevenly all over the country.

Over the past 10 years, Romania has maintained its first place of the annual incidence rate of reported trichinosis, ahead of Bulgaria and Spain, in comparison with other EU countries, as reported by the Surveillance Systems and Epidemiological

Owerview in the annual Report of the European Centre for the Prevention and Control of Infections (ECDPC, 2011).

Analyzing the report on developments in parasitic diseases issued by the National Institute of Public Health, we notice that in 2010, the annual incidence rate of human trichinosis decreased by 50%, compared to 2009. Romania is second in the EU. Questions are still being asked regarding the seriousness with which the legislative measures of prevention and veterinary control of meat offered to the population are complied with (INSP, 2011).

In Brasov County, the number of human trichinosisis cases has been steadily decreasing in the last decade.

The minimum incidence of the disease in Brasov was recorded in 2010, when nobody was hospitalized for infectious diseases (Costache et al., 2011).

The study showed that the number of people who consumed infected meat products, but who did not develop the disease was higher than the number of people who got sick and hospitalized; that suggests a so-called epidemiological iceberg.

Also the maximum number of consumers was also recorded between 1998–2001 (381 cases – 70%), with a gradual decrease in subsequent years (Costache et al.).

The situation is similar in the case of patients hospitalized to be treated. The maximum incidence occured between 1998–2001 (276 cases – 70%). Compared to the doctoral study conducted by me in Brasov for the last 20 years (1993–2002) and comparing these results to the period of the epidemiological analysis of one decade, from 1998 to 2011, we notice that the number of people falling ill decreased almost by half over the decade; thus, the number of hospitalized cases fell from 791 cases to 333. There were only seven cases in 2014 (2).

The epidemiological statistics of trichinosis in County Brasov

An increased incidence of diseases in urban areas, approximately double, compared to that in rural areas has been found in Brasov County. The explanation could be the fact that the majority of the cities' inhabitants buy meat for the winter holidays in the street, without any veterinary examination (trichinoscopics).

An increased incidence of disease has been registered among poorly educated adults, but also among the gypsy population facing low socio-economic level and poor hygiene.

The statistics of Brasov County, in terms of seasonal distribution of trichinosis cases, show a maximum during winter months, due to Romanians' Christmas habits, and it is similar to that at the national level. It is different from the statistics collected in Europe, where, according to the data provided by Euro-Surveille, there is an increase in the number of trichinellosis cases during the summer months (Costache et al., 2011; ECDPC, 2011).

The average duration of hospitalization

Trichinosis is a disease with a strong impact from the economic, social and psychological points of view because both the diagnostic methods and the period of hospitalization are very expensive, which seriously affect the budget of medical establishments where patients are treated.

The lack of information and education of the patients' entourage make them reject the sick persons which may cause depression and isolation. Probably, if the first symptoms of illness (gastrointestinal disorders, diarrhoea, abdominal pain) were not completely ignored and treated as mere food poisoing, and if the patient addressed a doctor, an effective medical history could correlate the patient's symptoms to the consumption of raw or insufficiently cooked pork. The patient would be sent to a specialized medical center where his state of being would be quickly improved.

In my retrospective study, conducted between 1998--2011, most patients came to the hospital with severe and medium forms of illness (83.4%) in need of hospitalization for between eight and 28 days, as compared to those with abortive and asymptomatic forms of illness (16.8%) whose hospitalization was between one and seven days (Costache et al., 2011).

Incubation

Incubation represents the length of time between the moment of consumption and the first symptoms. As the diagram shows, in most of cases, clinical manifestations occur within the first two weeks after the consumption of the infested meat (Costache et al., 2011).

The average length of hospitalization for trichinosis

The analysis of the average length of hospitalization of clear trichinosis cases has shown that most patients need about two weeks of hospital recovery, in relation to the clinical severity of the disease:

- one week – 90 cases,
- two weeks – 152 cases,
- three weeks – 53 cases,
- four weeks – 38 cases (see figure 1).

Fig. 1: The average length of hospitalization in trichinosis

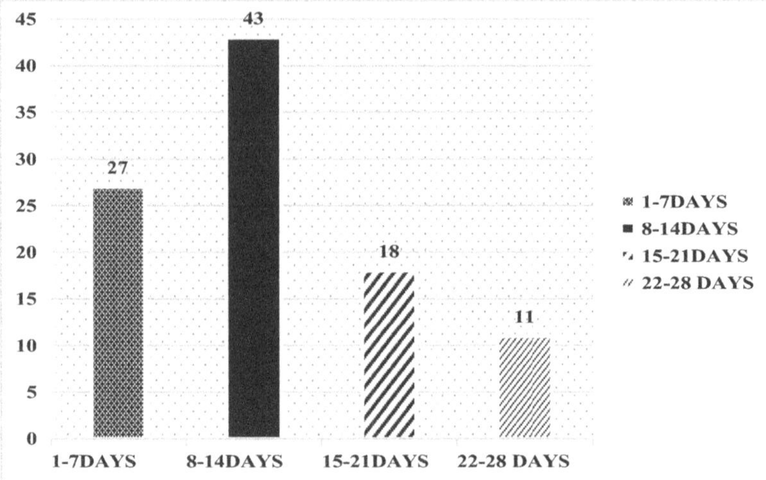

Source: Brasov Clinical Infectious Diseases Hospital

Clinical and economic management of infested patients

In the following paragraphs, I try to point out the economic advantages of the correct management of trichinosis disease, by reducing the costs of treatment for the patients who see the doctor at the very first manifestation of symptoms, not only when medical complications have begun to appear.

A general clinical examination of the patient by a specialized doctor is compulsory at his very admission to hospital. The doctor should carry out a full run of medical examinations of the etiologically targeted patient, followed by a preset specific laboratory examination package; this should be developed on the basis of an updated therapeutic diagnostic protocol widely supported at the national level specifically for trichinosis; the package has to be adapted to the patient's clinical form of severity and evolution of the disease.

Expenditure statistics resulting from patients' hospitalization

The hospitalization period for patients with severe, pronounced and average forms of the disease implies high costs because of the numerous analyses for the diagnosis; a brief inventory of the hospitalization expenses, including food, accommodation, administered drug therapy, medical procedures, sanitary materials, and medical labor is shown below (see figure 2, table 1).

Fig. 2: Expenditure statistics resulting from patients' hospitalization

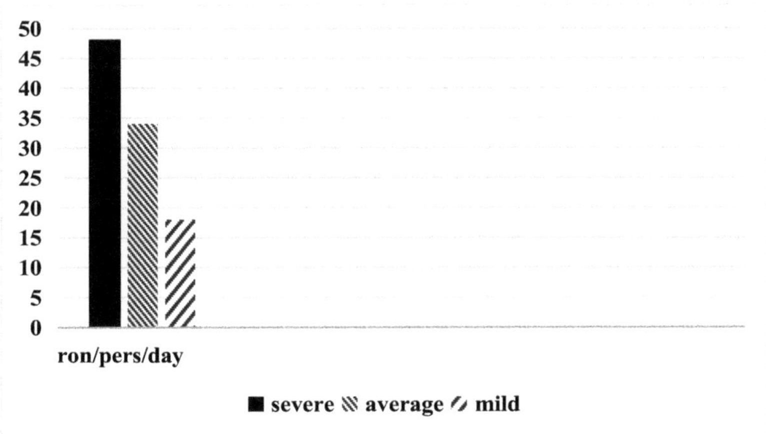

Source: Brasov Clinical Infectious Diseases Hospital

Table 1: Estimate of economic costs of the clinical forms of trichinosis

Clinical forms	Severe	Average	Mild	Total
Number of cases	7	31	14	52
Average hospitalization duration	14–22 (18)	7–19 (13)	2–12 (7)	2–22 (21)
HLG	21	62	14	97
*Costs- 15 ron	315	930	210	1,455
Blood smear	3	5	1	9
*Costs- 12 ron	36	60	12	108
VSH and Fibrinogen	7	31	14	52
*Costs- 19 ron	133	589	266	988
Total Bilirubin	4	1	2	7
*Costs- 8 ron	32	8	16	56
Serum protein electrophoresis	7 + 4 control = 11	28	10	49
*Costs- 25 ron	275	700	250	1,225
Urine analysis	4	20	2	26
*Costs- 10 ron	40	200	20	260
TGO	7 + 2 = 9	31 + 12 = 43	14	66

Clinical forms	Severe	Average	Mild	Total
TGP	14	43	14	71
*Costs- 8 + 8 ron	184	688	224	1,096
R.Elisa	3	23	1	27
*Costs- 78 ron	234	1,794	78	2,106
R.Western- Bloot	5	12	0	17
*Costs- 100 ron	550	1,320	–	1,870
RPL	7	31	14	52
*Costs- 60 ron	420	1,860	840	3,120
Abdominal ultrasound	7	27	2	36
*Costs- 16 ron	112	432	32	576
EKG	7	14	1	22
*Costs- 10 ron	70	140	10	220
Lung X-ray examination	1	10	1	12
*Costs- 15 ron	15	150	15	180
Infusions	26	20	1	47
*Costs- 10 ron	260	200	10	470
Food cost/patient	7*18 days	31*13 days	14*7 days	627
*Costs- 8 ron/day	1,008	3,224	784	5,016
Medication cost	7*18	31*13	14*7	627
*Costs- 20 ron	2,520	8,060	1,960	12,540
Cost of hospitalization days/ related expenses:	7*18	31*13	14*7	627
*Costs- 260 ron/day	32,760	104,780	25,480	163,020
Sanitary material costs	7*18	31*13	14*7	627
*Costs- 11,88 ron	1,497	4,788	1,164	7,449
Other specialty medical checking	4	1	0	5
*Costs- 80 ron	320	80	-	400
*Total Costs (ron)	40,681	130,003	31,371	202,055
*Total Costs/person (ron/person)	5,811.5	4,193.6	2,240.8	3,885.6

Source: Based on estimated expenses/person/hospitalization/day in Brasov Clinical Infectious Diseases Hospital.

Conclusions

Cost analysis (management) of trichinosis patients indicates that for hospitalizing severe and pronounced disease cases, the cost per patient is about 2.5 times higher than the costs for patients who see the doctor as soon as they have ingested probably parasitological contaminated food and would need only a prophylactic treatment.

Costs incurred by hospitalization of average, abortive and asymptomatic disease cases are almost double.

Hospitalization of trichinosis patients has burdened the hospital with about €4,500, that is €86.5 /patient, as compared to prophylaxis, which would have been no more than 50 Ron = €11, i.e. the examination cost of the slaughtered animal for a family.

Trichnosis is a costly disease requiring weeks, even months of treatment.

All these costs may be reduced to zero if a specific prophylactic treatment is applied by the general practitioner or the infection disease doctor as close as possible to the infestation, of course, always preceeded by the trichinosis test of pork immediately after being slaughtered.

It is absolutely compulsory that people eat only sanitary-veterinary tested products and subsequently process meat products by heating. It is also essential to educate people with respect to the risk of trichinosis disease, through the media as well.

All authorized organizations must take appropriate legislative measures in order to achieve nationwide food safety.

They must promote a healthy food policy, in full compliance with the health legislation in force that needs to be harmonized to the European one, to promote the science of healthy living.

Bioeconomy will contribute to enhancing global food security, to improving nutrition and health; it will create innovations based on biofuels and bio-products and will help agriculture, forestry, aquaculture and other ecosystems to adapt to climate changes.

References

1. Brown, Lestern R.: Lumea pe marginea prăpastiei – cum să prevenim colapsul ecologic şi economic. Earth Policy Institute, Editura Tehnică: Bucureşti, 2011, pp. 1–191.
2. Costache, Delia; Costache, Cristea; Bogdan, Alexandru T.: "A clinical and epidemiological prospective study of human trichinosis of patients hospitalized during 2004–2010 at Infectious Diseases Hospital of Braşov", Bulletin of the Transilvania University of Braşov, Series VI: Medical Sciences, Vol. 4 (53) No. 1, ISSN 2065–2216 (Print), ISSN 2065–2224 (CD-ROM), Brasov, 2011, pp. 97–105.
3. Dupouy, Camet J.; Murrell, Darwin K. (eds): FAO/WHO/OIE (Food and Agriculture Organization of the United Nations/World Health Organization/World Organisation for Animal Health) Guidelines for the surveillance, management, prevention and control of trichinellosis. Paris: OIE, 2007, p. 108.

4. European Center for Disease Prevention and Control. Surveillance Report. Annual epidemiological report, Reporting on 2009 surveillance data and 2010 epidemic intelligence data 2011, pp. 110–114, website: www.ecde.europa.eu.
5. Institutul Național de Sănătate Publică. Centrul Național de Supraveghere și Control al Bolilor Transmisibile. Raportul pentru anul 2010, Analiza evoluției bolilor transmisibile aflate în Supraveghere, România, București, 2011, pp. 37–39.
6. Ipate, Iudith; Brem, Gotfried; Bogdan, Alexandru T.; Monika, Gutscher; Seregi, Ianos; Tobă, George F.; Simona, Ivana et al.: Genes assisted selection as instrument of selection for the biodiversity and pooling the genetic diseases (Scientifical Papers, Animal Science and Biotechnologies), vol. 33–42 (1, 2), Editura Agroprint, 2009, România, București, ISSN: 1221–5287, p. 563.
7. Murrell, Darwin K.; Pozio, Eduardo: The worldwide Occurrence and Impact of Human Trichinellosis, 1986–2009, Abstract Book, 13th International Conference on Trichinellosis Changchun, China 1–6 August 2011, p. 37. website: http://www.ict13.org.

Maria MOLDOVEANU

The Romanian Centre for Comparative Economics and Consensus – NIER; e-mail: mmoldoveanu39@gmail.com

Paula NEACȘU

The Centre for Economic Information and Documentation – NIER; e-mail: cide90@gmail.com

Coordinates of Urban Culture in the Context of Sustainable Development of the Cities

Abstract: The paper deals with definitions of urban culture in relation to various fields: town planning, architecture, anthropology, urban sociology, cultural management.

The coordinates of urban culture – in the context of (economic, technological, social, ecological and cultural) integrated urban development – depend on the local context, the typology of cities and communities. Our research work deals with urban culture coordinates in large cities, where social polarization and economic stratification as well as the contrasting ways of living and mentalities are more obvious. Moreover, in cities we find most of the cultural institutions and creative industry organizations – spaces for creating the cultural contents and behavioral rules able to reshape the urbanity model. But there are problems concerning urban culture in localities lacking in economic units, resources, and productive businesses – towns which we could define by the well-known phrase "places where nothing happens."

Keywords: town, sustainable development, architectural heritage, urban culture, social inclusion, participation, urban consciousness, creativeness

Introduction

In various scientific contexts referring to the term "culture" or its dimensions, whether we discuss ethnology or town planning, art history or economic sciences, the most frequently used definitions are those on which we base our research of the concept of "urban culture."

Culture is analyzed as: human activity – "creation of spiritual values" (R. Vulcănescu); process – "economic process for including the individual in the sphere of cultural values" (D. Gusti); system – "system of creative activities in the spiritual domain, specific to the society," as well as "system of cultural goods that from the age style" (D. Gusti); value – "first of all, culture is the expression of the idea of value" (H. Rickert); product – "culture is the product of the mutual action between society and personality" (T. Parçons); state of mind – "state of mind produced by experience, instruction and secular education" (D. Gusti); totality – "totality of knowledge, attitudes and usual behavioural models which the member of a certain society share and transmit" (R. Linton); assembly – "assembly of meanings, intentional action and behaviours" (P. Sorokin).

According to B. Malinowski, an American anthropologist, as human activity, culture and culture sciences are "on top in our century's intellectual restlessness".

Most of the definitions contain the reference concepts of culture as well, e.g., nature, society, attitude, value, personality, knowledge, finality; others imply culture typologies worked out by several authors. Oswald Spengler mentions – besides the Chinese, Hindu and Arab culture – "the western or Fantastic culture," an expression of the European culture.

In other context, we find dichotomous typologies: material culture–spiritual culture, live culture–acquired culture, general culture–personal culture, academic culture–popular culture, etc. Some authors (like F. Chazel) blame the wish to order cultural behaviors around two poles, considering that the criteria too are opposed and express "dominance relations" (e.g., high culture, meaning elaborate culture–mass culture, urban culture–suburban/rururban culture), in a depreciatory sense of the last words.

Reflections on urban culture from literature

To European city planners, urban culture is a sum of preoccupations for cultural economic, social and managerial aspects of a city as an assembly of artistic manifestation and activities disseminating cultural values among the urban population, etc.

In an interview given to Urbanismul (2011), João Teixeira, a specialist in town planning and management, author of speciality publications (Statistical Atlas of Living in Lisbon), member of the Board of the European Council of City Planners, defines urban culture as "an iterative social and territorial process associating artistic manifestations and integrating methods such as communication, social and territorial inclusion and promoting culture in relation to the global citizen, places and urban identities." According to Teixeira, city planning as town regeneration, urban landscape design and social inclusion policies are issues pertaining to this process, which we consider as essential coordinates of urban culture.

The common vision of urban culture, as Maria Mănescu points out, is related to all culture projects and artistic (sports) ones taking place in urban areas. The term "urban culture" does not cover other aspects, such as identity, although the author thinks that there is a city language, an urban semiotics, as famous scholars (R. Barthes, F. Choay, etc.) say. After finding the semiotic elements established by the above authors, Maria Mănescu opts for metaphors to define urban culture: "While the urban ground is a text, the buildings, streets, parks are words, and words can be grouped harmoniously." City planners create texts and city dwellers are great readers, and "the binder of this chain of metaphors concerning the permanent relation between the reader and the text is urban culture" (10, p. 64).

Since towns are diverse and offer experiences and opportunities, the people involved show equally diverse perceptions and responses. Therefore, to understand urban culture, Ger Duijzings (an anthropologist) thinks that researchers must investigate human and social behaviors and interactions, responses to phenomena specific to crowds, individuals' mobility among places (e.g., neighborhoods) and non-places, i.e., anonymous areas such as railway stations, gas stations, malls, bus stops, which are not public areas in the true sense, since they limit some rights of the individuals.

Public spaces play a leading role in creating urban culture, through ideas disseminated and emotions generated by various events (shows, contests, anniversaries), through the psycho-cultural diversity of persons/groups frequenting public spaces downtown and uptown. Sometimes, even the city night life could be studied as a new experience and a distinct chapter of urban policies, as Luc Gwiazdzinski, a Portuguese of French origin, points out in *La ville 24 heurs sur 24.*

Most works define urban culture as an experience, as a "life aspect" as well as a response to urban opportunities (and difficulties, Şerban Văetişi).

The question is whether urban culture means "city culture" (i.e., of the inhabitants) or, more exactly, "cultures in the city." The paradox of the Romanian city, according to Vintilă Mihăilescu, an anthropologist, is that of a city which is being populated with postmodern urban cultures, before having a settled urban culture.

Defining urban culture as a sum of several cultures is accepted by other specialists (architects, city planners) as well: "... I think there is a culture of mine, of the neighbour, of everybody, acquired by socialisation and education" – according to A. I. Spoială, an architect – a culture consisting in the sum and, especially, "the interaction of urban cultures of all the social actors. Therefore, urban culture looks like an apparently articulated system allowing the society to function" (15, p. 65).

In our opinion, urban culture consists of all mentalities and behaviors of the people living in urban areas and all institutions and activities involved in creating and disseminating cultural products (symbolic goods and services), in urban awareness raising, in supporting the cultural life of urban communities.

During the signing of the Charter of Sustainable Cities in Leipzig (2007), the term "Baukultur" was launched; it means "culture of the built environment, of what is built, of building," which defines a type of urban culture.

The charter was prepared during Germany's EU presidency and was preceded by many studies and research works on the modernization of infrastructure, local economy development, employment policies for poor areas, education for sustainability, that is, for responsible utilization of resources and energy, etc.

The concept of Baukultur refers to all preoccupations about economic, cultural, technological, social, ecological aspects influencing city planning and building, and a successful sustainable development policy. Baukultur is a *sine qua non* condition for urban localities to overcome underdevelopment (Mariana Celac) and, equally, it implies the people's participation.

Methodologies, projects and projections

In compliance with the Leipzig Charter, some documents published in Romania (e.g., The Cluj-Napoca Declaration of the Romanian Order of Architects, 2008) support the participation of the citizens in developing the cities and in improving the quality of life in urban areas, which can be determined by raising awareness of "the right to architecture and landscape," the right to art (we would add), i.e., cultural heritage, public monuments, etc.

One year after launching the Leipzig Charter, the Romanian Union of the Architects (RUA) and other institutions and associations organized a debate session on "Culture and Urban Conscience" in order to identify the elements contributing to the formation of urban culture and to model the conscience of the urban population, as well as on the assessment of the capacity of public institutions and local administration structures to formulate coherent policies for architecture, heritage, landscape, sustainable development (Gabriel Pascariu, coordinator of the "Urban Observer" Project of the RUA).

In comparison with the pre-revolution period, G. Pascariu writes in "Jurnal de Bucureşti" that "the present urban landscape seems to have undergone a positive change. In fact, it is the expression of urban anarchy which is taking place and could be the expression of the anarchy of the society, institutions and interhuman relations. The people's behavior in the public area, in general, as they perceive it in the city where they live is the essence of urban culture"(A. I. Spoială).

In 2008, The Congress of the EC Local and Regional Authorities adopted The Manifesto for a New Urbanity that encourages the European territories "to build sustainable towns," cities of knowledge and cultural diversity. We have to understand what "sustainable cities" means, what implications they have for present and future generations, for the saving of natural resources and energy.

The sustainable development of cities requires the harmonization of economic policies with social and environmental policies, cultural policies, reasonable utilization of natural resources, urban heritage protection and stimulation of the people to participate in setting the objectives of integrated development of the cities and promoting new sustainability concepts – "stable economy," "ecological economy," economies in the interest of all the population, to satisfy the needs of each individual, with the least consumption of material resources and energy.

The sustainable economic development of our country has several purposes, among them – according to G. Zaman – permanent GDP growth which "implies a steady institutional effort of high efficiency, high increase of total productivity of the production factors, but mainly the fulfilment of the ecoefficiency criterion to achieve more by consuming less natural and human resources" (19, p. 9).

Several studies and statistical surveys show the role of culture in the economy of a country, a locality, in the rising economic weight of culture in the GDP, as well as its contribution to rising welfare and economic exchanges. In this article on "consensus européen sur le development" (2005), Stefano Manservisi shows that at a certain time the economic weight of culture, especially of the creative industries, in the GDP was higher than the weight of culture in the labor market (e.g., 6% compared to 5.1%).

Reaching a high level of available labor employment, besides keeping the inflation rate at acceptable levels (i.e., single-digit) is a priority target of economic sustainability.

The targets, based on strategic management principle, such as the good governance principle in a spirit of transparency and honesty, the citizens' participation in decision-making, access to information regarding the community and its concerns, strategic partnerships among institutions, equity among generations in using resources and development instruments, etc. help us to build sustainable cities, to implement social, cultural and environmental policies.

As we know, the culture domain exerts two kinds of influence on localities: economic (i.e., generating incomes and economic growth and jobs, "being an extraordinary basis for economic development and wealth creation," as people used to say before the global economic crisis, 7, p. 16) and non-economic, i.e., contributing to the improvement of knowledge and education, the structuring of the system of values, for information and expression of creative capacities, the development of cohesion and the assessment of the local/cultural identity, the promotion of new technologies in people's lives and the improvement of the quality of life as well. Therefore, the contribution of urban culture to the sustainable development of towns includes conceptions, ideas, information, knowledge, and values, models etc. created and circulated by cultural institutions pertaining to public institutions or creative industries.

Their activity is relevant in relation to culture domains, branches and symbolic products, and to the typology of cultural organizations.

Specialists in the culture management (Y. Evrard, F. Colbert, B. Cuadrado) classify cultural organizations and activities into two main branches: (1) arts and cultural services and (2) cultural/creative industries and cultural goods.

As regards the activity nature, the arts domain includes visual arts and performing arts, while the cultural industries include audio-visual goods/services, publishing, design and handicraftsmanship.

The cultural activities or the forms of art/culture are managed by several categories of organizations based in large cities, but in small number or even non-existent in smaller localities, where some type of institution (museums or art centres) or cultural industry (local TV stations or show agencies) can – to some extent – meet the need of information, cultural knowledge, entertainment of the local people.

The cultural activities in the visual arts domain such as painting, sculpture, photography – according to other opinions, architecture and cultural heritage, as well – are managed by museums, cultural centers, art galleries.

The cultural heritage with its two dimensions, tangible heritage (movable – icons, books, and immovable – monuments, archaeological sites) and intangible heritage (rituals, social customs, oral traditions, and cultural practices) is the expression of a concept cumulating creations and social contents, characteristics and potentialities.

The cultural heritage contains the most significant sources of knowledge, information and artistic values; therefore, it cannot exclusively be related to the past and antiquities as it should be understood as a synthesis of the past, the present and the future. In this respect, the communication and dissemination of contents should be supported by competent organizational practices and structures, such as museums, archives, art galleries and libraries.

Besides the social, educational and communication functions the heritage contents may have a significant economic potential when included among tourism activities. The framework convention (2005) regarding the value of cultural heritage for the society considers cultural heritage as a source of sustainable development. At the same time, the contemporary museums are increasingly involved in town sustainability and in successful managerial practice. The case study presented below is a good example.

A case study: "The Museum of History in Bucharest" – story, not fiction

The new vision of the present managerial team "draws inspiration from cultural anthropology" (Adrian Majuru, director).

Designed as an interactive museum as well as an interdisciplinary activity space, the "Museum of History in Bucharest" "combines great history with anonymous history, chronology with thematic perspectives" and provides an imaginary travel depicted on several panels as well as smart mechanisms (like the "counterclockwise" clock) – a story about time, time loss, frame overlapping (day and night), and not about the contents proper.

Story, but not fiction, says the manager, when also referring to the urban space/point where the embassies, as relevant partners, told their own stories.

What people achieved with the Bucharest Museum, located in a heritage building (the Şuţu Palace), from the acquisition to the exhibition and communication of values, from using new technologies to modeling urban awareness and cultural mentality of the visitors, implies keenness in judging, professionalism, innovative management, etc.

The heritage goods are organized with scientific discernment. The historical heritage section contains over 25 collections, such as numismatics, photography, ancient books, maps and plans, decorative art (metal, china), icons and service objects, as well as collections called "Nottara," "Theodor Amman," etc.

The inestimable value of the collections, accessible by means of new technologies, is revealed by their contents. The numismatic collection contains medals and seals – Ottoman, Austrian and Russian coin thesaurus as well as seals of the great noble families in our country.

The Bucharest Museum includes other museums and memorial houses, many successfully reinserted into the cultural life of Bucharest, based on a modern anthropological and managerial vision.

The museum organizes previews and symposiums, concerts and attractive shows (for example, the "Time" multimedia show), book launching and art conferences, conferences on Bucharest, on "Architects and Architecture One Century Ago," on the Minovici brothers and other personalities.

A top museum usually issues cultural/scientific publications, so the Bucharest museum could not do otherwise: the volume called "Bucharest – History and Museography Materials" and the "Journal of Archaeological and Numismatic Research" are remarkable scientific instruments.

Conclusions

Many scientific papers, debates, conferences approach the museum issues in relation to cultural heritage. At the 2009 International Conference on Art and Culture Management (AIMAC), specialists examined the evolution of culture management as a scientific discipline and the cultural research activity in the last decades by country, domain, activity, author, organization etc., and revealed the studies presenting the activity of the museums in relation to the heritage development: "The community's involvement in preserving the historical and artistic heritage of a small Brazilian town" or "The role of art museums: difficulties in promoting them and the artistic heritage."

As regards the arts domain, including visual arts and related organizations and activities, we point out that this domain also includes the performing arts – the most visible ones at the urban culture level, in our opinion.

The performing arts sector includes theater, dancing, opera, music, circus, puppet shows managed either by cultural organizations such as related artistic companies, as well as independent companies.

At the AIMAC, specialists proved that theater was the most relevant cultural activity in the performing arts field, while the theater, music and film festivals have the greatest impact on local economies and on the revival of central city areas and neighborhoods where industrial ruins were turned into complex cultural areas.

Romanian researchers consider the town regeneration between urban culture coordinates and present positive aspects and less successful ones. Şerban Văetişi thinks that urban regeneration and reconversion of former industrial spaces produced "a class of terrace consumers" which is less interested in city history and the cultural potential of the area, so a new underground art and a new services and entertainment culture emerged.

Considering the experience with the Historical Central Area of the Capital City and the Central Area of Cluj-Napoca, Şerban Văetişi thinks we can understand Zukin Sharon's idea in "The Culture of Cities" that culture is stronger and is one of the main occupations in the urban area in the context of industrial decline and internet expansion.

The new cultural/creative industries feed "the symbolic economy" of the cities and contribute to their sustainability. But the architect thinks that there is a small cultural elite consisting of creators and urban public, interested and involved in activities such as exhibitions, previews, festivals, magazines, book launchings, street art, etc. This is a segment of young people, informed, open to positive solutions and aware of the urban problems, of the need to involve citizens in reshaping the public space and developing the community. Văetişi thinks that "reasonable, critical and creative utilization of the public space could be a good start for a new urban culture."

References

1. Boştenaru Dan, M.: "Spaţiul verde redescoperit." Urbanismul, nr. 12–13, 2012.
2. Constantinescu, M./Arţăreanu, M./Eliad, S.: "Aspecte de artă în Bucureşti." Urbanismul (serie nouă), nr. 18, 2014.
3. Dewey, P.: "From arts management to cultural administration." Conference Paper, 2013.
4. Grodach, C.: "Before and After the Creative City: The Politics of Urban Cultural Policy in Austin." Journal of urban affairs, 34 (1), 2012, p. 81–97.
5. Gwiazdzinski, L.: La ville 24 heures sur 24. Regards croisés sur la société en continu. Editions de l'aube: Paris, 2002.
6. Krier, R.: Urban Spaces. Ed. Rizzoli: New York, 1979.
7. Leblanc, M.: La culture à Montréal. Impacts économiques et financement privé. Montréal, 2009.
8. Lynch, K.: Imaginea oraşului. Editor Registrul Urbaniştilor din România, trad. Alexandru-Ionuţ Petrişor, Bucureşti, 2012.
9. Manservisi, S.: Consensus européen sur le développement. Commission européenne, 2005.
10. Mănescu, M.: "Semiologie, urbanism, cultură urbană." Cultura urbană, editat de Registrul Urbaniştilor din România şi revista Urbanismul, Bucureşti, 2011.
11. Moldoveanu, M.: "Contribuţia culturii la dezvoltarea sustenabilă a aşezărilor urbane" (I). Caiete critice, nr. 11 (313), FNSA: Bucureşti, 2013.
12. Niculae, L.: "Spaţiul public, de la zonificare la spaţiul pentru toţi." Urbanismul (serie nouă), nr. 18, 2014.
13. Pumain, D.: "Les systèmes de villes." In Encyclopédie de géographie. Ed. Economica: Paris, 1992.
14. Radoslov, R./Branea, A. M./Bădescu, Ş. et al.: Creştere organică – Studii de amenajare a teritoriului, urbanism şi design urban. Ed. Orizonturi Universitare: Timişoara, 2010.
15. Spoială, A. I.: "Eu şi cultura mea urbană." Urbanismul (serie nouă), nr. 9, 2011.
16. Văetişi, Ş.: "Coordonate ale culturii urbane." Urbanismul (serie nouă), nr. 9, 2011, p. 47.
17. Sapoval, Y.-L.Les activités culturelles, les industries créatives et les villes. pdf, http://www.ville.gouv.fr/IMG/pdf/urbact-villes-culture-2008_cle16a848.pdf. Zaman, G.: "Abordări teoretico-metodologice ale dezvoltării durabile în România. Principii, criterii şi exigenţe la nivel internaţional." in Zaman, G./Vasile V. (coordinators), "Transferul tehnologiilor şi investiţiile – priorităţi ale dezvoltării durabile," Academia Română, INCE, IEN, 2005.

Maria MOLDOVEANU

The Romanian Centre for Comparative Economics and Consensus, NIER, e-mail: mmoldoveanu39@gmail.com

Valeriu IOAN-FRANC

The Centre for Economic Information and Documentation, NIER, e-mail: cide90@gmail.com

Innovative Management and Priorities of Urban Policies

Abstract: The paper presents priorities of urban policies in relation to innovative management and the strengths of this kind of strategic approach. In fact, urban policies are policies for managing the cities and the urban as a way of being. They define the planning benchmarks and directions for the sustainable development of the urban area.

Cities are made up of several components/sub-systems on which sectoral policies focus (e.g., demographic, social, municipal, cultural, environmental). Therefore, at the city level, we speak about a mix of urban policies and not one policy. A priority of urban policies is the regeneration of municipal heritage, especially of the architectural heritage – of "iconic buildings" – as symbols of collective memory. The European cities which signed the Leipzig Charter undertake projects to effectively regenerate and use the architectural heritage as a development axis. Also, it is very necessary to create and value public spaces – elements of the urban framework – as places bearing value and symbols required for creatively living together.

Culture is another priority of the urban policy. Studying the relation between culture and city regeneration provides several benchmarks for formulating public policies and ensuring economic sustainability of the urban world. The entire dynamics of the urban area – from the municipal policy to the development of a creative economy and high technology acquisition – leave their mark on cultural policies, on their targets and functions. The assessment of the outcome of the innovative activity reveals the managerial efficiency in its multidimensionality: material, environmental, cultural, economic, institutional, etc.

Keywords: city, sustainability, innovative management, urban policy, architectural regeneration, efficacy

Introduction

In the last decades, cities have undergone unprecedented quick changes in the basic components – for example, economic, territorial, demographic, social – in environment, in education as well as in city planning and management practice.

The outskirts of the modern cities "are increasingly elastic and discontinuous". The resources – water, air, food, clime – are scarce, and energy is, as we know, the major problem; city expansion causes many dysfunctions, food supply is dependent on hypermarkets and long distribution chains at the global level, while the number of localities trying to turn wasteland into farms and of those trying vertical agriculture is very small.

The capacity of cities to provide strategic services and to develop symbolic goods industries is inequal; the same goes for access to capital and technological innovations. That is why some cities cannot play a role in the global environment.

Major demographic changes as well as people's/the masses' mobility along with the multinationals' dominance cause the gradual diminution in authenticity and identity of urban localities as well as a "dilution" of the "spirit of the place."

To preserve characteristics ensuring uniqueness and independence, and to create new economic models and new forms of social manifestation in order to develop "complete" strong neighborhoods able to solve everyday problems, to revive the local production and to identify proper forms of expressing their local identity, the cities need – according to specialists from the Terreform Urban Research Center of New York, coordinated by Michael Sorkin – a mix of urban policies for the modernization, diversity and autonomy, equity and sustainability of the urban communities.

Literature

Carl Grodach from the University of Texas, Arlington, says that the structures and rules of urban policies are influenced/determined by material resources, on one hand, and by "economic imageries" on the other hand, i.e. symbols, speeches and specific practices, aimed to legitimize an institutional order.

Urban policies take advantage of the institutional heritage of management structures, but they are strongly influenced by local factors (including, for example, interests of the authorities, interests of the cultural management, etc.) as well as specific contextual factors, among which Grodach includes the local economy (economic development level), local institutions and political factors, urban space organization and geographic context, interaction among municipal actors, between administrative entities and various interested groups or even institutions displaying certain economic interests, such as the interests of the commercial sector of culture.

In his paper "Before and after the creative city...", published in the Journal of Urban Affairs (2012), C. Grodach points out that urban development is based on top technologies and smart growth, on cultural or creative industries.

In the creative industries – especially the book industry, architecture industry, IT industry, design industry, etc. – we may identify groups of interests which often guide urban policies through negotiations with the local administration representatives in accordance with their personal interests.

In the last decades, there have been non-governmental organizations (self-called elitist/vanguard organizations, for example, the "Social Dialogue Group") or individuals and groups of interests within certain institutions (for example, the Romanian Cultural Institute, ministries) in Romania which tried, and sometimes even succeeded, to direct, in their own interest, public resources destined for urban development and cultural production.

Brief conceptual approaches

As we wrote in an earlier paper, "the strategy for sustainable development of the cities requires complex, anticipatory, visionary measures, harmonisation of the economic policies with cultural and environmental policies, reasonable utilisation of natural resources, protection/conservation of the architectural heritage, stimulation of competitiveness, participation and innovation" (Moldoveanu, 2013).

Innovative capacity is a characteristic of the human being which can be identified, educated and stimulated "by a motivation intrinsic to the activities carried out." Innovation has been studied by researchers from various fields such as science and engineering, economics, technology, management, marketing, etc. They formulated over 60 definitions of innovation, each of them bearing the mark of the reference domain. For them, innovation means "creation of a new organizational structure," "introduction of new products, ideas, processes, procedures within an organization, group or social structure," "introduction of a new method of action or products with new/improved features," etc. A relatively comprehensive approach defines innovation as "implementation of a new or improved product (or service), introduction (in an organization), of ideas, processes or procedures new to that unit." According to some researchers, there is no definition to comply with the specific features of various domains. But, in any context, innovation can be assessed by the following benchmarks:

- innovation study: creation, implementation, etc.;
- social context: organization, social system, etc.;
- innovation means: ideas, technology, etc.;
- innovation nature: novelty, improvement, etc.;
- type of innovation: product, service, process, etc.;
- purpose of innovation; success, competitiveness, etc.

Innovation results are perceived in accordance with people's needs and attitudes. Some researchers think that innovation in the public sector usually raises trust and satisfaction of the people. The assessment of results implies new objective criteria. Authors who studied the relation between innovation and its effects on urban policies and urban cultural institutions (e.g., Mateusz Lewandowski) point out that efficacy is the basic criterion of result assessment.

Essentially, urban policies are the management policies of cities and of the urban as a way of living. They define the development directions and urban planning benchmarks.

Cities (as systems) consist of several component structures (i.e., sub-systems) on which sectoral policies (e.g., economic, demographic, social, municipal, cultural, environmental) are focused. Therefore, there is a mix of urban policies and not one policy.

In relation to city planning and architecture, sociology and city management, the public space is a concept having many meanings. So, "public space is the non-built part of the public domain for public utilization", it is "a component of free, open or outdoor spaces (...) also including spaces such as streets, squares, boulevards, covered crossings and green areas (parks, gardens, squares ...) or spaces with plants (promenades), rivers," etc. as mentioned in the "Dictionnaire de l'urbanisme et de l'aménagement", Paris (2010, p. 334).

For Romanian researchers, the public area is "an element of the built urban framework which reflects better, faster and more exactly the changes taking place in the society, the evolution of technologies (...), as well as politics, level of living, culture and civilisation of the human groups pertaining to it" (22, p. 4). The author's views on "the image of the experienced public space," expressed in very expressive essay terms, add to the knowledge of the implicit issues included in the specialists' definitions; for example, the public space is "geometry which organizes life, builds bridges that brings us together or separates us," a "daily universe that contains its own routine and preserves surprise," "the recall of the transition along with the recall of staying," "places with preserving memory," etc. (Niculae, 2014, p. 38).

Both the classic definitions and the images-ideas reveal the multifunctionality of public spaces, their significance and role in the city's life, their capacity to axiologically communicate, to reflect values and customs, community practices, features of the environment, tensions in the social environment, "the capacity to link and separate things," as pointed out by Ali Madanipour, city planning professor and researcher at the University of Newcastle (UK), the author of valuable books in the field ("Public and Private Spaces of the City", "Urban Design", "Space and Society",etc.). In an interview given to Cătălina Ioniță, architect and urban designer, A. Madanipour says that "the public space is the basic ingredient of social life," a space able to bring people together and help them be aware of themselves and the others...."

In her book "Green Space Rediscovered", Göttingen, 2010, Maria Boştenaru Dan writes: "Permanently threatened to be replaced with speculative constructions, green spaces should be re-valued, rediscovered, protected and arranged, managed with inventiveness and vision related to city planning" (Boştenaru, D. M., 2012 p. 59).

The book consists of two parts: "Urban gardens and the landscape around the city" and "The Frankfurt Green Belt" (where the Water Museum and the Museum Garden were designed) deals with the lasting green landscape: "Building gardens means living stories. Stories come to end but gardens never do" (Boştenaru, D. M., p. 58).

Projects and projections

Of course, alternative values and visions concerning the evolution of the urban world are very useful, but the priorities of the policies for the cities' sustainable development should be assumed by the entire community and all managerial structures in charge.

One of the urban policy priorities is, in our opinion, the regeneration of the municipal heritage, especially the architectural heritage prevailing in the central part of the cities – regeneration policies focused on the recovery of central zones of the urban localities, on buildings of cultural, historical and architectural importance, facing physical worsening and other aggressions (e.g., caused by developers and homeless people).

Some European cities assumed the regeneration and utilization of the architectural patrimony as an axis of development, including them (with the help of several generations of architects) in various ecological issues and urban design.

Architects think that "iconic buildings" – symbols of the collective memory – could be included in promotional projects as an expression of esthetic values, of the community and the perennity.

Looking for a better management of the urban equipment, the managerial structures of the city face a dilemma:

- to either demolish dilapidated buildings and to erect new ones;
- or to preserve, restore, re-equip and introduce dilapidated architectural buildings in the municipal and tourism circuits, and to turn the industrial buildings out of service, located in peripheral neighborhoods, into multifunctional spaces: exhibition halls, recording studios, second-hand books shops, art galleries, designers' and artists' workshops, entertainment agencies, other public services.

In this context, we could analyze and select as targets of the urban regeneration policies many other creative, educational, training and cultural production activities.

A good example known by the European urban management, mentioned at the 2005 OECD Conference, is Manchester, especially the Northern Quarter. When the city was dominating the world's trade in textiles, there was a large area of workshops and warehouses in the neighborhood. When the trade went into decline, the area was marginalized. But in the 1990s, the North Quarter Association was created on the initiative of the dwellers and the local enterprises. Along with the municipality representatives, the Association assumed the regeneration project, by improving pedestrian traffic, creating new enterprises and public art programs. Today, there are film and TV studios in the Northern Quarter, design studios, recording studios, music distribution shops and other services related to the creative industries.

The experience of the Northern Quarter proves that the Manchester project is a success owing to the periodical consultation of the residents and their participation, besides urban actors and creative experimentators, in transforming/regenerating the city center. Similarly, the success of the Helsinki Project – covering a quarter of 30,000 residents – can be explained by the inclusion of culture in the program of urban regeneration and rigorous management of the people's participation. Both cases prove that the adaptation of the projects to the people's needs and a common existential ideal could ensure what we call participative urban planning.

According to Romanian city planners, urban regeneration and urban expansion are two co-existing concepts (e.g., Simona Dobrescu). Sometimes, the restoration of a quarter or parts of a quarter implies the *de facto* expansion of the urban area or at least the extension of its influence to the neighborhood; the urban itself is defined as a complex system evolving and expressing itself in time and space. The dynamics of this system implies spatial expansion either by joining/adding peripheral zones or by "conversion of farm land" or "diffusion in periurban area."

C. Sârbu defines expansion as a quasi-permanent process when the urban and the urbanity produce increasingly complex rules for the community's functioning with developments on the political, political and administrative planes, and with new cultural and information values, including the extraurban territory (Sârbu, 2014, p. 46).

Actually, expansion means "exit beyond the limits (especially spatial ones) as well as the expansion of the city and its outskirts, larger urbanized areas." According to other opinions, metropolization is a form of expansion just like "the parcelling in the existing outskirts" or illegal building of residential quarters on the outskirts.

All these actions and other forms of expansion have complex influences (economic, political, geopolitical, social, ecologic, cultural, etc.) that must be professionally managed at all levels of urban management.

The concept of "quality of the place" – in close relation to the "public space" – plays a leading role in urban regeneration and expansion.

Being considered a "place bearing functional and symbolic values" (Sapoval, Y.-L., 2008, p. 35), public spaces are very necessary for the city residents' life and activity, including "creative living together" – as some authors wrote.

The Programme for Management and Redevelopment of the European Cities (URBACT) points out that "urban regeneration implies creation of public spaces as well".

As mentioned above, green spaces (parks, gardens, squares as well as green belts) represent an important category of public spaces. They were considered early measures for restoring the relation with nature, for reconnecting urban localities to natural resources and implicitly "improving the living conditions in a modern city."

Created or discovered, located in central areas (e.g., gardens, squares) or on the outskirts, similarly to a belt for limiting the uncontrolled growth of the cities, green spaces provide not only relaxation and silence, not only beauty and emotion, but also opportunities for stimulating human interactions and activities, especially those related to arts, entertainment and urban design.

In the last years, similar projects (e.g., Our Tower, in Iași) have been carried out, mostly by young people involved in restoring abandoned buildings, for valuing an urban area "in ruins" and turning it into an attractive zone with many facilities for the residents. Irrespective of the local actors involved in revaluing the public spaces, be they buildings of historical or architectural value or green spaces, some expertise is necessary. The experts' diversity varies by city, project, managerial vision; we refer to architects and city planners, anthropologists and economists – as urban regeneration includes a *sine qua non* economic regeneration – to culture sociologists and experts in social issues, adding to them artistic personalities from the area or innovative youths, just like the young people who started the above project in Iași.

Culture is central to urban regeneration. The study of the relation between culture and physical regeneration of the cities provided several benchmarks for formulating public policies and ensuring the economic sustainability of the urban world.

According to the 2013 Report of the UNESCO Statistical Institute, culture exerts two kinds of influence:

- economic: it generates incomes and trade, contributes to economic growth and welfare, creates jobs and stimulates labor competitiveness;
- non-economic: it helps to improve the knowledge and education level, to restructure the system of values and to form creative abilities, to assert local/regional identity and to provide models of urban organization, to promote new technologies and improve the quality of life.
  - Both the commercial sector of culture (e.g. publishing houses, antiques shops, festivals, TV stations, art galleries, recording studios, cultural tourism) and the public culture institutions (e.g., museums, libraries, art exhibitions, cultural centers) play a decisive role in implementing policies for sustainable planning of the European territory, as provided by documents issued by the Council of Europe Conference of Ministers responsible for Spatial/Regional Planning (CEMAT), as follows:providing access to information and knowledge for all residents;
  - promoting cohesion by balanced development of the urban space;
  - protecting and valuing natural zones and cultural heritage, as important factors for asserting the identity and attractiveness of the European territory, and for developing an urban economy and stimulating creativeness.

Conclusion

Resizing urban space by the policy for architectural heritage regeneration, by functional reconversion of abandoned zones, by development of the economy and of the cultural production and creative industries, and the local policies for city development, living, education, quality of the environment, etc. leave their mark on urban culture, especially on cultural structures and activities. Actually, the dynamics of the urban space and the effects on everyday life lead to the reorientation and resizing of the cultural policies, of the targets and functioning of the cultural organizations, especially when there is an innovative managerial vision of the cultural system.

Carl Grodach – in a study on urban policies and cultural policy in Austin, Texas – reveals the role of the managerial vision of the local authorities and the contribution of the city community to the economic and cultural development of urban localities. Actually, the extraordinary evolution of Austin and the rapid development of the region began when the authorities recognized the importance of arts and culture for the economic development of the city, and to exploit and improve its image of "world capital of live music." In the early 1960s, the city was famous for its country music and blues, and for the musical institutions.

Following the decisions of the local management, the number of live music places increased, business in music were started, musicians were financed and the contribution of the musical industry to local development and to the city image was recognized, so that Austin adopted the title of "cultural capital of the world." All actions related to music were assumed by the city leadership as "development goods." Structures and services were created to support the fulfilment of the city objectives, such as to projects of the Mayor's Action Group, which provided the strategic basis for the city development and set the economic development targets, thus stimulating small businesses, creative economy and investments in science, research and high technology. The new development projects included the cultural facilities of the city and carried on the strategy for keeping Austin "as a magnet for arts, culture and creativeness" – key factors for asserting the cultural identity of the urban area. The Austin community supported the authorities in all actions for cultural heritage conservation and fulfilment of the program for the smart growth of the city, so that Austin "became a high technology centre from a little university town", thus proving the efficacy of innovative management in several forms: cultural efficacy, economic efficacy, urban system efficacy, material efficacy, responsibility-based bahavior efficacy.

References

1. Boştenaru D., M.: "Spaţiul verde redescoperit." Urbanismul 12–13, Bucureşti, 2012.
2. Brookink, A.: Intellectual Capital: Care Asset for the Third Millennium Enterprise, Ed. International Thomson Business Press: New York, 1996.
3. Chandler, K. A.: "Rethinking the use of the case study in the arts management classroom." Journal of Arts Management, Law and Society 29 (4), 2000, pp. 244–269.
4. Choay, F.: "Pentru o analiză structurală a percepţiei urbane." In Urbanismul, utopii şi realităţi, Ed. Paideia-Simetria: Bucureşti, 2002.
5. Constantinescu, M./Arţăreanu, M.i/Eliad, S.: "Aspecte de artă în Bucureşti." Urbanismul (serie nouă) 18, Bucureşti, 2014.
6. Cooper, J.: "A multidimensional approach to the adoption of innovation." Management Decision 36 (8), 1998.
7. Damanpour, F.: "Organizational complexity and innovation: Developing and testing multiple contingency models." Management Science 42 (5), 1996, pp. 693–713.
8. Dewey, P.: From arts management to cultural administration, Conference Paper, 2003.
9. Dictionnaire de l'urbanisme et de l'aménagement, Presses Universitaires de France: Paris, 2010.
10. Dicţionar de economie, Ed. Economică: Bucureşti, 1999.
11. Dicţionar de geografie umană, Ed. Corint: Bucureşti, 1999.
12. Gainer, B./Padanyi, P.: "Applying the marketing concept to cultural organizations: An empirical study of the relationship between market orientation and

performance." International Journal of Nonprofit and Voluntary Sector Marketing 7 (2), 2002, pp. 182–193.
13. Garrido, M./Camarero, C.: "Assessing the impact of organizaţional learning and innovation on performance in cultural organizations." International Journal of Nonprofit and Voluntary Sector Marketing 15 (3), 2010.
14. Grodach, C.: "Before and After the Creative City: The Politics of Urban Cultural Policy in Austin." Journal of Urban Affairs, 34 (1), 2012, pp. 81–97.
15. Ianoş, I.: "Oraşul ca sistem şi sistemul urban." Sisteme urbane, editat de Registrul Urbaniştilor din România şi revista Urbanismul, Bucureşti, 2012.
16. Kozuch, B.: Interesul public în teoria şi practica organizaţiilor poloneze, Varşovia, 2004.
17. Lynch, K.: Imaginea oraşului, editor Registrul Urbaniştilor din România, trad. Alexandru-Ionuţ Petrişor, Bucureşti, 2012.
18. Mănescu, M.: "Semiologie, urbanism, cultură urbană." Cultura urbană, editat de Registrul Urbaniştilor din România şi revista Urbanismul, Bucureşti, 2011.
19. Mănescu, M.: "Un alt fel de a citi oraşul: traseul cultural Verona." Cultura urbană, editat de Registrul Urbaniştilor din România şi revista Urbanismul, Bucureşti, 2011.
20. Moldoveanu, M.: "Contribuţia culturii la dezvoltarea sustenabilă a aşezărilor urbane" (I). Caiete critice 11 (313), FNSA: Bucureşti, 2013.
21. Montal, P./Noisette, P.: "Une définition de l'espace public". In Dictionnaire de l'urbanisme et de l'amenagement, Presses Universitaires de France: Paris, 2010, pp. 334–336.
22. Niculae, L.: "Spaţiul public, de la zonificare la spaţiul pentru toţi." Urbanismul (serie nouă) 18, Bucureşti, 2014.
23. Radoslov, R./Branea, A. M./Bădescu, Ş. et al.: Creştere organică – Studii de amenajare a teritoriului, urbanism şi design urban, Ed. Orizonturi Universitare: Timişoara, 2010.
24. Sârbu, C.: "Expansiune urbană, dinamică teritorială." Parcelări şi extinderi de oraşe, editat de Registrul Urbaniştilor din România şi revista Urbanismul, Bucureşti, 2014.
25. Sârbu, C.: "Un sistem urban aparte: Brăila-Galaţi." Sisteme urbane, editat de Registrul Urbaniştilor din România şi revista Urbanismul, Bucureşti, 2012.
26. Stan, A.: "Oraşul ca poezie. The city as a poem." Cultura urbană, editat de Registrul Urbaniştilor din România şi revista Urbanismul, Bucureşti, 2011.
27. West, M. A./Farr, J. I.: "Innovation at work." In West, M. A.; Farr, J. I. (Ed.), Innovation and creativity at work, Psychological and organizational strategies, Ed. John Wiley & Sons: Chichester, 1990.
28. Wilson, I./Boyle, E.: "The role of partnerships in the delivery of local government museum services," The International Journal of Public Sector Management, 17 (6), 2004, pp. 513–533.
29. Sapoval, Y.-L.Les activités culturelles, les industries créatives et les villes.pdf, http://www.ville.gouv.fr/IMG/pdf/urbact-villes-culture-2008_cle16a848.pdf.

Ileana-Andra MĂRCULESCU

Doctoral student, Romanian Academy,
email: peridot.andra@gmail.com

Collaborative Consumption

Abstract: We belong today to a hyper-industrial society where we witness, sometimes with no power to intervene, rapid changes in all areas, when the adaptation rule ("the species that do not adapt, disappear") becomes even more valid. Although we refer to a relatively new concept, but with ancestral roots, a prospective niche – the collaborative consumption – becomes more and more manifest. Offering a larger access to products, services, talent and experience, as compared to the possibilities given when each person is a unique owner, the collaborative consumption favors the bond between people, goods and services, which results in the creation of communities, organizations and new models of activity, both private and public. In their turn, these "peer to peer" models (from person to person) determine new opportunities not only for the persons included in the model, but also for communities, corporations and even governments, which should reconsider their consumption strategies as regards the positions of purchaser, seller, creditor, tenant, but without ignoring the profit.

Keywords: consumption, collaboration, loan, network, technology, internet

Introduction

"Society is more and more characterised by 'nothing'. Ever more people seek satisfaction in consumption, but it became clear that it cannot offer the meanings and rewards previously obtained by work. On the contrary, no matter how much we consume, we are only plunging into frustration. The object of our consumption is the commercial 'nothing' consisting of an amorphous amount of things that come from nowhere and are produced anywhere. We no longer have time. This is the paradox: we are so busy that we got rid of everything that had significance for us, and the replacements will no longer give us the satisfactions we used to obtain from what we left aside. We dove headfirst into nothingness. But what are we going to do when this prosperity age ends, as it can already be anticipated?" (Ritzer, G., 2010).

How have we reached this point? Easily: we consumed more quickly than we produced!

Therefore, something had to happen! Crises (be they political, economic or social), information and communications technology, the ever wider use of the internet and of the latest gadgets make us remember Marshall McLuhan's "Global Village" and Alvin Toffler's "Future Shock".

And we cannot contradict them. Today we are part of a hyper-industrial society where everything is astoundingly rapidly changing and the adaptation rule ("the species that do not adapt, disappear") seems even more valid.

This is why, with the impetuous technologic progress, the consumption civilization – backed by marketing in the frantic attempt to keep up with it – determined much greater acquisitions than to cover normal needs, mainly in the most developed areas in the world, but not only there. Thus, huge quantities of resources stockpiled, which were no longer needed, while, paradoxically, the crisis loomed on the horizon.

But, as contradictions give rise to progress, an idea arose in the "global village": the idea of rethinking the allotment of available resources – the "sharing economy", i.e. the joint use of resources.

This is how the collaborative economy appeared, as a socio-economic system developed in order to jointly use resources.

Collaborative consumption, part of collaborative economy

As a system, the collaborative economy refers to the joint production, distribution, trade and consumption of goods and services, by individuals or groups of persons.

As a component part of the collaborative economy, the collaborative consumption as a phenomenon represents a system of socio-economic understandings in which participants have joint access to goods and services.

The "common economy" concept differs from the classical consumption system by the ownership of the consumed good or service, as not all the participants must be the owners of the utilized goods or services. Offering a larger access to products, services, talent and experience, as compared to the possibilities given when each person is a unique owner, the collaborative consumption favors the bond between people, goods and services, which results in the creation of communities, organizations and new models of activity, both private and public. In their turn, these "peer to peer" models (from person to person) determine new opportunities not only for the persons included in the model, but also for communities, corporations and even governments, which should reconsider their consumption strategies as regards the positions of purchaser, seller, creditor, tenant, but without ignoring the profit.

The common factor of all the organizations participating in the collaborative economy is the reconsideration of what we do not (ordinarily) use, as a value-creating opportunity, by an as efficient as possible utilization.

Being in a continuous evolution, the collaborative consumption is based on transparency, trust, authenticity, mutual help and, last but not least, human contact.

Starting from this, we can differentiate two trends: on the one hand, the re-use of the overcapacity of infrastructure, assets, talents and experience through new technology networks, communities and platforms; on the other hand, the re-defining of waste (assets considered unusable) as an opportunity for re-use and/or redistribution.

Thus, more and more models were developed with the help of the information technology, building on-line platforms that were set up and maintained for "collaborative" purposes.

The collaborative economy is manifest in various areas: from production – crowd-sourcing, the practice of engaging a local or regional 'crowd' or group for a common goal – to crowd-testing, and crowd-funding – which may be the most representative one if we consider such platforms as Indiegogo (www.indiegogo.com) or Kickstarter (www.kickstarter.com), which attracted huge funding from persons all over the world.

But the most economically flexible and easily scalable one (from local to global) is the "sharing economy." It allows for whoever has a product or asset which is not permanently used to become an entrepreneur, whenever he wants it, by using communications platforms.

Of course, we all remember the holidays when we lodged in a room at the seaside, for instance, or the commute by hitch-hiking. The new information technologies allow for the setting-up of interactive networks and platforms, whereby the "occasional" entrepreneur interacts with his "client" so that both of them attain their goal when, how and to the extent they want.

It may seem a sort of barter, which reminds us of early capitalism, but which becomes a kind of "extramural" capitalism as it occurs at irregular times.

Starting from the well-known witticism "I need a hole in the wall, I don't need a drilling device" and in order to better understand how the collaborative consumption operates, it is enough to look around us, to the neighbor to whom we lend our car, or who hangs washing on the line we fixed, to the children riding the tricycle given by the neighbor whose children no longer use it, or – if we are to become nostalgic – to the older times' rental of video cassettes which all of us watched at the only neighbor who owned a video recorder! Let us not mention the former "CAPs" (agricultural production cooperatives), with some political nuance, which are sometimes remembered with nostalgia ...

Today, when most of us "cannot breathe without the internet," the collaborative consumption manifests like a virus which "infected" most of us: we read digital books, we watch digital movies, we use virtual recipes of all kinds, without pondering who "owns" them.

Even when we want to redecorate our home or renew our clothes, or even when we need medicine or simply want to understand the meaning of an unknown word, the simplest and easiest way is to search on Google!

This is undoubtedly the most used form of collaborative consumption.

If we try to classify the collaborative consumption within theoretical parameters, we must start by setting some benchmarks:

First, it is necessary to own such goods or services that allow for the commencement of the collaborative consumption circuit. It is like in the market economy: "in order to give something, one must own such something."

Once we know the subject, we need a predicate: "we have something to offer" and we want "to make it known."

Remaining in the sphere of grammar, building a complex sentence requires some adjuncts: what it is, what it does, what can be said about what we have to offer. In fact, this is the basic requirement of the collaborative consumption, which ensures the trust between the owner and the user.

Of course, as we already mentioned, we can consider the collaborative consumption as a return in time, but we must remain anchored in reality, because the information technology has become indispensable like air or water in each and every area. The positive part is that such information technology ensures the public access of seekers (users) to what is available (merchantable). It is important that we renounce any preconceived ideas.

Although we refer to a relatively new concept (albeit with old roots), we can remark that it occupies a niche with a strong future, which has already been subjected to a lot of comments.

The term "collaborative consumption" seems to have been first defined by British analyst Ray Algar in a report on the rational and efficient consumption of resources in 2007, a report presenting the need that most people should reach equilibrium between their own interests and the wellbeing of the community they are part of.

Lisa Gansky herself can be considered as a model of collaborative consumption. Recognized as a successful entrepreneur, she generously shares her ideas about "The Mesh: Why the Future of Business Is Sharing," trying to explain "why sharing represents the future of business:" "traditional business follows a simple formula: to create a product or a service, to sell it and to collect the money; but a fundamentally different model has developed over the last few years, where consumers have more options, more instruments, more information and more power" (Gansky, L., 2011).

Steven Johnson, in his "Future Perfect: The Case for Progress in a Networked Age," tells us how progress is possible and how our future is really bright. The book emphasizes the significance of joint work and how the collaborative economy represents the key to human achievements, which can change the world, from governments to research and development. The main idea that Johnson promotes in "Future Perfect" is that productivity and innovation are best achieved through the collaborative efforts of a peer network rather than the restrictive structure interested in competition or profit. Johnson (anecdotally) presents his idea as a new political movement, avoiding the traditional ideas of the governing circles. Using stories that highlight successful peer networks, such as the emergency call system used in New York City that allows residents to call in issues that need to be addressed throughout the city, or also the story of a system developed by a small group of men in 18th century Britain, that offered incentives to citizens who could help foster innovation in manufacturing and the arts. Johnson also uses examples of failed systems and projects, and then analyzes the cause of the failure to determine how to learn from their mistakes. He shows us that in a hierarchical organization, all of the intelligence is kept at the center of the network, leading to decision-making being non-inclusive and stifling the flow of information. The story of the Legrand Star, the inefficiently designed French railway system that uses Paris as a central hub for all passenger trains, is his main illustration of a failed system. All these stories promote Johnson's idea of a decentralized peer network, one where there is not a clear group or location that has more power or control than another. Johnson argues that a large, diverse group of non-experts will generally make larger leaps in innovation than a small group of experts (Johnson, Steven 2012).

Morten T. Hansen, in his "Collaboration – How Leaders Avoid the Traps," emphasizes what many leaders inherently know: in today's competitive environment, companywide collaboration is imperative in ensuring success, even if it is difficult to achieve. In fact, most collaborative "peer to peer" efforts of companies end by wasting time, money and resources. How can the managers of these companies avoid the costly collaborative traps and obtain the wanted results? Hansen teaches us in his book: by a "disciplined collaboration," for which he offers a practical framework and the instruments to be used by managers in order to assess when to collaborate – and when not to, so as to avoid failures, how to identify the barriers that need to be addressed, how to encourage the people to buy, by making them aim at a lofty goal, how to set up a "T-shaped management" ensuring the collaboration by the work within and across units simultaneously, and to build small, but agile and efficient networks throughout the organization. Based on an extensive research work, thorough case studies and numerous interviews, the "Collaboration" offers practical advice and useful instruments so as to obtain good results in organizational collaboration. The conclusion: a poor collaboration can actually end up being worse than no collaboration at all (Hansen, M. T., 2010).

Referring to the phenomenon of downshifting (still tentative in our country), Aurora Liiceanu pointed out in an interview: "when you have much money and keep working like a robot, when you have more than you need, it is crucial to reconsider what you need (materially and spiritually)".

Rodica Ianole, in her paper "Behavioural Economy – Conceptual Analyses and Experimental Applications," "considers collaborative consumption one of the great socio-economic ideas, with a huge potential in profoundly changing consumption as it allows persons to create added value from shared open resources in such ways that balance personal interest with community welfare". She points out that "Time" magazine placed collaborative consumption among the ten ideas to change the world (Ianole, R. 2015).

Concrete benchmarks

But let us return to the immediate reality:

One of the commonest manifestations of collaborative consumption, which can be found all over the world as well as in Bucharest, is "bike-sharing" – the joint use of bicycles, which is in fact a means to move quickly and inexpensively from one place to another in a crowded city. It is a pilot program, "I'Velo Urban," of the Green Revolution Association, which together with its partners (Raiffeisen Bank and Kaufland Romania) launched an automated bike-sharing service. According to the representatives of this project, more than 200 bicycles can be rented through a subscription and they are available 24/7 in all weather. Users can ride the bicycle for a maximum 30 minutes several times a day, on the basis of a (daily/monthly/yearly) subscription.

If the bicycle is returned after the 30 minutes are up, additional costs are to be paid. "The I'Velo Urban is intended for those who want to use a bicycle instead of the underground, bus or other transportation means in Bucharest. Its users are open, mobile persons, interested in taking exercise, who like to try new things and to understand the things around them. They can be foreign tourists or expats. Commonly, they are over 20 and up to 45. They can be men or women, with medium or higher education. Many of them own a bicycle as well. For instance, a user can use the underground to go to work but during his break he goes to a meeting by the bicycle taken from the automated station" (Andreescu, I., Communication & PR Coordinator, Green Revolution Association).

Another form of collaborative consumption, more and more frequently used, is the so-called "co-working," whereby one shares with other professionals the office rent, the costs of utilities and storage, etc., so that the final costs are lower than with a traditional office building. It is generally preferred by freelancers, various professionals and small businesses. IT or communication experts have been using such solutions – so-called hubs – for several years in Romania as well, in Impact Hub, Connect Hub, Cluj Coworsinessesk and others. A hub has an open space where one can rent an office, plus meeting halls and socializing areas. Besides the low costs, working in the same environment with other professionals can bring new ideas and fruitful partnerships.

Such a co-working area is Nod Makerspace in Bucharest, which was specially designed for those who want to develop, test and implement ideas. It was opened in a former communist factory in 2015 by architects Florin Cobuz and Tamina Lolev. This creative community center includes studios, production workshops, cultural and leisure areas for architecture, design, handicrafts, fashion, advertising, film, photography, software, visual arts and performing arts. Its founders planned to democratize creative design, engineering, manufacture and education. "The idea of a makerspace came from the greater awareness of the need of those who want to implement their ideas but do not have the available resources, such as space, tools, funding, and people to work with or to learn from. The market response was positive, confirming our intuition for the need to create such a co-working space."

The community consists of about 80 active members from creative industry fields: architecture and interior design, object design, manufacture and prototypes, scenography, graphic design and illustration, communication, IT and engineering. The developed projects are quite various, from the design to the production of design objects and furniture, prototypes by means of 3D prints and interactive devices. "The occupancy of the space in the co-working area is about 70%. As the work is organised by the programming of the special equipment and the access is 24/7, the members can arrange a flexible work programme, and the flow of users is so as to allow each member to carry out his activity according to his needs" (Cobuz, 2016).

Of course, the most spectacular form of collaborative consumption is "car sharing," which has already become a trend.

The first "car sharing" programs – the joint use of cars – brought significant savings to their users, but such a service also provided environmental benefits as it reduced the inefficient use of resources.

Sociologists appreciate that today youngsters do not wish to buy cars as much as their parents wished, and the large car manufacturers realized this change in consumption behavior and entered the short-term rental niche. In the United States, BMW launched the car sharing service ReachNow, Daimler holds Car2Go, General Motors has Maven, and Ford holds GoDrive.

"Car sharing" programs have developed since 2011 in numerous European cities, such as Munich, Paris, London, Barcelona or Amsterdam, which involved the collective use of cars as part of what many consider as the beginning of a new era in Europe's history: the era of a rational and efficient use of resources.

Let us take the example of Amsterdam, the capital city of the Netherlands, where an innovative car sharing programme was launched (Car2go). The program is designed to be easy to use and not to pollute the town as it offers only electric-powered vehicles. In fact, any person who registers in this program can locate the nearest electric vehicle by means of the Car2go website or a smartphone application, then he uses his member card to unlock the car and is ready to use it for as long as he needs it; parking is free all over the city and, to end the rental, the car is left in a parking lot, not having to bring it to the garage or to charge it.

Many European governments encourage the development of such programs by promoting their advantages and by funding projects that support this concept.

The car-sharing system reached Romania as well, allowing its subscribers to search for the nearest car through a smartphone application, to drive such a car where they need to go, within a certain area, and to leave it in a legal parking lot. For instance, one year after its launch in Cluj-Napoca, Pony Car Sharing now has approximately 3,500 users. Most of them are youngsters between 23 and 35 years of age, who are technology enthusiasts and use the cars during the day to go to and from their office, or customers who prefer to rent a car in the evening or on the week-end either to go to a club with friends or to go to or from the airport. Starting from the experience in using this service abroad, entrepreneurs understood that anybody would prefer to choose his own route, music or temperature in the car, in the same time cutting his transportation expenses and contributing to the reduction of traffic jams and pollution in the city. "There are studies showing that for each car in the car-sharing programme about 5–7 personal cars remain at home. Thus, the crowd in the streets and parking lots is reduced. As the fleets of such services use only new cars, with low fuel consumption and exhaust emissions, the pollution in those cities reduced significantly."

Statistical data reveal that car sales decreased wherever such a service was active. "Forecasts for 2020 show a drastic decrease of car sales to individuals. Such a service is highly advantageous for those using their personal cars for short trips, mainly within the city. If at the end of the month you calculate the costs of the personal car versus the costs of the shared car, you can easily see that the cost of a shared car is at least 20–30% lower." As regards the less pleasant aspects of this type of collaborative consumption, "until now the shared cars suffered light accidents, scuffed bumpers, broken or split mirrors.

Usually, the community helps us to discover quite quickly the accidents or the cars parked illegally; when people see a car parked on a privately rented place or cars left in awkward places or positions, they call us immediately; one of our employees or even the users move the cars; we do our best to take action in such instances within 30 minutes. As regards the cleanness, by means of the card existing in the car, users can wash it, receiving bonus minutes for such action. "An average number of 50 cars were available in this service until recently, but their number increased by 30 at the end of November. Users want to find a car very quickly. A larger fleet will allow us to have a car 5 minutes away from them, within the service area." A variant of the car sharing service with premium electric cars has been brought to Bucharest as well. It is dedicated to companies, office buildings and residential complexes.

"In practice, a company will be able to rent a car and to decide, by means of an application, upon their users. In their turn, through the same application, such users will be able to reserve the car when they want. Several packages will be available, depending upon the needs of each company or residential complex. We contemplate launching a car sharing service similar with the Cluj one in Bucharest, too, in about one year" (Ghindeanu, 2016).

A special and quite controversial niche of the collaborative consumption related to car sharing ("carpooling," "ride-sharing," "lift-sharing") is the on-line platforms that allow the real time connection of potential drivers with potential passengers who want to go in the same direction, giving them the possibility to travel safely at a low cost (Uber, BlaBlaCar). Such applications are available for smartphone; each passenger can see the driver's picture and name as well as the registration number of the car before that car reaches him.

Moreover, the route can be monitored by an on-line map (GPS), thus making sure that he reaches the destination safely. There can be pre-defined destinations, which the company collaborators make available for users. In their turn, the interested persons can choose to divide the trip (and, implicitly, its cost) among several passengers. In his turn, the owner (who is also the driver) of the car can choose to cooperate with the company during an established period of time, in his spare time or on the way to/from the office or other destinations, which is in the interest of both parties. Although some legal aspects are still to be clarified, we see an increase both in the number of the collaborators of these companies (we could call them drivers-partners) and in the number of users.

If we think of it, this is in fact the recognition of the old practice of the persons who work at a great distance from home, for instance, or who commute: the persons going from the same place to the same place gather and contribute to (or divide) transport expenses, to the benefit of all of them. The difference lies in the fact that they know each other, while the car-sharing platforms require a "monitoring," a "control," as an alternative to the controversial taxi companies, or a new style of transport, which is safer and more civilized.

"The social evolution of the internet saw several stages: first, it allowed programmers to write a joint code, the result being the Linux operating system. Then, people were able to share their experiences by means of Facebook, while content designers used YouTube to share their achievements. Now we are on the verge of the fourth stage, when people realise they can use the same technology to share all kinds of off-line, everyday products. This could have an as great an impact as the Industrial Revolution by the way in which it changes our perspective over ownership" (Botsman, Rogers, 2010).

This is why an ever larger number of sharing consumption sites has been developed lately, in areas that were unconceivable to our grandparents or even our parents.

"LandShare," for instance, connects people who want to grow plants with those who have land to share.

"AirBnB" is a homestay network in which people host travellers in their spare rooms at reasonable prices. In October 2007, Brian Chesky and Joe Gebbia moved to San Francisco and, because they could not pay the rent, they rented their living room to tourists who could not afford a hotel room. Moreover, they offered them breakfast as well. In 2008, a third person joined them and together they launched the website Airbedandbreakfast.com, which subsequently became Airbnb.com. Now, its database includes properties in 192 countries, i.e. 34,000 towns. The site functions as a social network. Each owner has an account where he describes his offer: the price per night, the number of available places, the facilities, pictures of the location, the house rules, etc. Also, this profile includes a map of the location and a calendar of available dates. It also includes a section where the owner can write a few words about himself.

The verification is made through scanned identity documents, by code-verified telephone, by email etc. In their turn, upon leaving, tenants write a comment on the owner's profile, describing their experience in that location, and they can give marks from one to five for cleanness, communication, location, etc. In addition to the "rent," tenants must pay a security deposit, which differs depending on the flat, and which is blocked before lodging and reimbursed upon leaving. Some owners ask for a cleaning fee as well. The accommodation money is transferred to the owner only the day after the tenant leaves, and in case of any problem the Airbnb staff can be contacted to solve it. If the reservation is annulled, the money can be fully reimbursed – if such annulment is made within a certain period of time – or the accommodation cost for one night, or even 50% of the entire cost, is collected.

"Toygaroo" is a website that connects people who want to rent out used toys, allowing subscribers to offer their children access to more toys than they could purchase.

"Artsicle" allows art lovers to rent paintings or sculptures for a monthly fee, the members of this program can find the right artwork for them without having to buy such pieces, although they have this possibility as well.

In tourism, the classical tourism agencies are replaced by platforms such as "Booking," which allow tourists to reserve their journeys more easily, combining the best quality/price ratio with detailed information about locations, transportation and accommodation means, significant price reductions such as early booking or highly advantageous last-minute deals. Of great help are websites such as

"Trivago.ro," which compare the prices of over 700,000 hotels on more than 150 relevant sites. And all this is free of charge, "at a click distance."

We should not overlook the most popular sites, such as "LaJumate.ro," "Olx.ro," and "Mercador.ro," Romanian ad websites, which facilitate selling and buying goods and services in local communities and in the vicinity, at advantageous prices. The ads are free of charge and the users are not obliged to create an account to publish them.

And above all are social networking websites (Facebook being the king) and all kinds of forums.

Conclusions

Due to its popularity among the general public, although the new concept of "collaborative consumption" disagrees with the basic principles of the traditional economic model (the use of a product entails its ownership, and transactions are usually between a person and an organization), what we can synthesize by the term "disownership" is the collaborative consumption, which will allow people to get what they want without owning it.

Thus, more and more new business opportunities occur.

The access to a product becomes more desirable than owning such a product, first and foremost for financial reasons. We can spend less if we pay only for what we consume instead of owning a good.

This style of consumption significantly reduces the numerous negative effects of overconsumption, both as regards over-accumulation (beyond the actual consumption needs), and as regards the environmental protection and long-lasting development.

Implicitly, this type of consumption forces a significant increase in the quality of products and services, in the level of competition, also ensuring an efficient use of resources, time and space.

The final result? Savings!

Of course, it is not all beer and skittles. Collaborative consumption cannot be seen as a universal remedy. It also has its shortcomings.

One of them, especially in our country (but not only), is trust or rather the lack of trust. Social networking or ratings could be of help in this area, when we refer to official sites, or forums which generally gather divided opinions.

There are sites the administrators of which resort to the insurance of the rented goods and offer damages, or take collaterals which are returned if no problems occur.

The mentality of most of us (especially with us Romanians) can also be an obstacle in the way of collaborative consumption. Many of us are still hesitant about this type of consumption, either because of our attachment to the goods we own (which receive sentimental value), or because of our fear of poverty (inherited from past times), conservatism ("maybe we will need it one day"), selfishness ("why should other people also have...?"), or the "misery loves company"-syndrome. Our chance resides in youngsters, who are more receptive to this style of living, to technology, to novelties, to a "chummy" lifestyle and to getting more income with minimum effort (but only if they are not going to submit to the Downshifting Phenomenon!).

Collaborative consumption can also act as a brake for certain products and services, when consumers borrow more than they purchase, thus determining the downturn of actual sales. An example is the discography, cinematography, software piracy, a phenomenon very difficult to overcome.

However, "by its flexible and individual-centred character, the collaborative economy shall assert itself as a form of human action belonging both to the 21st century and to the digital economy, it will develop our creativity and it will bring us incomes in various ways and intensities, specific for each of us. As an 'extramural' capitalism, it will certainly have its stars and its losers, it will prove a great opportunity for the daring people and a shot of hope or optimism for all the others" (Bonciu, Bâlgăr, 2015).

References

1. Bonciu, Florin; Bâlgăr, Ana-Cristina – article published in "Economistul" magazine no. 39–40, 2015.
2. Botsman, Rachel, Rogers, Roo – "What's Mine Is Yours: The Rise of Collaborative Consumption," Harper Collins (New York), 2010.
3. Cobuz, Florin "Ziarul financiar", 22 July 2016.
4. Dăianu, Daniel – "Why does globalisation breed to so many passions?, Secolul 21 – Globalisation and Identity 7–9, 436–438 (2001).
5. Gansky, Lisa – "The Mesh" (Business within a network), Public Publishing House, 2011.
6. Ghindeanu, Demis, "Cariere" magazine, no. 233, December 2016.
7. Hansen, Morten T. – "Collaboration" ("Collaboration – How Leaders Avoid the Traps, Create Unity, and Reap Big Results"), Curtea Veche Publishing House, 2010.
8. Ianole, Rodica – "Behavioural Economy – Conceptual Analyses and Experimental Applications," University Publishing House in Bucharest, 2015).
9. Johnson, Steven – "Future Perfect: The Case for Progress in A Networked Age," Penguin Books (Riverhead), 2012.
10. Young, Stephen – "Moral Capitalism: Reconciling Private Interest with the Public Good," Romanian translation by Mihaela Moga and Bogdan Diaconu, Bucharest: Curtea Veche Publishing House, 2009.
11. Liiceanu, Aurora – "The Downshifting Phenomenon" – interview taken by Eugen Dumbravă – http://frumoasaverde.blogspot.ro.
12. McLuhan, Marshall – "The Gutenberg Galaxy"– Bucharest, Political Publishing House, 1975 (Romanian translation by L. and P. Năvodaru).
13. Ritzer, George – "The Globalization of Nothing" – Humanitas Publishing House, 2010.
14. "Cariere" magazine.
15. "Economistul" magazine.
16. "Ziarul Financiar."

Mihail DIMITRIU

"Victor Slăvescu" Centre for Financial and Monetary Research, Romanian Academy, e-mail: dimitriu689@gmail.com

Harmonisation of the Financing Structure with the Objective of Sustainable Development at the Micro Level. Specific Aspects of Companies in the Real Economy of Romania during 2007–2014

Abstract: The decision to structure the capital presumes choosing a mix of debts and own capitals to ensure a sustainable economic development, in agreement with the evolution of the limitations imposed by the economic, social and natural environment. The theories of capital structure provide the basic directions in this respect. However, a particular theory will not be enough to deal with all these problems. On the one hand, the macroeconomic scenario plays a significant role; on the other hand, internal factors, specific to the company, are at the forefront. Thus, one of the most important problems of companies in Romania refers to the evaluation and selection of models and policies of capital structure in accordance with their current and prospective activity.

This paper provides a descriptive analysis by components of the financing structure, using data from the accounting balance sheets of companies from the real economy of Romania, in 2007–2014. Conclusions include possible scenarios of evolution of Romanian companies in relation with the factors of influence at the macro- and microeconomic levels.

Keywords: working capital, requirement of working capital, financial state

Introduction

In a modern economy, the requirement of resources usually exceeds the possibilities for procuring them. Also, while resources have a limited character, the demand for resources is increasing continuously. The resources, as elements of wealth of a nation, include the financial resources as well as material, human, information and currency resources.

The financial resources represent the totality of monetary means required for the achievement of the economic and social objectives within a given period of time.

At the national level, financial resources include: the financial resources of public authorities and institutions; the financial resources of public and private companies; the financial resources of non-lucrative organizations; the financial resources of the population.

Between the financial resources of society and public financial resources, there is a relation as between the whole and the part, because the financial resources of a society are much more comprehensive. Besides public financial resources, the financial resources of the society also include private financial resources. In this paper, we aim to analyze some aspects regarding the private financial resources of companies, and the balance which exists (or not!) between available funds and the requirement for financial resources. The theories of capital structure provide the basic directions, even though a single particular theory is not capable of encompassing all these issues. On the one hand, the macroeconomic sector plays a significant role, on the other hand, internal factors, specific to the company play an important role too. Thus, one of the most important problems of companies from Romania is the evaluation and selection of the models and policies of capital structure in accordance with their current and prospective activity.

1. Literature review

The financing structure is one of the most controversial and interesting problems of corporate finance, and it was brought up for discussion by researchers with the outstanding work of Modigliani and Miller (1958). Many theories regarding the financing structure were developed using their theoretical framework.

The paper of Modigliani and Miller (1958) was the theoretical basis for subsequent research on the theory of the financing structure. The contribution of different financial researchers and economists further developed financing structure theories, particularly by considering the fiscality (Modigliani and Miller, 1963), the cost of bankruptcy (Stiglitz, 1972; Titman, 1984), the agent cost (Jensen and Meckling, 1976; Myers, 1977; Jensen, 1986), the personal taxes (Miller, 1977) and information asymmetry (Ross, 1977; Myers and Majluf, 1984; Myers, 1984). Theoretical discussions regarding the financial structure of the company appeared in financial theory as three different approaches: the traditional approach, the Miller-Modigliani approach and the modern approach.

1.1. The traditional (classical) theory

According to the traditional pattern, debt has a lower cost than the own funds because it is less risky. Therefore, a moderate increase in debt can reduce the overall cost of using financial resources, because a less expensive resource is replaced by a more expensive one. The traditional pattern relies on the following observations:

The yield rate increases with the rate of indebting because the financial risk increases; when the indicator of debt increases beyond a particular point, the yield rate demanded by the shareholders increases.

The cost of financing by debts remains stable up to a particular level of indebting, then the yield rate demanded by the shareholders increases due to the risks assumed by indebting.

According to this theory, the mean weighted cost of the capital decreases up to a certain point, and then it increases as the level of indebting increases. The optimal capital structure will be at the minimal level of the mean weighted cost of the capital. This traditional pattern doesn't consider the fiscality and ignores tax saving which can be achieved due to indebting[1].

1.2. The Modigliani & Miller approach

I. Theory of financial structure irrelevance (model without fiscality)

The pattern developed by Modigliani and Miller (MM) in 1958 is one of the underlying theories of the explosive growth of financial science and practice. This model regards the neutrality of the financing policy in relation to the value of the company and with the cost of capital[2]. Unlike traditional theories, the MM approach is a construction relying on hypotheses which characterize an ideal situation, which is far from being proved by reality. The conclusion is that the value of an indebted company is equal to that of an unindebted equivalent company, i.e. the value of a company is independent of its level of indebtedness (proposition 1). Thus, the market value of a company is independent of the structure of capital and is determined by capitalizing the expected gross operational result at a constant rate, corresponding to the risk class of the company[3]. Proposition 2, regarding the cost of own capital, expresses the fact that the mean weighted cost of the capital of a particular company varies with the ratio of the debt to own capitals; it is not influenced by the level of indebtedness. Therefore, two propositions of the MM theory show that both the value of the company and the cost of capital are independent of the structure of capital, therefore, the structure of the capital is irrelevant.

II. The Modigliami-Miller model in the presence of fiscality

Five years after their original paper, in 1963, Modigliani and Miller published a second paper in which they introduced fiscality. Resuming the problem of the structure of capital, Modigliani and Miller developed the previous theory, analyzing the effect of fiscality on debts and on own capitals, comparing the value of a company without debts with the value of a similar company which had debts in the composition of the permanent capital[4].

---

1 Brezeanu, Petre, Management financiar, *Managementul deciziilor de finanţare*, Ed. Universităţii Româno-Britanice, Bucureşti, 2005 p. 46.

2 Dragota, Mihaela, *Decizia de investire pe piaţa de capital*, Ed. ASE, Bucureşti, 2006, p. 65.

3 Modigliani, F.; Miller, M. H., *The Cost of Capital, Corporate Finance and Theory of Investment*, pp. 268–269.

4 Ivanescu, Dan Nicolae, *Factorii determinant ai structurii financiare*, Editura ASE, Bucureşti, 2007, p. 13.

The conclusions of the two economists are formulated in two propositions:

Proposition 1: The value of a company with debts is equal with the value of a company without debts from the same class of risks, plus the gain due to the effect of financial leverage. This gain is obtained by multiplying the interest rate with the tax rate on company profit and it represents the fiscal saving. As the fiscal saving increases with the rate of indebtedness, the company may increase its value by replacing own funds with debt.

Proposition 2: The cost of own capital of a company with debts is equal to the cost of capital of a company without debts from the same class of risks, plus a risk premium which depends on the difference between the cost of own capital of a company without debts and the cost of borrowed capital, the rate of financial leverage, and profit tax rate.

This theory suggests that for a 100% rate of indebtedness, the mean weighted cost of the capital is minimal, and the value of the company is maximal, i.e. maximal indebting is necessary in order to benefit from the advantages provided by fiscal saving[5]. In the hypothesis of taxation, the financial structure is no longer neutral because, while the interest can be deducted from taxable profit, the mean weighted cost of the capital for a company with debts decreases with the decrease in the real cost of interests with fiscal savings, therefore; the financial structure influences the value of the company[6]. However, it is unrealistic to consider that the managers must work to increase the rate of indebtedness up to a higher limit, so as to maximize the total value of the company. As the rate of indebtedness increases, the position of the company in relation to its business partners changes, and the value of the company decreases automatically, because of the higher financial risk and the implicit risk of bankruptcy. In other words, the value of the indebted company increases with the actual value of fiscal savings and decreases with the value of bankruptcy costs[7].

III. Extensions of the theory of the optimal capital structure (personal tax)[8]

In a paper published in 1977 in the Journal of Finance, M. H. Miller takes into account company fiscality and the personal fiscality of the investor[9]. Miller's model

5 Tudose, Mihaela-Brandusa, *Gestiunea capitalurilor întreprinderii. Optimizarea structurii finaciare*, Ed. Economica, Bucureşti, 2006, pp. 129–132.

6 Dragota, Mihaela, *Decizia de investire pe piaţa de capital*, Editura ASE, Bucureşti, 2006, p. 47.

7 Dinesh Prasad Gajurel, "Capital Structure Management in Nepalese Enterprises," Master's Degree Thesis, Kathmandu: Faculty of Management, Tribhuvan University, 2005.

8 Tudose, Mihaela-Brandusa, *Gestiunea capitalurilor intreprinderii. Optimizarea structurii financiare*, Ed. Economica, Bucureşti, 2006, p. 134.

9 Petre Brezeanu, *Management financiar. Managementul deciziilor de finanţare*, Ed. Universităţii Romano-Britanice, Bucureşti, 2005, p. 47.

(1977)[10] changes some of the conclusions of the classical model of Modigliani and Miller, by taking into consideration the fiscality on the personal incomes of the investors as well.

Companies which develop strategies based on non-indebtedness or on a low indebtedness rate will have as a "market" those investors whose income levels place them at higher taxation levels, while companies with heavy debts will find investors among people with lower taxable incomes. In other words, companies paying high rates of dividends will be preferred by tax-exempted investors or by investors with lower taxable income, while companies which are not paying high rates of dividends will be preferred by investors with higher levels of taxable income.

In conclusion, Miller's theory says that companies with less debts will attract shareholders whose taxation rate on personal income exceeds the taxation rate on company profit and, vice versa, investors with lower taxation rates will prefer corporate indebtedness to personal one[11].

1.3. Current theories on capital structure

Other trends, emerged in the 1970s, such as the theory of signal and agency, allow us to analyze practices of company financing and of establishing the financial structure by taking into consideration potential conflicts between different holders of financial titles: managers, shareholders and creditors. Besides, the trade-off theory and the pecking order theory, as well as a recent one, the market timing theory, also appeared.

I. The trade-off theory[12] – also called the theory of balancing fiscal advantages from indebting and bankruptcy costs – appeared following the criticisms at the theory of F. Modigliani and H. M. Miller. The new elements introduced in research were profit tax, deductibility of expenditure with interest rates and the cost of financial difficulties (the bankruptcy cost); thus, the theory capitalizes on the fiscal advantage of financing by indebting.

The classical version of the trade-off theory was founded by A. Kraus and R. H. Litzenberger (1973); according to this theory, the optimal level of indebtedness reflects a balance between the fiscal advantages of indebtedness and bankruptcy costs. They have shown that, for a specific period of time (for instance, one year), the market value of an indebted company is equal to the market value of a company with no debts, plus the updated value of the fiscal advantage of indebtedness, minus the updated value of bankruptcy costs. Later on, S. Myers (1984) said that a company which follows the hypotheses of the trade-off theory sets a target rate

---

10 Miller, M.H., "Debt and taxes", *Journal of finance*, no. 2, 1977, pp. 261–275.

11 Dragota, Mihaela, *Decizia de investire pe piaţa de capital*, Editura ASE, Bucureşti, 2006, pp. 84–85.

12 In some works in Romania, the formulation provided by the theory of compromise, "balance," based on the translation of "trade-off," is used.

of indebtedness (implicitly a target/optimal financial structure); the target rate of indebtedness can be determined by trading off the bankruptcy costs against the advantages obtained by reducing the tax on the profit from interests.

Also, J. Scott (1977) made contributions to the development of this theory. Admitting that a higher rate of using the borrowed funds amplifies the bankruptcy risk and the financial risks, he says that the theory proves its applicability to the big companies, capable of generating larger profits. On the other hand, R. Pettit and R. Singer (1985) said that the trade-off theory loses applicability to small companies, less susceptible of having big profits.

As a final development, the trade-off theory postulates that a company will borrow up to the moment when the marginal value of the fiscal advantages of the loans is balanced by the increase in the updated value of bankruptcy costs (Myers, 2001; Brealey et al., 2006).

II. The agency theory founded by M. Jensen and W. Meckling (1976) relied on the prerequisite that the previous theories are theoretically unlikely and impossible to be tested empirically. The new research vision is that between the shareholders and the agents, there is an agency-type relation; the managers – as agents for the shareholders – have to act in their interest. The managers, however, don't always act according to the interest of the shareholders; rather they aim at private benefits (higher wages, bonuses, job safety and drawing in assets or cash flows). Although the shareholders can deter such transfers of value (by supervising, monitoring and through control mechanisms), the perfect monitoring of the managers is yet to be accomplished. Furthermore, these mechanisms generate specific costs which don't only decrease company's incomes, but also influence the capital structure.

The founders (Jensen and Meckling, 1976) showed that the optimal structure of capital was the result of a trade-off between benefits (management discipline) and agency costs under the conditions of increasing financing by indebtedness (when the shareholders assume additional risks).

Subsequent researches by M. Harris and A. Raviv (1990) showed that the divergent interests of managers and shareholders may also be the result of disagreements on the decision of continuing the activity. They showed that while shareholders (the creditors) will want to liquidate the company when the cash flows are not enough, managers will always want to go on with the activity. Synthesizing, it was shown that the level of indebtedness is directly proportional to company value, with a probability of default, with available cash flows and with the managerial reputation, and that the level of indebtedness is inversely proportional to the development opportunities and with the probability of reorganizing the companies in default.

Analyzing the problem in terms of company size, it was shown that in the case of small companies, the conflicts of interest between shareholders and creditors can be particularly serious; this happens because most of the small companies' managers are also the owners (which means null or very low agency costs). In such situations, the creditors may ask for additional collaterals (Ang, 1992).

Thus, the structure of assets is analyzed in direct correlation with the costs of possible financial difficulties; if a company invests mainly in corporeal assets (lands and fixed means), the possible costs induced by possible financial difficulties will be lower; however, a company making investments mainly in non-corporeal assets will have higher costs induced by possible financial difficulties.

Subsequent developments, considering the company as a heterogeneous gathering of interests, have shown that the source of inter-agent conflicts lies in the separation of management from finance, of property from control. From this perspective, the capital structure is significantly influenced by the existence and functioning of mechanisms of corporate governance. Although most studies in this field analyzed the situation in developed countries, some also surveyed the developing or transition countries (in which they showed that the mechanisms of corporate governance were practically inexistent).

III. The pecking order theory was launched in 1961, based on the idea that the order of the financing sources is important, not their proportion (which resulted from an exhaustive study of how US companies set their capital structure).

The traditional version of the theory relies on the idea that the company can't set a target value for debt. Myers (1984) introduced an expanded version of the theory in the context in which the asymmetric information between managers and investors causes costs of adverse selection (defining the financing hierarchy for new projects).

This theory has been subsequently developed as an alternative to the trade-off theory (Myers and Majluf, 1984). Companies prioritize their sources of financing for new projects, in conditions of asymmetric information, first preferring internal financing, and then debt, lastly raising equity.

The novelty was the asymmetry of information, which means that managers are more easily informed on the state of the company than external investors. The underlying hypotheses of the pecking order theory are that the capital markets are perfect; there are no transaction costs; the market value of shares depends on the information available on the market; the company has investment opportunities which it has to finance. Starting from these hypotheses, the theory postulates that companies prefer internal financing when available, and if external financing is required, the available means will be selected according to their level of risk.

Because it is presumed that the investors don't know the true value of the assets and of the development opportunities, they cannot correctly assess the shares issued by the company to finance new investments. Concretely, if companies have to finance new investment projects by issuing shares, their undervaluation could be so large, that the new investors would obtain a higher value for their shares than the net updated value of the new project, which means a net loss for existing shareholders; consequently, even if the net updated value of the project is positive, it will be dropped; underinvestment can be avoided by using other sources of financing which are not strongly undervalued by the market (internal funds, riskless loans and even low-risk loans). Thus, according to the pecking order theory, companies first use internal funding, then low-risk loans, lastly raising equity as a last resort.

Subsequent research (Halov and Heider, 2006) showed that big companies were confronted with lower adverse selection costs than smaller companies (in a context of risky debts). Considering that smaller companies are less "transparent", M. Psillaki (1995) shows that they incur higher costs due to information asymmetry, as also concluded by R. Pettit and R. Singer (1985) who, assuming that the classification of a company was based on periodical financial statements, said that small companies usually have higher costs due to information asymmetry.

More recently, for the developed countries, J. Chen (2004) and N. Delcoure (2007) developed a "new pecking order theory" characterized by funding economic units from unassigned profit, own capital and, lastly, long-term debts.

IV. Theories based on the correlation between capital structure and company strategy rely on two classes of models which explain capital structure depending on the factors associated to company organization and to industrial strategy. The first model deals with the relation between capital structure and growth strategy on the market for goods and services. The second one deals with the relation between capital structure and the characteristics of inputs and outputs from the production system.

This approach relies on the influence of debt on the strategic variables and on the relations between suppliers and consumers. The strategic variables are price and amount. The company strategy is thus determined to influence the attitude of competitors. This is why capital structure influences the strategy and results of any company at market equilibrium. Regarding the characteristics of the production process, the capital structure can have an effect on the availability of a good or service and on the process of negotiation between directors and suppliers.

J. A. Brander and T. R. Lewis (1986) show that, within a competitive economy, oligopolies are tempted to be more indebted than monopolies. J. Glazer (1989) supports this result and shows that debt tends to accumulate in the long run. However, with tacit understanding, debt is reduced and the indebting capacity increases with demand elasticity.

Theoretically, the models established on organizational and industrial considerations provide very interesting results for choosing a capital structure. Both models explain the relation between capital structure and the characteristics of the offer, demand and power of competition within a sector or branch of activity. The main results of these debates have shown that leverage increases when the product manufactured by the company is not unique and doesn't require special knowledge (Titman, 1984; Titman and Wessels, 1988), when it is proportional to the elasticity of the demand for the product (Maksimovic, 1988), when the workers manufacturing the good are polyvalent (Sarig, 1998), when the brand image of the good is not a basic concern for the company.

All the theories grounded on the correlation between capital structure and the production factors market (goods and merchandises) include new coordinates in research: role of non-financial actors and design of the financial structure ("the stakeholder theory"), industrial organization and the strategic management of the companies. A. Istaitieh and J. M. Rodriguez-Fernandez (2006) showed that the influences between the production factors market and corporative financial decisions are bilateral; the two have also shown that there are correlations between financial structure and the level of industrial concentration (horizontal/vertical integration), as well as between financial structure and the policy in the field of competition.

The theoretical research in this field revealed conflicts of interest not just between the agents within a company (between managers and shareholders, for instance), but also between the agents outside the company (such as those between the competitors and consumers).

M. Campello (2003) points out that only some of the theoretical formulations have been examined empirically, and their direct testing is a hard task, because it is difficult to determine whether transformations in the competition were due to the funding decisions of a particular company. Supposing that the timing, extent and consequences of macroeconomic shocks cannot be fully predicted by the market competitors, M. Campello analyzed the sensitiveness of sales increases to the change in the rate of indebtedness of different industries. His conclusion is that financial structure can affect company performance on the market, because different sources of funding affect the competitive capacity of companies.

Looking back, we can say that the validity of a theory is derived from its resistance to attempts of contradicting it; however, the resistance to criticisms was not the only pattern of theory validation; in order to make progress in research, there was no strict limitation to the negative heuristic (relying on denials, rejections, criticisms), the positive heuristic being also used, which complemented and improved the financial theory (new variables introduced in analysis, as shown above).

Transformations in the global society reoriented (even stimulated) the fundamental research on financial theory. The research was directed towards the effect of macroeconomic conditions on the decision to select a particular mix of funding sources. For instance, crises required reconsideration of the risks involved in various forms of funding, which a company might assume. The mutations in the structure of company funding and their impact on the risks aimed at the manner of managing the sources of funding and the fund use in terms of cash flow (Minsky, 1992), the analysis of financial fragility, not just at company level, but also at the level of the national economy, in the context of different stages of the economic cycle – refreshment, boom, crash (Foley, 2003) – the description of so-called moments of dynamic processes, using the balance of net financial flows and coefficients (rates) of liquidity and solvency at company level and at the aggregate level as analytical instruments (Dieci et al., 2005; Sordi and Vercelli, 2006, 2010; Vercelli, 2009), the role of risk management instruments in conditions of capital market integration, because the increase of risk level generates vulnerability (Brezeanu and Al Essawi, 2011).

These new directions reveal that, under the conditions of a higher impact of macroeconomic factors on the financial structure of companies, companies will have to adopt a more prudent financial policy to support risk minimization for an easier control of financial vulnerability.

Sustainable development was another new and radical challenge for human society at the beginning of the 3rd millennium B. C.. Correlated with this underlying problem, there is an operational problem: funding a sustainable economic activity. Thus, in financial matters, the concerns dropped out the preoccupation for optimality in favor of sustainability. The analyses (Dinga, 2009) aimed at both the sustainability of funding sources, and the design of a sustainable funding portfolio, able to include different sources of funding which enable decision-makers to choose (according to economic and financial context) an adequate funding package. Similarly, A. Sen (2010), admitting that funding through debts is neither stable, nor sustainable, claimed that the world's economic and financial system needs a more prudent funding, to support a more stable, although feeble, rate of growth.

After four decades of agitation regarding the fundamentals of company funding theories, accepting S. Myers' postulate (2001) that no theory is universally valid, and admitting that there is no reason to justify the emergence of such a theory, the researchers reoriented themselves towards the level of empirical analyses, trying to bring evidence in favor of previously formulated theories. Thus, we witnessed a shift of concerns from the theoretical to empirical analysis, when the area of econometric models (used to evaluate the direction and intensity of influences) increased considerably.

In the context of the transformations which have marked the economic and social life after 2007, we are witnessing the reorientation of research towards company funding: the impact of funding through debts on the financial vulnerability of the company. The old challenge (proportion of debt in the whole funding of the company) was ignored and made room for a new challenge (financial vulnerability of the company); the new target was the research of the real effect of funding in the context of new micro- and macroeconomic coordinates.

2. Determination of the working capital and of the need for working capital for companies from the real economy in Romania

Irrespective of its source, financial resources are seen in a dual manner within companies, as capital (actual or potential source to be used in the economic circuit of the company) and as a source (debt). Any company needs working capital (requirement of working capital) for its current activity and, at the same time, it can generate, by the existence of the fixed capital, a flow of financial resources (working capital); the theoretical aspects of these concepts are mentioned in the appendix.

Based on the data from balance sheets of companies from the real economy of Romania, the two basic indicators which influence financial balance were determined. In order to reflect the impact of external sources on the requirement for working capital (credit, mainly) we eliminated from the calculations the value of credit as reflected in the annual balance sheet of companies.

a. For companies ranked by size

- For large companies

The chart below shows the evolution of working capital and the requirement for working capital for the large companies from the real economy in Romania, in 2007–2014.

Fig. 1: Evolution of working capital and of the requirement for working capital (average values per company) for large companies from the real economy in Romania, 2007–2014 (chain index)

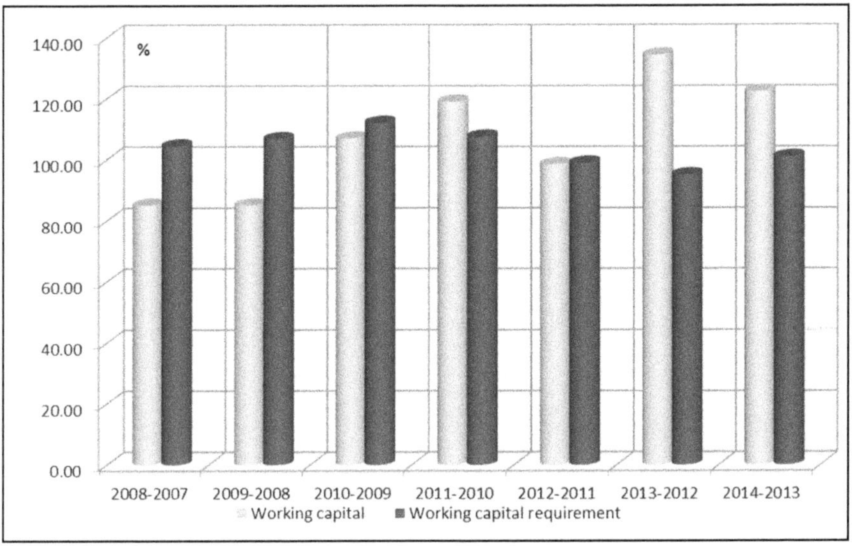

Source: Own calculations, using data from balance sheets of active companies from the real economy in Romania, in 2007–2014; data from the Ministry of Public Finance.

- For SMEs

The chart below shows the evolution of working capital and the requirement for working capital for small and medium companies from the real economy in Romania, in 2007–2014.

Fig. 2: Evolution of working capital and of the requirement for working capital (average values per company) for small and medium companies from the real economy in Romania, 2007–2014 (chain index)

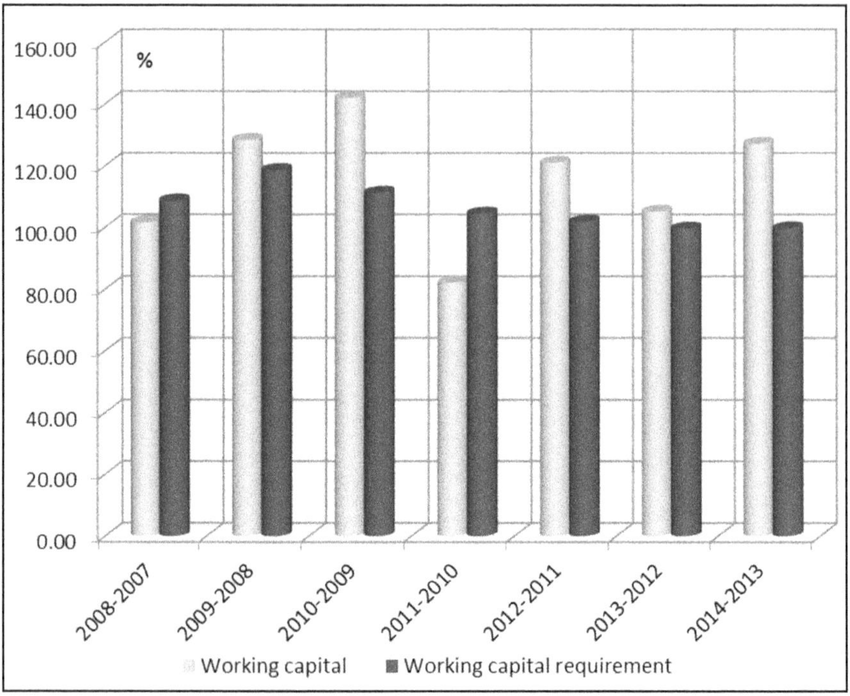

Source: Own calculations, using data from balance sheets of active companies from the real economy in Romania, in 2007–2014; data from the Ministry of Public Finance.

- For micro-companies

The chart below shows the evolution of working capital and the requirement for working capital for micro-companies from the real economy in Romania, in 2007–2014.

Fig. 3: Evolution of working capital and of the requirement for working capital (average values per company) for micro-companies from the real economy in Romania, 2007–2014 (chain index)

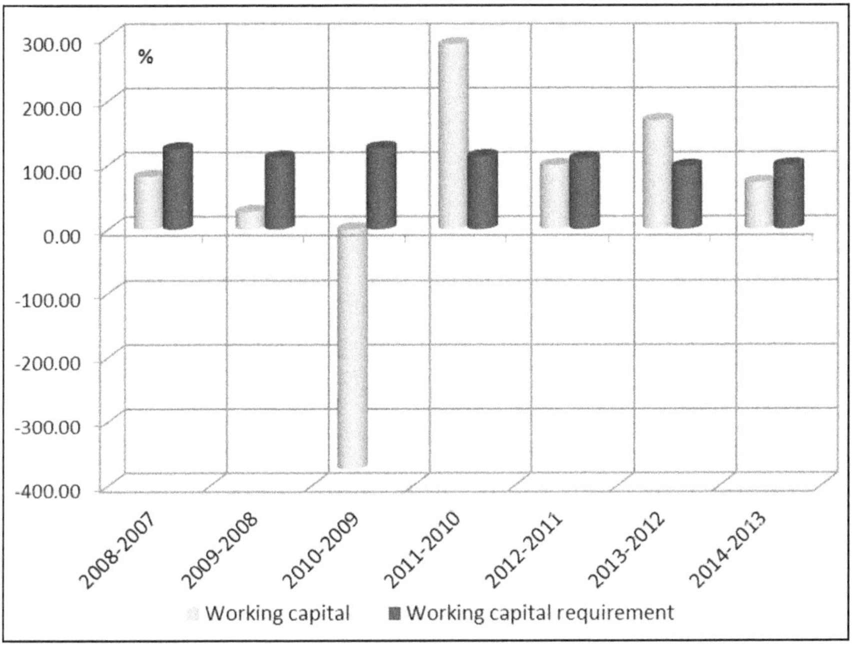

Source: Own calculations, using data from balance sheets of active companies from the real economy in Romania, in 2007–2014; data from the Ministry of Public Finance.

The comparative analysis of these charts shows that, on average, there is an imbalance between the requirement for working capital and the working capital, which reflects the volume of external sources required to reach financial balance.

b. For companies ranked by area of activity

The area of activity is a major factor for the structure of working capital and for the requirement for the working capital of any company. The table below shows the rate of global financing of companies from the real economy in Romania (excluding the impact of crediting).

Table 2: Rate of global financing of companies (average per company) from the real economy in Romania by branch, 2007–2014 (%)

No. crt.	Branch	Period							
		2007	**2008**	**2009**	**2010**	**2011**	**2012**	**2013**	**2014**
1	Agriculture, forestry and fishery	11.54	10.83	12.23	14.3	13.01	14.475	12.83	12,88
2	Extractive industry	11.63	5.26	−0.14	−3.01	−4.15	−2.04	−1.15	−0,65
3	Processing industry	5.89	2.58	2.01	3.6	1.03	0.78	3.18	3,86
4	Production and supply of electric power, heating, gases, warm water and conditioned air	17.62	18.25	14.35	3.72	5.11	5.84	1.42	6,38
5	Water supply, city cleaning, garbage disposal, decontamination activities	2.81	23.94	46.12	52.18	50.69	49.09	53.63	65,12
6	Constructions	11.54	12.51	11.18	10.62	9.95	10.25	2.17	9,31
7	Wholesale and retail car and motorcycle repair	7.78	6.06	5.48	6.38	5.53	6.29	6.95	9,48
8	Transport and storage	27.7	22.76	16.42	11.97	8.91	17.82	25.79	33,73
9	Hotels and restaurants	−6.85	−9.22	−10.66	−10.75	−12.73	−11.09	−10.13	−6,25
10	Information and telecommunications	10.49	5.3	3.4	5.71	−5.43	5.17	9.1	20,72
11	Real estate, leasing and services to companies mainly	−1.93	3.77	−4.08	−6.1	−15.56	−23.04	−22.32	−23,55
12	Professional, scientific and technical activities	19.46	18.31	18.16	19.81	17.82	23.45	24.83	32,3
13	Administrative activities and services, support services	56.13	45.01	13.21	14.85	43.54	36.99	37.83	47,83

No. crt.	Branch	Period							
		2007	**2008**	**2009**	**2010**	**2011**	**2012**	**2013**	**2014**
14	Education	10.71	3.3	3.02	42.42	40.86	31.42	23.75	44,9
15	Healthcare and social assistance	2.85	−0.86	−6.27	−11.79	−10.36	−9.72	−4.45	0,2
16	Shows, culture and leisure activities	4.46	6.42	5.68	1.43	−0.58	−9.5	2.84	5,21
17	Other activities of the national economy	−12.2	−15.53	−21.92	−24.16	−23.04	−20.7	−19.19	−19,31
Real economy – total		**10,37**	**8.91**	**6.96**	**6.72**	**5.91**	**6.17**	**7.34**	**10.25**

Source: Own calculations, using data from balance sheets of active companies from the real economy in Romania, in 2007–2014; data from the Ministry of Public Finance.

There are branches where the level of global funding increased significantly during the analyzed period (such as water supply, city cleaning, garbage disposal, decontamination activities, + 62.31%), but there are also branches with negative evolutions (real estate, – 21.62%). This situation is due to the evolution of the crediting process which, in its broad sense (including commercial credit), was translated into increase in short-term debts.

According to previous analyses (see the project Financial state of Romania, 2015, "Victor Slăvescu" Centre for Financial and Monetary Research, the Romanian Academy), the general situation of the real economy of Romania is as shown in table below.

Table 2: Dynamics of the self-funding rate, of the general indebting rate and of the debt rate for companies from the real economy, 2007–2014 (%)

No.	Indicator	2007	2008	2009	2010	2011	2012	2013	2014
1	Rate of self-funding	14.37	13.77	15.57	17.55	17.50	20.46	30.99	31.71
2	General indebting rate	371.84	391.80	322.73	283.17	293.77	258.73	203.06	192.15
3	Debt rate	164.28	160.38	105.20	73.87	72.57	58.85	69.01	68.29

Source: Calculated using data from the Ministry of Public Finance (annual financial statements of active commercial companies from the real economy in Romania).

After the accession of Romania to the European Union, within a period of seven years, the rate of self-funding doubled among the companies from the real economy, and the rate of debts decreased significantly.

If we refer only to the size of total debt of the companies from the real economy and compare it to the nominal GDP of Romania, the situation is as shown below.

Table 3: Ratio of total debt of the companies from the real economy to the nominal GDP of Romania in 2007–2014 (%)

No.	Period	Current debt of the companies from the real economy	Medium and long-term debt in the real economy	Total debt in the real economy
1	2007	73.54	45.74	119.29
2	2008	71.08	43.88	114.96
3	2009	74.87	40.13	115.01
4	2010	82.62	37.61	120.23
5	2011	90.81	38.82	129.63
6	2012	88.71	36.12	124.83
7	2013	81.28	35.65	116.93
8	2014	77.09	33.20	110.29

Source: Calculated using data from the Ministry of Public Finance (annual financial statements of active commercial companies from the real economy in Romania) and from the National Bank of Romania (monthly bulletins, 2008–2015).

We notice that the current debt in the real economy amounted to 77.09% of the GDP, in 2014, 9% less than in 2007.

Although in the long term, i.e. 2007–2014, the companies active in the real economy in Romania improved their financial state, to be able to really speak of sustainable development within the real economy of Romania, there should be a balance between working capital and the requirement for working capital, which still has to be achieved (both in terms of the structure by branches, and in terms of territorial structure).

c. For companies grouped by regions of development

The location of the company is a factor of influence in the analysis of the working capital structure and requirement. The table below shows the evolution of the rate of average global funding of the companies from the real economy of Romania, by region of development, in 2007–2014.

Table 4: Rate of average global funding of companies from the real economy of Romania, by region of development, in 2007–2014 (%)

No. crt.	Region of development	Period							
		2007	**2008**	**2009**	**2010**	**2011**	**2012**	**2013**	**2014**
1	Northwest	6,32	5,52	7,63	4,38	6,67	7,16	7,46	11
2	Northeast	2,45	6,77	7,84	6,42	5,21	5,66	7,71	8,88
3	Southwest	1,38	2,51	6,6	6,7	6,88	8,28	-6,21	-1,75
4	Southeast	7,77	5,48	5,09	5,78	7,33	7,13	3,22	11,06
5	South	4,35	4,12	6,54	7,36	5,72	7,77	6,46	8,61
6	Center	5,84	3,95	5,68	7,57	5,36	7,26	6,66	10,25
7	West	4,29	4,72	3,3	0,98	3,31	4,7	4,98	5,49
8	Bucharest-Ilfov	13,89	11,46	7,53	7,29	6,15	5,97	8,92	11,31
Real economy – total		**10,37**	**8,91**	**6,96**	**6,72**	**5,91**	**6,17**	**7,34**	**10,25**

Source: Own calculations, using data from balance sheets of active companies from the real economy of Romania, 2007–2014; data from the Ministry of Public Finance.

There are regions where the rate of global funding decreased, such as the Southwest or Bucharest-Ilfov, but there are also regions where this indicator increased significantly, such as the Northeast (+ 6.43%).

Some conclusions

The final conclusion is that the evolution of theories dealing with company funding are marked by contemporary science – the development of new theories to overturn the traditional (this is how we passed from the classical theory of financial structure neutrality to the theory of non-neutrality, or from the maximization of positive effects of indebting to a more prudent funding to support a moderate, yet stable and sustainable, growth; Tudose, 2012). Because research in this area increased over the years, we had to make a selection of the most representative ones, which means that our study is not exhaustive. The somehow sterile presentation of these theories (showing just the founders and the most representative contributions) may bring up the criticism of incomplete scientific fundamentals, when it actually is just the limitation of space. Beyond these limits, the opinions we presented here preserve their representativeness.

Although in the long term, i.e. 2007–2014, the companies active in the real economy of Romania improved their financial state, to be able to really speak of sustainable development, within the real economy of Romania, there should be a balance between the working capital and the requirement for working capital, which still has to be achieved (both in terms of the structure by branches, and in terms of territorial structure).

References

1. Armendariz de Aghion, B., Morduch, J. (2005), The Economics of Microfinance, London, The MIT Press.
2. Atrill, P. (2011), Financial Management for Decision Makers, Sixth Edition, Pearson Education Limited.
3. Barbera, R., The Cost of Capitalism, McGraw-Hill Professional, 2009.
4. Berk, J., Morzo, P. (2013), Corporate Finance, Third Edition, London, Pearson.
5. Bierman, H., Jr., Smidt, S., (1980), The Capital Budgeting Decision. Economic Analysis of Investment Projects, Macmillan Publishing Co. Inc., New York.
6. Cooper, G. (2010), The Origin of Financial Crises: Central Banks, Credit Bubbles, and the Efficient Market Fallacy. Harriman House Ltd., London.
7. Minsky, H. P. (2008), Stabilizing and Unstable Economy, McGraw-Hill, New York.
8. Minsky, H. P. (2013), Ending Poverty: Jobs, Not Welfare, Levy Economics Institute, New York.
9. Ogden, J., Jen, F., O'Connor, P. (2003), Advanced Corporate Finance. Policies and Strategies, Prentice Hall.
10. Rogers, S. (2009), Entrepreneurial Finance: Finance and Business Strategies for the Serious Entrepreneur, Mc-Graw-Hill, SUA.
11. Ross, S., Westerfield, R, Jaffle, J. (2012) Corporate Finance, McGraw Hill.
12. Toporowski, J., Tavasci, D. (2010), Minsky, Crisis and Development, Palgrave Macmillan.
13. Titman, S.; Martin, J.; Keown, A. (2010), Financial Management. Principles and Applications, International Edition, Pearson Education.
14. Tirole, J. (2006), The Theory of Corporate Finance, Princeton, NJ., Princeton University Press.
15. Vernimmen, P. (2002), Finance d'enterprise, 5 edition, Paris, Dalloz.
16. Booth, L., Aivazian, V., Demirguc-Kunt, A., Maksimovic, V., (2001) Capital structure in developing countries, Journal of Finance, vol. 56: pp. 87–130.
17. Cassidy, J. (2008), "The Minsky Moment. Subprime mortgage crisis and possible recession," The New Yorker, 4 February.
18. Frank, M. & Goyal, V. (2003), "Testing the pecking order theory of capital structure." Journal of Financial Economics, vol. 67: pp. 217–248.
19. Frank, M. Z. & Goyal, V. K., (2007) Capital Structure Decisions: Which Factors are Reliably Important? (10 October). Available at SSRN: http://ssrn.com/abstract=567650.
20. Miroslav, M. (2003), "What Does the Risk Appetite Index Measure?" Working Paper No. 2003–23, Bank of Canada.
21. Modigliani, F., Miller, M. (1958), "The Cost of Capital, Corporation Finance and Theory of Investment." American Economic Review, vol. 48.
22. Modigliani, F., Miller, M. (1963), "Taxes and the Cost of Capital: A Correction." American Economic Review, vol. 53.

23. Nivorozhkin, E. (2005), "Financing choices of firms in EU accession countries." Emerging Markets Review, vol. 6.
24. Stiglitz, J. (1969), "A re-examination of the Modigliani-Miller theorem". The American Economic Review, vol. 59.
25. Titman, S., Wessels, R. (1988), "The determinants of capital structure choice". Journal of Finance, vol. 43.

Simona FRONE

Institute of National Economy, 050711, Bucharest,
Casa Academiei Române, Calea 13 Septembrie nr. 13, sector 5,
E-mail: frone.simona@gmail.com

Issues and Trends of Eco-innovation. Promoting the Green Economy in Romania

Abstract: In this paper we present, in a synthetic way, the most important research outcomes of the project on "The role of innovation in promoting a green economy in Romania." First, we outline the main features and principles of the green economy and especially the necessity for increasing resource efficiency, for implementing and monitoring all the latest strategies of sustainable economic growth in the European Union and consequently, in Romania. A conceptual and empirical analysis of eco-innovation follows, introducing the concept of eco-innovation parks. There is a pointing to the positive direct correlation between eco-innovation parks (EInvP) and resource productivity revealed by recent national and international surveys as well as by our own research. In the second part of the paper, we analyze some of the latest national and European trends and issues of eco-innovation. The conclusions and recommendations of the paper outline some progress, but also some difficulties in eco-innovation promoting the green economy in Romania, as well as the expected prospects and policies.

Keywords: sustainable development; green economy; circular economy; industrial symbiosis; eco-innovation parks

Introduction

In this paper, we resume the research dedicated to sustainable economic growth and resource efficiency by adopting a new research objective: substantiation and analysis of concepts, principles and implementation issues related to the green and circular economy. The secondary objective of the paper is a deeper analysis of the concepts of eco-innovation and eco-innovation parks that have the potential for playing a major role in the transition to a green economy in Romania, through the implementation of industrial symbiosis as an advanced form of circular economy.

The methodological approach will be based on literature, especially on some recent documents issued by the European Commission, our own theoretical and empirical research outcomes reviewed and developed from new points of view, and on a case study. In the case study we show an example of good practice, within the ecosystem of industrial symbiosis in Suceava, which, in accordance with our conceptual framework, can be considered an eco-innovation park (EInvP).

1. Literature review

Green economic growth is not just a better approach to economic development. On the contrary, it is considered the only way to ensure sustained economic growth in the long term (EEA, 2013). The United Nations Environment Programme (UNEP) developed a working definition of a green economy as one resulting in improved human well-being and social equity, while significantly reducing environmental risks and ecological scarcities (UNEP, 2012).

In its simplest expression, a green economy can be one which is low carbon, resource efficient and socially inclusive. Increasing resource efficiency is perhaps the most important reason for green economy. If we carry on using resources at the current rate, by 2050 we will need, on aggregate, the equivalent of more than two planets to sustain us, and the aspirations for a better quality of life will not be achieved.

As shown in table 1, the green economy requires gradual changes in resource efficiency, investment in clean technologies, the development of alternative products, services and materials, and the ability to obtain value from unavoidable waste (UNIDO, 2013).

Table 1: General background concepts of present research

Concept	Definition or characteristics
Eco-efficiency (resource-efficiency)	Eco-efficiency may be acknowledged as a more general expression of the concept of resource efficiency – minimizing the resources used in producing a unit of output – and resource productivity – the efficiency of economic activities in generating value added from the use of resources. Eco-efficiency is achieved through the delivery of "competitively priced goods and services that satisfy human needs and bring quality of life while progressively reducing environmental impacts of goods and resource intensity throughout the entire life cycle to a level at least in line with the Earth's estimated carrying capacity" (WBCSD).
Resource productivity	Resource productivity is defined as the ratio of GDP to domestic material consumption. Domestic material consumption measures the total amount of material directly used by an economy, such as biomass products, metal ores, fossil fuels, non-metallic minerals, petroleum resources, etc. and it is equal to domestic material extraction plus imports minus exports.
Industrial ecology (IE)	Industrial ecology explores the assumption that the industrial system can be seen as an ecosystem. Industrial systems, just as natural ecosystems, can be described as a particular distribution of materials, energy, and information flows. Furthermore, the entire industrial system relies on resources and services provided by the biosphere, from which it cannot be dissociated. Industrial ecology suggests using the design of natural ecosystems to guide the redesign of industrial systems and offers opportunities and solutions to turn industrial parks into eco-industrial parks.

Concept	Definition or characteristics
Circular economy	In a circular economy, the value of products, materials and resources is maintained in the economy for as long as possible, and the generation of waste minimized. It is an essential contribution to the EU's efforts to develop a sustainable, low carbon, resource efficient and competitive economy, ultimately the green economy (COM/2015/0614 final).
Green economy	In a green economy the growth in income and employment is driven by public and private investments that reduce carbon emissions and pollution, enhance energy and resource efficiency, and prevent the loss of biodiversity and ecosystem services. The UNEP working definition of a green economy: an economy that results in improved human wellbeing and social equity, while significantly reducing environmental risks and ecological scarcities.

Source: Own synthesis mainly based on references.

An essential concept for green economy is eco-innovation. Eco-innovation is a key concept that provides economic efficiency by saving energy and resources, in order to ensure efficient growth in terms of environmental assets and in people's benefit. This can create sustainable gains for society in a long-term vision regarding issues of resource and of environmental conservation and a strong support from both public authorities and citizens. Thus, technological innovation and eco-innovation are complementary ways to ensure sustainable economic development (Constantinescu, A., Frone, S., 2014).

Eco-innovation involves technological advance in a new model of development that entails a change in social behavior. Moreover, another important concept of our research is the circular economy (as a form of green economy) that proposes the re-use of resources involved in products whose shelf life has come to an end or which lose their usefulness, in order to make new objects of the same or even better quality.

As stated by F. Bonciu (2014): "we can understand that the essence of the circular economy is to maintain and recycle energy and material resources as much as possible within the economic system. In order to have a functioning economic system in an optimal way it is necessary to secure an efficient inter-linkage among industrial processes, various industries and activities."

The EC action plan for the circular economy (COM/2015/0614 final) actually states that "it is important to promote innovative industrial processes. For example, industrial symbiosis allows waste or by-products of one industry to become inputs for another."

As argued in this paper, eco-innovation parks and the related industrial symbiosis offer such an innovative approach to production and consumption by promoting circular economy and increasing business, innovation and development opportunities for all responsible and environmentally sound businesses and authorities from an area or a region.

2. Objectives and trends relating to eco-innovation in the EU and in Romania

The initiative entitled "A Resource Efficient Europe", which is important in promoting a green economy, recognizes the role that eco-innovation can play, detailing the support provided to do this through a series of EU policy instruments. In terms of the trends and issues of eco-innovation, most important or pressing for sustainable development in Romania, they are raised by the reports of the Eco-Innovation Observatory (EIO), analyzed and completed with own comments and results.

While these issues of poor or inefficient resource management and low propensity to invest and cooperate for sustainable production and consumption were signalled in the previous edition, it is important to point out that the last EIO Country Profile report on Romania (EIO, 2015) specifically raises the issues of barriers and drivers to circular economy and targeted eco-innovation in Romania.

According to the latest EIO Country Profile (EIO, 2015), Romania ranks 18th in the Eco-Innovation Scoreboard (Eco-IS), obtaining a score of 87.1. This indicates it is below the overall EU-28 average score by 13%. However, it is encouraging that our country has advanced three positions since 2013, from the previous rank of 21 to the current rank.

The best accomplishment is the fact that Romania ranks above the EU average in terms of eco-innovation activities, with an average score of 138 (38 points above the EU average score of 100). This has been a positive improvement since 2013, and the high score is shown in figure 1.

Fig. 1: Components of the eco-innovation composite index for Romania, 2015

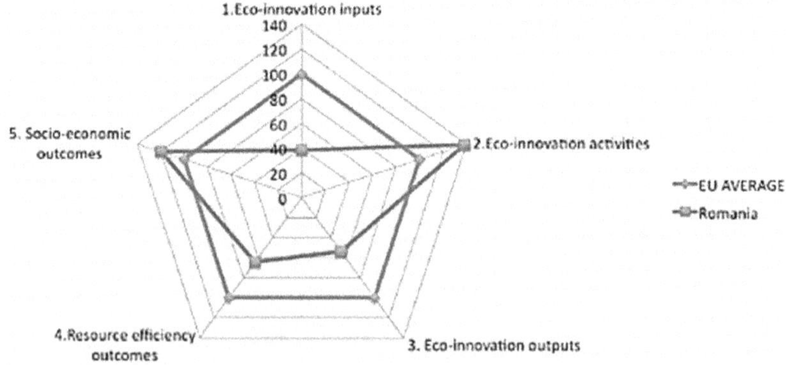

Source: Figure 4 in (EIO, 2015)

As may be noticed in figure 1, the highest contribution to the progress of Romania's eco-innovation score is given only by some eco-innovation activities and socio-economic outcomes. Romania's performance in achieving resource efficiency is stagnating, according to the latest data, as the economy remained on average 40% less resource efficient than the EU. Material productivity, measured in euro per kilogram (€/kg), amounted to 0.66 €/kg in 2013. The (EIO, 2015) report also confirms some of our recent research outcomes (Frone, S., Frone, D. F., 2015) in showing that due to the increase in EU-level average material productivity, the gap is widening between the Romanian and the EU average (EU reached 1.93 €/kg average resource productivity in 2013).

However, the total score for socioeconomic outcomes is now 20% above EU average performance (figure 1). There are two indicators composing this sub-index which have improved due to increased data availability and are not comparable to previous EIO reports: the employment in eco-industries is 4.26% of total employment in Romania in 2014, and this level ranks Romania at 68% above the EU average level of 2.53% of total employment in 2014; the eco-industries' revenue in Romania is 2.99% of the total revenue across sectors, as compared to the EU average turnover of eco-industries amounting to 2.2% of the total turnover in 2012.

The Green Business Index 2015, measuring the companies' environmental responsibility for 2014 (Green Revolution, 2015), provided a deeper analysis of the eco-innovative and environmental behavior and approach of the Romanian enterprises. The main issues from the report include:

- Companies show weak environmental awareness and weak levels of transparency and communication on environmental issues. In terms of cost assessment, companies do not measure or do not want to declare the costs and benefits obtained through their environmental management practices.
- The surveyed companies do not monitor their resource use systematically, so they are not able to take measures to improve their environmental performance.
- A notable change is the increase in companies' use of renewable energy sources. Now 9.3% of the surveyed companies predominantly use renewable energy sources, while for 18.5% of the companies, less than 50% of their energy use comes from renewables.
- The majority of the surveyed companies (57%) do not use recycled resources as production materials at all, while for another 16.3%, recycled resources make up less than 2.5% of their production materials.
- A rising number of companies have started implementing waste management policies: 83% in 2014, which is an increase of 15%, compared to 2013. Although all of them also have a policy for minimizing their waste production, but only 60% took actual measures. However, this is a promising trend towards a more sustainable use of resources.

On the other hand, confirming the findings that eco-innovation activities are on the rise in Romania (EIO, 2013), there are islands of eco-innovation at the grassroots level that have gradually accumulated. These have the potential for reaching a critical mass, and possibly have positive spillover effects on further fields of economic activities in time.

3. Eco-innovation parks – vectors of transition towards a green economy

In this section, we would like to emphasize the importance of eco-innovation and analyze its characteristics through the perspective of eco-innovation parks as well as some new concepts and policies related to the implementation of sustainable development strategies in the EU and in Romania also for the transition to a circular economy and eco-efficient use of resources.

In a green economy, all economic organizations and parties are interested in developing more efficient ways of production and more performant environmental management systems. These measures and developments are essential to significantly reduce pollution and waste, to save water reserves and other natural resources or critical ecosystem services.

In the contemporary society, strict environmental regulations and increasing market variability also force economies to be innovative and to create new production models. The study (ERA-NET ECO-INNOVERA, 2014) "International survey on Ecoinnovation parks. Learning from experiences in the spatial dimension of eco-innovation" describes European and non-European industrial parks implementing eco-innovation (technologies, processes and services) or industrial symbioses.

According to the definition by Lowe (1997), an eco-industrial park (EIP) is a community of manufacturing and service businesses seeking enhanced environmental and economic performance through collaboration in managing environmental and resources issues, including energy, water and materials. By working together, the community of businesses seeks a collective benefit that is greater than the sum of the individual benefits each company would have realized if it had optimized its individual interests.

Such collaborative patterns in industrial areas, also known as eco-industrial networks, industrial symbioses or industrial ecosystems, are only one type of spatial eco-innovation applicable to an EIP. Consequently, the eco-innovation parks (EInvP) are basically eco-industrial parks (EIP) which also embed research and development institutions pro-actively involved in technological innovation dedicated both to economic and environmental objectives, such as the increase in resource efficiency (table 2).

Table 2: Concepts of spatial eco-innovation and green (circular) economy

Concept	Definition or characteristics
Eco-innovation	Eco-innovation is any form of innovation aiming at significant and demonstrable progress towards the goal of sustainable development, by reducing impacts on the environment or achieving a more efficient and responsible use of natural resources, including energy. Collaboration among project partners (private and academia) for research and development is an important element for eco-innovation.
Eco-innovation park (EInvP)	The term "eco-innovation park" is used to define both eco-industrial parks and eco-innovative areas combining residential and industrial activities. Eco-innovation parks are optimized from an environmental point of view (e.g., piloting installations and processes that incorporate environmental technologies and services) and are open to continuous improvement (e.g., collaboration with institutions of research and development).
Industrial symbiosis	Industrial symbiosis (IS), as part of the industrial ecology research field, focuses on the flow of materials and energy from local and regional economies. Industrial symbiosis traditionally engages separate industries in a collective approach to a competitive advantage involving physical exchange of materials, energy, water, and/or by-products as well as services and infrastructures shared at the industrial park scale to reduce environmental impact and overall production cost (Mansard, 2011).
Industrial ecosystem	The broadest application of industrial ecology's analogical approach is to describe manufacturing complexes as "industrial ecosystems." This idea suggests a web of interaction among companies, so that the residuals of one facility become feedstock for another. Industrial ecosystems aim to minimize inefficiencies and the amount of waste created by mimicking natural ecosystems in industrial systems.

Source: Own synthesis mainly based on references.

In recent approaches, EInvP may be only considered the EIP which present the combination of at least two measures leading to economic and environmental gains. Planned or implemented eco-innovative solutions in the parks are principally linked to materials, energy and water issues as reflected by the occurrence of the five main eco-criteria: waste management; energy efficiency; water management; materials flow; renewable energy.

In our empirical research we have focused on the role and significance of EInvP in promoting the rise of resource efficiency (i.e., to increase resource productivity, which is the main indicator for monitoring this issue in EU 2020 strategy documents (EC COM (2011) 21) and for green growth in the European Union. To perform a data analysis and regression, we selected data from the database of the European countries in the survey, only EU member states. A total of 180 EInvP have been identified in 18 countries of the European Union (see figure 2).

The main conclusion of our previous approach (Frone, S., 2015) was that (for the 16 European countries of the analyzed sample) a regression output indicates that there is a direct positive correlation between the number of eco-innovation parks EInvP in a country (the explanatory variable x) and the national indicator of resource efficiency, measured by resource productivity (the determined variable y) RP (expressed in Purchasing Power Standards).

Fig. 2: Resource productivity RP and the number of eco-innovation parks EInvP in selected EU countries (2013)

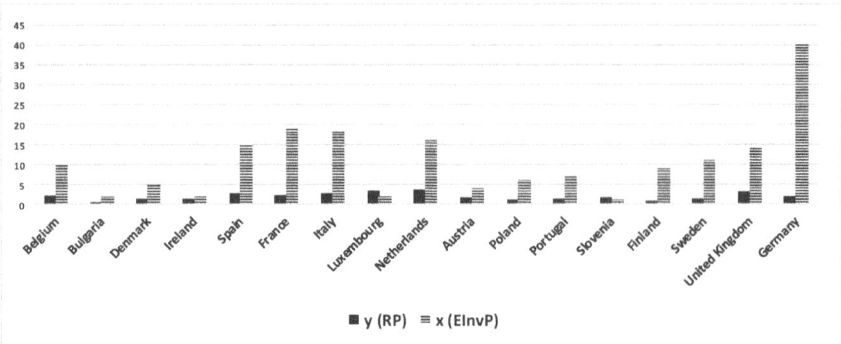

Source: Own computations based on data from ERA-NET ECO-INNOVERA, 2014.

Nevertheless, the importance of creating and developing eco-industrial parks, namely eco-innovation parks (EInvP), is not limited to their potential for increasing resource efficiency. The case study also resulted in other conclusions concerning the topic of the various advantages and benefits of these eco-innovation parks.

4. Promoting circular economy through industrial symbiosis in the ECOREG pilot EInvP

An important aspect in the creation and development of eco-innovation parks (EInvP) is not just their potential for increasing resource efficiency (Frone, 2017), but also for the implementation of new modern synergic and circular business models. In practice, using industrial symbiosis as an approach to commercial operations – by using, recovering and redirecting resources for their re-use – means that resources remain in productive use in the economy for a longer period.

As a case study, we shall analyze here the main features, objectives and outcomes of this pilot Romanian EInvP named Application of Industrial Ecosystems Principles to Regional Development (ECOREG) in Suceava County, according to the official reporting (nisp-ecoreg.ro). The main objective of the ECOREG Project was to test the application of industrial symbiosis (IS) principles in the area of Suceava County (the focal area of the project), also allowing for regional symbiotic development with neighboring counties. This entails the reuse of resources and by-products from one production cycle into another, thus creating mutually beneficial partnerships between companies in various sectors.

Basically, it is a new way of looking at economic activity, in which environmental concerns (so expensive) are turned into profit-making opportunities and benefits (not necessarily material) through the establishment of symbiotic partnerships between companies from various industries. The wastes/by-products of the work unit become resources for another activity, thereby reducing the consumption of raw materials, the amount of waste generated and the associated environmental impact in the entire area of the eco-innovation park.

The ECOREG project objectives meet the requirements for local, regional and national sustainable development, as they are environmental, economic and social. Thus, the project to create this eco-industrial park presents these specific objectives (nisp-ecoreg.ro):

i. **Environmental objectives:** reduction in raw material consumption, energy, utilities, by **2–5%** for all units through implementing innovative tools and instruments; reduction of waste generation and pollutant emissions by **5–20%** for all units; conversion of wastes/by-products into resources (secondary materials); significant reduction of environmental impact by developing result-based programs at the level of industrial units.
ii. **Economic objectives:** increase in economic efficiency (through technological improvements, reduction of production costs); reduction in environmental expenditure.
iii. **Social objectives:** creation of new jobs; improvement of public image and of interrelation between industrial units; preservation and improvement of tourism potential of the pilot area.

The industrial ecosystem ECOREG project was implemented in Romania, in Suceava County, with financial support of the European Union through the LIFE+ Programme. The total project budget was €880,700, out of which: LIFE+ Programme, 41.48% of project's value; Co-financing Ministry of Environment, 17.3% of project value; Ministry of Economy, 22.53% of project value; in-kind contribution of each partner, 18.69% of project value.

The main environmental drivers and the mechanisms of the multiple industrial synergies functioning in the ECOREG are described and analyzed more in detail in Frone, S. (2017). Therefore, a new economic body is created, actually an EInvP with increased efficiency in the use of matter and energy. In the context of the economic crisis, these actions contributed to the maintenance of jobs and the development of sustainable economic activities with the protection of the environment, the more so as it aimed to identify new directions for action to improve the performance of the operators.

The economic impact of implementing the ECOREG industrial ecosystem in the Suceava region is given by: reducing production costs by processing waste (cheaper than raw materials); reducing waste disposal costs by 20–30% on average per company (as shown in the synergy sheets for the finalized synergies); reducing the penalties for environmental non-compliance and other economic benefits through the sale of waste.

The outcomes of the ECOREG project are impressive: over 200 economic and social units from various fields and industrial sectors have been included in a regional symbiotic network; 568 resource flows and 200 synergies were identified; 114 synergies were completed, involving 13 waste categories; a quantity of over 530,000 tons of waste was involved in the synergies, out of which: 30,000 tons of construction and demolition waste; over 500,000 tons of wood waste; 232 tons of animal and food waste; 25 tons of plastic waste; 20 tons of electrical and electronic equipment waste; a surface of over 2,500 ha of forest was preserved, following the replacement of raw wood materials with other types of waste; the reduction in GHG emissions by more than 130,000 tons of CO_2, following the replacement of virgin materials with alternative resources.

Conclusions

The green or ecological economy represents an economic paradigm sprung from the requirements of a sustainable economic development, to which other challenges were added in recent years, since economic and financial or natural resources crises have imposed an increased attention and concern for the efficiency in the use of all resources as part of a holistic approach.

Advantages of a circular economy, which by recycling avoids the exhaustion of resources, are amazing. Basically, if a linear economy leads the global society toward collapse as it accelerates the exploitation of resources (which are limited, not infinite), a circular economy has the reversed effect of ensuring the existence and increased prosperity grounds for the human race in the future. Although industrial ecology has emerged as a form of eco-innovation required by sustainable development challenges, the principle of industrial symbiosis has been replicated and developed with much more dedication and interest during the financial and economic crisis (2009–2012) at the European and global level. Implementation of future patterns of industrial ecology in eco-industrial parks will turn them into EInvPs needed for promoting an effective resource-saving, environment-friendly and circular economy in the European Union as well as in Romania.

However, we showed that, taking into account recent trends and issues of eco-innovation in Romania, there are a lot of aspects to improve in order to align with European Union trends in this field, which is essential for sustainable development and systemic green economic restructuring.

In Romania, over 95% of waste is stored and for increasing their recycling rate, many opportunities are offered to develop the circular economy. As illustrated in sections 2 and 4, there are some bottom-up initiatives from the civil society and the private sector which really identified opportunities in this respect. But a pro-active policy, a coordinated and systematic approach to public management is needed to develop the circular economy in a sustainable way in Romania and to reap significant economic and environmental benefits.

The conclusions of the extended research show that the planning, implementation and development of eco-innovation parks is necessary especially in Romania, with a view to sustainable economic development towards a green growth. Romania's priorities include the greening of production processes and consumption, increased investment in RDI activities, and the strengthening of cooperation between the public and private sectors in tackling environmental challenges.

Future research will be dedicated to the identification and implementation of specific indicators for the monitoring of circular economy in Romania.

References

1. EEA (2013), European Environmental Agency, "Green economy, Towards a green economy in Europe," EEA Report No. 8/2013, http://www.eea.europa.eu/publications/towards-a-green-economy-in-europe.
2. Bonciu, F. (2014). "The European economy: From a linear to a circular economy." Romanian Journal of European Affairs, 14 (4), pp. 78–91.
3. COM (2015) 614 final: "Closing the loop – An EU action plan for the Circular Economy," European Commission, Brussels, 2015.
4. Constantinescu, A., Frone, S., 2014: "The role of technological innovation in sustainable economic development," Scientific Papers International Conference on Knowledge Society, in Journal of Knowledge Management, Economics and Information Technology 2014, Vol. 4 Issue 1.1 https://ideas.repec.org/a/spp/jkmeit/spicks14013.html.
5. EIO, 2013: "Country Profile Romania 2013," Eco-Innovation Observatory, Brussels, 2013 http://www.eco-innovation.eu/images/stories/Reports/EIO_Country_Brief_2013_Romania.pdf.
6. EIO, 2015: "Country Profile Romania 2014–2015," Eco-Innovation Observatory, Brussels, 2016 http://www.eco-innovation.eu/images/stories/2015_country_reports/romania_eco-innovation_2015.pdf.
7. ERA-NET ECO-INNOVERA, 2014: International survey on Eco innovation parks. Learning from experiences on the spatial dimension of eco-innovation. Federal Office for the Environment and the ERANET ECO-INNOVERA, Bern. Environmental studies no. 1402.
8. Frone, S., 2015: "The Eco-Innovation Parks: Vectors of Transition to A Green Economy," Annals of the "Constantin Brâncuşi" University of Târgu Jiu, Economy Series Special Issue ECO-TREND 2015, pp. 27–35.
9. Frone, S., 2017: The Role of Eco-Innovation for Promoting a Green Economy, LAP LAMBERT Academic Publishing, D-66111 Saarbrücken, pp. 44–54; http://www.nisp-ecoreg.ro/industrial_symbiosis.aspx.
10. Green Revolution, 2015: Green Business Index Report 2015, https://www.gbindex.ro/wpcontent/uploads/2015/11/Raport-Green-Business-Index-2015.pdf.

11. Lowe, E. A., 1997: "Creating by-product resource exchanges: strategies for eco-industrial parks." Journal of Cleaner Production 5, pp. 57–65.
12. Massard, G., 2011. "Les symbioses industrielles: une nouvelle stratégie pour l'amélioration de l'utilisation des ressources matérielles et énergétiques par les activités économiques," Ph.D. thesis, Université de Lausanne.
13. UNEP (2012), "The Business Case for the Green Economy. Sustainable Return on Investment," United Nations Environment Programme, 2012.
14. UNIDO, 2013: "Green growth: From labour to resource productivity. Best practice examples, initiatives and policy options," 2013.

Otilia Teodora CIUTACU

Ph.D., RNP Romsilva, 9A, Petricani St., MC 023841, Bucharest, Romania, otilia.ciutacu@yahoo.com

Ioan I. GÂF-DEAC

Senior Lecturer Ph.D., Research, III, NIER/Romanian Academy, Calea 13 Septembrie, No. 13, MC 050711, Bucharest, Romania, editurafmp@gmail.com

Normative Economy and Interventionist Policies to Achieve Efficiency in the Field of Natural Resources

Abstract: The exploitation and utilization of natural resources is desirable conduct scientifically and objectively. In this framework, normative economics provides specific methods and ways of operation. Using the best economic methods is only hypothetical, since the course of practical operation and recovery process just tends to be increasingly more representative, according to one method or another. Normative economy of natural resources leads to economic positivity accepted in conventional production and reproduction. In the space of normative economics, value manifests parametrically. Relativity of variation in size of value of resources and goods is given, for example, by increasing taxes to achieve controlled distribution and to encourage or discourage consumption, or by minimizing taxes, when we intend to create conditions to encourage a certain type of consumption. Normative economics is demanding answers to questions concerning "what to produce with certain resources at our disposal," "how to produce those products" and "for whom to produce" (who consumes). In such a situation, it requires knowledge and understanding of the functionality of markets in competition. It is also necessary to identify the balance and efficiency of resources under transformation by understanding the differences in the markets in which we can operate with a set of interventions to ensure procedural efficiency.

Keywords: normative economics, interventionist politics, producer, consumer, taxes, natural resources

Introduction

Political economy can be: 1) positive/descriptive economics and 2) normative/prescriptive economy. John Neville Keynes defines the relationship between "positive" or descriptive economics and "normative" or prescriptive economics (Keynes, 1993, p. 43). The results stemming from economics are used to formulate economic policies or government programs. On the other hand, regulatory issues affect the sense of positive economic developments. Positive economics offer an objective or scientific explanation on the functioning of the economy by making statements about facts and relationships. On this basis, assumptions are made about the behavior of the economic agents. Normative economy offers prescriptions or recommendations based on value judgments, often personal, related to macroeconomics aimed at evolving trends, identifying what will be.

In fact, "normative economics is a perspective on economics that reflects normative judgments or opinionated reactions toward economic projects, statements, and scenarios. Unlike positive economics, normative economics heavily concerns itself with value judgments and theoretical scenarios and economic statements that present 'what ought to be' rather than facts and cause-and-effect statements. Normative economics expresses judgments about what may result of economic activities if public policy changes are done" (Normative Economics Definition, Investopedia).

1. Normative economics elements in natural resources economy in Romania

The exploitation and utilization of natural resources in Romania is desirable to be made scientifically, objectively. Romania exploits more than 80 kinds of mineral resources, from alabaster, geothermal and natural waters to gold and silver ore, quartz, limestone, marble, lignite and molybdenum ore or uranium etc. The patrimony of renewable resources consists of untapped mineral reserves estimated to be over 20 billion tons: iron ore (58.6 million tons), non-ferrous ores (potential resources 2.21 billion tons), salt (16.96 billion tons), non-metallic minerals (292.8 million tons), sand and gravel (456.9 million tons), ornamental rocks (34.5 million tons, of which 6.39 million tons of marble). We identified 1,900 non-energy deposits such as: metallic minerals (polymetallic ores, copper, iron, precious metals, molybdenum, manganese, etc.), industrial minerals (talc, bentonite, diatomite, salt, feldspar, kaolin, peat, etc.) and mineral construction materials (andesite, granite, marble, sand, clay, limestone, chalk, quartzite, sandstone, gravel, gypsum, National Agency for Mineral Resources in Romania)

Normative economics provides specific methods and ways of operating. The use of the best methods is only hypothetical, since the course of practical operation and recovery processes tend to be increasingly more representative, according to one or another imposed method. Normative economics of natural resources leads to conventionally accepted economic positivity in production and reproduction. In the space of normative economics, value manifests parametrically.

The relativity of variation in size of value of resources and goods is given, as an example, by increasing taxes to achieve controlled distribution, to encourage or discourage consumption, and by lowering taxes when we intend to create conditions to encourage a certain type of consumption. Normative economy is demanding answers to questions concerning "what to produce with certain resources at our disposal," "how to produce those products" and "for whom to produce" (who consumes). In such a situation, it requires knowledge and understanding of the functionality of markets in competition. It is also necessary to identify the balance and resource efficiency under transformation by understanding the differences in the markets in which it can operate with a set of interventions to ensure procedural efficiency.

2. Interventionist policy formulation and implementation. Literature review

Typically, we consider that Romania should resort to situational economic analysis in natural resources, as a prerequisite for the formulation of intervention methods and techniques for the management and/or correction of the exploitation and recovery. The basic restrictions recognized in the activities aimed at the exploitation and utilization of the country's natural resources is found in environmental policies. Legislative provisions and administrative measures (shares) represent inputs in the resource processing system. Environmental policies are periodically or quasi-permanently reviewed with economic methods, aiming at acting balance and anticipated effectiveness.

The analyses conducted for this paper show that in Romania, in the sphere of normative economy, there is a quasi-excessive legislative process compared with juridical normativity in the economies in the region.

Iulian Anghel (2011) states that "in Romania there is now in effect a huge number of legal acts, individual and international – 95 618 in January 2011, of which only 1958 issued before 1989." Legislative changes occur in the transformation that led the country to a market economy after 1989. Another motivation is given by specific legislative wishes of governments in their succession to power.

Vasile Puscas (2006, p. 97), Romania's former chief negotiator with the EU, points out that "Romania has adopted most (EU) laws, and has to apply them. Romania does not need so many laws. The focus should be on fewer and better laws that do not change from day to day." This phenomenon causes legislative inflation and, as such, overregulation in various fields, plus legislative unpredictability. Romania ranks first among states in the region in terms of number of legislative changes, with 490 laws in 2014/2016, of which more than a third have an impact on the business environment. G. Abraham (2016), from the EEC Grayling Public Affairs Practice Group, shows that almost 40% of all legislative changes made in Romania in 2015 had a direct impact on the business environment, close to the level recorded in the region, 36%.

According to the DEX '09 (2009). interventionism means "orientation of an economic policy consisting in state intervention in order to steer the economy to the set objectives."

Another opinion is that the bankruptcy law is an interventionist legislative measure. This interferes with the freedom of people or to businesses and exploit natural resources in order to establish the terms of a loan. Specific bankruptcy regulations are in Law 85/2006 on the insolvency procedure, published in the Official Gazette no. 359 of 21 April 2006, and Government Emergency Ordinance no. 86/2006 on the organization of insolvency practitioners, published in the Official Gazette no. 944 of

22 November 2007. The main goal of modern bankruptcy is to liquidate debtor assets, pay the costs and creditors or the debtor to discharge any outstanding obligation.

"Interventionism means that the government wants to do more, it wants to intervene in the market" (von Mises, 1995).

Punitive interventionist policies turn out to be less feasible if compared to the operational interventionist policies of a situational construction, e.g. for not harming the environment. Operational asymmetries in the context of achieving objectives or a horizon of development are eliminated by official institutions (government, budget, development banks) which bear the cost differences arising from the exploitation and utilization of natural resources that prove to be of "strategic importance." Subsidizing can be 1) final or 2) temporary (with recovery of support). Market imperfections, uncontrollable endogenous preferences, risks, limiting standards or the need to mandatorily achieve certain levels of standard products and services from natural resources etc. can be countered by deploying subsidy.

3. Interventionist policies on natural resources found in normative economics in Romania

Formalizing the general system of natural resources in Romania involves identifying the characteristics of systematizing economic and legal/normative factors (Gâf-Deac., 2007, pp. 248–250), as follows:

- Theoretical bases of economic exploitation of natural resources: the limits of knowledge; Neo-Malthusian theory; Hotelling's rule; zero extraction costs; void extraction costs; exploitation of natural resources at different costs; exploiting accumulations with unexploitable areas; completing and exploration of the natural resources' fund.
- Exploitation of natural resources under uncertainty: reserves of natural resources under conditions of uncertainty; uncertainty of production costs; time uncertainty for innovative resources; uncertainties relating to price and elements of options theory.
- Imperfect competition: monopoly on natural resource reserves; oligopoly in the field; monopoly on unworkable reserves; cartels for natural resources and competitive actions; capacity limitations (e.g. OPEC).
- Natural Resources Taxes: taxes on sales; exponential growth of taxes; tax policies and agreement between producers and consumers; taxation and optimal levels of extraction; a single reservoir exploitation by several owners and optimal taxation.
- Empirical analyses of the exploitability of natural resources.
- General operation and exploitation of natural resources: economic growth based on natural resources; equity in natural resources exploitation; rational use of natural resources over time; the role of ethics in equitable distribution of consumption resources between generations (utilitarianism, egalitarianism, elitism); optimal use of exploitable resources (utilitarianism and egalitarianism).
- Exploitation of natural resources in the open economy.

- Natural resources in national accounting: measuring the contribution of natural resources to the public welfare; participation in national net production; participation in sustainable development.

Considering the completely finite existence in absolute physical volume of natural resources, (Gâf-Deac, 2007, pp. 248–250) [3], in Romania it is possible – in relation to the multitude of elements: resources, their distribution area, the operating cost and the selling price for consumption – to formalize optimal sufficiency (S_{optim}) in terms of normative economy by the model:

$$\left.\begin{cases} M(E_r) = \{E_r^i\} \\ S \in D \\ C \leq P \\ V_f[M(E_r^i)] \neq +\infty \end{cases}\right\} \rightarrow S_{optim} \quad (1)$$

However, we infer that if the set of completely finite resources-elements in absolute physical volume is high quantitatively (dimensionally), the final cost of mining-recovery can be typically lower than the possible price the sale sequences (figure 1).

Fig. 1: Dependence of the total cost for natural resources' exploitation and utilization of the completely finite amount in absolute physical volume in the normative economics in Romania

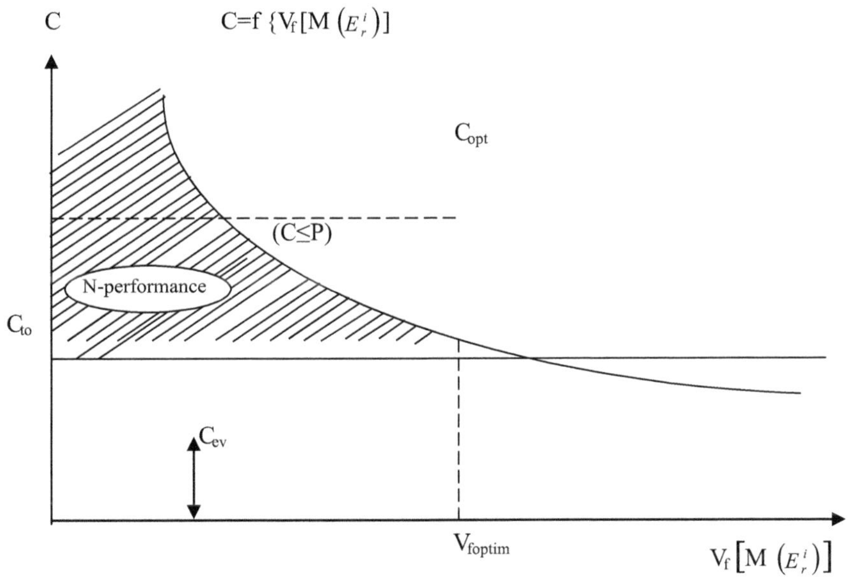

C = total cost; C_{ev} = extraction-recovery cost; C_{opt} = optimal cost; C_{to} = optimal total cost; P = price of sale marketing;

$V_f[M(E_r^i)]$ = completely finished resources in absolute physical volume.

In the above analytical framework, we can identify maximum sufficiency (S_{max}) and the minimum one (i.e. insufficiency, $S_{min} = I_s$), in relation to operational prices (P_{op}) and non-operational ones ($P_{n\text{-}op}$), i.e. the minimum total costs (C_{min}) and maximum ones (C_{max}), as follows:

$$\begin{cases} V_f[M(E_r^i)] \rightarrow MAX \rightarrow C_{min} \rightarrow P_{op} \rightarrow S_{max} \\ V_f[M(E_r^i)] \rightarrow MIN \rightarrow C_{min} \equiv C_{max} \rightarrow P_{n\text{-}op} \rightarrow S_{min} \equiv I_s \end{cases} \quad (2)$$

The conflict between values and consumption in the system of natural resources exploitation in the normative economics of Romania persists because the "economic" is still, in a conventional way, confronted with the "environment," instead of both being interconnected to the flow of production and reproduction. A wrong idea is that "environment" determines "insufficiency" of natural resources or formalize a certain sufficiency.

4. Conclusions

Normative economics ensures scheduled methods and ways, conventionally accepted and expected in the exploration and exploitation of natural resources in Romania.

It identifies the relativity of the size of the final value of resources and goods from natural resources.

The value variation is more dynamic through implemented solutions to "what to produce," "how to produce" and "for whom to produce."

We believe that identifying the balance and efficiency of natural resources processing means "knowledge for intervention."

However, we notice that administrative policies in the operation and exploitation of natural resources in Romania are less feasible in relation to operational policies, to formalize proceedings.

Damaged viability of the market of resources and goods from natural resources is negative (–) as regards the average cost per protected/rehabilitated unit of environment and positive (+) as regards the research and alternatives to counter pollution (damage) of the environment.

Sufficiency of natural resources in Romania results from physical geological and ecosystem reality. We affirm that sufficiency of natural resources is characterized by operational relativity given by normative economics. However, one can never achieve the full operation and exploitation of finite state resources.

The normative economics of Romania is useful for formalization of conceptual modeling of the sufficiency of natural resources and identification of a non-performance zone caused by the ratio of total operating recovery cost to fully finite resources in absolute volume.

References

1. Abraham, G., – Grayling AcTrend Report 2016 Third edition., Grayling Central & Eastern European Public Affairs Group., 20 November 2016.
2. Anghel, I., – România, ţară guvernată de 95.000 de acte normative. Cum scăpăm de "nebunia" legislativă?, Ziarul Financiar, Bucharest, 2 February 2011.
3. Gâf-Deac, I. I., – The legal and economic systems resources in the new economy, Editura Infomin Deva, 2007, pp. 248–250.
4. Keynes, J. N., – Philosophy of economics. Anthology, Editura Humanitas, Bucharest, 1993, p. 43.
5. von Mises, L., – Economic Policy. Thoughts for Today and for Tomorrow, Free Market Books, Bucharest, 1995.
6. Puşcaş, V., – European Negotiations. A Case Study: Romania's Accession to the EU. Gorizia, IUIES, 2006, p. 97.
7. Law no. 85/2006 on insolvency proceedings, published in Monitorul Oficial al României no. 359 din 21 April 2006.
8. Government Emergency Ordinance no. 86/2006 on the organization of insolvency practitioners, published in Monitorul Oficial al României no. 944 din 22 November 2007.
9. **,- National Agency for Mineral Resources, Annual Report, Bucharest, 2015.

Irina A. CHERVINSKAYA

Institute of Economics, National Academy of Sciences of Belarus,
Surhanova str., Minsk, 220072, Belarus

Identifying Commercial Risks by Means of an Anti-dumping Regulation, using as an Example the Republic of Belarus

Abstract: In this article, the risks of exporters due to specific protection measures of modern trade policy are analyzed, using as an example the Republic of Belarus. The set of risks is divided into two groups: non-specific risks that are typical of the majority of states, and specific risks that are typical for "non-market economies." The price conjuncture of the Belarusian products export is analyzed. The results confirmed the high vulnerability of its major constituents to anti-dumping proceedings. Mechanisms minimizing the threat of anti-dumping proceedings in respect of Belarusian producers-exporters are suggested. Approaches to improving economic practices and normative legal provisions are suggested.

Keywords: anti-dumping regulation, risk, non-market economy, normal price, transition economies

1. Introduction

Growth of international trade and openness of national economies are a key feature of the current stage of development of the world economy. Increasing their participation in the international division of labor causes dependencies on the results of export-import operations. This creates not only a possibility of increasing specialization and efficiency of the national economies, but it also forms a prerequisite for increased competition. A lack of competitiveness of transitive economies is a serious threat to national businesses and industries.

The problem becomes more acute in the face of declining global economic growth. An opinion that free trade does not always ensure the development of national economies is widely spread in economic science. A practical implementation of this position is the formation of trading blocs, and the development of non-tariff regulation mechanisms. These actions are intended not only to provide interaction with the global market, but also to maintain a necessary level of protection on the internal markets, and to minimize threats to the national economies.

There are two main groups in the structure of foreign trade risks of the Republic of Belarus:

a. Non-specific risks. This is the kind of risks that are common to the majority of countries that are members of modern global trade. These include the reduction of tariff barriers, the liberalization of foreign trade regulations, as well as the implementation of approved domestic market protection measures against exporters. This reflects an increasing role of the World Trade Organization.

b. Specific risks that are typical for "non-market economy" countries. The Republic of Belarus is one of them. These risks are associated with the biased use of anti-dumping measures against exporters, an insufficient level of dedicated experts, and certain features of the anti-dumping regulation practice.

2. Literature review

The high vulnerability of non-market economies has been the subject of several studies. As a rule, researchers concluded that absence of market economy status is an increasing factor for probability of detection of dumping in anti-dumping proceedings and implementation of appropriate measures. This point of view is reflected in scientific works by J. M. Finger, H. K. Hall, D. R. Nelson (1982), P. K. M. Tharakan, and J. Waelbroek (1994).

Russian researchers A. Isayenko and A. Shcherbakov (2002) conclude that the status of the country's transition causes a lot of flexibility in the realization of anti-dumping proceedings. In other words, it contributes voluntarism, which leads to a relatively higher probability of a negative decision for the defendant. They determine several key factors that have a significant impact on the results of the anti-dumping investigation:

- a "non-market economy" status for a country, whose exporters are accused of dumping;
- high concentration of national industry;
- total import.

Belarusian scientists A. A. Bakanov and L. A. Zhulego (2003) agree with a possible discriminatory use of dumping detection procedures for non-market economies. However, they point out that in some cases, the defendants do not use all available legal options to prevent the application of anti-dumping measures. The Congressional Budget Office conducted a study in 1996. It pointed out that 18% of the total number of US anti-dumping measures at the end of 1995 were applied against non-market economies. However, they held only 6% of total imports in this country. In addition, data was presented that the average anti-dumping duties for countries with a market economy has been lower than that of countries with non-market economies for the period of 1955–1975. This ratio also illustrates higher vulnerability of this category of the countries to anti-dumping proceedings(CBO, 1996).

3. Foreign trade risks for exporters

The foreign trade risks of exporters may be described in more detail.

Non-specific risks

a) Reduction of tariff barriers and liberalization of foreign trade conditions that reflect the importance of the World Trade Organization.

The possibilites for using protectionist mechanisms are limited by international treaties, a legal and regulatory framework of the WTO. At the same time, the current level of tariffs for WTO members is quite low. Its increasing is a difficult or even impossible action. The possible changes can not ensure an adequate level of protection of domestic products.

Belarus is not a WTO member; it is affected by the WTO international trade rules. Participation of domestic exporters in international trade requires economic and legal compliance with WTO principles. The existing obligations do not allow for the full utilization of tariff and non-tariff barriers. The Republic of Belarus is a member of the Eurasian Economic Union. Therefore, it is necessary to comply with the terms of contracts and to maintain the level of customs tariffs. The results of the negotiations of the Russian Federation and the Republic of Kazakhstan on joining the WTO determine the value of the customs tariffs of the Eurasian Economic Union.

b) Implementation of the WTO allowed measures against Belarusian enterprises.

According to WTO rules, to protect domestic producers from having to compete with foreign companies, participating countries can use only the "allowed measures" to certain goods and services used in accordance with rather stringent regulations. The list of the allowed measures is rather short:

- anti-dumping measures;
- compensation measures;
- special protective measures.

The anti-dumping measure is a popular tool for counteraction against competitive foreign goods. The reason for the popularity of anti-dumping measures is their simplicity. The procedure for anti-dumping measures is regulated by Article VI of the GATT and the Agreement on Implementation of Article VI of the GATT. Their application consists in the implementation of anti-dumping duties or voluntary price obligations taken by exporters.

Dumping itself is not forbidden and its use does not lead to immediate sanctions. However, dumping distorts the conditions of fair competition and may adversely affect the working conditions of producers in the importing country. Therefore, a prerequisite for the application of anti-dumping measures is the existence of damage or threat of damage to domestic industries.

c) The problems of biased anti-dumping measures against Belarusian exporters.

Traditionally, economists consider anti-dumping measures as an instrument for the protection and promotion of competition in the international trading system. However, in many economic studies, there is a widely represented opinion that the presence of dumping is not always a demonstration of unfair trading practices, because dumping may appear as a way of preventing so-called "predatory pricing" in foreign trading.

The pressure group contains the domestic producers in import-competing industries. It turns out that anti-dumping actions are the most powerful tools for their protection, due to a number of reasons, including the fact that the findings on dumping damage followed by the protective actions are taken at the discretion of the authorities.

In almost any industry, there is a good chance to prove the dumping threat if a well-grounded petition is provided. Governments tend to make decisions in favor of the implementation of protectionist interests. Ease of anti-dumping law implementation is provided by the opacity of administrative protection instruments involved in responding to the protectionist demands of domestic producers.

d) Possible distortion when using a constructed normal value.

According to the WTO rules, dumping is considered the sale of goods for export at prices lower than the "normal value." As an indicator for normal value, the price for identical goods in the domestic market of the exporting country is used the most often. In a market economy, the normal price is determined based on the price of shipping products, taking into account transport expenses, physical characteristics of the goods, sales and insurance conditions. This is done in order to make it comparable with the price of similar products shipped for export.

However, there is a number of exceptions allowing the use of other methods for the calculation of a "normal price", including, first of all, the "constructed price" method. This can happen if the domestic market of the exporting parties does not contain models of goods similar to the ones imported, if sales in the domestic market are insignificant compared to the export value, and in case of product realization in the domestic market at prices that do not cover the production expenses.

Specific risks

Non-market economy status of the country

Determination of the normal price for a non-market economy has its own specific features. The WTO recognized the right of importing countries to use alternative approaches to the "normal value" measurement for countries that do not have market economy status. Moreover, even the entry into the WTO is not a guarantee of non-use of these alternatives if the country does not have "market" status.

There is no uniform approach to defining the non-market economies in the world. Thus, the United States do not have a list of countries that are considered non-market.

The decision on whether an exporter represents a market or non-market country is made in each case mainly on the basis of the statements expressing dissatisfaction of the company. The US Commerce Department allows defendants to challenge the country's evaluation comparing with other non-market economies or to prove that a particular company operates in the mode of a market economy, even if the whole country in general is defined as the non-market economy (WTO agreement, p. 104).

According to European Union normative legal documents, receiving market economy status requires compliance with certain criteria. Among the countries with a "non-market economy", the European Union currently counts the Republic of Belarus, and also Albania, Armenia, Azerbaijan, Vietnam, Georgia, Kazakhstan, China, Kyrgyzstan, Moldova, Mongolia, North Korea, Tajikistan, Turkmenistan and Uzbekistan (EC, 2016).

The threats associated with the use of an comparable country in the "normal value" calculation

The provisions of the GATT WTO give freedom to individual countries to develop their domestic law to determine the normal value in the context of anti-dumping legislation. However, in general, there is no incompatibility between procedures adopted by countries and WTO requirements, which are the primary source for anti-dumping legislation of individual countries.

In the United States, the "constructed normal value" method is used. According to this method, the manufacturer must document actual expenses. At the next stage, an analog country is chosen. At the third stage, expenses are transferred to the cost value using the prices for resources in the appropriate analog country. The costs are added to the estimated selling, general and administrative expenses equal to 10% of the costs, as well as the profit rate of 8%.

The approach used in the European Union is similar to the US'. Initially, the analog country is chosen. Subsequently, a similar procedure based on constructing the normal value may be applied. Using the market prices or prices of exports to third countries is also a possible approach.

The first step in the determination of the "normal value" in the domestic market is the choice of methodology for its calculation. Moreover, for the countries with "non-market economy" there is a high probability that it is impossible to determine an adequate (i.e. the market) price for the relevant goods. In this case, there are two alternative approaches to its definition:

- the method of analogy to the export value of the goods from a third country;
- the method of constructed value.

Often the choice of method defines whether dumping would be found or not. For the countries with a "non-market economy" the country selected as an analog does not need to strictly comply with all requirements. This leads to applying unreasonably high anti-dumping duties.

Use of the zeroing method in dumping determination

A good example of procedure falsification while determining the normal value for goods imported from countries recognized as non-market economies can be the manipulations with the dumping margin calculation procedure carried out using the "zeroing method." Comparison of the normal product value and its selling price in the importing country is made separately for each transaction. Then the results are summarized, and the average factor is determined. Based on that, the dumping margin is calculated as the difference between the obtained normal value and the price in the importing country. In case the obtained normal value exceeds the price in the country of import, such excess is reflected in the procedure for the dumping margin calculation. But when the value of the normal price appears less than the selling price of goods in the country of import, the contribution of a single transaction is zeroed.

The peculiarity of this method lies in the fact that if at least one transaction is ignored, then the desired dumping will be inevitably found by unscrupulous competitors. This approach results in the actions showing signs of the violation of free market principles declared in the regulations of the WTO. The practice of implementing such procedures leads to a voluntary increase of the dumping margin, which opens opportunities for the unwarranted applying of protective duties.

Other risks for the Belarusian economy in the anti-dumping context

Many of the problems which foreign enterprises faced are related to a lack of knowledge about the anti-dumping legislation and procedures, as well as to the requirements to immediately respond, in English, to detailed technical questionnaires. The lack of reporting in line with international standards causes serious problems.

The main problems arising during anti-dumping proceedings involving the producers from developing countries, in addition to the lack of the "market economy" status, are the following:

- poor knowledge of the importing country's laws and procedures of anti-dumping proceedings;
- in countries with a non-market economy, due to its specificity, the price level does not always correspond to the real cost of production, which can increase the probability of a sale at prices lower than normal, leading to a higher level of the dumping margin than in countries with a market economy;
- poor knowledge of the foreign language of representatives of the respondent firms, making it difficult to construct the argument for protection;
- mismatch between the national accounting system and the standards of the international financial reporting system. This leads to difficulties in the rapid provision of information (justified according to specific requirements) on the structure of expenses for production being the object of the proceedings.

Currently, the legal basis for measures protecting the domestic market of the Eurasian Customs Union is a number of international treaties in force within the integration association. First of all, it is the agreement on the application of special protection, anti-dumping and compensating measures against third countries to regulate certain import issues from third countries [3]. According to it, the decision on the application of anti-dumping, compensation and protection measures are made by the responsible body – the Eurasian Economic Commission. Thus, the Republic of Belarus cannot independently impose anti-dumping measures against third countries. They should be used in coordination with the other members of the integration union, preceded by an investigation. However, the Eurasian Customs Union mechanisms do not provide a coordinated response to anti-dumping sanctions against member-states used by third countries.

On the contrary, the European Union countries actively resort to these protection measures against exports from third countries. Moreover, the prices of commodities in the vast majority of large Belarusian export items to the European Union are much lower than the world average.

Table 1: The main products of the Belarusian export to the European Union

Harmonized system codes	Commodity groups	World average export prices, $	Belarusian export prices, $	Belarus' share in global exports
310420	Potassium chloride for use as fertilizer (excluding tablets or similar forms, or in packages with a gross weight of ≤ 10 kg)	292	291	20.9%
721420	Bars and rods, of iron or non-alloy steel, with indentations, ribs, groves or other deformations produced during the rolling process	446	365	3.1%
310520	Mineral or chemical fertilizers containing the three fertilizing elements nitrogen, phosphorus and potassium (excluding tablets or similar forms, or in packages with a gross weight of ≤ 10 kg)	409	322	4.4%
310210	Urea, whether or not in aqueous solution (excluding pellet or similar forms, or in packages with a gross weight of ≤ 10 kg)	291	263	1.1%

Harmonized system codes	Commodity groups	World average export prices, $	Belarusian export prices, $	Belarus' share in global exports
440710	Coniferous wood sawn or chipped lengthwise, sliced or peeled, whether or not planed, sanded or end-jointed, of a thickness of > 6 mm	160	119	0.5%
721710	Wire of iron or non-alloy steel, in coils, not plated or coated, whether or not polished (excluding bars and rods)	818	423	3.1%
151411	Low erucic acid rape or colza oil "fixed oil which has an erucic acid content of < 2%," crude	768	661	2.6%

As you can see in table 1, the prices for Belarusian products are lower than the world average prices. Note that the price of "Potassium chloride for use as fertilizer" is close to the world average export price. But only the Russian Federation has an average export price of potassium lower than $263 per ton. This price ratio leads to a high treat for Belarusian export commodities.

Conclusions

Summarizing, the current trends in the world trade form a number of foreign trade risks for the Belarusian economy, requiring improvement of the economic practice, as well as the adaptation of legislation. In this structure, there are non-specific and specific risks. One of the key factors threatening Belarusian exporters is the lack of "market economy" status of our country.

The analysis of the price conjuncture of the Belarusian export has confirmed the high vulnerability of its major components for anti-dumping proceedings, excepting products related to oil and petroleum products. This is primarily due to the lower prices of Belarusian exporters compared to the prices of similar goods and exporters from countries having the market economy status.

Under these conditions, a key focus of the domestic exporter protection is providing the "market economy" status for the Republic of Belarus. There are a number of actions that reduce the amount of anti-dumping investigations against the subjects of foreign economic activity of the Republic of Belarus:

- accession of the Republic of Belarus to the WTO as a full member. This will mean that the Anti-dumping Code, which is part of the GATT, would be applied to Belarus;

- inclusion of provisions for compensation of the lawyer service expenses for customers in the case of anti-dumping procedure excitations in the text of contracts upon supplying said contracts;
- providing scientific instruments for the prediction of the anti-dumping procedure emergence, calculating wherever possible by analyzing the dynamics of domestic production, demand, consumption, exports and considering all this in conjunction with forecasts for the global, regional and sectoral economy.
- coordination of deliveries for certain geographic markets through joint efforts of domestic producers and traders.

Minimizing of the anti-dumping investigation probability against the Belarusian exporters and effective responses to possible anti-dumping measures by other countries suggest training of specialists, providing state, legal, and information support for domestic producers and exporters.

References

1. Agreement on implementation of article VI of the general agreement on tariffs and trade, World Trade Organization [Electronic resource]. Access mode: http://www.wto.org/english/docs_e/legal_e/19-adp.pdf.
2. Bakanov, A. A., Zhulego, L. A.: Anti-dumping measures against non-market economies: some conceptual problems and an example, ECOWEST, no. 4, 2003, p. 637–668.
3. CBO (1996): Antidumping Action in the United States and Around the World: An Analysis of International Data, Washington, Congressional Budget Office.
4. European Commission http://europa.eu/rapid/press-release_MEMO-16-61_en.htm Brussels, 13 January 2016.
5. GATT, World Trade Organization [Electronic resource]. Access mode: http://www.wto.org/english/docs_e/legal_e/gatt47_e.pdf.
6. International Trade and Market Access Data // World Trade Organization [Electronic resource]. Access mode: https://www.wto.org/english/res_e/statis_e/statis_bis_e.htm?solution=WTO&path=/Dashboards/MAPS&file=Tariff.wcdf&bookmarkState={%22impl%22:%22client%22,%22params%22:{%22langParam%22:%22en%22}}.
7. Isaenko, A., Shcherbakov, A. (2002): The causes of the disproportionate use of anti-dumping / The final report, Moscow, Economics education and research consortium – Russia and CIS. [Electronic resource]. Access mode: http://www.eerc.ru/default/download/creater/working_papers/file/c7535ef6fd71946a08f3889e6efb1bce91adc985.pdf.
8. Finger, J. M., Hall, H. K., Nelson, D. R. (1982): "The Political Economy of Administered Protection" American Economic Review 72, pp. 452–466.
9. Tharakan, P. K. M., Waelbroek, J. (1994) Anti-dumping and Countervailing Duty Decision in the EC and USA: An Experiment in Comparative Political Economy, European Economic Review, p. 171–193.

Sorin-George TOMA

Faculty of Administration and Business, University of Bucharest, tomagsorin62@yahoo.com

Paul MARINESCU

Faculty of Administration and Business, University of Bucharest, paulmarinescu1@gmail.com

Ionut CONSTANTIN

Faculty of Administration and Business, University of Bucharest, ionut.constantin@drept.unibuc.ro

Entrepreneurship and Economic Growth

Abstract: Countries compete not only for markets, human resources, technology or investments, but also for growth and development in a very dynamic economic environment. Economic growth has always constituted a leading concern for governments, policymakers, and researchers. There is a broad consensus around the necessity of a growth-oriented economic policy in all countries of the world. The paper builds on a vast body of literature that highlights the importance of economic growth in a highly competitive global environment and the various ways entrepreneurship may contribute to growth. The main objectives of this research are to briefly define the concepts of entrepreneurship and economic growth, and to emphasize their relationship. The methodology is based on a quantitative research. The paper shows that entrepreneurship and economic growth represent two multidimensional and interconnected concepts.

Keywords: entrepreneurship, economic growth, global entrepreneurship index, gross domestic product

Introduction

The last decades have witnessed the rapid expansion of globalization, communication, and technology all over the world. The playing field of global economy has become wider and the competition among companies, cities, countries, or regions has increased at unprecedented speed. Countries compete not only for markets, human resources, technology or investments, but also for growth and development in a very dynamic economic environment (Vietor 2007).

The world economy is projected to grow by 2.7% in 2017 (World Bank 2017), supported especially by the high economic performance of developing countries such as

China and India (National Intelligence Council 2017). In fact, the increasing shift in global economic power towards emerging market economies, which will gradually enlarge their share of world gross domestic product (GDP), has begun since the end of the last century (Hawksworth, Audino and Clarry 2017).

As competitiveness is generally viewed as a key factor in raising the overall level of prosperity of a nation, all countries should establish their objectives in the field of economic growth. In this respect, robust economic growth and shared prosperity have to be top priorities on the political agenda of any government (Porter, Rivkin and Desai 2016).

Economic growth has always constituted a leading concern for governments, policymakers, and researchers. There is a broad consensus around the necessity of a growth-oriented economic policy in all countries of the world (Rodrik 2007). Economic growth contributes to the improvement of people's wellbeing (e.g., education, health, housing, income, life expectancy, etc.) and helps governments in achieving various objectives related to economic, social, and environmental issues (e.g., reducing poverty, advanced health care, enhancing employment, low-carbon emission, etc.).

Government may affect economic growth through numerous means and actions, such as the accumulation of physical and human capital, pro- or anti-natalist measures, the speed of technological progress, the maintenance of the rule of the law, the practice of planning, taxation, regulation, or the overall size of government (Acemoglu 2009; Weil 2009). At the European Union (EU) level, governments have agreed to implement the "Europe 2020 strategy" that put at its core a smart (the role of knowledge and innovation within the economic system), sustainable (the need for a greener and more competitive economy) and inclusive (the importance of a high-employment economy) growth (European Commission 2010). Along this line, the EU member states have been advised to pursue policies that support growth both in the short and in the long term, and to prioritize reforms that increase productivity (European Commission 2016; Organisation for Economic Cooperation and Development 2016). The reason is that productivity represents the main source of economic growth. Higher productivity typically comes from new ways of doing things (e.g., new production methods, new management techniques, new skills among workers, etc.) and from new companies (e.g., start-ups) that replace the old companies (Cochrane 2016).

The academic interest in economic growth is not new, as it has constituted a major concern for economic thinkers since the emergence of classical economy (Thirlwall 1972). There is a plethora of studies on economic growth and its relationships with other main concepts such as entrepreneurship, innovation and technology (Mowery and Rosenberg 1995; Feldman, Link and Siegel 2002; Brown and Ulijn 2004; Wong, Ho and Autio 2005; Maradana, 2017). Among them, the research regarding the connection between economic growth and entrepreneurship represents a major concern for theoreticians, especially in the last decade (van Stel 2006; Minniti 2007; Prieger et al. 2016; Naudé 2016; Ferreira et al. 2017).

The paper builds on a vast body of literature that highlights the importance of economic growth in a highly competitive global economic environment and the various ways entrepreneurship may contribute to growth. This rather new approach that differs from the traditional views reveals the need to relate entrepreneurship to economic growth.

The main objectives of this research are to briefly define the concepts of entrepreneurship and economic growth and to emphasize their relationship. The paper utilizes a quantitative research that describes and explains the two abovementioned concepts, and seeks to validate the connection between them. The data used for this descriptive research were collected through desk research based on a significant literature review. The main sources were books, reports and journal articles, mainly from the areas of economics, business and entrepreneurship, and were found in libraries and electronic databases. The paper attempts to contribute to the current business literature by demonstrating the relationship between entrepreneurship and economic growth through the analysis of several specific key indices.

1. Literature review

Defining the main concepts and their connection is beneficial for what is to come in the next section of the paper. Both notions, entrepreneurship and economic growth, are to be found in numerous studies and scientific research.

- There is a broad array of definitions of entrepreneurship in literature as the concept is rather complex and covers many entrepreneurial activities. The taxonomy of entrepreneurial theories can be concentrated into three distinct intellectual traditions as follows (Hébert and Link 1989): the German tradition (e.g., J. A. Schumpeter), the Chicagoan tradition (e.g., F. Knight), and the Austrian tradition (e.g., I. Kirzner). Schumpeter considers that entrepreneurship refers to the undertaking of new ideas and new combinations (e.g., innovations) because it expresses the creativity of human beings (Schumpeter 1934). He also distinguishes various manifestations of entrepreneurship such as the introduction of new goods/methods of production or the creation of new organizations. In his turn, Knight asserts that entrepreneurship deals with risk and uncertainty. Later, Kirzner stresses that the entrepreneurial process can be summarized as acting upon a previously unobserved profit opportunity (Kirzner 1973). In recent times, researchers suggest different approaches as follows: "Entrepreneurship is the manifest ability and willingness of individuals, on their own, in teams, within and outside existing organizations, to: perceive and create new economic opportunities (new products, new production methods, new organizational schemes and new product-market combinations) and to introduce their ideas in the market, in the face of uncertainty and other obstacles, by making decisions on location, form and the use of resources and institutions" (Wennekers and Thurik 1999, pp. 46–47).
- "Entrepreneurship is a process of exploiting opportunities that exist in the environment or that are created through innovation in an attempt to create value" (Brown and Ulijn 2004, p. 5).

- Entrepreneurship is "the process whereby an individual or group of individuals, acting independently of any association with an existing organization, creates a new organization" (Ács and Armington 2006, p. 8).

Thus, entrepreneurship constitutes essentially a human process that harnesses various resources (e.g., creativity) and brings something new (e.g., organization). Secondly, it allows the entrepreneur to create/identify and exploit opportunities that exist in the environment. Thirdly, entrepreneurship may lead to value creation under risky and uncertain conditions.

The theories of economic growth emerged more than two hundreds years ago. A. Smith stated that there is no limit for economic growth, whereas D. Ricardo considered that the growth potential is limited by the availability of economic resources (Holcombe 1998). Prior to World War II, C. Clark analyzed the shift from primary to secondary and tertiary industrial structure and related to economic growth (Clark 1940). After the war, S. Kuznets stated that the essence of growth is that trends, over time, are dominated by the appearance of numerous changes in technology, institutions, and tastes (Kuznets 1966). In the same period, W. W. Rostow identified the five stages of economic growth as follows: the traditional society, the preconditions for take-off, the take-off, the drive to maturity, and the age of mass-consumption (Rostow 1960). In his view, the take-off requires the existence and the successful activity of some group which is prepared to approve innovation (e.g., entrepreneurs).

In his turn, W. A. Lewis investigated the kinds of institutions that favor growth, and the relationships between attitudes and institutions. He concluded that economic growth depends on the attitudes related to work, to wealth, to invention or to adventure, and the greatest growth appears in societies where "men have an eye to the economic chance, and are willing to stir themselves to seize it" (Lewis 1961, p. 23).

Later, the Solow model econometrically linked physical capital with (unskilled) labor in order to explain economic growth (Solow 1971), whereas others revealed the importance of technical change (Pasinetti 1983) and technology's contribution to growth and competitiveness (Mowery and Rosenberg 1995; Acemoglu 2009). Some authors established the interdependence between the changes in social organization and values (e.g., urbanization promotes values favorable to entrepreneurship) and economic growth (Adelman and Morris 1973), and others took into consideration elements such as strong business confidence, greater professionalism of management or better education (Scott 1998; Acemoglu 2009). Starting from the fact that growth implies the increase of a real or nominal economic variable, economic growth represents:

- "An increase in a nation's or an area's capacity to produce goods and services coupled with an increase in production of these goods and services" (Greenwald 1973, p. 186) that is measured by the annual rate of increase in GDP.
- "The steady process of increasing productive capacity of the economy, and hence of increasing national income" (Bannock, Baxter and Rees 1977, p. 132).
- "The rate at which the national income of a country increases" (Adam 1993, p. 171).

- Economic growth constitutes, therefore, a valued concept and is determined by different factors such as population, natural resources, physical capital, social organization, technology or entrepreneurship. A plethora of research has analyzed the relationship between entrepreneurship and economic growth and concluded that: Entrepreneurship may affect economic growth in several ways. First, the entrepreneurial activities lead to the introduction of key innovations within the economy, play an important role in the early stages of industries, enhance knowledge and increase productivity (Wennekers and Thurik 1999; Holtz-Eakin and Chihwa 2003; van Stel, Carree and Thurik, 2005; Audretsch, Keilbach and Lehmann 2006). Second, entrepreneurship often conducts to technological change that is beneficial for growth (Holcombe 1998; Ács and Audretsch 2005). Third, it may determine the expansion of the financial system, one of the economic growth engines (King and Levine 1993).
- Economic growth influences entrepreneurship. Economic growth provides more opportunities and, as a consequence, entrepreneurs become more interested in acting on them (Prieger et al. 2016). It may determine the enlargement of human networks (e.g., personal contacts) that offer the entrepreneur the opportunity for obtaining more and better resources (Burt 1995). Also, economic growth often creates a social milieu favorable to the dissemination of the entrepreneurial initiatives and culture.

In sum, there is an interconnection between entrepreneurship and economic growth. Entrepreneurship leads to growth and vice versa.

2. Linking entrepreneurship to economic growth

- During the time, several indices have become representative both in literature and the economic world. In order to validate the connection between entrepreneurship and economic growth, this section of the paper presents the relationships among the Global Entrepreneurship Index (GEI), economic freedom, ease of doing business and total early-stage entrepreneurial activity (TEA = percentage of the adult population between the ages of 18 and 64 years who are in the process of starting a business or who have just started a business which is less than 42 months old) for the year 2016 (table 1). The GEI 2016 analyzes 132 countries of the world and comprises three sub-indices (Ács, Szerb and Autio 2016): entrepreneurial attitudes (opportunity perception, startup skills, risk acceptance, networking, cultural support),
- entrepreneurial abilities (opportunity startup, technology absorption, human capital, competition),
- entrepreneurial aspirations (product innovation, process innovation, high growth, internationalization, risk capital).

The Index of Economic Freedom measures ten aspects that are grouped into four broad categories (Miller and Kim 2016): rule of law (property rights, freedom from corruption), government size (fiscal freedom, government spending), regulatory efficiency (business freedom, labor freedom, monetary freedom), and market openness (trade freedom, investment freedom, financial freedom). In its turn, the ease of doing business captures the following 11 dimensions of business regulation (World Bank 2017): starting a business, dealing with construction permits, getting electricity, registering property, getting credit, protecting minority investors, paying taxes, trading across borders, enforcing contracts, resolving insolvency, labor market regulation.

The top ten countries in the GEI 2016 are mostly from the Anglo-Saxon (four countries) and Nordic (three countries) countries and belong to the innovation-stage of development. The United States, Canada and Australia lead the ranking. It is interesting that, taking into account the economic freedom, the ease of doing business and the TEA, the majority of these countries hold lower positions in the rankings.

Table 1: Indices of entrepreneurship in the world, 2016

Rank	**Global Entrepreneurship Index**		**Economic freedom**		**Ease of doing business**		**Total early-stage entrepreneurial activity**	
	Country	**Score**	**Rank**	**Score**	**Rank**	**Score**	**Rank**	**Score**
1	United States	86.2	11	75.4	8	82.45	24	12.6
2	Canada	79.5	6	78.0	22	78.57	12	16.7
3	Australia	78.0	5	80.3	15	80.26	15	14.6
4	Denmark	76.0	12	75.3	3	84.87	n/a	n/a
5	Sweden	75.9	26	72.0	9	82.13	51	7.6
6	Taiwan	69.7	14	74.7	11	81.09	44	8.2
7	Iceland	68.9	20	73.3	20	78.91	n/a	n/a
8	Switzerland	67.8	4	81.0	31	76.06	44	8.2
9	United Kingdom	67.7	10	76.4	7	82.74	41	8.8
10	France	66.4	75	62.3	29	76.27	60	5.3

Sources: Ács, Szerb and Autio 2016; Miller and Kim 2016; World Bank 2017; Global Entrepreneurship Monitor 2017.

In spite of the fact that the best entrepreneurial countries of the world do not have the most entrepreneurs, they have well-functioning entrepreneurial ecosystems and the best entrepreneurs (Ács, Szerb and Autio 2016). These countries own some of the highest GDP, GDP per capita (table 2), and incomes in the world. Also, most of them obtain good performances in the global competitiveness ranking.

Table 2: Indices related to economic growth of the most entrepreneurial countries in the world, 2016

GDP at PPP 2016 estimation		GDP per capita at PPP 2016 estimation	GDP growth 2016 estimation	Global Competitiveness Index 2016	
Country	**Value ($ bn)**			**Rank**	**Score**
United States	18,560	57,300	1.60	3	5.70
Canada	1,674	46,200	1.20	15	5.27
Australia	1,189	48,800	2.90	22	5.19
Denmark	264.8	46,600	1.00	12	5.35
Sweden	498.1	49,700	3.60	6	5.53
Taiwan	1,125	47,800	1.00	14	5.28
Iceland	16.15	48,100	4.90	27	4.96
Switzerland	494.3	59,400	1.00	1	5.81
United Kingdom	2,788	42,500	1.80	7	5.49
France	2,737	42,400	1.30	21	5.20

Sources: Central Intelligence Agency 2017; Schwab 2016.

Several main ideas should be revealed on the basis of the above indices and rankings. First, entrepreneurship is practically a worldwide phenomenon. Second, it is the outcome of the capitalist system, as free societies provide numerous and varied opportunities for individuals and, therefore, encourage entrepreneurship. The improvement of economic freedom leads to achieving faster economic growth (Miller and Kim 2016). Third, entrepreneurship appears as a key element of a competitive economy. Fourth, the best entrepreneurial countries of the world are wealthy and prosperous nations, as growth is maximized when burdensome and redundant regulations are eliminated and business freedom is valued. Fifth, their entrepreneurial ecosystems promote the entrepreneurial activities, provide a stable regulatory framework, support innovation and boost technological changes. Sixth, the best entrepreneurial countries of the world tend to have lower levels of income inequality on average. Seventh, governments play a major role in establishing more business-friendly regulations in order to create an energizing playing field for doing business.

As the GEI correlates relatively high with GDP (Ács, Szerb and Autio 2016) entrepreneurship is to be seen as an important factor in determining and stimulating economic growth. In its turn, economic growth may create favorable conditions for the development of entrepreneurship. More and more governments around the world understand that entrepreneurship constitutes an engine of economic growth and, therefore, they recognize the need to establish well-functioning markets through simple and transparent regulations.

Conclusions

Economic growth has remained a highly debated topic both in the economic and academic world. On the one side, cities, countries, regions and blocks of countries compete for growth and development at a global level. On the other side, economic growth represents a highly debated topic among researchers, academics and policymakers all over the world. In this respect, the recognition of the importance of entrepreneurial activity on economic growth has been emphasized in numerous research, especially in the past decades.

The paper contributes to the enrichment of the scientific literature from the economic and business domains. From a theoretical standpoint, it brings some clarifications regarding the two concepts. First, the work demonstrates that entrepreneurship and economic growth are two complex and rather multidimensional notions. Second, it explains the relationship between entrepreneurship and economic growth, pointing out that on the one hand, entrepreneurship leads to economic growth, and on the other hand, economic growth influences entrepreneurship, as shown in other studies (Ács and Audretsch 2005; Prieger et al. 2016). Third, the work shows that the best entrepreneurial countries of the world are wealthy societies and growth-oriented economies.

Further research could be carried on in order to expand the analysis of the factors that determine the interconnection between entrepreneurship and economic growth.

References

1. Acemoglu, Daron: Introduction to Modern Economic Growth. Princeton University Press: Princeton 2009.
2. Ács, Zoltán J./Audretsch, David B. (eds.): Handbook of Entrepreneurship Research. Kluwer: Boston 2005.
3. Ács, Zoltán J./Armington, Catherine: Entrepreneurship, Geography, and American Economic Growth. Cambridge University Press: New York 2006.
4. Ács, Zoltán J./Szerb, László/Autio, Erkko: Global Entrepreneurship Index. The Global Entrepreneurship and Development Institute: Washington, 2016.
5. Adam, John H. (ed.): Longman Dictionary of Business English. Longman: Harlow 1993.

6. Adelman, Irma/Morris, Cynthia T.: Economic Growth and Social Equity in Developing Countries. Stanford University Press: Stanford 1973.
7. Audretsch, David B./Keilbach, Max C./Lehmann, Erich E.: Entrepreneurship and Economic Growth. Oxford University Press: New York 2006.
8. Bannock, Graham/Baxter, Ron E./Rees, Ray: The Penguin Dictionary of Economics. Penguin Books: Middlesex 1977.
9. Brown, Terrence E./Ulijn, Jan (eds.): Innovation, Entrepreneurship and Culture: The Interaction between Technology, Progress and Economic Growth. Edward Elgar: Cheltenham 2004.
10. Burt, Ronald S.: Structural Holes. Harvard University Press: Cambridge 1995.
11. Central Intelligence Agency: The World Factbook 2017. Central Intelligence Agency: Langley 2017.
12. Clark, Colin: Conditions of Economic Progress. Macmillan: London 1940.
13. Cochrane, John H.: "Economic Growth." In Moore, John N. (ed.): The Presidential Debates: Issues and Questions for the 2016 Elections and Beyond. Carolina Academic Press: Durham 2016.
14. European Commission: Europe 2020 – A strategy for smart, sustainable and inclusive growth. European Commission: Brussels 2010.
15. European Commission: Council recommendation on the economic policy of the euro area. European Commission: Brussels 2016.
16. Feldman, Maryann P./Link, Albert N./Siegel, Donald S.: The Economics of Science and Technology: An Overview of Initiatives to Foster Innovation, Entrepreneurship, and Economic Growth. Springer: New York 2002.
17. Ferreira, João J. et al.: "Effects of Schumpeterian and Kirznerian entrepreneurship on economic growth: Panel data evidence". Entrepreneurship & Regional Development 29 (1–2), 2017, pp. 27–50.
18. Global Entrepreneurship Monitor: Global Report 2016/17. Global Entrepreneurship Research Association: Massachusetts 2017.
19. Greenwald, Douglas (ed.): The McGraw-Hill Dictionary of Modern Economics. McGraw-Hill: New York 1973.
20. Hawksworth, John/Audino, Hannah/Clarry, Rob: The long view: How will the global economic order change by 2050? PricewaterhouseCoopers: London 2017.
21. Hébert, Robert F./Link, Albert N.: "In Search of the Meaning of Entrepreneurship." Small Business Economics 1 (1), 1989, pp. 39–49.
22. Holcombe, Randall G.: "Entrepreneurship and economic growth." The Quarterly Journal of Austrian Economics 1 (2), 1998, pp. 45–62.
23. Holtz-Eakin, Douglas/Chihwa, Kao: "Entrepreneurship and economic growth: The proof is in the productivity." Center for Policy Research, Working Paper No. 50, 2003, pp. 1–30.
24. King, Robert G./Levine, Ross: "Finance, entrepreneurship, and growth: Theory and evidence." Journal of Monetary Economics 32 (3), 1993, pp. 513–542.
25. Kirzner, Israel M.: Competition and Entrepreneurship. University of Chicago Press: Chicago 1973.

26. Kuznets, Simon: Modern Economic Growth: Rate, Structure and Spread. Yale University Press: New Haven and London 1966.
27. Lewis, William A.: The Theory of Economic Growth. George Allen & Unwin: London 1961.
28. Maradana, Rana P. et al.: "Does innovation promote economic growth? Evidence from European countries." Journal of Innovation and Entrepreneurship 6 (1), 2017, pp. 1–23.
29. Miller, Terry/Kim, Anthony B.: 2016 Index of Economic Freedom. The Heritage Foundation and Dow Jones & Company: Washington 2016.
30. Minniti, Maria (ed.): Entrepreneurship: The Engine of Growth. Volume 1 – People. Praeger Publishers: Westport 2007.
31. Mowery, David C./Rosenberg, Nathan: Technology and the Pursuit of Economic Growth. Cambridge University Press: New York 1995.
32. National Intelligence Council: Global Trends: The Paradox of Progress. National Intelligence Council: Washington 2017.
33. Naudé, Wim: "Is European entrepreneurship in crisis?". IZA Discussion Paper 9817, 2016, pp. 1–10.
34. Organisation for Economic Cooperation and Development: Going for Growth Interim Report. OECD: Paris 2016.
35. Pasinetti, Luigi L.: Structural Change and Economic Growth: A Theoretical Essay on the Dynamics of the Wealth of Nations. Cambridge University Press: Cambridge 1983.
36. Porter, Michael E./Rivkin, Jan W./Desai, Mihir A.: Problems Unsolved and a Nation Divided: The State of U.S. Competitiveness 2016. Harvard Business School: Boston 2016.
37. Prieger, James E. et al.: "Economic growth and the optimal level of entrepreneurship." World Development 82 (C), 2016, pp. 95–109.
38. Rodrik, Dani: One Economics, Many Recipes: Globalization, Institutions, and Economic Growth. Princeton University Press: Princeton and Oxford 2007.
39. Rostow, Walt W.: The Stages of Economic Growth. Cambridge University Press: London 1960.
40. Schwab, Klaus (ed.): The Global Competitiveness Report 2016–2017. World Economic Forum: Geneva 2016.
41. Schumpeter, Joseph. A.: The Theory of Economic Development. Harvard University Press: Cambridge 1934.
42. Scott, Maurice F.: A New View of Economic Growth. Clarendon Press: Oxford 1998.
43. Solow, Robert M.: Growth Theory: An Exposition. Clarendon Press: London 1971.
44. Thirlwall, Anthony P.: Growth and Development. Macmillan: London and Basingstoke 1972.
45. van Stel, André/Carree, Martin/Thurik, Roy: "The Effect of Entrepreneurial Activity on National Economic Growth." Small Business Economics 24 (3), 2005, pp. 311–321.

46. van Stel, André: Empirical Analysis of Entrepreneurship and Economic Growth. Springer: New York 2006.
47. Vietor, Richard H. K.: How Countries Compete: Strategy, Structure, and Government in the Global Economy. Harvard Business School Press: Boston 2007.
48. Weil, David N.: Economic Growth. Pearson Education: Boston 2009.
49. Wennekers, Sander/Thurik, Roy: "Linking entrepreneurship and economic growth." Small Business Economics 13 (1), 1999, pp. 27–55.
50. Wong, Poh K./Ho, Yuen P./Autio, Erkko: "Entrepreneurship, innovation and economic growth: Evidence from GEM data." Small Business Economics 24 (3), 2005, pp. 335–350.
51. World Bank: Global Economic Prospects: Weak Investments in Uncertain Times. International Bank for Reconstruction and Development/The World Bank: Washington 2017.
52. World Bank: Doing Business 2017: Equal Opportunity for All. International Bank for Reconstruction and Development/The World Bank: Washington 2017.

Marina BĂDILEANU

Center of Industry and Services Econnomy, National Institute for Economic Research "Costin C. Kiriţescu", Romanian Academy, email: badmarina@yahoo.com

Svetlana CIUMAC

Institute of Legal and Political Research (ICJP) of Academy of Sciences of Moldova, email: svetlanaciumac@gmail.com

Luminiţa Izabell GEORGESCU

Center of Industry and Services Econnomy, National Institute for Economic Research "Costin C. Kiriţescu", Romanian Academy, email: georgescu_izabell@yahoo.com

Regional Shifts of Multinational Public Utility Companies

Abstract: The regional development of public utilities services' supply depends on a number of factors, such as: endowment with natural resources of the region, the level of economic development, the urban/rural ratio, degree of compliance with local communities to EU directives (for instance, drinking water supply and access to sewerage networks) etc. At the same time, the interest of specialized multinational companies for one region or another is determined by criteria that include, besides the above-mentioned, other factors such as existing infrastructure, the demand for public utilities, the availability of tax or financial incentives (green certificates in renewable energy) etc. The paper aims to map out the evolution of regional interest of these companies, their financial and accounting situation, their concern for social responsibility of corporate governance depending on the area they serve, etc.

Keywords: multi-national companies, regional distribution, electricity, water supply

Introduction

The industrial structure and organization of public utilities vary considerably, according to their degree of vertical or horizontal integration and competition. In several countries, these industries are dominated by large multinational companies. Property types are quite complex, involving a combination of private, state or community owned units. The expansion of these activities indicates the huge interest in accessing new markets through the acquisition of other national business areas or by extending the operations to new territories. The result of mergers and takeovers is a market ruled by a small number of public utility giants diversifying their range of services, from electricity to natural gas, telecommunications, water, and recycling.

The overall objective of this paper is to assess, from a historical perspective – economic and legislative – the evolution of ownership structure of some public utilities in Romania. Features regarding electricity, thermal energy and water supply have been presented in numerous studies elaborated by our economic research institutes, departmental research units or by specialized ministries. The novelty of this paper is to define the historical milestones from legislative and economic perspectives.

1. Literature review

Jamasab, Mota, Newbery and Pollitt (Jamasab et al., 2005) conducted a comprehensive, critical study addressing the energy sectors' reform in developing countries, with the stated aim to test the extent to which reality and empiric evidence justify the economic or ideological background of the reform process initiation.

Buzar concludes that most countries simply have no other political option than to follow a pre-determined path in the energy, housing and social welfare areas. Generally, this includes energy liberalization, reduction of social welfare and delegation of social policies to private actors. The author argues that these processes are supported by a synergy complex between global powers and central governments, making efforts to influence neoliberalism in an inevitable way, specific to post-socialist transformation (Buzar, 2007).

Aspects such as the comparative effectiveness of public owned natural monopolies versus private ones, the benefits of competitive systems versus economies of vertically integrated units, currently attract many controversies. Joskow concludes that in practice, the benefits of each reform must at least compensate for increasing transactional costs of vertical separation (Joskow, 2002).

Pollitt believes that economic efficiency of large energy companies registers no significant differences, according to the type of property. He also examines the effects of competition, economies of scale, vertical structure and regulations on energy systems' efficiency (Pollitt, 1995). Evidence suggests that all these factors influence the costs equally, regardless of ownership structure.

Different opinions shared in the economic literature, regarding the efficacy of privatization and competition promotion in network industries, revealed some weaknesses in the competitiveness assessment methodologies for energy systems in relation to their new international dimensions driven by the internal energy market creation. These can be summarized as follows: ignoring strategic, long-term vision in order to estimate the effects of liberalization and competitiveness; lack of appropriate methodological tools for assessing the degree of competitiveness expressed by the degree of concentration of production and distribution, price competitiveness, consumer response and the effects of entry barriers; lack of transparency.

2.1. Highlights of changes in ownership structure of the Romanian energy industry

Romania transited, after 1989, from a planned economy, to a market economy, gradually passing towards restructuring public utilities[1]. From the inside, the main drives included the need to increase efficiency throughout the lifespan of a power supply to consumers and preventing the state budget from accumulating huge debts that the energy system imposed upon several industrial late payers. According to most decision-makers, this could be achieved by promoting competition between energy generators and suppliers and encouraging private investment. The way of achieving reform goals, however, was different from the one pursued by the developed EU countries. The year 1998 marked the first stage of vertical disintegration of the Romanian power system: the separation of distribution and electricity generation. The most important energy company, Termoelectrica, quickly reducing its size by horizontal disintegration, and reducing its annual contribution to total energy production, disappeared from the market. In 2001, the distribution company Electrica, also separated horizontally and divided into eight separate entities, privatized later. Distinction between distribution and supply activities was first made in 2003 and, in 2008, the separation of the distribution and supply businesses was completed.

In subsequent years, the main objective of the Romanian energy sector reform was the privatization of distribution. ENEL SpA paid only €43.4 million for 51% of Electrica Dobrogea (a company with 1,894,699 consumers in 2006; €2.51 per share) and €69 million for a 51% stake in Electrica Banat (a company with 2,841,437 consumers in 2006; €2.92 per share). In Romania, in 2006, the year before the last privatizations were carried out, Italian ENEL held 35.6% of the energy distributed in Romania, the German company E.ON 12.3%, the Czech company CEZ 12.2% and the Romanian company Electrica less than 40% (Romanian Government, 2004, 2005).

---

1 In the period before 1989, three essential stages could be identified: the one marked by the adoption of the 1924 Energy Law, which reflected the liberal doctrine "by ourselves" and restricted the right to "concession only to Romanian citizens and companies," thus fencing the foreign capital access to the Romanian energy market (Gusti, 1938); the one subjected to the Law on Energy of 1930, reflecting the "open doors" policy that lifted the prerequisite of Romanian nationality of concessions, making no distinction between foreign and local capital (Iovanelli, 1975); finally, the one subsumed to the socialist doctrine based on the intensive development of the sector.
From 1948, beginning with the nationalization of the means of production, the organization of large state-owned regional companies started, and the 1950 provisions on electricity included in the 1930 Law on Energy were replaced by those based on the new socialist concept. The new legislation provided that "the right to produce, transport, distribute and sell electricity only belonged to the state," which was exercised by the Ministry of Electricity.

The main transformations of the institutional-legislative framework governing the Romanian energy system during the transition and integration into the EU periods concerned the vertical and horizontal separation of activities, the introduction of competition among electricity producers and suppliers, the privatization of distribution and price liberalization. The creation of the energy suppliers' market has been inadequately prepared from an institutional point of view and forced by interest groups. The regulatory agency has failed to ensure transparency, to monitor the activity of suppliers so that this new energy segment might become indeed a useful tool for the real opening of the energy market.

2.2. The behavior and performance of electricity suppliers

The analysis of the suppliers market was conducted based on information from the balance sheets of companies, provided by the Ministry of Finance (www.mfinante.ro). The net profit shown in the balance sheets has been converted into euro using the average exchange rates published by the National Bank of Romania (www.bnr.ro). The evolution of financial indicators presents the following (fig. 1):

Fig. 1: Net profits of last resort suppliers in Romania, in 2008 and 2011–2015 years (Mil.€)

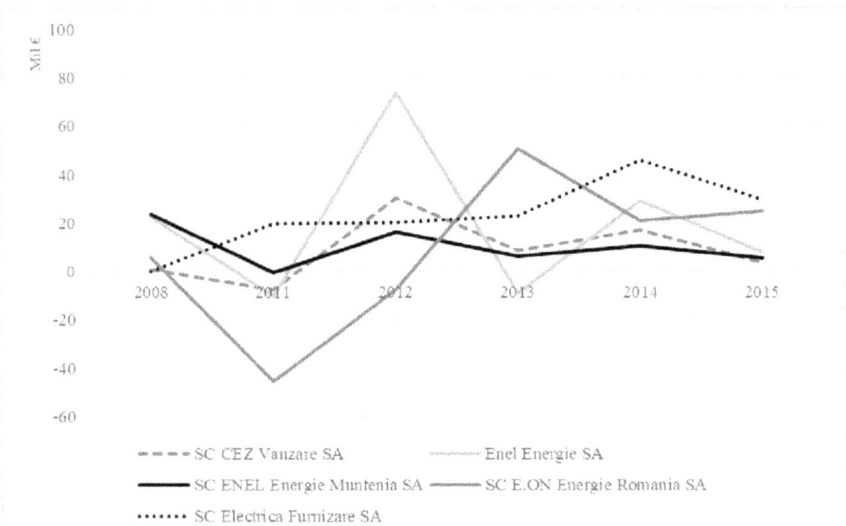

Source: Authors, based on data from www.mfinante.ro

- the Czech CEZ Vanzare SA obtained a profit of under €1 million in 2008, after which, every year, it suffered losses until 2012 when it managed to obtain a net profit of approx. €30 million, this being the most prolific year in the analyzed period;

- the Italian company Enel Energie obtained, in 2008, a net profit of about €22.5 million (only on the energy supply side), and in 2014, nearly €30 million; with its other company, Enel Energie Muntenia, the group succeeded in generating a €23.7 million profit in 2008. The only unfavorable year for Enel Energie Muntenia was 2011;
- the German group E.ON was the most dynamic company, according to multiple structure changes of its component units operating in the country. Thus, in 2007, E.ON Energie Romania SA, based in Bucharest, distributed and supplied electricity and registered losses of nearly €1.5 million. The same year, E.ON Energie Romania SA, based in Targu Mures, distributed and supplied gaseous fuels, at a profit of €22.4 million. The first firm was dissolved in 2008 through a merger. E.ON Moldova Furnizare appeared. On 2 November 2010, the German group launched its project to become "legally an integrated energy service provider, serving 1.5 million natural gas consumers and 1.4 million electricity consumers in the north." In the article posted on www.eon-gaz-romania.ro, entitled "Together for our customers" it is said that "E.ON ... continued in 2010 its plans to strengthen the important position the company holds in Romania." These plans have materialized in 2011, with losses of over €45 million. It is no less true that the year 2013 brought to the integrated company a net profit of approx. €50 million.
- the Romanian company Electrica Furnizare SA registered a positively constant evolution during the past years, scoring its best results in 2014.

2.3. The behavior and performance of central heating companies

Most companies that manage cogeneration power plants are insolvent or in liquidation. Moreover, companies producing electricity and heat that passed to the administration of local councils face a precarious financial situation because of low investment capacity of the new owners.

At the end of 2014, in the area of heat supply, excluding the one produced in cogeneration, there were 90 service providers still operating, compared to 109 in 2006. Of the 48 companies for which we have data from the Ministry of Finance, 32 (67%) recorded financial losses in 2014 (fig. 2). The highest could be found at RADET Bucharest, over €72 million, which, moreover, at the end of 2016, entered into insolvency, together with the main producer of thermal energy ELCEN Bucharest. The total net losses of these companies make up a sum of €100 million, and the degree of indebtedness ranged between 12–1600%.

Fig. 2: Net profits and losses of the central heating companies, in 2014 (RADET Bucharest is not included in this figure) (Mil.€)

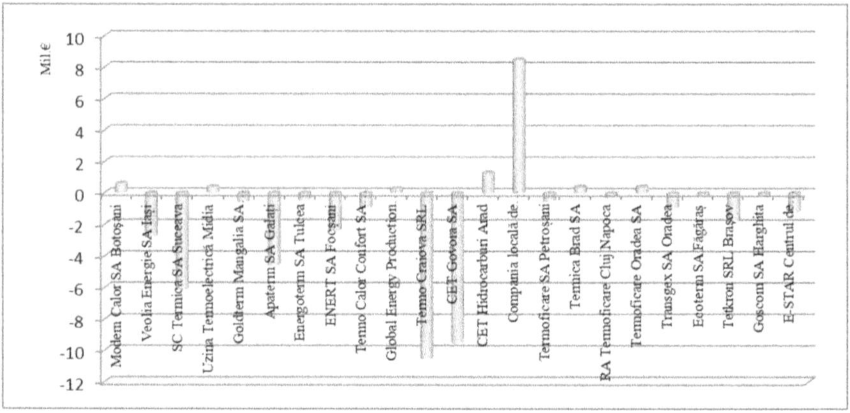

Source: Authors, based on data from www.mfinante.ro.

Given the many negative aspects that characterize the centralized heat supply, we decided to make a short trip into another area of public services, namely central water supply.

2.4. Behavior and performance of centralized water suppliers

The economic and financial analysis of regional water companies based on the balance sheets available on the website of the Ministry of Finance revealed the following:

- All 40 analyzed companies reported profits in 2013, the first ranked being Apa Nova (belonging to the French group Veolia) with almost €30 million, followed by Aquatim SA Timisoara with nearly €5 million (fig. 3);
- Profit rates ranged in 2013 from approx. 20% to 0.3%;
- In the same time, all companies registered debts, Apa Serv SA Piatra Neamt and Apa Nova

Fig. 3: Net profits/losses of the regional water companies, in 2012 and 2013 (Mil.€)

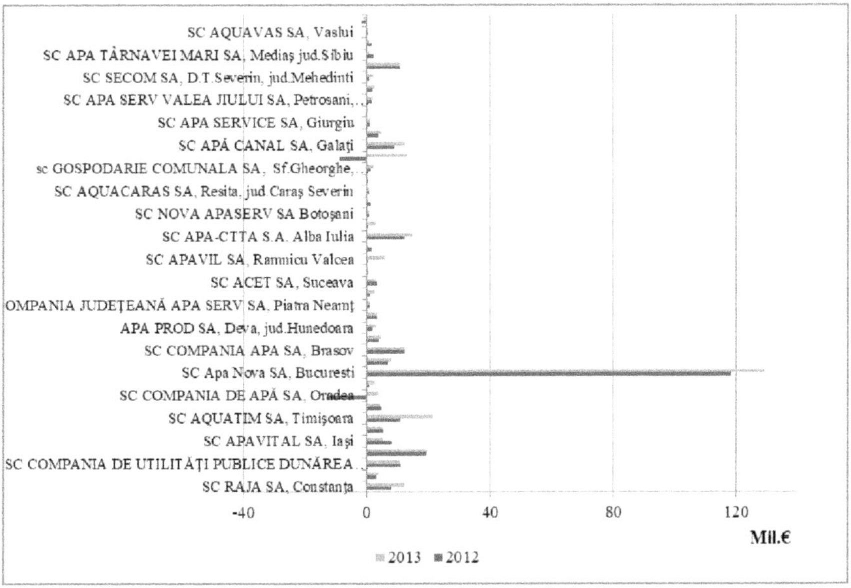

Source: Authors, based on data from www.mfinante.ro

In the next two years, 2014 and 2015, Apa Nova has located a net profit of more than €30 million yearly, due to the fact that the company is benefiting from the advantages of greater scale economies (the highest density of population per kilometer of network), and applies the highest prices nationwide for water distribution.

Conclusions

The analysis of the three public utility areas revealed some distinct issue categories and a series of similarities and differences (table 1).

Table 1: Some similarities and differences between three public network services: electricity supply, centralized heat supply and water supply

Electricity supply	Centralized heat supply	Centralized water supply
Privatization of the companies has not led to increased investments in energy efficiency	EU Directives recommendations have not led to increased investment in high efficiency cogeneration	EU directives have imposed the extension of networks and the compliance with strict deadlines
Natural monopoly is maintained by the lack of exploiting the possibilities of consumer eligibility	Urban centralized monopoly was overthrown by the promotion of individual heating sources	Natural monopoly is maintained in urban areas and extends to the rural ones
Main consumer is industry	Main consumer is population	Main consumer is industry
All companies are profitable	**The majority of centralized heating companies are insolvent or under liquidation**	**The majority of companies is profitable**
The generation is separated from transport, distribution and supply	The generation is separated from distribution	Activities have an integrated character
The share of expenditures in population's money incomes was, in 2015, 3.92%	The share of expenditures in population's money incomes was, in 2015, 0,62%	The share of expenditures in population's money incomes was, in 2015, 2.37%

Source: Authors based on data from INSSE, Tempo-online program.

For electricity: resizing the international energy system was accomplished in a single direction from the outside inwards, with the atomization of the system components contributing to the growth of large European energy groups; if the Romanian generation sector is struggling for survival, being subjected to continuous transformation more or less coherently, the distribution sector takes full advantage of its privileged position of being close to the customer. The small companies' participation in the spot market has led to increased competition and reduced operating costs, while increasing transaction costs and reducing investment capacity. The level of energy prices, the drop in revenues and the inequalities in their distribution have led us to a decrease in consumption and, implicitly, a decline in capacity utilization, to an inefficient and unsustainable use of energy resources.

For thermal energy: faulty operation of companies that provide centralized heat supply; decline of the part of the population supplied through centralized heat sources; very low access of the population, especially in rural areas, to these services; consumption structure of rural population by type of energy carriers burdened by the preponderance of firewood. The precarious situation of district heating plants passed to the local council management was emphasized. Also highlighted was the planned investments' low degree of return, and especially for the ones made from own sources and European funds, caused by the local public authorities', as well as the operators' low interest, and the lack of a correct substantiation of investment plans, based on the real needs and possibilities for their realization.

Drinking Water: Romania is characterized by very low drinking water consumption from centralized sources. We emphasized the poor quality of services provided by the water supply and sanitation companies, and limited access of the population to these services. The study revealed several aspects that characterize the functioning of regional drinking water supply companies in Romania: the profitability of regional companies and high profit rates; the existing huge economies of scale in Bucharest, doubled by the highest water prices.

References

1. Buzar, Stefan: Energy Poverty in Eastern Europe: hidden geographies of deprivation. Ashgate Publishing Company 2007.
2. Gusti, Dimitrie et al.: Enciclopedia României. vol. IV Economie naţională. Ed. Imprimeria Naţională a Moldovei 1938, p. 130.
3. Iovanelli, Marcela Felicia: Industria româneasca 1934–1938. Editura Academiei Republicii Socialiste România: Bucureşti 1975, p. 124.
4. Jamasab, Tooraj/Mota Raffaella/Newbery, David/Pollitt, Michael: Electricity sector reform in developing countries: a survey of empirical evidence on determinants and performance. World Bank Policy Research Working Paper 3549, 2005.
5. Joskow, Paul: "Electricity Sector Restructuring and Competition: A transaction-cost Perspective," 2002. Cited in Jamasab, Tooraj/Mota Raffaella/Newbery, David/Pollitt, Michael: Electricity sector reform in developing countries: a survey of empirical evidence on determinants and performance. World Bank Policy Research Working Paper 3549, 2005.
6. Pollitt, Michael: Ownership and Performance in Electric utilities: The International evidence on Privatization and Efficiency. Oxford University Press, 1995.
7. Romanian Government: Legea energiei. Monitorul Oficial nr. 143, 4 July 1924.
8. Romanian Government: Legea asupra energiei. Monitorul Oficial nr. 148, 7 July 1930.
9. Romanian Government: Decretul pentru producerea, transportul si vânzarea energiei electrice. Buletinul Oficial nr. 31 din 31 March 1950.
10. Romanian Government: Legea energiei. Monitorul Oficial nr. 511 din 16 July 2003.
11. Romanian Government: Hotărârea Guvernului nr. 1000/2004 privind unele măsuri pentru derularea şi finalizarea privatizării şi modificarea şi completarea. Strategiei de privatizare a societăţilor comerciale filiale de distribuţie şi

furnizare a energiei electrice "Electrica Dobrogea" – S. A. şi "Electrica Banat" – S.A. Monitorul Oficial nr. 629 din 10 July 2004.
12. Romanian Government: Nota de fundamentare – O.U.G. nr. 114/14-07-2005, Ordonanţa de urgenţă a Guvernului nr. 114/2005 privind unele măsuri pentru derularea şi finalizarea privatizării societăţilor comerciale filiale de distribuţie şi furnizare a energiei electrice "Electrica Moldova" – S.A. şi "Electrica Oltenia" – S.A. Monitorul Oficial nr. 668 din 27 July 2005.
13. National Institute of Statistics, Tempo-online, www.insse.ro (accessed in February 2017).
14. Ministry of Finance, www.mfinante.ro (accessed in February 2017).

Cosmin SĂLĂŞAN, Păun Ion OTIMAN, Vasile GOŞA,
Nicoleta MATEOC-SÎRB

Romanian Academy – Branch of Timisoara, Research
Centre for Sustainable Rural Development of Romania,
cosminsalasan@gmail.com, otiman@acad.ro,
gosavasile@gmail.com, mateocnicol@yahoo.com

The Link Between the Native Potential for Rural Development of a Territory and the Expectations of its Relevant Actors

Abstract: The place and the role of native or endogenous potential in terms of rural development is frequently placed in a central position when different analysis tools are employed and used to justify the orientation of a series of interventions, particularly when public funding is consistently used. The rationale behind this "natural" link points to the problem-solving by local readiness and normal expectations aiming to highlight not only the needs, but the most fitted interventions for the territory. In our approach, these elements are analyzed in a comparative manner between two significantly different territories, in terms of favorability and suitability of different interventions and development support instruments. The expectations and the interventions (as project intentions) related to rural development in a Community Led Local Development approach following the specific actions of animation and information led to a uniform knowledge and understanding, in which the actors had the freedom to express their immediate future project-based actions. The analysis considers the general orientation of preferences, the readiness (including own financial contribution) and the link with the territory's potential. Furthermore, it compares the two territories in both agriculture and rural development potential and expectations. The conclusions lead beyond the usual lack of understanding or incomplete information passed to local actors and expose the genuine orientation at community level, but individually promoted.

Keywords: rural development, endogenous potential, territorial favorability, Community-Led Local Development

Introduction

The relatively limited experience rural Romania, regarding community-led local development, leaves place for the research question – is there any type of link between the native development potential and intentions of a rural region and the expectations of this territory's relevant actors? To this purpose, the choice of period has excluded pre-accession efforts in rural development, since the programming approach of the period had no consistent input from local communities, being mainly a collection of development opportunities programmed together. The first programming period of Structural and Complementary Funds and Instruments, although started with a considerable delay, had a dedicated component within the National Rural Development Programme (NRDP), namely the fourth program axis, LEADER.

The administrative approach was not using the expression "community-led" back in 2007, but based on the history of the LEADER Community Initiative and the specific implementation setup, the later Local Development Strategies were developed by typical animation, information and consultations activities. The preparation approach was not uniform and was depending, to a large extent, on the consultants and their knowledge and practices. The current program has introduced as compulsory the specific working tools in the preparation phase, ensuring a relevant participation of the territories' population to the formulation and validation of further Local Development Strategies. In order to ensure the relevance of the research approach and validate the findings, the selection of the analyzed territories considered critical the use of these specific tools in community-led initiatives during the first programming period for one of the selected territories. The comparison choice was aiming to highlight any potential differences between micro-regions with experience from the first program, and micro-regions with no experience and, if possible, with limited contact to the previous program (NRDP 2007–2013) while selected and active within the frame of the current program (NRDP 2014–2020).

Targeting the native potential of the territories, the choice allowed the introduction of three variables differentiating the micro-regions: the natural favorability for agriculture and non-agricultural rural economic activities; the infrastructure and general logistic framework, including the proximity to large urban centers; and the general economic wealth and recent developments in all economic sectors in the micro-regions and neighboring regions. The final choice of territories introduced one micro-region with no previous history in LEADER approach, with limited experience in rural development and project based activities, relatively low natural favorability for agriculture and related activities (mostly high hills and less fertile valleys), neighboring former industrial urban centers with low economic growth over the past two decades.

The other territory was the opposite profile, with a considerably high natural favorability for all types of agriculture, well-placed in a flat and fertile environment with a good history in both large-scale cereals production and traditional and regional products, well-linked with booming urban centers, with good knowledge and sound experience in different project-based developments and successful in the previous LEADER programming period. No difference was introduced in terms of infrastructure and general logistic framework in order to avoid biasing the findings and the observations. The options and the opinions of the relevant local actors were collected with a structured questionnaire containing seven simple questions with open answers. The participation was voluntary for the entire questionnaire (one A4 sheet, single-sided) or for any of the contained questions. The application was based on individual answers, always following information and animation meetings specific to the support for finalization of the Local Development Strategies as part of sub-measure 19.1 of the NRDP 2014–2020. The collected answers were anonymized and encoded for further processing, measured and interpreted as further presented in the following sections of the paper.

1. Literature review

Earlier research from the period of Romania pre-accession to the EU (Salasan 1999, pp. 23–24) highlight the need to extend from the much-needed agricultural development and rural economic investments (Otiman 1999, pp. 10–12) towards a reasonable and inclusive approach. Moving from the state scale to the region's level (Mantino 2011, pp. 28–31) does improve the relevance and the fitness of the development choices, yet enhancing the territorial approach within the Common Agricultural Policy (CAP) frame could reinforce the architecture of the policy by adding a holistic view (resources and potential of rural) and a tool for coordination and integration of policy interventions (Mantino 2011, pp. 35–36).

A later collection of implementation experiences in selected regions of the EU (European Parliament COMAGRI 2015) highlight a transversal diversity of expectations from the CAP with no connection to the participatory development of a rural future and no obvious link to the particular resources available locally. The Swedish Research Council for Environment, Agricultural Sciences and Spatial Planning underlines that "territorial initiatives are ideally based on the assumption that local factors can be linked up to regional, national and global levels [...] At the same time, rural research focused on policy must tackle practical questions in the borderland to evaluation. An independent critical review of all the funds that go to rural industries and the rural population must be established [...]" as early as 2006 in its Research Strategy (Swedish Research Strategy 2006, pp. 27–28). The Romanian NRDPs, together with the Romanian Regional Operational Programme, for the programming periods 2007–2013 and 2014–2020, include an analysis without establishing a link between the people and the territory they live in, manage and modify by use of own or in combination with public funds. This paper tries to establish a link between the resources of a territory, the knowledge of its actors and the design of future developments.

2. Materials and method

Sub-measure 19.1 of the NRDP and its implementation setup offers the perfect grounds to regroup all relevant actors of a dominantly rural micro-region by bringing together local authorities representatives, NGOs, rural entrepreneurs in local businesses, farmers and private natural persons interested in the immediate future development of their territory. The choice of questions was strictly linked to the content and the information passed and discussed during the animation and information meetings. The link justifies the analysis of recent knowledge, placed in the expectation frame of the stakeholders and relevant rural actors.

Considering the deployment methods used during the sessions, mainly brainstorming, questions and answers, debate, projections and estimations, the questions tried to capture the interest of different possible developments in an existing and structured intentional environment. This manner avoids fresh intentions resulted from the newly acquired knowledge as result of opportunity reactions. The interest, with respect to the research question, is to retrieve the development expected and intended before the meeting and not the result and the impact of new possibilities and opportunities from future available resources.

The questionnaire:s seven questions were: Q1: What projects do you expect to implement with the support of the future Local Action Group (LAG)? Q2: What is the total value/amount for each of these projects? Q3: What is the level of your own financial contribution that you are prepared to allocate for these projects? Q4: If, for any reasons, you should select one single project of the ones mentioned above, which one would that be? Q5: What projects would you recommend to your friends, relatives, acquaintances or neighbors? Q6: What innovative projects do you expect to see implemented in your LAG? Q7: What cooperation projects do you expect to see implemented in your LAG? The first four questions maintain this requirement by the link introduced between potential intentions, the requested amount, the eventual own contribution and the priority where more than one intention is mentioned.

The understanding of the community-led local development process and environment is captured by the fifth question, and the complementary development of the territory by innovative and cooperation projects is recorded by the last two questions. The total of seven questions presented in detail with the respective results in the third section of the paper were considered sufficient to illustrate any differences in approach between the two selected territories and to highlight any possible link between the native potential for rural development and the qualified opinions and expectations of its relevant local actors.

3. Results and observations

The two selected micro-regions are named following the mix of their general favorability and are presented further as the favorable (FLAG) and less favorable (LFLAG) in order to facilitate the differentiation and with no other connotations or judgements regarding their potential. The FLAG questionnaire exercise returned 152 completed questionnaires, and the LFLAG had 162 questionnaires returned, all answers being analyzed and presented below. The first question gave each participant the possibility to indicate one or more (up to three) different intentions of development by projects expected in the following period within the frame of the Local Action Group, meaning within the boundaries of the precisely defined territory. As the results show in tab. 1, the large majority indicated a minimum of two different project intentions.

The FLAG has, in decreasing order, 64% of intentions aiming at modernizing agriculture, non-agricultural activities, services and rural affairs, fruit production, physical public infrastructure and conditioning and storage, with 53% of the answers for the first three options. From the same FLAG respondents, 62% target a project in non-agricultural activities, services and rural affairs, modernizing agriculture, animal husbandry, physical public infrastructure, cultural and social infrastructure, with the first three options covering 83% of total expressed options. Almost 30% of the respondents from the same territory aim at a third possible project in non-agricultural activities, services and rural affairs, physical public infrastructure, modernizing agriculture, animal husbandry, association and producer groups, with almost 40% of the answers for the first three intentions.

The LFLAG respondents indicated in a large majority, intention for one project (75%), with 70% choosing a second intended project, and 30% even indicating the intent for a third project. In different combinations and shares, the LFLAG's options target agricultural infrastructure, agro-tourism, animal husbandry, fruit production, non-agricultural activities, services and rural affairs, with the first three covering systematically 50% of the options. One interesting observation indicates that, except for the agro-tourism option due to the high suitability for this type of services given the profile of the region, the other options of the LFLAG are basically oriented towards agricultural production, while in the case of the FLAG, the diversification of the rural economy, the association, conditioning and storage of the agricultural production, the social and cultural infrastructure raise a considerably higher interest, most likely due to the developments from the previous programming period and the general level of development of the region. This difference is also supported by the financial level indicatively allocated to the projects and the capacity to co-finance the intended projects as detailed presented in tab. 2 and 3.

Table 1: Results from the first question, What projects do you expect to implement with the support of the future LAG?

Favorable LAG	**Less Favorable LAG**
Q1. What projects do you expect to implement with the support of the future LAG? (first option)	
64% of respondents indicate their first investment in: a. modernizing agriculture b. non-agricultural activities, services and rural business c. fruit production d. physical public infrastructure e. conditioning and storage	75% of respondents indicate their first investment in: a. agro-tourism b. agricultural infrastructure c. support for young farmers d. animal husbandry e. fruit production
Q1. What projects do you expect to implement with the support of the future LAG? (second option)	
62% of respondents indicate the interest for a second project in: a. non-agricultural activities, services and rural business b. modernizing agriculture c. modernizing animal husbandry d. physical public infrastructure e. cultural and social infrastructure	70% of respondents indicate the interest for a second project in: a. agro-tourism b. agricultural infrastructure c. support for young farmers d. animal husbandry e. fruit production

Favorable LAG	Less Favorable LAG
Q1. What projects do you expect to implement with the support of the future LAG? (third option)	
28% of the respondents gave a third project option in: a. non-agricultural activities, services and rural business b. physical public infrastructure c. modernizing agriculture d. modernizing animal husbandry e. association and producer groups	Almost 30% of the respondents gave a third project option in: a. agro-tourism b. agricultural infrastructure c. support for young farmers d. animal husbandry e. fruit production f. non-agricultural activities, services and rural business

Source: Authors' own primary data.

While the LFLAG's respondents target ⅔ of the projects under €50,000 and we can assume that the 20% of projects going above €100,000 are indicated by the local authorities, the respondents from the FLAG target mainly large projects with ⅔ above €50,000 and even ⅓ above €100,000 EUR (tab. 2). The same type of observation is valid for the level of co-financing for the proposed projects, where the large majority from the FLAG indicated 10–50%, and almost ⅕ going for 50% or more, while in the case of the respondents from the LFLAG, only ¼ are willing to contribute with 10%, and those going above this level represent only 2% of total respondents!

Table 2: Results from the second question, What is the total value/amount for each of these projects?

Q2. What is the total value/amount for each of these projects?	
Favorable LAG	**Less Favorable LAG**
Almost ⅓ of respondents target an investment of €20–50,000 for the main investment	Almost ⅓ of respondents target a main investment of €20–40,000
More than ¼ (27%) of respondents aim for €50–100,000.	Another ⅓ of respondents aim for €50,000
Another ⅓ of respondents go above €100,000 and even €200.000	Only ⅕ of respondents go above €100,000

Source: Authors' own primary data.

The amounts and the levels of financing coupled with the co-financing are mainly outside the boundaries set by the NRDP and the EU Regulation in the case of the LFLAG, and this observation is valuable, as the actors were not thinking inside the box within the strict limitations of the opportunities. Their expectations are not considered non-realistic, on the contrary; they are a good reflection of their inner financial potential in close connection with the project intentions.

Table 3: Results from the third question, What is the level of your own financial contribution that you are prepared to allocate for these projects?

Q3. What is the level of your own financial contribution that you are prepared to allocate for these projects?	
Favorable LAG	**Less Favorable LAG**
Only 5% of respondents go for 5% or less in co-financing their project intentions	⅓ of total respondents consider 2% as own co-financing
30% of respondents target 10% co-financing	Another ⅓ expect 5% as co-financing
46% of respondents aim at 10–50% co-financing	Approx. ¼ of respondents are ready to contribute 10% co-financing
18% of respondents go for 50% or more (even 85%) of co-financing	Only 2% of respondents are willing to contribute with more than 10%

Source: Authors' own primary data.

The fourth question aims to introduce a priority pressure in order to collect the most important aspects and the validity of the first options as indicated for the first question (tab. 4). The options expressed by the respondents do support the findings highlighted on the results of the first question, for first option as well as for all the three options cumulated. The FLAG targets more new developments, and to a certain extent we can read this as a follow-up development to the previous programming period (NRDP 2007–2013), continuing to invest in diversification of rural economy and entrepreneurship, modernizing agriculture as a need for increasing competitiveness and conditioning and storage facilities for the agricultural goods. On the other side, the LFLAG respondents are also loyal to their initial options with agro-tourism and basic agricultural production.

Table 4: Results from the fourth question, If, for any reasons, you should select one single project of the ones mentioned above, which one would that be?

Q4. If, for any reasons, you should select one single project of the ones mentioned above, which one would that be?	
Favorable LAG	**Less Favorable LAG**
a. non-agricultural activities, services and rural business b. modernizing agriculture c. conditioning and storage d. social and cultural infrastructure e. modernizing animal husbandry	a. agricultural infrastructure b. agro-tourism c. animal husbandry d. fruit production e. support for young farmers

Source: Authors' own primary data.

The responses to the fifth question should indicate, as designed, the understanding of both the traditions of the territory as well as the knowledge about the programmed circumstances (tab. 5). The FLAG respondents would recommend to their peers, particularly to the young ones (support to young farmers), to invest in modernizing agriculture and diversification of the rural economic activities outside agriculture. The LFLAG respondents surprisingly indicate crop production (cereals) before other types of agricultural production. This type of recommendation can be read either as complementary to the respondents' needs or as an easy step-in for the newcomers in the rural and agricultural economy of the territory.

Table 5: Results from the fifth question, What projects would you recommend to your friends, relatives, acquaintances or neighbors?

Q5. What projects would you recommend to your friends, relatives, acquaintances or neighbors?	
Favorable LAG	**Less Favorable LAG**
a. modernizing agriculture b. non-agricultural activities, services and rural business c. support for young farmers d. fruit production e. modernizing animal husbandry	a. crop production (cereals) b. animal husbandry c. fruit production d. support for young farmers e. agro-tourism and agricultural infrastructure

Source: Authors' own primary data.

The expectations in terms of innovative projects for both territories indicate the same observation: lack of understanding in terms of innovation needs and potential impact (tab. 6). The finding is not surprising, since most administrative clerks in program implementation have difficulties in seeing and understanding innovative projects. However, a positive surprise is the indication of environmentally related innovative projects in the case of the FLAG. Most other answers from both territories are correlated to the expected developments by own projects and possible complementarities or even synergies.

Table 6: Results from the sixth question, What innovative projects you expect to see implemented in your LAG?

Q6. What innovative projects you expect to see implemented in your LAG?	
Favorable LAG	**Less Favorable LAG**
a. non-agricultural activities, services and rural business b. physical public infrastructure c. social and cultural activities d. agricultural infrastructure e. alternative energy f. environment	a. agro-tourism b. crop production (cereals) c. social services d. industrial development e. photovoltaic energy f. agro-food market

Source: Authors' own primary data.

The results of expectations from the cooperation projects is slightly different, marking the difference between the favorable and less favorable LAGs. If, in the case of the LFLAG, the expectations are connected to the general development, as indicated earlier, for the FLAG the exchange schemes and know-how comes as the most important. This is a powerful indication of precise knowledge in terms of needs and enabling processes, and could be the result of previous experiences and from past cooperation projects outside the previous NRDP framework.

Table 7: Results from the seventh question, What cooperation projects you expect to see implemented in your LAG?

Q7. What cooperation projects you expect to see implemented in your LAG?	
Favorable LAG	**Less Favorable LAG**
The most important cooperation directions identified for the future LAG point to:	The most important cooperation directions identified for the future LAG point to:
a. exchange techniques and know-how b. physical public infrastructure c. social and cultural activities d. association and producer groups e. ecological agriculture	a. exchange of experiences b. cooperation between LAGs at EU level c. agro-tourism d. agro-food market e. crop production (cereals)

Source: Authors' own primary data.

A very positive observation at the general level is that all respondents gave coherent answers in the questionnaires and no copy had to be excluded from the analysis. Also, since the application of the questionnaires happened punctually in every locality of each territory, there were no mainstreamed answers, nor orientations given by limitations (such as natural factors) or potentially favoring attractions or local opportunities. This observation highlights the scale of the exercise, maintaining the level of the entire territory in the attention of the participants and respondents, helping them make the choice in the complete frame of the micro-region, particularly in the case of the region were no previous LAG was functioning and the knowledge related to it was completely absent.

Conclusions

The different choices expressed by the respondents illustrate a good knowledge of local potential, its availability and suitability to be enhanced by rural development interventions within the current support framework (NRDP 2014–2020). The advanced and qualified formulations of the immediate and medium-term development are closely connected with the location and its favorability, assuming that a complete inventory of the local resources of all types is known and assumed by all relevant local actors.

In the case of the FLAG, the impact of the previous programming experience is highly visible. In their particular case, an extra effort was performed during the animation and information sessions in order to separate the two programs and their objectives, tools and specifications. The general setup of the NRDP 2014–2020, in terms of contained measures, had little to no influence at all since at the time of data collection, most measures were not finalized and their intervention was unknown to the public. As the answers indicate, the availability of investment resources is linked to the territory's richness as well as possibly connected to previous investments and/or experiences.

The considerable distance in volumes and levels seems to be connected to the inner capacity to support projects as well as to ongoing developments exclusively supported from own resources. This observation is corroborated by the answers of all respondents from both territories. The information, as a resource, might prove essential in a balanced strategic development, particularly in the programming phase, such as in the design of the Local Development Strategies as core of the future LAGs, when well-informed local actors can link the endogenous potential to rational/reasonable development opportunities. These observations and interpretations allow for the conclusion that answers the research question, indicating that there is a close connection and a number of links between the native potential (natural, and not only) of a territory and the intentions and expectations of the relevant actors in rural development.

References

1. Mantino, F., Developing a Territorial Approach for the CAP, A Discussion Paper, Institute for European Environmental Policy, 2011, pp. 2--31, pp. 35–36.
2. Otiman, P. I., Restructurarea agriculturii şi dezvoltarea rurala a Romaniei în vederea aderarii la Uniunea Europeană – un punct de vedere, Agroprint P. H., 1999, Timisoara, pp. 10–12.

3. Sălăşan, C., Europenizarea polictii agricole româneşti, Coman Ramona, Dobre Ana Maria, Politici Publice Româneşti, Institutul European, 2007, Iaşi, pp. 23–24.
4. European Parliament COMAGRI hearing 15 September 2015, The territorial implementation of the Common Agricultural Policy: contributions and views from European Regions, 2015, Brussels.
5. Ministry of Agriculture and Rural Development, Agency for Financing the Rural Investments, Measure M19 LEADER, Sub-measure 19.1 Preparatory Support, Applicant's Guide and Appendixes, 2016, Bucharest.
6. Ministry of Agriculture and Rural Development, National Rural Development Programme 2007–2013, consolidated version, 8 February 2008, Bucharest.
7. Ministry of Agriculture and Rural Development, National Rural Development Programme 2014–2020, 2016, Bucharest.
8. Ministry of Regional Development and Public Administration, ROP Framework Implementation Document, 2010, 2011, 2012, 2013, 2014, Bucharest.
9. Ministry of Regional Development and Public Administration, Regional Operational Programme 2014–2020 Romania, 2016, Bucharest.
10. The Swedish Research Council for Environment, Agricultural Sciences and Spatial Planning, Research Strategy 2006, Knowledge concerning rural development, 2006, Stockholm, pp. 27–28.

Elisabeta ROȘU

Institute of Agricultural Economics, betty_rosu@yahoo.com

Regional Competitiveness in Romania

Abstract: Regional competitiveness is the way in which regions promote, attract and support economic activity to achieve a high standard of living for its inhabitants. Thus, regions have no other option than to strive to be competitive, to survive in the new global market in order to face new competition. This study aims to substantiate a methodology for evaluating rural competitiveness in regional profiles. Thus, the analysis is an assessment of competitiveness of Romania's eight rural development regions versus national competitiveness. This evaluation was conducted using an index of competitiveness, which included a series of indicators to measure competitiveness considered representative.

Keywords: regional competitiveness, Romania, index of regional competitiveness

Introduction

Starting from the notion of "competitive advantage" (Porter., M, 1990, p. 75) another notion imposed itself, with specific features, that of competitiveness. Competitiveness can be studied both at firm level and at the local, regional or national level.

From the economic point of view, competitiveness is associated with productivity, or the efficiency with which resources are transformed into goods and services.

When it comes to competitiveness at the micro level, assessment is mainly on account of supply, competitiveness concerns on price and competitiveness through quality.

However, macroeconomic competitiveness level differs substantially from that of the microeconomic level. Competitiveness of a country depends on the ability of institutional and economic support to increase productivity and innovation. From national competitiveness, gradually attention was directed toward regional competitiveness.

So "regional competitiveness might be defined as the success with which regions compete with one another in some way" (Kitson, M., Martin, M., Tyler, P., 2004, p. 992).

The main objective of the present study is to substantiate a methodology for assessing regional competitiveness. The study is an analysis of the competitiveness of eight development regions of Romania, in relation to national competitiveness.

This evaluation was made by using a competitiveness index adapted to the local particularities, which included a number of indicators available in the data sources and considered representative for measuring competitiveness.

Two questions have been formulated to which the answers were sought during the analysis: how competitive are the eight development regions of Romania in relation to the national average, and what differentiates them in the fight for competitiveness.

Literature review

According to World Economic Forum, the concept of competitiveness involves both static components and dynamic components, and the "Global Competitiveness Report published since 1979 aims to serve as a neutral and objective tool for governments, the private sector, and civil society to work together on effective public-private collaboration to boost future prosperity" (WEF, 2016–2017, p. 6). The methodology developed by the WEF for calculating the Global Competitiveness Index (GCI) has in view the aggregation of twelve pillars grouped into three categories of sub-indices: basic requirements index, efficiency enhances and innovation and sophistication factors (WEF, 2016–2017, p. 4).

In the latest report of the World Economic Forum 2016–2017, the competitiveness of 138 economies was analyzed using 100 indicators. The first three ranks were taken by Switzerland, Singapore and the United States, and the last were taken by Chad, Mauritania and Yemen. Romania was ranked 62, with a score of 4.3 overall competitiveness index of a maximum 7 points (WEF, 2016–2017, p. xiii). The score obtained by Romania in the last years did not change very much, yet Romania's position in the ranking changed each year.

At the European Union level, in 2010 was published the first report regarding regions' competitiveness, containing evaluations on regional disparities and identifing the main factors contributing to the competitiveness improvement in territorial profile. In 2013, the study was remade and reviewed regarding indicators used in the calculation of the Regional Competitiveness Index (RCI).

The indicators that describe the regional competitiveness evaluated at the level of EU regions are grouped into three categories, as follows: the base sub-indicator (including indicators referring to institutions, macro-economic stability, infrastructure, health, primary education); efficiency sub-indicator (tertiary education, labor market efficiency, market size); innovation sub-indicator (technological training, business complexity, innovation; EU, JRC, 2013, p. V).

The conclusions of the 2013 report on regional competitiveness indicate that at the EU level, competitiveness has a strong regional dimension, as within each member state, there are development regions with different competitiveness levels.

The most competitive region of the EU was the region of Utrecht in Holland, which obtained a maximum of 100 points (EU, JRC, 2013, p. 128). Three of Romania's development regions were situated in the last places. The Southeast Development Region is in position 265 out of 266 of the report in the hierarchy of EU regions, with a regional competitiveness index of only 0.1 points. Two other development regions, Southwest Oltenia and Center, obtained the same rank, places 258 and 259 with the same number of points, 4.2 (EU, JRC, 2013, p. 131).

In the study "The evaluation of rural competitiveness in creating a policy of rural development in Croatia", published in 2012, the authors build a rural competitiveness index. The rural competitiveness index was composed of a set of 16 indicators, grouped into four components: human resources, the economy of non-agricultural and agricultural sectors and other gainful activities in agricultural households. The calculation formula for the rural competitiveness index was:

$\mathbf{X_i = 100\ (x_i / X) / (p_i / P)}$, where:

x_i – the variable chosen for the zone studied;
X – the variable chosen at the country level;

p_i – the number of inhabitants in the studied zone;
P – the number on inhabitants at country level

Starting from the described study, a team from the Institute of the Agricultural Economics[1] adapted and adjusted this model. In the case of the present study, I myself calculated an index of regional competitiveness to measure the competitiveness of all eight development regions of Romania.

The indicators from the Croatian model were not available in sources or official statistics in Romania. I have resorted to identifying other statistical data available and compatible in terms of statistical significance with unavailable indicators. Thus, the index of regional competitiveness was made up of four components with 16 indicators.

So, the first component – human resources – included the same indicators as the Croatian model, but not at the rural level: employed population, populations with higher education, young population and population density; the second component – economy of non-agricultural sector – has changed: turnover replaced gross value added (GVA) because turnover includes, besides the gross value added, the value of intermediary consumptions used to produce the goods and services traded; density of local active units replaced investments in durable goods because a higher density of local active units leads to an increased attractiveness to investors and investments; the other two indicators remained the same as in the Croatian model: value of exports and net average wages.

The third component – economy of agricultural sector – includes average farm size, value of exports and net average wages, the same as those in the Croatian model, with turnover and density of local active units replaced as in case of the component – economy of non-agricultural economy. The last component was replaced with a set of three indicators under the name specialization and innovation. "This last adjustment brought to the initial model was justified, on one hand, by the need to introduce in the study two of the pillars used in the well-known competitiveness evaluation models (WEF and EU) and on the other hand, this methodological decision to change the last set of indicators was motivated by the purpose and coverage area to which the present study has been subsumed" (Tudor, M. M, Chitea M. A., Rosu, E., 2016).

1 Monica Mihela Tudor, Mihai Alexandru Chitea, Elisabeta Rosu were the team who contributed to the adapted model in Romania's case. The model adapted was used in analyses at different territorial levels by each of the team members or in collaboration.

Table 1: Adapted model for competitiveness evaluation at county level

Variable – Original Croatian model	Variable – Adapted model
Group – Human resources	
Population employed in the rural area (pers.)	Employed population (thou. pers.)
Population with higher education (pers.)	Population with higher education (pers.)
Young population in the rural area (pers.)	Young population (pers.)
Population density (pers./km^2)	Population density (pers./km^2)
Group – Situation of non-agricultural sector economy	
GVA (euro)	Turnover (thou. euro)
Value of exports (€)	Value of exports (thou. €)
Investments in durable goods (€)	Density of local active units (no. of local active units/1,000 inhabitants)
Net average wages (€)	Net average wages (€)
Group – Situation of agricultural (primary) sector	
Average farm size (ha UAA/farm)	Average farm size (ha UAA/farm)
GVA (€)	Turnover (thou. €)
Value of exports (€)	Value of exports (thou. €)
Investments in durable goods (€)	Density of local active units (no. of local active units/1,000 inhabitants)
Net average wages (€)	Net average wages (€)
Group – Other gainful activities in agricultural households	**Group – Specialization and innovation**
Share of tourism households	Share of population employed in non-agricultural sectors
Share of handicraft households	RDI employees in 10,000 employed civilians
Share of processing households	Share of crop production value in total agricultural output value
Share of households that gain from other income generating activities	

Source: Adaptation of the model designed by O. Mikuš, R. Franić and I. Grgić, 2012.

Data was extracted from statistical sources of secondary data for the most recent year available in the official statistics – 2014. The only indicators for which data was extracted using previous years are: population with higher education (Census of population and dwellings, 2011) and average farm size (Structural Farm Survey, 2013).

Table 2: Data source for the indicators included in the adapted model for competitiveness evaluation

Group/Indicators	Source
Group – Human resources	
Employed population (thou. pers.)	NIS, Tempo on-line, TEMPO_FOM103D
Population with higher education (pers.)	NIS, Census of population and Dwellings 2011
Young population 0–20 years (pers.)	NIS, Tempo on-line, TEMPO_POP106A
Population density (pers./km²)	NIS, Tempo on-line, TEMPO_POP106A, Statistical yearbook – area in km²
Group – Economy of non-agricultural sector	
Turnover (thou. €)	NIS, e_Demos database
Value of exports (thou. €)	NIS, Tempo on-line, TEMPO_EXP101J
Density of local active units (no. of local active units/1,000 inhabitants)	NIS, Tempo on-line, TEMPO_INT101R, TEMPO_POP106A
Net average wages (€)	NIS, Tempo on-line, TEMPO_FOM106E
Group – Economy of agricultural sector	
Average farm size (ha UAA/farm)	NIS, Structural Farm Survey, 2013
Turnover (thou. €)	NIS, e_Demos database
Value of exports (thou. €)	NIS, Tempo on-line, TEMPO_EXP101J
Density of local active units (no. of local active units/1,000 inhabitants)	NIS, Tempo on-line, TEMPO_INT101R, TEMPO_POP106A
Net average wages (€)	NIS, Tempo on-line, TEMPO_FOM106E
Group – Specialization and innovation	
Share of employed population in non-agricultural sectors	NIS, Tempo on-line, TEMPO_FOM103D
RDI employees in 10,000 employed civilians	NIS, Tempo on-line, TEMPO_CDP102E
Share of crop production value in total agricultural output value	NIS, Tempo on-line, TEMPO_AGR206A

Each indicator was assigned a specific weight, equal to that of the other indicators from the group, and for each group, an intermediate value of index was calculated (SI) using the arithmetic mean. The values thus determined for each group of indicators (SI) were used for the calculation of the value of the Regional Competitiveness Index (RCI) by determining the arithmetic average of the values SI. It was considered that all components are equally important, having the same weight in expressing competitiveness.

Results and conclusions

For the calculation of the Regional Competitiveness Index of the eight development regions of Romania, we start from the premise that at national level, competitiveness is equal with 100. After the analysis, results revealed that the region Bucharest-Ilfov placed above the national average, followed by the region West. The explanation for obtaining an index of competitiveness so high for the Region Bucharest-Ilfov is that this region contains Bucharest Municipality, the capital of the country, in which most of the population is concentrated, with office headquarters, and developing activities both with non-agricultural and agricultural profile. The region West was propelled to second place from a competitiveness point of view through the economy of agricultural and non-agricultural sectors.

The other regions, Region Southeast, with 5.25% () and Region Northeast, with 25.69%, are () less competitive than Romania.

The analysis by components, which entered into the calculation of the regional competitiveness index, showed the fact that in the component of human resources, the region of Bucharest-Ilfov situated itself in first place, the indicators sustaining it strongly in this competition being the population density, the population with higher education and the employed population. The indicator with the smallest value within the region Bucharest-Ilfov, in this component, was the young population of 0–20 years old, an indicator which has registered the smallest value, compared to the other seven regions of Romania. In second place for this component was the region Northwest, which was only 0.47% less competitive than Romania for the human resources component, being sustained by the higher values of the indicators employed population and young population of 0–20 years old. In the last two positions for this component were the regions Southeast and Southwest, which were 9.84% and 10.1% respectively less competitive than Romania national average.

Table 3: Regional competitive index

Variables	Regional Competitivenes Indicator (X_i) Romania = 100							
	North-west	Center	North-east	South-east	South	Buc.-Ilfov	Sout-west	West
Human resources								
Employed population (thou. pers.)	108.24	103.00	85.18	93.17	88.08	129.71	94.90	108.93
Population with higher education (pers.)	97.89	93.98	69.77	82.45	74.31	213.24	85.02	107.18
Young population 0–20 years (pers.)	101.21	102.40	116.69	101.09	98.32	82.13	96.69	92.54
Population density (pers./km²)	90.77	82.63	106.34	83.95	106.82	1501.91	82.99	67.90
SI_1	**99.53**	**95.50**	**94.50**	**90.16**	**91.88**	**481.75**	89.90	**94.14**
Economy of non-agricultural sector								
Turnover (thou. €)	81.80	81.30	32.06	60.27	61.00	405.85	38.79	76.89
Value of exports (thou. €)	92.27	128.75	29.73	69.22	112.51	162.16	56.56	191.84
Density of local active units (no. local active units/1,000 inhabitants)	110.16	98.49	63.93	89.28	68.99	220.75	70.81	100.55
Net average wages (€)	87.04	88.26	84.44	86.76	93.31	140.74	90.62	94.20
SI_2	**92.82**	**99.20**	**52.54**	**76.38**	**83.95**	**232.38**	**64.20**	**115.87**
Economy of agricultural sector								
Average farm size (ha UAA/farm)	97.81	131.96	71.31	134.69	83.87	86.88	78.41	184.69
Turnover (thou. €)	72.40	80.17	69.33	132.19	150.60	124.85	49.86	114.92
Value of exports (thou. €)	45.57	39.14	9.27	171.89	44.10	434.07	26.00	77.86

Variables	Regional Competitivenes Indicator (X_i) Romania =100							
	North-west	Center	North-east	South-east	South	Buc.-Ilfov	Sout-west	West
Density of local active units (no. local active units/1,000 inhabitants)	100	105.61	80.89	142.69	114.60	49.43	80.89	132.58
Net average wages (€)	90.07	96.37	101.96	96.61	106.65	132.36	91.02	94.20
SI_3	**81.17**	**90.65**	**66.55**	**135.62**	**99.96**	**165.52**	**65.24**	**120.85**
Specialization and inovation								
% pop. employed in non-agricultural sectors	97.38	106.60	83.21	93.67	88.99	133.70	84.73	105.77
No. of RDI employees in 10,000 employed persons	57.64	74.31	71.76	32.94	65.49	315.88	47.25	84.70
% crop production value in total agricultural output value	94.54	90.68	96.02	104.05	106.65	109.85	104.14	100.01
SI_4	**83.19**	**90.53**	**83.66**	**76.88**	**87.04**	**186.48**	**78.71**	**96.83**
Regional Competitiveness Index **(RCI)**	**89.18**	**93.97**	**74.31**	**94.76**	**90.71**	**266.53**	**89.87**	**106.92**
Ranking	VII	IV	VIII	III	V	I	VI	II

Note: [1] – variable calculated using the formula: X = 100*(xi/Xi)/(pi/Pi);
[2] – variable calculated using the formula: X = xi/Xi*100

Source: Own calculations.

For the component of economy of the non-agricultural sector, excepting the region Bucharest-Ilfov, region West was 15.87% more competitive than the national average, being sustained by the exports' value. The same indicator, exports value, recorded above average in two regions: Center and South. The export's value, both in economy of the non-agricultural sector and in economy of agricultural sector, "certifies competitive advantage of regional economies on international markets" (Chitea, M., 2016).

The least competitive within this component were the regions Southwest and Northeast, where the exports' value and the turnover rate in the non-agricultural sector registered very low values.

As regarding the component of economy of the agricultural sector, the region Bucharest-Ilfov was situated in first place, although it is the region with the smallest total area, but also agricultural area in Romania, the explanation being that firms dealing with exports from this sector have their office headquarters in the region's territory. For this component, two development regions with large agricultural areas and big size farms were more competitive than Romania's national average: Southeast and West. Their competitiveness was sustained by three of the five indicators of the agricultural sector's component that are: the agricultural farm's medium size, the turnover rate and the density of the local active units in this sector. The region with the least competitive agricultural sector was Southwest.

For the component specialization and innovation, the only region more competitive than Romania's national average was the region of Bucharest-Ilfov, the competitiveness of which was fully sustained by the wage earners employed in the sector of research, development, and innovation. It is obvious that "the size of staff engaged in RDI provides comparative advantage of access to innovation" (Tudor, M. M., 2016).

The other development regions varied from being 3.17%, in case of the region West, up to 23.12%, in case of the region Southeast, less competitive than Romania's national average.

Conclusions

The study had as its main goal the assessment of the competitiveness level of the eight development regions of Romania. The approach was concretized into the adaptation of a model for assessing competitiveness developed in Croatia in the year 2012, a pattern which was modified in function for the availability of statistical information from Romania and on recent theoretical developments in assessing the competitiveness advanced by well-known international forums.

The study provided the answer to the first question, namely: there are regional disparities regarding competitiveness, with the eight development regions of Romania having different degrees of competitiveness. Two Romanian development regions – Bucharest-Ilfov and West – are more competitive than the national average. The other six regions are less competitive than the national average, between 5.25% (region Southeast) and 25.69% (region Northeast) less competitive than Romania's national average.

The most competitive region of the country is Bucharest-Ilfov, which, although it is the smallest region by territorial size, concentrates a big number of inhabitants, of which a significant percentage is working in the RDI sector, and where there are office headquarters of firms developing activities both with an agricultural and non-agricultural profile.

With the smallest value in the regional competitiveness index, the region Northeast is in last place in the fight for competitiveness. Even if it has human resources, especially from the category of age between 0–20 years old (indicator with 16.69% higher than the national average), they are weakly trained from a professional point of view and not attractive on the labor market, so that both the agricultural and non-agricultural sectors are weakly competitive.

Except for the region Bucharest-Ilfov, which obtained values over the national average for all components entering in the final calculation of the regional competitiveness index, the sector of agricultural economy has strongly sustained the competitiveness of two regions: Southeast and West. Also, the region West was sustained by the economy of the non-agricultural sector. On the other hand, in two regions, Northeast and Southwest, the economy of the two sectors registered values much under the national average.

The answer to the second questions in the study is: in the fight for competitiveness, the eight development regions of Romania are differentiated by the results of the economy of the agricultural and non-agricultural sectors.

References

1. Chitea, M.: "Territorial competitiveness in the development region South-East. Case study: Buzău county" in Agrarian Economy and Rural Development – Realities and Perspectives for Romania, 2016, ISSN 2285–6803, ISSN-L 2285–6803, p. 291, available at http://www.symposium.iceadr.ro/arhive/arhiva-2016/volum-2016.
2. Mikuś, Ornella/Franić Ramona/Grgić Ivo: "The evaluation of rural competitiveness in creating a policy of rural development in Croatia," Journal of Food, Agriculture & Environment, 2012, ISSN: 1459–026, Vol. 10, Issue 2, pp. 962–969, Publisher: WFL, available at http://world-food.net/the-evaluation-of-rural-com petitiveness-in-creating-a-policy-of-rural-development-in-croatia/.
3. Kitson, Michael/Martin, Ron/Tyler, Peter: "Regional competitiveness: an elusive yet key concept?", Regional Studies, 2004, availale at https://michaelkitson.files.wordpress.com/2013/02/kitson-marrtin-tyler-rs-2004.pdf.
4. Porter, Michael: "The Competitive Advantage of Nations", Harvard Business Review, March–April 1990, available at https://www.clustermapping.us/sites/default/files/files/resource/The%20Competitive%20Advantage%20of%20Nations%20HBR.pdf.
5. Tudor, Monica Mihaela/Chitea, Mihai Alexandru/Rosu, Elisabeta: "Competitiveness and Inovation in Rural Romania" paper presented at 14th ERDN Conference, Budapest 3–5 October 2016.
6. Tudor, Monica Mihaela: "Evaluation of rural competitiveness – cases study Romania" in Agrarian Economy and Rural Development – Realities and Perspectives for Romania, ISSN 2285–6803, ISSN-L 2285–6803, p. 5, available at http://www.symposium.iceadr.ro/arhive/arhiva-2016/volum-2016.

7. National Institute of Statistics (NIS) (2013) – Census of population and Dwellings, 2011, http://www.recensamantromania.ro/rezultate-2/.
8. NIS (2013) – Structural Farm Survey, 2010, http://www.insse.ro/cms/files/RGA2010/.
9. NIS, database e-Demos, http://edemos.insse.ro/portal/.
10. *NIS, database TEMPO on-line, http://statistici.insse.ro/shop/.
11. European Commission, Joint Research Centre – Scientific and Policy Reports (EU, JRC, 2013), – EU Regional Competitiveness Index, available at http://ec.europa.eu/regional_policy/sources/docgener/studies/pdf/6th_report/rci_2013.
12. ***World Economic Forum (WEF, 2016–2017), The Global Competitiveness Report 2016–2017, available at https://www.weforum.org/reports/the-global-competitiveness-report-2016-2017-1/.

Zizi GOSCHIN

The Bucharest University of Economic Studies, Institute of National Economy, email: zizi.goschin@csie.ase.ro

Elena DRUICĂ

University of Bucharest, email: elena.druica@faa.unibuc.ro

Ana-Maria GRIGORE

University of Bucharest, email: ana.grigore@faa.unibuc.ro

Spatial Analysis of Regional Variation in Self-Employment Density in Romania

Abstract: The steady increase in the number of self-employed persons in Romania in the last two decades illustrates the growing entrepreneurial spirit, especially among young people, but might also be the consequence of worsening labor market circumstances in the context of recent global crisis and slow economic recovery, as self-employment might be an alternative solution when jobs are scarce. Responding to the information needs of the decision-making process in this area and given the high variation in the regional density of self-employment in Romania, our paper seeks to explore its underlying factors of influence, both during and following the recent economic crisis. To this end, we applied appropriate methods of spatial analysis that take into account the spatial autocorrelation patterns exhibited by our data. We tested various model specifications and found the spatial models to be a better fit for the data, compared to classic regression. In line with the mainstream literature, our annual estimations, covering the interval 2008 to 2014, pointed to gross domestic product (GDP) per capita as the main factor of influence on the distribution of self-employment density across Romanian counties. Another positive determinant is the share of young persons in the total population of the county, while foreign direct investments (FDIs) exert a negative effect.

Keywords: self-employed person, spatial model, county, Romania

Introduction

Lacking large capital, new entrepreneurs usually start a small business, either as a self-employed person or a micro-firm. Each option has its own advantages and drawbacks. Self-employment requires high entrepreneurial qualities, a marked propensity for independent activity, and a strong risk-taking disposition. In return, the self-employed persons get hold of significant advantages, such as lower income taxes and smaller contributions for health and unemployment insurances, a flexible work schedule, complete decision-making independence (being their own boss), ownership of the entire profit, etc. but have to endure the considerable risk-related drawbacks of any independent economic activity.

A self-employed person (PFA) is a natural person authorized to conduct commercial activity. According to Government Emergency Ordinance no. 44 of 2008 on commercial activities, these are individuals authorized to undertake any form of commercial activity permitted by law, using mainly their own workforce. The steady increase in the number of self-employed persons in Romania is an indication of the growing entrepreneurial spirit, especially among young people, but might also be the outcome of worsening labor market circumstances in the context of recent global crisis and slow economic recovery, as self-employment might provide an alternative solution when jobs are scarce.

The maps in figure 1 display the territorial distribution of the number of self-employed persons per 1,000 inhabitants in 2008 and 2014. These maps reveal big disparities in self-employment density, with a visible and persistent dominance of some counties in West and Center regions, while in the East and South (except for Bucharest Municipality) self-employment is less extensive. Despite some changes in the regional density of self-employment, the overall picture remains largely stable between 2008 and 2014, with both high- and low-density counties unchanged during this interval. This suggests regional stability in self-employment propensity, due to factors of influence that need to be identified.

Fig. 1: Density of self-employed persons by county, 2008 and 2014

(2008) (2014)

Source: Authors' processing in Geoda 1.7.

Creating the appropriate regional policy design in this sector requires good data and information on the territorial characteristics and distribution of entrepreneurial activity. Responding to the information needs of the decision-making process in this area and given the high variation in the regional density of self-employment in Romania, our paper seeks to explore its underlying factors of influence, both during and following the recent economic crisis. To this end, we applied appropriate methods of spatial analysis that take into account the spatial autocorrelation patterns exhibited by our data.

Literature review

According to OECD, self-employment is defined as "the employment of employers, workers who work for themselves, members of producers' co-operatives, and unpaid family workers. Self-employment may be seen either as a survival strategy for those who cannot find any other means of earning an income or as evidence of entrepreneurial spirit and a desire to be one's own boss" (OECD, 2016).

Hatfield (2015) noticed that self-employed workers across Europe have traditionally reported higher levels of job satisfaction than employees, emphasizing some nonpecuniary benefits of the greater autonomy and flexibility of being your own boss. However, freedom has its own cost: a more sustained investment of work and a constant fight with the purpose of obtaining income, which is much fiercer than when you have a job in an already formed structure. Hamilton (2000) assessed that, oddly enough, a surprising number of entrepreneurs remain in business despite their obvious lesser earnings compared with their former jobs.

Taking into consideration the fact that self-employment can bring the necessary flexibility to the labor market and can help to create jobs and develop skills, "the Europe 2020 strategy recognizes entrepreneurship and self-employment as key for achieving smart, sustainable and inclusive growth" (EC, 2016).

Jacobsen (2015) has shown that governments are encouraging young people to become self-employed, but the results are rather modest. While 14% of European workers are self-employed, the rates among young people remain low in the EU, on average just over 4%. The politics of encouraging entrepreneurship may be a solution to take into account for the problem of youth unemployment (Cojocaru, 2014).

The Romanian people's inclination of starting a business as a self-employed person is around 2%, half compared to the number of 4 active companies per 100 inhabitants (Paul, 2016). The data from the trade register reveal that the medium lifespan of a limited company is less than 10 years, while a self-employed person lasts for less than 6 years (Business Ideas, 2015). Entrepreneurship in Romania is still under construction (Marchis, 2011), and we can assert that it is a journey full of obstacles (Cojocaru, 2014) and setbacks.

Anton and Onofrei (2016), using data provided by the Global Monitor Entrepreneurship, have conducted an analysis of the entrepreneurial profile of the Romanian economy and, surprisingly, the results of the study reveal a positive attitude towards entrepreneurship (48% of the population expressing a desire to work on their own in comparison with the European average of 37% – here we must note a serious reserve concerning the figures, knowing the fact that the survey subjects in Romania are usually reluctant to answer according to their inner beliefs), but also that the economic and financial crisis that started in 2008 has severely affected the entrepreneurial environment. The sad reality is that over 50% of the newly established initiatives do not survive in the critical 42-months-period (Tocan and Chindris, 2014). In this context, any initiative that will improve the business environment (better financing solutions, a coherent education of the human resource, substantially less bureaucracy and others) will be salutary.

In their turn, Tudor and Bisa (2016) conducted a study on a sample of 37,593 Romanian companies, clustered in 182 sub-industries and 35 industries, during 2008–2013, and they discovered that small enterprises getting a turnover of €100,000–500,000 are the most affected by economic recession, having the highest insolvency risk. Burcea et al. (2011), analyzing the effects of the crisis at the regional development level, has shown that there are significant differences among the Romanian development regions. The fact that the effects of the economic and financial crisis have not been equally felt in the entire country has also been revealed by Visinescu and Micuda (2011): "the counties that are better connected to the global economy feeling the full effects, while the less developed areas being less affected. Thus, the least affected by the crisis will be the country's southern and eastern counties, mainly agricultural, rural and still predominantly tributary to traditional economic relations, which have the lowest contribution to the GDP" (Visinescu and Micuda, 2011, p. 5).

Burcea (2012) has shown that "the entrepreneurship activity has the potential to respond to the challenges of an environment in a continuous change and ensures both local and regional development" (Burcea, 2012, p. 314). Also, entrepreneurship could be an alternative by which market failures – and we are talking here about environmental, financial and social disruptions – can be improved (Stefanescu and On, 2012). Using a sample of 45 countries, Beck et al. (2005) have found a strong association between the importance of SME's and the GDP per capita growth.

Method, variables and data

Our analysis on the regional determinants of regional density of self-employed persons (PFA) in Romania uses classic and spatial regression models. We start from a classic regression model:

$$\boldsymbol{PFA}_i = \boldsymbol{a} + \sum_k \boldsymbol{b}_k \boldsymbol{X}_{ki} + \varepsilon_i \qquad (1)$$

where X_k are the explanatory variables (displayed in table 1) and $\boldsymbol{\varepsilon}$ is the error.

We further test for spatial dependence in regional density of self-employed persons with Moran's I indicator (Anselin and Rey, 1991):

$$\boldsymbol{MI} = \frac{\boldsymbol{n}\sum_{i=1}^{n}\sum_{j=1}^{n}\boldsymbol{w}_{ij}(\boldsymbol{x}_i - \overline{\boldsymbol{x}})(\boldsymbol{x}_j - \overline{\boldsymbol{x}})}{(\sum_{i=1}^{n}\sum_{j=1}^{n}\boldsymbol{w}_{ij})\sum_{i=1}^{n}(\boldsymbol{x}_i - \overline{\boldsymbol{x}})^2} \qquad (2)$$

where x_i and x_j represent the number of self-employed persons per 1,000 inhabitants in regions i and j respectivelly, $\overline{\boldsymbol{x}}$ is the average, and w_{ij} are spatial weights capturing the interdependence between county j and county i. We use a first-order queen contiguity matrix, i.e. $w_{ij} = 1$ if regions i and j are neighbors and $w_{ij} = 0$ otherwise. A permutation test is applied to validate the statistic significance of the results (Anselin and Rey, 1991).

Spatial dependence can be corrected with spatial models which include it in the specification (Anselin, 2005; LeSage and Pace, 2009). The spatial autoregressive model contains a spatial lag of the dependent variable ($\sum w_{ij} PFA_j$):

$$PFA_i = a + \sum_k b_k X_{ki} + \rho \sum_j w_{ij} PFA_j + \varepsilon_i \quad (3)$$

while the spatial error model includes the spatial dependence in the error term:

$$PFA_i = a + \sum_k b_k X_{ki} + (\lambda \sum_j w_{ij} \varepsilon_j + v_i), \quad (4)$$

where v_i are the uncorrelated errors. The final choice of the best model for our data is based on the Lagrange multiplier test.

Table 1 describes the variables included in the final specifications of the models. We tested more explanatory variables and rejected the ones that were not able to provide significant estimations.

Table 1: The variables

Variable name	Description	Data source
PFA	Number of individual entrepreneurs per 1,000 inhabitants	National Institute of Statistics and own computations
W_PFA	Spatial lag of the dependent variable PFA	Own estimation using GeoDa software
FDI per capita	The foreign direct investments stock per capita (€)	The National Trade Register Office and own computations
GDP per capita	Gross Domestic Product per inhabitant (€)	Eurostat database
Young	The share of population aged 25–45 years (%)	National Institute of Statistics and own computations

GDP per capita was included in the model as the traditional proxy for regional market size and level of development. Well-developed counties provide better business opportunities and tend to fuel higher entrepreneurial activity, therefore we expect a positive influence of this variable. The FDI flows into a county should have a positive impact on the economic activity, but empirical evidence on its economic impact is mixed.

Given that certain age groups are more inclined towards independent activity and private initiative, we included the share of population aged 25–45 among the explanatory variables. By the age of 25, most persons have ended studying and are economically active.

We used various data sources for the analysis: the TEMPO database of the Romanian Institute of National Statistics, the Eurostat database and National Trade Register Office. In order to increase comparability among counties, we computed per capita values where appropriate.

Results and discussion

Applying the Geoda software (Anselin et al., 2006) for spatial analysis, we tested for the spatial dependence in PFA density by computing Moran's I indicator of spatial autocorrelation and by building LISA spatial clusters maps. Both spatial methods clearly showed that self-employment density is marked by high spatial dependence, i.e. its level in a certain county is directly influenced by PFA density in the surrounding counties. Specific permutations tests that have been used for these methods confirmed the statistical significance of the outcomes.

Fig. 2: LISA spatial clusters maps for self-employment density and the associated significance maps, for selected years

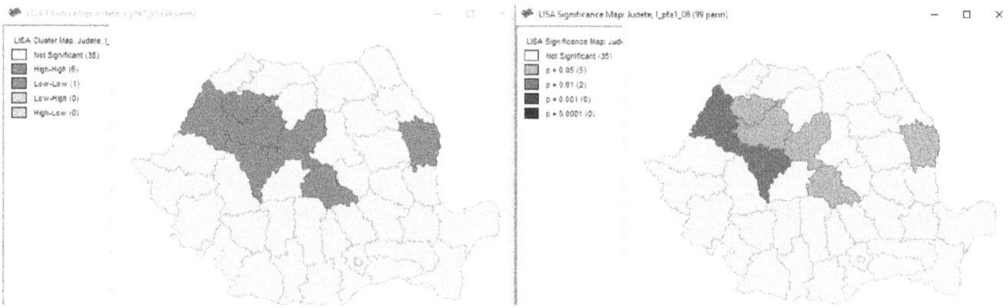

(2008)

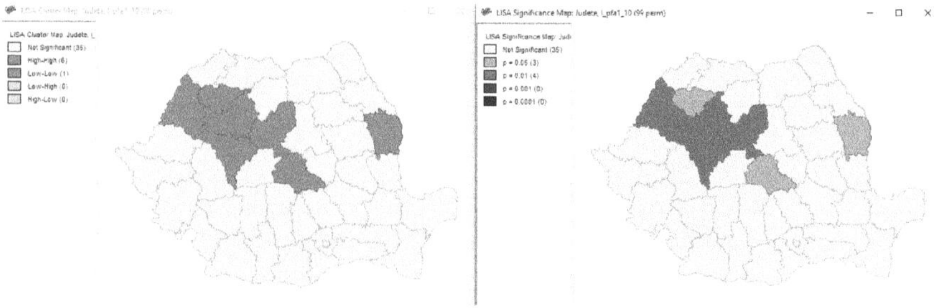

(2010)

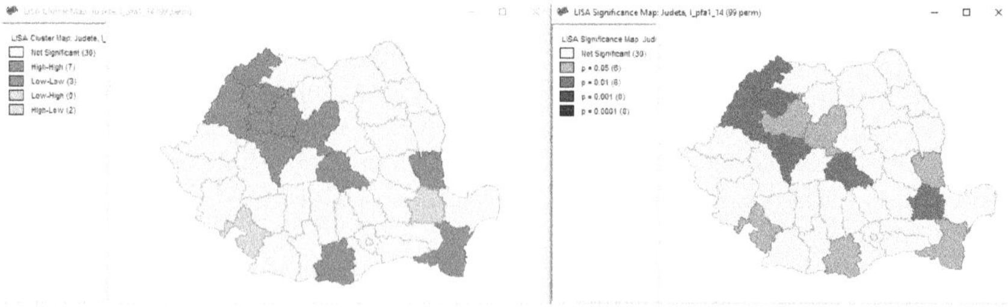

(2014)

Source: Authors' processing with GeoDa software.

The results from estimating the coefficients of the models (1), (3) and (4) are presented in table 2. Statistical tests indicated that spatial models are better suited for our data, except for 2008. Our annual estimations, covering the interval 2008–2014, pointed to GDP per capita and FDIs stock per capita as good predictors of self-employment density in Romania for most of the period under investigation. In line with the mainstream literature, GDP per capita plays a major role in explaining regional inequalities in self-employment density. It seems indeed to be the most stable factor of influence, as it is highly significant in each year of the interval 2008–2014. Well-developed counties provide better business opportunities on a larger market, therefore supporting higher individual economic activity.

Table 2: The determinants of regional self-employment density, 2008–2014

Variables	2008 Classic model*		2009 Spatial lag model**		2010 Spatial lag model**	
	Coeff.	**Prob.**	**Coeff.**	**Prob.**	**Coeff.**	**Prob.**
W_PFA (spatial lag)			0.5182	0.0003	0.5698	0.0000
Constant	2.1482	0.2111	−0.2332	0.9059	0.2408	0.9024
GDP per capita	0.0232	0.0000	0.0152	0.0000	0.0127	0.0001
FDI per capita	−0.0029	0.0012	−0.0017	0.0030	−0.0090	0.0270
Statistics	**Value**	**Prob**	**Value**	**Prob**	**Value**	**Prob**
R-squared	0.4431		0.5017		0.4759	
Log likelihood	-103.816		-99.9694		-100.872	
F-statistic	15.512	0.0000				
White test	10.6162	0.0595				
Breusch-Pagan test	7.4147	0.0027	1.7610	0.4146	1.4799	0.4771
Spatial dependence: Likelihood Ratio Test			8.6005	0.0034	10.2578	0.0013

Variables	2011 Spatial error model**		2012 Spatial lag model**		2013 Spatial error model**	
	Coeff.	**Prob.**	**Coeff.**	**Prob.**	**Coeff.**	**Prob.**
W_PFA (spatial lag)			0.5693	0.0000		
Constant	6.9375	0.0000	−0.1613	0.9344	8.2813	0.0000
GDP per capita	0.0129	0.0005	0.0145	0.0004	0.0050	0.0387
FDI per capita	−0.0013	0.0201	−0.0014	0.0108		
Young					49.4283	0.0431
LAMBDA	0.6551	0.0000			0.6995	0.0000
Statistics	**Value**	**Prob**	**Value**	**Prob**	**Value**	**Prob**
R-squared	0.4591		0.4390		0.4622	
Log likelihood	−100.1893		−101.163		−91.2844	
Breusch-Pagan test	1.4942	0.4735	1.3017	0.5216	2.0619	0.3567
Spatial dependence: Likelihood Ratio Test	13.6030	0.0002	10.7223	0.0011	15.1763	0.0001

Variables	2014 Spatial error model**	
	Coeff.	**Prob.**
Constant	2.4620	0.1718
GDP per capita	0.0047	0.0081
Young	60.6047	0.0380
LAMBDA	0.6770	0.0000
Statistics	**Value**	**Prob**
R-squared	0.4198	
Log likelihood	−97.5187	
Breusch-Pagan test	0.2676	0.6049
Spatial dependence: Likelihood Ratio Test	15.1606	0.0001

*OLS estimation
**Maximum Likelihood Estimation

According to our expectations, the results indicate that another positive determinant of self-employment is the share of young persons (25–34 age group) in the total population of the county. Although young persons should have a higher propensity to be self-employed because they are naturally less risk-adverse and more inclined towards independent activity and initiative, the "Young" variable was statistically significant only in the last two years of the period, namely 2013 and 2014. This outcome suggests that employment opportunities diminished in the post-crisis labor market environment and young persons are motivated, more than other age groups, to become self-employed.

In opposition to the previous two factors that positively impact the distribution of self-employment density across Romanian counties, the FDIs stock seems to exert a negative effect. The literature showed that FDIs is a mixed factor of influence, as it might impact the economic growth and entrepreneurial activity both positively and negatively. Although a credible proxy for business opportunities, since FDI flows can enhance the economic performance of the firms, they might negatively affect the individual entrepreneurs in the same county, who face stronger competition on the local market. Our empirical analyses showed that after the economic crisis, FDIs seem to have lost their impact on self-employment distribution in Romania.

Conclusions

Given the high variation in the regional density of self-employment in Romania, and the need to identify its underlying factors of influence, our paper undertook a spatial analysis on the self-employed persons, both during and following the recent economic crisis. To this end, we applied appropriate methods of spatial analysis that have taken into account the spatial autocorrelation patterns exhibited by our data. We tested various model specifications and found the spatial models to be a better fit for the data, compared to classic regression.

In line with mainstream literature, our annual estimations, covering the interval 2008–2014, pointed to GDP per capita as the main factor of influence for the distribution of self-employment density across Romanian counties. Another positive determinant is the share of young persons in the total population of the county, while FDIs exert a negative effect. Given that FDI flows favor medium and large firms and increase competition, they might negatively affect the individual entrepreneurs.

Addressing the marked entrepreneurial inequalities revealed by our study represents an important economic policy challenge. Regional development strategies should devise effective ways to boost entrepreneurial activity in socially and economically disadvantaged regions, as a means to foster employment and income, and support for self-employed persons could be an important part of the solution.

References

1. Anselin, Luc: Exploring Spatial Data with GeoDaTM: A Workbook, Spatial Analysis Laboratory Department of Geography. University of Illinois, Urbana, 2005, available at: http://sal.agecon.uiuc.edu.

2. Anselin, Luc/Rey, Serge: "Properties of Tests for Spatial Dependence in Linear Regression Models." Geographical Analysis, 23, 1991, pp. 112–131.
3. Anselin, Luc/Ibnu Syabri and Youngihn Kho: GeoDa An Introduction to Spatial Data Analysis. Geographical Analysis 38 (1), 2006, pp. 5–22.
4. Anton, Sorin G./Onofrei, Mihaela: "Public policies to support entrepreneurship and SME's," Transylvanian Review of Administrative Sciences. No. 47 E, 2016, pp. 5–19, available at: http://www.rtsa.ro/tras/index.php/tras/article/viewFile/468/457.
5. Beck, Thorsten/Demirgüç-Kunt, Asli and Levine, Ross: "SMEs, Growth and Poverty: Cross-Country Evidence." Journal of Economic Growth, vol. 10 (3), 2005, pp. 199–229.
6. Burcea, Marin/Toma Sorin-G. and Papuc Razvan: "The Effects of the Economic and Financial Crisis on the Romanian Entrepreneurship." "Ovidius" University Annals, Economic Sciences Series, Volume XI, Issue 2/2011, pp. 162–168, available at: http://stec.univ-ovidius.ro/html/anale/RO/cuprins%20rezumate/volum2011p2.pdf.
7. Burcea Marin: "Romanian Entrepreneurship in the Years of Economic Crisis: A Regional Approach." "Ovidius" University Annals, Economic Sciences Series, Volume XII, Issue 1/2012, pp. 314–317.
8. Cojocaru, Florentina-G.: "Young Entrepreneurs – promoters of economic development." Strategii manageriale, no. 4 (26), 2014, pp. 563–570.
9. European Commission: "Supporting entrepreneurs and the self-employed," available at: http://ec.europa.eu/social/main.jsp?catId=952, retrieved 18 November 2016.
10. GeoDa software: "The Center for Spatial Data Science (CSDS)," University of Chicago, available at: http://spatial.uchicago.edu/.
11. Hamilton, Barton, H.: "Does entrepreneurship pay? An empirical analysis of the returns to self-employment," Journal of Political economy, Vol. 108, No. 3, June 2000, pp. 604–631.
12. Hatfield, Izzy: "Self-employment in Europe." Institute for Public Policy Research, JPMorgan Chase&Co., 2015, available at: http://www.ippr.org/files/publications/pdf/self-employment-Europe_Jan2015.pdf?noredirect=, retrieved 18 November 2016.
13. Idei de Afaceri: "Portretul antreprenorului roman si in ce domenii activeaza. Cat traieste un SRL romanesc?" April 2015, available at: http://ideideafaceri.manager.ro/articole/dosare-de-afaceri/portretul-antreprenorului-roman-si-in-ce-domenii-activeaza-cat-traieste-un-srl-romanesc-13911.html, retrieved 16 November 2016.
14. Jacobsen, Henriette: "Self-employment seen as possible exit door for jobless youth." EurActiv.com, September 2015, available at: https://www.euractiv.com/section/social-europe-jobs/news/self-employment-seen-as-possible-exit-door-for-job less-youth, retrieved 17 November 2016.
15. LeSage, James, P./Kelly, Pace R.: Introduction to Spatial Econometrics, Boca Raton, CRC Press, 2009.

16. Marchis, Gabriela: "Study Regarding Romanian Entrepreneurship," Euro-Economica, Vol. 30, No. 5, 2011, pp. 129–136.
17. National Institute of Statistics: "TEMPO database – time series," 2016, available at https://statistici.insse.ro/shop/.
18. OECD: "Self-employment rate", available at: https://data.oecd.org/emp/self-employment-rate.htm, retrieved 15 November 2016.
19. Paul, Andreea: "Mai multe firme, mai puţine PFA-uri în 2016", Stiripesurse.ro, November, 2016, available at: http://www.stiripesurse.ro/mai-multe-firme-mai-pu-ine-pfa-uri-in-anul-2016-topul-jude-elor_1164134.html, retrieved 18 November 2016.
20. Stefanescu, Daniela/On, Angela: "Entrepreneurship and Sustainable Development in European Countries before and during the International Crisis." Procedia – Social and Behavioral Sciences, Volume 58, October, 2012, pp. 889–898, available at: http://www.sciencedirect.com/science/article/pii/S1877042812045296.
21. Tocan, Madalina/Chindris-Vasioiu, Oana: "The development of Romanian entrepreneurship – a possible solution to attenuate the crisis effects and to resume economic growth." Knowledge Horizons. Economics, 2014, pp. 160–165.
22. Tudor, Liviu/Bisa, Cristian: "The Effects of the Economic Recession on Romanian Entrepreneurship: A Change Management Perspective." Journal of Entrepreneurship: Research & Practice, Vol. 2016 (2016), pp. 1–13.
23. Visinescu, Sorin/Micuda, Dan: "Romanian SME's sector through crisis: the effectiveness of government policies and the present situation." Munich Personal Repec Archive, 2011, pp. 1–8.

Ioan I. GÂF-DEAC*

Senior Lecturer PhD., Research. III, INCE/Romanian Academy, Calea 13 Septembrie, No. 13, MC 050711, Bucharest, Romania, editurafmp@gmail.com

Otilia Teodora CIUTACU

PhD., RNP Romsilva, 9A, Petricani St., MC 023841, Bucharest, Romania, otilia.ciutacu@yahoo.com

Co-location and Economic Growth in Clustered Areas

Abstract: Co-location of natural resources subsystems with productive subsystems, social and infrastructural areas lead to a new economic report, measured by indicators of economic prosperity. Research literature has revealed significant links between co-location and prosperity rate. To quantify a clustering profile, the use of resources is an useful conceptual and practical immersion in at least three projects, namely: a) flow elements for developing new sector, which highlights how to build a cluster, to acquire as principal "dynamic" characteristic, b) elements of knowledge flow and assimilation of opportunities within a cluster; c) analysis of stream elements at different scales and at different levels of comparison of the corresponding operational cluster. Being considered "higher level" in relation to industrial leadership in a complex, a logical cluster is ranked with comparative higher chance of success in almost all cases of its existence and functioning. On the fundamental expression, cluster phenomenon may be included in the evolutionary stages of the "new economy" toward a "knowledge economy." Authors of the research literature expresses the observation that "confidence in the applied clustering phenomenon in a national economy is growing", although structural operationalization of clusters starts to break down those productive economy in distinct geographic industrial areas.

Keywords: co-location subsystems, economic growth, decay productive economy, cluster

Introduction

The definition of co-location, according to Lexicon FT (2016), in the modern vision, refers to the fact that "in a sign of the rush for speed in trading, exchanges are building huge data centres where traders, members and non-members alike, can place computers containing their trading algorithms next to an exchange's matching engine, which matches buy and sell orders." Moreover, co-locate means "to locate or be located in jointly or together, as two or more groups, (...) or the like; share or

* Corresponding author. Tel.: +4076978875, *E-mail:* editurafmp@gmail.com.

designate to share the same place." In the same context "co-location facilities are built to capitalize on the economies of scale achieved through shared bandwidth, power and disaster resistant facilities. In co-location facilities, customers only own the server and related hardware and procure all other services based on a monthly billing cycle" (Techopedia, 2016).

The definition of a cluster can also be found in the Romanian legislation (HG 918:2006 – the Impact Program) and The European Commission's Communication COM (2008) 652/2008 –Towards world-class clusters in the European Union – Implementing the broad-based innovation strategy (Cosniţă, Guth, 2010).

On the other hand, considered "higher level" in relation to industrial leadership in a complex economy, the cluster is seen as a logical network with superior comparative chance of success of its existence and operation. The basic expression may includ clustering phenomenon in evolutionary steps toward the "new economy", toward a "knowledge economy."

Co-locations and clusters boost economic growth. The combination can be considered the most favorable for sustainable economic growth.

1. Literature review

Co-location subsystems/systems in specific areas, specialized in productive subsystems, social and infrastructural areas, lead to a new economic report, measured by indicators of economic prosperity. A. Marshall (1980) found significant links between co-location and the prosperity rate.

In preoccupations for economic growth, considered to be legitimate as an objective to human societyevolution, M. Porter (1990) stresses that both practitioners and strategies preparers must observe the potential contributory in the new co-location, as clustering prerequisite for local, national, zonal, regional and global areas. On this occasion, he identified the conceptual re-positioning between co-location as the snew trend, and established and classically recognized industry leaders in the area of the general economic resource holder.

Further, in the same spirit, D. A. Wolfe and M. S. Gertler (2004) shows that quantifying the clusters results, provides useful economic resources for general practice immersion streams in at least 3 projects, namely:

1) elements' flow to create a dependencies sector (this flow shows the birth of a cluster, to acquire as main "dynamic" feature);
2) elements' flow of knowledge and assimilation of opportunities (located within a cluster);
3) elements' flow analysis at different scales and different levels of operability compared to the related cluster.

R. Martin and P. Sunley (2004) expresses the observation that "confidence in the applied clusterian phenomenon in a national economy is growing," although the structural operationalization of clusters starts to break down those productive economies in distinct geographic industrial areas.

The central principle of the clusterian phenomenon, found in literature worldwide, is related to the opportunity of creating a closeness between industry and innovative companies. Identifying sources of competitive advantage can be achieved using strategic management, both in terms of endogenous and exogenous companies (Tallmanet al., 2004). Reference proximity of facilities become common places of knowledge dissemination and effective practices in the productive processes of exploitation and valorization of resources.

2. Sustainable competitive advantage in co-locations

Expanding research, it can be concluded that in Romania, the possible operationalization of clusters is aimed at creating a sustainable competitive advantage. Achieving this objective requires the development of models for clusters that, through quasi-infinite resources, used to lead to the maintaining in the same area the producers and consumers, including natural resources, on an imposed level, ordered through performance. Since clusters involve the delimitation of areas, it is considered that for the Romanian economy to become suitable, geographical zoning, based on differentiated and varied natural distribution of each type of resource in the ecosystem, is essential.

Since 2008, the Romanian Ministry of Economy carried out a wide effort meant to identify the existing and emerging clusters in Romania, which materialized in four main ways: the clusters from the industrial policy document; the Inov Cluster Project, by disseminating the concept of innovation clusters and the examples of good international practice; the cluster mapping exercise; generating potential competitiveness poles. The model used was that of Pro Wood, 21 clusters succeeding, integrated in the cluster, 15 of which are found in 2011 in the new Romanian Cluster Association (RCA). A mapping of Romanian clusters has been developed in 2011, resulting in a number of 35 clusters: agro-food, automotive, wood industry, IT, electro-technical industry, etc. (Cosniţă, D., Guth, M., 2010).

Cs. Nagy's study (2014) concludes that "economic geography during an era of global competition involves a paradox. It is widely recognized that changes in technology and competition have diminished many of the traditional roles of location. Yet clusters, or geographic concentrations of interconnected companies, are a striking feature of virtually every national, regional, state, and even metropolitan economy, especially in more advanced nations." We agree with the author's view that "in Romania we need to make the distinction between natural clusters and public clusters. The public clusters (industrial parks, scientific and technological parks) have been established by law, but only few of them are realistically operative. The natural clusters, on the other hand, can be searched by means of statistical analysis and qualitative analysis". However, in Romania, experience has proved that the three natural partners of the "triple helix" model (companies, universities and research institutes, local and regional public authorities) not only do not cooperate, but they also do not know each other and do not get to discuss with one another. In this context, innovation is a necessary critical component of ensuring long-term economic growth. Expanding research and considerations in the field and advancing the thesis that governmental public role in designing and imposing economic growth in Romania, based on co-location and resources in clusters, should be reflected mainly through the following conceptual, strategic aspects (Gâf-Deac, 2007), we suggest:

- Declaring innovative processes priorities of national importance;
- Governmental context implications for overall economic exploitation and utilization of resources;
- Ameliorating the widely misleading information content on the Romanian economy, and eradicating statements with incomplete or imperfect information from economic productive processes, making them non-redundant;
- Oligopolistic market development based on circulation effects of technical progress of the news in general knowledge, namely in the field of advanced technologies;
- The recognition and introduction of systemic behavior in the general innovative process in Romania, with a complex multi-criteria and innovation approach;
- Evaluating the competitive level reached the and re-classification of Romanian enterprises (companies) on a national, or at least regional level;
- Formalizing the process of organizational literacy by creating and disseminating knowledge and best industrial-productive practice;
- Promoting distinctive, according to the proximity (formalizing the connection with proximity in clustered areas, in co-location);
- Development of strategic management discipline in co-locations;
- Identifying imbalances from monopolistic advantages applied by enterprises in the context of use of resources, involving quantitative and qualitative differentiated input-output in disparate, isolated or single business areas.

So, for Romania we propose introducing a sustainable competitive advantage in companies whose business is mainly based on resources in co-locations and clusters. Scientific investigations on the competitive edge, with a possible application in Romania in co-locations and clusters, indicate that it usually is found and measured within the company (enterprise) located in the network, derived from all the resources and network and entity capacity.

According to J. A. Mathews (2003), the resources may be entirely tangible (e.g., technology, capital goods, raw materials, etc.) or non-tangible (e.g., know-how, intellectual property rights, patents, trademarks, etc.). It is noted that globalization determines the access of all higher firms to increasingly numerous resources. In this context, capability as a defining element of sustainable competitive advantage refers to the ability of the entity (company) to use the resources at its disposal for co-locations and clusters. Competitiveness clusters and co-locations in Romania can count on at least two types of benefits derived from:

a) interdependencies of a commercial nature, found in the real economy, when formal values are exchanged between the actors of co-locations and clusters (licensing, alliances, acquisitions and sales values changed sides from producers to consumers);

b) interdependencies of a non-commercial nature, based, according to M. Storper (1993), in the "shared knowledge not covered by their movement in a market,".

I noticed that in co-locations and clusters in Romania (2015), technologies, knowledge (know-how), labor and other elements such as capital, considered the classical-vision exogenous variables, become variables with a pronounced endogenous character. Knowledge, as a catalyst in the process and technological progress, is non-opposable and free reproductive in co-locations and clusters. Even if any restrictions were imposed, knowledge could not remain strictly exclusive to one company, or totally enclosed. However, knowledge in non-rivalry with non-knowledge in co-locations and clusters suggests the manifestation of non-perfect competition in the production of knowledge that ensures technological progress. Non-perfect competition in the race for new knowledge underlies new investment instruments, which include infrastructure transformation, innovation bearing in co-locations and clusters.

On the other hand, co-locations and clusters have a noted concern for investing in knowledge. Typically, this capital investment targets especially complex horizons to be achieved in knowledge, or powerful innovative stages too advanced or out of reach of single, isolated, SMEs, since they do not have the financial strength, applicable mainly in research. Mentioned characteristics are defined by P. Krugman (1998) [4] as centripetal forces, because they "attract or repel additional economic activity in the area/co-locations and clusters in which the company operates." However, through co-location and clustering, old ties of the company are filled with new bonds, formed through commercial requirements, which in turn are central to the life of the entity through supply-demand ratio (access to new markets) and inputs-outputs.

3. The new economic growth in co-locations and clusters

Results from research in the field, indicate that market signals are what determine the behavior of firms located in reactive co-locations and clusters. The economic literature is frequently reminded of the existence of a "collection of resources" (A. M. Rugman and A. Verbeke, 2002), leading to advancing the argument that it is possible to effectively use it in the industrial-productive and economic vision based on resources. Any reaction or pro-active attitude of firms in co-locations and clusters inevitably leads to some imbalance, the opposite action awaiting a favorable response to the general economic use of resources.

The competitive advantage in co-locations and clusters lies in this context, in the capacity for decision-making and acquiring resources, for accumulating and using the general resources and capabilities they provide. In fact, it can be seen that the co-location and clustering process described, plus the protection and development of a competitive advantage, can be considered as having innovative industrial-productive valences and economic environment. Co-location firms and clusters operating with such process elements should benefit from an environment facilitating and generating organizational learning. The determinants model for new growth in co-locations and clusters refers in this context to the ways in which entries (inputs) and transformations come into outputs, directed and supported by feasible knowledge and not necessarily by labor or capital mustered through the physical infrastructure (C. Jones, 1998).

4. Research Method

Figure 1 introduces a proposed generalized co-location subsystem productive economic cluster in Romania, based on our formula.

Fig. 1: Formalizing cluster/co-location model for productive-economic subsystem in Romania

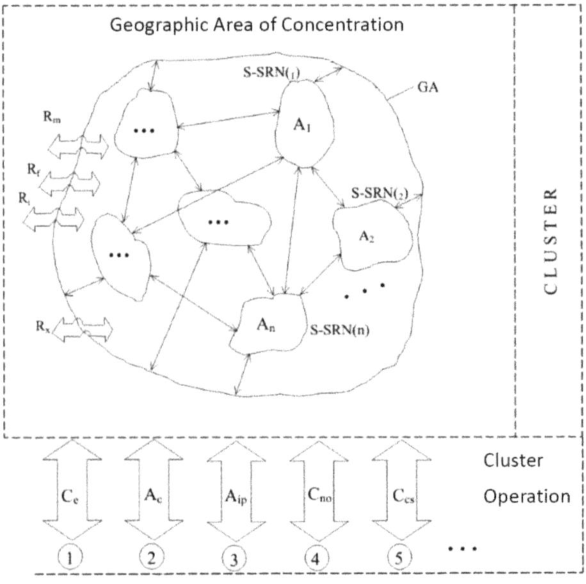

Source: Gâf-Deac I.I., 2007.

SRN = resources system;
S-SRN(1),...,S-SRN(2) = subsystems;
A_1; A_2,...,A_n = partition agglomerations (groups of interconnected companies and institutions);
GA = autonomy;
R_m; R_f; R_i,...,R_x = relations material, financial, informational, etc.;
C_c = competition between competitors on the market;

A_c = threats from new competitors;
A_{ip}= threats from replacement with new products;
C_{no} = negotiating capacity of the offering;
C_{cs} = the purchasing power of those calls.

The classification or concrete designation of any proposed cluster follows taxonomic laws (science of classification), using specific analyses (cluster analysis).

To configure the cluster, pass the measuring multidimensional distance between objects. The obtained general metric space provides the opportunity to identify the objects' features and "close enough" values to indicate different types, or a general typology of this crowd. The decision-maker or analyst – usually a collective – relies mainly on the choice of variables to induce a certain typology of co-location or cluster (figure 2).

Fig. 2: Premises for formalization of multidiminesionale metric spaces by distances between objects and variables related to a cluster of economic-productive subsystem in Romania

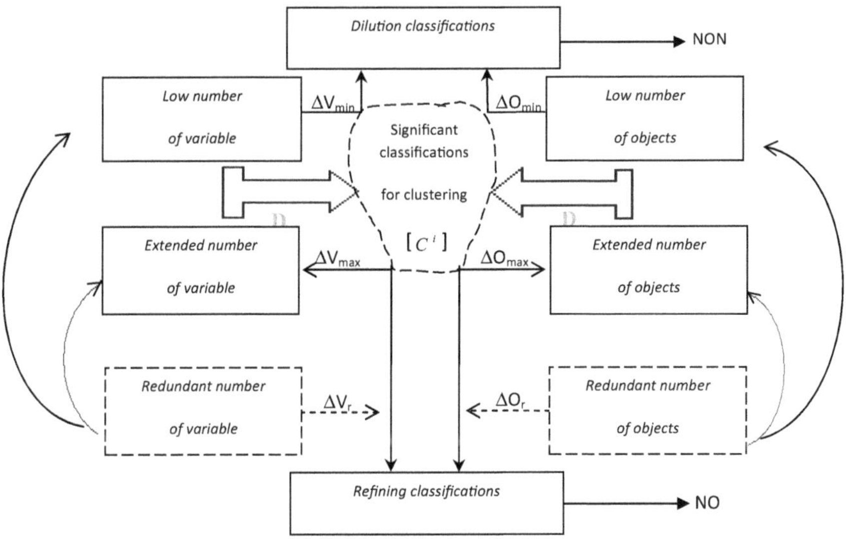

Source: Adapted Gâf-Deac I.I., 2007, 2016 [2].

We believe it is necessary to configure the significant clustering classifications (Gâf-Deac I.I., 2007), based on the optimal choice of the number of variables (nV_{optim}) in co-location (of the subset containing the alternative "low" and "extended"), respective to the objects (mO_{optim}) (in the same context of alternatives):

$$\begin{cases} \{\Delta V_{min} * \Delta V_{max}\} \rightarrow n\ V_{optim} \\ \{\Delta O_{min} * \Delta O_{max}\} \rightarrow m\ O_{optim} \\ \{\Delta V_r * \Delta O_r\} \rightarrow zero \end{cases} \quad (1)$$

which gives rise to the contours and content of the cluster $\left(C_c^i\right)$ in its quasi-final stage:

$$\{nV_{optim} * \ m\ O_{optim}\} \rightarrow \left(C_c^i\right) \quad (2)$$

This formula is now capable, when applied, of identifying the forces that shape competitiveness, using a concentration of a critical mass of variables (goods resources, manufacturers, institutions, etc.) and quantitative variables, respectively quality. As such, it may suggest controlling measures (investments, restructurings, etc.) to develop forces that shape competitiveness in that it captures the majority of the cluster/co-location with superior performance that can express the competitive edge.

5. Conclusions

- Defining cluster in a multi-partition system, as an aggregate of subsystems, suggests a certain degree of autonomy for the studied area, which can be achieved and which should manifest itself as competitive, and more competitive in the general economic national or regional and global field.
- It is considered that at the present stage of Romania's economic productive subsystems, the competitive forces are not treated significantly and erroneously.
- Using clusters in the new context and actionable methodology, it proves to be useful to consider the direct distinct potential of Romania's economy, its competitors inside and outside, tenderers, consumers (buyers) and substitutable products. Thus, the general flow of opportunities for competitive behavior in the new economy is identified through co-locations and clusters.
- It can be concluded that sustainable competitive advantage in co-locations and clusters is the concept originally introduced in the Romanian economy, from industrial-productive vision based on general economic resources. The concept is operational only when accompanied by a pre-existing type of previous economic system, namely that based on a market economy introduced in Romania after 1989.
- This functional parallelism in co-locations and clusters, the binomial "economically-sustainable competitive advantage," helps reduce costs and therefore enables more efficient transactional activities, mostly related to commercial operations group interdependencies.
- At the same time, Romanian economic entities no longer operate exclusively on traditional imperatives of efficiency, but also with inputs with low cost, forming chains of distribution, polarization or labor specialization, and know-how, looking only into one so-called "common industrial atmosphere."

- In fact, co-locations and clusters intend to counteract another phenomenon of utmost importance because of its consequences, i.e. globalization, which reduces more than just the role and importance of proximity in commercial interdependencies.
- Clusters and co-locations will continue to operate with powerful new skills, especially in the sphere of noncommercial interdependencies through sustainable competitive advantage.
- However, co-location and proximity of the clusters remain objective factors which enhance expression of interdependence of the two categories (commercial or noncommercial).

References

1. Cosniţă, D., Guth, M.:Clusters and Potential Clusters in Romania – A Mapping Exercise, German Government by the GTZ and the Romanian Ministry of Economy, Bucharest, February 2010. pp. 8–11.
2. Gâf-Deac, I. I.:The legal and economic systems resources in the new economy, Ed. Infomin Deva, 2007, pp. 248–250.
3. Jones, C.: Introduction to Economic Growth, W. W. Norton & Co, New York, 1998, pp. 45–46.
4. Krugman, P.: What's New About the New Economic Geography, Oxford Review of Economic Policy, no. 14 (2), 1998.
5. Marshall, A.: Principles of Economics, MacMillan, London, 1980, p. 213.
6. Martin, R., Sunley, P.: Deconstructing Cluster: Chaotic Concept or Policy Panacea, Journal of Economic Geography, 3:1, 2002.
7. Mathews, J. A.: Competitive Dynamics and Economic Learning: An Extended Resource-Based View, Industrial and Corporate Change, 12/1 2003, pp. 115–145.
8. Nagy, C.: Clusters In The Romanian Economy, M. Eminescu University of Timisoara, 2014, p. 3.
9. Porter, M.: The Competitive Advantage of Nations, The Free Press, New York, 1990, p. 112–114.
10. Rugman, A. M., Verbeke, A.: Edith Penrose's Contribution to the Resource-Based View of Strategic Management, Strategic Management Journal, no. 23 (8)/2002.
11. Storper, M.:Regional "Worlds" of Production: Learning and Innovation in Technology Districts of France, Italy and the USA, Regional Studies, no. 27/1993.
12. Tallman, S. et al.: Knowledge, Clusters and Competitive Advantage, Academy of Management Review, vol. 29/2, 2004, p. 258.
13. Wolfe, D. A., Gertler, M. S.: Clusters from the Inside and Out: Local Dynamics and Global Linkages; Urban Studies, WD, 2004, p. 111.
14. ***,- http://lexicon.ft.com/Term?term =co_location, last accessed 23 November 2016.
15. ***,- www.techopedia.com/definition/26557/colocation-facility, last accessed 23 November 2016.

Gabriela-Cornelia PICIU

"Victor Slăvescu" Centre for Financial and Monetary Research, Bucharest, Romania, gabriela_piciu@yahoo.com

Iudith IPATE

"Acad. David Davidescu," Centre for Study and Research in Agro-biodiversity, ipate.iudith@gmail.com

Addressing an Environmental Risks Matrix

Abstract: The paper presents the main steps to the identification and definition of the sources and targets of the financial flows required for the diminution and complete removal, if possible, of pollution as well as the reconstruction of the financial mechanisms and instruments of environmental protection aiming at the environment consumers; the elaboration of the managerial construct as a subsystem and of the integrative financial architecture oriented toward the institutionalization, instrumentation and holding responsible the participants in control, and toward diminution and removal of environmental risks.

Risks related to the use of products sometimes cause the discontinuation of the products by manufacturers, while risks concerning so-called "free" goods, i.e. air and water pollution, have become a reason for criminal responsibility. As economic theory is about to abandon the concept of "free" goods, i.e., to introduce the concept of inferred values to be accounted for, "free risk" should be accepted as risks caused by humans, which must respond to the generator thereof, particularly those who produce dangerous goods.

Keywords: pollution, environmental risks, impact of risks, financing needs, quantified risk

Introduction

It is obvious that human activity is currently leading to environmental damage. For this reason, we have identified patterns of development that preserve the environment's endurance capacity, of reduction of environmental risk, as the only way is to reduce the intensity of pollution caused by human activity.

In our opinion, economic development can be sustained only if it ensures environmental protection. Otherwise, the gradual erosion of the environment will hinder economic growth.

The place of the pollutant is obvious in the "human system," but lately Environmental Economics emerged and developed in our country which, while acting as a subsystem of the economic system, by the products and services provided by the economic agent, reduces the pressure of the human system on the environment system.

1. Literature review

Risk is defined as the probability of exposure of man and goods to a particular hazard of a certain size. Risk is the likely casualties, the number of casualties, damage to property and economic activities by some natural phenomenon or group of phenomena in a certain place and a certain time. Values at risk are the population, properties, roads, economic activities etc., in a particular area.

An action is said to be risky if there are several possible outcomes that can be derived from it, and if these results may be attached objectively to known probabilities. The probability characterizes the degree of possibility of generation, by a certain human action, of a result under set conditions (Fishburn, 1982, p. 15).

The risk is therefore distinct from uncertainty in that there is a plurality of results which can't be determined with objective probability.

Human decisions and actions that accept a loss are at risk because there is more than one possible outcome and the odds can be calculated. In the event that the objective likelihood of obtaining a result can't be determined (not known), the decision shall be adopted in an uncertain situation, rather than a risky one, even if the "form" of the possible outcome is known.

Economic activity is a distinct category of human activities through which man appropriates the natural resources offered by the environment in order to meet his needs. This appropriation has evolved in form and content from simple resource collection, when resources needs substantially corresponded to resources, to the complicated transformation of resources, streamlined and instrumented transformation, in this case needs being substantially different as comparing with the resources. In this evolution, the goods produced by man to meet his needs are natural goods extracted from the environment, from the natural ecosystem, and transferred to the human ecosystem, for human consumption, irrespective of its nature.

2. Description of the problem

In Romania, the ERA (Environmental Risks Assessment) shows several trends such as:

- Environmental issues were amplified and sharpened, accidents and environmental disasters are becoming increasingly severe, covering large territories.
- Nearly full economic freedom caused accidents with environmental implications of local, regional, national and even international significance.
- Legislative and institutional changes led to a slow response of the institutions to issues of environmental risks.
- The scarcity of financial resources led to a "motivation" of organizational links involved in environmental risk protection for low activity.
- The structure of the economy, in general, and of industry, in particular, requires resources that may cause the environmental risk of depletion of the materials.
- Economic downturn led to a reduction or improvement of parameters that define the "state of the environment."

When referring to small and medium businesses, we notice that the phenomenon of ecological risk is not a prerogative of large enterprises, and quality standards of the products, restrictions related to environmental risks, are the same in small and in large companies.

Small and medium businesses are disadvantaged in the institutional process related to production, treating effluent pollutants, developing clean technologies. It is the task of government authorities to pay greater attention to these types of businesses, to help them in the ecological survival through financial incentives, technology transfer, and access to resources or less polluting sources, administrative and financial incentives.

3. Analysis of ecological risks

Generative economic activities and decisions represent a dialog between man and nature, constituting praxis, with the following meanings relating to man and nature: depletion of natural resources, environmental damage, human artefacts expansion (artificial environment) and distortion of the existential substance property.

Environmental pollution, causing polluting effects and risks, affects the natural ecosystems, destroying the natural biological support of the human ecosystems.

In the process of environmental or ecological risk protection, one can distinguish among five defining components: polluters, pollutants, decision-makers, environmental policy and environmental funding. Funding sources of insurance cover the financial resources to support environmental protection policies against risks.

Environmental hazards and their effects on the environment generate environmental costs, costs in different terms: very long, long, medium, short. Costs may be operating costs and capital costs, costs of prevention, recovery, consolidation, direct costs and indirect costs, autonomous or associated costs, internal costs and external costs, etc.

Achieving these costs implies financial resources to ensure the financing of environmental policies required by these costs.

In this respect, we can define five sources of financing: environmental funds that should be raised independently and be associated with decision-makers specializing in environmental issues (environmental organizations); suprastate, state or local government budgets; voluntary contributions of the associations of various informal communities; financial contribution from polluting and polluted firms, for example, contribution to technological conversion; philanthropic participation (sponsorship, donations).

Determining the funding sources is a crucial problem of the funding policy, as funding the construction of a matrix, taking into consideration all taxonomy, can help clarify many mysteries of stray funds.

Using matrix calculations, we determine the coefficient of financial coverage of environmental risks detailed by risk factors and funding sources (table 1).

Table 1: Matrix of the risk

Funding sources/risk source	**State budget**	**Local budgets**	**Private Funds**	**External loans (repayable funds)**
Risk source is the industry	X11	X12	X13	X14
Risk source is the agriculture	X21	X22	X23	X24
Risk is transport	X31	X32	X33	X34
Risk are the households	X41	X42	X43	X44

Source: Author's calculations.

X i = total financing sources at j level

For i = 1 – risk source is industry;
i = 2 – risk source is agriculture;
i = 3 – risk source is transport;
i = 4 – risk source is household;

Yj = funding needs by source; j = 1, 2, 3, 4, 5.

j = 1 – source of funding is the state budget;
j = 2 – source of funding is local budget;
j = 3 – source of funding is private funds and bank loans;
j = 4 – source of funding is external funds and borrowings.

The system of equations can be written in the restricted form of: $s_{ij} = x_{ij}/X_j$ or $x_{ij} = s_{ij} \cdot X_j$
Writing matrix above relationship is obtained:

$$\begin{pmatrix} x_{11} & x_{12} & x_{13} & x_{14} \\ x_{21} & x_{22} & x_{23} & x_{24} \\ x_{31} & x_{32} & x_{33} & x_{34} \\ x_{41} & x_{42} & x_{43} & x_{44} \end{pmatrix} = \begin{pmatrix} s_{11} & s_{12} & s_{13} & s_{14} \\ s_{21} & s_{22} & s_{23} & s_{24} \\ s_{31} & s_{32} & s_{33} & s_{34} \\ s_{41} & s_{42} & s_{43} & s_{44} \end{pmatrix} \bullet \begin{pmatrix} X_1 \\ X_2 \\ X_3 \\ X_4 \end{pmatrix}$$

Dynamic matrix may allow to highlight the evolving relationships, while providing the possibility of treating econometric correlations and interdependencies between factors, sources of risk and funding sources of these risks.

Analysis of ecological risks may be based on quantitative methods, stochastic methods to quantify the dispersion of possible values in the form of predictions of cost/time, or qualitatively, through a formal investigation based on accumulated knowledge and methods of diagnosis using checklists.

Environmental risk impact on the environment factors can be written as: $IRT = \sum IF$ where: IRT = total risk impact and IF = flow risk impact.

Obviously, one can express the impact of each risk factor on all environmental factors, the impact of all risk factors on an environmental factor, or the impact of each risk factor on each environment factor by means of the rates and the coefficient of impact (RRIR and CIR):

$$RIRi = \frac{IFi}{\Sigma IFi}$$

where: RIRi = rate impact of a risk factor on all environmental factors

i = risk factors of industry, agriculture, transport, households,
i = 1, 2, 3, 4.

To express the impact of all risk factors on an environmental factor, we use the following formula:

$$RIRj = \frac{IFj}{\Sigma IFj}$$

where: j = environmental factors: water, air and soil, subsoil, biodiversity
j = 1, 2, 3, 4.

$$CIRij = \frac{RIRi}{RIRj}$$

Sources of risks generate, by the risk factors, risk flows affecting specifically differentiated the delimitative areas.

Risk flows mean to produce pollution, activating forms of pollution affecting human and natural ecosystems.

There are five groups of risk flows: fuels generated in one way or other by burning; manufacturing, usually from industrial sources; quarrying; consuming, generated in part by housework; erosive, generated by agriculture, and more.

Harmful emissions are producing fuel flows, which can often be characterized as forms of chemical, thermal, radioactive and even noise risk factors. Erosive flows often take on the effects of other flows, strongly affecting natural bio systems, or environmental factors, such as soil (agriculture being a direct source of these flows).

Pollution flows cause important risks differentiated by environmental factors. One can build this matrix, including the risk factors and environmental factors, at the intersection of two dimensions highlighting the environmental risks.

4. Financial expression of the risk factors

To establish the financial expression of the risk factors, one must first determine the components involved in environmental funding in order to diminish or eliminate the effects of risks.

These components include: sources of pollution, risk factors, funding sources. The whole strategy for environmental protection reduces the risks causing short-term effects.

Financing needs to cover all the ecological risks, which is a maximal funding level, denoted by FRTM, and financing needs, revealed by the economic entities and other decision-makers involved, representing an appropriate level, denoted by FRSE.

Also, the funding is denoted by FSF. Knowing that the financing provided by financing sources (FSF) usually does not cover the funding, we may write:

$$FS < FRTM \text{ and } IRT = \sum IF$$

$$FSF < FRTM \text{ and } FRSE < FRTM$$

The difference between borrowing and provided financing is a size denoted by ΔF, so:

$$\Delta F = FRTM - FSF$$

FRTM is revealed borrowing information

FSF is financing, achieved by means of existing funding sources

Financing revealed by business entities is included in the total financing requirement.

The difference between financing provided by sources of financing (SF) and borrowing revealed by economic entities, and relating the difference to borrowing will get the funding gap:

$$DEF = \frac{FSE - FRTM}{FRTM}$$

FNTM borrowing is revealed in the informational VT.

Thus, we can determine the rate of funding extended (RFE), by the following relation:

$$RFE = \frac{FSF}{VT}$$

or

$$RFE = \frac{FSF}{FRTM}$$

In this case, the financing rate can be calculated as follows:

$$RFE = \frac{\sum FSF}{\sum FRT}$$

This rate shows that part of the total risk to which funding sources were allocated, in order to prevent and eliminate the environmental risks.

These relationships can be synthesized in a multiplicative algorithm showing the final dual relationship between sources of risk and funding sources, between risk and finance risk mitigation.

5. Conclusions

Integrated risk management is based on the assumption that all phases of management localization, prevention, mitigation, protection and the institutional element can be exploited from a global and complementary resource, so that the management process is optimized.

Although integrated assessment and management of environmental risk considers all risks, the level of detail may vary in each case, depending on predetermined priorities.

Quantified risk assessment is a probabilistic process. There are many questions associated to this risk quantification. Among the most important sources of uncertainty, one may mention the mathematical models to estimate the consequences of accidents due to environmental risks.

References

1. Bradley, May; Plummer, Ryan: "Synthesis Accommodating the Challenges of a Climate Change adaptation and Governance in Conventional Risk Management: Adaptive Collaborative Risk Management (ACRM)," Ecology and Society, vol 16 no. 1, 2011, p. 27.
2. Fishburn, Peter C.: "Foundations of Risk Measurement Effects of Gains on Risk," Journal of Mathematical Psychology 25, 1982, pp. 228–229.
3. Fishburn, Peter C.: "Foundations of Risk Measurement Risk and Probable Loss," Management Science 30, 1984, p. 21.
4. Goulder, Lawrence; Parry, Ian W. H.: "Instrument Choice in Environmental Policy", Review of Environmental Economics and Policy, Oxford University Press for Association of Environmental and Resource Economists, vol. 2 (2), 2008, pp. 152–174.
5. Hansjürgens, Bernd; Antes, Ralf: Economics and Management of Climate Change – Risks, Mitigation and Adaptation, Springer, 2008, pp. 132–138.
6. Harris, Jonathan M.: "The Economics of Global Climate Change – A GDAE Teaching Module on Social and Environmental Issues in Economics," Global Development and Environment Institute, Tufts University.
7. Herring, Horace; Sorell, S.: "Energy Efficiency and Sustainable Consumption – The Rebound Effect," Energy, Climate and the Environment Series, Palgrave MacMillan, 2010.
8. Huppes G.: "Realistic Eco-Efficiency Analysis. Why We Need Better Eco-Efficiency Analysis – From Technological Optimism to Realism," Technikfolgenabschätzung – Theorie und Praxis Nr. 3, 16. Jg., Dezember, 2007, pp. 38–45.
9. Parascandola, Mark: "Epistemic Risk: Empirical Science and the Fear of Being Wrong," Law, Probability and Risk," vol. 9 (3–4), 2010, pp. 201–214.
10. Peterlini, Edward: Innovative Technologies for Intermodal Transfer Points, Competitive and Sustainable Growth Programmed, 2010, pp. 1–23.

11. Piciu, Gabriela; Manolescu, Gheorghe; Dimitriu, Mihail: "The financial impact on the natural environment. Zonal Studies," Financial Studies vol 1. – (23), 2003.
12. Piciu, Gabriela (coordinator): "Risk assessment financing investment projects aimed at environmental protection," research project of "Victor Slăvescu" Centre for Financial and Monetary Research, 2002.
13. Piciu, Gabriela; Manolescu, Gheorghe; Dimitriu, Mihail; Băltărețu, Camelia: "The financial impact of the ERA on the behavior of economic subjects," research project, "Victor Slăvescu" Centre for Financial and Monetary Research, 2003.
14. Piciu, Gabriela Cornelia (coordinator): "Financing costs and internalisation of negative externalities on Natural Environmental Protection," research project of "Victor Slăvescu" Centre for Financial and Monetary Research, 2010.

Cătălin VOICA

Petroleum and Gas University of Ploiesti, Romania,
catalin.voica@upg-ploiesti.ro

Mirela PANAIT

Petroleum and Gas University of Ploiesti, Romania,
mirela.matei@upg-ploiesti.ro

Corina ENE

Petroleum and Gas University of Ploiesti, Romania,
ecorina@upg-ploiesti.ro

The Capital Market's Actors and Financial Education. The Romanian Case

Abstract: The international crisis revealed that the financial world was so complex that even qualified investors and rating agencies could hardly properly evaluate the financial products, especially the new ones that are very complex and sophisticated. The article is focused on the importance of financial education for capital market consumers/investors who must acquire specific skills. This is the first step that leads to financial literacy and the final result is an adequate financial behavior of investors. Even the consumers from the developed countries face the lack of financial literacy, but in former communist countries, the level of financial education is very low. The consequences of the lack of financial literacy are long-term, and the wellbeing of consumers is affected. Therefore, the financial consumers must be helped to become more resilient. Public authorities like financial supervisory authorities and institutions like stock exchanges could support this by improving financial regulation and consumer protection frameworks and promoting suitable financial products. The authors analyzed the activities of the capital market's institutions from Romania and proposed specific measures in order to improve the financial education of the investors.

Keywords: financial education, stock exchanges, financial supervisory authority, consumers, investors

Introduction

US companies realized decades ago that the existence of employees who had solid financial knowledge and made right decisions on contracting a bank loan, buying a home or on initiating an investment plan for the period after retirement, was an essential asset for the efficient functioning of these companies. The efforts made by private companies (Volosevici, 2013) were sustained by public authorities, who wanted to have, on the financial market, informed consumers able to make right decisions, considering the risks and costs of financial products and prevention of financial fraud. In this way, investor protection is provided against companies from the sector that, desiring to maximize profits, tend to sell complex financial products to clients without warning them of the potential risks. So, in the US, the financial education movement appeared in the 1960s, and expanded rapidly in the 1990s, and is closely linked to the consumer protection movement.

Studies conducted worldwide have shown the limits of financial education programs. Financial knowledge is not sufficient for making good decisions, as other important aspects are attitude, opinions or values that every investor trusts. Investor confidence in their knowledge and skills are essential for initiation of transactions in the financial market. For this reason, financial education should be made from the perspective of behavioral finance: "Financial education programmes are not the only approach to helping people manage their financial futures. Research in behavioral finance has shown that powerful psychological and behavioral traits such as inertia and lack of will-power reduce the effectiveness of financial education programmes" (BRA, 2014). Investors make irrational decisions in some cases, if we consider the classic profitability-risk criterion. But these investment decisions are determined by certain psychological and environmental factors such as risk aversion, inertia, lack of trust or overconfidence in acquired knowledge and skills, procrastination or cultural sensitivities (IOSCO, CR03/2014).

More and more investors access financial products available on the capital market. Unlike the banking market, the stock market is characterized by a high degree of innovation and the existence of complex financial products that are difficult to evaluate even by the institutional investors. The international financial crisis demonstrated the existence of toxic financial products that created huge losses, not only to individual investors, but also to investment funds, banks or insurance companies. On the other hand, the financial crisis led to a dramatic drop in investor confidence in financial institutions and market-specific mechanisms. Therefore, financial education programs currently have a new component, namely restoring and promoting investor confidence, especially in the integrity of capital markets (IOSCO, R09/2014). The activity of investors is threatened by the use of fraudulent securities offerings such as the Ponzi scheme, pyramid schemes, advance fee fraud, high-yield investment programs. For this reason, the interest areas of financial education programs promoted by IOSCO developed and included "investment knowledge and understanding, financial skills and competence, and a design, delivery and measurement program," also aiming at protecting investors against financial fraud (IOSCO, 2015).

1. Literature review

Internationally, several studies have been conducted on the necessity and importance of financial education. Diversification of financial products, increasing their complexity, and the privatization of pension and social insurance, as well as international financial crisis, have required to raise the awareness of the population on key economic and financial concepts (Hastings, Madrian Skimmyhorn, 2013; Van Rooij, Lusardi, Alessi, 2011).

Financial education should not only focus on the investment process, but also on the saving process. On the one hand, the financial education programs must aim at increasing the savings rate and, on the other hand, attracting low-income and vulnerable people to the financial system (Klapper, Lusardi, Panos, 2012). In this way, through financial education, the financial inclusion goals set at the European level could be met. Studies have shown a weak financial culture worldwide, regardless of the level of development of that country and the fact that this phenomenon mainly affects women and seniors (Lusardi, Mitchell, 2011). People with a more solid financial education are investing in the stock market where more complex financial products are available (Lusardi, Mitchell, 2014). The financial education programs should be individualized by vocational categories and must focus on changing the behavior of consumers/investors in the financial market, and not just on the mere transmission of information (Lusardi, Mitchell, 2007).

2. Financial Education – Approaches at Global and Regional Level

A fair and competitive financial sector can function effectively only if customers of the financial institutions are financially educated, receive clear, accurate and complete information before making their decision and have access to adequate appeal mechanisms.

After the financial crisis of 2007–2009, particular attention was given to improving consumer financial literacy – as a critical component of consumer protection, which became an essential policy objective in countries all over the world.

At the global level, the Organisation for Economic Co-operation and Development (OECD) is one of the main international organizations working on enhancing financial consumer protection, including financial education, through its International Network on Financial Education (INFE), developing various research tools to support the designing of national strategies for financial education.

As the Organisation for Economic Co-operation and Development (OECD) stated, sound and adequate consumer protection and financial literacy are key-instruments (OECD, 2009) for:

(1) ensuring that financial markets are serving the broad population, including low-income households/borrowers;
(2) improving the efficiency of the retail financial market; and
(3) ensuring long-term stability in the financial system.

Financial consumer protection targets retail customers, establishing clear rules of conduct for financial institutions. At a general level, financial consumer protection aims to ensure that consumers (World Bank, 2012):

(1) receive information to allow them to make informed decisions;
(2) are not subject to unfair or deceptive practices; and
(3) have access to appeal mechanisms to resolve disputes.

At present, the effective protection of consumers of financial services is a challenge for national and global stakeholders, as there are several international initiatives establishing principles to follow in this area. Initiated more than ten years ago, the international community's efforts and concerns in this field have been amplified in recent years:

- In September 2010, Consumers International (CI), the not-for-profit world federation of consumer groups, launched a new global campaign calling for fairer financial services. CI made many efforts in the field of financial education, considering that the access to stable, secure and fair financial services was important for each consumer (Consumers International, 2013).
- In 2011, the theme chosen by CI for the World Consumers Rights Day was reflected by the motto "Our money, our rights" – an issue of great interest for consumers around the world needing access to safe, fair and competitive financial services (CI website, 2016).
- In October 2011, following the joint efforts made by the OECD, collaborative structures and relevant international organizations, the G20 released and endorsed its High-Level Principles on Financial Consumer Protection.

These principles referred to the following issues and areas of interest (OECD, 2011):

1. Legal, regulatory and supervisory framework
2. Role of supervisory bodies
3. Equitable and fair treatment of consumers
4. Disclosure and transparency
5. Financial education and awareness
6. Responsible business conduct of financial services providers and authorized agents
7. Protection of consumer assets against fraud and misuse
8. Protection of consumer data and privacy
9. Complaints handling and clarification
10. Competition

Subsequently, the G20/OECD Task Force on Financial Consumer Protection was created to support the implementation of the High-Level Principles.

- In 2012, the World Bank established a set of 39 good practices for financial consumer protection, applicable to the entire range of consumer financial services, which can be used by interested parties to further develop financial consumer protection principles at different levels. These practices were designed to function mainly as a diagnosis tool in order to identify consumer protection issues throughout the financial sector (World Bank, 2012).

- In 2013, G20 finance ministers and Central Bank governors called for the OECD to prepare a progress report on the development of national strategies, resulted in a joint publication "Advancing National Strategies for Financial Education."
- In June 2014, CI launched a financial services pilot e-learning course in order to provide consumer associations with the necessary tools to influence national financial services policies and practices.
- In 2015, the OECD/INFE published the OECD/INFE Policy Handbook on National Strategies for Financial Education as a follow up to the OECD/INFE High-Level Principles on National Strategies for Financial Education, aiming to support governments and other actors in the implementation of national strategies in this field (OECD, 2015).
- In November 2015, the OECD publishes "Core Competencies Framework on Financial Literacy for Youth," a document containing objectives and key components of the international framework designed to be applicable to the youth aged 15–18, establishing the basic necessary level of financial literacy which allows them to safely participate in financial life.
- In August 2016, OECD issued "Core Competencies Framework on financial literacy for Adults," a document containing a series of financial literacy outcomes considered universally relevant for the financial well-being of adults and youth (aged 18+).

Many authors (Rutledge, 2010; Aprahamian, 2010) point out that weak financial literacy undermines both consumers' ability to protect their financial assets and the development of the financial sector. In this context, the financial capability needs to be improved by financial education, so consumers can make well-informed financial decisions.

But financial education is not a substitute for adequate regulation, the two approaches being complementary (Aprahamian, 2010).

In the European Union (EU), consumer protection and financial literacy are regarded as key issues for a sound financial market, therefore 'consumer financial capability' is an important issue which allows consumers to make well-informed choices (ECRI, 2006) and to feel confident about their being adequately protected. Actually, the financial protection of consumers permanently represents a part of the objective of the EU in developing a single market for financial services.

The proper functioning of the EU market for financial services depends on the Commission's commitment to ensure a high degree of consumer protection, focused on areas of high interest for the consumers, such as: bank accounts, consumer credit, mortgage credit and the distance marketing of financial services.

In the EU, the interests of consumers and retail investors are represented by The Financial Services User Group (FSUG), providing advice to the Commission and ensuring that consumer interests are taken into account in relevant EU financial legislation.

One of the key preoccupations of the European Parliament is to enhance the consumers' protection within the financial markets. These issues are addressed by the 2014–2020 Consumer Program and by recent European Parliament resolutions regarding stronger consumer protection, better financial education and improved financial literacy (European Parliament, 2014).

Consumer trust in financial markets can increase – thus sustaining their development – by combining rules for financial firms with sound programs of financial education for consumers. In this context, financial literacy initiatives provide consumers with knowledge and skills to understand both the risks and rewards of using financial products and services and their legal rights and obligations in this area.

Emerging markets, where most consumers tend to be vulnerable in terms of consumer protection (Rutledge, 2010), need special attention as financial service contracts and the inherent risks are difficult to understand.

Another notable initiative on the international capital market is made by the World Federation on Exchanges – WFE. Thus, in 2015, the Financial Literacy & Education Initiative was launched by the WFE and brought together over 30 exchanges – WFE members. The programs aimed at young people (pupils and students), and the initiation of this project was prompted by the need to promote transparency and confidence in stock markets. New generations must be prepared, given the intense globalizing trends on capital markets and the velocity of the financial crises' spread at international level (WFE, 2015).

The international financial crisis demonstrated the importance of the protection of investors in the capital market. Therefore, at the European level, the legislation was revised in 2014 (new regulations were adopted – the Markets in Financial Instruments Directive – MiFID II and the Markets in Financial Instruments Regulation – MiFIR) in order to improve the functioning of the capital market and to increase investors' protection. These regulations and their implementing rules (ESMA, 2016) will be enforced in 2018. Investors' protection requires emphasized transparency of activities on capital market. This is done by requiring issuers to provide continuous information to holders of securities and potential investors about important events occurring within the company, but also through the efforts of the stock exchanges and financial supervisory authorities that publish information on the characteristics, profitability and risk of financial products traded on different segments of the capital market.

3. Financial education on the capital market in Romania

The Romanian capital market is small, compared to other markets in Central and Eastern Europe, and the operations performed are mainly speculative; this market fulfills its function of financing companies and public institutions to a small extent. Reduced liquidity, frequent oscillations, the herd behavior of investors, reduced offers from the two exchanges, the lack of financial education, the frauds that rocked capital market (the best known being the case of the National Fund of Investment) caused a reduced involvement of retail investors in this market, and the banking market was preferred (Alexandru, Caragea, 2011; Anghelache, Anghel, 2015 Trenca, Petria, Pece, 2015).

Institutions of the Romanian capital market are involved in taking measures for the reclassification of the capital market as an "emerging market" (now the Romanian market holds the status of "frontier market"). The Financial Supervision Authority (FSA) initiated a large reform of the capital market called STEAM (Set of Actions towards Establishing and Acknowledgment of the Emerging Market Status) in 2014. Along with ambitious goals such as increasing the implementation of corporate governance principles at the level of its capital market's entities, raising visibility of the Romanian companies listed on the stock market by the possibility of indirectly listing them on other capital markets, development of local bonds market (primary and secondary bonds/municipal and corporate), we find an increase in market liquidity and attraction of new investors to the capital market.

This last objective is achieved through specific measures, one of them being the creation of an educational program for the capital market. This program aims at organizing conferences/presentations for:

- categories of investors from the most representative cities (e.g., Bucharest, Timisoara, Constanta, Iasi, Brasov, Cluj-Napoca);
- government and parliament members;
- courts' representatives and managers of the top 50 companies that are not listed on the capital market in Romania.

The Bucharest Stock Exchange runs an extensive financial education campaign as part of its CSR (corporate social responsibility) actions promoted by this entity. The "Fluent in Finance" program was launched in 2015; first conducted in large companies, it now includes individuals and students.

The Sibiu Stock Exchange (Sibex) launched a financial education program in 2013, as the management team realized that the stock market had well-trained specialists, but a limited number of investors. That is why several courses to popularize financial products traded on Sibex among retail investors were developed.

Conclusions

In most developed countries, public authorities have realized the importance of financial education, not only for consumers/investors but also for economic stability in general. Therefore, national strategies for financial education were launched and the leading role belonged to public authorities such as the Ministry of Finance, the Central Bank or the Financial Supervision Authority, involving also consumer and investor associations from the financial market. In Romania, the National Authority for Consumer Protection and the Romanian Consumer Protection Association took the initiative to launch such a strategy for the period of 2012–2017; the project has not been completed although it was publicly debated.

Financial education is a long process that should be based on a national strategy that provides both resources and clear objectives and should begin in the earliest childhood. For this reason, the cooperation between the financial authorities and the ministry of education is essential. Changing consumer behavior in the market must be accompanied by an ethic attitude of financial institutions that must provide consumers with information regarding the risks of financial products and higher transparency from issuers and public authorities acting on the financial market.

The capital market is characterized by a higher complexity compared to other segments of the financial market. The future merger of the Bucharest Stock Exchange and the Sibiu Stock Exchange will intensify efforts of these institutions to attract new retail investors, which are boosted by financial education programs implemented by the FSA.

References

1. Alexandru, Antoniade-Ciprian, and Nicoleta Caragea. "Financial Crisis from the Trust and Loss Aversion Perspective in Emerging Romanian Capital Market." Theoretical and Applied Economics 7, no. 7, 2011, pp. 101–110.
2. Anghelache, Constantin, and Madalina-Gabriela Anghel. "Analysis Model of the Capital Market in Romania." Knowledge Horizons. Economics 7.3 (2015): pp. 65–73.
3. Aprahamian, Arabela, Building Financial Capability to Strengthen Consumer Protection, Riga, Latvia, 13 May 2010, ppt presentation.
4. BRA (Boston Redevelopement Authority). "Financial Education Report 2014, A Review of Financial Education Practices in the United States & Observations on Applications to Immigrant."
5. CI (Consumers International). In Search of Good Practices in Financial Consumer Protection, February 2013.
6. CI (Consumers International). http://www.consumersinternational.org/our-work/financial-services/key-projects/financial-education/.
7. ESMA (European Securities and Markets Authority). 2016, https://www.esma.europa.eu/regulation/mifid-ii-and-investor-protection.
8. ECRI (European Credit Research Institute). Consumer Financial Capability: Empowering European Consumers, 2006, available at http://www.ecri.eu/new/system/files/FinCap_Workshop_I_papers.pdf.
9. European Parliament. Consumer Protection Aspects of Financial Services, Directorate General for Internal Policies, IP/A/IMCO/ST/2013-07 February 2014, available at http://www.europarl.europa.eu/studies.
10. Hastings, Justine S., Madrian, Brigitte C. and William L. Skimmyhorn. "Financial literacy, financial education, and economic outcomes." Annu. Rev. Econ. 5.1, 2013, pp. 347–373.
11. IOSCO (International Organization of Securities Commissions). Strategic Framework for Investor Education and Financial Literacy, Consultation Report, CR03/2014.
12. IOSCO (International Organization of Securities Commissions). Strategic Framework for Investor Education and Financial Literacy, Final Report, R09/2014.

13. IOSCO (International Organization of Securities Commissions). "Survey on Anti-Fraud Messaging," Final Report FR 06/2015.
14. IOSCO (International Organization of Securities Commissions). "Sound Practices for Investment Risk Education," Final Report, FR 21/2015.
15. Hong, Harrison, Jeffrey D. Kubik, and Jeremy C. Stein. "Social interaction and stock-market participation." The journal of finance 59.1, 2004, pp. 137–163.
16. Klapper, Leora F., Annamaria Lusardi, and Georgios A. Panos. Financial literacy and the financial crisis. No. w17930. National Bureau of Economic Research, 2012.
17. Lusardi, Annamaria, and Olivia S. Mitchell. "Financial literacy and retirement preparedness: Evidence and implications for financial education." Business economics 42.1, 2007, pp. 35–44.
18. Lusardi, Annamaria, and Olivia S. Mitchell. Financial literacy around the world: An overview. No. w17107. National Bureau of Economic Research, 2011.
19. Lusardi, Annamaria, and Olivia S. Mitchell. "The economic importance of financial literacy: Theory and evidence." Journal of Economic Literature 52.1, 2014, pp. 5–44.
20. OECD (Organisation for Economic Co-operation and Development). Financial Literacy and Consumer Protection: Overlooked Aspects of the Crisis, June 2009, available at http://www.oecd.org/daf/fin/financial-markets/financialconsumer-protection.htm.
21. OECD (Organisation for Economic Co-operation and Development). G20 High-Level Principles on Financial Consumer Protection, October 2011, available at: http://www.oecd.org/daf/fin/financial-markets/financialconsumerprotection.htm.
22. OECD (Organisation for Economic Co-operation and Development). National Strategies For Financial Education OECD/INFE Policy Handbook, 2015 available at http://www.oecd.org/finance/financial-education/nationalstrategiesforfinancialeducation.htm.
23. Rutledge, Susan. Consumer Protection And Financial Literacy: Lessons From Nine Country Studies, 2010, http://elibrary.worldbank.org/doi/abs/10.1596/1813-9450-5326.
24. Trenca, Ioan, Petria Nicolae, and Pece Andreea Maria. "The herding behavior on small capital markets: Evidence from Romania." The Annals of The University of Oradea, 2014, p. 793.
25. Van Rooij, Maarten, Annamaria Lusardi, and Rob Alessie. "Financial literacy and stock market participation." Journal of Financial Economics 101.2, 2011, pp. 449–472.
26. Volosevici, Dana. "Corporations-between Governance and Social Responsibility: the European Commission Approach." Economic Insights Trends and Challenges (2013), pp. 121–135.
27. World Bank, Good practices for financial consumer protection, 2012, Washington, DC, available at http://documents.worldbank.org/curated/en/583191468246041829/Good-practices-for-financial-consumer-protection.

28. World Federation of Exchanges. World Exchanges Launch Global Financial Education & Literacy Initiative, 2015, https://www.world-exchanges.org/home/index.php/news/world-exchange-news/world-exchanges-launch-global-finan cial-education-literacy-initiative.

Cristian CIUREA

Bucharest University of Economic Studies & Romanian Academy Library (BAR), Bucharest, Romania, cristian.ciurea@ie.ase.ro

Florin Gheorghe FILIP

Romanian Academy – INCE & BAR, Bucharest, Romania, ffilip@acad.ro

New Results on Creating Virtual Exhibitions in the Cultural Sector

Abstract: The paper presents new research results achieved in the development of virtual exhibitions in cultural institutions. The economic aspects of virtual exhibitions implementation are presented in order to highlight the benefits of these applications to cultural institutions. The role of virtual exhibitions in the promotion of cultural heritage collections is described. The key aspects of development process of virtual exhibitions are revealed using dedicated tools and programming languages. The paper describes the most recent implementations of virtual exhibitions, created with a dedicated software available at the Romanian Academy Library. A study is conducted on a virtual exhibition in order to measure the user experience and user behavior in the application.

Keywords: virtual exhibitions, cultural heritage, mobile technologies, digitization

1. Introduction

The current research focuses on the involvement of new information and communication technologies in the cultural sector and on the results achieved by using computer science tools in cultural heritage valorization and promotion. Modern informatics technologies have generated new concepts in the cultural sector, such as virtual exhibitions. In the literature review of the paper, we have defined the concept of virtual exhibitions, taking into account the definitions from the specialty literature in the recent years.

We paid special attention to the influence of mobile technologies in the development and implementation of virtual exhibitions in the cultural heritage area. The exponential evolution of mobile technologies in the recent years has changed the way we communicate and collaborate in all activity fields, including the cultural field, where it is now possible to access cultural collections from everywhere in the world and at any time.

The penetration of modern informatics technologies in the cultural sector offers new possibilities of knowledge, promotion and valorization that didn't exist before.

For example, the implementation of virtual exhibitions can attract young people to discover a specific part of their history, to enrich their general knowledge about the history and specific culture of their country.

The digitization of collections from cultural institutions (galleries, libraries, archives, and museums) ensures the awareness, valorization and preservation of national cultural heritage.

The modern informatics technologies provide not only a better understanding of the cultural content, but promise more real visitors for cultural institutions. The objective of virtual exhibitions is not to get current visitors outside the cultural institutions, but to stimulate them to come back to explore the physical collections.

2. Literature review

There are many valuable papers and books that were published in recent years on the cultural heritage sector, especially on the topic of the exploitation and promotion of existing cultural heritage collections from European museums and libraries (Styliani et al., 2009; Dziekan, 2012). There were also European projects that involved many cultural heritage institutions and helped them to valorize their beautiful collections and make them available to the public around the world. One of these recent projects was AthenaPlus (http://www.athenaplus.eu), which also involved the Romanian Academy Library that contributed with the digitization of rare and old manuscripts and the development of some virtual exhibitions (Ciurea & Filip, 2016b; Filip et al., 2015).

The European cultural heritage is seen now as a strategic economic resource for the countries that preserve this heritage and for the whole Europe (EC, 2015). Nowadays, the cultural heritage has become not a public funds consumer, but a public and private funds producer. This could happen because of the development of information and communication technologies that generated new concepts, such as virtual exhibitions, and new ways to promote the cultural heritage.

One of the main problems in the exploitation of cultural heritage on a digital basis is the very small number of digitized items. There are a lot of cultural items that need to be digitized in the next years in order to use them as digital content. Statistically, at this moment only 10% of the European cultural heritage have been digitized, and the remaining 90% must be digitized in the next years (Ciurea & Filip, 2016a; Stroeker et al., 2013).

3. The impact of virtual exhibitions in the cultural field

Based on Corovic et al. (2014), we can define a virtual exhibition as an entity that translates the information about physical cultural objects, which are presented in a digital or virtual way, and makes this information available to the public from anywhere and at any time, in a effective and efficient manner.

But, a virtual exhibition is not only "another way" to show cultural content with the help of a new technology, as was the case with Eminescu's digitized manuscripts

(Dumitrescu et al., 2010). It has a dynamic character, meaning that it can be updated with new content at any time, and it has a variety of forms and presentations. In this way, a virtual exhibition is considered more than a digitized collection or an eBook (Filip et al., 2015).

When creating a virtual exhibition, it is very important to present the content in an attractive manner to the public in order to arouse their interest. So, it is not enough to select the content to be presented, but to make it available in a beautiful way. A virtual exhibition can include educational and cultural content that can be very useful for the young people to develop their knowledge.

There are some special characteristics of virtual exhibitions that distinguish them from a website or mobile application. These characteristics are as follows:

- a virtual exhibition represents a substitute for the physical guide or catalog of a real exhibition;
- a virtual exhibition can incorporate multimedia content, which makes it dynamic for the users;
- a virtual exhibition can be developed and implemented for mobile devices, enlarging the possibilities for access to a wide number of users.

In addition to the main objective of a virtual exhibition, which consists in the promotion and valorization of cultural heritage collections, another objective is to allow the visitors to experience alternative routes for exploration and navigation through the cultural content, and also to offer opportunities that visitors were not able to find in a physical exhibition (Lepouras et al., 2004).

When implementing a virtual exhibition, it is mandatory to pay attention to the target public. The development of a virtual exhibition implies people from different fields, including specialists from cultural institutions (librarians, museum specialists, archivists) and specialists in information and communication technologies (analysts, web designers, web developers, programmers). Their collaborative work leads to this special result, represented by the virtual exhibition. A virtual exhibition should have many features in order to be accepted by the target public. For example, it must have a user-friendly interface, but at the same time, it must provide the most attractive digital copies of the cultural objects. In the digital world, it is very simple to provide feedback for a software product, including virtual exhibitions. In the case that a user is not satisfied with the virtual exhibition and he writes a negative review for the application, then many other potential users will not install or open the application because they believe that it is not attractive.

Virtual exhibitions can be designed and developed to be used both on personal computers and on mobile devices. Nowadays, all the web applications are designed to be accessed from devices of different screen sizes. These kind of web solutions are called applications with responsive interface, and they also allow access from mobile devices. The controls from the interface are adapted to screen size, in order to be accessed from different types of mobile devices (smartphones and tablets). But, for a better experience on mobile devices, a virtual exhibition must be implemented as a native mobile application. In this case, the application offers possibilities to access hardware functionalities of the mobile device, such as different sensors and localization services. As a native mobile application, the virtual exhibition can be standalone and can be accessed without permanent access to the Internet. The disadvantage of native mobile applications is that they must be implemented for each type of operating system (Android, iOS, Windows Phone). In this situation, differences in design and functionalities of the mobile application can show up, because of the interoperability of the operating systems.

As presented in figure 1, we expect, at the same time with the development of a big number of virtual exhibitions, to increase the number of physical visitors of cultural institutions. The main role of virtual exhibitions is to promote some special collections that are not well known by many people, and in this way to attract them to visit the cultural institutions. By growing the number of visitors, cultural institutions will grow their revenues, based especially on some entry fees payed by the visitors. If cultural institutions increase their incomes, then they not will require so many public funds from the government to pay their initial and running costs. In this way, cultural institutions will become financially independent and the public funds contribution from the government will decrease.

Fig. 1: The evolution of cultural institutions based on number of virtual exhibitions

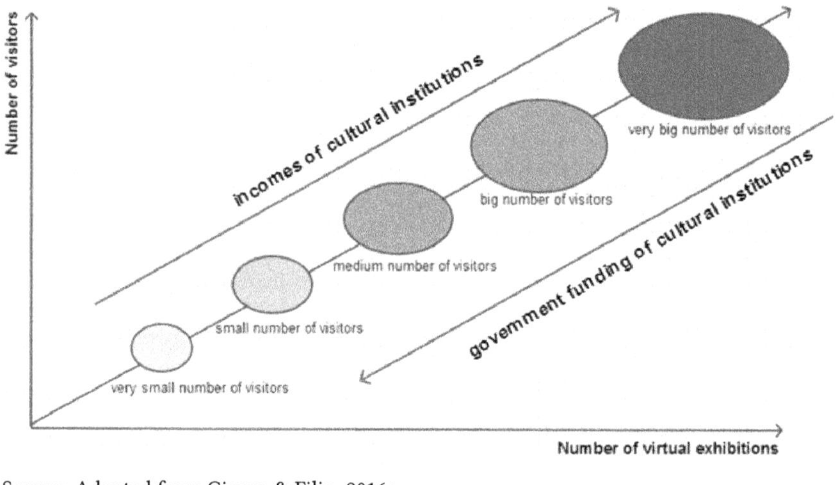

Source: Adapted from Ciurea & Filip, 2016a.

In terms of number of visitors of cultural institutions, there are some aspects that need to be clarified. It is difficult to count the number of single visitors of a cultural institution in a certain period of time, because institutions don't keep a database with personal information of their visitors. We can obtain a number of visits in a period of time, based on the number of tickets paid by visitors or other counting ways. Certainly, there are people that visit a cultural institution many times during a period of time, and they cannot be counted as distinct visitors.

A recent study on the cultural behavior of the Romanian people was conducted in 2015; 38% of the total number of people participating in this study have not read any books in the last year, and only 16% declared that they participated in cultural events often. As for young people aged between 14–30 years, only 48% said that they visited museums and cultural exhibitions, and only 35% went to the library to study (Ciurea & Filip, 2016a).

4. Current implementations of virtual exhibitions at the Romanian Academy Library

During the AthenaPlus Project (http://athenaplus.eu), when the Romanian Academy Library was involved as a partner in the project consortium, an exciting tool was developed to create virtual exhibitions, named MOVIO (http://wiki.athenaplus.eu/index.php/MOVIO; Natale et al., 2014). This software solution allows to create virtual exhibitions, which are available online on the Internet, which can be exported as native mobile applications, especially for iOS and Android mobile operating systems.

Recently, at the Romanian Academy Library we have designed and implemented six virtual exhibitions with the help of MOVIO, namely:

- Constantin Brancoveanu – Prince of Wallachia (http://movio.biblacad.ro/BRANCO/);
- Greek Coins – Constantin Orghidan Collection of the Romanian Academy Library (http://movio.biblacad.ro/COINS/);
- Seals – The history treasure (http://movio.biblacad.ro/SEALS/);
- Ştefan Luchian – Illustrator (http://movio.biblacad.ro/LUCHIAN/);
- Saint Antim Ivireanul (http://movio.biblacad.ro/ANTIM/);
- To other worlds – Painting exhibition of Vasilica CHIFU (http://movio.biblacad.ro/CHIFU/).

Figure 2 below presents some screenshots from the first three virtual exhibitions described above. These virtual exhibitions are already implemented and available at the Romanian Academy Library, which is the provider of cultural objects. In the figure, we present the main pages of the following virtual exhibitions: Constantin Brancoveanu – Prince of Wallachia, Greek Coins – Constantin Orghidan Collection of the Romanian Academy Library, and Seals – The history treasure.

Fig. 2: Three virtual exhibitions implemented with MOVIO

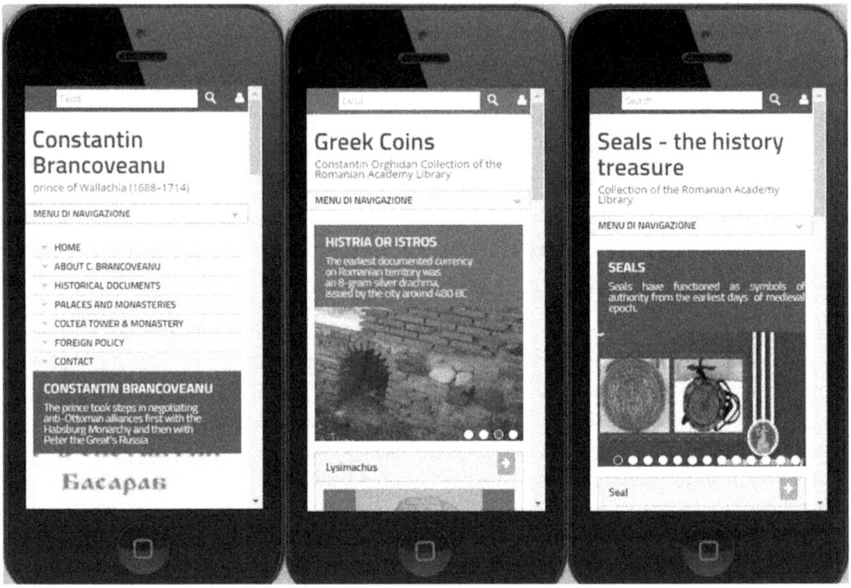

Source: Ciurea & Filip, 2016.

Another important feature of the MOVIO tool is that it is a semantic content management system, which allows users to create their own ontologies, and also to use them immediately without having some specialized knowledge in the field.

Figure 3 presents some screen captures from the other three virtual exhibitions implemented at the Romanian Academy Library. These virtual exhibitions are as follows: Ştefan Luchian – Illustrator, Saint Antim Ivireanul, and To other worlds – Painting exhibition of Vasilica Chifu.

Fig. 3: Other three virtual exhibitions implemented with MOVIO

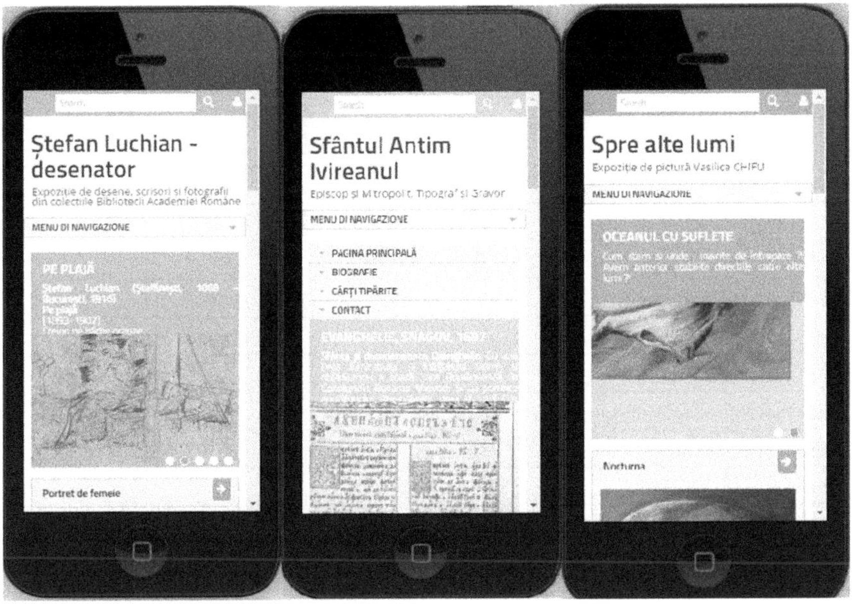

Source: Ciurea & Filip, 2016.

In the future we plan to implement other virtual exhibitions at the Romanian Academy Library, because there are many beautiful collections that can be digitized and promoted to the public, some of them unknown to the young people.

5. Experimental results on the user experience in a virtual exhibition

All virtual exhibitions presented above have similar characteristics and offer similar user experiences, because they are created with the same tool, on the same platform, namely MOVIO. In order to discover what users think about a virtual exhibition implemented with MOVIO, we conducted a survey and we have processed the results.

The objective of the survey was to find what is the user experience with a virtual exhibition created with MOVIO, and after that to measure the user behavior in the application.

The proposed survey was applied to a number of around 100 students for the virtual exhibition Constantin Brancoveanu – Prince of Wallachia, with the help of an online questionnaire. The respondents declared that they used the virtual exhibition as a mobile application on their smartphones and tablets. Table 1 below presents the statistics of the responses, taking into account the most important quality characteristics of the virtual exhibition.

Table 1: Statistics of the survey results

Characteristic measured	Satisfied	Unsatisfied
Contents of home page	71%	29%
Graphic design of main page	79%	21%
Download speed of images	65%	35%
Navigation in the application	68%	32%
Graphic layout of pages	84%	16%
Navigation between pages	75%	25%
Multimedia content	67%	33%
Personal information requested	58%	42%
Network usage	51%	49%
Storage space needed	88%	12%

Source: Based on Feliciati & Natale (2008), Ciurea & Tudorache (2014).

Based on the data presented in table 1, the spider diagram of figure 4 shows that the satisfactory answers are greater than the unsatisfactory answers for each characteristic analyzed.

Fig. 4: Graphical representation of the satisfaction degree on the use of virtual exhibition

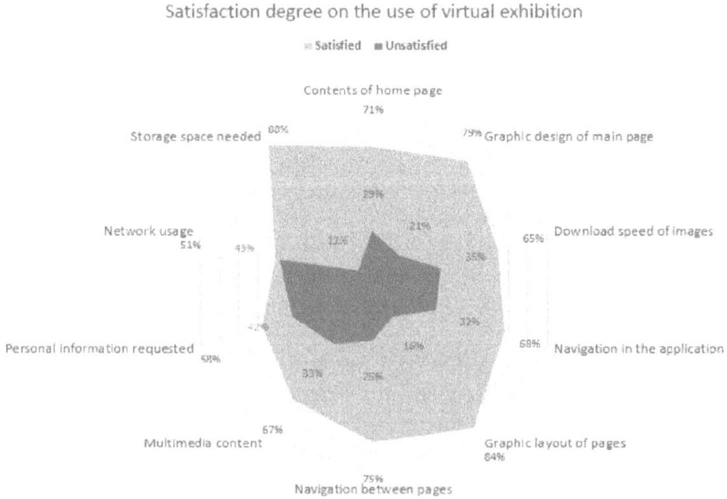

The results of the survey demonstrates that, as a whole, users are satisfied with the experience in the virtual exhibition. The results can be useful for software developers to make future improvements in the users experience in the application.

6. Conclusions

Virtual exhibitions are just the beginning of the revolution made by modern information and communication technologies in the cultural field. Certainly, there will be other projects and concepts that will appear in order to reveal this (r)evolution. In the next years, when the number of digitized documents will increase in cultural institutions, new opportunities of exploring the cultural heritage cam be offered. Cultural institutions need to adapt to these changes in order to satisfy the needs of the modern society.

The main contribution of the paper is to reveal the importance of cultural heritage collections, both from cultural and economic points of view, by using new information and communication technologies. The research limits consists in the incipient results obtained until now in the literature regarding the impact of virtual exhibitions in the development of cultural institutions. The future research directions imply a case study that will be conducted at the Romanian Academy Library concerning the implementation of a new virtual exhibition, the dissemination of the virtual exhibition to the target public, and then the analysis of the number of real visitors that will come to see the physical exhibition, based on the attractions from the virtual exhibition.

References

1. Ciurea, Cristian; Filip, Florin Gheorghe: 2016a, "New Researches on the Role of Virtual Exhibitions in Digitization, Preservation and Valorization of Cultural Heritage," Informatica Economică, 20 (4), pp. 26–33.
2. Ciurea, Cristian; Filip, Florin Gheorghe: 2016b, "Using Mobile Technologies to Promote and Valorize the Cultural Heritage in the Knowledge Based Society," Proceedings of 3rd International Conference Economic Scientific Research – Theoretical, Empirical and Practical Approaches, ESPERA 2015, 3–4 December 2015, Bucharest, Romania, in Luminita Chivu et al. (eds.): Economic Dynamics and Sustainable Development – Resources, Factors, Structures and Policies, Peter Lang: Frankfurt a. M.
3. Ciurea, Cristian; Tudorache, Catalin: 2014, "New Perspectives on the Development of Virtual Exhibitions for Mobile Devices," Economy Informatics, 14 (1), pp. 31–38.
4. Corovic, Ljubica; Vuksan, Vesna; Sofronijevic, Adam: 2014, "Virtual exhibition as a medium for presenting scientific and cultural heritage to international audiences: Dorde Stanojevic – a rector who lit up Belgrade," The 9th SEEDI Conference: Digitisation of cultural and scientific heritage, Belgrade, Serbia, 15–16 May.

5. Dumitrescu, Gabriela; Filip, Florin Gheorghe; Ioniţă, Angela; Lepădatu, Cornel: 2010, "Open source Eminescu's manuscripts: a digitization experiment." Studies in Informatics and Control, 19 (1), pp. 79–84.
6. Dziekan, Vince: 2012, Virtuality and the Art of Exhibition. Curatorial Design for the Multimedia Museum, Chicago, IL: The University of Chicago Press.
7. EC 2015, Getting cultural heritage to work for Europe, Report of the Horizon 2020 Expert Group on Cultural Heritage, 2015, Available at: http://www.kowi.de/Portaldata/2/Resources/horizon2020/coop/H2020-Report-Expert-Group-Cultural-Heritage.pdf.
8. Feliciati, Pierluigi; Natale, Maria Teresa (eds.): 2008, Handbook of cultural web user interaction, First edition (September 2008), MINERVA EC Project.
9. Filip, Florin Gheorghe; Ciurea, Cristian; Dragomirescu, Horaţiu; Ivan, Ion: 2015, May, "Cultural Heritage and Modern Information and Communication Technologies," Technological and Economic Development of Economy, 21 (3), Taylor & Francis, pp. 441–459.
10. Lepouras, George; Katifori, Akrivi; Vassilakis, Costas; Charitos, Dimitris: 2004, "Real Exhibitions in a Virtual Museum," Virtual Reality, 7 (2), pp. 120–128.
11. Natale, Maria Teresa; Minelli, Sam Habibi; Dierickx, Barbara; Ongaro, Paolo; Piccininno, Marzia; Ugoletti, Daniele; Saccoccio, Rubino; Raggioli, Alberto: 2014, "Exhibiting Intangible Cultural Heritage using MOVIO: a multilingual toolkit for creating curated digital exhibitions, made available by the AthenaPlus project," ICOM 2014 – Access and Understanding – Networking in the Digital Era: Intangible Cultural Heritage, Available at: http://www.cidoc2014.de/images/sampledata/cidoc/papers/H-2_Natale_Minelli_et-al_paper.pdf.
12. Stroeker, Natasha, Vogels, René, Jan Nauta, Gerhard, de Niet, Marco: 2013, September, Report on the ENUMERATE Thematic Surveys on Digital Collections in European Cultural Heritage Institutions, Available at: http://www.enumerate.eu/fileadmin/ENUMERATE/documents/ENUMERATE-Thematic-Survey-2013.pdf.
13. Styliani, Sylaiou; Fotis, Liarokapis; Kostas, Kotsakis; Petros, Patias: 2009, "Virtual museums, a survey and some issues for consideration," Journal of Cultural Heritage, No. 10, pp. 520–528.

Andrei Silviu DOSPINESCU

Center for Industrial and Services Economics, Calea 13 Septembrie, nr. 13, Bucharest, 050711, Romania, e-mail: andrei@mail.ince.ro

Nicoleta HORNIANSCHI

Center for Industrial and Services Economics, Calea 13 Septembrie, nr. 13, Bucharest, 050711, Romania, email: hornianschi@yahoo.com

The Contribution of Total Factor Productivity, Capital and Labor Force to the Output Growth of the Romanian Manufacturing Subsectors

Abstract: Analyzing the drivers of output growth at the sectoral level facilitates the understanding of the Romanian industry growth profile and the economic factors that affect sectoral and structural evolutions. With this in mind, the paper identifies the contribution of total factor productivity, capital and labor force on the output growth for ten manufacturing subsectors of the Romanian economy. The contributions of the paper are twofold. From a methodological and statistical perspective, the paper calculates the capital stock for ten manufacturing subsectors using the permanent inventory method and builds a Cobb-Douglas production function for each of the ten subsectors as well as estimates of total factor productivity. From an applied perspective, the paper builds profiles and clusters of the Romanian manufacturing subsectors with similar behaviors in terms of the impact of production factors on output. This facilitates an understanding of the impact of economic policies affecting capital and labor force on the subsectors evolution.

Keywords: growth accounting, permanent inventory method, manufacturing subsectors, total factor productivity, capital, labor force

Introduction

The paper analyzes the drivers of output growth at the level of the manufacturing subsectors, for 1995–2015, in terms of the factors that played a key role in increasing production. The identification is based on the neoclassical exogenous growth theory. Therefore, it takes into account: a) the accumulation of capital; b) population growth and employment and c) technological progress.

The objective of the study is to identify the contribution of total factor productivity, capital and labor force on the output growth for ten manufacturing subsectors of the Romanian economy, and to build profiles and clusters with similar behavior in terms of the impact of production factors on output.

1. Literature review

Using capital and labor as determinants of production has a long tradition and is at the central of exogenous growth theory (Solow 1956, Swan 1956, Lucas 1990). The availability of statistics on employment and gross capital formation correlated with the difficulty to capture other factors influencing production such as, for example, institutional factors which led to the widespread use of the Cobb-Douglas function or related functions exhibiting constant elasticity of substitution (CES). An example in this sense is the use of the Cobb-Douglas production function to determine potential output and the cyclical position of the economy (Congressional Budget Office (CBO, 2001), Havik et al. 2014, Burns et al. 2014).

The estimation of the neoclassical production function is confronted with a number of challenges extensively presented in the literature, of which the most important are the assumptions about the values of the output elasticities of capital and labor and the estimation of the capital stock.

The output elasticities of capital and labor reflect technology factors, characteristics of the production process as well as characteristics of the analyzed economy (degree of capitalization of the economy for example). Different values are used in the literature (see Burns et al. 2014, Shrine et al. 2010, Gălăţescu et al. 2007, Dobrescu 2006) reflecting the authors' assumptions as well as specificities of the analyzed economy. In countries with a low share of the gray economy, employment elasticity can be estimated using the ratio between earnings and gross value added (GVA). The approach is not preferred in the case of the Romanian economy, because it does not take into account the income of family workers and freelancers, leading to an underestimation of labor elasticity. It was preferred in this context to use a value of 0.65 for the output elasticity of labor and, consequently, a value of 0.35 for the output elasticity of capital consistent with studies that take into account the specificities of the Romanian economy (see Dobrescu 2006, Alter et al. 2010).

Estimations of the capital stock for Romania were made particularly in the context of estimating potential gross domestic product (GDP) and the output gap (Dobrescu 2006, Shrine et al. 2010, Galatescu et al. 2007). The novelty of this paper is represented by the reconstitution of the capital stock data series at sectoral level. The estimation method used was the perpetual inventory method (Meinen et al. 1998, Bergoeing et al. 2002) which takes into account the depreciation of capital stock and the gross fixed capital formation. The quality of the estimates depends to a high degree on the value used for the capital depreciation rate. To this end, estimates made by Galatescu et al. (2007), Dobrescu (2006), Shrine et al. (2010) for the Romanian economy. In the literature (see Capros 2013, Fragkiadakis et al. 2012, Mohora 2006), different values are used at the sectoral level reflecting variation in the technical characteristics between sectors. In this context, the paper uses specific capital depreciation rates for the Romanian economy (see Timmer et al. 2012), reflecting the characteristics of the Romanian manufacturing subsectors.

2. Model description

The impact of production factors on the output growth of ten Romanian manufacturing subsectors was estimated based on the exogenous growth theory using the Cobb-Douglas production function.

The Cobb-Douglas production function captures the role of capital, labor and total factor productivity in the production process. The approach assumes constant returns to scale (CRS) and constant elasticity of substitution (CES).

$$y_t = A_t L_t^{\alpha} K_t^{\beta} \quad (1)$$

Where A represents the total factor productivity, Y subsector output, L labor, K capital stock and

$$\beta = 1 - \alpha$$

Alpha and beta are the output elasticities of labor and capital and are determined by specific technologies and economic conditions. Studies relevant to Romania use a value of 0.65 for alpha (Dobrescu, 2006; Shrine, 2010 and Galatescu et al., 2007), which is also used in this paper.

Y represents the output of the manufacturing subsectors in constant 1995 prices.

Labor is represented by employment at the level of the manufacturing subsectors.

The estimation of the capital stock was the main challenge. For the Romanian economy estimations were done, especially in the context of estimating potential gross domestic product (GDP) and the output gap (Dobrescu 2006, Shrine 2010 and Galatescu et al. 2007). The novelty of the work is the reconstitution of the data series at sectoral level. The method used to this end was the perpetual inventory method. The method takes into account the depreciation of the capital stock and the gross fixed capital formation.

$$K_t = K_{t-1}(1 - \delta) + FBCF_t \quad (2)$$

Where K represents the capital stock, δ represents the capital depreciation rate, FBCF represents the gross fixed capital formation.

The quality of the estimations depends to a high degree on the value used for the depreciation rate. Taking into account the specific literature for Romania (Galatescu et al. 2007, Shrine et al. 2010), a capital depreciation of 5% was used for the whole economy. The technical characteristics vary between sectors. Given this, the reconstruction of the data series at the sectoral level required the use of specific rates that were taken from the World Input-Output Database (WIOD) estimates for Romania (see Timmer et al. 2012).

Total factor productivity was calculated by rearranging equation (1) which led to the following identity:

$$A_t = \frac{Y_t}{L_t^{\alpha} K_t^{\beta}} \quad (3)$$

Where A represents the total factor productivity, Y subsector output, L labor, K capital stock and $\beta = 1 - \alpha$.

The analysis of the impact of production factors on output growth at the subsector level was calculated based on the rearrangement of relation (1).

$$\ln(y_t / y_{t-1}) = \ln(A_t / A_{t-1}) + \alpha \ln(L_t / L_{t-1}) + \beta \ln(K_t / K_{t-1}) \tag{4}$$

The 'k-means clustering' algorithm (Everitt and Hothorn 2009, MacQueen 1967) was used for grouping the analyzed subsectors based on the impact of the production factors on output growth.

3. Results. Subsector clustering

Total factor productivity had the highest impact on output growth for the ten manufacturing subsectors under investigation followed by capital. The contribution of labor was negative for the majority of the subsectors. This reflects the impact of the Romanian manufacturing sector restructuring process in the analyzed period.

Table 1: Contribution of production inputs to the output growth (1995–2015)

Subsector	Total factor productivity	Capital	Labor force
Food, beverages and tobacco products	0.058	0.016	–0.03
Textiles	0.006	0.014	–0.002
Tanning and dressing of leather, manufacture of footwear	–0.012	0.027	0.01
Wood, products of wood and cork, except mobile	0.075	0.025	–0.027
Paper and paper products; printing and reproduction of recorded media	0.045	0.023	–0.033
Chemical industry	0.02	0.004	–0.03
Manufacture of rubber and plastic	0.02	0.024	0.012
Manufacture of machinery and equipment n.c.a.	0.058	0.004	–0.048
Manufacture of electrical and optical equipment	–0.004	0.015	0.019
Manufacture of transport equipment	0.049	0.028	–0.012

Source: Own calculations based on relation 4.

The application of the clustering algorithm led to a series of results which should be interpreted with caution. The identified impact includes both fundamental economic mechanisms reflecting, for example, capital or labor intensive industries, as well as market distortions, numerous in the transition to a market economy.

In what follows, we will identify only those results that are consistent with economic theory and which can be correlated with the realities of the Romanian economy.

Table 2: Subsector clustering based on total factor productivity, capital and labor

Subsector	Centroid		
	Total factor productivity	**Capital**	**Labor force**
Food, beverages and tobacco products	3	2	1
Textiles	2	2	2
Tanning and dressing of leather, manufacture of footwear	1	3	2
Wood, products of wood and cork, except mobile	3	3	1
Paper and paper products; printing and reproduction of recorded media	3	3	1
Chemical industry	2	1	1
Manufacture of rubber and plastic	2	2	3
Manufacture of machinery and equipment n.c.a.	3	1	1
Manufacture of electrical and optical equipment	1	2	3
Manufacture of transport equipment	3	3	2

Note: Lowest contributions are recorded in the first centroid and the highest in the third.

Source: Own calculations.

The contribution of total factor productivity reflects both the role of the economic restructuring process and the impact of investments. The highest contributions were recorded in subsectors like manufacture of machinery and equipment not classified in other subsectors (n.c.a.), characterized by successful privatizations as in the case of Dacia and extensive restructuring as in the case of Roman Brasov, where the work force decreased from 20,000 employees in 1989 to about 8,600 in 2003.

Regarding the capital contribution, the results indicate that in periods of massive restructuring, characterized by annual changes in labor of more than 20%, changes in capital stock were comparatively much lower. For those capital-intensive subsectors characterized by massive labor force adjustments, lower capital contribution to growth does not reflect the technical characteristics of the subsector, but the extensive restructuring process.

In terms of the labor force contribution to output growth, the highest contributions were obtained for subsectors with a positive dynamics of employment. For example, in the manufacture of electrical and optical equipment, the labor force grew by 80% between 1995–2015, compared with manufacture of machinery and equipment n.c.a., where it contracted by 60%. Consequently, the labor force contribution reflects the major restructuring that took place in the Romanian manufacturing subsectors.

4. Conclusions

The highest contribution to the output growth, for the ten analyzed manufacturing subsectors, was recorded for total factor productivity followed by capital. The labor force contribution was negative for the majority of subsectors. The hierarchy reflects the extensive restructuring of the Romanian manufacturing subsectors, characterized by massive labor adjustments.

The application of the clustering algorithm led to a series of results correlated with the restructuring process.

The ratio of net investment to industrial production was a good indicator of the total factor productivity contribution to the subsectors' output growth.

Massive labor adjustments have played a key role in the negative contribution of labor to the output growth for the majority of the analyzed manufacturing subsectors.

The restructuring process in traditional capital-intensive subsectors decoupled the capital impact from the technical characteristics of the analyzed subsectors. Consequently, analyses aiming to capture the impact of investment in terms of technical characteristics of the subsectors (e.g., investment in equipment) should use the specific capital stock series with caution.

References

1. Alter, M. Ciprian N./G. Bobeică: "Estimating potential GDP for the Romanian economy. An eclectic approach," Romanian Journal of Economic Forecasting, 3, 2010, pp. 5–25.
2. Bergoeing, R./Kehoe, P./Kehoe, T./Soto, R.: "A Decade Lost and Found: Mexico and Chile in the 1980s," Review of Economic Dynamics, 5, 2002, pp. 166–205.
3. Burns, A./Van Rensburg, T. J./Dybczak, K. and Bui, T.: "Estimating potential output in developing countries," Journal of Policy Modeling 36, 2014, pp. 700–716.
4. Capros, P./Van Regemorter, D. /Paroussos, L. /Karkatsoulis, P. /Revesz, T. / Fragkiadakis, C. /Tsani, S. /Charalampidis, I.: "GEM-E3 Model Documentation. JRC Scientific and Technical Reports," 2013, EUR 26034 EN.
5. Congressional Budget Office: "CBO's method for estimating potential output: An update", CBO papers, 2001.
6. Dobrescu, E.: "Double Conditioned Potential Output," paper presented at The 28th General Conference of The International Association for Research in Income and Wealth, Cork, Ireland, 22–28 August 2004.

7. Everitt, Brian S./Hothorn, Torsten: A Handbook of Statistical Analyses Using. R. Chapman and Hall/CRC, 2nd edition, 2009, ISBN-10: 1420079336.
8. Fragkiadakis, K./Paroussos, L./Kouvaritakis, N./Capros, P.: "A Multi – Country Econometric Estimation of the Constant Elasticity of Substitution." Presented at the Final WIOD Conference: Causes and Consequences of Globalization, Groningen, The Netherlands, 24–26 April 2012.
9. Galatescu, A. A./Radulescu, B./Copaciu, M.: "Potential GDP Estimation for Romania," National Bank of Romania Occasional Paper no. 6, 2007.
10. Genty, A./Inaki, A./Neuwahl, F.: "Final database of environmental satellite accounts: technical report on their compilation," WIOD Deliverable 4.6, Documentation, 2012, available at http://www.wiod.org/ publications/ source_ docs/ Environmental_Sources.pdf.
11. Havik, K./Mc Morrow, K./Orlandi, F./Planas, C./Raciborski, R./Roger, W./Rossi, A./Thum Thysen, A./Vandermeulen, V.: "The production function methodology for calculating potential growth rates & output gaps," Economic Papers 535, 2014.
12. Hodrick, R. J./Prescott, E. C.: "Postwar U.S. Business Cycles: An Empirical Investigation," Journal of Money, Credit and Banking, 29 (1), 1997, pp. 1–16.
13. Lucas, Robert: "Why doesn't Capital Flow from Rich to Poor Countries?". American Economic Review 80 (2), 1990, pp. 92–96.
14. MacQueen, James B.: "Some Methods for classification and Analysis of Multivariate Observations." Proceedings of 5th Berkeley Symposium on Mathematical Statistics and Probability 1, University of California Press, 1967.
15. Meinen, G./Verbiest, P./de Wolf, P.P.: "Perpetual Inventory Method. Service lives, Discard patterns and Depreciation methods," OECD, 1998, Available at https://www.oecd.org/std/na/2552337.pdf.
16. Mohora, M. C. "RoMod: a dynamic CGE model for Romania a tool for policy analysis," Erasmus Universiteit, 2006, available at http://sar.org.ro/wp-content/uploads/2013/01/Romod-A-dynamic-CGE-Model-for-Romania.-A-Tool-for-Policy-Analysis.pdf.
17. Solow, R. M.: "A contribution to the theory of economic growth." Quarterly Journal of Economics (Oxford Journals) 70 (1), 1956, pp. 65–94.
18. Swan, Trevor W.: "Economic growth and capital accumulation." Economic Record (Wiley) 32 (2), 1956, pp. 334–361.
19. Timmer, M. P./Dietzenbacher, E./Los, B./Stehrer, R. Ş./de Vries, G. J.: "An Illustrated User Guide to the World Input–Output Database: the Case of Global Automotive Production," Review of International Economics, 23, 2015, pp. 575–605. http://ec.europa.eu/eurostat/data/database [Accessed at 19 October 2016].

Appendix 1

Fig. A.1: The output dynamics for ten Romanian manufacturing subsectors (1996–2015)

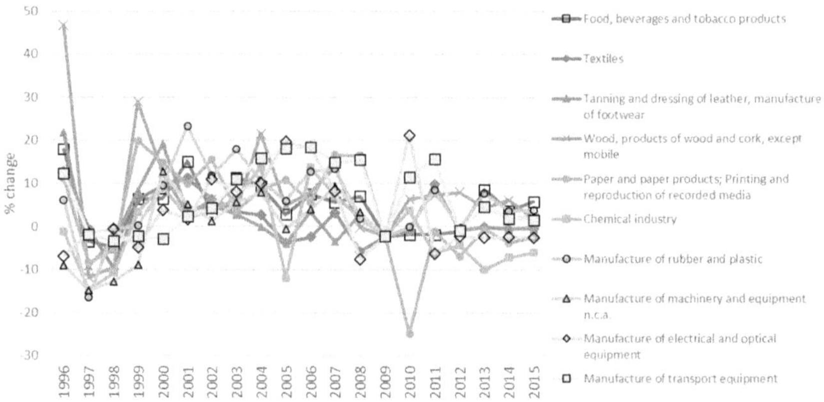

Source: Own calculations based on the World Input-Output Database (WIOD) and Eurostat.

Fig. A.2: The capital stock dynamics for ten Romanian manufacturing subsectors (1996–2015)

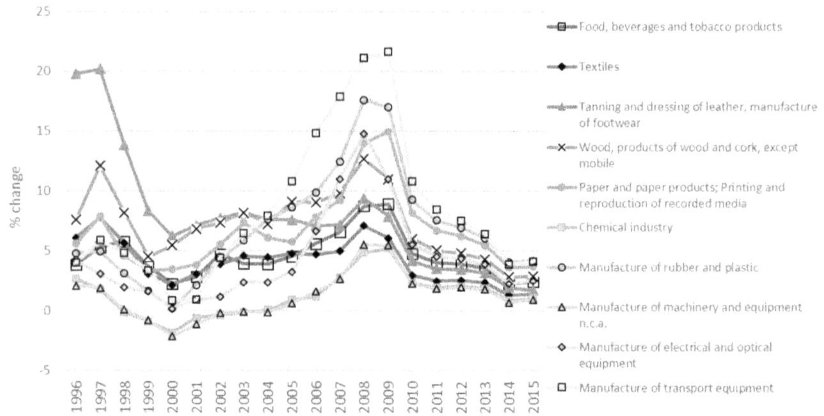

Source: Own calculations based on World Input-Output Database (WIOD) and Eurostat.

Fig. A.3: The labor force dynamics for ten Romanian manufacturing subsectors (1996–2015)

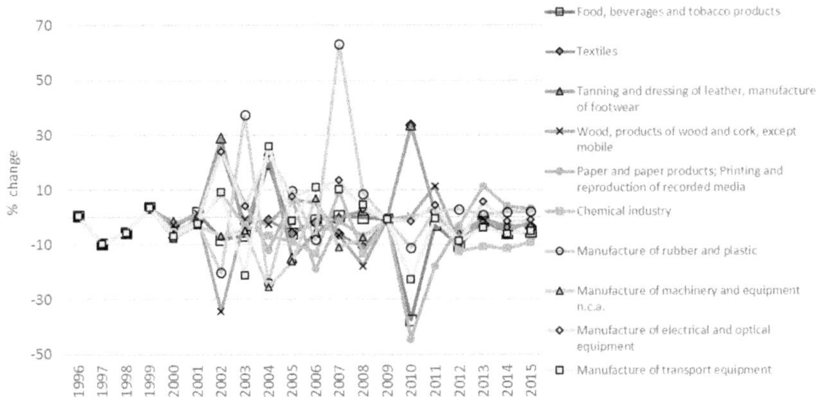

Source: Own calculations based on World Input-Output Database (WIOD) and Eurostat.

Raluca Elisabeta BOZGA, Daniela Nicoleta BĂLEANU

Centre for Industry and Services Economy, INCE
“Costin C. Kiriţescu,” Academia Româna; Calea 13 Septembrie
nr. 13, sector 5, Bucharest 050711, Romania
ralucaelisabeta@yahoo.com

The Evolution of the Romanian Drug Industry – Past and Present

Abstract: The drug, medicine or pharmaceutical industry is a branch of the chemical industry producing organic synthesis substances or bio-derived products useful in human health care. The purpose of this work is to analyze the evolution of the drug industry in Romania, since the appearance of the first production units up to present days. The main changes in this sector are investigated: starting businesses, development of their product portfolio etc. Data are presented chronologically, giving details regarding the production structures and the main Romanian producers before 1989, the transformations induced in this industry by the political and economic changes that occurred in Romania after 1989 (the evolution of older companies, the creation of new companies, data regarding the evolution of the drugs market and the main competitors).

Keywords: drug industry, evolution, market

1. Introduction

The drug or pharmaceutical industry is tightly related to the health care of a population and, in the same time, presents important economic incentives. In the past centuries, when the circulation of goods was more controlled, it also presented strategic importance, particularly in what regards the base medicines and vaccines. Presently, in the epoch of globalization, when the circulation of medicines is unrestrained, the dominating factor is the economic one. The consumption of medicines per capita increased continuously, and so did the government's expenses in this domain.

For Romania and other developing countries, providing the population with pharmaceutical products involves important financial efforts in foreign currencies. On the other side, a strong national pharmaceutical industry represents an important source of revenue, as it is representing a very profitable sector. Published data are evidencing that, in 2014, the overall revenue of the pharmaceutical industry in the world, exceeded $1 trillion Global Pharmaceutical Industry, 2014). In view of these aspects, we consider that an analysis of the evolution and actual state of this sector in Romania is an interesting subject, both from social and economic points of view. This paper examines the Romanian pharmaceutical industry and drug market, from historical perspectives, present state and the future evolution.

2. Literature review

The medicines represent an important and effective way to ensure the health of the people, which explains the growing number of studies focused on the discovery and development of new products, the evolution of this industry. The evolution of the drug industry in Romania, along with the evolution of other industrial branches, was described in different published monographs (Iovanelli, 1975; Opritescu, 2005; Florescu, 1972). A short study regarding the progress of pharmaceutical production in Romania was published by Stancu (2008).

Data on the production, import and export of medicines in different periods are also published in existing works (Enciclopedia Romaniei, 1938; Dezvoltarea industriei in RPR, 1960). Details on the progress of the Romanian drug industry during the period of 1945–1971 are given by Florescu (1972). The present drug market analysis, its potential and the development trends of the pharmaceutical industry are published by different authors (Industria farmaceutică în România, 2012; Somanescu, 2015).

3. The period before 1918

The pharmaceutical industry evolved as a spin-off from the dye industry in the late 19th century. The first drug factories appeared in Switzerland: Ciba (1850), E. Sandoz (1886), Hoffman-La Roche (1896). In Germany, the old dye factory Bayer began producing pharmaceutical products at an industrial scale in 1897. The first product manufactured was aspirin, under the name "Aspirine." In the same period, the first large drug factories appeared in the USA: Pfizer & Co. (1849), P. A. Sharp and Dohme L. (1860), and Medicines Vera-Park Davis & Co. (1862).

In Romania, the beginning of the drug industry was closely linked to the development of the chemical industry, the organization of medical and pharmaceutical schools, adoption of the legislation and standards for pharmaceutical preparations and drugs control and drafting of Romanian Pharmacopoeia.

The first reported units for drug production were operating at laboratory scale. The first one was "Chemical-Pharmaceutical Laboratory" founded by Al. Iteanu in Bucharest at the end of the 19th century. This laboratory produced various pharmaceutical formulations and "rigorous injectable dosage vials perfectly sterilized" (Stancu, 2008). Another laboratory was registered in in Cluj in 1904, by Bela Pater. This laboratory set up an experimental station for the study of medicinal plants, in order to recover their active principles. Practically, the existing data are not evidencing an industrial production of medicines in Romania before 1918. Only in this period, the first chemical factories appeared, producing the basic chemicals and creating the premises for the production of drugs.

In 1884, there was a glue production workshop in Bucharest, that operated using animal bones as raw material. This workshop also started producing soap in 1911. The soap factory Stella was also built in 1884. Another glue factory, the Fritz Sledinsky factory, was created in the same period, situated between Podul Mihai

Bravu and Podul Vitan Barzesti. Among the first chemical plants are mentioned the chemical fertilizers factory Mărăşeşti (1890) and the sulphuric acid factory Valea Calugărească (1902). In the same period (1896), two gunpowder production units for the Romanian army are mentioned, located in Bucharest (the areas Grozavesti and Dudeşti-Cioplea, respectively). By 1913, this second factory was producing sulphuric acid too. In the same period, the first factories for acetic acid were constructed in Dărmăneşti-Bacau (G. Stirbey factory, 1904), in Bucharest (Dr. Casiner factory, 1893) and in Mogosoaia (Victor Teclu factory, 1905).

It should be recalled that in 1903, the most important branch of economy was the food industry, which represented approximately 30% of all companies, while the chemical industry represented only 16%, the manufacture of medicinal products appearing later.

4. Period of 1919–1944

In the interwar period, the necessary drugs were still predominantly imported. Due to the lack of specialists in the field of drug synthesis and limited resources for the production, the national medicine production was limited to laboratories for drug conditioning and formulations following existing recipes. These laboratories were reproducing the product formulas of foreign companies (called "specialties," basically 'generic drugs'). The drug production units mentioned in the publications of those times consisted mainly of larger industrial laboratories and workshops. The name "factory" could be really attributed only to a small number of production units created later in this period.

In Cluj, in 1920, a "Therapy Laboratory" was established in addition to the pharmacy "Unicorn," specializing in the production of opotherapeutic-pharmaceutical drugs. In 1923, this laboratory became the "Factory Egger & Co" after merging with the Austrian company of the same name, which subsequently bought the shares in 1931. Lateron, the same plant was named "Ufarom – Romanian Pharmaceutical Works" and thereafter, "Napochemia."

In the same period, "Pharmaceutical Laboratories Réne Dunod" (1924) was set up in Bucharest by associating with the representatives of eleven French companies, later organized as a joint stock company, "Lutetia" (1928). Also, for the purpose of the cultivation and exploitation of medicinal plants, the cooperatives "Adonis" in Cluj (1926), "Romania" in Bucharest (1927) and "Digitalis" in Orastie (1929) were set up. The phytotherapeutic industry (production of plant-derived medicines) was also represented through "Vorel laboratories" in Piatra Neamt, established in 1919. In April 1921, the "Dr. I. Cantacuzino" institute was founded, specializing in research and production of serums and vaccines.

The values of imported pharmaceutical products in the years 1936 and 1937 were 280.8 thousand lei and 240.8 thousand lei, respectively. Further details regarding the import situation are presented in table 1.

Table 1: Import of drugs in the period 1936–1937

Product	**1936**			**1937**		
	tonne	**thousands lei**	**lei/kg**	**tonne**	**thousands lei**	**lei/kg**
medicines prepared	106	39,724	375	59	20,426	346
drugs for injection	8	9,143	143	17	15,026	883
medicinal tablets	7	4,722	675	10	6,122	612
specialties for injections	53	94,042	1,774	58	93,524	1,612
specialties in tablets	43	55,810	1,298	62	80,277	1,295

Source: Enciclopedia Romaniei, vol. 2, 1938, table 5, p. 1014.

5. Period of 1944–1990

In 1945, the pharmaceutical laboratories were nationalized, their evolution having different pathways. In 1947, under Law no. 189 for the establishment and operation of Industrial Offices, published in the Official Gazette no. 129 of 10 June 1947, the Industrial Office of Pharmaceutical and Specialty Chemical Products S. A. was founded, which was composed of 30 enterprises. In July 1948, in line with the coordination and organization of economic activity, the industrial enterprises were structured by branches. With the prior approval of the Council of Ministers, industrial centrals were created at the level of industrial branches and groups of enterprises, following the type of production. As result, the Industrial Office of Pharmaceutical and Specialty Chemical Products S.A. was dissolved and its tasks and assets were taken over by the Industrial Central of Enterprises for Chemical Synthesis and Processing (Florescu, 1975).

In the pharmaceutical industry, the new organization considered companies on the basis of the technological process and nature of their products, by repealing the workshops for conditioning and packaging. After 1950, the drug industry increased its volume, production and assortment, with new sections being built. Thus, compared with 1950, the production of drugs had increased in 1954 by 337% for synthetic products, 351% for lozenges and tablets, 338% for solutions for internal use, 152% for ampules, 209% for opotherapeutic extracts, 487% for vegetal extracts, 229% for ointments and 202% for tinctures. In 1954, about 400 new medicines were fabricated (Stancu, 2008).

After 1950, new drugs factories appeared: Antibiotice Iasi, Sintofarm in Bucharest (an enterprise for drugs and dyes) and Armedica Targu Mures, much later. Also new plant units for herbal products were expanded or created. In the same time, the production of veterinary drugs and the opotherapeutic products (heparin, insulin, enzymes etc.) were organized. In Iasi, a plant for broad-spectrum antibiotics through biosynthetic technologies was constructed, in Cluj a modern production chloramphenicol plant was built, and in Bucharest, a modern center for drug synthesis and conditioning. In 1965, the production of drugs was 2.3 times higher than in 1959. In 1970, the branch faced reorganization again, and the Industrial Central of Medicines, Cosmetics, Dyes and Varnishes was created, which included six drugs factories: the Enterprise for Medicines Bucharest, "Sinteza" Oradea, "Terapia" Cluj-Napoca, Antibiotics Iaşi, "Sintofarm" Bucharest and "Biofarm" Bucharest. Also, the Chemical-Pharmaceutical Research Institute was created and developed, a network of research and design for this area, where technologies for the production of medicines have been developed. Since 1974, the institute was expanding and opening new centers in Iasi, Cluj and Brasov.

The drug production value in 1970 was about 37.5 times higher than in 1950. In this period, the active substances used in the production of drugs were produced entirely in Romanian factories (Intreprinderea de medicamente Bucuresti, Terapia-Cluj). Another producer was "Sinteza" Oradea, which was manufacturing, besides drugs, a wide range of products like inorganic pigments, paints and varnishes, insecticides, auxiliary products for the plastics industry, liquefied gas and automotive chemicals.

6. The period after 1990

After 1990, as a result of the policy adopted by successive governments, the privatization of existing enterprises was enforced. Many units were closed, buildings demolished, and machinery sold for scrap. Two Romanian-owned companies that have survived are Antibiotice Iasi and Biofarm Bucharest.

The Romanian drug factories that were operating in 1989 and their actual status are shown in table 4, where the main stages of their evolution are mentioned. It should be noted that, today, practically all enterprises producing medicines in Romania, are basically a conditioning of active substances imported from other countries.

After 1990, some previously existing laboratories were also developed to exploit the *spontaneous flora*, and new ones were established. These were among the first units manufacturing pharmaceuticals in Romania, where medicinal flora is represented by around 800 species, of which 283 have proven therapeutic properties. Before 1990, there was only one company in this area, Plafar; today, there are dozens of private companies in charge of the cultivation, processing and exploitation of medicinal and aromatic plants. Among the best-known manufacturers are Hofigal Bucharest, founded in 1990, which is producing homeopathic products and phytotherapeutic galenical, Dacia Plant Brasov, a producer of natural medicines, Fares Deva and Exhelios Timisoara.

The Romanian pharmaceutical market was dominated by domestic output in the six factories already mentioned, coordinated by the Ministry of Chemical Industry. After 1990, private producers also appeared: Europharm Brasov, Helcor Baia Mare, Labormed Bucharest, Pharmatech Targu Mures, Sindan Bucharest etc., their number reaching 168 in 2015. These factories are producing drugs from different therapeutic groups operating in certain areas of the country.

The production of drugs in the period of 1993–2004 is illustrated in table 2, which shows an increase in production by almost 70 times in this period.

Table 2: The production of drugs during 1993–2004 (thousands lei)

	1993	1994	1995	1996	1997	1998	1999	2000	2001	2002	2004
Prod.	111	274	368	465	1,075	774.5	981.8	2,073.4	4,589.8	5,903.3	7,775.7

Source: National Institute of Statistics (NIS) – production of main industrial products, serie PRODROM.

The number of people working in this sector has decreased by almost 38% in the period of 2000–2015 (table 3).

Table 3: Number of the employees working in pharmaceutical industry

Year	Thousands	Year	Thousands	Year	Thousands	Year	Thousands
2000	187.5	2004	136.1	2008	106.6	2012	114.5
2001	166.1	2005	122.8	2009	103.5	2013	116.3
2002	152.5	2006	119.3	2010	95.8	2014	118.2
2003	140.8	2007	111.8	2011	105.0	2015	123.2

Source: National Institute of Statistics, data processing platform online tempo, number of employees at the end of the national economy activities NACE Rev. 2, accessed 10 October 2016.

The total number of drug manufacturers present on the market in Romania was 184 in 2011, but only 10 players were at the top, accounting for almost 60% of this market.

Of the top pharmaceutical manufacturers in 2006, only seven companies were Romanian (Antibiotice Iasi, Biofarm Bucharest, Iasi Fiterman Pharma, Biotehnos Ilfov, Romvac Company Voluntari, Arena Group in Bucharest and Hofigal Export Import from Bucharest). This situation changed in 2014, when the top Romanian manufacturers of drugs were Terapia, Europharm (closed in December 2015), Zentiva, Antibiotice Iasi, Sandoz, and Biofarm. Table 5 presents the exclusive rank of Romanian drugs manufactures.

Note that Antibiotice has been overtaken (formerly 4), and Biofarm was down to position 8 (from 2). The only company that managed to climb a few ranks in 2014 was EEL Bio Targu Mures, which showed increases in terms of turnover and profits.

As for turnover, the situation in the period of 2012–2014 shows that the 20 largest local manufacturers of drugs (including veterinary) recorded a turnover of over €560 million in 2013, up 11%, as compared to 2012. It should be recalled that factories generally produce generic medicines using active substances from import.

The Romanian pharmaceutical market is currently dominated by foreign companies. In the top 20, there is only one Romanian company, Antibiotice Iasi (table 6). The total drug market in 2014 was 11.7 billion lei, down 4.7% compared to the corresponding period of 2013 (Somanescu 2015).

The top in 2016 was unchanged from previous years, Abbvie, whose turnover reflects the increase in sales of products used in the treatment of hepatitis C, hovering in first. The following places are occupied by Sanofi (including Zentiva) and Novartis (including Sandoz). Sun Pharma (including therapy) occupies position 6, and Antibiotice Iasi position 12.

Conclusion

The paper presents data on the history of the Romanian pharmaceutical industry. In chronological order, the emergence and evolution of drug manufacture is described.

Table 4: The actual situation of the earliest manufacturers of drugs

Name initial / Current	History	References
TERAPIA/ Daiichi-Sankyo	- 1921 set up in Cluj-Napoca as a small laboratory - 1991 manufacture and sale of pharmaceutical products for humans and animals - 1996 privatized, its shares being controlled by individual and institutional investors - 1997–2002 listed at the Bucharest Stock Exchange - 2003 acquired by an investment fund led by Advent International - 2004 listed at the Bucharest Stock Exchange - 2006 Ranbaxy acquires 96.7% of company shares - 2008 becomes the property of Daiichi-Sankyo.	www.zf.ro/.../ istoria-celor-mai-vechi-10-producatori-de-medicamente-cele-mai-vechi https://ro.wikipedia.org/wiki/Terapia_(companie
Biofarm	- 1921 established - 1936 company Gedeon Richter from Timisoara, with laboratories and shareholders of Societăţii Române pe Acţiuni, start the production in two units in Bucharest - 1948 becomes a state enterprise and in 1956 establishes a new division, medicine factory Galenica, specializing in plant extracts, tinctures, pure substances, veterinary products - 1969 merger of Fabricile de Medicamente Galenică and Biofarm creates Intreprinderea de Medicamente Biofarm - 1969 Biofarm brand launched, a producer of natural raw materials of plant and animal origin - 1997 company privatization - 2005 listed on the Bucharest Stock Exchange	www.biofarm.ro, https://ro.wikipedia.org/wiki/Biofarm

Name initial / Current	History	References
Antibiotice Iaşi	- 1953–1955 Chemical factory no. 2 built in Iasi - 1959 begins production of streptomycin (active substance) and the first forms of finished goods - name change to Fabrica de Antibiotice - producing antibiotics through semi-synthesis and biosynthesis - 1990 becomes joint stock company - 1997 listed at the Bucharest Stock Exchange - 2002 second largest producer of nystatin	https://ro.wikipedia.org/wiki/Antibiotice_Iaşi
Uzina de Medicamente Bucureşti, (Sanofi)	- 1962 established - performs synthesis of different active substances and conditioning of human medicines - 1963 begins production of vitamin C, novalgin and piramidon - 1967 creates divisions: ampoules and tablets - 1980 reaches a portfolio of over 600 products - 1990 name change to Sicomed factory - 2000 privatized - 2005 aquired by Zentiva. - 2009 acquired by Sanofi	www.zentiva.ro/about-us/history www.zf.ro/.../fabrica-de-medicamente-zentiva-a-ajuns-la-50-de-ani-algocalmin-si-ger
Sintofarm	- 1946 founded through anonymous company Nitranil, a producer of chemical-pharmaceuticals through synthesis - 1969 Fabrica Chimică Sintofarm created by merging four units: Sintofarm, Getica, Reactivul and Sin. - 1973 Întreprinderea de Medicamente and Coloranţi Sintofarm founded - 1971–1975 produces cholesterol-lowering drug - 1986–1990 modernization of production processes - 1999 drug synthesis abandoned, becomes a majority private company - 1999 detergents and disinfectants technologies are assimilated - 2003–2004 develops the sector of pharmaceutical dosage forms	www.sintofarm.ro/
Armedica (Gedeon Richter) România	- 1985 established - 1998 aquired by Gedeon Richter Plc. Hungary - 2001 name change to Gedeon Richter Romania - 2005 exports drugs to Hungaria, Russia, Moldovia and EU countries	www.gedeon-richter.ro/ro-ro/pages/OurCompany.aspx

Table 5: The top Romanian drug companies between 2012–2014

2014	Company/Group of companies	Turnover (€ million)			Net profit / loss (million euros)			Employees		
		2014	2013	2012	2014	2013	2012	2014	2013	2012
1	Terapia SA	117.4	113.3	105.8	19.4	24.7	21.7	859	801	783
2	Europharm SA	96.0	N/A	104.0	−2.0	N/A	11.1	213	N/A	254
3	Zentiva SA	88.8	65.7	54.4	12.2	9.1	7.2	488	484	531
4	Antibiotice SA	72.0	72.1	68.4		7.1	6.1	1,465	1,465	1,465
5	Sandoz SRL	69.2	60.7	58.6		4.9	5.8	270	257	225
6	Bio EEL SRL*	31.7	X	X		X	X	165	X	X
7	Labormed-Pharma SA	30.8	32.1	19.8		−4.1	−25.4	241	235	269
8	Biofarm SA	28.9	26.9	23.6		5.8	4.7	380	360	340
9	Infomed Fluids SRL	26.1	25.0	27.1		0.8	1.7	418	409	
10	Gedeon Richter Romania	25.7	27.0	27.6		−10	−6.6	548	544	550

Source: Data presented in this ranking taken from the website of the Ministry of Finance. Figures were calculated at the average BNR 4.44 lei/€ (2014) and 4.41 lei/€ (2013).

Table 6: The top pharmaceutical companies with the highest sales in the period 2014–2016

2016	Company	2016 (millions lei)		2015 (millions lei)		2014 (millions lei)	
		Quarter II	Total estimated	Quarter I	Total estimated	Quarter. IV	Total estimated
1	Abbvie	497.0	932.0	70.4	298.0	78.8	298.0
2	Sanofi*	204.3	815.0	220.5	862.8	226.2	852.0
3	Novartis**	147.4	586.3	187.3	698.6	200.5	713.5
4	Servier***	138.0	550.0	178.4	705.4	182.7	697.9
5	Pfizer	142.8	538.7	145.6	622.3	167.9	627.7
6	Sun pharma****	132.9	517.5	X	X	X	X
7	Hoffmann la roche	114.2	492.9	192.4	801.7	211.2	
8	Glaxosmithkline	124.4	489.6	153.0	553.8	135.0	492.8
9	Astrazeneteca	100.1	379.9	134.7	527.6	132.0	489.4
10	Merck&co	78.5	322.5	97.7	396.7	103.8	412.5
11	Krka	78.6	297.3	103.1	383.5	101.2	364.2
12	**Antibiotice SA**	**74.0**	**291.9**	**74.4**	**273.0**	**72.8**	**257.4**

Source: Abrihan, R., Forbes, 2015.

Presentation is accompanied by data relating to production, the range of products made, number of employees etc. The study showed the following features in the evolution of this branch of the chemical industry:

- the period before 1949 is characterized by the appearance of workshops and laboratories specializing in the production of medicines. The market was still dependent on imports, domestic production covered only a small part of the needs of the population;
- the period of 1949–1990 is characterized by development of existing units and building of new ones. This is a period when, in spite of existing difficulties (restrictions on imported raw materials, packaging, lack of publicity, restricted access to information), some products were exported.
- after 1990, new private units with both Romanian and foreign capital were created. However, the chemical synthesis of active pharmaceutical compounds disappeared. From this point of view, the existing pharmaceutical industry became tributary to the imported active substances used in the drug production.

References

1. Abrihan, R., Topul celor mai mari producători farma, după primul trimestru din 2015, Forbes.
2. Topul celor mai mari producători după primul trimestru din 2015, 2015, http://www.forbes.ro/topul-celor-mai-mari-producatori-dupa-primul-trimestru-din-2015-39268.
3. Constantinescu, N. N.: Istoria economica a Romaniei. Vol. 2, 1939–1989, Ed. Economica, Bucureşti.
4. Florescu, M., Industria chimica si petrochimica, Editura Tehnica, 1972.
5. Iovanelli, M. F., Industria romaneasca 1934–1938, Bucureşti: Editura Academiei Republicii Socialiste România, 1975.
6. Opritescu, M., Istoria economiei, Editura ASE, 2005.
7. Stancu, E., Din istoria farmaciei românesti interbelice, NOEMA VOL. VII, 2008, pp. 61–71, www.crifst.ro/noema/doc/200801_06.pdf.
8. Şomănescu, C., Companiile farmaceutice care au avut cele mai vânzări în 2015 – analiză Cegedim, ECONOMICA.net, 2015, https://www.google.ro/#q=piata+farmaceutica+din+romania+2016.
9. Puscas, V. et al., Dezvoltarea si modernizarea in Romania interbelica 1919–1939 (culegere de studii), Editura politica, Bucuresti, 1988.
10. Dezvoltarea industriei in RPR, Editura stiintifica, 1959.
11. Gusti, D., Enciclopedia Romaniei, vol. II, cap. Industrie, 1938, pp. 1010–1030.
12. Direcţia Centrală de Statistică, Industria in Republica Socialistă România, Bucuresti, 1960.
13. Institutul de Prognoză Economică, Industria farmaceutică în România: principalele tendinte si impactul asupra societătii si economiei, 2012, http://www.lawg.ro/files/assets/userfiles/files/Industria%20Farmaceutica%20din%20Romania.pdf.

Dr. Frantz Daniel FISTUNG

The Center for Industrial and Services Economics-Romanian Academy,
13 September Blvd., nr. 13, Sector 5, Bucharest, 050711, Romania,
e-mail: dfistung@yahoo.com

Teodor POPESCU

The Center for Industrial and Services Economics-Romanian Academy,
13 September Blvd., nr. 13, Sector 5, Bucharest, 050711, Romania,
e-mail: axel_me5678@yahoo.com

Transports, One of the Key Pillars of the Romanian Development, 1918–1989

Abstract: After 1918, Romanian transport significantly increased with direct influences on national economy. In that respect, during 1918–1989 we can observe a movement from a less planned development of road and naval transportation toward a rapid growth of the road transport and the emergence of a new type of transport, by air. Particular characteristics gave the evolution path for each of the transportation areas but, in our opinion, for that time period the major influences on the evolution of transport was related to three important historical events: a) the territorial union in 1918, when several territories under foreign jurisdiction joined to form Romania, b) the Second World War, when during 1940–1944, Romania ceded some territories to foreign administration and c) the communist period, after 1945. Highlighting the mutual influences between the economic and social development of Romania and the evolution of the transport network represent the principal goal of this working paper. We divide our investigation period into two: the one before communism, and the communist period. A major conclusion of our research investigation is that transport shows permanent growth during that period, but shares of the specific transport modes, in total, have changed significantly, showing the historical importance given to each of them. The general socio-economic and political conditions influenced that evolution, but several situations, such as the poor quality of the transport infrastructure, were due to inadequate management of the sector, or even worse, the disinterest in modernizing and permanently adapting the Romanian transport networks to meet the period's requirements.

Keywords: Transport modes, economic history of transport, transport infrastructures

Introduction

In the history of Romanian development, transport has been always a key factor, being itself influenced by the period's particularities. In that respect, starting with the (re-)integration of ancient Romanian territories from the west, east and north parts of the country, in 1918, united Romania created favorable conditions for the modernization of "historical" modes of transport (such as roads, rails or naval) and, at the same time, favored the development of a new mode, for that times: air transportation. This working paper aims to pinpoint the particularities and the development stages of the Romanian transport network during 1918–1989, and also to discover some mutual influences between transport development and the Romanian socio-economic growth. The research was based on national statistical data, and also on many other documents of those times. The most important conclusion of the analysis is that during the analyzed period, no matter the socio-economic and territorial situation, the Romanian transport network has been modernized and developed. That evolution has in turn influenced the Romania's economic growth. Also, in that period, fluctuations on the share of modes, in the transport sector have been observed, underlining the importance given, at distinct points, to a particular mode over other transport types.

Literature review

The analyses of the 1918–1989 events and their effects produced on national and international levels have been presented in many documents from that period, but also in more recent ones. Among the most notable, we can mention the extremely valuable works "Romanian Economy – The XX century" (Postolache, T., 2001), Romania's history in data (Giurescu, D. C., 2003), and "Romania's economic evolution, statistical-historical researches 1859–1947" (Axenciuc, V., 1997). All these and many others presents data and detailed analyses regarding the historical-economic time period of Romania, after 1918. Also, authors such as Th. Gâlcă (1930), I. Cristea, O. Ionescu, V. Stanciu (1980), C. Bungețianu (1934) or I. Tătar and V. Chiriac (1994) published some very interesting studies regarding specific stages and characteristics of the evolution of transport modes in Romania during 1918–1989. However, in the Romanian specific literature, there is a lack of working studies presenting detailed particularities and causes of the Romanian transport network evolution, mode by mode and/or as an integrated system, due to the historical, economical and political conditions, but also due to the national needs for the country's development.

The economic environment and its influences on the Romanian transport network during 1918–1944

Territorial and institutional transformations starting after 1918 had a major influence on Romania's entire economic development.

In that period, transport registered an important development process, reaching a share of 6. 4% in GDP[1] in 1938. Comparing 1938 with 1912, the contribution of transport to the national income rose up to 25%, and the social product up to 29.4%,

1 In the Statistical Yearbook of the Socialist Republic of Romania (SRR; 1968) this indicator was defined as "Specific Weight of the material production branches in the

reaching $70 million[2]. Unfortunately, due to the Second World War (SWW), the contribution of transport to the total social product followed a strong trend downward and continued to do so for a long time after the end of the SWW.

The communist period, based on the Stalinist economic principles, was developed on the vision of the national economy as a unique corporation, and on a strategy that wanted to switch the national economy from mostly agrarian to an industrial one. Industrialization involved the relocation of many rural inhabitants to the city, and also important efforts for urbanization, tuition and professional training (Tudor-Pavelescu, A., 2007).

In that context, after the end of the SWW, Romania went through many and profound political and economic transformations. We underline the 1945 agrarian reform, the 1947 monetary reform and the Sovroms[3] development. Also, on 11 June 1948, the Grand National Assembly voted on Law nr. 119, for the nationalization of industrial corporations, banks, mining, assurance and transportation firms, aiming to obtain a strong "socialist economic estate" and to start the process for leading the planned national economy and the application of a later policy of "forced industrialization" (Ilie, C., 2015).

As we said before, all these territorial and political evolutions had major influences on the general evolution of the Romanian economy. Unfortunately, the economic growth intensity prognosis made by the communists was not always translated in a permanent positive development in transport. Thus, the share of transport in total social product declined from 4.2% in 1950 to 3.9% in 1955, to 3.5% in 1960 and only 3.3% in 1967[4]. The same downward trend is mirrored for the share of transport in national income, from 6.5% in 1938 to 4.3% in 1950, to 3.7% in 1950 and only 4.2% in 1967. If we take the year 1938 as a reference, in monetary terms and related to the social product dynamic, transport decreased to 58% in 1948, but after that moment, it has a spectacular growth from 79% in 1950 to 201% in 1960 and 420% in 1967, meaning four times the 1938 value. Later, the situation changed for the better.

---

total social product" (http://opac.biblioteca.ase.ro/opac/bibliographic_view/189098;jsessionid=BEC6A71BE10FA8E79F787356546B7F8B).

2 In 1938, the exchange rate was 136.2 lei/$, according to "The social product, production expenses and national income of Romania in 1859, 1900 and 1912. Comparisons between 1938 and 1912" by Ion Răvar and Mihai Capătă, published in Romanian Statistical Revue nr. 6/2013.

3 Sovroms was a Romanian-Soviet Union mixed corporation, established in 1945, with the main goal to manage Romanian debt to the Soviet Union. In fact, this was the most cynical form for the exploitation of general goods and resources of Romania by the Soviets. Sovroms was dissolved in 1956 (source: http://dictionary.sensagent.com/sovrom/ro-ro/, accessed 10 November 2016).

4 Source: Statistical Yearbook of Socialist Republic of Romania, 1968, p. 114, available at: http://opac.biblioteca.ase.ro/opac/bibliographic_view/189098;jsessionid=BEC6A71BE10FA8E79F787356546B7F8B, accessed 16 October 2016.

So, from 1970 on the Romanian social product dynamic was permanently positive, as was the share of transport in the social product (table 1). Moreover, if the social product of Romanian economy has quadrupled in that period, the share of transport from that indicator grew rapidly to almost six times, in comparable prices, reaching 5.1% of Romania's social product in 1989, a share about 60% higher than that from 1970. This means that the transport sector had a faster growth than the general economic development.

Table 1: Dynamics for some relevant indicators of the Romanian economy, 1970–1989

INDICATOR	**U.M.**	**YEAR**					
		1970	**1975**	**1980**	**1985**	**1987**	**1989**
Social product	Billions of lei	523.4	863.7	1,250.9	1,939.9	1,960.7	1,931.4
National income	Billions of lei	212.1	361.9	508.7	672.0	697.2	632.6
The contribution of transport to social product	%	3.2	4.2	5.2	4.8	4.8	5.1
The contribution of transport to national income	%	4.0	5.8	7.0	6.4	6.6	7.5

Source: Statistical Yearbooks of SRR, 1978, 1983 and of Romania, 1990.

In table 1, we see the same directions of evolution for national income, social product or transport shares, but at various amplitudes, much more obvious for national income compared with social product. However, the percentage increase in transport rates to national income and social product, combined with the strong growth of these macroeconomic indicators, underlines once again the increased speed of development of transport, compared with the Romanian economy in general. Also, the analyzed data underscores the increased size of the production expenses related with the added value created, which shows a poor competitiveness of the Romanian economy during that period. However, the share of productive expenses in the total social product, related to transport, doesn't grow significantly between 1938 and 1989 (from 48.9% to 51.8%). At the same time, the national income share in the social product, related to transport, displays the opposite evolution (from 51.1% in 1938 to 48.2% in 1989).

Table 2: The dynamics of the most representatives transport indicators during 1938–1989 (%)

INDICATOR	YEAR							
	1938	1948	1955	1960	1970	1975	1980	1989
Goods	100.0	90.7	241.6	448.5	1,481.7	2,322.3	2,676.4	2,730.4
Passengers	100.0	103.9	357.0	377.9	906.2	1,554.9	1,817.8	1,791.1
Goods traffic	n.d.	n.d.	184.0	260.0	1,000.0	1,600.0	1,900.0	2,900.0
Passengers traffic	n.d.	n.d.	151.0	142.0	308.0	499.0	578.0	720.0

Source: Statistical Yearbooks of SRR, 1978, 1983, of Romania, 1990 and author processing.
Legend: n.d. – no data

The analyzed data highlights major tendencies in transport development process during the 1938–1989 period. The first is linked to a poor allocation of resources towards the development of the sector until the seventh decade, while the second highlights the strong growth in transport activities over the last two decades of the communist era. Obviously, as we already mentioned, not all modes of the transport sector had the same intensity of development (table 2). In that context, the goods transportation subsector rose faster that the passengers subsector. This was because of the general development of the economy that required increasingly more freight transportation, especially for import/export activities.

Nevertheless, the positive evolution of the economic indicators presented in table 2 far exceeded the size of the investments made in the transport sector, which can be explained by a weak support for the modernization of the sector at the levels required by the market. In that respect, statistical data shows that transport registered in 1965 9.4% of the total investments attracted to the Romanian economy, and only 9.9% in 1981. That means an increase of half a percentage point for the share of transport sector investments in the total national economy, over 15 years (table 3).

Table 3: Dynamic of the transport investments' share in the national economy in some European countries during 1965–1981 (%)

COUNTRY	1965	1970	1976	1981
ROMANIA	9.4	10.6	10.9	9.9
BULGARIA	6.7	8.7	11.2	12.2
CZECHOSLOVAKIA	11.3	12.4	14.0	11.2
GERMAN DEMOCRATIC REPUBLIC	9.4	8.7	10.5	8.6
HUNGARY	13.1	11.6	11.6	11.8
POLAND	11.5	13.1	11.3	9.8
SOVIET UNION	10.0	9.8	11.4	12.1

Source: Statistical Yearbooks of SRR, 1978, 1983.

Comparing table 3 data, Bulgaria and even the Soviet Union had positive and almost linear rythms for transport investments, with major increase rates (82% and 21%), and in the same period, all the other countries had non-linear evolutions and, basically, a decreased value at the end of the analyzed period.

Table 4: Evolution of the share of transport modes, in the total of the sector, for goods and passengers during the period 1938–1990 (%)

Transport mode	**YEAR**						
	1938	**1950**	**1960**	**1970**	**1980**	**1989**	**1990**
Goods							
Total, of which:	**100.0**	**100.0**	**100.0**	**100.0**	**100.0**	**100.0**	**100.0**
Rail	56.2	71.3	30.8	16.6	12.5	10.8	9.8
Road	38.0	24.0	66.1	81.6	85.2	85.5	87.3
River	2.8	2.3	0.8	0.3	0.6	1.3	0.5
Maritime	1.3	0.4	0.1	0.4	0.7	1.3	1.3
Air	-	-	-	-	-	-	-
Passengers							
Total, of which:	**100.0**	**100.0**	**100.0**	**100.0**	**100.0**	**100.0**	**100.0**
Rail	94.1	90.7	74.6	47.6	25.1	35.2	34.2
Road	4.9	8.8	24.9	52.0	74.6	64.4	65.5
River	0.9	0.4	0.3	0.1	0.1	0.1	0.1
Maritime	0.1	0.1	-	-	-	-	-
Air	-	-	0.1	0.1	0.2	0.3	0.2

Source: Statistical Yearbooks of SRR, 1978, 1983, and of Romania, 1990.

Even in these conditions, we can say that in the second half of the 20th century, the industrialization process of the Romanian economy and the investment boom led to significant changes in the transport system, encouraging faster or slower development of a particular mode of transport than others on the specific internal market.

So, if in 1938, goods transported by rail had a share of 56.2% in the total of goods carried, and goods transported by road had a share of 38.0% in the next period, the situation has changed dramatically. Indeed, the transports development process show us that in 1989, the share of the goods transported by rail, in the total of goods carried, fell to only 9.8%, while the carriage of goods by road rose up to 87.3% (see table 4).

The same tendencies exist for passenger transportation, where rail share, in the total of the sector, fell from 94.1% in 1938 to 34.2% in 1989. In the same period, the share of passengers transported by road rose from 4.9% in 1938 to 65.5% in 1989.

Table 5: Evolution of the share of transport modes in the total of the sector, for goods and passengers traffic during the period 1938–1990

(%)

Transport mode	YEAR						
	1938	1950	1960	1970	1980	1985	1989
Goods traffic							
Total, of which:	-	**100.0**	**100.0**	**100.0**	**100.0**	**100.0**	**100.0**
Rail	-	83.4	83.6	51.2	43.1	34.9	29.9
Road	-	0.5	4.0	5.5	6.7	13.1	11.1
River	-	7.3	3.6	1.4	1.3	1.1	1.4
Maritime	-	6.7	4.5	39.9	45.8	48.6	55.1
Air	-	-	-	-	0.1	-	-
Passengers traffic							
Total, of which:	**100.0**	**100.0**	**100.0**	**100.0**	**100.0**	**100.0**	**100.0**
Rail	96.6	94.1	87.2	66.5	46.3	55.3	56.8
Road	1.9	4.5	11.5	29.4	47.9	38.5	37.0
River	0.5	0.2	0.3	0.3	0.2	0.1	0.1
Maritime	0.9	1.1	0.3	0.1	-	-	-
Air	0.1	0.1	0.7	3.7	5.6	6.1	6.1

Source: Statistical Yearbooks of SRR, 1978, 1983, and of Romania, 1990.

All others transport modes (naval, air) had a positive evolution, but their weight, in the sector, was very small (between 0.1% and 2.8%). That means that in the analyzed period, favorable transportation conditions, such as the existence of the Danube River and the Black Sea coast, have been neglected by the Romanian authorities (especially those from the communist period) in favor of road and rail transportation development. That was, in my opinion, a big political mistake. The same evolution cannot be observed for the traffic of goods and passengers during 1938–1989 (table 5).

The obvious differences for specific transport indicators presented in tables 4 and 5 can have, a few explanations:

- While the share of the volume for goods transported on the seaways, in total, has seen the same values in 1938 and 1989, the traffic of goods was, in 1989, over eight

times higher than that of 1938, which can be explained by increasing transport distances and the addressing of new commercial markets.
- Starting in the 60s and 70s, the weights for road carriage of goods and passengers, in total, exceeded those of rail transport, while the rail traffic of goods and passengers remained prevailing. This fact underlines, mainly, the use of rail transport for both goods and passengers, especially on the long routes.
- The air transport traffic of passengers has increased by more than 60 times during 1938–1989, on the basis of modernization and the development of a specific transport fleet, but also through intensifying business relations and tourism between more distant geographical areas.

Defining elements for the evolution of each mode of transport during 1918–1989

In the analyzed period, road modernization activities were permanently done, with some syncopation due to historical and economic situations. Until the end of SWW, the evolution of road transport had some particularities (Fistung, D., 2016):

- After First World War, the national framework has been majorly increased by adding networks within the new territories.
- In 1920–1947, the major features were: insufficient roads (even in areas with stronger economic activity) and the lack of an appropriate car park.
- The development of a proper road network was insufficiently supported. The legislative framework, including the provisions relating to the construction and maintenance of roads, were effective only after the Great Union. Thus, during in the interwar period, the development of the road network and specific parks for trucks, buses, cars, motorbikes etc. continued, but insufficiently, compared to the needs of Romania both for population and military goals.
- During SWW, road transport suffered damages that were reflected in the future process of restoration. Three quarters of the number of vehicles were destroyed or damaged, and much of the roads have deteriorated due to military transport (heavy vehicles). Some roads even became unusable in particular sectors.

During the communist era, the road sector's development has seen an impressive growth, both in terms of infrastructure and vehicle fleet. The unique party policy relating to transport support was, in our opinion, a pretty good one, for that period of time. As a major effect, Romania came to have a dense road network, in relation to surface or population, better than many Western countries from Europe. The major problem was, however, a lack of continuity and interest in proper modernization and maintenance, which has led to the degradation of a good part of the national road network.

The most important mode of transportation in Romania until the 1960s, was, however, rail transport. After that moment, it was outrun by the road. Among the most important milestones of the developments in rail transport during 1918–1989, we can emphasize that:

- From the administrative point of view, the adopted solutions led to a continuous improvement of the national railway sector situation.
- Even though there were not too many favorable factors during that period, the Romanian policy in the field of construction of rolling stock made possible the removal of massive imports, and the development of a specific competitive domestic industry.
- The territorial development of railways has not been balanced, the most important routes being in the former Austro-Hungarian Empire territory.
- From the economic point of view, rail activity became one of the leading sectors in terms of national work force employed, on the basis of the increased level of demand for related industries' products.
- There was a permanent shortage of public funds in proportion to needs for maintenance and modernization of the Romanian railway network, in accordance with the requirements of national and international trends.

As a conclusion, in the period under review, despite the obstacles encountered, the trend regarding key indicators of railway transport in Romania has been, at all times, positive. Romania's communist state policy has been consistently favorable to the development of railway transport, with priority over other modes. At the end of the analysis' period, Romania had an extensive rail network, balanced in terms of space, but unfortunately increasingly less modernized in recent years, even though there is a real support from entrepreneurial and creative areas.

For shipping developments in the period under review, a few comments can be made:

- After 1918 and until the outbreak of SWW, shipping in Romania (river and maritime) has experienced a permanent favorable evolution (for example, maritime transport has seen an increase of almost three times of the volume of transported goods and of 1.5 times in term of passengerstransported).
- During SWW, if the early activities on the Danube River were not impeded, starting from August 1944, traffic on the Constanta port and on the maritime Danube was practically non-existent, due to the withdrawal of Soviet troops, and the river was almost entirely used for the transport of materials and petroleum products to the conflict areas.
- The Communist Party's policy has been beneficial for shipping in Romania, especially after 1968, when development and modernization of 32 inland ports was begun, starting from Sulina and until Moldova Veche.
- A special remark is the one relating to maritime fishing activities. The communist era policy has led to the development of strong specialized fleets. As a consequence, at the end of 1989 the Romanian maritime fishing fleet had 62 ships, of which 48 were trawler-freezers, 12 freezer vessels and 2 oil tanks, which situate Romania, worldwide, in seventh position in the group of countries with vessels

trawling over 2,500 tons and fifth in the group of countries that own carrier freezer vessels.

Air transportation has made great achievements during the interwar period and after that. Analysis of the evolution of the main indicators of civil aviation from Romania, from 1946–1980, allowed us to highlight the following conclusions (Fistung, D., 2016):

- Air transport activity was enacted in 1920. From that time until 1990, Romanian air transport had a generally positive evolution.
- The emergence and evolution of TAROM Company was an important moment in the history of air transport. Founded at the end of 1954, TAROM succeeded in only six years in significantly increasing the length of its lines both internally, where the network ensuring fast and direct links to all zones of the country was basically doubled, as well as externally, where the increase was almost ten times in only five years, from 1,300 km in 1955 to 12,600 km in 1960.
- Increasing activity efficiency of TAROM and other companies operating in Romania has led to the situation that in 1989, the volume of goods transported by air increased by 12.3 times over that in 1938, and the number of passengers by 57 times.

After 1980, the aviation industry from Romania manifested the same tendency that existed in the entire national economy to assimilate all parts and subassemblies intended for the aeronautical industry in indigenous production. The first flight with the ROMBAC 1–11, built in Romania, took place in the year 1982. In 1988, the Romanian aeronautical industry achieved its first aircraft subsonic jet, "IAR-99 Soim," which was a fully Romanian project.

Conclusions

One of the most important conditions for the consolidation of the national economy and modern market development was the creation, development and modernization of a competitive national transport system after 1918. The development of industry, agriculture, commerce and the connection of the national economy with Europe and worldwide through railways, roads (cars), ships and airways can be considered key factors for Romanian economic and social modernization, especially in the aftermath of the Great Union. It is obvious that the evolution of the goods and passenger transports were a reflection of the expansion of services rendered or, in other words, a reflection of the support of transport to the economic activity, on the exchange of goods and on the people's movement. So, transport was a key and permanent factor for Romania's economic modernization and growth, both at national and international levels.

In that respect, we can underline that for the period under review, in this study, the data highlights important values of some specific transport indicators in direct correlation with the general economic condition of the country. Thus, there are positive trends for transport's contribution to both the total social product (for example, from 3.2% in 1970 up to 5.1 in 1989) and the national income (for example, from 4.0% in 1970 up to 7.5% in 1989). These developments not only highlight the important place transport occupies in the Romanian economy, but also the permanent support it has received for development and modernization. Obviously, political-administrative changes have influenced the generally development of transport, but a major trend can be contoured. Thus, after 1918 and until the end of the communist era, the dominant modes of transport were rail and road. Moreover, it can be affirmed that, at the beginning of the analyzed period, in united Romania, the main transportation is carried out by rail. Gradually, this mode's importance has decreased and an important share of it is assumed by the road transport which, in the late 80s, became the main mode of transport, even though the end of the communist era imposed numerous restrictions on the purchase for fuel and vehicles, which affected the evolution of this mode. Alongside this trend, we can also distinguish positive evolution periods for shipping, especially during the communist era, or for air transportation, whose period of occurrence can be "identified" with that of the appearance of a united Romania.

However, the general economic situation, in different stages of the Romanian society's development, created various conditions and premises for faster development of one specific transport mode over the others, such as, for example, the road over rail or ship.

All these facts show us not only the important place of transport in the Romanian socio-economic development, but also the economy's counter-reaction by permanently supporting the development and modernization of transport networks, fleets and activities.

The general conclusion of the analysis is that, for a period of seven decades, between 1918 and 1989, transport was permanently developed, with relevant changes of the share of modes in total. These evolutions were influenced not only by territorial and socio-economic factors, but in certain circumstances by inadequate managerial policies or, even worse, a disinterest expressed in the modernization and adaptation of the transport policies to the period's requirements.

References

1. Axenciuc, V., 1997, Introduction to the economic history of Romania – The modern era, Tomorrow Romania Foundation Publishing House, Bucharest.
2. Bungețianu, C., 1934, The Central Europe Railways, Universul, Bucharest.
3. Cristea, I., Ionescu, O., Stanciu, V., 1980, Air transport for goods and passengers, Technic Publishing House, Bucharest.
4. Fistung, D., 2016, "Seven decades of transport development in Romania: 1918–1990," Study CEIS-INCE, Romanian Academy.
5. Gâlcă, Th., 1930, River and maritime navigation in Romania, Graphic Arts Institute "Lupta," Bucharest.
6. Giurescu, D. C. (coord.), 2003, Romania's history in dates, Enciclopedic Publishing House, Bucharest.

7. Ilie, C., 2015, Communist Romania: economic aspects of Communism in Romania, available at: http://www.comunismulinromania.ro/index.php/romania-comunista-aspecte-economice-2/, accessed 15 August 2016.
8. Postolache, T., 1991, Romanian economy – The twentieth Century, Romanian Academy Publishing House, Bucharest.
9. Tudor-Pavelescu, A., 2007, PCR and intellectuals in the early years of the Ceaușescu regime (1965–1972), National Archives of Romania, Bucharest.
10. ***, Statistical Yearbook of SRR, 1968, Central Statistical Directorate, Bucharest.
11. ***, Statistical Yearbook of SRR, 1978, Central Statistical Directorate, Bucharest.
12. ***, Statistical Yearbook of SRR, 1983, Central Statistical Directorate, Bucharest.
13. ***, Statistical Yearbook of Romania, 1990, The National Commission For Statistics, Bucharest.
14. ***, Vienna treaty, 1940, Universul/1 September 1940, available at: https://ro.wikipedia.org/wiki/Dictatul_de_la_Viena, accessed 09 August 2016.

Cecilia ALEXANDRI

Institute of Agricultural Economics, Bucharest, Romania,
email: cecilia@eadr.ro

Lucian LUCA

Institute of Agricultural Economics, Bucharest, Romania,
email: luca@eadr.ro

Romanian Agriculture Support Scenarios for the Next 20 Years

Abstract: Romania's accession to the European Union has brought predictability to the support to agriculture, due to the multi-annual financial programming of European funds, and the total public funds destined to agriculture have continuously increased and will continue to increase until the year 2020. The three projected scenarios for the evolution of agriculture in the next 20 years (optimistic, realistic and pessimistic) took into consideration a wide range of economic, social and demographic evolutions, and mainly the future of the Common Agricultural Policy, which featured stability and increased financial support in the optimistic scenario, similar financing to the current period in the realistic scenario and a drastic diminution of financing in the pessimistic scenario.

Keywords: Common Agricultural Policy, direct payments, rural development, national budget, Romania

Introduction

The prospective approach developed in this paper consisted in defining short-, medium- and long-term scenarios, to which certain levels of the main performance indicators could be associated in relation to food security and agriculture in Romania, under an ampler project aiming to define a national development strategy for the next 20 years. For the agricultural and rural development sector, the goal of the approach is to identify to what extent Romania can get closer to the agricultural performance, living standard and food and nutrition quality specific to the developed European countries. The gaps are significant at the moment, and there is no certainty that they will be recovered quickly.

The importance of European funds, both for the support for agricultural investments and to farmers' current incomes, made the defining elements of the three scenarios taken into consideration be related to the future Common Agricultural Policy. In this respect, the optimistic and even the realistic scenario started from the hypothesis of continuation of the generous European funding received by the

Romanian agriculture and rural area. It should be mentioned that the funding started in the pre-accession period and continued with the financial allocations received under the two CAP pillars, from EAGF and EAFRD funds, under the financial programming of 2007–2013 and 2014–2020. Thus, the agricultural sector has been one of the main beneficiaries of Romania's EU membership, the European funds providing stability and predictability of financial support to farmers.

1. Literature review

The succession of the Common Agricultural Reforms in the recent decades makes discussing the possibility of a new reform shortly after the previous one plausible. A recent analysis (Swinnen, 2015) of the CAP 2013 Reform also includes certain questions about the future CAP post-2020, the conclusion being that the agricultural policy will continue to be an area under EU competence, as a materialization of the need for public policies caused by the complexity of challenges in the agricultural, food and rural sectors. As no consensus exists among member states on a particular aspect of CAP that should be reformed, the eventual post-2020 reform will represent a set of pragmatic adjustments of current structures and measures, which could include the sustainable management of forests, stimulating farmers to better manage the environmental problems, and a greater focus on innovation and modernization so as to comply with the environmental standards without the need for annual subsidies. The reform suggestions of experts in agricultural policies target the diminution of direct payments so as to release several funds for rural development and narrow the disparities between the member states through the continuation of the harmonization process initiated by the 2013 Reform.

Yet the future Common Agricultural Policy does not depend only on the European Commission proposals, but also on the position of certain key member states, referring to the directions of CAP reform, to which the European Parliament contributions are added. In the post-Brexit context, the positions of France and the Netherlands are of particular importance.

In the first half of 2016, under the Dutch presidency of the European Union, a document was submitted for discussion by member states (Netherlands presidency, 2016) that investigated the possibility of shifting from the Common Agricultural Policy to a Common Agricultural and Food Policy. This new approach starts from the changes that were made in the last decades at global agriculture level, meaning industrialization and intensification of agri-food supply, internationalization of food suppliers, increase in importance of multinational corporations, as well as an increased involvement of seed, fertilizer or pesticide suppliers. In this context, the European solidarity acquires new meanings, in interaction with a higher market orientation of agriculture, as well as with ensuring rural area viability through the contribution of family farms. Agriculture and food integration into a single policy would extend its field of action from the primary sector to the entire food chain, even though the farmers' position in this chain remains a topic of interest for policy makers.

With a similar approach to that of the Dutch government, a group of Dutch researchers made a proposal (Fresco & Poppe, 2016) for CAP post-2020, including 5 pillars: pillar A for income support (an important direction would be the diminution of direct payments by capping and better targeting); pillar B for ecosystem services based on contracts (with the idea of allowing the management of contracts by regional authorities); pillar C for rural development (which would promote innovation for competitiveness); pillar D for food policy (addressed to consumers, retail sector and food industry); pillar E for monitoring, reflection and research.

In its turn, France also launched a programmatic document (French contribution, 2016) militating for a competitive, sustainable and resilient agriculture, which aims to address the multitude of problems European agriculture is facing: food security, economy, employment, environment, territory and resilience. The answer to these problems, in the vision of France, is represented by a strong and ambitious Common Agricultural Policy, which should have three main objectives: to contribute to growth and job creation, based on innovation and transition to new production patterns; to respond to environmental and climate challenges, and to ensure stability in rural areas; to strengthen the sector resilience so as to be able to face a broad category of risks. These objectives could be pursued through intervention measures grouped under three axes: axis for growth, jobs and competitiveness in the European supply chains (agricultural, food and non-food); axis for environmental public goods and development of territories, mainly of areas with natural handicap; axis for resilience, so as to be able to cope with sanitary, climate and economic risks.

In addition to the discussions in the Council of the European Union, with the increasing importance of the European Parliament in adopting the European agricultural policies, the CAP reform ideas are also discussed at the level of the European Parliament Committee on Agriculture and Rural Development, where a set of three studies was presented (European Parliament, 2016), dedicated to the future of direct payments, future market measures and future rural development.

In the study on the future of direct payments, it is considered that the current system is neither sustainable in the long term, nor designed to respond to the present and future challenges of the European agricultural sector; another structure for the future direct payments is proposed (and an indicative budget for 2025), on the basis of a set of principles that should lead to an increased effectiveness of interventions. The proposed principles refer to: targeting payments to specific objectives; restructuring the payments under a single CAP pillar; phasing out decoupled payments during a transition period; redirecting savings to spending more on risk management and climate actions; replacing the area payments by contracts between farmers and authorities; replacing the eco-conditionality and greening payments with the obligation of enrollment into an environmental scheme; allocation of budgets to member states on the basis of performance and needs.

As regards the future of market measures and of risk management schemes, it has been proposed that all the policy instruments that influence prices and income stability be reassembled into a single framework as a third pillar of CAP. Another suggestion is to condition eligibility for payments from basic scheme and emergency aids from the reserve fund on the contribution to an income stabilization instrument.

The study on the future of rural development considers the diversity of rural areas and the way in which their needs are reflected in the rural development programs as crucial aspects for a future reform, the increased focus on territorial aspects, mainly in the poor regions, extending the beneficiaries of interventions to all persons in the rural areas, support to certain participatory actions, including certain measures with social impact, putting into value the LEADER approach potential.

2. Analysis of expenditures for agriculture from European and national funds

Romania's EU membership brought predictability to the support for agriculture and rural development, due to multi-annual financial programming of European funds, with positive impact on the increase of agricultural production and farmers' incomes. Complementing the EU funds, the state budget contribution to the financial support to agriculture has significantly increased, reaching €1 billion per year in the post-accession period, with a slightly decreasing tendency since 2012. The total public funds to support agriculture continuously increased, exceeding €3 billion in each of the last three years (figure 1), cumulating the support provided from the state budget funds (through the budget of the Ministry of Agriculture and Rural Development – MARD), from the funds of CAP Pillar 1 (European Agricultural Guarantee Fund – EAGF) and of CAP pillar 2 (European Agricultural Fund for Rural Development – EAFRD).

For Romania, the European funds destined to agriculture will continue to increase until the year 2020, which will lead to total allocations – from European and from national funds – of about €4 billion annually. The increase of support to agriculture is due to the increase of direct payments (CAP pillar 1), which were estimated at €1.77 billion for the year 2016 and at €1.90 billion for 2019. These allocations are the result of negotiations from CAP 2013 Reform, and the cumulated amounts to be received by Romania for the period 2015–2020 comprise €10.85 billion for direct payments and €8.12 billion for payments from NRDP 2014–2020.

Complementarily, the MARD budget provided for amounts of around €1.19 billion in 2016, reaching €1.26 billion in 2019. The state budget finances two main categories of support to farmers, the measures falling in the category of state aid and the national co-financing for the European programs for agriculture and rural development. Besides these, MARD budget also finances the operation of institutions from the agricultural sector (central and territorial structure of MARD, payment agencies inclusively).

Fig. 1: Evolution of support to agriculture and rural development from national and EU funds in the period 2002–2015, effective payments per calendar years

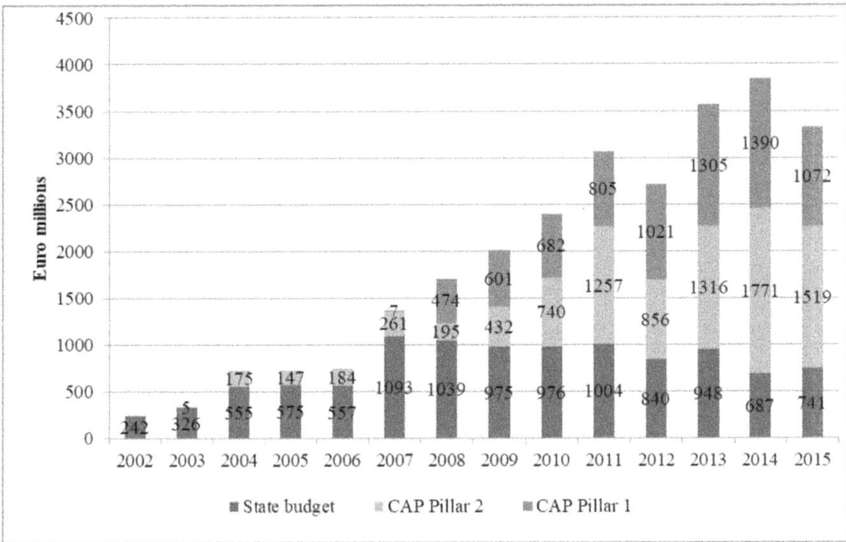

Source: Authors' processing of MARD data.

The instruments from the state aid category represented more than half a billion € in the year 2015, the most important being the complementary national payments for the livestock sector (bovines and sheep), the transitional national aid for the crop production sector, the support for diesel oil and the compensations for drought, plus smaller scale interventions, such as subsidies for insurance premiums, funding the breeds improvement program, support to organic farming or the payments under the life annuity scheme. According to the DG AGRI statistics, in 2014 Romania accounted for 1% of total state aid paid at EU level. It is obvious that Romania can increase this type of support, in compliance with the European legislation and on the condition of national funding availability.

The national co-funding of European programs presupposes a contribution from the state budget, generally for CAP pillar 2 (rural development programs). For NRDP 2014–2020 throughout the entire programming period, a national co-financing of €1.34 billion is needed. This represents 14% of total public funds allocated to NRDP, which places Romania among the member with the lowest co-financing (for instance, France has a 50% co-financing for the period 2015–2020, among the highest in the EU).

The EU funds allocated to Romania in the period 2015–2020 for covering the direct payments are divided between several payment schemes, the most important being the simplified area payment scheme (with 51% of total), followed by the greening payments (30%), the coupled support payments (12%), redistributive payments (5%) and supplementary payments to young farmers (2%).

The European funds destined to finance the market measures are used by each state to the extent that interventions are needed at European level, defined by the various common market organizations. Romania used this financial resource for measures such as the reconversion of vine plantations, support to producer groups in the vegetables and fruit sector, promoting agricultural products on third markets. Of course, Romania has the possibility to benefit more from these funds, with an increasing share of marketed production.

The funds of CAP pillar 2 have been programmed according to the rural development policy for the period 2014–2020 to support the 6 priorities, defined at European level with CAP 2013 Reform, namely: knowledge transfer and innovation; improving the competitiveness of farmers; organization of the food chains; preservation of ecosystems; efficient use of resources; social inclusion.

3. Three scenarios on financial allocations for agriculture

The specificity of the Romanian agricultural sector, compared to other sectors of the economy, is given by the importance of European financing, to support both agricultural investments (through the rural development programs) and farmers' current incomes (through direct payments). Among the elements that can outline the different scenarios on the financial allocations for Romania's agriculture one can mention, as an extreme event with low probability, the possible dissolution of the European Union (which would implicitly mean CAP disappearance); another event, yet with higher probability, would be the progressive diminution of funds allocated to CAP in the next periods of budgetary planning under the pressure of the states advocating the "public money for public goods" approach, to the detriment of the perspective that relies on supply management and market regulation. Thus, three scenarios can be considered here, corresponding to different levels of financial allocations.

The optimistic scenario assumes that at European level, the importance of agriculture will be recognized, from the multiple perspectives of food security, economy, employment, environment, territoriality and resilience, which will make the future CAP be structured around three main objectives: contribution to economic growth and job creation, addressing the challenges of climate change and ensuring stability in rural areas, strengthening the resilience of the agricultural sector and risk management. In this case, Romania would be an important beneficiary of CAP funds, and the technical and economic performance of the Romanian agriculture would significantly improve in the long term. Such a favorable situation means, in terms of public funding, an additional support for agriculture and rural development.

The realistic scenario envisages CAP operation along the current directions in the next 20 years, with total financial allocations at EU level decreasing slowly, yet with an increase of convergence between Romania and the old member states, as regards both the financial support level and the average yields and labor productivity. The estimates corresponding to this scenario will ensure the necessary funds for investments in the priority sectors from a food security perspective.

The pessimistic scenario takes into account the hypothesis of the European Union continuing to operate for the next 20 years, yet it has in view a diminution of CAP funding through re-allocation of funds to other destinations (environment preservation, combating poverty, labor retraining). In this case, the amounts estimated as necessary for ensuring the Romanian agricultural sector's convergence should largely come from the national budget.

4. Estimating the financial allocations for agriculture

Having in view the debates on the future Common Agricultural Policy, which are still at the beginning, and taking as reference the position of France, the officials of which consider that a strong European agricultural policy is indispensable for the European Union, we estimated the level of public expenditures for agriculture and rural development at values comparable to the current ones, both as regards MARD budget contribution and the contribution of the two CAP pillars. While the funds to be received by Romania for direct payments after 2020 were estimated to increase, following the convergence process initiated with the CAP 2013 Reform, the rural development funds were estimated to decrease, as a result of solving certain structural problems of agriculture and rural areas. The sums allocated from the state budget were estimated to slowly increase, the increase being lower than GDP increase, which will lead to the diminution of the share of expenditures for agriculture in GDP, in the long term.

4.1. Estimating the direct payments to farmers

In the case of direct payments, the optimistic scenario takes into consideration a consensus at European level, around the position of France, on the importance of agriculture, from a food security perspective inclusively, which presupposes maintaining a high level of subsidies to farmers, even though throughout the two decades, the decoupled payments will be replaced by payments under risk management instruments. For Romania, the convergence of direct payments could be accelerated (in the first decade), and compensations for the variations of production could be higher (in the second decade). The pessimistic scenario presupposes a drastic diminution of amounts for direct payments in the long term, which will also make irrelevant the effort to equalize the level of direct payments level between the old and new member states. At the same time, it is also possible that the national states will take over the obligation to ensure part of the support provided through the Common Agricultural Policy, under the form of co-financing the support schemes under pillar 1, according to the pillar 2 co-financing pattern. The realistic scenario describes the situation of certain CAP reforms that will lead to the gradual diminution of funding direct payments at European level, which in Romania's case will be compensated by the process of payments convergence between member states. In 2014, for instance, the direct payments received by a Romanian farmer were estimated at €107/ha, while those received by a French farmer at €281/ha. For the 2020 horizon, for which allocations have already been made, the differences between the three scenarios are given by the absorption level, this being complete in the optimistic scenario and around 95% in the pessimistic scenario.

Table 1: Scenarios on annual allocations for direct payments (€ million)

Scenarios	2020 Horizon	2028 Horizon	2038 Horizon
Optimistic	1,903	2,100	2,600
Realistic	1,850	2,000	2,400
Pessimistic	1,800	1,700	1,300

Source: Authors' estimations.

4.2. Estimating the payments for rural development

In the case of funds allocated to rural development, the optimistic scenario considers that the gap between the rural areas from Romania and those from the old member states can be recovered only with significant EU financial support, in line with the ambitious objectives of the recent programmatic documents (Cork Declaration 2.0). The pessimistic scenario assumes that a greater part of the necessary funds for rural development will be covered from national sources (yet without fully covering the necessary funding), against the background of allocating the EU funds to other priorities, or of a diminution of EU contribution as a result of incomplete use of funds from previous programming periods. The realistic scenario provides for slightly decreasing annual allocations to rural development, as far as Romania is making progress as regards general economic growth (which will also lead to a higher national contribution to rural development funds). For the 2020 horizon, the differences between scenarios are given by the incomplete level of EU funds absorption.

Table 2: Scenarios on annual allocations for rural development (€ million)

Scenarios	2020 Horizon	2028 Horizon	2038 Horizon
Optimistic	1,142	1,200	1,000
Realistic	1,100	1,000	8,00
Pessimistic	1,000	800	700

Source: Authors' estimations

4.3. Estimating the payments from the state budget

The efficient running of European funds also presupposes significant national budgetary allocations. After getting close to €1 billion allocated annually to the budget of the Ministry of Agriculture and Rural Development (MARD), starting with the year 2011, the indicative amount foreseen for 2020 is more than €1.2 billion, which could be supplemented in case of an opportunity for strategic investments (for instance for rehabilitation of the irrigation system), or it could be diminished in the case of difficult economic situations, yet without creating difficulties for the national programs providing support to farmers or the European programs for which co-financing is needed, according to CAP. Thus, MARD budget has a complementary role to the European funds, and in the case of the pessimistic scenario a larger national contribution may be needed, so as to compensate for the diminution of EU funds.

Table 3: Scenarios on the annual allocations from the state budget (€ million)

Scenarios	2020 Horizon	2028 Horizon	2038 Horizon
Optimistic	1,142	1,200	1,000
Realistic	1,100	1,000	800
Pessimistic	1,000	800	700

Source: Authors' estimations.

Conclusions

The projections on the public support for Romania's agriculture developed in this study started from the specificity of the agricultural sector of the European Union, the evolution of which is strongly linked to the Common Agricultural Policy (CAP), as regards supplementing farmers' incomes through direct payment schemes as well as providing public financial support to farmers' private investments under the rural development programs. All three proposed scenarios (optimistic, pessimistic, and realistic) considered the hypothesis of CAP continuation, yet with different financing levels. In the current European context, complicated by post-Brexit uncertainties, the anticipation of the future evolutions of the Common Agricultural Policy is an operation that deserves the attention of a country like Romania, as net beneficiary of European funds for agriculture.

The scenarios developed in this study started from certain assumptions on how to cover the financing requirements for Romania's agriculture. The realistic scenario had in view CAP operation along the current directions in the next 20 years, with total financial allocations at EU level slightly diminishing, yet with increasing convergence between Romania and the old member states. The pessimistic scenario assumed that the European Union will continue to function for the next 20 years, but has in view CAP funding diminution through the reallocation of money to other destinations. The optimistic scenario presupposes that the importance of agriculture will be recognized at European level, which will ensure future CAP funding in accordance with the ambitious objectives assumed. In this case, Romania could be an important beneficiary of CAP funds.

Acknowledgements

This study benefited from financial support under the project Romania's Development Strategy for the Next 20 years, funded by the "Patrimoniu" Foundation from the Recurrent Fund of Donors, aiming to provide support to the Romanian Academy for cultural and scientific activities.

References

1. European Parliament: Research for AGRI Committee – CAP reform post-2020 – challenges in agriculture: workshop documentation, 2016.
2. French contribution (for EU Council): A reformed CAP for competitive, sustainable and resilient agriculture, French contribution to the 29/30 May informal Council of the post-2020 CAP, 2016.
3. Fresco, Luise O./Poppe, Krijn J.: Toward a Common Agricultural and Food Policy, WUR, Wageningen, 2016.
4. Netherlands presidency (of EU Council): Food of the future – the future of food, discussion paper of the Netherlands presidency, 2016.
5. Swinnen, Johan (edited by): The Political Economy of the 2014–2020 Common Agricultural Policy. An imperfect storm, CEPS, Brussels, 2015.

Camelia TOMA, Camelia GAVRILESCU, Crina TURTOI

Institute of Agricultural Economics,
email: cameliatoma2004@yahoo.fr

Increase of Value Added for Agricultural Products – An Analysis of the Implementation of Measure 123 in the NPRD 2007–2013

Abstract: The analysis is following the degree of attaining the goal of Measure 123, from a financial and physical point of view, but also of the efficiency, regional distribution, the type and profile of the beneficiaries of European funds for investments in the field of agri-food processing. The statistical data processing from the European reports for financing monitoring have put into evidence, at the end of the year 2015, a financing rate of 88% from the measure's allocation at European level. In Romania, there were signed contracts for which payments were made, the share of which exceeded 90%. Because of the prolonged period of making investments, 9% of the projects were transferred to financing from the new NPRD. From total measure, 86% of the projects with 89% of the value are in the agri-food industry sector, the rest (14%) of the number and value are coming from the sector of wood processing, the renewable energy production and bio-fuels for self consumption and other sectors. From the sector of food industry, the highest share is represented by investments in storage, processing of cereals, and bakery with 555 projects (59%) with a value of over €300 million. In the regions South and South-East, the most projects (39%) are concentrated with 45% of the measure's value.

Keywords: European Funds, financing rate, agri-food, regional distribution

Introduction

The goal of this study was that of making an x-ray of the way in which the Romanian business environment in the agri-food processing domain answered and put into value the financial support offered through the NPRD 2007–2013 and of the way in which the Romanian authorities contributed to the success of this measure's implementation.

The authors of this paper chose to realize an analysis of Measure 123, implementing "increase of value added at agricultural and forestry products," as the increase of enterprises' competitiveness in agri-food processing, and marketing of agricultural products represented a very important goal in implementation of the rural development plan of 2007–2013, both of the European Union (5% of total EFARD budget and 15% from axis I), as well as that of Romania (8% of the total financial allocation and 25% from axis I).

1. Stage of problem knowledge

According to some studies (Mereuță, C., 2014), the food industry represents one of the few sectors in which the share of Romanian capital exceeds 60%; the value added realized by the food industry also represents almost one quarter of the total value added of the processing industry.

From the published dates (Nițulescu, G., 2016), the food production sector and the beverages sector in Romania realize each year 8.72 million tons of food products, of which 13.8% are exported. The share of expenditure for cost of the logistical services in Romania for the food products is estimated to be 55%, the rest being allocated to the secondary logistics (shops and wholesales). The food industry in our country represents 27% of the total value of agricultural production. It is dominated by a number of 50 big companies, representing less than 1% of the total of around 8.400 firms active in this domain, which realize over 40% of the Romanian agricultural sector. The food industry ensures over 180,000 jobs, that is 11.6% of the total number of employees in the Romanian industry and 2.1% from the total work force in Romania.

Among the most important sectors of the food and beverages industry there are:

- Meat industry and that of meat products, which through the 92 companies in the field realized, in 2014, a total business of 10.81 billion lei (€2.4 billion),
- The market of non-alcoholic beverages and that of mineral waters, with a value estimated at the rate of turnover of 4.52 billion lei (€1 billion), increasing by 5.23% compared to the year 2013,
- The milling and baking industry, the value of turnover rate of which increased by 8.34% in 2014, as result of the reduction of VAT to 9%, reaching around €900 million (55 active firms), and
- Milk and dairy products' industry, with a total business of 3.84 billion lei in 2014 (about €885 million) rolled in by 36 companies.

We must specify the fact that in the statistical data above there are also included the processing units already present, which accessed and had projects financed from European funds for investments in the modernization of some technological processes or the expanding of some production capacities. The processing units newly founded, being in the stage of investment-making in the reference year 2014 (statistical data regarding the main sectors of the food industry), are not included in the "Xray of the Romanian food industry."

According to statistical data supplied by the official institutions with the NPRD monitoring on 2007–2013, the total value of Measure 123 was of €2.92 billion, of which €1.63 billion came from private co-financing, and the rest from public sources, European and national (fig. 1).

Fig. 1: Sources of financing Measure 123 from RNDP 2007–2013

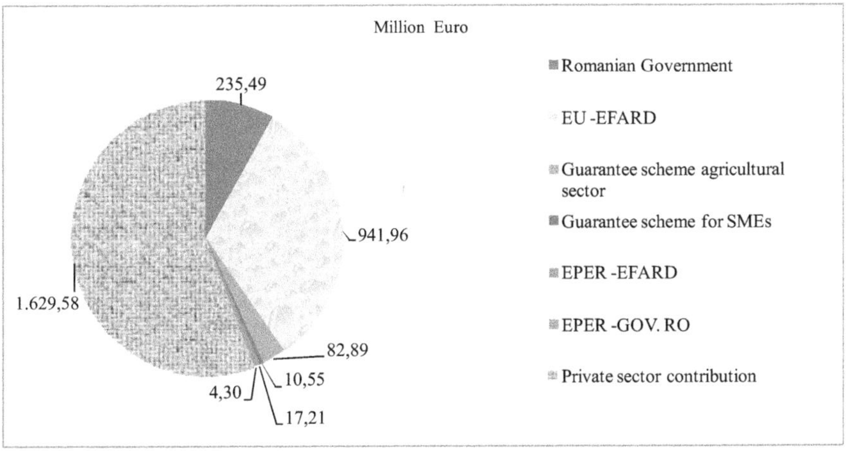

Source: Annual progresses Report – RNDP 2015, www.madr.ro.

The sums allocated from the budget of the European Fund for Agriculture and Rural Development represent 33% from the public financing allocated to the measure, those from the national budget making up 11%, and the private co-financing of the support beneficiaries is 56% from the total financial of the measure.

2. The goals and eligibility conditions of Measure 123

The general goal of Measure 123 was the increase of competitiveness of the enterprises for agri-food and forestry processing, made by the improvement of the general technical and economic performance, the improvement of the marketing performance and a better utilization of the human resources and other production factors.

The specific goals hinted to:

1. Introduction and development of technologies and procedures to obtain new competitive agricultural and forestry products;
2. Adapting of the enterprises to the new community standards, both in the stage of processing and in distribution of the obtained products;
3. Improvement of enterprises' incomes supported by the increase of value added of the agricultural products;
4. Increase of value added of forestry products as well as of the economic efficiency and micro-enterprises activity, through development and modernization of equipments, processing technologies and processes.

The eligible beneficiaries for the support granted through Measure 123, for the investments targeted to the increase of value added at agricultural products, were:

- Microenterprises and the Small and Medium Enterprises, as well as family enterprises/individual enterprises;
- Other enterprises, which have less than 750 employees or a turnover rate not exceeding €200 million;
- The processing agricultural cooperatives for agricultural products, the Co-operative Companies of Marketing and the groups of producers formed by commercial companies and processing agricultural cooperatives for agricultural products, which have as a goal the common selling of agricultural and forestry products.

Through the projects financed, the beneficiaries of the financial support were obliged to respect the technical conditions (for the improvement and optimization of the production flows, of the capacities of processing, storage, conditioning, packaging and marketing), economic-financial conditions (the reduction of production costs, the increase of gross value added and of efficiency for utilizing the resources and a better cooperation on horizontal among processors, the units supplying raw materials and the selling sector), as well as environmental conditions and food safety (reduction of polluting emissions and wastes, the increase of the degree of utilizing the energy from renewable sources, used only for own needs, improvement of safety at the workplace and of hygiene conditions, improvement of the quality of processed products and traceability).

The realization of investments was supported at the level of the whole territory of Romania, and non-reimbursable funds were granted to beneficiaries for investments in tangible assets and/or intangible ones in the agricultural domain.

There were not financed any investments for: sugar-beet processing without allocated quota, tobacco processing, units of rendering, investments in research activity in the domain, and neither were the investments supporting the wholesale directly.

In order not to be overexposed with the investments from Measure 121, the SMEs, which were both producers of raw agricultural material and processors, were obliged to respect the condition that at least 10%, but not more than 50% from the raw material processed and/or stored come from own production.

The priority sectors were considered: milk and dairy products; meat, meat products and eggs; cereals; vegetables, fruits and potatoes; oilseeds, honey and wine.

Out of the non-priority sectors, the biggest share was held by the sectors "cereals and combined fodders," followed by "sweets and sugar products," "sugar free foods" and "other foods."

The minimum processing capacity for micro-enterprises of slaughtering and meat processing was 4–5 bovines/day, respectively 80–100 bovines/month, 7–8 pigs/day, respectively 140–160 pigs/month, and a minimum quantity of 2 tones of milk per day for the collection and processing of milk.

The grants maximum ceilings (€/project) varied from €3 million for associative forms, to €2 million for micro-enterprises, SMEs and big enterprises, and €200,000 for micro-enterprises for meat and milk processing, and the minimum value was €5,000 per project. The quantum of the grants support was, in general, 50%, with some exceptions, for example the region Bucharest-Ilfov (40%), and 25% for the big enterprises.

3. Implementation of Measure 123

Measure 123 was structured in function of the sectors of activity (processing of agri-food products, processing of forestry products, and production of renewable energy from sources others than natural ones, as sun, wind, geo-thermal etc.) and in function of the financial sources and schemes of state aid (tab. 1).

Table 1: Situation of projects and the value of investments, grouped by measure and schemes of state aid

Measure and schemes of State aid	Number of projects handled	Number of selected projects	Number of contracted projects	Investments value, € million	Public value, € million
Measure 123 -classic	1,762	961	524	1,198	438
XS 13/2008 Agro	247	215	147	154	56
XS 28/2008 Forest	177	157	87	84	33
N578/2009 Agro	310	230	140	194	70
N578/2009 Forest	143	62	37	51	18
TOTAL	2,639	1,625	935	1,681	615

Source: Annual progresses Report – NRDP 2015, www.madr.ro, own calculations.

In 2008–2013, within the 25 sessions for handling the projects, from the total of 2,639 projects 62% were selected and 35% were contracted. From the total value of the expenses for investments, 37% were represented by public expenses.

The "classic" Measure and the schemes of state aid destined for the food industry supported almost 88% of the total number of projects contracted, and 92% of total investments' volume of Measure 123 (fig. 2).

Fig. 2: Distribution of projects contracted within the Measure 123 classic, in function of the priority domain

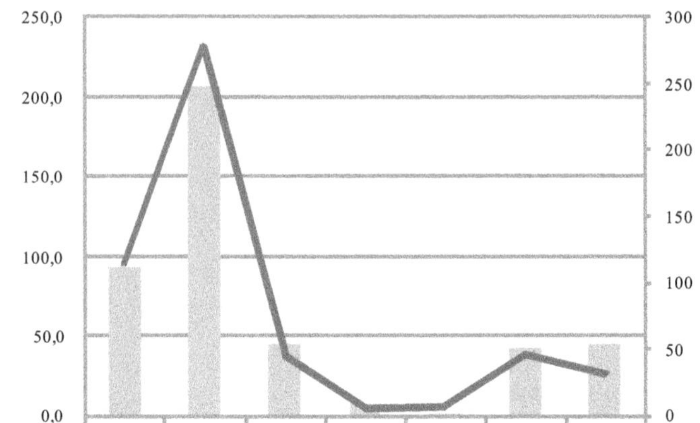

	Milk and milk products, meat, meat products and eggs	Grain	Vegetables, fruit and potatoes	Oilseeds	Honey	Wine	Non-prioriy sectors
Value -mil Euro-	92,7	206,8	44,1	6,4	0,8	42,2	44,6
Projects -no.-	114	278	44	5	6	46	31

Source: Annual progresses Report NRDP, 2015, www.madr.ro, own calculations.

Within the priority domains, 524 projects were contracted with a value of €437.5 million. The highest share was registered by the projects in the domain "cereals," representing half of the number and value, followed by the domains "milk" and "meat" with 22% of number and 21% of the value of priority domains.

The unit average costs from public funds, of over €1 million, was registered in domains "non-priority sectors" with €1.4 million, "oilseeds" with €1.3 million and "vegetables, fruits and potatoes" with €1 million.

The other non-agricultural sectors, such as "renewable energy" and "bio-fuels", have registered average values/projects between €1.7 and €3 million (fig. 3).

Fig. 3: Unit cost per project, € million, for Measure 123

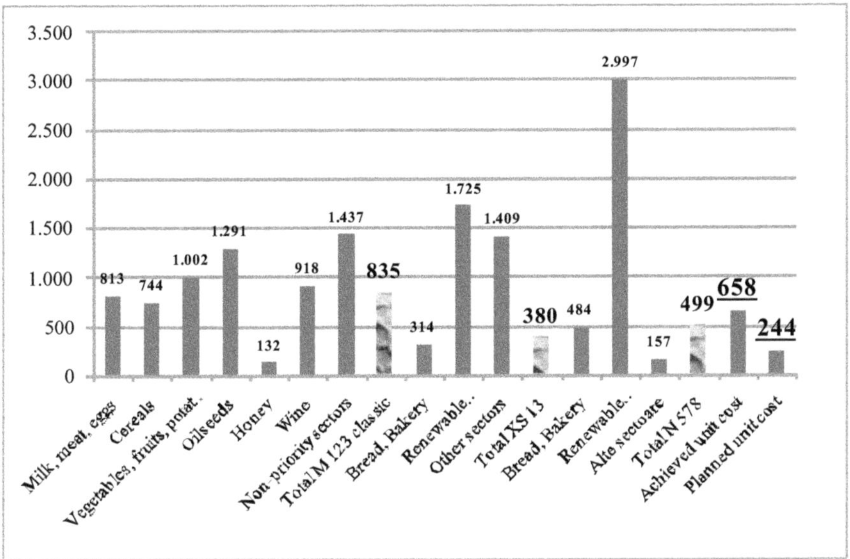

Source: Annual progresses Report – NRDP 2015, www.madr.ro, own calculations.

Per total measure, the financial support had a reduced efficiency, as the unit cost realized was situated over the unit cost programmed for the support of one enterprise, a fact explained through the accessing of the measure by enterprises which handled projects with values of almost the maximum permitted by the measure's chart, so only 32% of target was obtained.

From the total of 935 contracted projects, 81% were micro-/small enterprises, 18% were medium and only 1% were big enterprises, and from point of view of the production type processed, conventional raw materials and technological processes were used in 94% of the projects and only 6% were ecological (fig. 4).

Fig. 4: Distribution of projects from Measure 123, by types of beneficiaries and by production type

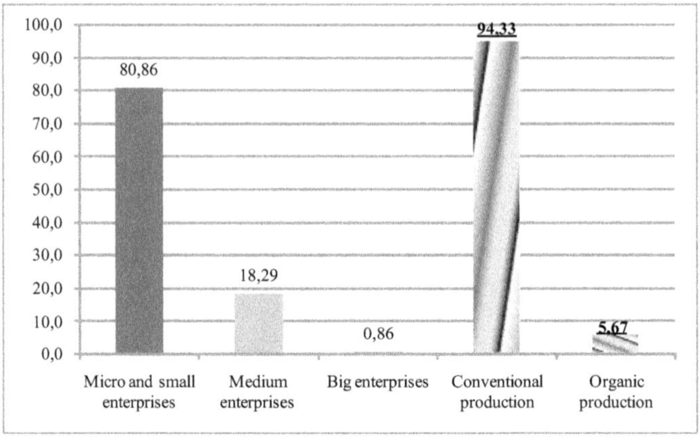

Source: Annual progresses Report – NRDP 2015, www.madr.ro, own calculations.

In regions South and South-East, 39% from the number of projects were financed and 45% of the public value allocated for the measure. The weakest represented is the region South-West Oltenia, with only 7% of the projects' number and 2.7% of the total value, contracted from public source. We consider that the region Bucharest-Ilfov cannot be compared with the rest of regions, predominantly rural and intermediary, where the necessity of investments in the agri-food industry is a priority (fig. 5).

Fig. 5: Regional distribution of projects contracted on Measure 123

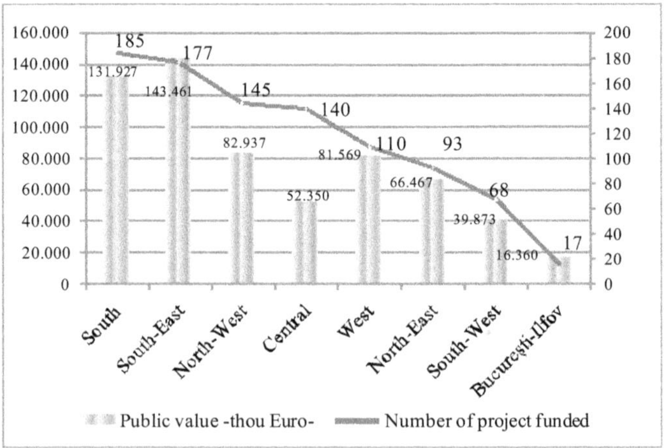

Source: Annual Progresses report – NRDP 2015, www.madr.ro, own calculations.

Cumulatively, until the end of 2015, payments of €503.4 million were made for the projects financed, the contribution of EFARD representing €439 million (87%).

The rate of financial execution was around 70% of the allocation of €720 million. To the payments made for the investments projects, the payments afferent to the guarantee schemes in value of €49 million were added, the contribution EFARD being 80%.

Thus, the total payments made for the investments projects and for the guarantee schemes were in value of €552.8 million, respectively €478.5 of EFARD.

By sectors, the financial execution rate – the highest – was registered by "forestry," followed by the "food industry" and "mixed sector" (fig. 6).

Fig. 6: The rate of contracted projects' financing, by sectors, € million

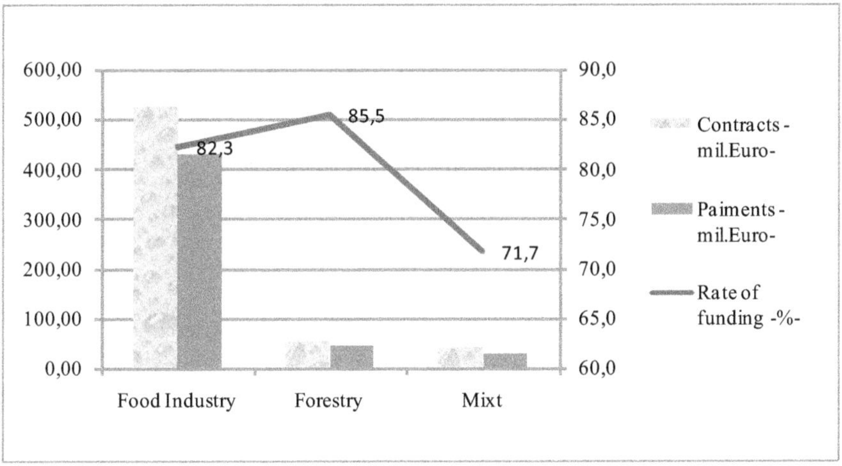

Source: Annual progresses – RNDP 2015, www.madr.ro, own calculations.

The average regional financial execution was manifested relatively different. Region South registered the highest rate of financing. Paradoxically, region South-East, where the biggest public sums were contracted, registered the lowest financing rate (69.6%; fig. 7).

Fig. 7: Financing rate of contracted projects, by development regions, € million

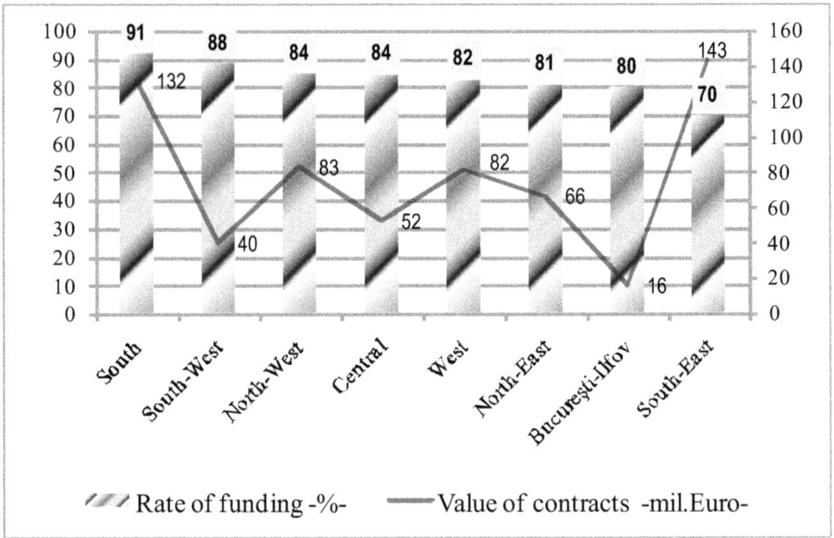

Source: Annual progresses Report – RNDP 2015, www.madr.ro, own calculations.

Within this measure, 571 financing contracts were canceled.

At the level of the financing domains of the sector of agri-food industry (123-Classic, XS 13 and N578A), 485 projects were canceled (some in developing, others before starting the payments), of which 71.6% at the request of beneficiaries, 27.2% for breach of contractual clauses and 1.2% out of insolvency or bankruptcy reasons.

Of the reasons that led to the cancellation of contracts, on behalf of the private beneficiaries, we mention: lack of co-financing, the big number of controls and verifications and re-verifications made on artificial conditions, which discouraged the beneficiaries who considered them excessive and preferred to go to other co-financing sources, and the launch of the new RNDP in more advantageous conditions.

Other reasons that led to the cancellation were: financial blockages of economic agents, insolvency or their bankruptcy, difficulties regarding the obtaining of banking liquidities.

The public authorities admitted the emergence of some dysfunctions in the procurement process as result of the poor performance of the procedure (offers' demands wrongly made, erroneous assessments etc.).

The main impact of the big number of cancelled projects was represented by the disengagement from payments of the funds which were blocked in these projects. In order to avoid disengagement, the authorities have over-contracted and granted advancements for other eligible projects.

4. Conclusions

This measure was realized at only one third of the established target, both per total measure, and at the projects accessed by micro-enterprise and SMEs, with 13.6% at the level of big enterprises, 50% at the associative forms and 8% of the target for the restructuring of some enterprises.

The share of investments from total public value was of 94%, and by the end of 2015, 66% of total number of projects of the measure were finalized.

This measure registered a significant number of cancelled contracts, of which three quarters at the request of beneficiaries and one quarter for breach of contractual clauses.

Regions South and South-East are in the first places, both for number and value of realized projects, and the regions South-West and Bucharest-Ilfov are in the last places.

A reduced efficacy of 32% of the target was found, as the unit cost realized was 2.7 times higher than the projected unit cost.

References

1. Mereuţă, Cezar: "Priorităţi strategice ale dezvoltării României la orizont 2025" in: http://www.contributors.ro/economie/prioritati-strategice-ale-dezvoltarii-romaniei-la-orizont-2025/, 2014.
2. Niţulescu, Gabi: "Radiografia industriei alimentare româneşti" in: http://www.roaliment.ro/editia-1/radiografia-industriei-alimentare-romanesti/, 2016.
3. ***Comisia Europeană, 2016, Al 9-lea raport financiar al Comisiei către Parlamentul European şi Consiliu privind Fondul european agricol pentru dezvoltare rurală (FEADR) exerciţiul financiar 2015, Bruxelles, 30 September 2016 com (2016) 632 final.
4. ***Comisia Europeană, 2016, CELEX_52016DC0632_RO_TXT.pdf, www.ec.europa.eu/agriculture/rural-development-2014-2020.
5. ***MADR, 2016, Raport anual de progrese PNDR 2015, August; www. madr.ro.
6. ***MADR, 2016, Situaţia proiectelor depuse la 18 August 2016 prin PNDR 2007–2013, www. madr.ro.
7. ***MADR, 2016, "Stadiul implementării PNDR 2014–2020 la data de 20.10.2016," www.madr.ro.
8. ***MADR/APDRP/AFIR, Ghidul solicitantului pentru Măsura 123, Versiunea 9 din ianuarie 2013, www.madr.ro.

Donatella PRIVITERA

University of Catania, Department of Educational Sciences, Italy,
email: donatella.privitera@unict.it

Food Citizenship and Community Gardens. A Case Study in Italy

Abstract: The study highlights the practice of urban agriculture, especially community gardens. Using qualitative methods, this investigation aimed to gain an understanding of how a community garden may facilitate social capital stocks of members. An example as case study is the municipality of Catania, in the South of Italy, an urban context characterized by few public green spaces. The finding is that gardens are places where both attitudes and practices can change in the process of engagements of the citizens. In a world where questions of sustainability are increasingly driven by cities and their residents, the community gardens help identify areas of social and transformative food potential as well as concern.

Keywords: Sustainability, social inclusion, local governance, municipal incentives

Introduction

Actually it's relevant to discuss the role of community-based initiatives in the creation of sustainable green cities. The study is embedded in the framework of urban food system research to explore community gardens as places to practice active citizenships. Also, the manuscript explores the concept of social capital within the context of an urban community garden in order to understand the significance of the social connections made through this natural and common space. The term community garden generally refers to "open spaces which are managed and operated by members of the local community, in which food or flowers are cultivated" (Guitart et al., 2012, p. 364). They have a range of critical functions in cities, including social, health and environmental functions, and build alternative food initiatives with, and not for, marginalized communities (Hall, 2011). In much of the literature, as well as in public discourse, community gardens are portrayed as spaces of anti-gentrification activism and struggle for the right to the city (Aptekar, 2015). It aims to relate spaces, practices and imaginaries of foodscapes by analyzing the genesis and the state of art in the city.

The challenge in describing a project or a real urban gardens, is linked to the fact that it is a space for growing vegetables, and a more complicated social urban process that takes shape through the dynamics of the community who takes part, the environment, the political and social context administrative. Green spaces, as well as woods and natural meadows, wetlands or other ecosystems, represent a fundamental component of the urban ecosystem. Green urban areas facilitate physical activity and are important to mental health and relaxation, and form a refuge from noise. The urban gardens represent a resource for individuals and families, but also an organizing concept for new ideas and practices on quality of life, urban sustainability, and the relationship with the environment and nature.

Experience shows that urban gardens can generate a wide range of benefits within the community, and build multiple outcomes, integrating individual, social, environmental and economic in relationship with nature, providing a quality space for physical exercise, health and nutrition, environmental education, personal growth, friendship, capacity development, the expression of culture, inclusion and social cohesion, the local economy and more. Some of these benefits are tangible, like access to fresh food and fruits for home consumption, or giving shape to open air areas for this practice; others are intangible benefits, such as cultural or spiritual practices of the people. Italy, unfortunately, does not seem to follow the example of other countries, but urban gardens are improving, considering all their potential environmental functions. However, their role in contrasting not only unauthorized development, but also urban planning with no care for green urban spaces, is often neglected and scarce. In fact, many years ago, groups of citizenships were emerging in all major cities of Italy. They are the "guerrilla gardeners" (www.guerrilagardening.it), a group of enthusiasts that decided to interact positively with the urban space through small demonstrations of green acts. Guerrilla gardening is actively opposed to urban decay, acting against the neglect of green areas. The principal activities of the community are remodelling and beautifying spaces, with plants and flowerbeds, if there's some neglected land to transform of the city. The social movement was born in Italy in 2006, but it is an international network of independent activists, fighting against globalized commerce and the strict rules of urban planning to improve the quality of open space (Reynolds, 2008). The community is the hub where guerrilla gardeners from around the world are sharing what they are up to, plotting and planting.

Before presenting the empirical results, a short literature review on which questions of spatial and conceptual boundary-making have been prominent, where cities are as places of nature, and on green common spaces. An examination of the literature showed that there have been many publications on the subject of urban gardens as a use of land in the cities, but few have presented evidence of the effectiveness of its social implications. An example as case study is the municipality of Catania, in the South of Italy, an urban context characterized by few public green spaces.

1. Literature review

It's of note that there is an emerging recognition of people actors as crucial to biodiversity conservation, where urban gardens play an important environmental role by bringing back nature to the heart of the city, sometimes requalifying vacant and residual spaces, contributing to building communities capable of addressing new social demands (Rubino, 2007). The proximity of people, businesses and services associated with city living means that there are benefits associated with urban living, also in terms of sustainability and resource use. At the same time, urban gardens can very well be a valid instrument to grant better alimentary safety, to prevent environmental degradation and property speculation (Ghose, Pettygrove, 2014). The sharing of work and new lifestyles position themselves as alternatives to the individualism typical of the cities. Moreover, it provides a reason to create small experiences of aggregation and solidarity. Community gardens have, through successive waves of garden movements, fulfilled various needs for communities, including supplementing food supplies, fostering individual independence, and bringing green space within the decaying urban landscape (Kurtz 2001; Lawson 2005).

Actually, many community gardens and urban agriculture initiatives are driven by activism, focused on procuring community food security and food justice (Hall, 2011), where the role of urban agriculture is in self-empowerment and learning, and in constituting ways to achieve food justice (Tornaghi, 2016). The space of community gardens has multiple expressions in images, memories, emotions, identity, and everyday practice (Einzerberg, 2012). The most physically salient aspect of the symbolic meaning of the gardens is their constitution as carriers of cultures within the city, such as culinary preferences, customs, foodscapes, and social interactions. These practices also stimulate ecological networks, in order to protect the health and safety of consumers and farmers, by exploiting all the possibilities of the rudimentary tools used, largely obtained from recyclable materials (Rusciano, Cirvero, Scarpato, 2016).

Otherwise, taking care of an urban garden involves taking responsibility for our urban environment, as well as for the future and the following generations (Ferris et al., 2001). In fact, cultivation in urban spaces contributes to the reduction of the environmental footprint of the cities and requalifies unused or degraded urban areas, promoting a green and sustainable environment through consumption of locally grown food and connecting people to ideas, expertise, and partners who share a passion for creating vital places. But the garden is not always seen only as an environmental good, but a chance to focus on the types of relationships and engagements that are possible in such a context, because, as in other environmental debates, we need to continue to find ways to go beyond dualisms, while continuing to analyze why they remain so resilient and appealing (Head, Muir, 2006).

2. Findings

Urban gardens are a growing phenomenon, especially in the north of Italy. According to National Institute of Statistics data (2015), 64 cities offer the opportunity for managing urban gardens, an increase of 27.3% in surface in four years, for a total of over 1.6 million m^2. The promotion of this practice helps contain land consumption and to preserve green areas present between the built-up areas from decay, but also to achieve certain social objectives (training, therapy, socialization and intergenerational and intercultural integration). The gardens are available in almost all the cities of the north, more than two of three cities in the center (such as Florence and Rome), while in the south they are rarer: less than one city of five (in Naples and Cagliari among the great common).

In the present study, we analyze the different realities of community gardens in the municipality of Catania. Catania is a city characterized by medium socio-economic development levels, and a lack of public green spaces and services where urban agriculture and community gardening efforts can develop. Currently, the public green spaces are about 2.2 m^2 per capita, much less than the minimum amount stated by the national legislation (9 m^2; Martinico et al., 2014). In the municipality of Catania (fig. 1), an example of community gardening is located in the suburbs of the city (Librino), which hosts the largest social housing scheme built in the late 1970s with 36,000 inhabitants.

A planned new settlement was designed to provide a high-quality, low-density residential environment in a garden setting, an urban project by Luigi Piccinato (1964) and Kenzo Tange (1970). They imagined Librino had to be nice, clean and not to become a degraded place full of unwanted people: it was like a dream in which everyone who chose to set up cooperative housing societies to create their own spaces of liveability in a modern city believed.

Nevertheless, Librino has been born sick and deprived. There will not be place – for a long time – for any kind of dream or plan. Drafts of policies, one public project has followed another, always with a top-down approach. Many associations and local parishes become pioneers of the fight against decay, rebuilding identities and spaces, not only involving well-known practices, but also moving towards a real, strong will of planning for themselves as well as their own life spaces. Librino evokes spaces expelled from the city because inconvenience. It combines in itself all the negative characteristics of the great device satellite areas: marginality and problematic mobility, segregation, socio-economic distress, disorientation, lack of relational spaces.

In September 2016, the municipality of Catania initiated a pilot project in Librino, aiming to respond to current social aspects, as well as smaller-scale intra-urban garden suburbs. "Green" creativity was used as a tool of local empowerment and socio-cultural revitalization. The institution aims to create new social public green spaces (more than 3.5 ha) that are assigned to associations or private persons to cultivate small land pieces. Part of these areas will be available for urban agriculture that contributes to the production of food at local level, and at the same time reduces maintenance costs for the municipality. Also, based on some practical implications, it will be presented related to the monitoring of policy effects related to community gardens, entrepreneurial activities and urban sustainability.

It is a fine example of community that involves not only the young people of associations and of the neighborhood, and aims at the environmental qualification of the area. The plots of land, ranging between 20 and 200 m^2, are managed with the aim of spreading the green culture and stimulating participation in community life, through a non-profit agricultural production.

In August 2016, seven gardens were assigned to four families, one to a school and two to cultural associations. Each garden has free water for irrigation, and assignees will be able to buy seedlings at subsidized prices, bulbs, seeds, saplings, fertilizers and natural pesticides. The social community are followed in their activities by the Office for Ecology, with the cooperation of agriculture associations. For each garden – assignment lasts four years with renewal – an annual fee must be paid, established by the municipality. The lots for community gardens, reserved for retirees and people in socially disadvantaged conditions, as well as those for the families, do not exceed 200 m². For educational-training, gardens and associations, where theoretical activities and practices will take place, can be assigned to neighboring lots, up to a maximum of 2,000 m².

Fig. 1: Land-use map for the study area in Catania (Italy)

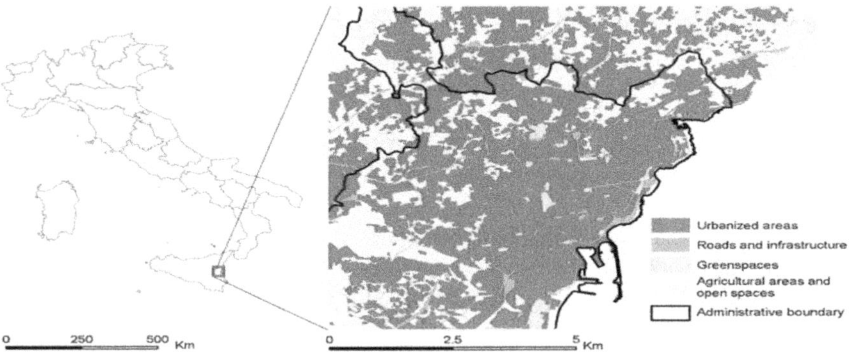

Source: Martinico et al. (2014).

The trade is only allowed to cover the costs of training-work projects. The gardens will be cultivated directly by beneficiaries or their family, without paid labor.

The parcels of land are assigned for a period of five years to residents in the municipality of Catania, upon payment of an annual fee, and if you are in one of the following categories: pensioners no younger than 60 years, handicapped compatible with the activities to be developed, unemployed, homemakers, adult citizens, all residents in the municipality; not suitable are those who are already farmers or who have plots of land in the municipality. Each family can be given a single vegetable garden, and associations of disadvantaged or disabled persons can also receive concessions. The assignment is obviously personal and cannot be transferred to others, and in case of death or renunciation of the assignee, it is handed over to another subject on the list, and cannot be granted through inheritance. Whoever receives the plot of land cannot use private paid labor, except under certain conditions such as a disease, but can use the family's help.

The assignment may be revoked in the event of bad maintenance conditions or carelessness in crops, or in case of abandonment. After the assignment period, the one who got the land must leave camp without any kind of law on it. The costs for the cultivation and maintenance and cleaning of the gardens are a responsibility of the assignee, who cannot make a different use of the land received under their management. Vegetables and flower plants can be cultivated on an annual cycle, herbaceous perennials and small fruits. The purpose of upgrading was to put these spaces available to the community for commercial and cultural activities, of course, encouraging cultural exchanges and integration. In the end, the project involved associations, individual citizens including foreigners, committees, and religious leaders.

The garden is arranged following traditional criteria, in order to enhance the local products, such as tomatoes, horticultural products and eggplants, as well as several fruit trees.

Discussion and Conclusions

The important role of community-based initiatives in the creation of sustainable green cities seems to be in line with common ideas of involvement and sustainability in the new project of Catania. Through the lens of lived space, the community gardens support the social status of a community of residents, and provide an alternative lived experience within the modern urban environment of the neighborhoods of Catania.

The policy work and administrative support related to community gardens, entrepreneurial activities and urban sustainability, seem to stimulate various forms of grass-root initiatives in Catania. A positive agenda seems to include both private and community-oriented initiatives, even though there are also indications of difficulties in coordinating bureaucracy and interests of small organizations.

In Catania, community gardens are good examples of the right to public space, but they are not developed enough as sites for demonstrating the urban environment as "the commons." They represent a "social use-value." The usefulness of the gardens that become the allotment gardens lies in accomplishing tasks purely for environmental sustainability, as a support for the administrations to create local governance.. In fact, from the analysis of the case study, relating to the environmental approach of the city of Catania in respect to community gardens, emerges a management focused on the redevelopment of the degraded area, promoting social inclusion, but still with serious environmental deficit. It has been enjoyed a favorable support from active citizens, substantially excited about the activities and projects implemented, even though they are not missed obstacles due to a delicate social environment. It seeks to empower the participants, so that they can manage their lives and in relation to the work done in the gardens themselves, regardless of the support of institutions. The community gardens could be presented as an instrument to ensure food security, to combat environmental degradation and speculation (Ghose, Pettygrove, 2014). The traditional food is also well known and requested by consumers, which are interested by the link between product and territory.

Urban gardens may contribute to lower human pressure on natural resources by reducing the pollution and mitigating the environmental alterations, although in terms of CO_2 reduction, urban gardens have a negligible impact, and are inferior to other forms of cultivation (Cattivelli, 2016). The regulatory path faced by the city of Catania is to meet this demand for accessibility of the land, although it is still anchored to limited initiatives and not fully supported, however, that they have contributed to the renewal of public green management is indeed a desirable enhancement, an empowerment of the people involved with the local administration's support.

Local governments, in cooperation with the central, and active citizens have been an opportunity for encouraging such practices at a small social cost, benefiting from advantages in terms of reputation. In this way, local communities can create territorial social responsibility, which becomes shared and participatory. However, it is necessary to spread the information about the possibility of buying an urban garden and the existence of subsidies also in the perspective of requalification of the urban areas.

References

1. Aptekar, Sofya: "Visions of Public Space: Reproducing and Resisting Social Hierarchies in a Community Garden." Sociological Forum 30 (1), 2015, pp. 209–227.
2. Cattivelli, Valentina: "Not just food: the (new) importance of urban gardens in the modern socio-economic system. A brief analysis," in Nobile, Maurizio (ed.): World Food Trends and the Future of Food, Ledizioni, Milano, 2016, pp. 122–134.
3. Eizenberg, Efrat: "Actually Existing Commons: Three Moments of Space of Community Gardens in New York City." Antipode 44 (3), 2012, pp. 764–782.
4. Ferris, John/Norman, Carol/Sempik, Joe: "People, land and sustainability: Community gardens and the social dimension of sustainable development." Social Policy & Administration 35, 2001, pp. 559–568.
5. Ghose, Rina/Pettygrove, Margaret: "Urban community gardens as spaces of citizenship." Antipode 46 (4), 2014, pp. 1092–1112.
6. Guitart, Daniela/Pickering, Catherine M./Byrne, Jason: "Past results and future directions in urban community gardens research." Urban Forestry and Urban Greening, 11, 2012, pp. 364–373.
7. Hall, Billy: "The Garden is Always Greener…." Catalyst: A Social Justice Forum 1 (1), 2011, pp. 86–113.
8. Head, Lesley/Muir, Pat: "Suburban life and the boundaries of nature: resilience and rupture in Australian backyard gardens." Transactions of the Institute of British Geographers 31 (4), 2006, pp. 505–524.
9. Kurtz, Hilda E.: "Differentiating Multiple Meanings of Garden and Community." Urban Geography 22 (7), 2001, pp. 656–670.
10. Lawson, Laura: "The City Bountiful. A Century of Community Gardening in America." University of California Press, Berkeley, 2005, pp. 1–382.
11. Martinico, Francesco/La Rosa, Daniele/Privitera, Riccardo: "Green oriented urban development for urban ecosystem services provision in a medium sized city in southern Italy". iForest 7, 2014, pp. 385–395.
12. Reynolds Richard: On guerrilla gardening: a handbook for gardening without boundaries. Blomsbury, London, 2008.

13. Rusciano, Vincenzo/Civero, Gennaro/Scarpato, Debora: "Urban Gardens and environmental sustainability: an empirical research of Campania region," International Conference, Ecological Performance in a Competitive Economy, Bucharest, 9–10 March 2017 Proceedings, Quality-Access to Success, 18, 2017, pp. 376–381.
14. Rubino, Adalgisa: "The allotment gardens of the Ile de France: a tool for social development." Journal of Mediterranean Ecology 8, 2007, pp. 67–75.
15. Tornaghi, Chiara: "Urban Agriculture in the Food-Disabling City: (Re)defining Urban Food Justice, Reimagining a Politics of Empowerment." Antipode, 2016, pp. 1–21, doi 10.1111/anti.12291.

Dan-Marius VOICILAȘ

Romanian Academy, Institute of Agricultural Economics – Bucharest, voicilas@eadr.ro

Camelia Anişoara GAVRILESCU

Romanian Academy, Institute of Agricultural Economics – Bucharest, cgavrilescu@eadr.ro

The Romanian Agriculture Challenges – Organic Products

Abstract: Organic farming is one positive and complex way to give a proper response to the many environmental problems posed by the agricultural sector in its continuous efforts of increasing output, efficiency and competitiveness on both EU and international markets. The interest of the EU for organic farming and products has grown in the last decades and the members have promoted farming and consumption of organic products as a response to increasing chemical use in farming and consequently to the pollution of soil and water, as well as of agricultural and food products. Romania showed interest in organic farming since the pre-accession period, when it started implementing the acquis communautaire in this field, and organic farming appeared in the general picture of agriculture. The paper presents the analysis of the recent evolutions in the Romanian organic farming, as well as the development and implementation of the EU and national regulations in the field. Also, it highlights the past, present and future challenges, the ways of removing obstacles and dealing with threats. The results show that the consumers' response has been increasingly positive, although the higher prices for organic food remained a barrier to a wider expansion of demand.

Keywords: agriculture, organic products, challenges, Romania

Introduction

Organic farming ("ecological" in the Romanian version, or "biological" agriculture) is a modern practice to grow crops animals and to produce foodstuffs which is fundamentally different from conventional farming. The role of this agriculture system is to produce much cleaner food, more appropriate to the human body metabolism, but in full correlation with the preservation and development of the environment in respect to nature and its laws. The process and procedures for obtaining organic products are regulated by strict production rules and principles, enforced by the EU and national legislation, which start with the quality of the land and ends with the effective final food product. Organic farming does not use synthetic fertilizers and pesticides, growth stimulants and regulators, hormones, antibiotics or intensive animal raising systems. Genetically Modified Organisms (GMOs) and their products are forbidden in organic farming legislation. The European Union laid a special focus upon obtaining crop or livestock products based upon organic farming procedures; and it provides incentives for those willing to practice organic farming. Coming back to old procedures is not at all simple, as the rules are very strict, so that the final product should be completely natural and ecological.

In contrast to that, nowadays, the market gives us products that seem to be designed on the computer, large-sized, with perfect shapes and charming colours, as if coming from an unreal world; big, good-looking fruits, all having the same size; vegetables, full of colour and appetizing, with the same picture aspect, as if cut from a magazine. But beyond these exterior aspects, pleasantness to the eye, there is something else, which is disappearing, that some of us have completely forgotten. It is the essence, the contents, the texture, it is that "something" enchanting not only the eye but also the other senses. This is ... the taste. So, a few additional questions are: are the products of today still tasty? Are the products of today still healthy? Most knowledgeable consumers' opinion is that most often, these products have almost nothing in common with their natural taste. About the quality, it is hard for consumers to give a prompt answer and they need help from specialists, from different fields. This is the reason why we considered it useful to conduct the study, and we are trying to show the needs of the consumers and present a clear picture of the recent trends, from economics point of view. This subject is relevant and important for all European countries, having in view the EU regulations.

1. Literature review

During the years, the subject was studied intensively by many authors, from different countries. Also, EU regulations gave the opportunity for producers and researchers to focus on the production of organic products, and they produced different studies regarding the quality of products.

According to IFOAM (International Federation of Organic Agriculture Movements), the definition of organic agriculture is "... a production system that sustains the health of soils, ecosystems and people. It relies on ecological processes, biodiversity and cycles adapted to local conditions, rather than the use of inputs with adverse effects. Organic Agriculture combines tradition, innovation and science to benefit the shared environment and promote fair relationships and a good quality of life for all involved" (IFOAM, 2008). According to the same organization, organic farming is based upon four principles:

a) Principle of Health: "Organic Agriculture should sustain and enhance the health of soil, plant, animal, human and planet as one and indivisible;"
b) Principle of Ecology: "Organic Agriculture should be based on living ecological systems and cycles, work with them, emulate them and help sustain them;"

c) Principle of Fairness: "Organic Agriculture should build on relationships that ensure fairness with regard to the common environment and life opportunities;"
d) Principle of Care: "Organic Agriculture should be managed in a precautionary and responsible manner to protect the health and well-being of current and future generations and the environment" (IFOAM, 2008).

A SWOT analysis of organic farming (Burghelea et al., 2016) shows many advantages at ecologic, social and economic levels. The disadvantages are mainly economic, related to increased costs due to the loss of productivity during the conversion period, to the use of more extensive technologies, to the extra costs of certification and to unfair competition of fake products.

The analyses of the evolution of the market for ecological products based on quantitative market research, which used questionnaires, were carried out by several authors. Among these, we would like to highlight the study conducted in Romania, in 25 counties, by Dinu et al. (2014), which highlights the population's perception of organic products and market structure based on age, gender, or income criteria.

A detailed analysis of organic agriculture in Romania was carried out in 2007 (Voicilas, 2007a, b), highlighting the development stages of this sector during the pre-accession period, as well as the main perspectives and challenges. This study was later supplemented with information on the transformation of the sector after Romania's accession to the EU (Voicilas, 2009).

In many new member states, such as Bulgaria (Agapieva, 2015), Poland (Gołaś, 2016), or Romania (Voicilas 2009; Voicilas & Alboiu, 2014), organic agriculture developed significantly after EU accession, but due to the domestic consumers' lower purchasing power, most of the products were sold to richer Western countries (Germany, United Kingdom, Austria, etc.).

For our present analysis, we used other previous research of the authors as well, which was updated and developed. For updating, we use statistical data provided by the National Institute of Statistics of Romania, the Ministry of Agriculture and various publications in the field.

2. Legislation and institutions

The legal basis of the organic farming system was established in the 1990s by the Commission Regulation (EC) no. 2092/1991, regarding organic farm production and the indications for their presentation as agricultural and agri-food products.

At the national level, together with the signing of the Association Agreement and the initiation of the EU accession negotiations, the Romanian legislation had to get in line with EU legislation. Following this process, at present, the Romanian legislation complies with EU requirements and orientations.

The main normative acts are: Government's Emergency Ordinance (OUG) no. 34/2000 on the organic agri-food products, approved by Law no. 38/2000; Government's Decision no. 917/2001, for the approval of the methodological norms for the application of provisions from OUG no. 34/2000 regarding organic agri-food products; Joint Order no. 417/2002 and no. 110/2002 of the Minister of Agriculture and of the President of the National Authority for Consumers' Protection; Order no. 70/2002 of the Minister of Agriculture on the establishment of the Commission for Organic Farming Development in Romania; Order no. 527/2003 of the Minister of Agriculture for the approval of the Rules on the inspection and certification system and the accrediting conditions for the inspection and certification of bodies in organic farming; Order no. 721/2003 of the Minister of Agriculture for the approval of rules on the import and export of organic agri-food products; Order no. 153/2006 regarding the approval of the componence of the Commission for the accrediting of inspection and certification of bodies in the organic farming sector, which inspects and controls the operators on Romania's territory; Order no. 317/2006 regarding the modification and completion of the Annex to the Order of the Ministry of Agriculture and of the President of the National Authority for Consumers' Protection no. 417/110/2002, for the approval of specific labelling rules for organic agri-food products; OUG no. 62/2006 for the modification and completion of OUG no. 34/2000 on organic agri-food products; Law no. 513/2006 on the approval of OUG no. 62/2006 for the modification and completion of OUG no. 34/2000 regarding organic agri-food products; Order no. 219/2007 on the approval of rules regarding organic farmers' official registration.

They provide information, rules and norms necessary in this field, like: the authority responsible for organic farming; the general rules and principles of organic production; the duration of the conversion period; the inspection and certification system; the list of accepted products to be used in organic farming practice; the list of ingredients and processing methods that can be used in the preparation of organic foodstuffs; sanctions etc.

The governmental policy is elaborated and coordinated by the Ministry of Agriculture and Rural Development (MADR), under which the Office of the National Authority for Organic Products (ANPE) is operating, which is the authority in charge of the organic farming sector. ANPE is collaborating with different agencies, education and research institutions, foundations, among which we can list the following:

- The Academy of Agricultural and Forestry Sciences – ASAS;
- Higher education institutions, agricultural research institutes and stations;
- The National Organic Farming Federation, whose activity is based on the "sustainable development principle," a development type which should not disable the next generations' access to a clean environment.

3. Romanian organic products before European Union accession

Data supplied by MADR reveal the increasing importance of the organic sector for domestic producers. The positive evolutions of areas, livestock herds and production subject to organic farming practices prove the existing potential, initiative, development prospects and increasing demand of consumers (see tables 1 and 2).

Table 1: Areas and livestock herds before EU accession

Item	2000	Index (year 2000=1.00)					
		2001	2002	2003	2004	2005	2006
Total area, out of which:	**17,438 ha**	1.65	2.51	3.28	4.23	6.33	8.20
- Cereals	**4,000 ha**	2.00	3.00	4.00	5.12	5.52	4.08
- Pastures and fodder crops	**9,300 ha**	1.51	2.15	2.58	3.37	4.55	5.51
- Oilseeds and protein crops	**4,000 ha**	1.58	2.50	3.90	5.02	5.65	5.97
- Vegetables	**38 ha**	2.63	18.40	5.26	7.89	11.58	18.95
- Fruit (apples, cherries, sour cherries)	-	-	**50 ha***	2.00	4.00	8.64	5.84
- Spontaneous flora collection	**50 ha**	2.00	6.00	8.00	10.00	352.60	774.00
- Other crops	**50 ha**	6.00	16.00	18.00	18.00	97.68	242.00
Livestock, out of which:							
- Dairy cows	**2,100 heads**	2.52	3.10	3.43	0.33	3.86	4.71
- Sheep and goats	**1,700 heads**	2.18	1.76	1.88	1.88	23.82	50.69

Note: for fruit, base year is 2002.

Source: Calculations based on MADR data.

Both land areas and the number of animals increased in the investigated period. The trend is increasing and the perception of these crops as an alternative activity and income source is positive. Comparing the objectives established by the government's strategy with the field results, we could say that the objectives were achieved (Voicilaş & Alboiu, 2014). Thus, the bases were created for the development of this activity and for the exploitation of market niches, both in the domestic and world markets.

Table 2: Romanian organic production before EU accession

Item	2000 production	Index (year 2000=1.00)					
		2001	2002	2003	2004	2005	2006
Total cereals production, out of which:	13,502 t	1.81	2.39	2.25	6.46	9.77	12.34
- Cereals,	7,200 t	1.74	2.22	2.00	5.69	7.64	6.73
out of which.: export	-	-	-	-		1.56	2.55
- Oilseeds and protein crops,	5,500 t	1.31	2.00	2.27	6.73	8.29	13.29
out of which: export	-	-	-	-		1.23	2.26
- Vegetables	600 t	6.67	6.67	3.33	5.00	12.00	14.51
- Fruit (cherries, sour cherries)	-	-		1.50	2.50	5.00	1.70
- Spontaneous flora collection,	200 t	2.00	1.50	1.60	22.50	83.74	124.81
out of which: export	-	-	-	-		3.74	-
- Other crops	2 t	150.00	400.00	450.00	600.00	3,175.00	5,520.50
Animal production, out of which:							
- Cow milk	58,367 hl	1.09	1.59	1.58	1.59	1.71	1.92
- Sheep and goat milk	701 hl	2.48	1.94	2.10	2.57	19.26	22.11

Note: for fruit, the base year is 2002; for exports base year is 2004.

Source: Calculations based on MADR data.

As in the case of land areas and livestock, productions continuously increased in the investigated period. Although the production levels are much higher than those obtained 5–6 years ago, the domestic supply cannot totally meet the demand yet, which makes it possible for the imported organic products to penetrate the Romanian market. At the same time, Romanian organic products are mainly exported to Western Europe (Germany, Italy, Switzerland, Netherlands, for example) and attempts are being made to penetrate the U.S. market. Wild berries, either organic or non-organic, have a much higher export price, and the price is even higher if these are organically certified (i.e. the volume of the exports of fruits in 2004, in Germany and Italy, was 800 tons). According to this statistical evidence, organic farming can be considered a dynamic sector in Romania, with an increasing trend in recent years, both in crop and livestock production (Voicilaş & Alboiu, 2014).

4. Romanian organic products after European Union accession

In this section of the paper, we present the evolution and characteristics of the market after EU accession. For our analysis, we took into consideration the number of farmers involved in organic production and areas cultivated. According to the statistical database, the areas under organic production are split into: arable, permanent crops of pastures and fodder, permanent crops of orchards and grapevine, spontaneous flora. In the next table, we present the evolution of the indicators in the period of 2007–2014.

Table 3: Romanian organic areas and producers after EU accession

Item	2006	Index (year 2006=1.00)								
		2007	**2008**	**2009**	**2010**	**2011**	**2012**	**2013**	**2014**	**2015**
No. of certified operators	**3,409 persons**	1.12	1.23	0.95	0.93	2.85	4.56	4.46	4.24	3.59
Area in arable land	**55,605 ha**	1.17	1.55	1.98	3.29	4.14	5.18	5.42	5.20	4.42
Area under permanent crops – pastures and hayfields	**51,200 ha**	1.13	0.90	0.77	0.62	1.53	2.07	2.03	1.87	1.48
Area under permanent crops – vineyards and orchards	**294 ha**	3.24	5.16	6.36	10.52	14.17	26.47	31.97	32.10	37.81

Source: Calculations based on MADR data.

In all cases, the evolution had a positive trend. The areas under organic agriculture increased fantastically, due to facilities accorded by the Ministry of Agriculture and EU funds at the producers' disposal on one side, and on the other side due to change of the classification of organic producers (this was mainly due to the existing support measures for the period conversion granted under art. 68 of Regulation (EC) nr. 73/2009 laying common rules for direct support schemes for farmers under the common agricultural policy and establishing certain support schemes for farmers). In the same time, the number of organic operators increased in the same rapid way (about 15,000 registered operators in 2014). To support this assertion, we want to exemplify the evolution of two groups of crops: cereals and vegetables (figure 1 and 1 b).

Except for the slow growth before EU accession, in both cases, we observe a different speed of growth after accession, a rapid one in the case of cereals and a slow evolution at the beginning, then a fast growth, in the case of vegetables. These evolutions are explained by the specific rules in the field, which must be followed by the organic farmers during the conversion period, the characteristics of the crops and their attractiveness. Also, the preferences of the farmers are important and the facilities offered. All these aspects must be taken into consideration when we analyze the activity in the field.

5. Market challenges

The largest markets for organic agri-food products are USA, Germany, France, UK and Italy. Romania ranks 19 in organic sales in EU-28 (Gavrilescu et al., 2016).

The organic market has good perspectives not only in developed countries. Also, the Romanian market has a good potential, even if different obstacles still make the development harder. The objectives in the short, medium and long term, which can contribute to the improvement of the competitiveness of the Romanian organic sector in the next period, can be synthesized as followed:

- The increase in the number of operators in this sector, receiving financial support from Romanian government programs;
- Increase of the role of non-governmental organizations (NGOs) in this sector through programs for the development of trade with organic products;
- Increase in the number of exporters who are actively involved in programs for organic agricultural trade development in less-favored areas;
- Support provided to organic commercial farms, so as to be more active on the market;
- The association of small organic farmers so as to co-operate in the marketing of organic products;
- The increase in the number of municipal and regional organizations directly involved in the implementation of national programs;
- The increase in the number of local processing units and foreign direct investment projects;
- The increase of investments in related activities in rural areas;
- The increase in the number of employees in the units which are implementing organic farming regulations;
- The increase of investments in the activities related to exportable organic products from less developed rural areas;
- The increase of organic farm output;
- The increase in the number of new companies involved in export activities with primary and processed organic agricultural products;
- The increase in the number of optimal operation modules by the association of crop and livestock farms;
- The development of processing capacities for the organic farming sector;
- Capacity improvement in terms of products and value added;
- The development of services for organic production;
- The diversification of cultivated species and of the range of processed products.

Fig. 1 (a, b): Areas under organic production

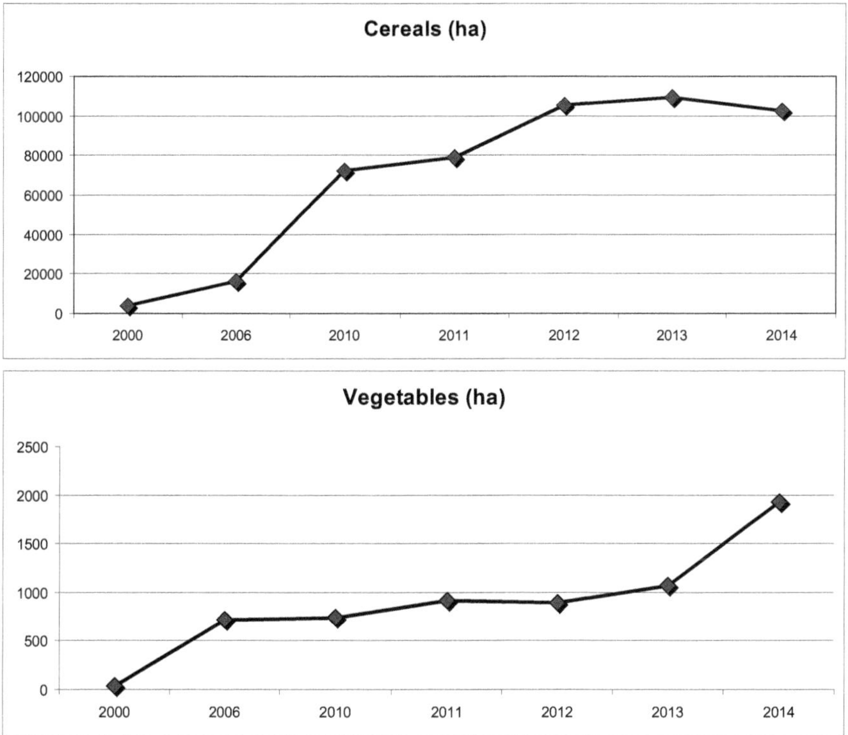

Source: Calculations based on MADR data.

Unfortunately, not all producers are satisfied with the evolution of this market and with the government's involvement in the activity of supporting organic farming. In the opinion of some farmers who had initiatives in this field, organic agriculture became a non-efficient business in Romania, not because the outlet is not large enough, but rather because the government has not shown interest in this activity so far.

The lack of financial support from the state, in addition to the extreme weather phenomena in the last years, is the main factor which determines the producers to think about giving up their business. In many reports made by producers or in the communications at scientific events organized by them, it is mentioned that farmers are confronted with the problem of higher production costs as well as with the problem of product distribution.

For Romania, organic agriculture represents a market niche that is still insufficiently exploited, with a definite and real development potential for the agricultural sector (Dinu et al., 2014).

6. Conclusions

The main conclusions from this analysis, as regards the ways in which we can contribute to the improvement of the competitiveness of the Romanian organic sector in the next period, which is considered an important niche market, are as follows: the increase of the number of operators in this sector, receiving financial support from the Romanian government programs; the association of small organic farmers so as to co-operate in the marketing of organic products; an increase in the number of municipal and regional organizations directly involved in the implementation of national programs; an increase in the number of foreign direct investment projects and investments in related activities in the rural area; an increase and diversification of organic farm output; capacity improvement in terms of products and value added; the development of services.

On the other hand, the development of the Romanian organic market is under the condition of two factors. The first factor is the premium price of the organic products, which restricts demand in countries where consumers do not have high purchasing power. The second factor is the education, and more specifically awareness, of organic products. As consumers become more educated and informed on food issues, they are more inclined to buy organic products, whether it is because of factors like food safety, concern for the environment, or health reasons. Except for these two factors, which are not strictly linked to the field, there are other obstacles which can influence the future development, like: high cost of certification, high production cost, extreme weather conditions, difficulties in distribution, high rate of forgery, and low degree of producers' organization.

Due to growing demand and supply, international trade flows of organic agri-food products are expected to increase in the coming years, stimulated also by the new trade facilities between EU-28, USA and Canada, opening good perspectives for the Romanian organic production.

References

1. Agapieva, Valentina: "Trends in the development of organic farming in Bulgaria." Scientific Papers. Series "Management, Economic Engineering in Agriculture and Rural Development," 15 (2), 2015, pp. 9–12.
2. Burghelea, Cristina/Uzlău, Carmen/Ene, Corina Maria/Topor, Dan: "Prospects for organic farming in Romania." Scientific Papers. Series "Management, Economic Engineering in Agriculture and Rural Development," 16 (1), 2016, pp. 73–78. [Available at: http://managementjournal.usamv.ro/pdf/vol.16_1/Art12.pdf].
3. Dinu, Toma Adrian/Stoian, Elena/Micu, Marius Mihai/Condei, Reta/Niculae, Ioana: "Study regarding consumption of organic products in Romania." Scientific Papers. Series "Management, Economic Engineering in Agriculture and Rural Development," 14 (2), 2014, pp. 113–118. [Available at: http://managementjournal.usamv.ro/index.php/scientific-papers/62-vol-2-2014/599-study-regarding-consumption-of-organic-products-in-romania].

4. Gavrilescu, Camelia/Florea, Adina/David Saida/Popescu, Alin/Mateoc-Sirb, Nicoleta: "Agri-food organic products – A fast increasing market." Journal of Biotechnology, 231, Supplement, 10 August 2016, p. 94. [Available at: http://www.sciencedirect.com/science/article/pii/S016816561630596X].
5. Gołaś, Jakub: "Development of organic farming in Poland – economic and legal aspects." Scientific Papers. Series "Management, Economic Engineering in Agriculture and Rural Development," 16 (1), 2016, pp. 165–174.
6. IFOAM: Principles of organic agriculture [Available at: https://www.ifoam.bio/en/organic-landmarks/principles-organic-agriculture].
7. MADR (Ministerul Agriculturii şi Dezvoltării Rurale): ***, Baza de date a Ministerului Agriculturii şi Dezvoltării Rurale.
8. Voicilas, Dan-Marius: "Organic farming." In: Ionel Iuliana (coord.): Non-conventional farming economics, ISBN 973-8432-75-8, Terra Nostra, Iasi, 2007 (a), pp. 88–149.
9. Voicilaş, Dan-Marius: "Alternatives of rural development – organic farming." In "Multifunctional agriculture and rural development (II) – Rural values preservation," Institute of Agricultural Economics-Belgrade, ISBN 978-86-82121-48-0, Ed. DIS Public DOO, Belgrade-Beocin, Serbia, 2007 (b).
10. Voicilaş, Dan-Marius: "New challenges for Romanian agriculture – organic farming." In: Neuwirth Julia, Wagner Klaus (eds.): "Multifunctional territories: Importance of rural areas beyond food production," vol. 6, "Rural areas and development," ERDN, IERIGZ-PIB, ISBN 978-83-7658-096-8; 3-901338-29-2, Warsaw, Poland, 2009, pp. 125–143.
11. Voicilaş, Dan-Marius/Alboiu, Cornelia-Florentina: "Applied EU quality schemes and organic products on Romanian market." Journal Economics of Agriculture, 61 (2 April–June), Institute of Agricultural Economics & Balkan Scientific Association of Agrarian Economists, Belgrade, Serbia, 2014, [Available at: http://www.ea.bg.ac.rs/images/Arhiva/2014/Broj%202/8%20EP%202%202014-8.pdf].

María RIVERA, Carmen GARCÍA, Miriam LÓPEZ, Raquel PASTOR, José Antonio NAVARRO

Technical University of Madrid, Calle Ramiro de Maeztu, 7, 28040 Madrid, Spain

Adrian TUREK RAHOVEANU

University of Agronomic Sciences and Veterinary Medicine of Bucharest, 59 Mărăşti Boulevard, District 1, 011464 Bucharest, Romania

Magdalena TUREK RAHOVEANU

"Dunărea de Jos" University of Galati, 47 Domnească Street, 800008 Galaţi, Romania

Corresponding author: turek.adrian@managusamv.ro

Organic Aquaculture to Meet Global Fish Demands: Feasibility and Opportunities

Abstract: This paper offers a global view of fish supply and demand. Based on trends in each country or group of countries for the production of capture fisheries and aquaculture and those for the consumption of fish, driven by income and population growth, IFPRI's newly improved International Model for Policy Analysis of Agricultural Commodities and Trade (IMPACT model) simulates outcomes of interactions across countries and regions and makes projections of global fish supply and demand into 2030. Projections are generated under different assumptions about factors considered as drivers of the global fish markets.

Introduction

The growing population in recent decades has caused increasing demands of food and traditional fuels for family daily use, leading to serious problems of resources exploitation, forest destruction and environmental pollution. Traditional fuels such as wood and coal for cooking are becoming increasingly scarce and expensive, and can contribute to deforestation. Large numbers of households engage in farming, and agricultural waste poses a threat to the environment due to fresh animal dung being discharged into open gutters and community waterways. An increasing population leads to intensive agricultural aquaculture practices, damaging the environment.

For organic agriculture, the USDA's National Organic Standards Board (NOSB) presented a definition in 1995: "Organic agriculture is an ecological production management system that promotes and enhances biodiversity, biological cycles and soil biological activity. It is based on minimal use of off-farm inputs and on management practices that restore, maintain and enhance ecological harmony." The principal guidelines for organic production are to use materials and practices that enhance the ecological balance of natural systems and that integrate the parts of the farming system into an ecological whole. Organic agriculture practices cannot ensure that products are completely free of residues; however, methods are used to minimize pollution from air, soil and water. Organic food handlers, processors and retailers adhere to standards that maintain the integrity of organic agricultural products. The primary goal of organic agriculture is to optimize the health and productivity of interdependent communities of soil life, plants, animals and people.

Diminishing fishery harvests, wild fish food-safety issues, environmental concerns, increased fish consumption, and the increasing market share of organic foods have combined to focus attention on "organic aquaculture." Consumer demand may well drive the organic production of finfish, shellfish, and other aquatic species into the mainstream during the next decade. Organic aquaculture has attracted the attention of researchers from several academic disciplines as well as that of environmental advocates and entrepreneurial innovators. A small number of "certified" and noncertified organic fish and microalgae products have made it to the retail market place in the developed countries. While the regulatory specifics still need to be addressed, this new organic market niche has significant potential for growth in the future (Boehmer et al., 2005).

The World Bank Group (WBG) Agriculture Action Plan 2013–15 summarizes critical challenges the global food and agriculture sector is facing. Global population is expected to reach 9 billion by 2050, and the world's food-producing sector must secure food and nutrition for the growing population through increased production and reduced waste.

Production increase must occur in a context where resources necessary for food production, such as land and water, are even scarcer in a more crowded world, and thus the sector needs to be far more efficient in utilizing productive resources. Further, in the face of global climate change, the world is required to change the ways to conduct economic activities.

Fisheries and aquaculture must address many of these difficult challenges. Especially with rapidly expanding aquaculture production around the world, there is a large potential of further and rapid increases in fish supply, an important source of animal protein for human consumption. During the last three decades, capture fisheries' production increased from 69 million to 93 million tons; during the same time, world aquaculture production increased from 5 million to 63 million tons (FishStat). Globally, fish currently represents about 16.6% of animal protein supply and 6.5% of all protein for human consumption (FAO, 2012). Fish is usually low in saturated fats, carbohydrates, and cholesterol and provides not only high-value protein, but also a wide range of essential micronutrients, including various vitamins, minerals, and polyunsaturated omega-3 fatty acids (FAO, 2012). Thus, even in small quantities, provision of fish can be effective in addressing food and nutritional security among the poor and vulnerable populations around the globe.

In some parts of the world and for certain species, aquaculture has expanded at the expense of natural environment (for example, shrimp aquaculture and mangrove cover) or under technology with high input requirements from capture fisheries (for example, fishmeal). However, some aquaculture can produce fish efficiently with low or no direct input. For example, bivalve species such as oysters, mussels, clams, and scallops are grown without artificial feeding; they feed on materials that occur naturally in their culture environment in the sea and lagoons. Silver carp and bighead carp are grown with planktons proliferated through fertilization and the wastes and leftover feed materials for fed species in multispecies aquaculture systems (FAO, 2012). While the proportion of non-fed species in global aquaculture has declined relative to higher trophic-level species of fish and crustaceans over the past decades, these fish still represent a third of all farmed food fish production, or 20 million tons (FAO, 2012).

Further, production efficiency of fed species has improved. For example, the use of fishmeal and fish oil per unit of farmed fish produced has declined substantially, as reflected in the steadily declining inclusion levels of average dietary fishmeal and fish oil within compound aquafeeds (Tacon and Metian, 2008). Overall, a 62% increase in global aquaculture production was achieved when the global supply of fishmeal declined by 12% during the 2000–08 period (FAO, 2012).

Many of the fishers and fish farmers in developing countries are smallholders. The Food and Agriculture Organization (FAO) estimates that 55 million people were engaged in capture fisheries and aquaculture in 2010, while small-scale fisheries employ over 90% of the world's capture fishers (FAO, 2012). To these small-scale producers, fish are both sources of household income and nutrients, and sustainable production and improved efficiency would contribute to improving their livelihoods and food security. Sustainably managing marine and coastal resources, including fish stock and habitat, would also help building and augmenting resilience of coastal communities in the face of climate change threats.

One important feature of this food-producing sector is that fish is highly traded in international markets. According to the FAO (2012), 38% of fish produced in the world was exported in 2010. This implies that there are inherent imbalances in regional supply and regional demand for fish, and international trade – through price signals in markets – provides a mechanism to resolve such imbalances (Anderson, 2003).

Therefore, it is important to understand the global links of supply and demand of fish to discuss production and consumption of fish in a given country or a region, while understanding the drivers of fish supply and demand in major countries and regions essential in making inferences about global trade outcomes. Developing countries are well integrated in the global seafood trade, and flow of seafood exports from developing countries to developed countries has been increasing. In value, 67% of fishery exports by developing countries are now directed toward developed countries (FAO, 2012).

This report offers a global view of fish supply and demand. Based on trends in each country or group of countries for the production of capture fisheries and aquaculture and those for the consumption of fish, driven by income and population growth, IFPRI's newly improved International Model for Policy Analysis of Agricultural Commodities and Trade (IMPACT model) simulates outcomes of interactions across countries and regions and makes projections of global fish supply and demand into 2030. Projections are generated under different assumptions about factors considered as drivers of the global fish markets. This report reflects a collaborative work between the International Food Policy Research Institute (IFPRI), the FAO, the University of Arkansas at Pine Bluff, and the World Bank. This work builds on the publication "Fish to 2020" by Delgado and others (2003).

Throughout the report, the discussions are centered around three themes: (1) health of global capture fisheries, (2) the role of aquaculture in filling the global fish supply-demand-gap and potentially reducing the pressure on capture fisheries, and (3) implications of changes in the global fish markets on fish consumption, especially in China and Sub-Saharan Africa.

Methods

Systematic review of scientific papers, searching in Google Scholar, without date limit and only papers in English and Spanish. Gray literature accessed through manual search in the Albert R. Mann Library, Cornell University. No restrictions were made by study design. Abstracts were reviewed and in the necessary cases the full articles, finally taking into account all articles which included aspects related to aquaculture and deleting the rest.

Searching for original studies, the database was consulted using the keywords "organic aquaculture" and "global fish demands." Additionally, bibliographical references of selected articles were analyzed in order to rescue other potential studies for the review. These articles were also located through Google Scholar.

Inclusion and exclusion criteria: in the gray literature search was included all kinds of different documents, provided by societies and professional associations which included aspects related to aquaculture. Regarding systematic reviews and scientific studies, it has been applied as an inclusion criterion that studies had to incorporate conclusions on the future of aquaculture. The main exclusion criterion was that the articles had only local information.

Data extraction: After the initial search, 178 studies were found, although 167 were excluded due to not being relevant to the purpose of this review. So finally, the 11 documents listed in the literature were selected.

Results

The remarkably dynamic character of the aquaculture sector stands out in the results and underscores the tremendous contribution that will likely be made by the

Asian region, in particular, in meeting the growing world seafood demand in the next 20 years. The growth of global aquaculture production is projected to continue at a strong pace, until it matches the production of capture fisheries by the year 2030. China will likely still be at the top of the producer list of major fish species, but other Asian countries/regions (particularly SEA, IND, and SAR) will likely become stronger contributors of future aquaculture growth. Species such as shrimp, salmon, tilapia and carp are seen to grow fairly rapidly over the projection horizon, with projected annual average growth rates well in excess of 2% a year over the 2010–30 period. This represents a strong contrast with the stagnant nature of capture, whose growth in the model is kept at exogenous rates that reflect its historical patterns of production.

Other pelagic will likely continue to be the most important category for use in producing fishmeal and fish oil. The supply of these fish-based feeds is projected to grow at a steady pace, although nowhere near as quickly as the overall trajectory of aquaculture production that unfolds until 2030. Much faster growth in aquaculture production than in fishmeal supply toward 2030 reflects our assumption that there will continue to be steady improvements in the feed and feeding efficiency within the aquaculture sector.

While such technological improvements are exogenously imposed in the model, rather than endogenously determined, this trend is reflected in the historical data.

Dissemination of best management practices will likely continue from more advanced regions – for example, Scandinavia for salmon aquaculture – throughout the industry.

This will likely come about as a result of competition for quality, the pressures of sustainability certifications, and the purely economic drive to lower costs per unit production of output as much as possible. The fishmeal price that is projected to steadily rise over the projection horizon to 2030 represents a continuing imperative and driver for technological change and efficiency gains. This is also reflected, in FAO results, in terms of the increasing use of fish processing waste for reduction into fishmeal and fish oil. Use of such "free" feedstock will likely increase, especially as fishery operations become more consolidated and vertically integrated within the industry. All in all, it is likely that technological change surrounding feed production and feeding practices will enable aquaculture to become more efficient and sustainable in nature as we move into the medium- to long-term horizon.

In FAO projections for 2030, the prices of all fish products continue on a slightly increasing trajectory into the future, which is consistent with what the FAO observes in other global food commodity markets and projections. This reflects the "tightness" of market conditions that they expect to prevail across a number of food categories, given the steady demand for growth of food and feed products that is expected to continue on a global level toward 2030 and beyond. This, in turn, is driven by steady growth in emerging economies like China, India, and the faster-growing countries within the Latin American and Sub-Saharan African regions.

As was the case in the earlier "Fish to 2020" study, a good deal of production and consumption growth and volume is expected to continue to be centered in China. The projections also highlight a number of Southeast Asian countries increasing their aquaculture supply in order to meet the growing food fish demand of regions such as China, as well as their own internal consumption needs. The model predicts that the fishmeal to fuel the future growth of Asian aquaculture will largely be imported from Latin America, which will likely continue to produce a surplus of feed for both fish and livestock production.

One of the illustrative scenarios that the FAO explores points toward important sources of feed for aquaculture: fish processing waste that can be reduced, along with whole fish, into fishmeal and fish oil. The projected sizable increase in fishmeal production and reduction in world prices suggests this as a promising source of change within the industry. Increased use of processing waste will likely help relieve the pressure on marine stocks in the future as well. This kind of development could be one of the factors that leads toward the "faster growth" scenario simulated for aquaculture worldwide, in which a greater pressure on fishmeal markets (in the absence of any other technological change) and higher prices for fishmeal, fish oil, and their ingredient fish species are projected.

The disease scenario for shrimp aquaculture in Asia shows, by design, a very dramatic initial decline in shrimp production, but the shocks even out toward 2030, as the industry recovers. The shift in trade patterns would be the main mechanism through which the Asian production loss is made up, by additional production from other regions, especially Latin America. However, given the size of the aggregate shock to the market, Latin America would not be able to fill the initial global supply gap. Given the projected tightness of shrimp markets due to the continuing growth in global demand, such large-scale disease outbreaks will likely cause substantial impacts on the global market.

The scenarios focusing on capture fisheries show potentially dramatic changes in production and distribution of production across regions. The effects of restoring global capture fisheries will be positive in all aspects – both in production and consumption across all regions. This contrasts with the climate change scenario, where some regions gain in productivity due to more favorable biophysical conditions than other regions. This result underscores the importance of understanding and properly measuring the region-specific environmental changes, including ocean temperature and acidity levels that would occur under various climate change projections, and their implications on regional fisheries.

The fact that there remains a large degree of uncertainty and inconsistency across various climate model projections, in terms of the degree and direction of these effects, underscores the importance of resolving these issues before meaningful interpretations can be given to their simulated effects on capture fisheries and, more broadly, on global fish markets. This also shows the growing need to manage fisheries in a precautionary fashion, given all the unknowns surrounding climate change.

A scenario on the demand side illustrates the effects of accelerated food preference changes among consumers in China. Substantially increased demand for high- and medium-value fish species within China would shift the global fish trade. The trade position of China for these products would shift from either small net exporter or large net importer to a solid net exporter by 2030. As a result, fish consumption would be reduced in every other region by 1–32%.

Each of these scenarios helps to illustrate important dimensions of the world fish economy that might be substantially affected by technical, environmental, or socio-economic change, and how sensitive the model results are to those shifts. They also help point to areas that should receive closer attention in future work, such as sourcing of alternative feedstock for fishmeal, and which countries and regions could be significant game changers in the industry as it evolves over the next 20 years.

Discussion and possible future directions

The series of comparative analyses presented in the model projections provided by OECD-FAO (2012) in "Fish to 2030: Prospects for Fisheries and Aquaculture" gives them a degree of confidence in the model's ability to reproduce the observed dynamics of the global fish markets. However, the model shows some difficulty in generating consistent price projections, despite its success in reproducing their supply, demand, and trade volumes. In particular, for shrimp, crustaceans, and other freshwater and diadromous categories, the model does not reproduce the sharply falling price trend over the 2000–08 period. However, they are confident that the model has captured reasonably well the features of each of these markets at the regional and global level.

As is often the case with a large and detailed model, this model contains a necessary degree of simplification, so that the model is consistently clear in the construction and framework, tractable in its computational properties, and easily modifiable to introduce exploratory scenarios. Although there may be some features specific to certain segments of the fish markets that have not been fully incorporated in our representation of fish supply and demand relationships, they feel that this has not compromised the overall fidelity of the model to its original goal of representing the basic drivers of change and capturing the dynamics in the global fish markets to 2030.

Nonetheless, there are areas where improvements can be made on the model representation, especially when additional and better data become available.

Aquaculture Growth Rates

One set of parameters that can be improved is exogenous growth rates of aquaculture production. Except for those related to feed and price-driven supply responses, the dynamics of aquaculture are approximated by their historical trends observed in aggregate statistics. Given the sheer number of combinations for country and fish species represented in the IMPACT model, case-by-case investigation of aquaculture expansion potential is not conducted. For example, each country faces species-specific and overall capacity constraints for aquaculture that are driven by geographical characteristics, such as soils, topography, climate, and water availability (Pillay and Kutty 2005; Boyd, Li, and Brummett 2012). Without sufficiently controlling the culture environment (for example, putting fish in greenhouses), aquaculture of certain species is simply infeasible in certain countries. If country-level information is compiled, that information can be incorporated into the model by fine-tuning the growth rate parameters. Alternatively, capacity constraints may be explicitly specified within the model.

Capture Growth Rates

Similarly, the representation of the dynamics of capture fisheries can be improved. In this study, the harvest of capture fisheries is treated as entirely exogenous, and their trends are determined using the aggregate statistics. Use of fishery-specific information about capacity and trends will likely improve the model predictions and expand the scope of analysis. While the state of world fisheries are periodically assessed and reported by the FAO, many fisheries, especially those in developing countries, are not currently assessed. However, tools are available to infer the state of unassessed fisheries. For example, Costello and others (2012) provide a regression-based predictive model of the state of unassessed fisheries. While efforts at the University of Washington aim at quantifying the variability in management systems around the world to evaluate which particular attributes lead to more successful outcomes for fish populations and fisheries (see, for example, Melnychuk, Banobi, and Hilborn 2013), recently developed Fishery Performance Indicators (FPI) can be used for rapid assessment of fisheries that are not formally assessed (Chu, Anderson, and Anderson 2012). Interacting the IMPACT model with an ecological simulation model may be an alternative way to characterize the dynamics of capture fisheries.

Trends in Consumption Demand

Consumption trend is another area where country- or region-specific parameters could be improved. In this study, the dynamics of demand for food by individual consumers is driven solely by growth in per capita income, and resulting per capita consumption demand is scaled up for each country or region by the total population, whose trend is exogenously given. All other changes in consumption in the model are purely price driven, which is regulated by price and income elasticities of demand that are fixed throughout the projection horizon. However, factors such as affluence and urbanization as well as concerns for health, environment, and other ethical and social values are considered to affect consumer preferences (FAO, 2012) and, hence, own and cross-price elasticities and income elasticities of demand. Where available, country- or region-specific updates in elasticity estimates could be incorporated to reflect observed trends and shifts in consumer preferences.

Linking with Ecosystem Model

As the FAO has pointed out in earlier discussions, there could have been greater detail brought to the analysis of capture fisheries if an ecosystems-based framework had been used to replace our simple treatment of the sector in the IMPACT model. In earlier conceptions of the "Fish to 2030" study, it was envisioned that the IMPACT model could be linked to a marine ecosystems model such as those within the Ecopath with Ecosim (EwE) family of models (Christiansen and Walters, 2004a, 2004b). The EcoOcean model (Alder et al., 2007), for example, is built on the EwE modeling platform and provides global-level projections of capture production potential across all of the FAO fishing regions. This model could potentially be linked to IMPACT. Since the EcoOcean model takes into account the quantity and value of marine fishery landings, the effort required, and the ability of the ecosystem to regenerate itself, it would have provided a much more dynamic feedback to the market-driven demand for capture species in IMPACT – especially since it relates to the demand for whole fish that are reduced for fishmeal for the aquaculture sector. Since it was designed to project ecosystem impacts of longer-term environmental change, such as climate change, it could have been used to extend the projections to a longer horizon (for example, to 2050).

Linking with an ecosystem model could allow them to address a much wider range of policy-relevant questions by combining questions of trade and agricultural policy with questions of environmental management and technology adoption in fisheries. There would be considerable value added, created by developing a robust link between a market-based, global food supply and demand model, such as IMPACT, and ecological process models for fisheries, such as EcoOcean. Such a link enables the study to a) examine more closely the effects of climate change-induced changes in aquatic ecosystems and ocean conditions, the resulting impact on the productivity of marine ecosystems, and how that affects global fish market dynamics; and b) gain a better sense of how global supply and demand for fish products would be impacted by the ecological collapse of certain fisheries due to various causes, including overfishing, climate change, or a combination of ecological factors. While "Fish to 2020" included such a scenario, it was not underpinned by this kind of detailed biophysical modeling.

Consumption and Trade Data

At the time of model preparation, production data from the FishStat database were available through 2009, whereas consumption and trade data from FAO FIPS FBS were available only up to 2007. Lack of more recent data for the consumption/trade side has posed a limitation in the calibration exercises for these series.

More importantly, the use of FAO FIPS FBS data determines the level of disaggregation of fish species, which limits the scope of analysis in this study. For example, the level of species aggregation dictated by the FAO FIPS FBS data precludes the analyses of most dynamic fish markets, such as for tilapia and Pangasius, mainly due to limitation of trade raw data availability for these species.

Furthermore, the FAO FIPS FBS data are geared toward understanding the supply consumption balances of food commodities; for that reason, trade is expressed in terms of "net export." However, fish is traded heavily and extensively both in the form of fish and processed seafood. Allowing the model to represent fish trade for processing purposes would require substantial changes to the code, and obtaining consistent series of trade and consumption for fish and seafood would require a more complicated data preparation. But it may be a possible direction to go in to improve the model representation.

Overall Data Quality

The FAO has tried, as much as possible, to maintain a close match between the model projections and the existing data for the calibration period. However, a complete congruence is not possible as the development of the fish part of IMPACT relies on three different datasets that are not mutually consistent. As a result, much time has been spent identifying the sources of discrepancy and reconciling them to re-construct a plausible and consistent picture of the global fish markets. For example, there are many cases in which positive fishmeal production is observed (based on IFFO data) in countries where there is no recorded "reduction" of whole fish (in FAO data), and the converse. To a lesser degree, discrepancies are also identified between the more detailed production data from the FAO's FishStat database and the more aggregated consumption and trade data from the FAO FIPS FBS database. It is desirable that these two important datasets are updated in tandem, so that they can be more readily used together. Unfortunately, at present, it is not technically possible, because data sets are updated sequentially starting with production series, then trade series, and then consumption series. Furthermore, as many countries do not report trade data that are as highly disaggregated by species as production data, trade and consumption series are necessarily more aggregated. The FAO has initiated an effort to encourage member countries to report disaggregated fish trade data.

Undoubtedly, this would be a desirable goal for anyone working on fish supply and demand studies, within the FAO and within the wider research community. Investment in consistent fisheries data seems especially sensible, given the parallel modeling work that the FAO undertakes in collaboration with the OECD (OECD-FAO, 2012). In many ways, their effort in this study to reconcile across the datasets is, by itself, a valuable contribution toward that goal and will hopefully form a basis for further work within the FAO and its partner organizations.

Conclusions

Organic fish farming is a new concept still in the early stages of development, that strives to re-establish a proper balance in aquaculture systems, for the benefit of the fish, the environment and the consumers. Organic fish farming systems and standards that define them are likely to witness considerable evolution and refinement over the years.

However, for the moment, three basic issues have to be conformed with for setting up standards. Nutrient cycling within closed systems, following the law of return, is a central organic principle. Also, the use of pesticides, dyes and antibiotics, which are conventionally used in aquaculture, are not to be permitted.

Water, which is both soil and air to the fish, is the critical issue, the quality of which plays an important role in the quality of the product. Standards must be established for the quality and purity of the incoming and outgoing water in terms of environmental impact.

The feed, consisting of fishmeal, fish oil, cereal-based products, vitamins and minerals etc. should be organically produced. It is not an easy task to bring down and remove the level of organo-chlorine pollutants in the marine fish that are used for conversion into fishmeal. National standards would have to be set up, which the farmers and exporters who seek eco-labeling will have to abide by.

Consumer and market studies confirm a growing demand for both organic food products and for fish and related food products coming from conventional aquaculture.

Despite the unresolved status of the certification and labeling of organic aquatic animals and plants in the U.S., the parallel successes of both the organic livestock and conventional aquaculture markets have encouraged producers involved in both sectors to explore niche markets for organic aquacultural products. There are documented trends in the growth of other organic livestock sectors, and in the sales of "natural," hormone-free, and antibiotic-free fish and shellfish. This increasing demand has started to drive producer and retail interest in aquacultural products that have a "certified organic" label. "Burgeoning consumer interest in organically grown foods has opened new market opportunities for producers and is leading to a transformation in the organic foods industry," summarizes a current U.S. Department of Agriculture (USDA) Economic Research Service (ERS) report. It further clarifies the organic market situation: "Once a niche product sold in a limited number of retail outlets, organic foods are currently sold in a wide variety of venues including farmer's markets, natural product supermarkets, conventional supermarkets, and club stores. Many U.S. manufacturers and distributors are specializing in processing and marketing organic products, while some longtime manufacturers of conventional products have introduced organic items to their product lines. As a result, an ever-widening array of organic agricultural and food products is now available" (Dimitri and Greene, 2002, p. 1). U.S. aquaculture is also a growing sector of the agricultural market, although experiencing considerable international competition. Recent ERS reports have supported this point. In the October 2003 USDA Aquaculture Outlook, author David Harvey observed that "although beset with questions about the production of aquatic species, aquaculture is expected to continue to grow as a source of fish, shellfish, and mollusks. The potential for aquaculture production to expand and compete with wild harvest seafood and other livestock products is readily evident in the continued growth in imported aquaculture products."

Additionally, in the subsequent Aquaculture Outlook, Harvey reported: "With a stronger domestic economy and higher prices for livestock and poultry products, domestic aquacultural production is expected to increase. Imports of foreign aquacultural products are also expected to expand, but at a slower rate than seen over the last several years."

Consumer demand for fish will also play a role in the future of aquaculture. ERS projections point not only to increased per capita consumption of fish in the U.S., but to growth in the number of older Americans, who traditionally eat more fish than younger people. "Fish and fruits are predicted to lead the increase in total consumption, with about 30-percent growth over the next two decades" (Biing-Hwan, 2003).

In a Food and Agriculture Organization (FAO) report from 2002, Brister and Tacon attempt to approximate the current international production for organic aquaculture.

"Although no official statistical data are available concerning the global production of certified organic aquaculture products, it is estimated that total production in 2000 was only about 5,000 metric tonnes, primarily from European countries." Later in the report, this estimate is used to chart potential future production: "Based on current estimates of certified organic aquaculture production and an anticipated compound annual growth rate of 30 percent from 2001 to 2010, 20 percent from 2011 to 2020, and 10 percent from 2021 to 2030, it is estimated that production will increase 240-fold from 5,000 tons in 2000 to 1.2 [million] tons by 2030. Such a production of certified aquatic products would be equivalent to 0.6 percent of the total estimated aquaculture production in 2030." This analysis parallels the outlook for organic and aquacultural production in the U.S. and may encourage U.S. producers to enter this market.

References

1. "Fish to 2030: Prospects for Fisheries and Aquaculture," report released by the World Bank, Food and Agriculture Organization of the United Nations (FAO). World Bank Report Number 83177-Glb, December 2013, Full-text online: http://www.fao.org/docrep/019/i3640e/i3640e.pdf.
2. The Future of Fish: Issues and Trends to 2020, by Christopher L. Delgado, Nikolas Wada, Mark W. Rosegrant, and Mahfuzuddin Ahmed. Washington, DC; Penang, Malaysia: International Food Policy Research Institute (IFPRI); WorldFish Center, 2003. Full-text online: http://www.ifpri.org/pubs/ib/ib15.pdf.
3. "Organic Aquaculture: Completing the First Decade," by S. Bergleiter. 7th IFOAM International Conference on Trade in Organic Products: 2003 Mainstreaming Organic Trade: New Frontiers, Opportunities and Responsibilities, 6–8 November, Bangkok, Thailand, 2003.
4. Full-textonline:http://www.greennetorganic.com/downloads/IFOAM%20speaker%20presentation%20-PDF/Presentation_Seminar%20E_Stefan%20Bergleiter.pdf.
5. Aquaculture News & Opinion, Cyber-Help for Organic Farmers, A Rural Capacity Building Through Organic Agriculture Project, by The Rural Capacity Building Through Organic Agriculture (RCBTOA) Project. Ongoing updates. Full-text online: http://www.certifiedorganic.bc.ca/rcbtoa/services/organic-aquaculture-newslinks.html.

6. Aquaculture Outlook, by David J. Harvey. Semi-Annual Publication. Full-text online: http://usda.mannlib.cornell.edu/reports/erssor/livestock/ldp-aqs/.
7. "Aquaculture Production Forecast to Grow, but Many Uncertainties Loom," by David J. Harvey. Aquaculture Outlook, LDP-AQS-18. Washington, DC: U.S. Department of Agriculture, Economic Research Service, 9 October 2003. Full-text online: http://usda.mannlib.cornell.edu/reports/erssor/livestock/ldp-aqs/2003/aqs18.pdf.
8. "Domestic Aquacultural Production Higher and Imports Up," by David J. Harvey. Aquaculture Outlook, LDP-AQS-19. Washington, DC: U.S. Department of Agriculture, Economic Research Service, 12 March 2004. Full-text online: http://usda.mannlib.cornell.edu/reports/erssor/livestock/ldp-aqs/2004/aqs19.pdf.
9. "Organic Aquaculture: Current Standards and Future Prospects: Chapter 6," by Albert G. J. Tacon and Deborah J. Brister. Organic Agriculture, Environment and Food Security, edited by Nadia El-Hage Scialbba and Caroline Hattam. Environment and Natural Resources Series, 4. Rome, Italy: Food and Agriculture Organization (FAO) of the United Nations, 2002. [NAL Call Number: QH540.E68 no. 4] Full-text online: http://www.fao.org/DOCREP/005/Y4137E/y4137e06.htm.
10. Outlook for Fish to 2020: Meeting Global Demand, by Christopher L. Delgado, Nikolas Wada, Mark W. Rosegrant, Seit Meijer, and Mahfuzuddin Ahmed. Food Policy Report. Washington, DC; Penang, Malaysia: International Food Policy Research Institute (IFPRI); WorldFish Center, October 2003. Online information/reviews: Additional materials related to this topic available at http://www.ifpri.org/media/fish20031002.htm, Full-text online: http://www.ifpri.org/pubs/fpr/pr15.pdf.
11. Recent Growth Patterns in the U.S. Organic Foods Market, by Carolyn Dimitri, Catherine Greene, and U.S. Department of Agriculture, Economic Research Service. Agriculture Information Bulletin, no. 777. Washington, DC: U.S. Department of Agriculture, Economic Research Service, September 2002. [NAL Call Number: 1 Ag84Ab no. 777] Full-text online: http://www.ers.usda.gov/publications/aib777/.
12. U.S. Organic Farming in 2000–2001: Adoption of Certified Systems, by Catherine Greene, Amy Kremen, and U.S. Department of Agriculture, Economic Research Service. Agriculture Information Bulletin, no. 780. Washington, DC: U.S. Department of Agriculture, Economic Research Service, April 2003. [NAL Call Number: 1 Ag84Ab no. 780] Full-text online: http://www.ers.usda.gov/publications/aib780/.

Mihaela KRUZSLICIKA

Institute of Agricultural Economics, Romanian Academy,
Calea 13 Septembrie, nr. 13, 050711 Bucureşti, România,
e-mail: mkruzslicika@gmail.com

Variability of Grain Production in Romania – A Regional Perspective

Abstract: The paper attempts to investigate the variation of factors determining the grain production variation across regions in Romania on a comparative basis with the main grain producing countries in the European Union.

Romania's total grain production largely depends on the weather conditions, resulting in a strong production instability nationwide, with variations from year to year, against the background of modifications of cultivated areas and average yields. Thus, the paper investigates the variation of these factors, i.e. areas and productivity, which are the main determinants of production stability.

Grains have a significant share in human and animal consumption, and under these conditions, the investigation of grain production stability is important, as a stable production can cover the domestic consumption needs, attenuating price volatility.

In order to attenuate the errors that can appear in the utilization of variation coefficient that can lead to an overestimation when we analyze the trend data series, the Cuddy-Della Valle instability index was used in the paper. Calculating the variability of average wheat and maize yields per hectare, across counties, we noticed that the counties with high yields also have the highest variations.

Keywords: agriculture, production, cereals, stability, Romania

Introduction

The paper aims to deepen the study of factors variation that determines the stability of cereal production across counties in Romania; in order to reach this goal, data series for eleven years (2005–2015) were used on the evolution of areas and cereal productions in Romania, at regional level. Comparisons at country level with certain grain producing countries from the European Union were made: countries with low volatility (France, Germany etc); countries with economic policies similar to Romania's (Poland). For the analysis of instability, we used the Cuddy-Della Valle instability index (Cuddy and Della Valle, 1978; Della Valle, 1979), which expresses variability in the time series with trend.

As this uses the R^2 determination coefficient, which has the role of removing the trend influence from the time series, it is expressed in percentages and varies by the instability intervals as follows: low instability between 0–15, medium instability between 15–30 and high instability, higher than 30. The index represents a modification of the variation coefficient application, when the time series show a trend, which is a frequently met situation.

$$I_x = CV(x)\sqrt{(1-R^2)}$$

Where: R^2 is the determination coefficient.
CV(x) is the variation coefficient.

The Cuddy-Della Valle instability index was calculated for the production of cereals (wheat and maize) at county level and the results were filtered for the extraction of the county with the highest and lowest production volatility. The production and productivity were correlated with each of the above factors, establishing the relevance for each of them. The data were taken from the National Institute of Statistics and from the Ministry of Agriculture and Rural Development. For the international comparisons and those linked to the production value we used EUROSTAT data. International databases were also consulted, coming from the United States Department of Agriculture, Foreign Agricultural Service, Office of Global Analysis, the Directorate General for Agriculture and Rural Development of the European Commission (DG AGRI), FAO as well as many other sites; the Romanian and European Commission legislation was analyzed.

1. Literature review

In the specialty literature, the factors that determine production stability are investigated; the cultivated areas and productivity are analyzed as main determinants of production stability, as well as the natural factors (rain, wind, soil, and weather), structural factors such as farm structure, structure of agricultural production, technological and economic factors: inputs as prices and infrastructure. External factors, such as agricultural policy or policies in general or the demographic factors also influence production stability.

In "The National Strategic Framework for the Sustainable Development of the Agri-Food Sector and of the Rural Space in the period 2014 – 2020 – 2030," evaluating the present situation of agriculture and of the Romanian rural area, the authors state that the instability of the agricultural production is generated mainly by the extreme weather conditions, combined with the non-performing production technologies. These elements, together with the wrong working of the agri-food chains, are leading to imports, mainly of milk, vegetables and fruits, for covering the population's consumption. Among the causes we can mention also the low inputs' consumption, an example being the fertilizers, which in Romania represent 41.17% of the European average, of 119 €/ha (Romania's Presidency, The Presidential Commission for Public Policies for Agriculture Development, 2013).

In volume I of the "Development Strategy of Romania in the next 20 years", the authors consider that "the agricultural production – through its quantity, quality, but also stability – influences the welfare of a country. Within this strategy, in order to increase Romania's agriculture role as food security supplier, the following target indicators were established: diminution of production variability in cereals, vegetables and fruit production, of agricultural production variability implicitly." Having in view the reference values, it is estimated that, in the short term, a slight improvement of the present situation will take place, for the period of 2010–2014, the cereal production variation is calculated at 21%, but in the medium and long term, the instability of agricultural production, with regard to the stability of the agricultural supply through the variation coefficient, will be significantly lowered as a result of the measures that will be implemented, getting close to or reaching the value of the variation coefficients of agricultural production in France. At the horizon of the year 2023, the variation of cereal production in Romania will reach 8%, close to that of France. In the French agriculture, the variation coefficient for cereals was 6.88% for the period of 2007–2011(Vlad, Ionel-Valentin, 2015).

As regards the effect of weather factors, in the PhD thesis "Researches on the improvement of environment quality by landscape management and irrigation works," A. Chiper stated that agricultural production is affected by extreme weather conditions, thermic shock affecting the crops, mainly in the growing period, but also by the genetic features of the crop plants, with tolerance to cold, drought or floods (Chiper, Alexandru-Marian, 2012).

In the agronomical literature from our country, reference is most often made to the wheat and maize varieties – intensive type, high-yielding varieties, early and productive varieties, with very good yield stability, tolerant to unfavorable weather and soil conditions, having good milling and baking qualities, and their importance in the selection for production stability; the biological diversity can increase the stability and total production of any ecosystem, hence it is an important and necessary pre-condition for the sustainable agriculture development. The natural ecosystem must be protected for biodiversity preservation.

2. The analysis of cereal production instability across counties on the basis of the Cuddy-Della Valle method

For the long-term data series with trends, the variation coefficient can lead to instability overestimation, as this can indicate high instability at time series that have a constant trend but do not vary very much from one calculation interval to the other. That is why it becomes necessary to use the Cuddy-Della Valle instability index for the purpose of our analysis, as this uses the R^2 determination coefficient, which has the role of removing the trend influence from the time series. Out of these considerations, we shall next present the results after the calculation of the instability degree through the Cuddy-Della Valle method.

Fig. 1: Distribution of the Cuddy-Della Valle index for the average production, at national level

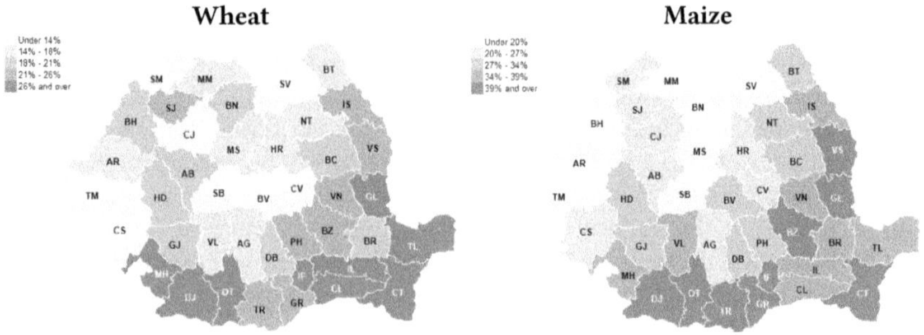

Source: Processing and calculations based on tempo-online data, National Institute of Statistics, Bucharest 2016.

Fig. 2: Distribution of the Cuddy-Della Valle index for the total production, at national level

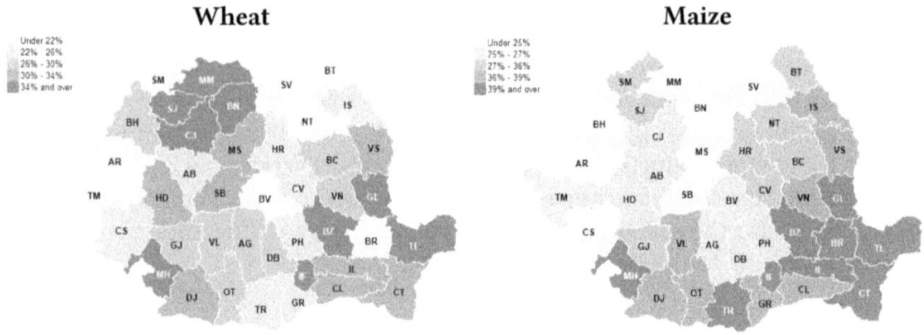

Source: Processing and calculations based on tempo-online data, National Institute of Statistics, Bucharest 2016.

The highest instability of cereal yields can be found in the counties Tulcea (36.9%), Buzău (36.2%) and Galaţi (35.5%), while at national level the index value is 22.9%. For the wheat crop, the county where the yields have the highest instability is Tulcea, with the instability index 38.4%, followed by the counties Călăraşi (32%) and Galaţi (30.9%). The counties with the highest instability of maize yields are Buzău (49.4%), Constanţa (45.1%) and Galaţi (41.6%).

At the opposite pole we can find the counties with the lowest instability of cereal yields: 13.1% for Harghita and Suceava, Covasna with 13.7%, followed by Timiş, with 14.2%. For the wheat yields, County Suceava is in first place with 9.7%, followed by Caraş-Severin with 10.7% and Braşov with 13.9%. In maize, the first place is held by County Mureş with 15.9%, followed by Bistriţa-Năsăud with 16.5% and Maramureş with 16.9%.

As regards the areas, the county with the highest stability of cereal production is Dâmboviţa (3.1%), followed by Gorj (3.6%) and Suceava (4%); County Iaşi also has quite a similar value (4.1%). The most stable wheat productions are found in the counties Ialomiţa (7.1%), Timiş (7.9%) and Giurgiu (8.1%), and the most stable maize productions are in Iaşi (4.2%), Gorj (4.4%), Sibiu (4.9%) and Galaţi (5.3%). The most unstable areas cultivated with cereals are in the counties Ilfov (23.8%), Cluj (20.6%) and Vaslui (18%), while the nationwide value is 4.3%. For the areas cultivated with wheat, the highest instability can be found in the county Cluj (41.4%), followed by Bistriţa-Năsăud with 37.7% and Sălaj with 36.6%. The counties with the greatest instability of the areas cultivated with maize are Ilfov (33.9%), Constanţa (25.2%) and Covasna (21.1%). County Brasov is a relevant example as regards the total wheat production, which is relatively low (the last eleven-year average is 46,088 tons) yet with high stability, this county ranking first in the 41 counties from Romania, with the most stable wheat production and second with the most stable yields. We also bring into discussion the example of County Cluj, which is at the opposite pole, with the highest instability as regards the areas cultivated with wheat and also production (42,723 tons is the last eleven-year average).

3. Comparisons with the main cereal producers in the European Union

Compared to the main cereal producers in Europe, we can notice high variations in the cereal productions, which are mainly caused by the low yields in the main crops. We included in the study countries like Germany, France and Italy, as the first three great producers of cereals in Europe, as well as Poland, due to the comparable size and socio-political evolution, which is relatively similar to that of Romania. For all the data categories used in the present study we used both the variation coefficient and the Cuddy-Della Valle instability index to highlight the differences between the two values, when the time series feature trends.

From table 1 we can notice that Italy has the lowest variation of cereal production, with the variation coefficient 7.8%, and the Cuddy-Della Valle index 7.2%, while Romania has the highest variation coefficient with 24.4% and a Cuddy-Della Valle index of 22.7%. France and Poland have relatively low variation coefficients, 8.3% and 9.3%, respectively.

Table 1: Production of cereals in the main producing countries in EU-28, thousand tons

	Germany	France	Italy	Poland	Romania
2006	43,475	61,613	18,787	21,776	15,741
2007	40,632	59,382	18,812	27,143	7,787
2008	50,105	70,142	20,459	27,664	16,778
2009	49,748	69,862	15,892	29,827	14,801

	Germany	France	Italy	Poland	Romania
2010	44,039	65,444	17,036	27,512	16,651
2011	41,921	63,695	17,955	26,767	20,777
2012	45,396	68,335	17,169	28,544	12,773
2013	47,757	67,242	16,872	29,702	20,842
2014	52,011	72,632	18,047	31,945	22,026
2015	48,867	72,085	16,148	28,003	18,623
2016	45,496	55,325	16,426	30,241	18,571
Variation coefficient	7.9%	8.3%	7.8%	9.3%	24.4%
CDV index	**7.8%**	**8.3%**	**7.2%**	**8.2%**	**22.7%**

Source: Processing of data from DG AGRI 2016.

From the analysis of the data from table 2, we can see that the areas cultivated with cereals have varied very slightly, being around 5,278 thousand hectares. The variation coefficient is 2.9%, with the Cuddy-Della Valle index 2.2%, among the lowest in Europe.

France has a variation coefficient quite close to that of Romania (2.3%), and a Cuddy-Della Valle index of 2.1%; higher variations of the areas cultivated with cereals were found in Italy (7.1%) with a CDV index of 6%.

Table 2: Variation of the areas cultivated with cereals, thousand hectares

	Germany	France	Italy	Poland	Romania
2006	6,702	9,031	3,575	8,381	5,109
2007	6,572	9,072	3,701	8,353	5,121
2008	7,038	9,646	3,814	8,599	5,201
2009	6,909	9,357	3,215	8,583	5,270
2010	6,595	9,219	3,225	7,638	5,028
2011	6,501	9,178	3,173	7,803	5,212
2012	6,527	9,371	3,361	7,704	5,430
2013	6,534	9,453	3,306	7,480	5,410
2014	6,469	9,575	3,207	7,485	5,431
2015	6,526	9,519	3,082	7,512	5,452
2016	6,355	9,592	3,194	7,785	5,397
Variation coefficient	3.0%	2.3%	7.1%	5.6%	2.9%
CDV index	**2.7%**	**2.1%**	**6.0%**	**4.4%**	**2.2%**

Source: Processing of data from DG AGRI 2016.

We can conclude that the variation of the areas cultivated with cereals does not explain to a great extent such a high variation of the cereal production.

We can see that the grain cereal yields in Romania are well below those obtained in the great cereal producing countries of Europe (table 3). Thus, the average yield in Romania of 3.18 tons per hectare is only 45% of the yields obtained in Germany (7.01 t/ha) and France (7.04 t/ha), but comparable to that of Poland (3.56 t/ha).

However, from the point of view of the instability in obtaining such yields, Romania is in last place among the investigated countries. Thus, while Germany ranks second as regards the stability of yields per hectare, with a CDV index of 6.8%, after Italy, which has an average yield of 5.26 t/ha in the investigated period of 2006–2016 and a CDV index of 4.3% (the smallest), Romania has the largest value of yield instability in all the analyzed countries (22.6%). By comparison, Poland, although its grains cereal yields quite similar to that of Romania, 3.56 tons per hectare, has an instability index significantly lower than Romania (8.6%).

Table 3: Average grain cereal yields per hectare, t/ha

	Germany	**France**	**Italy**	**Poland**	**Romania**
2006	6.49	6.82	5.26	2.60	3.08
2007	6.18	6.55	5.08	3.25	1.52
2008	7.12	7.27	5.36	3.22	3.23
2009	7.20	7.47	4.94	3.48	2.81
2010	6.68	7.10	5.28	3.60	3.31
2011	6.45	6.94	5.66	3.43	3.99
2012	6.95	7.29	5.11	3.70	2.35
2013	7.31	7.11	5.10	3.97	3.85
2014	8.04	7.59	5.63	4.27	4.06
2015	7.49	7.57	5.24	3.73	3.42
2016	7.16	5.77	5.14	3.88	3.44
Variation coefficient	7.6%	7.5%	4.3%	12.5%	23.5%
CDV index	**6.8%**	**7.5%**	**4.3%**	**8.6%**	**22.6%**

Source: Processing of data from DG AGRI 2016.

In order to quantify the influence of these years, with extremely low yields, we made a simulation, by considering the yields of these years being within the limit of the yearly average of 3.46 tons per hectare. The results obtained are important, as they isolate all the other elements that could influence the yields, such as: technical endowment with regard to agricultural equipment, and fertilization and pest control treatments; thus, only the weather dependency elements and the irrigation systems implicitly remain under discussion, assuming the hypothesis that the technical endowment, the fertilization and pest control treatments are within the annual average.

Thus, eliminating the absolute values of the yields from the years 2007 and 2012, we obtained, for the nine-year instead of an eleven-year interval, an average grain cereal yield of 3.46 tons per hectare, very close to that of Poland, of 3.56 t/ha. By replacing the obtained values of yields in the years 2007 (1.52 t/ha) and 2012 (2.35 t/ha) by the new calculated average of 3.46 t/ha, we obtain a CDV index of 10.6%, which reveals in this case a low instability of yields, its value being under 15% as medium instability threshold (table 4).

Table 4: Simulation for cereal yields per hectare, tons/ha

	Germany	**France**	**Italy**	**Poland**	**Romania**
2006	6.49	6.82	5.26	2.60	3.08
2007	6.18	6.55	5.08	3.25	**3.46**
2008	7.12	7.27	5.36	3.22	3.23
2009	7.20	7.47	4.94	3.48	2.81
2010	6.68	7.10	5.28	3.60	3.31
2011	6.45	6.94	5.66	3.43	3.99
2012	6.95	7.29	5.11	3.70	**3.46**
2013	7.31	7.11	5.10	3.97	3.85
2014	8.04	7.59	5.63	4.27	4.06
2015	7.49	7.57	5.24	3.73	3.42
2016	7.16	5.77	5.14	3.88	3.44
Variation coefficient	7.6%	7.5%	4.3%	12.5%	10.9%
CDV index	**6.8%**	**7.5%**	**4.3%**	**8.6%**	**10.6%**

Source: Processing of data from DG AGRI 2016.

Extrapolating the methodology used to the data series corresponding to the common wheat production and maize, we obtain the following results:

As regards the common wheat, we can notice that the utilized areas have low variation coefficient (3.4%). Countries with a lower variation coefficient than that of Romania are France with 2.6% and Germany with 2.9%, while Poland had a variation coefficient of 4.9% and Italy 8.9%.

As regards wheat production, the lowest instabilities are found in Germany, where the CDV index is 8.2% and the average production in the investigated period was 22,229 thousand tons, France with a CDV index of 9.8% and an average production of 36,078 thousand tons, and Italy, where the CDV index is 9.5% with the average production 3,162 thousand tons in common wheat. Poland has an average value of wheat production of 9,480 thousand tons, with a CDV index of 10.5%, while Romania has an average production of 6,386 thousand tons of wheat and the highest instability index (20.5%).

Analyzing the yields, we can see major discrepancies between Romania and the other countries, the national average yield being around 3.1 t/ha, much lower than that of Germany (7.24 t/ha), which is 2.34 times higher, and of France (7.08 t/ha, 2.29 times higher). Italy has an average yield of 5.34 t/ha, 1.73 times higher, and Poland has higher yields than Romania by 37%, up to the average value of 4.23 t/ha.

While the measures to reduce the impact of extreme weather effects upon the agricultural production, mainly in the case of drought, should represent a priority, we must not forget some other active measures as well, to determine an increase of yields to meet the European average.

In the case of maize, besides the already analyzed countries, we also took into consideration Hungary, this being one of the main European producers of maize grain, ranking fourth in Europe, with an average production of 7,253 thousand tons, next to France with 14,936 thousand tons, Romania with 8,597 thousand tons, and Italy with 8,574 thousand tons in the period of 2006–2016.

In the case of Romania, the areas cultivated with maize have varied very little in the investigated period, the variation coefficient being 6.6%, equal to the CDV index, the average cultivated area with maize being 2,497 thousand hectares. Only Hungary had a lower variation coefficient than our country (5.1%), while the great producers had higher CDV indices, e.g., France (7.3%) and Italy (8.2%). Poland had the highest instability index of the areas cultivated with maize (22.1%).

As regards the grain maize production, the most constant production, in time, was that of France and Italy, with a CDV index of 11.1%, while Romania, Hungary and Poland had the highest production variations. The instability indices had the following values: Romania 28.5%, Hungary 23.1% and Poland 27.1%. However, we should mention that Poland had such significant variations in maize production because it had a higher increase of the areas cultivated with grain maize, with an average yield of 6.17 t/ha and a CDV index of 16.8%.

Conclusions

The production instability in the two investigated products is much higher in Romania than at European level. This derives from the high instability of one of the investigated determinant factors, namely the average yields per hectare. The main causes of these significant variations that have had a negative effect on the stability of cereal production are the high dependency on weather conditions, as well as inadequate measures for the attenuation of these effects: lack of rainfall, drought, floods, but also the non-performant agricultural technologies, absence of irrigations, etc.

In Romania, the region with the highest cereal production is South-East; the highest production variability can be also noticed in this region. The most stable region is North-West with a medium variability level, while the most unstable region is South-East with a high variability level. At national level, the counties that are the greatest wheat and maize producers are the most exposed to high variations of yields.

The cereal yields, mainly in wheat and maize, are very low, compared to those of the great cereal producing countries in the European Union, and measures should be developed to narrow the yield gaps between Romania and the other countries. Nevertheless, one measure has the highest priority in comparison with other measures (increase of agricultural machinery fleet, performant equipment, fertilization and pest control treatments): this refers to the development of the irrigation system, mainly in the counties most exposed to extreme weather conditions with adverse effects for agriculture, as this has a determinant role in instability diminution. From our simulation, one can notice that the high agriculture dependency on weather conditions plays a most significant role in cereal production instability in our country.

References

1. Godfray, H.C., Beddington, J.R., Crute, I. R., Haddad, L., Lawrence, D., Muir, J. F., JPretty, J., Robinson, S., Thomas, S. M., Toulmin, S. 2010, Food Security: The Challenge of Feeding 9 Billion People. Science 12 Feb 2010: Vol. 327. Issue 5967. pp. 812–818 DOI:10.1126/science.1185383.
2. Chiper, A. M., 2012, Cercetări privind îmbunătăţirea calităţii mediului prin lucrări de amenajare peisageră şi de irigaţii. Teza de Doctorat Conducător de doctorat: Prof. Univ. Dr. Cîmpeanu Sorin-Mihai. Universitatea de Ştiinţe Agronomice şi Medicină Veterinară din Bucureşti. Facultatea de Îmbunătăţiri Funciare şi Ingineria Mediului.
3. Cuddy., J. D. A. and Della Valle, P. A., 1978, Measuring the Instability of Time Series Data. Oxford Bulletin of Economics and Statistics. 40: pp. 79–85. doi: 10.1111/j.1468-0084.1978.mp40001006.x.
4. Gerald G. Marten, 1987, Productivity. Stability. Sustainability. Equitability and Autonomy as Properties for Agroecosystem Assessment. Agricultural Systems 26 (1988) pp. 291–316.
5. Popa, G. M., 2015, Cercetări privind îmbunătăţirea tehnologiei culturii grâului în câmpia Găvanu-Burdea, în contextul schimbărilor climatice. Teza de doctorat. Universitatea de Ştiinţe Agronomice şi Medicină Veterinară din Bucureşti.
6. Voica, Maria, 2009, Genetica şi ameliorarea plantelor stabilitatea producţiei soiurilor noi de grâu şi triticale de toamnă la S.C.D.A. Piteşti-Albota. I.N.C.D.A. FUNDULEA. vol. LXXVII.
7. Vlad., I.-V. (coord.; 2015), Strategia de dezvoltare a Romaniei in urmatorii 20 ani. Hera Cristian, Otiman Paun Ion (coordonatori). Proiectul 5. Securitate si siguranta alimentara. Volumul I. Editura Academiei Romane. ISBN 978-973-27-2555-9. vol. 1–2015 ISBN 978-973-27-2556-6.
8. Vlad., I.-V. (coord.; 2016), Strategia de dezvoltare a Romaniei in urmatorii 20 ani. Hera Cristian (coordonator). Otiman Paun Ion (responsabil proiect) Proiectul 5.

Securitate si siguranta alimentara. Volumul II. Editura Academiei Romane. ISBN 978-973-27-2555-9. vol. 2–2016 ISBN 978-973-27-2615-0.
9. Vlad., I.-V. (coord.; 2016), Strategia de dezvoltare a Romaniei in urmatorii 20 ani. Hera Cristian (coordonator). Otiman Paun Ion (responsabil proiect) Proiectul 5. Securitate si siguranta alimentara.Volumul III. partea I. Editura Academiei Romane. ISBN 978-973-27-2555-9. vol. 3–2016 ISBN 978-973-27-2706-5.
10. ***United States Department of Agriculture. Foreign Agricultural Service. Office of Global Analysis. October 2016. http://apps.fas.usda.gov/psdonline/circulars/grain.pdf.
11. ***Directorate-General for Agriculture and Rural Development – Short Term Outlook – N° 16 http://ec.europa.eu/agriculture/markets-and-prices/short-term-outlook/index_en.htm.
12. ***Comisia prezidenţială pentru politici publice de dezvoltare a agriculturii (2013). Cadrul naţional strategic pentru dezvoltarea durabilă a sectorului agroalimentar şi a spaţiului rural în perioada 2014–2020–2030. Academia Română şi Academia de Ştiinţe Agricole şi Silvice "Gheorghe Ionescu Şişeşti". http://www.acad.ro/forumuri/doc2013/d0701-02StrategieCadrulNationalRural.pdf.
13. ***Programul Naţional de Dezvoltare Rurală 2014–2020. Ministerul Agriculturii şi Dezvoltării Rurale. versiunea a 4-a. octombrie 2016. http://www.madr.ro/docs/dezvoltare-rurala/2016/PNDR-2014-2020-versiunea-aprobata-25-octombrie-2016.pdf.
14. ***FAO, IFAD and WFP, 2014, The State of Food Insecurity in the World 2014. Strengthening the enabling environment for food security and nutrition. Rome. FAO. http://www.fao.org/3/2ae5ab78-c75c-4203-a727-98a15056a3a1/i4030e.pdf.
15. ***INSSE Tempo online. INS. Bucureşti.
16. ***Eurostat database.

Mariana GRODEA

Institute of Agricultural Economics, Bucharest, Romania,
email: marianagrodea@yahoo.com

Beef Availability in Romania – A Long-Term Analysis from a Self-Sufficiency Perspective

Abstract: From the perspective of reaching food security, for Romania, beef meat (accounting for 10% of the total meat consumption structure, in the year 2015) is important both for dietary diversity and for the complex contribution to the valorization of the country's agricultural resources, through the export of live animals inclusively. With a decrease by 45% of (live weight) beef production, in the period of 2007–2014, the Romanian beef sector cannot capitalize on the opportunities provided by the European Single Market. Having in view that self-sufficiency in beef was down from 96% in 2007 to 82% in 2014, and to 79% in 2015, the purpose of the paper is to identify new opportunities for relaunching meat production, through investments, in the long term. The analisys is based on the assessment of financial necessities on the three horizons, short-term (2025), medium- (2038) and long-term (2038), both for measures implemented from the National Rural Development Planfor 2007–2013 period and for the measures financed from the Ministry of Agriculture and Rural Development budget.

Keywords: Self-sufficiency in beef, investments, production

Introduction

Having in view the 79.6% self-sufficiency in beef in the year 2015, which implies a chronic deficit in the consumption of this product, this paper aims to identify new opportunities for relaunching the Romanian consumption in order to reach a self-sufficiency level of 89.6% at the 2038 horizon, from the perspective of cattle raising sector stabilization, in the context of the European market stabilization.

The alternative to raise cattle for beef in Romania is considered by experts (Neață, 2015) as an immediate income source for producers who cannot obtain milk according to high quality standards, mainly in the context of the removal of the milk quota starting 1 April 2015. That is why the spirit of entrepreneurship must be stimulated, mainly in the young rural people.

Even though the beef and "baby beef" is not a traditional product in the Romanian consumers' diet (only 10% of the total meat consumed is represented by this meat type), the fact that about 35% of the cattle herds in Romania are of Simmental type – very suitable for beef production – the beef sector seems to have good prospects, as beef has a great growth potential compared to the other meat assortments; yet consumption will grow only gradually, with the increase of people's incomes and level of education on nutrition (Șerbănescu, 2014).

1. Literature review

According to the Food and Agricultural Organization (FAO, 2012), about 870 million people suffer from the lack of basic foodstuffs (out of which 81% are living in southern Asia, Sub-Saharan Africa and eastern Asia), in spite of the fact that sufficient potential exists to feed the entire world population from the world agricultural production. That is why the redistribution of foodstuffs across different continents represents one of the main problems of today's society.

At the same time, about two thirds of the meat animals throughout the world depend on cereals and soybeans (FAO, 2006). This demand for animal feeding means that people compete against farm animals for food. On the other hand, the increase in food prices in recent years has been determined by the economic growth in the long term, in several developing countries, which (a) has put increasing pressure on crude oil and fertilizer prices, due to the intensive nature of their economic growth resources and (b) led to an increase in meat demand, and hence in the demand for animal feed (FAO, 2011).

In this context, food self-sufficiency as part of food security should be understood as the capacity of a country to cover its population's consumption needs from domestic production, avoiding as much as possible imports from other countries (Minot and Pelijor, 2010).

Another author (Kazuo, 2008) analyzes food security from the agricultural potential perspective, i.e. the number of persons that can be fed from one hectare of agricultural land. Thus, according to this author, Australia can feed 0.1 people, USA – 0.8 people, France – 2.9 people, Germany – 4.5 people, Japan – 10.5 people. He also advocates that the diversity of the agricultural potential was the result of different support levels to farmers, in the form of subsidies. Thus, while in Europe, about 50% of the agricultural income comes from direct payments, in other countries such as Japan, this share is around 20%.

Other authors (Beun and Sheppard, 1980) consider that the calculation modality of self-sufficiency in meat must take into consideration the fact that a part of the meat quantity obtained from domestic production is based on imported feed, and hence the self-sufficiency level must be adjusted by a feed-meat conversion ratio.

A comparison with certain European countries with regard to self-sufficiency in beef reveals different situations. Thus, in the year 2013, while in Poland, the self-sufficiency significantly increased to 416% (from 125% in 2003), in other countries such as the Czech Republic, Hungary and Slovakia, self-sufficiency ranges from 106% to 130% (Slaboch and Kotyza, 2016). According to the two authors, Poland's situation is a result of the significant decrease of beef consumption, from 7 kg/capita in 2003 to 1.6 kg/capita in 2013 (– 77%), against the background of the massive rise of exports and of non-attractive prices on the domestic market, corroborated with a weak domestic supply in quality terms.

2. Methodology

Short-term (2025), medium-term (2028) and long-term (2035) targets for the production of meat were established, on the basis of an analysis model (of food balance sheets) used by the National Institute of Statistics, in conformity with the FAO and Eurostat methodologies; the main indicator, for which levels corresponding to the three time horizons were proposed, was the utilizable production, from which we can obtain the available supply (by adding imports and deducting imports). The ratio of utilizable production to available supply, expressed in percentage terms, represents the self-supply level (indicator that expresses the self-sufficiency rate for the respective product).

The method used for the development of scenarios on self-sufficiency increase was based on statistical calculations of the yearly average increase rate, rate of increase and the dynamics index of utilizable beef production, beef imports and exports. These were correlated with the trends of the period of 1990–2015, calculated on the basis of information from the "Food Balance Sheets" and "Population's Consumption Availabilities" from the National Institute of Statistics. At the same time, FAO long-term forecasts on the evolution of production, demand, import and export were taken into consideration (World Agriculture Towards 2030/2050) and of population (EUROSTAT), 2024 Prospects for EU agricultural markets.

The financial needs for the beef cattle sector, for the three time horizons, were estimated through the analysis of the way in which the NRDP 2007–2013 measures were developed, as well as the evaluation of the impact of future measures funded under NRDP 2014–2020.

3. Data and estimation results

From Romania's food security perspective, beef (accounting for 10% in the structure of total meat consumption, in the year 2015) is an important product, both for dietary diversification and for the complex contribution to the valorization of the country's agricultural resources, through the export of live animals inclusively.

The comparison of beef consumptions of the different European countries reveals quite significant differences across countries. Thus, Italy ranks first, with 25.4 kg/capita/year, being one of the European countries with the greatest number of cattle farms, and with the largest exports of beef in the region. The consumption of this country is 15 times higher than that of Poland (1.6 kg/capita/year) and about 4 times higher than that of Romania (6.3 kg/capita/year).

The production of beef from cattle slaughtered in slaughtering units (carcass meat), in EU-28, in the year 2014, was 7.3 million tons, the main producers being France (19%), Germany (15%), the United Kingdom (12%) and Italy (10%), all these making up 56% of total beef production of EU-28 (EUROSTAT, 2015). Romania ranks 20th on this list, with a beef production in carcass meat of 29.2 thousand tons. The poor quality of carcasses from Romania is given by the fact that 77.9% come from slaughtering adult animals, out of which 49.5% cows, as against the EU average of

30%. Other negative aspects in Romania, as compared to the European Union, refer to the following:

- the share of calves under eight months old that are slaughtered in slaughtering units is 18–20%, compared to 5% in the European Union;
- the slaughtering weight of calves under eight months old is extremely low, only 45 kg/head, compared to 137 kg/head in the European Union;
- Romania massively exports calves of 120–150 kg live weight, mainly to Italy and Croatia, instead of fattening them up until they reach 650 kg, to be exported afterwards.

In this context, the analysis of self-sufficiency in beef in the period of 1990–2015 reveals that this had an oscillating evolution throughout the investigated period (figure 1), with the lowest value in the year 2006 (75%), and the highest in 1993 (106%).

Fig. 1: Evolution of self-sufficiency in beef, 1990–2015 (%)

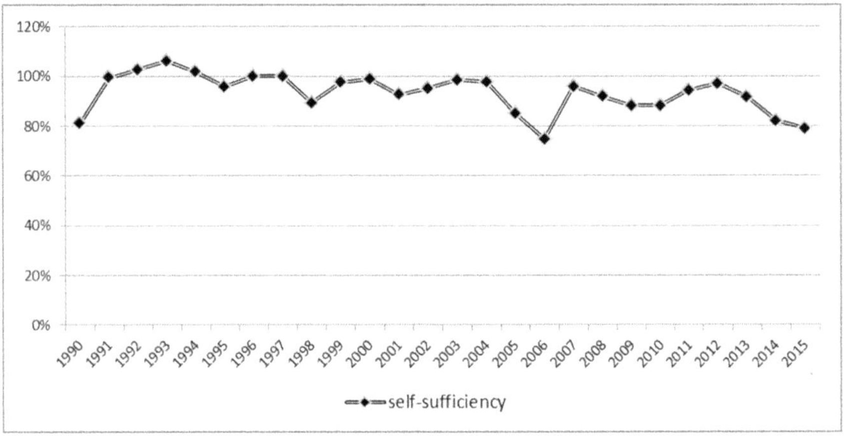

Source: Calculations based on Food Balance Sheets 1990–2015 – National Institute of Statistics.

The situation for the year 2006 can be explained by the fact that in that year, prior to its accession to the European Union, Romania had the highest level of imports from the period of 1990–2013 (53.9 thousand tons). This is because the average import price of frozen meat was down from €1.68/kg in 2005 to €1.47/kg in 2006 (−12%), with 98.9% of imports coming from non-EU countries (Brazil). In the year 1993, the quantitative exports, mainly of live cattle, had the highest volume from the period of 1990–2013 (19,000 tons), as a result of the geographic reorientation of trade flows to the developed countries of the European Union.

3.1. Targets proposed for beef in the short (2025), medium (2028) and long (2035) terms

Considering a desirable improvement of self-sufficiency in beef to 89.6% towards 2035, table 1 presents the short-, medium- and long-term targets (for production, imports and exports). In estimating these targets, we took into consideration the national evolutions (1990–2015) and the European (EC, 2016) and world (OECD/FAO, 2015) forecasts for the period of 2015–2026. Thus, the European institutions expect an increasing world demand for beef, due to the evolutions in the developing countries, which favors the increase of EU exports. In the medium term, at European Union (EU) level, it is estimated that beef production will resume its downward trend, with the production in 2026 slightly under the production obtained in 2014.

Thus, the resulted indicators, as presented in table 1, reflect the increase of utilizable production in the period of 2015–2035 by 23,100 tons (23.4%), of exports by 4,000 tons (46.9%), while imports will decrease by 7.300 tons (–21.5%).

Table 1: Target indicators for beef (in fresh meat equivalent)

	u.m.	Baseline situation (2015)	Short term (2025)	Medium term (2028)	Long term (2035)
Utilizable production	thou. tons	99.0	101.0	111.1	122.1
Import	thou. tons	33.9	31.8	29.3	26.6
Export	thou. tons	8.5	6.7	8.9	12.5
Supply availability	thou. tons	124.4	126.2	131.5	136.3
Self-supply level	percentage	79.2	80.1	84.5	89.6

Source: Own calculations.

These estimated targets were based on two hypotheses, which mainly refer to the support to the cattle raising sector under the MARD programs, i.e. the *de minimis* aid for purchasing heifers from specialized beef breeds (measure launched in 2014), transitory national aids, coupled support schemes in the beef sector (2015–2020), which add to the support under the NRDP 2014–2020 measures for the improvement of the general performance of agricultural holdings (investments on agricultural holdings), improvement of small-sized farm management and market orientation increase (support to the development of small farms), and increase of the number of young farmers who start an agricultural activity for the first time as heads of holdings (support to setting up of young farmers).

The assessment of indicators (production, import, export) on the three horizons had at basis statistical calculations, regarding the yearly average increase rate of the usable production, import and export of beef on short time intervals.

The result of beef production increase will be reflected in the increase of yearly average consumption per capita from 6.3 kg in 2015 to 6.9 kg in 2028 and to 7.3 kg in 2035, against the background of improving the meat quality produced on specialized farms.

3.2. Funding sources in short term (2025), medium term (2028) and long term (2035)

Starting from the present situation, i.e. a level of supply from domestic beef production of 79.2% (2015), the estimates of the necessary investments for reaching the proposed targets were based on the following hypotheses, supporting the long-term development of the cattle raising sector:

- Continuation of financial support from EU and national funds
- Continuation of the cattle farm consolidation process
- Speeding up the investment rate in performant technologies, new machinery and equipment, modernization of farm buildings and the genetics of animals (the investments target the increase of the share of commercial farms for young cattle fattening (with more than 36 animal heads) from 13% in 2014 to 25% in 2025, to 50% in 2028 and to 80% in 2035).

The investments in performant technological systems for beef cattle raising (feeding and maintenance) can be supported under NRDP 2014–2020, with an estimated amount of €85 million from public funds for investments in the period of 2016–2025; this amount should be increased in the period of 2026–2028 (€131 million) and in 2029–2035 (€235 million). Part of these amounts could also be covered by the payments to farmers from areas with natural constraints, mainly cattle raisers from the mountain areas.

Conclusions

The proposed targets can be reached if:

- Productivity per animal increases (large weight gains, feed consumption diminution, improvement of carcass quality and composition, higher slaughter yields)
- This is feasible through investments in the genetics of animals, namely the utilization of specialized cattle breeds for beef production in the crossing with local breeds
- Thus hybrids can be obtained adapted to our country's conditions with great weight gain, with high quality carcasses and a very good conversion of fodders obtained on pastures and meadows
- The economic farm size increases (standard output value), having in view that, at present, 82% of the cattle farms have an economic size under €8,000, out of which 33% are in the category €2,000–3,999, which makes them non-eligible for access to EU funds by farmers

- The investments in performant technologies, new machinery and equipment and modernization of farm buildings are intensified.

Reaching the proposed targets for beef is an ambitious objective that could be facilitated both by financial allocations for investments and by the initiation of national programs for the specialization of small farms that own beef cattle, mainly in the hilly and mountain areas, which are ideal areas for raising cattle.

However, the increase of beef production through the increase of herds is not always the most economical solution, as this presupposes additional costs for animal shelters, feeding and care. It would be desirable to obtain high yields by increasing the productivity per animal, i.e. increase of body weight, higher weight gains, diminution of feed consumption and improvement of carcass quality and composition.

References

1. European Commission: "EU Agricultural Outlook, Prospect for the EU agricultural markets and income 2016–2026," https://ec.europa.eu/agriculture/sites/agriculture/files/markets-and-prices/medium-term-outlook/2016/2016-fullrep_en.pdf, 2016.
2. EUROSTAT: "Meat production statistics," http://ec,europa,eu/eurostat/statistics-explained/index,php/Meat_production_statistics#Beef_and_veal_,28bovine_meat,29, 2015.
3. Food and Agricultural Organization: "Report on food deprivation towards the achievement of Millennium Development Goal (MDG) on hunger reduction," http://www.fao.org/fileadmin/templates/ess/documents/food_security_statis tics/working_paper_series/WP008e.pdf, 2006.
4. Food and Agricultural Organization: "What's feeding our food? The environmental and social impact of the livestock sector," https://www.foe.co.uk/sites/default/files/downloads/livestock_impacts.pdf, 2006.
5. Food and Agricultural Organization: "The state of food insecurity in the world," http://www.fao.org/docrep/014/i2330e/i2330e00.htm, 2011.
6. Food and Agricultural Organization: "The State of Food Insecurity in the World," ISBN 978-92-5-107316-2, http://www.fao.org/docrep/016/i3027e/i3027e.pdf, 2012.
7. Kazuo, S.: "For National Cooperation in Increasing Food Self-Sufficiency Rate," Symposium for revitalization of agriculture, http://www.japan-press.co.jp/pdf/special_june_2008.pdf, 2008.
8. Minot, N. / Pelijor, N.: "Food security and food self-sufficiency in Bhutan," International Food Policy Research Institute, http://www.ifpri.org/publication/food-security-and-food-self-sufficiency-bhutan, 2010.
9. Neaţă, G.: "Vaca de carne este o alternativă profitabilă pentru zootehnia din România," Profitul agricol, http://www.agrinet.ro/content.jsp?page=321, 2012.
10. OECD/FAO (2015), Agricultural Outlook 2015–2024, http://www.fao.org/3/a-i4738e.pdf.

11. Sheppard, R. L. / Benn, N. J.: "Japanese Food Policy and self-sufficiency – An analysis with Reference to meat", ISSN 0110–7720, https://researcharchive.lincoln.ac.nz/handle/10182/995, 1980.
12. Slaboch, J. /Kotyza, P.: "Comparison of self-sufficiency of selected types of meat in the Visegrad countries," Journal of Central European Agriculture, 17 (3), p. 793–814, 2016.
13. Şerbănescu, I.: "Dinamică şi concentrare pe piaţa produselor din carne," Fabrica de carne, Revista specialiştilor din industria cărnii, http://www.fabricadecarne.ro/dinamica-si-concentrare-pe-piata-produselor-din-carne-2, 2014.

Iuliana IONEL

Institute of Agricultural Economics, Bucharest, Romania,
email: 48ionel@gmail.com

Impact of Coupled Subsidies on the Romanian Soybean Market

Abstract: In the paper, we quantified the impact of the government's Decision no. 219/2015 upon the soybean market in Romania in the year 2015. For this purpose, we collected data on the soybean areas, production and trade with soybeans and soybean meal, as well as the prices for these products, both domestic prices and foreign trade prices. Based on existing data, we also estimated the minimum coupled support received by farmers per ton of soybeans and per cultivated hectare.

The farmers who cultivated soybeans in the year 2015 could receive the amount of €373.3/ha, out of which total subsidy for soybeans €181/ton, of which €113/ton represented the national coupled support. If we compare the annual (2015) average soybean price without subsidy (€480/ton) and the import price (€434/ton), we could draw the conclusion that Romania does not have a competitive advantage in soybean cultivation. At the same time, we find out that by subsidizing the domestic soybean production, the exported soybean production increased to 95,000 tons, and with this export, we also exported the subsidy worth €10.735 million.

Keywords: Soybeans; coupled subsidies; import and export price

Introduction

The unfavorable weather conditions for soybean cultivation, mainly in Western Europe, corroborated with the low prices of soybean meal and beans on the international market, make the soybean crop non-attractive for Europe.

With the strong development of the European livestock sector in the late 60s and 70s, the trade with soybeans intensified, while the imports from Latin America increased each year. This trend has been recently stabilized at the level of about 37 million tons imported in the European Union (EU; James, 2014).

The imports mainly consist of genetically modified soybean, as 88% of the world production is based on this technology. In other words, EU imports production obtained on 13.5 million ha cultivated with soybean in order to cover its domestic demand. The only source of conventional soybeans for Europe is Brazil, which produces both Genetically Modified Organism (GMO) and non-GMO soybeans; yet in this country, too, the biotech penetration rate reached more than 91% in 2013, and the production has a rather seasonal character, depending on the demand for animal feeding.

In the EU, the adoption of agricultural biotechnologies is rather slow, due to the regulation system, which is based on an extremely complex risk assessment by the competent authorities, the European Food Safety Authority (EFSA).

However, the EU authorized dozens of genetically modified products for import and utilization in human food, cultivated in other parts of the world. Thus, in the last decade, EU became the largest net importer of agricultural raw materials. Many of these products are obtained based on agricultural biotechnologies, mainly soybean, maize and rapeseed for the production of animal feeds, and cotton for the textile industry.

Romania was, and continues to be, a net importer of soybean meal, this product having one of the top positions in value terms in the country's balance of trade. However, there was an obvious diminution of dependency on imports during the period when transgenic soybean was authorized for cultivation (1999–2006). While the soybean meal imports covered 11%–30% of protein consumption until the accession to the EU in 2007, in the year 2014, the imports covered 71% of the national consumption needs, i.e. 586,000 tons. The main suppliers of protein meal for Romania were Brazil and Argentina.

1. Literature review

The agricultural policy is a component of the economic policy, which after the Second World War was based on the interventionist conception of production subsidizing and control and support to farmers' incomes, both in Europe and in America. Governments' interventions influenced the demand/supply ratios and contributed to the periodical re-establishment of an agricultural market equilibrium in these countries. The cost of these interventions was and remains high, and the effects were not satisfactory in the long term and required fundamental reforms in the United States of America (USA) and the EU, depending on market evolutions (Delloite, 2008).

In the year 2013, the European Commission under the European Innovation Partnership for Agricultural Productivity and Sustainability (EIP-AGRI) set up the Focus Group on Protein Crops, to support innovation and research, aiming to increase protein crop yields and to support the development of the protein crops chain in the European Union. In the year 2014, the European experts evaluated the challenges of the protein crop chain and identified solutions that can be implemented through agricultural consultancy, referring to good practices, demonstrative plots, utilization of certified seeds, fostering the adoption of new seed varieties by broadening the European genetic base of crops through long-term investments in the European agricultural research.

The increasing demand for soybean proteins, which are certified as non-GMO for the food industry, animal feeds and as raw material for the pharmaceutical industry, can stimulate farmers to cultivate conventional soybean, which also represents the core of the European Commission about the crop diversification measures and the Greening policy.

The study conducted by Dima (2015) reveals an important development potential for the soybean crop in Romania, Bulgaria and the Republic of Moldova.

Per the study, the governments should increase the support for soybean production and for the processing industry for this crop. The study estimates that Romania, Bulgaria and Moldova have a total potential of soybean cultivation of about 0.8–1.0 million ha that could generate a production of more than 2 million tons, accounting for about 5% of the yearly consumption of the European Union, i.e. around 30% of the non-GMO soybeans that is utilized in EU each year.

2. Methodology

The general objective of the paper is to analyze the relevance, efficiency, effectiveness, impact and sustainability of coupled support intervention, from national funds, for soybean cultivation in the year 2015. To quantify the impact of the coupled subsidy for soybeans, we assessed the impact upon the internal market in the year 2015 on: crop area; average yield; total yield; price of beans on the internal market comparing to import and export prices, and, finally, we quantified if the subsidy has favorited the national animal production, or the organic animal production from the West European countries.

The selected method that we used is the cost-benefit analysis, which is often indicated in policy evaluation (Ashdown, 2002). The purpose of the cost-benefit analysis is to determine the costs associated with policy implementation, to determine the monetary value of the results of its implementation, the calculation of the cost-benefit ratio and to appreciate the policy effectiveness in economic terms (Stufflebeam, 2001). The cost-effectiveness analysis necessarily includes the analysis of production factor costs in order to determine the costs associated to the progress made in reaching each objective. For instance, the costs and effects of the implementation of two or more policies in order to reach the same objectives could be compared (Levin, 1983).

A policy could be appreciated as more adequate for cost-efficiency reasons in the case it had the same costs, but yielded better results compared to other similar policies. Or a policy might be more advantageous if it achieves the same objectives as another policy, but at lower costs. Usually, the cost-effectiveness analysis does not need the conversion of results into monetary terms, but a target must be established that includes measurable objectives. But the cost-benefit analysis goes further and tries to identify a wider range of results than those strictly associated with the objectives of the group to which it is addressed. This analyzes the relation between the financial intervention and the intensity of positive and negative effects upon the economic environment in general. In this respect, the financial inputs are quantified and each obtained result is identified.

3. Data and results

For the purpose of the paper, we collected data referring to the soybean areas and production in the period of 1990–2015, Romania's foreign trade with soybeans and soybean meal, as well as the prices for these products, both on the domestic market and in foreign trade. At the same time, based on existing data we estimated the minimal support obtained by farmers for soybean production and per hectare. We quantified the effect of soybean supply on the Romanian market based on the balance of the product.

Fig. 1: Soybean: area and production, 1990–2015

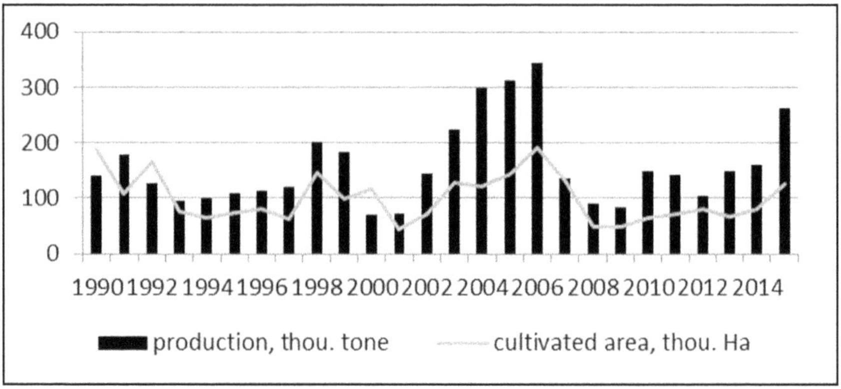

Source: National Institute of Statistics.

Soybean supply in Romania largely comes from soybean meal imports (60%), domestic soybean production (22%) and soybean imports (18%). To quantify the impact of imports upon the domestic market, we converted the imports to the average soybean production (olympic average) to estimate the number of soybean hectares that must be cultivated for self-sufficiency in soybeans. While in the year 2006, when the Romanian farmers cultivated GMO soybean, we imported the equivalent of 32,000 hectares, soybeans and meal; by the year 2015, the imports in hectares equivalent increased to 368,000 hectares, although the area cultivated with soybean also increased (by 47,000 ha) because of the introduction of the national coupled support for soybean.

As regards the prices of soybeans and soybean meal imports, one can notice that these are lower in Romania than in Rotterdam, as the quality criterion, i.e. the protein content, is not associated to prices.

Fig. 2: Soybeans prices 2004–2015, €/ton

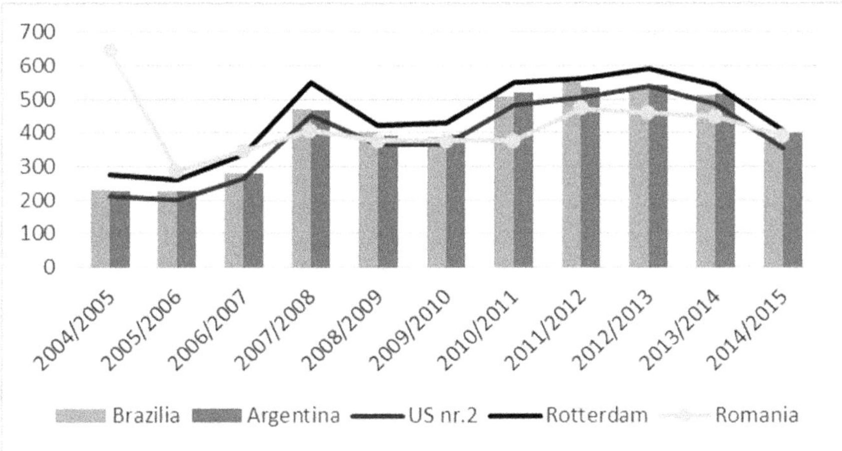

Source: United State Department of Agriculture, Foreign Agricultural Service, National Institute of Statistics.

Romania has a negative trade balance from the trade with soybean, which has recently grown larger as a result of the increase of vegetable protein demand destined for animal feeding in the industrial system.

Fig. 3: Romania: balance of trade with soybean and soybean products

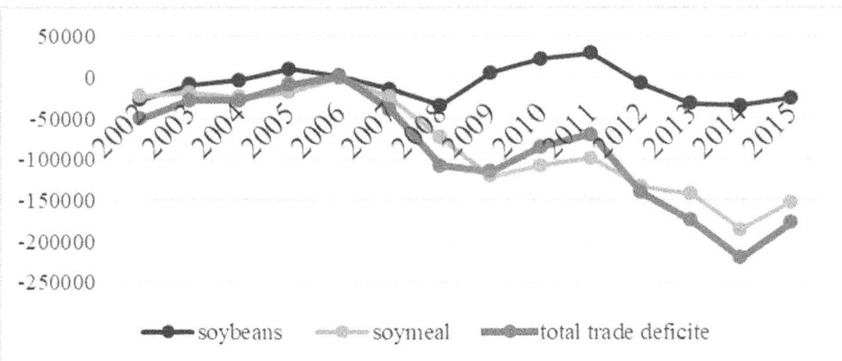

Source: Eurostat.

Romania's foreign trade with soybean in the year 2015 was dominated by imports from the non-EU countries of 158,000 tons, soybean exports to the EU countries of 55,000 tons and 38,000 tons to Turkey. The imports of soybean meal, as well as of soybeans, have a non-EU origin (445,000 tons), while the exports mainly go to the EU (135,000 tons).

According to the government's Decision 219/30.03.2016, the farmers who cultivated soybean in 2015 could benefit from several forms of support per hectare (according to table 1), such as: single area payment, redistributive payment, payment for environment-friendly agricultural practices, payment to young farmers, payment under the small farmer scheme, coupled support according to the National Transitory Aid 1 (NTA 1). Thus, farmers could receive a total amount of €373.3/ha for one hectare cultivated with soybean in the year 2015, out of which total subsidy for soybeans €181/ton, and national coupled support for soybean €113/ton.

Due to the coupled subsidy, soybean crop has become more attractive, for the farmers, than cereal. Thus, the the price for seeds used forseeding has increased, and the seeds' stocks exhausted during the spring of the year 2015.

At the level of the entire land area under soybean in the year 2015, all subsidy payments amounted to about €47.4 million, out of which €29.7million national coupled support.

Table 1: Subsidies paid to farmers who cultivated soybean, in the year 2015

	€/ha	**Soybean total (thou. €)**
Single area payment scheme	79.7	10,127
Redistributive payment	5–51.1	**
Payment for agricultural practices beneficial for the climate and the environment	59.1	7,509
Payment to young farmers	19.9	**
Simplified small farmer scheme		**
Total direct payments soybean (1)	138.9	17,636
National Transitory Aids (NTA 1)	191.9	**
National coupled support soybean (2)	234.4	29,770
Total soybean subsidy (1 + 2) * €/ha	373.3	47,406

Source: According to GD 2016 of 30 March 2016, *own calculations, **Lack of data.

If we compare the yearly average soybean price of €299/ton, practiced on the domestic market, to the import and export prices, we can draw the conclusion that Romania has a competitive advantage in soybean cultivation; but if we add the subsidy allocated per ton of product to the price practiced on the domestic market, we can notice that the price on the domestic market with subsidy included amounts to €480/ton, exceeding the import price of €434/ton.

Table 2: Romania: Soybean prices in 2015

	Soybean prices in 2015 (€/ton)
CIF import price (Constanţa)	391
FOB export price (Constanţa)	434
Price of domestic production	299
Soybean subsidy	181
Soybean price domestic production plus subsidy	480

Source: Eurostat, MARD, own calculations.

Thus, we can see that by subsidizing the domestic soybean production, soybean exports increased to 95,000 tons, and together with this export we also exported the subsidy worth €10.735 million (95,000 tons' soybeans export in 2015 x €113/ton subsidy).

Conclusions

The total budgetary effort for the coupled subsidies to the area cultivated with soybean in the year 2015 amounted to €29.770 thousand, to €113/cultivated hectares respectively. Subsidizing the soybean crop in the year 2015 determined the decrease of average yield per hectare (by 20% compared to 2014) with the increase of cultivated area (by 60%), while the total soybean production increased to 262,000 tons (by 30%). At the same time, soybean imports and exports increased by 66,000 tons and by 53,000 tons respectively, the balance of trade remaining negative.

The soybean prices, from internal production, with the subsidy included, are higher by 11% than the imported soybean prices, which shows that soybean subsidizing determines only the increase in the domestic soybean supply, and not an increased efficiency of the crop.

By subsidizing the domestic soybean production, the export increased to 95,000 tons, and with this soybean export we also exported the subsidy worth €10.735 million.

This means that in the year 2015, each Romanian contributed with €1.5 to the coupled subsidizing of soybean production, which finally went to export, to support the organic production of countries from Western Europe, and indirect the consumption of organic products of animal origin.

References

1. Dima, Dragos Costin (2015): "Soybean Crop in Romania, Bulgaria and the Republic of Moldova: Current Situation and Perspectives," Agriculture and Agricultural Science Procedia 6 (2015) 3–8 by Elsevier 2210–7843, 2015.
2. Stufflebeam, Daniel L. (2001): "Evaluation Models." NEW DIRECTIONS FOR EVALUATION, no. 89, Spring 2001, Jossey-Bass, A Publishing Unit of John Wiley & Sons, Inc.

3. James, Clive (2014). Global Status of Commercialized Biotech/GM Crops: 2014. ISAAA Brief No. 49. ISAAA: Ithaca, NY. ISBN: 978-1-892456-59-1.
4. Kee, J. E. (1995). Benefit-cost analysis in program evaluation. In J. S. Wholey, H. P. Hatry, & K. E. Newcomer, Handbook of practical program evaluation, pp. 456–488. San Francisco: Jossey-Bass.
5. Levin, H. M. (1983). Cost-effectiveness: A primer. New Perspectives in Evaluation, 4. Newbury Park, CA: Sage.
6. Ashdown, Jane (2002): What Is Cost-Effectiveness Analysis? New York University Barbara Hummel-Rossi, New York University, Journal of Reading Recovery Fall 2002.
7. Delloite (2008): "Raport de Evaluare Ex-Post a Politicii de Sprijin acordat producătorilor agricoli din sectoarele vegetal şi zootehnic pentru anul 2006," http://discutii.mfinante.ro/static/10/Mfp/evaluare/Anexa1_Rap_eval_politiciagricole.pdf.
8. Eurostat database, http://ec.europa.eu/eurostat/web/agriculture/data/database.
9. MADR website, www.madr.ro.
10. INSSE, http://statistici.insse.ro/shop/?lang=ro.

Radu REY[1], Adrian Radu REY[2]

Romanian Academy, "Costin C. Kiriţescu"
National Institute of Economic Research, Center for Mountain Economy "CE-MONT", Calea 13 Septembrie no. 13, Bucharest,
E-mails: cabinet_fmr@yahoo.com, radurey@yahoo.com

Predictions Regarding the Economic Implications, Market Development, Opportunities and Constraints of Capitalizing on Romanian "Mountain Products" in a Sustainable Vision

Abstract: The idea of capitalizing on certain "niche" food products with a high bio-energetic quality, obtained in the unpolluted mountain environment, stems from the developments that occurred due to population growth and pollution factors in the intensive production systems of large-scale agriculture and the agri-food industry practices regarding preservation, taste, and color, which can harm health. New regulation no. 1151/2012 and EC Delegated Regulation no. 665/2014 regarding "mountain products." Government Decision. no. 506/2016, which establishes the institutional framework and implements some measures for it, emerged in Romania. Romania, with about 2.9 million hectares of mountain and farmland, is interested in capitalizing on "mountain products," which are based on multifloral grass, ruminants, organic fertilizers and the difficult labor of small mountain farmers. "Mountain products" will be able to be sold nationally directly by farmers, if they form their "market." On a large scale, the capitalization internally and externally on "mountain products" requires the association with grade I and II cooperative systems. The main objective is increasing farmers' incomes and fighting poverty. The constraints are found in the low prices for meat, milk etc., the lack of organization in associative-cooperative forms and the predictable competitive reactions of the industrial actors.

Keywords: mountain product, organic fertilizers, cooperatives, markets, constraints

1 Corresponding author: Prof. Radu Rey. Mobile: (+40)745.507.537. E-mail: cabinet_fmr@yahoo.com.

2 Corresponding author: Ph.D. student Adrian Rey. Mobile: (+40)745.618.303. E-mail: radurey@yahoo.com, School for Advanced Studies of the Romanian Academy.

Introduction

The new guidelines generated by EU Regulation no. 1151/2012 (EP + EC)

Globally, new "concerns" manifest in relation to the rampant demographic evolution and the risks involved by food crises, hence the increasingly obvious need for the rational use of food sources, alongside conserving renewable resources and using sustainable solutions in the development process and in society's need to think preventively regarding the consequences of climate change, both in Europe and globally. In the context of the final document of the United Nations Conference on Sustainable Development with the 21st Agenda (mountains) and the Johannesburg Plan of Implementation (2002), which recognizes the fragility and importance of mountain ecosystems, and the great benefits to human society derived from the mountains, the UN General Assembly in November 2016 adopted the "Sustainable Mountain Development" Report, through which states are encouraged to undertake greater efforts to conserve mountain ecosystems, increase investments, combat poverty, provide education, encourage the initiatives of mountain communities, etc.

Regulation (EU) no. 1151/2012 – from 21 November 2012 (published in O. J. no. 3432/14, December 2012) on quality schemes for agricultural products and foodstuffs supplemented by EU delegated Regulation no. 665/2013 of the Commission from 11 March 2014 (O. J. of the EU L179/23 from 19 June 2014) modifying Regulation 1151/2012 regarding the conditions of use of the optional quality term "mountain product" have generated new guidelines designed to protect and boost a sustainable development of mountain areas – with at least two relatively different effects: for the mountain areas in developed countries in the EU – an effect of added opportunity, complementary to existing opportunities, well-practiced through "green," "bio" and "traditional" products (Boesch, M., et. al. 2008, Fleury, P., et. al., 2008) – subject to the existence of basic structures (highly productive animal breeds, adapted mechanization, hygienic stables, collection and use of organic fertilizers.

For the mountain areas in Romania (Caluseru, L., et. al., 2015), as well as in other emerging EU member countries with mountains from the Central-South-East European sphere, in a nuanced way, the new guidelines generated by the idea of agrifood "mountain products" do not come as an opportunity, but as a safeguarding solution for a great economy undergoing a process of degradation – with different stages, and in different segments.

Methodology

Observation of specific phenomena in different lengthy areas and periods, comparative research in long stages (1978–1988 and 2000–2015), in direct contact with the realities in the field, having as sources scientific papers, information obtained directly from mountain farmers, personal observations and experimental results, scientific debates on these issues, involvement in the creation of pilot entities and careful observation of the direct and collateral effects. Retrieving information and its inclusion in bio-economic concepts, use of certain research on associative-cooperative solutions, currently practiced in countries like Italy, Switzerland, France, Norway – adapting European experience to the environmental conditions and the specific stage and level of development associated with the mountain society's reaction to the prospect of "burning" bridges with impact in traditions and even in changing some mentalities, at the level of the ruling EU institutions. The correlation with the developments in thinking regarding the complex and differentiated issues of mountain areas was the overall methodology for the visionary sketching of the work.

Results and discussions

In the 3,520 mountain villages (658 administative units), of which 577 communes (relatively large in Romania, with approx. 800–1,300 family farms each – mostly small) with a total of arround 820,000 farms, at an average of approx. 4.5 ha/farm, including small plots of forest, accentuated forms of agricultural abandonment in young generations were recorded in 2016, with a tendency to accelerate, the aging of active mountain farmers and the weakening of the management and the capacity to adopt new, innovative approaches jeopardizing the continuity of the food production. The human depopulation phenomena are linked directly to the despoiling low prices practiced by "transformers" – whether these are large external companies or local industrialists and other intermediaries, using as inputs milk and meat, the consequences being found in states of increasing discouragement. For the first time in the last 26 years, the obvious apparition of disinterest for development is being registered in mountain villages. If in 1994 there were approx. 950,000 small and medium mountain households, in 2016 there were approx. 820,000 left – with a reduction of cattle of over 50%, and sheep with approx. 1 million heads, from 2.9 mil. to 1.9 mil., and profoundly negative effects on the families' food as well as on the valuable biodiversity of natural meadows and pastures through the disappearance of the essential contribution of the organic fertilizers to mountain agricultural practices (Otiman, P. I., 2006; Rey, R., 2013; Zaman, Gh. & Geamanu, M., 2014).

Mountain agricultural economy is based on four stable and interdependent factors (Rey, R., 2014): polifloral grass of meadows and pastures; herbivores (cattle, sheep, goats); organic fertilizers stemming from herbivores; the "mountain man" – the farmer/animal breeder, adapted to the harsh natural conditions.

It is important to note that the four essential factors of production are characterized by the fact that the energy required is almost entirely renewable and the sustainability is based on self-reproduction.

The herbaceous vegetation in mountain areas (fig. 1) shows differences depending on specific factors and the intensity of human intervention along the centuries, mainly through sheep and then cattle initially, through organic fertilizers. Mountain soils, pastures and hayfields are generally acidic with variations in pH intensity, on which a mosaic of plants evolved naturally – some being poor feed or not fit as feed – the most important being legumes (species of red and white clover, trefoil, etc.), followed by valuable species of grasses (Festuca sp., Phleum sp., Dactylis sp., etc.) or ubiquitous medicinal and fodder plants such as dandelions (Taraxacum officinale; Marusca, T., Dragomir, N., 2014). Summed up, the quality value of the basic food for herbivorous animals – which, through the multivitamins and mineral salts extracted from the soil and the added value brought by the medicinal plants, justify the customization and qualitative value of alimentary "mountain products."

Factoring in the absence of polluting factors, the water quality, the extensive livestock breeding and capitalization systems, in the end, we obtain a high quality of milk and meat, but with greater efforts and lower yields than those obtainable in the nearby high-fertility-areas of the plains/hills, defending the need for some compensation.

Photo 1: Polifloral meadow (photo Rey, R.) *Photo 2: Fertile soil – thin (photo Rey, R.)*

Worth mentioning is also the very thin topsoil (10–20 cm) – with a minimal reserve of humus, easily exhaustible if tampered with through "modern" methods for boosting grass production. Basically, faced with these natural realities, the grass production in mountainous areas should **not be forced** – under any consideration (Cojocariu, L., et al., 2016).

The selection and multiplication of plants with high nutritional value (achieved over long periods of time, through the essential and constant intake of organic fertilizers) was performed not always in the same way and with the same species of animals, but with similar effects (Marusca, T., 2013).

Sheep manure, which is capsule-shaped, could be spread relatively evenly across pasture or meadow surfaces simply through the grazing movements or/and by the flock remaining in the same place for several days, a method known as "grazing" (good practice). The result is found either in maintaining a convenient vegetable structure or in improving it through the added fertile substance brought by the sheep/goat manure which, when exposed to the moisture in the soil (rain, dew) combined with solar heat, being capsule-shaped, under anaerobic fermentation conditions, quickly reaches a state of "rotting", with a pH leaning toward alkaline.

Thus, the natural acidity of the soil is "tempered," it decreases slightly in intensity and the plants that evolve are those of great nutritious interest, with a higher amount of protein, such as perennial legumes, in the detriment of weak fodder species or those not consumed by animals, but with a high invasive capacity. Through the annual uninterrupted contribution of organic fertilizers, we maintain what we call functional biodiversity – valuable, created through a harmonious relation between mountain soil, grazing animals and the human interest for food, between man and nature, in a sustainable solution. A distinction needs to be noted regarding cattle: cattle dung is not capsular like in sheep, but has a much greater volume and is intensely acidic when falling to the ground – a situation unavoidable in grazing conditions. Practical observations show that the acidity of undispersed dung and cattle urine leads to the "burning" of the grass, its regeneration needing about a year, hence the appreciation that cattle are "creators" of grass on pastures less than sheep (Gruia, R., 2016).

This is, however, different in the case of pastures, since it is during the long stabling period that manure is collected, concentrated on platforms, where the fermentation can reach temperatures of over 70°C, and we get two results that contribute to the "quality of manure": the sterilization of parasitic and microbial factors and the "rotting," meaning the leaning toward the alkaline, and by spreading it in the meadows in spring, we achieve the contribution of nitrogen along with a slight reduction in the soil's natural acidity. The end result is providing a grass production increase and the preponderance, through the natural interspecies battle, of plant species with high nutritional value (legumes, grasses).

Urine from ruminants: a valuable organic fertilizer, rich in nitrogen, ignored

Fresh urine has an acidic pH – an effect which, on pastures, is alleviated by rain and the soil's water content. Traditionally, while grazing, urine from ruminants is not collected, and during the barn-bound winter, only cattle urine can be easily collected in pools. In the traditional system found in the Romanian mountains, stables are not provided with collecting basins, except sporadically, resulting in the loss of a valuable organic fertilizer, free and available in amounts of hundreds of millions of liters annually.

Inside the traditional mountain stables in the Romanian mountains, yet to be modernized and representing the majority in 2016, the effect of urine is harmful. Inside the stables, urine seeps under the floors daily in successive layers. Wooden gutters are not very effective, and the ventilation systems in stables are undersized, inefficient or missing. Thus, through the fermenting of the urine which has seeped into and under the wooden floors during the long period of being stabled, harmful gasses are given off, which are breathed in by animals as well as by farmers, with the effect of reducing the level of oxygen transported by the haemoglobin found in blood and the penetration of toxic gases, causing a significant reduction in the production of milk and meat.

Research conducted in the mountain area (50 stables) showed major concentrations, exceeding the maximum permitted for ammonia by 80%, significant overruns in carbon dioxide and hydrogen sulfide. The urine that is produced in the over 200,000 existing cattle stables in the mountain areas of Romania, in small- and medium-sized farms, is a valuable organic fertilizer, wasted (approx. 1,5 billion liters annually during the stabling period) by not organizing its collection in prepared pools in approx. 90% of the stables. The fact that the urine that drips, concentrated, onto the soil, induces negative environmental effects and can endanger human and animal health by polluting groundwater, should also be taken into consideration. A good management of urine, letting it age and ferment, with the effect of it attenuating from acidic to alkaline, and using it rationally mixed in with water in a ratio of 1:4–1:6 (associated with a rational use by dispersing it on meadows in fine layers that reach plant roots without the risk of polluting the water) can produce the effect of obtaining a supplementary crop of hay compared to the traditional one.

Photo 3: Traditional stable (photo Rey, R.)

The state of backwardness in mountain livestock raising is largely due to the focus in the last 70 years on the use of chemical fertilizers, of pesticides, on industrial technologies, deeply neglecting households/small and medium farms and implicitly mountain ones. The education system has abandoned or treated superficially the important problem of organic fertilizers.

In developed European countries, as well as Poland and Slovenia, it is very rare to find a stable lacking sanitation and ventilation, and especially without dung platforms and urine collecting tanks. In the Western sphere, due to increasing pressure from consumers for "organic" or bio-type food products, there was a "mutation" in the post-1985 period, also as a result of some worrying negative effects for human health, when the move was made to the application of the "conversion" – by giving up polluting chemical processing and granting, in the EU, "compensation" for the production losses (Rey. R., 2013).

Haylofts (hay barns) and aflatoxins

A worrying situation for Romanian mountain agriculture is the winter conservation system for hay, in stacks (haystacks) left mostly uncovered under the direct influence of rain and snow. The negative effects can be found in mechanical losses, and especially in the moulding of the hay which, once mixed in cow feed, can produce aflatoxins, which are transmitted through milk and can have bad effects on consumer health. The emergence of an aflatoxin "crisis" was required for a rude awakening (2010–2014), in order for this health problem to be officially taken into consideration.

For example, Austria has solved the problem of hay quality through a simple, relatively cheap and effective method: replacing haystacks (stacks) with haylofts built out of wood, placed directly on the meadows, so that the relatively dry grass can be immediately sheltered without the risk of being surprised by rain on the ground (when the invasion of mold is intense and inevitable) by depositing it directly into the hayloft – where it remains well-preserved until its use in animal feed. A "plus" brought by the existence of the haylofts has been the accumulation of seeds on the floors and the possibility of over-seeding meadows and a contribution to improving landscapes. In Romania, the hayloft solution evolved only in the Northern Carpathians.

Photo 4: Traditional outdated winter hay storage system (photo Rey, R.)

Photo 5: Hayloft (photo Rey, R.)

In summary

Approaching the idea of high-quality alimentary "mountain products" requires a complex of technical and organizational measures – which, in summary, refers mainly to several directions of progress specific to the mountain-type agricultural and food economy: enhanced support for livestock farmers – to construct, with priority: platforms for manure, urine (purine) collecting basins; hay granaries – in meadows, these simple constructs targeting both smaller farms and medium-sized and larger households. Being issues that concern both the animal production, environmental protection and the conservation of valuable biodiversity in mountain meadows, the financial and organizational efforts should interest both the Ministry of Agriculture and the Ministry of the Environment, invited to cooperate for a common interest issue.

This support needs to be accompanied by a process of modernizing the stables, complete with the machinery and systems necessary for manure and urine transportation and spreading technology. All the issues discussed above are the subject of the application of a "mountain policy," adapted to the existent realities and to the trends of the near future – arising from the new and great sustainable opportunity created by the idea of the alimentary "mountain product." An alignment in this new forward direction emerging in the agricultural economy also requires an effort to adapt from the part of the educational system. Especially in rural mountain education, in gymnasiums schools (from 577 mountain communes), the new subject of "rural mountain economy" with the organization of practical activities, by creating educational farms in a system of public-private cooperation should be suggested.

Economic issues

The essence of the application of EU regulations to high quality "mountain products" should be reflected in both the production of "added value" and especially in the urgent need for profit to return in the most direct and primary way to the producers of raw materials, the mountain farmers – by avoiding intermediaries as much as possible, thus being able to significantly improve farmers' incomes and to combat poverty. Romania, with a great mountainous area populated with humans and with century-old traditions in livestock farming, but also of cultural interest, has a constant and major interest (like the EU) in avoiding the further continuation of the state of marginalization of mountain agriculture and in developing a rational and balanced mountain policy, comparable to the plains/hills areas and directed towards conserving resources and values, applying effective and preventive measures for the imperative recovery and avoidance of the **depopulation of the rural mountain area** (3,520 villages), since it is well-known that mountain populations – younger generations, once removed from their natural environment, are not recoverable (except to a very small extent – the example of France, in the period after 1950, is enlightening).

The "mountain product" and predictable implications

Through Government Decision no. 506 of 20 July 2016, establishing the institutional framework and measures for implementing the EU Delegated Regulation no. 665/2014 of 11 March 2014, supplementing EU Regulation no. 1151/2012 of the European Parliament and of the Council regarding the conditions of use of the optional quality term "mountain product," the Ministry of Agriculture and Rural Development is designated as the **competent authority** for modifying the compliance of the data contained in the **specifications**, in order to grant the right to use the optional quality term "mountain product," to establish and manage the national register of "mountain products," as well as to verify the compliance with European and national legislation by the economic operators who have obtained the right to use the term (Gruia, R., et al., 2016).

Implementing, in practice, the idea of the high quality "mountain product," has **predictable implications**.

The EU-reserved term (McMorran, R. et al., 2015) and national "mountain product" schemes lack an explicit guarantee of product quality, beyond territorial quality associations. Still, it is validated by studies that the creation of a reserved term for mountain products based on clear definitions all over Europe (EU), and the potential to support the provision of positive externalities, add value to mountain products, and control misuse of the mountain term. But this is not sufficient to deliver durable results.

The efficiency of the mountain economy can be analyzed through the theory of positive and negative externalities, by which can be determined the positive or negative impact that each activity developed by individuals, companies or countries can have on the members of the entire society. Mountains can be associated with positive externalities, such as supply of freshwater to lowland areas, reservoirs of biodiversity, carbon sequestration, protection from natural hazards and provision of unique landscapes and opportunities for quality recreation, with associated health and well-being benefits (Robinson, R., 2009; Hopkins, A., 2009; NordRegio, 2004; Penati, C., et al., 2011).

In essence, the "mountain products" represent a positive externality of the mountian areas because they incorporate several factors that must be appreciated and properly remunerated by the whole society that benefits from them, such as: mountain producers preserve the cultural and natural landscape; mountain farming faces more challenges than in lower areas due to altitude, slope and weather conditions; products from the mountain areas are healthier, mainly because of the lack or reduced use of chemicals in the production process.

Agriculture and food production represent powerful cultural elements that are linking mountain environments with populations through long-established practices, such as traditional cheese-making and transhumance, associated with build heritage, songs, festivals and cultural landscapes (Macdonald, K. I., 2012).

A separation is needed for "mountain products" from similar products that are produced in the plains and hills.

In an early stage, the first beneficiaries will be the mountain farmers who will be able to process and capitalize on this type of product, alone or in small family associations, something that requires some organization and some investments in small processing workshops, which need to be authorized. For these producers, the capitalization on **the formation of the market** is essential and needs intense promotional actions. A central objective is to obtain an "added value," to compensate the direct producers' quality efforts and improve their family income. It is difficult to foresee the prices that will be practical for cheese, butter, meat, etc. – guaranteed "mountain products," an aspect that only the market itself will be able to decide. The first forms of (predictable) capitalization include target-selling directly through short chains – between farmers and consumers. Differences are also predictable in relation to the distances between producers and markets. The cities within the mountain area (81) are mostly small towns, with approx. 15–20,000 inhabitants, and the mountain products from the surrounding rural areas (10–15 UATs, with 8–12,000 small and medium farms) could only be sold in limited proportion, of approx. 3–5% compared to the actual production volume available for capitalization. The major concern is to solve the problem of capitalizing the whole offer as "mountain products," a situation that can, in time, turn the small mountain agriculture of Romania and other emerging countries into small "economic powers," generating high-quality food, contributing to the limiting or the avoidance of some food crises.

In the gr. I communal cooperatives formula, what becomes feasible is the collection of raw materials by the cooperative and negotiating a more advantageous contract with existing dairies or slaughterhouses[3].

The current realities (2016), in the absence of small food industries owned by the cooperatives, do not allow yet, on any possible level, for a high capitalization of "mountain products," directly benefiting mountain farmers.

Exiting this "trap" becomes realistic only by creating gr. II cooperatives, with their own independent capacity for transformation and capitalization, formed by the association of gr. I cooperatives with the necessary investments in: dairy factories, with a refining division – for "hard" cheeses – which allow capitalization for export to distant markets; midsized slaughterhouses, with charcuterie; mountain product factory – vegetables (berries, medicinal herbs, etc.); cold storage – for storing the final products and selling them throughout the year; a marketing service will analyze permanently both the level of possible internal prices, through their own stores, and the external offers, predictably significantly superior to the domestic market. A gr. II cooperative needs investments, through EU funds and national co-financing, in the context of a community policy which, for struggling mountain areas focused on capitalizing on "mountain products," should raise the current ceiling for grants from 50% up to 85–90%.

An agricultural cooperative mountain system becomes, inevitably, competitive, and could end the period which generated poverty and massive reductions in livestock numbers, with effects on mountain ecosystems through the degradation of valuable biodiversity created along centuries and, worst of all, visibly accelerating a process of depopulation of mountain villages.

Multiple new economic and social issues require the creation of a special protection system by governments within a multiannual strategy with a sustainable vision perspective.

In approaching the agro-mountain cooperative system, especially at the gr. II cooperatives level, it is rational to start by creating an experimental "pilot area,",

3 In Ardan village, in the commune of Sieu – Bistrita-Nasaud county, Romania, there are 2 cooperatives (milk, fruit). For the milk – ecologically approved, the cooperative negotiated and obtained the price of 1,85 lei/liter of plain milk (compared to 0,81 lei before the existence of the cooperative).

where research and innovation activities should also be conducted, an experiment that will highlight the entire complex of needs and ways to resolve them. Then we will be able to move on to the multiplication phase, in successive steps and with the necessary legislative, financial and organizational preparations, covering the mountain area in its entirety, being able to be appreciated on the horizon of 2035–2040, with the financial and organizational efforts demanded by the national and community interest (Rey. R., 2013).

A logical variation could be locating the experimental pilot area in the poorest part of Romania, the North-East region, where the livestock breeding and cultural traditions, although affected, are still present and where there are institutional and nongovernmental conditions able to assist in a creative process.

Conclusions

In the certain context of demographic growth and climate change, of the alarming spectrum of the exacerbation of "food crises," it becomes imperative that in the mountain areas, where through the natural conditions with still present traditions, for food, especially high quality food, to be produced, agricultural abandonment and the degradation of the biodiversity of natural pastures be avoided, and for a special and complex investment program to be adapted to the mountains' socio-economic specificity, to be applied, and capable of ensuring food for the population of the mountains as well as for the urban society, through sustainable means, in a context of harmonious equilibrium between man and nature, and with beneficial effects on the conservation of the mountain cultural fund. The alimentary agricultural economic system described could also be tested in other emerging countries with mountain areas from South-Eastern Europe (e.g., Bulgaria, Ukraine, other Carpathian countries, or the Balkan area).

It is necessary to extend social and economical comparative research to differentiated mountain areas, marketing studies on the sources and limits of valorization of "mountain products," organizational and legislative measures, needs and forms of support and compensatory measures with beneficial effects on producers, first of all, on consumer health and the preservation of the natural environment.

References

1. Boesch, M./Renner, E./Siegrist, D.: "Brandscaping:" From traditional cultural landscapes to "label regions:" A strategic scheme to achieve sustainable regional development in the Swiss Alps. Mountain Research and Development, 28 (2), 2008, pp. 100–104. Online at: http://dx.doi.org/10.1659/mrd.0950.
2. Caluseru, L., et al.: Rural development of Mountain areas in Romania, challenges and targets for the year 2020, DOI:10.5593/SGEM2015/B52/S23.104, online at: http://sgem.org/sgemlib/spip.php?article6498&lang=en.

3. Cojocariu, Luminita, et al.: Analysis of mountain grassland degradation affected by erosion and conservation measures, Agrobuletin AGIR, no. 21, 2016, pp. 24–31.
4. Commission Delegated Regulation (EU) No. 665/2014 of 11 March 2014, supplementing Regulation (EU) No. 1151/2012 of the European Parliament and of the Council with regard to conditions of use of the optional quality term "mountain product," https://www.fsai.ie/uploadedFiles/Legislation/FSAI_Legislation/2014/06_Jun_14/Reg665_2014.pdf.
5. Fleury, P., et al.: Implementing Sustainable agriculture and rural development in the European Alps. Mountain Research and Development, 28 (3), 2008, pp. 226–232. Doi: http://dx.doi.org/10.1659/mrd.1002.
6. Government Decision No. 506/2016 regarding the establishment of the national instituional framework and some measures for the application of Commission Delegated Regulation (EU) No. 665/2014 of 11 March 2014, supplementing Regulation (EU) No. 1151/2012 of the European Parliament and of the Council with regard to conditions of use of the optional quality term "mountain product" (published in the Official Journal of Romania on 26 July 2016).
7. Gruia, R.: Elements of mountain bioeconomics in the permaculture concept, with applications in carpathians, Journal of EcoAgriTourism, Publishing Transilvania University of Brasov, Romania, ISSN: 1844–8577 Vol. 11, Nr. 2, 2016, pp. 24–32.
8. Gruia, R., et al.: Mountain agri-tourism efficiency by the control of Qs procedures concerning cheese – case study, Journal of EcoAgriTourism, ISSN: 1844–8577, Vol. 12, Nr. 2 (33), 2016, pp. 161–171.
9. Hopkins, A., 2009. Relevance and functionality of semi-natural grassland in Europe – status quo and future prospectives, Report of the International Workshop of the SALVERE-Project 2009 at the Agricultural Research and Education Centre Raumberg-Gumpenstein, pp. 9–14.
10. Macdonald, K.I., 2012. "The morality of cheese: A paradox of defensive localism in a transnational cultural economy." Geoforum (In press, 2012), http://dx.doi.org/10.1016/j.geoforum.2012.03.011.
11. McMorran, R./Santini, F./Guri, F./Gomez-y-Paloma, S./Price, M./Beucherie, O./Monticelli, C./Rouby, A./Vitrolles, D. and Cloye, G.: "A mountain food label for Europe? The role of food labelling and certification in delivering sustainable development in European mountain regions." Journal of Alpine Research, 103–4, 2015. Online at: http://rga.revues.org/2654.
12. Marusca, T./Dragomir, N.: Mountain grasslands and their multifunctional role, Journal of Montanology, vol. I (1), 2014, pp. 7–20.
13. Marusca, T.: Gospodarirea durabila a pajistilor din zona montana, Editura Universitatii Transilvania, Brasov, 2013.
14. NordRegio, 2004. Mountain Areas in Europe: Analysis of mountain areas in EU member states, acceding and other European countries, Nordregio Report, 2004, Stockholm, Nordregio, p. 271, visited June 2012, http://www.nordregio.se/en/Publications/Publications-2004/Mountain-areas-in-Europe/.

15. Otiman, P. I.: Dezvoltarea rurala durabila in Romania, Editura Academiei Romane, 2006.
16. Penati, C., Berentsen, P. B. M., Sandrucci, A., De Boer, I. J. M., 2011 – "Effect of abandoning highland grazing on nutrient balances and economic performance of Italian Alpine dairy farms," Livestock Science, 139, pp. 142–149.
17. Regulation No. 1151/2012 of the European Parliament and Council of 21 November 2016, regarding quality systems of agri-food products, pp. 1–29, http://www.justice.gov.md/file/Centrul%20de%20armonizare%20a%20legislatiei/Baza%20de%20date/Materiale%202014/Legislatie/32012R1151.pdf.
18. Resolution of the European Parliament 2015/2279 (INI) of 10 May 2016 regarding the cohesion policy in the mountain regions of the EU, http://www.europarl.europa.eu/sides/getDoc.do?pubRef=-//EP//TEXT+TA+P8-TA-2016-0213+0+DOC+XML+V0//RO.
19. Rey, R.: "Mountain Product of High- biological Quality. Meadows' Poliflora, Organic Fertilizer and a Sustainable Mountain Economy," Procedia Economics and Finance, Volume 8, 2014, pp. 622–631, online at: https://doi.org/10.1016/S2212-5671(14)00137-3.
20. Rey, R.: "Muntii si secolul XXI. Studiu comparat al strategiilor europene privind zonele montane cu referire speciala la zona Carpatilor romanesti." Editura Terra Nostra, Iasi, 2013.
21. Robinson, R., 2009. Externalités positives des zones de montagne: valorisation par les politiques et les marchés, Rapport 2007, FAO, Euromontana, Brussels, p. 60.
22. Zaman, Gh./Geamanu, M.: "Eficienta economica in conditiile dezvoltarii durabile," Editura Fundatiei Romania de Maine, Bucuresti, 2014.

Vasile AVĂDĂNEI[a,b,1], Ioan SURDU[a,2]

[a]National Institute of Economic Research – Centre for Economics Mountain; str. 13 Septembrie, Bucureşti, România

Lidia AVĂDĂNEI[b,3]

[b]Creative and Innovation Business Incubation Center, str. Libertăţii, nr. 42, Roznov, jud. Neamţ, 617390

Mountain Peasant Household Between Employment and Entrepreneurship

Abstract: There is a great interest in maintaining and strengthening the traditional peasant farm as a reference unit in mountain development and to support the commercial consecration of mountain products. For the model to become operational it is necessary to make an assessment of the key elements that make it functional. It is necessary to build a model adapted to the economic and social variables. The aim of this study is to analyze the elements of the traditional mountain peasant farm and to integrate the requirements of competitiveness. There are taken into account cultural elements for conserving the specificity and traditionalism from montain rural areas. It also examines how the human resources system trails can integrate occupational reference, so that it can meet the challenges of economic and social integration in the food market. A testing of model result is equally an economic and cultural challenge.

Keywords: mountain development, entrepreneurship, mountaineering, mountain homestead

Motto: If a concept remains viable as it "becomes stale," it acquires a cultural value more consistent.

1. Preliminary issues

The peasant farm areas form the central unit of rural community from which we can build structures, relations, functions. They sum up the material and spiritual livelyhood, in accumulated forms that constitute the basic material for creating concepts and ideas generating sustainable development projects. In Europe, they were discussed as functional and competitive criteria of family farm (Mazzocchi et al., 2016).

1 vasilevadanei2004@yahoo.com, +40 721811362.
2 surdu.ioan@gmail.com, +40 727368054.
3 alidia_38@yahoo.com, +40 728994399.

We consider that it is necessary to define the starting point of our investigations in order to emphasize that a definition and a more detailed, and at the same time, systematic description of the peasant household as a whole living space, will highlight features that explain, much better and more informed, why rural projects approached "top-down," such as that from the National Plan for Rural Development (NRDP), are treated with caution by potential applicants.

It is necessary to define a full description of peasant farming and its complex structure, functionality and cultural role (Olaizola et al., 1998). It requires a convincing explanation of the fact that, essentially, the peasant household economy is a vital component for rural areas, that generates differences and specificity and may not be treated according to a global reference model regarding its place in postmodern society. Fassio et al. (2014) studied mountain family farms in terms of change and continuity.

Social and economic problems of mountain rural areas are reflected in macroeconomic approaches by keys other than those from the hilly and plain rural areas.

This study proposes a different approach toward the peasant household in terms of traditional paradigms and new paradigms from Western European mountain areas (Mathieu, 2010).

2. Working method

For collecting and interpreting data, several methods of investigation were used within some projects focused on communities from mountainous areas of County Neamt, consistsing of 22 communes. The data were collected by students from 8th to 12th class young people up to the age of 35 years, mature men (householders), elderly, and mayors of communes.

The activities of the authors were focused on the following topics:

- Support for entrepreneurial training (workshops, group; Avadanei et al., 2009);
- Evaluating, developing and fostering creativity (workshops, group; Avadanei et al., 2012);
- Measuring entrepreneurship in young people (questionnaires; Avadanei et al., 2010);
- What it means to be an entrepreneur in the mountain areas (workshops, group; Avadanei et al., 2013);
- Description of animal breeders' activities (interview; Avadanei et al., 2014);
- Young people's attitudes toward their professional future in their native villages (essay; Avadanei et al., 2016);
- Description of work in the community (interview): commune halls of Piatra Soimului, Tarcau, Tasca, Ceahlau, Farcasa, Pipirig, Hangu, Baltatesti, Vanatori-Neamt, Tazlau;
- Consulting publications (articles and studies) regarding mountain development (Rey, 1979, Neagu et al., 1996, Palic et al., 2005, Fitiu 2012, Florescu 2010, 2011); the Romanian Academy study "Ethnography Bistrita Valley", 1973.

Based on the synthesis of this information and appropriate correlations, the profile of a mountain peasant household was defined, delimited and described.

3. Conceptual Model

3.1. The mountain peasant household farm in the context of tetrahedral interpretation

Fig. 1: Tetrahedron with the fundamentals of the peasant household (orig. Avadanei, V., 2016)

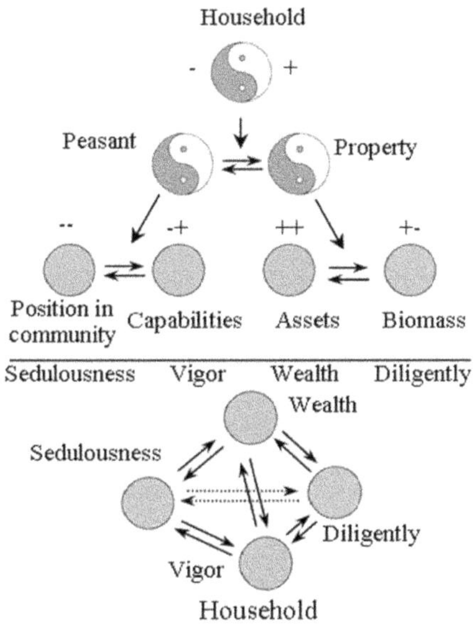

The tetrahedral approach toward the mountain peasant household is in agreement with tetrahedral thought patterns (Avadanei et al., 2016); applying double dichotomies at the household level has resulted in the components shown in figure 1, as follows: In the first division, peasant households consist of two components: "peasant" (with his family) and "property." The second division on the one hand defines the peasant's physical and intellectual "capabilities" and his "position in the community," and on the other hand, property (wealth) is given by the fixed material elements "assets" (land, buildings, tools) and agricultural and forestry "biomass" (which is produced during each annual cycle). Each of the four components of peasant household is defined synthetically by one keyword as follows: "vigor," "sedulousness," "wealth," "diligence." Under this structure is showed a tetrahedron filled with the interrelations between the four components.

Further studies could be deepened by approaching each of the four components or their combination take by two, by three and all four (interdisciplinary). Through systematic study, 15 categories of major themes are distinguished that give us a complete view on the subject.

3.2. Mountain peasant farm management

The term “management” is not exaggerated when considering a household in terms of resources. Hanna Astner (2015) believes that family resources are human, physical, financial and social. In the description of this paper, heritage/household capital is defined as being composed of the following elements:

a) Fixed assets, with long-term use in the production of other consumer goods. They are of an investment nature.
   - Land: in build-up area plots (yard, garden, orchard) and outside plots (field, meadow, forest, vineyard, orchard);
   - Construction/shed: house, barn, cages, pantry, cellar, workshop;
   - Tools: machinery, equipment, vehicles, agricultural machinery, artisanal devices;
   - Animal production; curent production, without sacrificing the animals.

   This is the wealth of households based on investment and maintenance activities.
b) Software assets consist of yields obtained annually which are valued internally and/or externally.

New assets created are made from: biomass produced annually by land (soil) through the action of light and solar heat, air and water; animal productions resulted from biomass; fruit, vegetables and products prepared from it with work contribution by the farmer and his family; during each annual cycle (especially in summer) both through natural food chains and anthropogenic production chains, useful plant and animal products are created, primarily for household consumption. In the mountains, diligence and skill compensate the low fertility of the land and disadvantages due to the most unpredictable climatic factors. Out of the diligence of the peasant and his family result the following newly created goods: the production of vegetables, fruits, grains (restricted), fiber production (flax, hemp), the number of large animals (cattle, sheep, goats, poultry – producing milk, eggs, meat, wool) production of young animals (calves, lambs, goats, chickens) which provide meat (through weight gain) and biological material replacement livestock. The animals were placed in this category because they have an obvious adherence to the solar cycle. They constitute the mobile food resources and their number can be changed through slaughter. Biomass production is determined decisively by the diligence of the family, soil quality and agro-meteorological conditions of each year.

Through this paper are identified and analyzed the main functions of peasant households in the context of sustainable development. Their detailed study revealed the following components and subcomponents:

- Social function: standard of living, wellbeing, health, culture, education. Here is concentrated the main motivation for work and moderation of family.
- Economic function: material wealth (land, house, outbuildings, tools), intangible assets (skill); biological assets (animals, poultry, trees), sources of existence (financial, non-financial). Basically, it is the support for work and family life, the driving force of evolution and existence. The relationship of exchange and equivalent value was created from the first division of labor and has continously increased in complexity and consistency. For a household based on self-sufficiency, economic function is debatable, because the weight of internal material flows ensure it proper functioning, without the need to convert goods into money or other financial resources. For comparison, the model urban fixed asset generically called "urban apartment" converts nearly all matter and energy flows into money.
- Ecological function: natural integration (waste, bioheritage, material heritage); biotechnology (artisanal), microbiology (artisanal). The householder, for millennia, has produced and managed natural products with reasonable integration cycles post-use. Moreover, some elements are found in ecological household function: manure storage space next to animal stables, pool purine (which after fermentation will be spread in the fields to increase soil fertility) and new ecological fossa.
- Technological function: tools, motorization, biological material. Rural technology is diverse and often surprising. In certain creative segments, the inventiveness of the farmer has created simple, but ingenious tools and facilities extremely useful in the household. However, this function has a significant share of outsourcing. Rural technological function has an important vocational connotation and can be performed only by certain people who have talent, are skillful and love their work, and spend a large portion of their time doing creative actions, usually to the detriment of common activities. Obviously, it creates prerequisites for a division of labor and elements for economic changes based on money.

Taking into account these functions, a four-dimensional model can be created regarding the annual activities carried out within the household. This model is centered around man's role in the household and what attributes he must possess, in order to be considered thrifty.

3.3. Man

Of course, the most important element of the household is the man (the husband). The family, "the basic cell of society," is directly linked to the household. The ideal structure of a family is considered as consisting of husband, wife, two children and an old man (Rey, 1979, Fernandez et al., 1998). The man (the husband) has the main position and he handles work "hard" in the household. The wife plays a complementary role and is generating stability. She deals with the "soft" activities, but replaces the man in specific activities when an emergency arises or when he is unavailable (out on business, hired for a job sufficiently well-paid; Hoop et al., 2014). Children are asked to participate in some household chores more readily. This contribution starts with a leading role in the context of educational process and becomes increasingly important to the point of marriage. It is a first step of intergenerational change in family farm (Cavichioli et al., 2014). Together, the husband and wife are authors and beneficiaries of how they generate and maintain a balance between wealth – fertility, values and position in the community. Elders also create stability through authority and wisdom (diversity of experiences they went through and the lessons they learned).

In light of current concepts and perceptions about work and social and economic life, we intend to better understand the role of the human factor in the household. From this point of view, we can define multiple roles that sit on the imaginary axis between the status of employee and entrepreneur status. The reason for this placement is due to a somewhat forced classification for the urban model. In this model, the household is represented by the apartment. It can be accepted as a "black box" with inputs and outputs. They are monetary support and can be described as follows: inputs are incomes resulted as wages (employee status) and/or profit (for the status of entrepreneur). With these, for personal needs are purchased goods or are paid services charges.

The application of this model for the rural household undergoes substantial changes. In the process is involved the household as a whole, by altering the decisive condition of "black box", with interface between internalandexternal faces. Sineiro-Garcia et al. (2014) defined the homestead flows from Galicia (Spain) and highlighted the factors that influence them.

The man (householder) uses his work, land, tools, and outhouses to get goods that satisfy his and family needs. These can not be strictly quantified, as comparing with the model definition of the urban household. Under these circumstances, taking into account the appropriate precautions mentioned above, a mixed positioning based on execution and decision roles is proposed for the rural householder (figure 2).

Fig. 2: Roles of family members in the rural household

The statute of the peasant
a. An employee at his own household (executant);
b. Administrator/manager (owner, tenant);
c. Manager (factor decision);
d. Entrepreneur (factor of initiative);
e. Businessman (capitalize and value the assets and liabilities of the household);
f. Investor (implement projects that increase his wealth)

From this point of view, the householder must possess the necessary skills (fig. 3) in order to be able to cope with specific challenges. It is true that many of these qualities are native. In fact, the post-modern society must find solutions in order to create informative, formative and educational support for householders.

Fig. 3: The qualities and features needed for a good householder

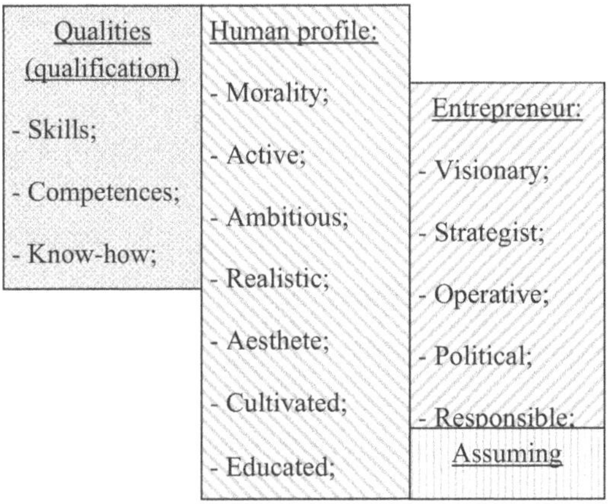

Developing entrepreneurial skills in rural areas will result in a more consistent compatibility and substantiation of economic models regarding household operation under more and more exigent conditions.

Thus, the predictability increases, many of the functional components may be quantified and formal correlations can be made in equivalent value terms of the internal physical flows and interconnections between them.

These qualities and features are valid for the head of household, wife and children, of course, in another distribution according to the current role and potential, the nature of activities performed differing for physical and intellectual capacities of any individual.

A significant advantage resulting from the complementarity of these traits to the husband and wife gives stability in the medium and long term for households.

4. Functional particularities

4.1. Functional territorial dimension

The scale of the activities related to the household pointed out a series of territorial special notes which are the subject of a concept called "area as possible action" (Hoffman, 1999). This is not a precise concept, but results in some energy optimization correlated with natural or artificial boundaries. Therefore, they were generically called "cages," placing some limits on the degree of freedom in the actions of the members of the family/household. In fig. 4 three categories of such "cages" are illustrated, and the levels of the optimization of the action described. Thus, there is a physical space, a social and a cultural area. The differentiation of each of them in levels determine, in fact, a particular psycho-sociological manifestation with an appropriate targeting of resources for the purposes of optimizing their consumption.

Fig. 4: Types of possible space of action (placing "cages

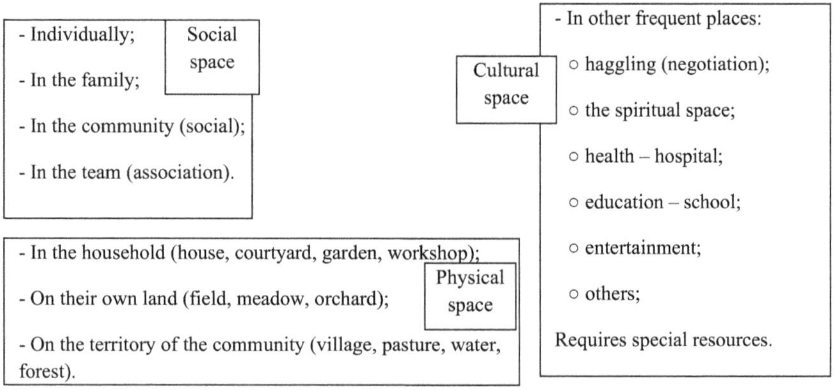

The behavior of the householder is differentiated according with the situation faced. However, the ability to manage the physical and intellectual energies for carrying out an activity or to obtain better results is differentiated and associated with the type of personality. There is also a meteorological constraint: most householders are striving to finish the agricultural work as soon as possible, because they do not know if in the next days the weather will be favorable. Under these circumstances the effort of scheduling suffers a compression which is reflected in the statuses of fatigue, stress, the change in lifestyle and even in feeding mode.

4.2. The dynamics of rural household

Work in the household comprises a succession of activities which concern the production and consumption of resources in a vital process to meet the needs in terms of predictability. For the continuity of the farm, the activities and the production of goods is the most important impact indicator, concerning the stability of the rural mountain communities. It takes into account the seasonal character and nature of the several activities on the components for the generation of resources and consumption, and the reserve of products (during the "dead" seasons) and rate of consumption. Also, continuity refers to the household transfer between generations. This is the reason why the life cycles of the family must be taken into account. It focuses on the head of the family (or on the surviving spouse, if one of them dies). The most relevant steps are:

- Marriage – the key moment; dowry – initial conditions;
- Taking over the inheritance from the previous generation;
- The richness/accumulation of new values and goods (via worthiness);
- Changing the inheritance to the next generation (offspring);
- Release from duty and responsibilities;

- The annual cycle (seasonal cycle based on the seasons of the year). It shall take into account the fact that there is a production season for living resources and a "dead" season which includes agricultural work or agricultural preparatory work. Material, financial and human efforts required during the year, are staggeringly different according to the season (Tocco et al., 2016). Diminishing of the human effort is supported by the new modern solutions, mechanization, automation and ICT. Consumption is differentiated for four specific seasons (for temperate climate zones): season of fresh food (summer), season of abundances (autumn), preserved products season (winter) and the sprouting season (spring). The rhythm of consumption is also important: it must be moderate and nutritionally balanced. In addition, the Christian faith has periods of religious fasting during which is selected and restricted the consumption of certain kinds of food (especial those of animal origin). To stay in good condition throughout the climatic cycles requires planning, as follows:
- Ordering of agricultural works during the climatic periods, as result of the experience of generations during hundreds of years;
- The management of the "dead" times (non-agricultural activities): carrying out non-agricultural activities, and the preparation for the next agricultural season;
- Activities planning: implementation of a timetable for the preparatory activities;
- Consumption (food, clothes, thermal energy): clothing, drawing up, the establishment of reserves and security management (perishability – fermentation, degradation).

Lifestyle correlation with the annual cycles (on the seasons)

Throughout history, the existence of people in a specified territory has been determined by the availability of resources to meet the living needs. When there was no mechanization, householder productivity was determined only by his own physical power in association with the works carried out by the domestic animals (traction). Under these conditions, the cultural pattern that he established for himself was "work first." Therefore, all things and all householder life was ordered according to this priority. Only in this way could he find pleasure in work, and win work values etc. Nowadays, the cultural pattern is still based on the priority of labor as a factor of stability and increasing living standards.

A lifestyle structured after the annual cycle (the seasons) was also established over several dozens of generations. Since rural mountain life involves work on extensive areas (agriculture, sewing, livestock) it was developed the concept of mobilities:

- The human resources were involved according to the "available space for action;"
- For tools, equipments, facilities and means of transport (the car, cart etc.) increase the area of action by contribution of pack animals which undertake a significant part of the human tasks. Under these conditions, the man is more rested and may carry out some activities in the workplace (away from home) or relax; the same effect appears in the help given by animals at the agricultural works: ploughing, weeding, mowing etc.

- The storage of fresh biomass in the form of hay (small haystack, mow, rick feed, rick, hay warehouse); here things are even more spectacular: storage of fodder resources (in particular of hay) for winter requires a special effort for transport. In the mountains, tiredness is amplified by work at the various levels of altitude. The compromise that is made consists in the building of wooden warenhouses for hay close to the place of production (haystacks made directly on the meadow) and moving the animals in winter, to feed them there with the stored hay. In this situation are allocated costs for building temporary shelters for the animals, but the effort of transport becomes significantly lower.
- The processing of agricultural or forest raw materials (at the mill, sawmill – artisanal tools for cutting logs); the necessary tools or equipments are expensive and it is not within the power of every man to make such investments. Considering this reality, the community encourages a local and skilled householder to build a mill or a sawmill because they call them up for these services against a barter payment or a toll payment. The volume of activity is sufficiently high, so that the developer can recover the investment within a reasonable period of time. It should be noted that the mill, e.g., is considered to be a service in rural areas and an activity of production in urban areas.

In this context of mobility already described, the householder makes a planning of warehouses depending on the productivity of the land, work, and the genetic value of the biological material (varieties of plant and animal). Taking into account the risks of climate change (rainy year/dry year), he can make an estimation on the volume of work and the production of biomass annually.

The planning in a household is modeled after the climatic cycles and aims for at least three directions of action:

- The preservation and storage of the products from one year to another and ensuring requirements;
- Phasing efforts to support the agricultural, forestry, zootechnical work after the biological cycles/productive and correlated with those seasonal products;
- Prioritizing activities by volume and emergencies (seasonal and climatic); complementarity with activities/non-agricultural production (when not in agricultural activities, household activities shall be conducted; Pascotto et al., 2004);
- Diversification of resources and improving the production of biomass: overseeding lawns, permanent meadows, seeds (improved varieties), animals (better-performing or more vigorous races), fertilizers for soil etc. (Costa et al., 2014, organic family farming).

In this context, were identified policies and strategies applied in the planning of the work/actions and the resources required for a mountain householder in each of the four seasons (Soares, 2016), as follows:

- in summer: produce and gather the resources (harvest), savings, pay debts (preparedness for the crisis);

- in autumn: sell weak animals/reformed, self-fertilizing shrubs first earth (reduces wastage);
- in winter: make purchases (animals, seeds, saplings), to engage works, grazing etc.;
- in spring: reap benefits from preparations for the cycle of the crop year (development).

4.3. The quantitative aspects

To speak about the household in quantitative terms means to draw up a balance sheet of material resources, financial, human and the information society. It is complex through diversity and the large number of random variables.

The equation of the annual balance sheet of material resources applied to the household level is:

$$(1)\ I - E + G = \pm\ Ac$$

where E = outputs, I = inputs G = generated (+)/consumped (−), Ac = accumulated

Table 1 presents the items that are subject to material balance for all four terms of equation (1). These elements are grouped into the following categories: lands (inside or outside build-up areas), construction (the house, outhouses), biomass (plants, animals), traditional processed domestic products, ○ non-food products, biomass energy (firewood), external services (mill, sawmill, mill machine, carpentry/joinery etc.).

The examination of the table shows a few remarkable aspects:

- the table expresses all the material and immaterial movements which are to take place in the household;
- "inputs and outputs" appear in the process of sale/purchase and have the effect of increasing or reducing the number/effects (to the interface);
- "generated" consists in the increase or reduction of the number in the household through propagation, respectively by slaughter (internal); the slaughter is done primarily for food; here can be taken into consideration and the risk of mortality;
- "accumulated" consists in the annual net result; it is actually household assets to be transferred from one year to the next;
- each item (article) has components in the four terms of the equation;
- most of the items shall be expressed in terms of physical units (pcs., kg, liters, etc.) for that destination in closed circuit and are subjects of barter; a reduced number of items are expressed in terms of monetary units (sales/purchase);
- each item corresponds to a value that represents the actual quantities of the various products passing through the household during a calendar year. The amount of the last column represents the wealth and fortune of the household. The social condition of householder within the community is established on the basis of the personal wealth.

- each item in table 1 can be associated with a monetary value, possibly after the price of the fair. Such an assessment provides a quantification value of the household, compatible with and equivalent to the urban economic models. Based on this quatification, an objectively comparative analysis can be done to evaluate what share of active and passive of the farmer's household shall be substituted for the natural units (and does not require the exchange in cash values).

The difference expressed by the monetary units, or directly resulting from the process of sale/purchase, strengthens the position of the household by ensuring some acquisitions of goods needed for non-agricultural activities, such as: school supplies for children, industrial objects inaccessible otherwise (crockery, tools, furniture), taxes and duties to the state, payment of some services, weddings, christenings, etc.

It is not usual for the householder to draw up a yearly income and expenditure budget for the household. But he can compare income and assets from a year with others and may make adjustments/necessary corrections for each of the items listed in table 1.

Drawing up a budget income and expenditure is an intellectual activity that is not common for the householder. Instead, he has developed a surprising memory and retains all details of the activity from the household.

For wealthier households, which can do this reckoning on "paper"(diploma) with a secondary education, he can make plans and even simulate possible scenarios, and can make decisions favorable to the development of his household. Thus, e.g., they can purchase animals raised for meat over the carrying capacity of the field or meadow and may increase their value via the acquisition of fodder so that the earnings are obtained only from the weight gain of animals and his labor.

In the circumstances described above, hardworking householders are found, with a more developed entrepreneurial spirit and who have the courage to live following the traditional pattern. This traditional pattern is based on a balanced and sober life and keeps the householder like in a corset, as a simple employee in their own household. By living this pattern, the motivational logic is also changing. The future of traditional mountain farms is decisively influenced by the proximity of consumers, since transportation costs over greater distances significantly increase the total cost of the product (Madelrieu et al., 2014).

Table 1: The components of a balance sheet of materials into a household

	Name articles	Inputs (money)	Outputs (money)	+ Generate (physical)	- Generate (physical)	Accumulated (money, physical)
A	Land - yard, garden, orchard (intravilan)	Purchase ,	Sale,	Inheritance	Dowry	Available
	Land - field, pasture, meadow, forest (extravilan)	Purchase ,	Sale,	Inheritance	Dowry	Available
B	Construction - home accessories (pantry, cellar, summer kitchen)	Purchase whole/parts, labor, materials	Sales whole/parts, labor, materials	Inheritance, Building	Dowry, pull down	Available
	Construction: mill, smokehouse, oven, workroom etc.	Purchase, labor, materials	Sale, labor, materials	Inheritance, Building	Dowry, pull down	Available
	Outbuildings: stable, cages, barn, warehouse,	Purchase, labor, materials	Sale, labor, materials	Inheritance, Building	Dowry, pull down	Available
C	Biomass vegetable (effective)	Buying seeds, fertilizers	The sale of the harvest field	Culture, Spontaneous	Harvest, grazing, mowing, Degradation	In vegetation
	Fruit trees and vines	Buying seedlings	Sale seedlings	Growth	Cleaning, cutting	In vegetation
	Biomass (primary processed) (vegetables, hay, fruits, grains, fibers - flax, hemp);	Purchase (deficit)	Sale (surplus)	Harvest. selling, drying, conditioning, swingle, combings	Degradation	Storage: stack, barn, pantry, cellar, attic,
	Animals, birds (effective)	Purchase (calves, piglets, chickens, lambs)	Sale (cows, sheep, pigs, poultry)	Multiplication increase growth	Slaughter for consumption	Number, Weight,
	Animals, birds (operation)	Milk, eggs, meat, wool	Milk, eggs, meat, wool	Milk production, egg, wool Meat production	Consumption, Processing	Available for consumption
	Horses, oxen	Buying foals, horses	Sale foals, horses	Traction services (horses, oxen)	-	Effective / Livestock
D	Processed food	Purchase (required)	Sale (surplus)	Grinding, Meat Preparation, Preparation cheese	Degradation	Available in the barn, pantry, cellar
	Food consumed in raw form	Purchase (required)	Sale (surplus)	-	Vegetables, fruits	Available in pantry
	Prepared food			Preparation (Gastronomy)	Consumption	
	Canned food	Purchase (required)	Sale (surplus)	Preparation: pickles, dried fruit, smoked meats, cheese	Consumption	Available in pantry, cellar
E	Textile crafts activities: spinning, weaving, stitching, sewing	Buy (materials)	Sale (finished products)	Clothing, footwear, carpets, mats, towels others	Use (wear), Exposure (decoration)	Dowry chest, clothing (summer, winter)
	Woodworking: carpentry, woodwork, farming tools, tools, crafts, coopers, wheelwrights	Buy (materials)	Sale (finished products)	Shed; Tails fork, rake, hoe, scythe, ax; Pots, tubs, bathtubs; Fences brackets dry hay, pot peg	Use (wear)	Dowry household (in use in reserve)
	Metal processing: the metal tools (forks, axes, spades, shovels), fasteners (nails, staples), horseshoes, wheel tracks etc.	Buy	Sale	Machining, thermal processing (forging), processing bending, impact; riveting, welding, grindstone	Use (wear)	Dowry household (in use in reserve)
F	Firewood (heating, cooking, etc.)	Firewood raw	Firewood cut	Cut to size, brushwood	Burning in fireplace or stove or oven	Storage timber
G	Outside the household: mill, mill machine, whirlpool, Smithy (farriery)	Purchase (services)	Sale (craftsmen)	-	Use (wear)	Dowry household (in use in reserve)

5. Exploiting the results

Applying equation (1) to items in table 1 leads to the following interpretations:

- the equation (1) is comprehensive and reflects the worthiness of the householder, the soundness of the household and his social position within the community;
- "inputs and outputs" constitute the extent of the entrepreneurial character of the householder, his courage and the challenge of coming to the market with his products (but not as Danila Prepeleac)[4].
- "Generated" (generic name for newly created product during a year) is especially the measure of the housewife's worthiness, of her ingenuity, the creative and innovative spirit (especially in the gastronomy); in other words, "generated" reflects the extent of domestic enterpreneurship.
- "Acumulated" means the measure of family worthiness; abundance can be found here (the difference between inputs and costs); here is measured the degree of regeneration of wealth (new and vigorous young, enduring outbuildings, increase in land, giving up old/used goods; here is kept the reserve assets for tomorrow's security of the whole family. "Acumulated" contains both results in physical units (nature), as well as in value units (money). It must be taken into account that "acumulated" is renewable and perishable and very rarely exceeds a shelf life of more than two years.

In fact, table 1 can be interpreted in the physical form (if each position is associated with one equivalent in nature – the number of heads, quantities, volume, etc.) or in value terms (if associated with the monetary equivalent). They give an image of the household in absolute value or by comparison from one year to the next.

However, the analysis is not complete and conclusive. The interpretations are made by association. Reasons:

- the monetary values does not reflect the structure, characteristics and productive qualities of the animals (breed, age, pedigree) or of plants (variety, soil, the relationship with the fertilizers, the diversity of flora meadows).
- for the expression in physical/natural units there is not a common measurement unit (number of heads, quantities, volumes, valorizing or internal devaluation, etc.)

At the European level, an equivalent unit of the characterization of the economic potential of one farm was found, on the basis of the statistical average calculated from the samples recorded in farms representative of all EU countries. Thus, for the program period of 2007–2013 were used UDE (units of economic development; Regulation (EC) No. 1242 / 2008), and for the programming period of 2014–2020,

4 Ion Creangă's fairy who went to the fair with two oxen and through successive damaging agreements, returned home with a paper bag.

VPS are used (standard production value or SO – standard output; EUROSAT CPSA/SB/714/2013).

Neither the first nor the second form of quantification favors the mountain household, because these units are based on a household from hilly and plains areas where mechanized works can be used in the field, also with the support of performing genetic biological material. The results are particularly high, and the coefficients are within the measure. In fact, as a result of the industrial model applicable to the farm rural areas, it can be said that the rural household of a hilly area can be assimilated to a farms/agricultural exploitation, but rural mountain household cannot. It follows that the model is detrimental to the mountain households which is based on lots of physical labor, higher costs and higher consumption (due to the extension of the cold-weather season), and the attributes of natural products are not recognized and appreciated.

The model of the rural mountain household can be assimilated to a farm oriented toward the performance in certain situations:

- If it has the attributes of a cooperative which puts in common certain movable or immovable property;
- If it is oriented toward an economic activity assessed in monetary values (because it works directly on the interface of sale/purchase, and with a more limited number of physical categories); the risks are significant (Jurt et al., 2014);
- It may be a simple rural household, located in the perimountain or depression area with access to more extensive lands (fields, meadows);
- It must produce more than the family needs and the surplus must be sold on the market; as such, they will be able to take into account the contribution to solve the world food problem.

A special category of rural householders with the status of entrepreneurs are to be found in several traditional non-agricultural activities. So, crafts are also taken into account: blacksmith, woodworker, carpenter, cooper, mason. The pursuit of these activities requires a special qualification, a vocation and, in particular, the transmission of "secrets" from father to son.

The entrepreneurship among young people must also take into account how to approach the farm activities (Parkinson et al., 2015). There are a lot of scientific papers describing attempts of mountain householders of associating agricultural activities with tourism (Warchalska et al., 2014). Other attempts relating to the approach of the farm from mountain areas with other components (Vogel et al., 2007).

Of course, there are other non-agricultural activities in the rural mountain area at present. They are not traditional, but needed (otherwise they would not have customers) and are a signal of modernizing rural life, bringing compensation for some breaks in the supply chain or in the value chain into traditional, economic and social landscape.

Conclusion

- The peasant farm is required as defined in order to be able to be classified (framed and integrated) in the community (community cohesion is given by the quality and the wealth of householders);
- Financial policies for rural development support must be reported to the ability of householders to put them to value for the benefit of the community;
- The micro-economic indicators associated with peasant households should support and substantiate the macro-economic indicators of development;
- The cultural life of the peasant household can be quantified and assessed in the monetary equivalent (with precautions) in order to strengthen the force and stability; the investment or its subsidizing should also be established for this component in conjunction with other criteria of compatibility;
- The conservation of the peasant household must contain elements of stability in relation with the external environment: the autonomy correlates with a series of interdependencies because so many of the traditional activities have been taken over by variants much more accessible and more acceptable (operations, materials, objects in current use). As a result, economic balance is hereby amended, and corrections and compensation are necessary.
- The transfer of the statuswhich we want for the peasant, from "employee in their own household" to "entrepreneur," requires professionalizing. This professionalizing must ensure the framing of the elements of traditional production with the contemporary world of consumption. If the required policies do not understand or do not accept that this is decisive, any action or attempt is futile. Therefore, it is not only the failure of policies, but also a gain of frustrations which supplies more solid reasons for the exodus of the population toward the city or to other developed countries.

A semantics valuation, which we recommend be taken into consideration when we make substantiations, and in further evaluation is the Romanian word "ortoman." This word appears in the ballad "Miorita," and the "Romanian language explicative dictionary" (DEX) given him a differing interpretation used in the course of time. We want to suggest that the term "ortoman" is a measure of the mountain entrepreneurs with strong historical roots. "Ortoman" can be placed in the top of Maslow's pyramid applied to the mountain householder. He is distinguished by a few attributes quite unique:

- Has proved his worthiness;
- Has managed to create a powerful genetic heritage in his animals;
- Has a high capacity of genetic renewal of the herd;
- Evolves in a very large possible action space (transhumance), overlaid on annual cycles (Jurt et al., 2014);
- Mobilizes resources and is able to respond to important commercial orders;
- His managerial performance can be compared to that of multinational companies;

- Realizes the huge advantage of food energy resources, in motion;
- Has in his service faithful animals, dedicated to some activities (flocks or sheep-fold guard): "dogs stronger and more devoted than men."

Unfortunately, literature places the peasant in a competitive hostile environment, in which not competition is predominant, but fraud. It is the answer to the question "Why has has there not been established a market economy in our country until now?"

As a matter of fact, in rural persons understanding, the term "entrepreneur" is associated with financiar speculation and not with the economic and social development.

However, a positive element remains for the term "householder," which associates the performance with honest work and with the seriousness, responsibility assumption and the refuse to accept a gain resulting from speculating a favorable conjuncture.

References

1. Astner, H., 2015, Entrepreneurship and Family as an Active Dimension of Context: the Co-creation of New Ventures, ICEIRD2015: International Conference for Entrepreneurship, Innovation and Regional Development, 18–19 June, Sheffield UK, Conferece proceedings, pp. 25–37.
2. Avădănei, V., Stângu, C., Iancu, E., 2009, START-up, cum se începe şi dezvoltă o afacere, Ed. Nona, Piatra Neamţ.
3. Avădănei, V., Avădănei, L., Tuduran, A., Bujor, O.C., Amagdei, D., 2010, Potenţialul antreprenorial şi de creativitate la graniţa dintre generaţii. Progrese în teoria deciziilor economice în condiţii de risc şi incertitudine, vol. XII, ed. I. Talabă, Ed. Tehnopress Iaşi.
4. Avădănei, V., Bujor, O. C., Avădănei, L., 2012, Aptitudini de creativitate ale tinerilor liceeni din judeţul Neamţ. Studiu, Ed. Răzeşu, Piatra Neamţ, ISBN 978-973-88108-0-8.
5. Avădănei, V., Bujor, O. C., Avădănei, L., 2013, "Secrete" şi "soluţii magice" în afaceri, Ed. Răzeşu, Piatra Neamţ, ISBN 978-606-8187-23-5.
6. Avădănei, V., Latu, L., Avădănei, L., 2014, Gastronomie în Munţii Neamţului, Forumul Montan din România – filiala Neamţ, ISBN 978-973-0-17839-5; (română, engleză – 2015, germană – 2015).
7. Avădănei, V., Avădănei, L., David, E., Marian, G., 2016, Comunicare asertivă prin abordare tetraedrică, in "Conferinţa internaţională, Progrese în teoria deciziilor economice în condiţii de risc şi incertitudine," vol. 27, ed. C. Alecu şi colab, Ed. Performantica Iaşi.
8. Avădănei, V., Horlescu B. C., Avădănei, L., 2016, Civilizaţia montană a judeţului Neamţ văzută prin ochii tinerei generaţii, Centrul de Incubare Creativ Inovativ de Afaceri.

9. Cavicchioli, D., Bertoni, D., Tesser, F., Frisio, D. G., 2014, What Factors Encourage Intrafamily Farm Succession in Mountain Areas?, Mountain Research and Development, 35 (2):pp. 152–160.
10. da Costa, C. A., Correia, P., Correia, H. E., Guine, R. P. F, Gouveia, J. P., Rodrigues, P., Teixeira, D., Tourino, L., Basile, S., 2014, Family and organic farming. New apprenticeship through m-learning. Practitioners' Track, IFOAM Organic World Congress 'Building Organic Bridges,' 13–15 Oct., Istanbul, Turkey.
11. Fassio, G., Battaglini, L. M., Porcellana, V., Viazzo, P. P., 2014, The Role of the Family in Mountain Pastoralism – Change and Continuity, Mountain Research and Development, 34 (4): pp. 336–343.
12. Fernandez, J. W., Fernandez, R. L., 2016, Under one roof: household formation and cultural ideals in an Asturian mountain village, Journal of family history, Volume 13, Lorand Soares, ciclul de conferințe "Responsabilitate și abilitate," Piatra Neamț (19 ian.), pp. 123–142.
13. Fitiu, A., 2012, Salvarea fermei ţărăneşti, Ed. Studia, Cluj Napoca.
14. Florescu, E., 2010, Textile populare de casă din zona Neamţ, Ed. Etnologică, Bucureşti.
15. Florescu, E., 2011, Arhitectura populară din zona Neamţ, Ed. Etnologică, Bucureşti.
16. Hoffman, O., 1999, Dezvoltarea durabilă și trecerea la sistemele economico – sociale antropo-centrice, in "Dezvoltarea în pragul Mileniului III," ed. V. Cândea, Ed. Europa Nova, Bucureşti.
17. Hoop, D., Mack, G., Mann, S., Schmid, D., 2014, On the dynamics of agricultural labour input and their impact on productivity and income: an empirical study of Swiss family farms, International Journal of Agricultural Management, Volume 3 Issue 4, pp. 221–231.
18. Jurt, C., Häberli, I., and Rossier, R., 2014, Transhumance Farming in Swiss Mountains: Adaptation to a Changing Environment, Mountain Research and Development, 35 (1): pp. 57–65.
19. Madelrieux, S., Terrier, M., Borg, D., Dobremez, L., 2014, Development trajectories of mountain dairy farms in the globalization era. Evidence from the Vercors (French Northern Alps), 11th European IFSA Symposium, April 2014, Berlin, Germany. p. 10.
20. Jon, M., 2010: "Diversity of Family Practices in Mountain Societies: Why?", Derouet, B., Lorenzetti, L., Mathieu, J., eds., Pratiques familiales et sociétés de montange, XVIe–XXe siècles. Basel: Schwabe Verlag, pp. 173–188.
21. Mazzocchi, C., Sali, G., 2016, Sustainability and Competitiveness of Agriculture in mountain Areas: A Willingness to Pay (WTP) Approach, Sustainability, 8, p. 343.
22. Neagu, V., Stanciu, Gh., 1996, România – Carta Europeană a Spațiului Rural, Ed. Ceres, București.
23. Olaizola, A. M., Manrique, E., Bernués, A., 1998, Family Types on Extensive Farming Systems in Less Favoured Mountain Areas of Spain, In: Doppler, W., Koutsouris A, editors. Rural and Farming Systems Analyses: Environmental Perspectives. Proceedings of the Third European Symposium of the Association

of Farming Systems Research and Extension in Hohenheim, Germany, 25–27 March, Weikersheim, Germany: Margraf Verlag, pp. 297–308.
24. Palicica, L, I., Palicica, M., 2005, Resursele umane şi pregătirea forţei de muncă în mediul rural, Ed. Orizonturi Universitare, Timişoara.
25. Parkinson, C., Southern, A., Howorth, C., Nowak, V., Young People and Entrepreneurial Cultures in 'Low- Income Communities,' ICEIRD2015: International Conference for Entrepreneurship, Innovation and Regional Development, 18–19 June 2015, Sheffield UK, Conferece proceedings, pp. 190–208.
26. Pascotto, S., De Ros, G., 2004, Diversification as a strategy for rural development: a case study in an EU mountain area, 87th EAAE-Seminar. Assessing rural development of the CAP, Vienna (Austria).
27. Rey, R., 1979, Viitor în Carpaţi, Ed. Scrisul Românesc.
28. Sineiro-García, F., Vázquez-González, I., García-Arias, A. I., 2014, Mountain Family Farms in Galicia, Spain: Challenges and Strategies, Mountain Research and Development, 34 (4): pp. 375–385.
29. Soares, L., 2016, ciclul de conferinţe "Responsabilitate şi abilitate," Piatra Neamţ (19 ian.).
30. Tocco, B., Davidova, S., Bailey, A., 2016, Part-Time Farming in Italy: Does Farm Size Really Matter?, 90th Annual Conference of the Agricultural Economics Society, University of Warwick, England.
31. Vogel, S., Maurer, O., Wytrzens, H. K., Larcher, M., 2007, Perceptions of mountain farming in South Tyrol: Cultural differences in a border region, Man in the lanscape across frontier – Igu-Lucc Central Europe Conference, Proceedings, pp. 209–220.
32. Warchalska-Troll, A., Troll, M., 2014, Summer Livestock Farming at the Crossroads in the Ukrainian Carpathians, Mountain Research and Development, 34 (4): pp. 344–355.
33. 1973, Etnografia Văii Bistriţei – zona Bicaz, Academia Română, colectiv Bicaz.
34. 2008, Regulamentul CE nr. 1242/.
35. 2013, Eurostat, CPSA/SB/714/.

Ion CUCUI

Prof., PhD, President of Dambovita Filiation of Academy of Romanian Scients, Valahia University of Targoviste, Associated Researcher CEMONT, email: cucui50@gmail.com

Dan Marius COMAN

Associate Professor, Faculty of economic science, Valahia University of Targoviste, email: cmnmarius@yahoo.com

Constantin Aurelian IONESCU

Phd. Student, Valahia University of Targoviste, email: aurel_eco_2006@yahoo.com

Mihaela Denisa COMAN

Research Assistant, Valahia University of Targoviste, Institute of Multidisciplinary Research for Science and Technology 130004, Targoviste, Romania, email: cmndenisa@gmail.com

Mountain Economy Under the Impact of Information and Communication Technologies

Abstract: Starting from the assumption that, at the global level, mountains cover 25% of the Earth's surface and are inhabited by more than 12% of the world population, and that mountain ecosystems are genuine reservoirs of biodiversity providing water, agri-food products, minerals, timber, building materials, and numerous energy sources, we should point out and emphasize the need to adjust mountain economy to the exhaustive expansion of information and communication technology. Information technologies represent an opportunity for economic entities in mountainous areas due to the services that give the possibility of creating web applications for electronic commerce, for product tracking and traceability, etc. Web applications are developed based on facile services provided by various companies, such as Microsoft, Oracle, which aim to bring technology closer to the business environment and especially to support those outsourced businesses. This paper aims to present mountain economy, given the development of information and communication technologies.

Keywords: Mountain economy, information technologies, communication technologies, web applications, e-commerce

Introduction

At the global level, mountains cover 25% of the Earth's surface and are inhabited by 12% of the population, forming reservoirs of biodiversity that provide water, agri-food products, minerals, timber, building materials, and numerous energy sources, which entails the need to highlight the connections between mountain economy and digital economy. The amount of goods and services provided by global mountain ecosystems supports, on average, half of human population and also maintains through its functions of regulating and rejuvenating, the entire Earth system (ICIMD, 2010, p. 5).

In Romania, 70% of the country surface is represented by mountainous and hilly areas, which point to the fact that mountain economy should rely on a durable development (Mitrache, Ş., 2000, p. 9–10) both on the whole and considering the component elements (for instance, eco-tourism), respecting man's current needs and demands without compromising the future generations' possibility to satisfy their own social needs. The development of mountain communities is a process involving the exploitation of their own resources in order to produce the best social and economic advantage for the entire community. The development of these communities implies the establishment of collaborations with governmental institutions (the government, public institutions, development agencies, agencies that manage structural funds) and the existence of local initiative, materialized in partnerships, able to identify and solve community problems, promoting these partnerships as projects, with a view to identifying solutions that lead the community to and engage them in a constant process development based on durable principles.

This process of constant development can be promoted and supported through the implementation of information and communication technologies, adapted to the specific nature of their activities. Furthermore, the mountain offers an illustrative way of thinking at historical levels, that has influenced over time the establishment and evolution of the historical course through the resources provided for the evolution of humanity (Hall, M., Kupper, P., 2014, p. 19). In order to achieve a sustainable development of mountain communities as well as to promote and capitalize the mountain products of a superior quality to the products of the plain and hill areas, within the process of globalization and the era of digitalization, the development of logistics and also the use the current information and communication technologies is impetuously necessary.

Simultaneously, the use of Information and Communications Technology Services and digital media contribute to changing both the daily life of the population, and the activities of economic entities, because it creates the framework for communicating, connecting and collaborating in a social context and also at work.

These technologies remove the space and time barriers and also exercise a liberalization of knowledge. The use of Information and Communications Technology Services generates various opportunities and benefits, highlighted in the present research, which can be a binder and an efficient possibility for exploiting them in the development of the mountain economy, as well as promoting the resulting products.

1. Literature review

Having established the aim of the paper, namely to present mountain economy in the context of the evolution of information and communication technologies, we deem it of great interest both at the national and global level, due to the ever-increasing integration of technology into contemporary man's daily life. The use of the Internet and of modern information and communication technologies generates significant economic benefits for all sectors by shaping the competitiveness framework of economic entities and highlighting the change in human mentality both at the individual and collective level. Thus, the integration of these technologies into mountain economy represents the framework for promoting and exhibiting national cultural values and products obtained through traditional methods in the mountain area. Scholarly literature abounds in data regarding the integration of information and communication technologies into most economic sectors (for example studies to improve supply chain management and selling in agriculture, Deichmann, et al., 2016, pp. 21–33; to increase access to services in rural communities Hodge, H., et al., 2016.; to develop rural tourism, Deuchar C., Milne S., 2016, p. 280, etc.), but we also identify the opportunity of utilizing them within mountain economy.

2. Rural economy and tourism, a basis for the development and progress of mountain economy

All countries worldwide, regardless of their level of economic and social development, support the development and progress of national economies. At European level, rural communities have suffered dramatic economic and demographic changes, namely: depopulation, aging population, migration of young people to urban areas, decrease in number of farmers and livestock breeders, etc. (ENRD, 2011). We find these negative changes also in Romania, especially in the mountain areas. We can affirm that the European rural development policy for 2014–2020 has a well-targeted mission to achieve sustainable food production, sustainable management of natural resources and climate action and balanced territorial development, a policy that is in line with the Europe 2020 strategy, focusing on research, innovation, employment labor, education, social inclusion, etc. (EPRS, 2015, p. 5).

Rural economy consists of five components: i) agriculture with the vegetal, animal and industrial production; ii) agrotourism, with emphasis on the specific traditions of each rural area; iii) forestry stock, fishing and hunting; iv) craftsmanship; v) transports, telecommunications and commercial activities. Within this system of rural economy, we may emphasize that rural areas can be characterized in terms of the following plurality of functions (Vincze, M., 2000, p. 9): i) economic function, which reflects all undertaken activities, such as: agricultural production, fishing and hunting, exploitation of natural resources and rural tourism; ii) socio-cultural function, which implies the preservation and promotion of cultural traditional values as well as of community values that regard aspects related to the rural way of life; iii) ecological function, which requires the protection of natural bases, such as land, water, air, as well as the protection of biodiversity and preservation of the specific character of the landscape. Having established the functions that rural areas fulfil, one may also point out the economic importance of products that can be exploited and promoted with real success both on the domestic market and internationally, accessory products supplied by the mountain forests of Romania.

The accessory products of the Romanian forestry stock are the material resources of vegetal nature, which are totally or partially attached, provided by shrubs, trees and forest soil, as well as the related lands, products that can be harvested and exploited as such or industrially processed by assortments, which, due to the plenty of vitamins, minerals and beneficial substances, help improve and diversify man's nourishment, the forage stock, or which are used in the pharmaceutical, chemical and cosmetic industries and to provide energetic materials, natural fertilizers and building materials (Milescu, I., 2006, p. 709).

According to their final destination, accessory products can be classified as: i) products for the food industry (mushrooms, forest fruit, seeds, etc.); ii) products for the pharmaceutical and cosmetic industry (medicinal plants, aromatic plants, etc.); iii) products used in the small-scale industry, craftsmanship (wattles, cones, Christmas trees, etc.); iv) products for the chemical industry producing resin and turpentine, lacquers, latexes and vegetable waxes, ethereal oils, etc; v) products which can be used as building materials (wattles, bark), natural fertilizers (leaves, bark), energetic resources (branches, bark), apiculture resources (melliferous plants).

In addition to these products supplied by mountain forests, another component, significant to both rural and mountain economy in general, is represented by fishing and hunting, two important activities that can be promoted and exploited for the development of a durable mountain economy. In Romania, the life environment of salmonids is represented by the streams in the montane and premontane areas, the alpine lakes and storage basins built on mountain rivers (Milescu, I., 2006, p. 771). Thus, Romanian mountainous aquaculture of salmonids consists of fish species such as: native trout, brook trout, lake trout, rainbow trout, huchen, grayling, etc. A controlled and efficient exploitation of these resources may lead to the growth and development of Romanian mountain economy.

Having previously described some of the products and activities that can be carried out in mountain rural areas, we shall continue our scientific research by presenting one component that has a major impact on mountain economy, namely tourism. The dynamics and complexity of transformations in all sectors of contemporary economic and social life undoubtedly reflect on mountain economy as well, with rural economy and tourism as its main components. Although Romania has a rich and diverse natural and entropic territory, as well as an old tradition in organizing trips – two arguments which should be sufficient to include tourism within the basic branches of Romanian economy – the managerial gap between economic entities belonging to the tourism industry of developed countries and Romanian companies is clear and almost unparalleled.

Romania should develop mountain tourism as an important part of its economic development policy, as it produces beneficial effects for employment, production and consumption, and thus establishing international relations becomes an incentive for progress and economic growth (Minciu, R., 2005). In a dynamic, modern economy, the supply of tourist activities cannot be considered attractive and competitive unless it complies with the customers' demands and motivations, the evolution of current trends and perspective on national and international tourist markets. Consequently, the tourist becomes the central factor of the tourism marketing mix (Bucur-Sabo, M., 2006, p. 24), which may influence the specific ways of strategic and tactical intervention both in defining the touristic product, setting the price and elaborating the distribution and promotion policy by using traditional alternatives, but mostly present-day information and communication technologies.

The integration of ICT services into the tourism marketing mix specific to mountain economy leads to the promotion and exposure of the entire area and of mountain biodiversity, corroborated with the expansion and development of the range of agro-industrial, pharmaceutical and cosmetic products which rely on the use of accessory products supplied by the forestry stock, cynegetic and viticultural funds related to the mountain area, towards potential national and international consumers.

Fig. 1: Tourism marketing mix

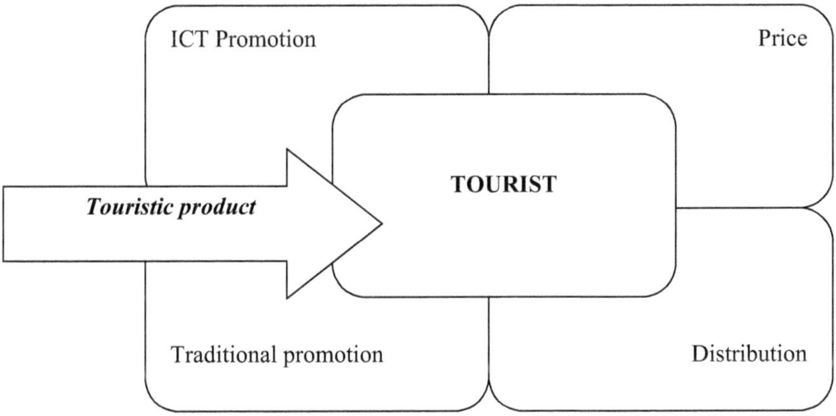

Source: Personal processing.

Achieving synchronization between the expansion of rural markets and the deployment of ICTs can lead to an increase in the number of people attracted to rural areas for the purchase of goods and the increase in farmers' financial returns. In other words, food tourism can provide an opportunity for the development of mountain rural communities coupled with a good promotion of locations and products through the use of websites, social networks, digital media tools and smartphone applications. By integrating these technologies, local producers can attract consumers to their location or develop online trade (ENRD, 2016, p. 10).

3. Information and communication technology services, a prerequisite for mountain economy development

As information and communication technologies, particularly the Internet, have changed the way in which economic entities communicate and transact, there are few domains that have not made any attempts to integrate these technologies into their own activity. However, economic entities in Romanian mountain areas are at a low level of adopting and implementing these technologies. It augurs well for all categories of mountain economy entities to get acquainted with these information and communication technologies, to find ways of implementing them in the sectors in which they operate. Although some economic entities have websites, it is necessary to integrate these services into the entity development strategy as an access channel to customers, a distribution channel of products and services or just a mere channel of distribution and dissemination of information, depending on the specific nature of the activity.

In present-day Romania, data transfer speed is optimal compared to the rest of the world; hence ICT can become the promoter of the development of electronic economy in all areas of traditional commerce in any region. Under these circumstances, electronic commerce is a concept that offers companies the chance to market their products worldwide, increasing the number of potential customers by removing geographical barriers and permanent availability to the product supply. Particularizing this idea, one may state that mountain tourism enterprises may choose the facilities provided by electronic commerce. This distribution channel has advantages as it shortens the chain of agents between supply and demand (avoiding travel agencies or tour-operators; Henke, B. G., 2004, p. 189).

Within this system of direct distribution, emphasis is laid on ICT which connects service providers from various industries associated with mountain economy with the supply that, in most cases, is distributed territorially at the level of a region, or country. Electronic commerce evolution is closely related to the increase in the number of Internet users and accessibility of this communication environment – trends that have been noted by numerous studies.

Online commerce or e-business is no longer used only by large companies (Jurnalul de afaceri, 2015). More and more medium- and even small-sized enterprises have understood the benefits of online business and the huge potential the Internet provides. There is an emblematic case study in which a major mobile network operator promoted a personage from the mountain area and the latter, as a result of the popularity gained due to the commercials of that company, instead of developing electronic businesses, went bankrupt when the traditional store opened in the capital Bucharest. Electronic commerce expanded by means of websites is an important tool for the development of an electronic economy, but also has a disadvantage related to a certain cost that has to do with the creation of hardware and software infrastructure.

According to the specific activity and the products or services supplied, any economic entity should use various means of promotion. In the modern age of online information and communication technologies, a sound marketing plan must be directed mainly by combining offline promotion (banners, posters, flyers, magazine ads, TV commercials, radio advertising, street billboards, etc.) with online promotion.

The result of this marketing mix is highlighted in figure 2. This promotion method consists in placing advertisements on various platforms such as Facebook, Google, LinkedIn, etc., taking into account the specific nature and the role of each of platform. The users' interest in social media tools prompted Facebook to launch Workplace, a communication tool designed for non-governmental businesses and organizations, which may replace the intranet, e-mail or other forms of on-the-job communication. Its explosive and long-term development points to the people's interest in short and concise information, which may anticipate the emergence of a hybrid mountain economy.

Fig. 2: Presentation of promotion channels

Online	**Offline**	**Press**
Website	Posters	Magazines/newspapers
Social networks	Flyers, brochures	Press releases
E-mail	Street billboards	Radio advertising spots
Blogs	Banners	TV commercials
Specialized sites	Stickers	E-banners on news websites
Video sites	BTL or guerrilla marketing	

Source: Personal processing.

4. Opportunities and prospects of implementing information and communication technology services for mountain economy

In recent years, online promotion has proved to be more efficient than offline promotion, owing to: audience targeting, (more diversified) communication channels, lower costs, manner of assessing campaign efficiency, real-time changes (if the message needs to be changed, this can be done without high costs).

Despite the positive aspects implied by the new technology as a channel of promoting mountain economy, and although it might become the most important means of introducing rural tourism locations on the potential market, there are also negative aspects that should be considered (Garcia Henche, B., 2004, p. 186). Within e-commerce, rural tourism portals enter a fierce competition against each other, which lowers the quality of services supplied. Another drawback of many Internet portals is the low speed in providing data to the beneficiary because of pop-up ads that slow down the search.

The use of ICT generates opportunities and benefits for the activity of economic entities, but also of the population as such (WEF, 2016, pp. 27–30): i) facilitate communication and social interaction between both civil society and the media, namely: economic, social, political, ideological, cultural and religious, facilitating a better understanding of them; ii) increase civic participation and facilitate the creation and development of communities; iii) the use of digital media contributes to increasing productivity, reorganizing work processes and increasing employee flexibility (Couceiro, A. C., 2016); iv). Computer technologies and digital media technologies facilitate the process of education and skills training.

The Internet age has created a market with a new type of consumer who is acquainted with information technologies, who uses various mobile devices that improve life quality. At the same time, this consumer lives in a world of speed, characterized by short conversations and abbreviations which make communication more efficient. Now, "customers have become more demanding of how we interact with them and how we treat them across segments, products and channels" (Gamble et al., 2008, p. 28). It is difficult for employees in the tourism industry to keep pace with the rapid information technology development. Therefore, personnel training is one of the vital components in successfully implementing computer systems in tourism. Despite the benefits of providing information efficiently and facilitating transactions, there is sometimes poor understanding of advantages of online card payments, and tourists still worry about credit card security in this type of transactions.

Conclusions

Integration of information and communication services into the development and promotion of mountain economy is a catalyst for the improvement of the entire national economy, because it allows the international promotion of Romanian socio-cultural values, traditions, customs, products and services. The growth of electronic commerce in mountain areas will be generated mainly by the rapid expansion of userbases of online and mobile services on emergent markets, expansion of commerce on mobile devices, improvement of delivery and payment options and expansion of autochthonous brands toward international markets. Integration of information and communication technology services into the tourism marketing mix specific to mountain economy entails the promotion and exposure of the entire mountain area and biodiversity, corroborated with the expansion and development of the range of agro-industrial, pharmaceutical and cosmetic products, which rely on the use of accessory products supplied by the forest, hunting and viticulture stocks, typical of the mountain area, toward potential national and international consumers.

Promotion activities, especially in online environment, are currently much more accessible; mountain communities can start up with a lower budget in order to be able to accurately analyze later which are their needs and which actions should be initiated for better results in the medium and long term. Now and in the future as well, information technology will still have a profound impact on tourism. The new technologies have changed the way in which customers search for information and buy touristic products and services. In this regard, the Internet has a huge potential, for it relies on the information flow, accepts the support of continuously developing multimedia, of information technologies and systems.

There is no clear solution or well-established steps when it comes to creating and successfully developing a brand online which should respect and reflect the socio-cultural, ethical and moral values that are specific to the Romanian mountain area. However, information and communication technologies offer a view to the future of Romanian mountain economy.

We consider that there is a need for change in the mentality of mountain communities regarding the expansion of the use of information and communication technologies, the opening of the population to the evolution of techniques and technology and the awareness of the high potential for their use for the evolution of the Romanian mountain economy and also the promotion and the externalization of both indigenous products and the beauty of Romanian native places and customs and traditions within an unlimited world of time and space barriers.

References

1. Bucur-Sabo, M., Touristic marketing, Ed. Irexon, Bucharest, 2006, p. 24.
2. Castellani, V., Sala S., Sustainable performance index for tourism policy development, Tourism management, 2010, 31.6: pp. 871–880.
3. Couceiro, A. C. Ecotourism potential clients' perceptions, practices and motivations-an exploratory study. Master's Dissertation in Management Faculdade de Economia da Universidade do Porto, 2016, p. 3, available online at https://repositorio-aberto.up.pt/bitstream/10216/86951/2/166301.pdf accessed 10 July 2017.
4. Deichmann, U., Aparajita G., and Deepak M., Will digital technologies transform agriculture in developing countries?, Agricultural Economics no. 47, S1, 2016, pp. 21–33.
5. Deuchar, C., Milne, S. 28 Rural Tourism and Small Business Networks in Mountain Areas: Integrating Information Communication Technologies (ICT) and Community in Western Southland, New Zealand, Mountain Tourism: Experiences, Communities, Environments and Sustainable Futures, 2016, p. 280.
6. EPRS, EU rural development policy, 2015, p. 5, available online at: http://www.europarl.europa.eu/RegData/etudes/BRIE/2015/568340/EPRS_BRI(2015)568340_EN.pdf.
7. ENRD, Emerging sectors of rural entrepreneurship, EU Rural Review N°10, 2011, p. 11, available online at: http://enrd.ec.europa.eu/enrd-static/fms/pdf/ED5808AC-994A-47AD-928F-0D3088716910.pdf, accessed July 2017.

8. ENRD, Smart and competitive food and drink supply chains, EU rural review No 22, 2016, p. 10, available online https://enrd.ec.europa.eu/sites/enrd/files/publi-enrd-rr-22-2016-en.pdf, accessed 11 July 2017.
9. Galluzzo, N., The development of agritourism in Romania and role of financial subsidies allocated under the common agricultural policy, Geographia Polonica 90.2, 2017.
10. Hall, M., Kupper P., Crossing Mountains: The Challenges of Doing Environmental History, RCC Perspectives, Munich, GERMANY, 2014, p. 19, available at http://www.environmentandsociety.org/sites/default/files/2014_i4.pdf, accessed 1 July 2017.
11. Henke, B. G., Marketing in rural tourism, Ed. Irecson, Bucureşti, 2004, p. 9–10.
12. Hodge, H., Carson, D., Carson, D., Newman, L., & Garrett, J., Using Internet technologies in rural communities to access services: The views of older people and service providers, Journal of Rural Studies, 2016.
13. Iancu, T. et al., Characterization of rural tourism activity in the mountain area, Scientific Research. Agricultural Management., Series 1, Vol. 19 (1), 2017.
14. International Centre for Integrated Mountain Development, Climate Change Vulnerability of Mountain Ecosystems in the Eastern Himalayas, Kathmandu, Nepal, 2010, p. 5, available at http://www.preventionweb.net/files/14744_cli matechangevulnerabilityofmountai.pdf, accessed 1 July 2017.
15. Kelles-Viitanen, A., The role of ICT in governing rural development. In: IFAD Workshop on What are the Innovation Challenges for Rural Development in Rome, 2005, p. 17.
16. MacDonald, D., et al., Agricultural abandonment in mountain areas of Europe: environmental consequences and policy response, Journal of environmental management 59.1, 2000, pp. 47–69.
17. Milescu, I., The Forestry Book, Ed. Universităţii Suceava, Suceava, 2006, p. 709.
18. Minciu, R., Tourism economy, 3rd Edition, Ed. Uranus, Bucurest, 2005.
19. Mitrache, Ş., Sustainable rural developlemt, Ed. Planeta, Bucureşti, 2000.
20. Naldi, L. et al. What is smart rural development?, Journal of rural studies, 2015, No. 40 pp. 90–101.
21. Neto, F., A new approach to sustainable tourism development: Moving beyond environmental protection, Natural resources forum, Blackwell Publishing Ltd, 2003. pp. 212–222.
22. Panagoret, D., Goldbach D., Social networks in marketing practice, International Jubilee Scientific-Practical Conference: "European Practices and National Reflection in the Planning," Svistov, Bulgaria, 24–25 aprilie, 2015 lucrarea, vol. I conferinta, ISBN 978-954-23-1058-7.
23. Gamble, P. R. et al., Revolution on marketing, Romanian translation by Carmen Pădurariu, Ed. Polirom, 2008, p. 28.
24. Rey, R., 'Mountain Product', of High-biological Quality. Meadows' Poliflora, Organic Fertilizer and a Sustainable Mountain Economy, Procedia Economics and Finance, 8, 2014, pp. 622–631.

25. Rey, R. Mountains and Eco-Economy. A New Attitude in the 21st Century. Economic Recession and Efforts in the Romanian Carpathians, Journal of Settlements and Spatial Planning, No. 1, 2012.
26. Thomson, A. A., Strickland A. J., Strategic Management, Concepts and cases, Ed. McGraw-Hill Higher Education, SUA, 2003.
27. Vincze, M., Regional and Rural Development, Ideas and Practices, Ed. Presa Universitară Clujeană, Cluj-Napoca, 2000, p. 9.
28. Jurnalul de afaceri, Nr. 23 iunie 2015, How important is online promotion for a company? available from: http://www.jurnaluldeafaceri.ro/cat-de-importanta-este-promovarea-online-pentru-o-companie/, accessed 12 December 2016.
29. Wymann Von Dach, S. et al., Investing in sustainable mountain development: Opportunities, resources and benefits, Sustainable Mountain Development Series. Bern, Switzerland: Centre for Development and Environment, University of Bern, with Bern Open Publishing, 2016, available online at http://dx.doi.org/10.7892/boris.74058, accessed 10 July 2017.
30. WORLD ECONOMIC FORUM, Digital Media and Society Implications in a Hyperconnected Era, 2016, available online at http://www3.weforum.org/docs/WEFUSA_DigitalMediaAndSociety_Report2016.pdf, accessed 10 July 2017.

Ioan I. GÂF-DEAC*

Senior Lecturer PhD., Research. III, INCE / Romanian Academy, Calea 13 Septembrie, No. 13, MC 050711, Bucharest, Romania, gafdeac@ince.ro

Otilia Teodora CIUTACU

PhD., RNP Romsilva, 9A, Petricani St., MC 023841, Bucharest, Romania, otilia.ciutacu@yahoo.com

Agglomeration Economies in Mountain Areas: Multi-Storeyed Montain Concentration in North-Eastern Romania

Abstract: Mountain economic productive activities inevitably are distributed in space. Economic policies, technologies and businesses in mountain areas target specific elements and induce spatial determinants, hosting geo-storeyed mountain economic productive activities. Location on a floor or other spatial positioning marks the profile of agro-mountain company. Inevitably, economic mountainous agglomeration occurs, since like in any case, perfectly symmetrical distribution of specific locations cannot be recorded. Overcrowding is characterized by levels of aggregation. The stairs are differentiated on heights of geographical/sub-geographical agglomeration, but essentially become dependent on externalities for business opportunities. You may find spatial distribution gradients of firms in a multistage mountain cluster. In a mountainous region, in our opinion, it is imperative to engender innovation spots. It appears that in the mountainous region capable of hosting a geo-multi-storied business infrastructure, as in northeastern Romania, there are some cumulative mechanisms, with which productive activities foodservice can be "crowded." Considering crowding as a self-consolidating economic zone or concerned mountain region, it is possible to identify thereof rational aspects as, the waste, dissipation, spread, disarticulation or desegregation equally lead to weakening economic zone or region under certain circumstances or de-localization effects.

Keywords: comparative advantage, competitive advantage, economic mountainous agglomeration, spatial distribution companies

Introduction

Development mountain research in Romania can delineate the socio-economic regions development. "In 1998, Romania has opted for a regional institutional structure (...) called regionalization without creating a regional level, or administrative

* Corresponding author. Tel.: +40769788751, *E-mail:* gafdeac@ince.ro.

regionalization" (Marcou, 2003, Davey, ed., 2003). The North-East region of Romania covers part of the old historical region of Moldova (figure 1).

Fig. 1: North-East region of Romania with mountainous geography

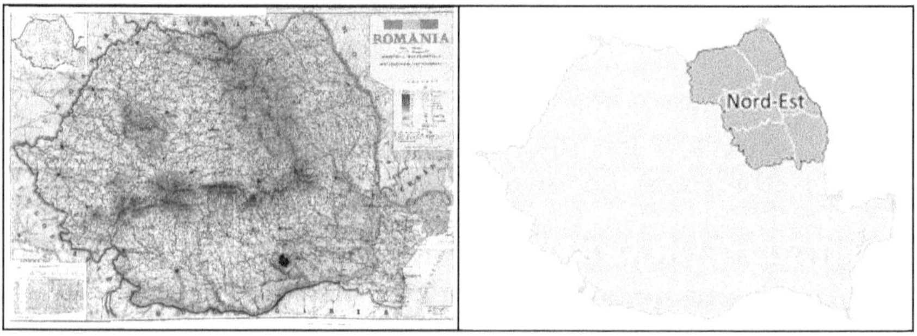

Source: ro.wikipedia.org/ google.ro/s [29].

The total area is 36,850 $km^{2,}$ with a population of 3.74 million inhabitants. It is the largest and most populated region of the country of the eight Romanian development regions and is characterized by 30% mountains, 30% Subcarpathian relief and 40% plateau. The Western Carpathians are like a wall, heights close to 2,000 m in the North (Pietrosu Peak, Rarău Peak, Giumalău Peak, Ocolaşu Mare Peak, Hăsmaşu Mare Peak), with height loss for South (Ciuc Mountains, Trotuş Mountains and, to a lesser extent, Vrancea Mountains). Maximum altitude is 1,907 m in Ceahlău Mountains (Ocolaşu Mare Peak) in County Neamt, and the minimum below 100 m, by the river Prut. Subcarpathian heights are 700–800 m.

GDP per capita in the North-East Region is 69.2% of the national level in 2014, the lowest compared to other regions in Romania (69.2% of the national level). It is the region with the lowest GDP/capita of the EU-28 regions (23.6%). The population density is 99.71 persons/km^2, higher than the national average of 91.3 persons/km^2. Economic productive activities inevitably are distributed in space. The region's economy is predominantly agrarian, especially to the north, although there are several industrial towns, the largest being Iaşi, Bacău and Suceava. Economic policies, technologies and companies in the area report targets specific elements on spatial determinants hosting economic productive activities. Today we can speak of the emergence and manifestation of a "new economic geography" (Ottaviano, G. I. P., Puga, D.,1997).

Implicitly, economic agglomeration occurs in mountainous areas, since like in any case perfectly symmetrical distribution of concrete production and consumption locations cannot be recorded. Overcrowding is characterized by levels of aggregation. Specializations lead to clustering of companies and in this way leverage technological externalities, from opportunities generated by agglomeration. The agglomeration scales are differentiated, but depend essentially on externalities considered opportunities. In an agglomeration, spatial gradient distribution of companies may be identified.

1. Literature review

The description of the situations to be developed, the economic problems and the developments over time in the mountain area is almost always complex, as there are factors, parameters and features in large numbers and with a high variety.

It is recognized that on the "checklist of Mountain Ecosystem Characteristics are: Complex climate with sharp vertical and seasonal varieties; Fragile geomorphology; Steep and elevated relief; Poor acid and shallow soils with high content of organic matter; Specific associations of pasture/forests; Specific economic orientation; Socioeconomic depression and peripherality; Mosaic of micro-situations; High proportion of threatened species; Disaster prone; Difficulty of agricultural sustainability" (Boyadgiev, T., et al., 1992).

It is stated that "it is predicted that by 2050 the world population will have reached nine billion. There is only a limited possibility of extending cultivated land in order to feed a population of that size. Agriculture, therefore, faces an enormous challenge of feeding several billion more people while maintaining ecosystems and their functions and conserving biodiversity" (p. 30), "diversity as a way of securing both food security and human existence" (p. 51; Breiholz, J., et al., 2011). This situation is associated with the fact that "... the terms on which mountain families can trade their products itself depends on the existence or otherwise of food security. (...) The political marginalization of mountain communities, (...) means that the interests of mountain communities play only a small role in determining national political economy agendas ..." (Nathan, D., Jodha N. S., 2002).

Fleischer (Fleischer, P., et al., 2009) believes that "Altitudinal span (from 600–2600 m) provides space for presence of altitudinal vegetation ranks. Together with wide spectrum of geoecological types, it forms conditions for unique biological and landscape diversity of territory", while "mountain ecosystems are characterised by steep environmental gradients such as temperature, atmospheric pressure, UV, precipitation and substrate and over relatively short geographic distances" (Körner, C., 2003).

Some authors like Pauli, H., et al. (2012), Stöcklin, J., et al. (2009) and Huntley, B. (1991), speak in their works about recent plant diversity changes in Europe's mountains, genetic diversity, phenotypic variation and local adaptation in the alpine landscape, or about how plants respond to climate change: migration rates, individualism and the consequences for plant communities, contributing to a more in-depth approach to mountain eco-development issues.

"The impact of tourism on mountain areas is often a matter of heated debate both in Poland and other countries" (p. 28). "The use of the point scoring evaluation to assess the degree of the environment transformation allowed indicating the areas with the largest and smallest intensification of human pressure" (p. 31; Swigost, A., 2005), and an "... inherent characteristic of the landscape, (...) is its dynamic nature. Landscapes change constantly over different temporal scales, from the ephemeral to the short (months and years), the medium (decades) and the long term (millennia and geological time). These changes are the result of interacting natural and cultural factors that act upon each other, often over different temporal scales" (Tsilimigkas, G., Kizos, T., 2014). Also, "soil characteristics are critical to plant growth. Soil morphological, chemical, physical and mechanical properties are essential when assessing agricultural potential of a given soil. However the variability of soils in the mountain slopes is extreme in the mountain slope" (Ndyeshumba, P., 1995).

It is noted that "many European countries define mountain areas according to constraints on agriculture. Altitude, length of growing seasons and slope are typical criteria" (Mountain Agenda, University of Berne, 2002, p. 6). It is important to consider that "about 10 percent of the world's population depends on mountain resources. A much larger percentage draws on other mountain resources, including and especially water. Mountains are a storehouse of biological diversity and endangered species" (UN Environment Programme, 2015).

Some studies, however, have suggested that the "agglomeration occurs when spatial concentration of one or more economic activities increases the size of the market and, thereby, a new spatial concentration of industries. Simultaneously, the dispersion favors the dissipation of economic activities within a given economic space. Agglomeration means concentration, dispersion means anti-concentration; they operate simultaneously, causing the geographic distribution of economic activity" (Clipa, R. I., Pohoaţă, I., Clipa, F., 2012).

At the global level, it is accepted that "mountains are an important source of water, energy and biological diversity. Furthermore, they are a source of such key resources as minerals, forest products and agricultural products and of recreation. As a major ecosystem representing the complex and interrelated ecology of our planet, mountain environments are essential to the survival of the global ecosystem" (UN Environment Programme, 2015).

On the other hand, "mountain ecosystems are, however, rapidly changing. They are susceptible to accelerated soil erosion, landslides and rapid loss of habitat and genetic diversity. On the human side, there is widespread poverty among mountain inhabitants and loss of indigenous knowledge. As a result, most global mountain areas are experiencing environmental degradation. Hence, the proper management of mountain resources and socio-economic development of the people deserves immediate action" (UN Environment Programme, 2015).

"Many of the world's mountains are marginal lands, with little potential for large-scale agriculture or other mono-functional uses. Mountain communities and families have traditionally overcome such limitations by diversifying and using complementarities. Thus, many mountain economies are characterised by use of land in various altitudinal belts and climatic zones, complementary income from other sectors such as small industry and tourism, and seasonal migration. Policy makers should build on the strength of such diversified systems" (Mountain Agenda, University of Berne, 2002, p. 11).

At the same time, "the results of the analysis of monthly, seasonal, and annual mean air temperature series from 10 meteorological stations distributed over North-eastern Romania for a 50-year study period 1961–2010" show that "the values of the statistically significant average slope varied until 0.93℃/decade for the positive slopes and until −0.29℃/decade for the negative slopes. (...) The spatial hierarchical cluster analysis suggests the existence of two distinctive groups. One of them consists of stations located at lower elevation and the other one includes stations that are located at higher elevation" (Piticar, A., Ristoiu, D., 2012). It is true that "a great diversity of cultures can be found in mountain areas" (Mountain Agenda, University of Berne, 2002, p. 15).

Geo-atmospheric climate of the interest's area is one of the reasons for tourism. By extrapolation we find that "the diurnal cycle of the aerosol number concentration showed the presence of two peaks (early morning and evening), during the transitional periods of boundary layer growth and collapse. (...) A decrease in aerosol number concentration was observed during the nighttime with the development of cold (downslope) mountain winds that force the low level warmer air in the valley to rise. The mountain valley wind mechanisms induced by the topography along with the valley geometry appear to have a strong control in the diurnal cycle of the aerosol size distribution" (Shrestha, P., Barros, A. P., Khlystov, A., 2010).

For the study area we think it is true that "atmospheric aerosol particles, or particulate matter (PM), are essential constituents in the atmosphere influencing issues such as atmospheric visibility, global climate, and human health" (Birmili, W., et. al., 2016). Therefore, "the rampant tourism development in the mountain valleys offered important alternatives to the historic boom-and-bust cycles of the region on one hand; on the other, it might change the character of the landscape and the social conditions that attracted visitors in the first place" (Yin, L., 2007).

2. Research Method. Data Collection and Preparation

Data was collected from a variety of state and local sources and processed in a graphical system. The method used can help planners to understand the dynamics of the tourism development in an area and its spatial effects. The North-Eastern mountains of Romania are renowned for nature tourism experiences. In this context it has developed a zoning diagram of multistage mountain development (figure 2)

Fig. 2: Zoning of multistage development in the mountains of North-Eastern Romania

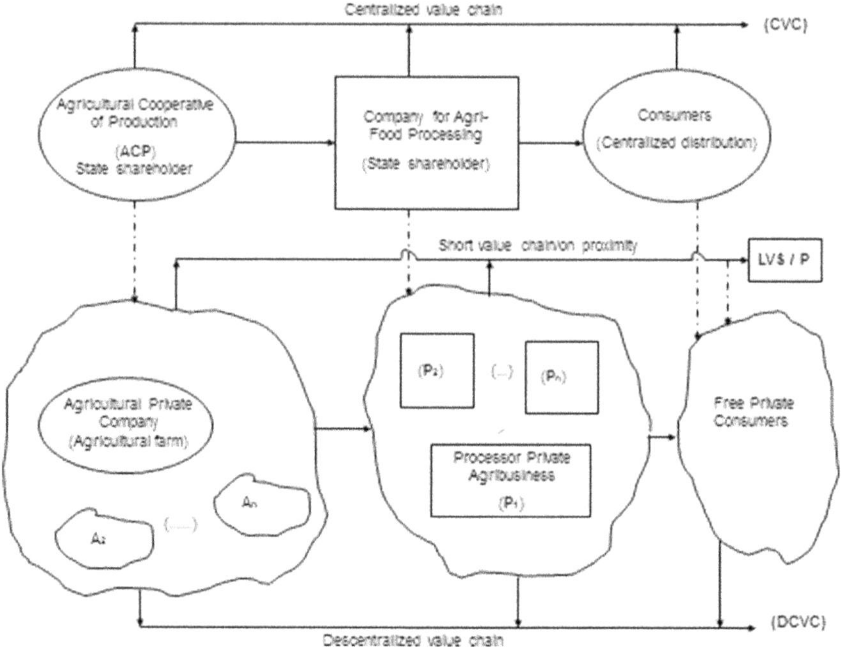

Source: Orig. Authors, 2016.

min(P) = reducing the number of inhabitants (low population density); max(B) = increase the business volume up to a maximum; min(E) = reduce to zero the number of enterprises (organizational entity); min(VR) = reducing the diversity of plant resources; min(F) = reducing diversity in fauna; max(QA) = increase air quality; min(W) = reduction of water resources; max(DT) = increasing difficulties of travel and transport.

Symbolic mathematical formalization to assess the level of development in mountainous Northeastern of Romania, based on empiric data processing area shows that currently (2016) the location of floor 2 of the development is below optimal level max/min.

$$\begin{aligned} &(i) \quad (RD)^{(-)}_{m} = \{min(P)^{*}\ min(E)^{*}\ min(VR)^{*}\ min(F)^{*}\ min(W)^{*}\ max(DT)\} \\ &(ii) \quad (RD)^{(+)}_{m} = \{max(B)^{*}\ min(E)^{*}\ max(QA)\} \qquad (1) \\ &(iii) \quad (RD)^{(+)}_{m} > (RD)^{(-)}_{m} \end{aligned}$$

Researching local statistical elements for the area of North-Eastern Romania was done to systematize the trends of the data characterizing the local mountain development.

Basically, we used the method of allocating the weight coefficients for a number of statistical elements of development characterization. In this context, the causal-dynamic character of development has been used, identifying the evolution of mountain areas in North-East Romania under the influence of internal (local) and external (regional, national and European) factors.

By the Laplace transformations, operational formalism deduces that "the primary dynamic operational model of the investigated system has a similar shape to the stationary model" (Cîrtoaje, V., 2013).

According to the same author, the secondary model is obtained by "introducing a size that mediates the entry-exit transfer."

In this framework, we opt for the convolution model in which the response is the result of the convolution product dependent on the entire evolution on time of the input signals and the responses that characterize the development with weights on the interval [0, t] or $[p_1, p_2, \dots p_{n-1}, p_n]$, respectively [0, …, 1].

Table 1: The characterization of the development of two mountainous levels in North-Eastern Romania, through important coefficients, evolutions in time and coefficients of weighting of certain activities and qualities of the environment and business (2017)

/	**(B_2)**	**(P)**	**(E)**	**(VR)**	**(F)**	**(W)**	**(DT)**	**(QA_2)**
$(RD)^{(-)}_m$ MF/UA 2	$(RD)^{(-)}_m < (RD)^{(+)}_m$	$(RD)^{(-)}_m < (RD)^{(+)}_m$	$(RD)^{(-)}_m < (RD)^{(+)}_m$	$(RD)^{(-)}_m < (RD)^{(+)}_m$	$(RD)^{(-)}_m > (RD)^{(+)}_m$	$(RD)^{(-)}_m < (RD)^{(+)}_m$	$(RD)^{(-)}_m > (RD)^{(+)}_m$	$(RD)^{(-)}_m > (RD)^{(+)}_m$
[0, t]	(+)	(−)	(+)	(+)	(+)	(+/−)	(+)	(+)
$[p_1, p_n]$	p(3)	p(2)	p(6)	p(2)	p(8)	p(2)	p(8)	p(9)
[0, 1]	0,20	0,15	0,20	0,15	0,65	0,15	0,90	0,90
/	(B_1)	-	-	-	-	-	-	(QA_1)
$(RD)^{(+)}_m$ MF/UA 1	$(RD)^{(+)}_m > (RD)^{(-)}_m$	$(RD)^{(+)}_m > (RD)^{0}_m$	$(RD)^{(+)}_m > (RD)^{(-)}_m$	$(RD)^{(+)}_m > (RD)^{(-)}_m$	$(RD)^{(+)}_m < (RD)^{(-)}_m$	$(RD)^{(+)}_m > (RD)^{(-)}_m$	$(RD)^{(+)}_m < (RD)^{(-)}_m$	$(RD)^{(+)}_m < (RD)^{(-)}_m$
[0, t]	(+/−)	(+)	(+/−)	(+/−)	(+/−)	(+/−)	(−)	(+/−)
$[p_1, p_n]$	p(8)	p(8)	p(5)	p(8)	p(5)	p(8)	p(1)	p(5)
[0, 1]	0,65	0,55	0,75	0,80	0,20	0,80	0,15	0,55

Note: MF/UA 1 = Mountain Floor 1 (under 600 m)/Altitude 1; MF/UA 2 = Mountain Floor 2 (over 600 m)/Altitude 2

Source: Authors, based on the processing of statistical data from the National Institute of Statistics of Romania, 2012–2016.

It can be noticed that of the eight activities and qualities of the environment and business in the mountain area of North-Eastern Romania, in five is registered the inequality $(RD)^{(-)}_{m} < (RD)^{(+)}_{m}$, and in three it is found that there is $(RD)^{(-)}_{m} > (RD)^{(+)}_{m}$ which demonstrates, as expected, that Mountain Floor 1 (under 600 m)/Altitude 1 is superior for development versus Mountain Floor 2 (over 600 m)/Altitude 2. However, it is noted that certain elements of the (MF/UA 2) are superior to those in (MF/UA 1), such as air quality and increased diversity of fauna.

These systematized observations show the relative discrepancy between the levels of comparative development of the mountain ranges in the studied area, confirming that at present, the competitive advantage of (MF/UA 2) is up to 15–17% in relation to (MF/UA 1). This competitive advantage, however, comes from the qualities and performance levels of the ecosystem that are objectively independent in the research area. However, it is important to emphasize that the comparative advantage of (MF/UA 2) can grow through managerial actions and decisions from the local community (figure 3).

Fig. 3: Floor medium of development, level of mountain development in the mountains of North-Eastern Romania

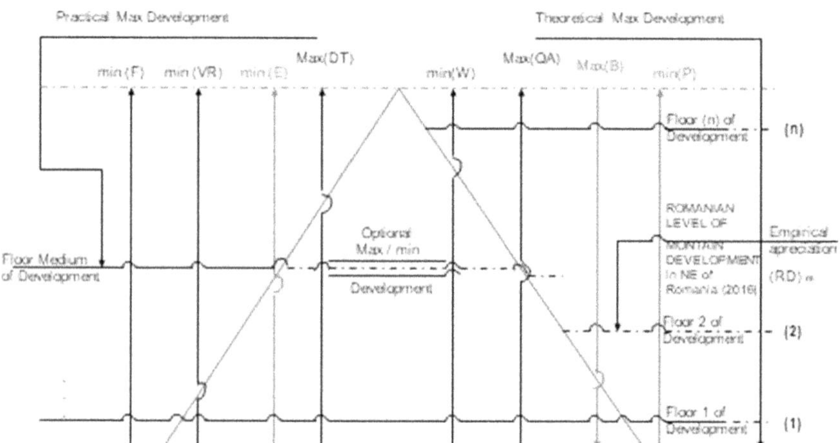

Source: Orig. Authors, 2016.

According to the Centre for Development and Environment (CDE), Institute of Geography, University of Berne, "local potential for innovation is a key factor in mountain development, requiring support for human resource development and capacity building" (Mountain Agenda, University of Berne, 2002, p. 11). If "decentralisation and local institution building are recognised as keys to sustainable development in mountain areas" (Mountain Agenda, University of Berne, 2002, p. 22), then "mountains are highly vulnerable to human and natural ecological imbalance" (UN Environment Programme, 2015).

Also, "environmental services provided by mountain forest ecosystems are crucial to people and economies" (Mountain Agenda, University of Berne, 2002, p. 21). We appreciate, by extension, that "there is also constant a balance that needs to be met between local needs and local capacity. (...) Sustainable Mountain Development within the context of mountain agriculture entails: Preservation and perpetuation of endangered traditional local breeds of animals and crops (i.e., agro-genetic resources); Promotion of ecological farming and the creation of a regional market for organic products, including marketing and promotional support through, for example, tourism; Development of national strategies for sustainable ecological agriculture and biodiversity conservation, including the development of guidelines to ensure that biodiversity issues are taken into consideration when national agricultural policies are developed; Establishment of a regional sustainable agriculture network" (Hugill, B., Ed., 2012, p. 31).

3. Managing economic clusters/agglomeration in mountain areas

It should be noted that "difficulty with predictions related to territorial development in the fact changes of this type are closely related to spatial developments are unpredictable in nonlinear whose causes" (Cojanu, V., 2009, p. 22) [8]. Comparable and unified knowledge of the volume and quality of accumulations of resources in mountain areas, facilitating communication on sub-floors, in floors and nationally, namely the creation of favorable investment system are elements that justify the need to address a knowledge framework for mountain reserves/resources (Bădescu, I. D., Bădescu, C. I., 2014).

Essentially, for the mountainous area in North-Eastern Romania, reassessment of resources, namely their placement in the new class, should be a priority. If this activitty is postponed again, may appear a blockage in the decision process to attract new investments in the exploration and exploitation of natural resources, particularly with agro-mountain. Moreover, the feasibility of exploitation underlying business projects and resources classification in the economic agglomeration emphasizes the role of mountain life and economy becomes a central axis of assessment in the referential system evaluation.

The main observation in context, is that the new recommended classification is not itself a supra-national framework-system because its development is based on the contribution of local concerned mountain communities. The internal dimension of eco-efficiency indicators, use of natural resources in economic agglomeration in mountain areas, including by focusing on multistage mountains in North-Eastern Romania, is a multidimensional analytical approach in research of national indicators. In North-Eastern Romania, exploitation of natural resources causes a quasi-continuous erosion of the environment and reduces its absolute bio-productive capacity. We find that, in fact, coordinating actions and anticipating the needs of production and consumption in the economic mountain agglomeration in North-East Romania, it does not have the operability required to be included at least in a "leading," "strong" strategy for sustainability. Therefore, the researched mountainous area needs a strategy for growth and jobs, but it must be characterized by sustainable use of natural resources.

In economic agglomeration in mountainous areas, by focusing on multistage mountains, as suggested in North-Eastern Romania, we believe it is useful to include in a recovery activities all types of natural resources. We are introducing an acceptance thesis of "circular economy," which proposes use of natural resources in the closed cycle of "extraction – production (processing) – consumer – regenerating of natural resource accumulations" (C_1; Gâf-Deac, I. I., 2007) [11]. As such, we recommend the use of natural resources through two closed conceptual cycles, respectively C_1: from extraction to recycling and C_2: the more added value to more feasible alternative use.

4. Re-shaping the natural potential by focusing on multistage mountains in North-Eastern Romania

The economic system operating in the multistage mountain concentration in North-Eastern Romania, found to be an economic agglomeration, is characterized by a certain evolutionary experience. Simultaneously, the mountain economy is characterized by experience and tradition of techniques designed to valorize the natural poential. Determination of procedures for resolving economic problems in mountainous areas is accompanied by schemes of actions, adapting to a variety of situations, articulating a certain degree of freedom for productive mountain activities.

We noticed that there is a certain coefficient of particular characterization of mountain economy. It may be a style and have some potential in financial and economic productive activity in economic agglomeration. Therefore, theoretical and practical mechanisms are needed in economic exercise, performed while in the economic agglomeration in mountainous areas.

The techniques, processes and methods of solving economic problems have varied, exerted in multistage mountain concentration to generate dynamic network connections, respectively resonate useful data entry, however distant it factors into action. Pseudo-rapid adaptation, manifested, for example, on the Romanian economy after 1989, through transition to a market economy, has been marked by uncertainty of theoretical knowledge and operational transition. The same thing can happen when imposing artificial development upon multi-storey mountain areas.

In reality, it is rather important to consider the Hegelian perception, which means that any idea is necessarily incomplete. By extension, the knowledge, including the economic and, in particular, that relating to the transition, is made through a series of successive inconsistencies that require solutions. We must increase the ability to define ignorance, conduct systematic screening exercises, circumlocution and explanation of uncertainties, or non-knowledge of eco-mountain development. It is possible to put into action and formulated problems for the mountainous area of North-Eastern Romania, leading to efforts to reduce domestic searches or the use of local thinking and practical commitment, self-explanatory in mountain multi-floors trails.

It advances the thesis that the Romanian economy, for the period after 1989, has not been judiciously advantageous by important heuristic value modeling, which will be applied in research on multi-storey mountain areas. Therefore, microeconomic research is considered useful based on integrated reasoning, respectively modular, articulated and composed. By inductive reasoning it is possible to build rules and laws arising from the review of a number of specific economic phenomena or events mountain areas (Gâf-Deac, I. I., 2007) [11]. Deductive reasoning can be obtained from a relationship, law, and from a general property known by performing customization, and used for individual cases. Analogical reasoning proposed to be practiced in Romania's mountain economy is the fact that the general is only hypothetically invoked. The mere existence of natural mountain resources in a country like Romania, with all the diversity of assortment, qualitative and quantitative flow, does not ensure their involvement in productive and economic development to determine itself, or self-development towards new horizons.

In North-Eastern Romania, we find that private traders or governments must face trial requirements and actions to curb the various difficulties in enforcing their natural resources trails. Of these, we can mention: cyclical demand for raw materials (can not ensure cyclical supply of resources both quantitative, qualitative); dependence on natural resources' exploitation of processing (production) and export of raw materials (in the area of technological processes which have particular size and structural density, depending on the level of achieved industrial-productive development); natural resource requirements different than the existing quantity target kinds; capital concentrated, major investments; reduced highlighting accumulation of resources or low knowledge of natural resources; dispersion of natural resources; manifest differences (mismatch intervals) between logistics companies equipment, transport and infrastructure in multi-floors mountainous natural resources; environmental actions are becoming more stringent and with a high degree of conditionality; attitudes of multi-storeys foreign owners of mountain natural resources do not always coincide with the interests of companies in the area; local owners' resistance where natural resources are not always streamlined on interest of firms in those multi-floors mountains.

5. The mountain's closed economy model and the open economy model in North-Eastern Romania

In the centralized economy, the state assumes an important role in the fields of: 1) production (production function); 2) procurement and management of goods and services; 3) creation and exploitation of intelligence structures of economic, social and political. A centralized economy is an economy formally closed. It is populated quasi-continuous with measurable economic agents. Every time $t_i = 0, 1, 2, \ldots$, generally, every economic agent is assigned a specific time divided into "labor" (t_m) and stationary/stop technology (t_o) (Gâf-Deac, I. I., 2010) [10]. Work time is the relationship:

$$t_m = 1 - t_0 \quad (2)$$

At the beginning of each period t_i, each economic agent is provided by the state, through allocation of capital k_i that will achieve production $P(k_i, t_m)$. At the end, the results are broken down into the consumer (P_c) and the resource endowment capital for the next period (P_k).

According to Bohacek, R. (2001) [3], production function of this type is a concave, continuously differentiable and homogeneous level one. With decreasing marginal productivity of capital is found that there is a finite maximum level of capital stock, always maintained by the state in every undertaking, given that labor must be kept employed (excluding unemployment).

Exogenous probability to achieved production is dependent on maintained labor and capital ensured to every economic agent. Always, in a centralized (closed) economy mentioned probability is strictly positive. The issue of each economic agent is to maximize rest time (t_0), the utility under restrictive budget. Social planning, relying on heterogeneous agents, under closed economy is linked to the ability of the economic planner to determine economic agents to carry out coordination and marketing of products from one another.

In a decentralized economy, new economic growth based on resources indicates that market signals are those that determine the behavior of reactive companies on exploiting natural resources and exploitation of the multi-floors trails. The economic literature frequently reminded of the existence of a "collection of resources" (Rugman, A. M. and Verbeke, A., 2002) [22], leading to advancing the argument that it is possible to effectively use the "collections" in industry – through a productive and economic resource based view. Any reaction or pro-active attitude of firms on mountain multi-floors, through the use of collection elements, inevitably leads to some imbalance.

The competitive advantage of a decentralized economy in relation to the centralized one resides, in this context, in the decision-making ability and the practice of acquiring natural resources, to accumulate and freely use general resources and capabilities they provide. In fact, it can be seen that the described process, plus the protection and development of a competitive advantage, can be considered having industrial-innovative valences in economically productive mountain.

Mountain multi-floors firms that operate with such process elements should benefit from an environment for a facilitator and generator of organizational learning. The access to knowledge is more advanced and widely spread. The company or even the eco-village will be characterized by innovation power, which in turn can place the entity in leadership positions in the clusterian area.

6. Conclusions

- In European Union countries, almost 16 million small and medium enterprises (99% of all enterprises in the EU) are in operation. The success of this formula is related to organizational focus, namely clusterian overcrowding in various fields, in which natural resources occupies the dominant place.
- In Romania, the density of small and medium enterprises is 13.8% per 1,000 inhabitants, compared with the density registered in EU countries, between 25 and 48 companies per 1,000 inhabitants.
- The size of the natural resources system in mountain areas gives freedom and flexibility for commitment valences in particular clusters, related to the field.
- The dominator "macroeconomic" needed to undergo adjustments or restructuring that influences microeconomic force elements to boost the economy.
- Conclusive evaluation of resources in economic agglomeration in areas of mountain shall be made within a "formulation framework," but we find that in order to be more efficient is necesary to group the resources in order to create the the conditions for a more precise, feasible approach, for economic exploitation and their recovery by multi-storey focusing.
- Resource-based vision recognition confirms the non-exclusivity of endogenous variables within a firm or sector related to natural resources in multi-floors trails. Any mountainous manufacturer considering the use of one or more resources, combining them and attracting new resources, which gives him heterogeneity to act, relies equally on exogenous variables in the eco-mountain economic growth.

Based on our research, the observations and the conclusions obtained, there are some recommendations:

- In the Romanian economy, based on the analysis performed for the North-Eastern Mountains, spatial hierarchical cluster analysis is useful in order to identify the competitive and comparative advantages between the development stages in relation to the altitudes and qualities of the mountainous environment;
- The North-Eastern Mountains of Romania are renowned for nature tourism experiences;
- It is feasible to use a method that takes into account the causal-dynamic character of the development, in order to identify the evolution of the mountain areas in North-Eastern Romania under the influence of the local, regional, national and European factors;
- We believe that in a first stage of development tactics, the multitude of comparative advantages of higher mountain ranges (from higher altitudes) can be increased through managerial actions and decisions in the local community.

References

1. Bădescu, I. D., Bădescu, C.I. -Conversion of the Systems: Post modern Desolation and the Deformation of the World; Epistemological problems of the theory of conversion, Ed. Mica Valahie, Bucharest, 2014, p. 112.
2. Birmili, W., et al. Long-term observations of tropospheric particle number size distributions and equivalent black carbon mass concentrations in the German Ultrafine Aerosol Network (GUAN), Earth Syst. Sci. Data, 8, 2016, p. 356.
3. Bohacek, R. Capital Accumulation in an Economy with Heterogeneous Agents and Moral Hazard, CERGE-EI, Prague, 2001.
4. Boyadgiev, T., et al. – Guidelines for the Integrated Management of Mountain Ecosystems, IIASA Working Paper, International Institute for Applied Systems Analysis, Laxenburg, Austria, WP-92-069, 1992, http:// pure.iiasa.ac.at/3630/, p. 5.
5. Breiholz, J., et al. – Mountain Gods and Wild Rice. Agrobiodiversity as a Basis for Human Existence. Contributions from China. In: Sustainability has many faces, No. 11, 2011, Deutsche Gesellschaft für Internationale Zusammenarbeit (GIZ), Eschborn, ISBN 978-3-00-034625-5.
6. Cîrtoaje, V. – The theory of automated systems. Analysis in the complex field, Ed. UPG Ploiești, 2013, p. 12.
7. Clipa, R. I., Pohoaţă, I., Clipa, F. – New Economic Geography and Regional Policy in Romania, Theoretical and Applied Economics, Bucharest, Vol. XIX /2012, No. 8/573, p. 7.
8. Cojanu, V. – Towards a competitive operational concept development at territorial level, Revista Transilvană de Ştiinţe Administrative, No. 1 (23)/2009, p. 22.
9. Fleischer, P., et al. – Risk Assessment of the Tatra Mountains Forest, Bioclimatology and natural hazards, Springer Science & Business Media B. V., 2009, p. 146.
10. Gâf-Deac, I. I. – New Economy between knowledge and risk – Ed. Infomin, Deva, 2010, pp. 37–42.
11. Gâf-Deac, I. I. – The legal and economic systems resources in the new economy – Ed. Infomin, Deva, 2007, pp. 162.
12. Hugill, B., Ed. – Sustainable Mountain Development in Central, Eastern and South Eastern Europe From Rio 1992 to Rio 2012 and beyond 2012, Mountain Partnership, mountainpartnership.org, p. 31.
13. Huntley, B. – How plants respond to climate change: migration rates, individualism and the consequences for plant communities, Annals of Botany, 1991, 67: pp. 15–22.
14. Körner, C. – Alpine plant life: functional plant ecology of high mountain ecosystems, 2nd ed. Springer, Berlin, 2003.
15. Marcou, G., Davey, J., ed. – Current Trends in Local Government Finance in Eastern and Western Europe, 2003.
16. Katsarova, I. – Economic, Social and Territorial Situation of Romania, Thematic Department Structural and Cohesion Policies, The European Parliament, Bruxelles, 2010, p. 9.

17. Mountain Agenda, Centre for Development and Environment (CDE), Institute of Geography, University of Berne, – Mountains of the World, Sustainable Development in Mountain Areas, The Need for Adequate Policies and Instruments, 2002, pp. 6, 11, 15, 21, 22.
18. Nathan, D., Jodha, N. S. - Globalization and Development of Mountain Communities, MacArthur Foundation, Asia Mountain High Summit, Kathmandu, 6–10 May 2002, p. 4.
19. Ndyeshumba, P. - Soil and Land Use Catenas. A Case Study of Amani Sub-Catchment, East Usambara Mountains, Tanzania, International Institute for Aerospace Survey and Earth, ITC Enschede, The Netherlands, 1995, p. 3.
20. Ottaviano, G. I. P., Puga, D.- Agglomeration in the Global Economy: A Survey of the "New Economic Geography," Discussion Paper no. 356, Centre for Economic Performance, London, 1997.
21. Pauli, H., et al. – Recent plant diversity changes on Europe's mountain summits, Science, 336: 353–355, 2012.
22. Piticar, A., Ristoiu, D. – Analysis of Air Temperature Evolution in Northeastern Romania and Evidence of Warming Trend, Carpathian Journal of Earth and Environmental Sciences, Volume 7, Number 4, 2012, pp. 24–25.
23. Rugman, A. M., Verbeke, A.- Edith Penrose's Contribution to the Resource-Based View of Strategic Management, Strategic Management Journal, no 23(8)/2002, pp. 324–326.
24. Shrestha, P., Barros, A. P., Khlystov, A. – Chemical composition and aerosol size distribution of the middle mountain range in the Nepal Himalayas during the 2009 pre-monsoon season, Atmos. Chem. Phys., 10, 2010, p. 11605.
25. Stöcklin, J., et al. – Genetic diversity, phenotypic variation and local adaptation in the alpine landscape: case studies with alpine plant species, Botanica Helvetica, 119: 125–133, 2009.
26. Swigost, A. – The transformation of the natural environment of the Polish and Ukrainian Bieszczady Mountains due to tourism and other forms of human pressure, Institute of Urban Development, Krakow, Poland, Tourism Research, No. 2/2005, p. 28, Sub-Carpathian Regional Government, www.umwp.podkarpackie.pl.
27. Tsilimigkas, G., Kizos, T. – Space, pressures and the management of the Greek landscape, Geografiska Annaler, Series B, 2014, Swedish Society for Anthropology and Geography, Human Geography, 96/2: pp. 159–175.
28. Yin, L. – Assessing Indirect Spatial Effects of Mountain Tourism Development: An Application of Agent-based Spatial Modeling, The Regional Analysis & Policy, Special Section: Tourism and Regional Science, JRAP 37 (3): 2007, p. 257.
29. ***UN Environment Programme, – Managing Fragile Ecosystems: Sustainable Mountain Development, available at: www.unep.org, 2015, last accessed 12 November 2016.

Romulus GRUIA

Transilvania University of Brasov –
Workstation CSCBAS/INCE – Romanian Academy and
CE-MONT/INCE – Romanian Academy; ecotec@unitbv.ro

Alexandru T. BOGDAN, George Florea TOBĂ

CSCBAS/INCE – Romanian Academy;
alecutbogdan@yahoo.com, tobageorgeflorea@yahoo.com

Radu REY

CE-MONT/INCE – Romanian Academy;
e-mail: cabinet_fmr@yahoo.com

Solar Energy and Biotransformation Dynamics in the Bioeconomic Model of Food Production with the "Mountain Product" as a Case Study

Abstract: The paper analyzes successive bioconversion of solar energy into other forms of energy specific to aliments, expressed through qualitatively superior characteristics and nutrients, in the context of economy and entropy that takes into account the environment, respectively by applying bio-economy principles. The problem of feeding the human population, with crisis potential in relation with demographic increase, may be widely solved by the bio-economic model of food production. As a "factory" of protein production, the perspective and operational context of animal breeding and farm field is thoroughly studied, which, similarly to bio-economic animal husbandry, will constitute in fact an intercession of equilibrium, of eco-efficiency and systemic efficacy and of perfect framing in nature demands, on the line of eco-development. There are exemplified aspects of application of the new paradigm in zones with a high degree of life and food production difficulty, respectively mountain zones. If they don't excel from a production quantity perspective, the zones with high altitude may offer bio-transformation in terms of quality and economic efficiency, from energetic point of view and related to the nutritive density of the "mountain product".

Keywords: bio-economy, biotransformation, eco-development, food production, mountain product

Introduction

Starting from Nicholas Georgesu-Roegen's basic ideas, the orientation towards biologic economy or bioeconomy practically means to surpass actual economy ("standard" economy) by its understanding, in the present case in relation with the alimentation field and especially through animal origin products of high quality, as a means for "man's life prolongation", whose fundamental aim and final product must be "the material flow of the pleasure to live." All this in the context of the collocation described by Georgesu-Roegen's Harvard magister, Joseph Alois Schumpeter, that "growth means to produce more, development, to produce differently," which might be economy transposition in and economy of the ontological dichotomy between "to have" and "to be" (Smyth, S. J., Aerni, P., Castle, D., Demont, M., Falck-Zepeda, J. B., Paarlberg, R., Phillips, P. W. B., Pray, C. E., Savastano, S., Wesseler, J., Zilberman, D., 2011; Bogdan, A. T., et al. 2014).

Taking into consideration the economic activity in general, it is observed, in essence, an evolutionist thinking as for bioeconomy, concerning the species' economic development, associated to nature's laws and, especially to the Law of Entropy (including to thermodynamic principles). What is remarkable is the definition and analysis of material and energy entropic transformations that constitute the fourth law of thermodynamics and was formulated by N. Georgescu-Roegen, with major applications in economy.

In this general context, the objective of the paper consists in the analysis, observation and research of a "eco-biotransformation" process for food, and the identification of this dynamic in food groups specific to every food level from a given ecosystem. More precisely, we will attempt to establish aspects of food eco-bioavailability and eco-biotransformation in order to sustain the bioeconomic model to produce food in different types of ecosystems (such as the mountain) and ranking it on basis of elements of eco-efficiency and systemic efficacy.

Working method

We studied the integronic dynamic of bio-transformations for direction of quality and economic efficiency through energetic modifications and nutritive density with applications for the "mountain product." There are taken into consideration technical-biologic and ecologic analysis of different types of food, considering bioeconomy principles. The environment enters into the food production equation through energetic analyses and the references to entropic dynamics from these systems.

Results and discussions

After a series of estimations (N. Georgescu-Roegen, 1979) it is considered that the resources of terrestrial energy do not exceed free energy received from the Sun in 4 days (!), which makes it extremely obvious that life on our planet quasi totally depends on solar energy. To conclude, economically and technologically, we must direct our attention towards solar energy flow. The field studies show that the entropy of the whole universe follows a natural and continuous process of entropic degradation, so that in essence, there is an irreversible process whose final is, for instance, the death of the living beings. But the continuity of life on Earth is ensured through the Sun's presence, i.e. it has continuity consequently to energetic recharge with low entropy from the Sun. This paradigm is considered to be the axis that may also sustain the perspectives of the sustainability of food production (Gilbert, S. F.; Sarkar, S., 2000; Gruia, R., Bogdan, A. T., Rey, R., Tobă, G. F., 2015).

By entropy growth the energy dissipates, disorganizes and becomes hardly accessible or unusable and even not handy or unavailable. In comparison, the utile available energy is an energy organized in a system. In this context, entropy is a sign of the steady tendency of growth towards the maximum of unusable energy until the whole energy becomes unusable. Low entropy means an organized structure in which energy is usable, and high entropy is the disorganized, chaotic state (Drăgan, I. C., Demetrescu, M. C., 1991).

The ever more numerous problems of feeding a population at worldwide level force us to decide between quantity and quality, between extensive, intensive and industrial production systems, between open, semi-open or closed organizational systems, the basic role being played by solar energy. The number of people that may live on Earth is directly proportional to the terrestrial banks of material and energetic resources (S) and inversely proportional to the speed of their consumption (r) and to the considered period (t), which may be expressed by the formula (Popescu, Gh., Filimon, R., 2009):

$$n = S/(r \times t).$$

Differently said, the larger the population will be, the shorter the life of human species on Earth will be. That is why, in order to prolong human species' life and even to save it, firm actions are necessary in all activity fields, and especially concerning food, i.e. in the agriculture branch, with all components, in at least four directions:

- conservation and saving the stock of terrestrial material;
- energy;
- the demographic control of the world population;
- the orientation of production technologies towards the preponderant use of the solar energy flow and
- profound understanding of the "biological & informational" evolution of human society (which includes also the 4th industrial revolution).

The food production, as economy itself, is a continuous processof transformation of low entropy into high entropy. The whole activity of obtaining food (especially of animal origin) is based on low entropy, respectively on a production with ordered structures. On the other hand, objects with high entropy, i.e. with dissipated material and energy in the environment, practically cannot be useful in the respective state.

In food production, aliments, as objects with high entropy (i.e. with dissipated material and energy in the environment), practically cannot be useful in the respective state; that is why the basic idea is to have access to more and more sources of material and energy with low entropy, which means an organized structure where energy is usable. Thus, the whole activity of obtaining food is based on low entropy, respectively on different agro-food productions, that are ordered structures. In the agro-zootechnical production process, especially in fragile zones such as the mountain ones, there must be considered that "a certain quantity of low entropy can be used only once," i.e. in conformity with the principle established by N. Georgescu-Roegen, we cannot use the same quantity of energy or of material twice, and, on the other hand, a certain quantity of energy and material dissipates, becoming wastes, residuum, garbage etc. (Wesseler, J., Spielman, D. S., Demont, M. (eds.), 2011; Gruia, R., 2016).

The solar energy flow "that we cannot regulate" and whose intensity diminishes in the very long term, slowly but constantly, at the same time with the Sun's entropic degradation and the Earth's finite reserve of natural resources, both represent the "dowry" we must have in view in the economic development, with all its branches (fig. 1).

Fig. 1: Groups of resources that man may count on in bio-economic activity

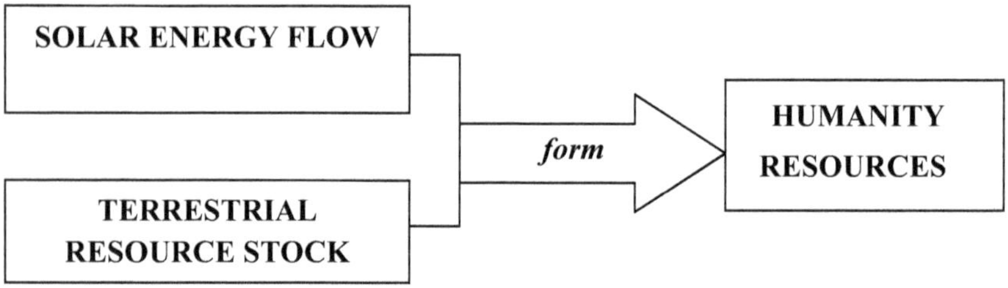

We observe the direct link between solar energy, entropy and the process of biotransformation from agro-ecosystems. Thus, we analyze food production systems, where entropy is the measure that indicates the organization degree of a system, by transforming order into disorder (Gruia, R., 2014).

In this context, bio-transformations and food in ecosystems lead to long-term solutions through a bioeconomic approach, in this case the "agro-zoo-food" production having a distinct specificity linked to: quantity/quality; low entropy/high entropy; productions/respectively wastes and residues etc. Starting from general to particular (food insurance), for the mountain agro-zoo-food production it becomes opportune to forecast population food insurance withprecaution. To achieve these analyses, we take into consideration that mountain economy and technology direct their attention towards solar energy flow (fig. 2).

It may be observed that "producers" from an ecosystem (vegetables) are consumed by phytophagous animals, which in turn are consumed by primary carnivorous animals, who become a food source for secondary carnivorous animals. These concatenations, where a series of organisms consume and are consumed, in essence represent the known food chain. Every organism that enters into the composition of the food chain constitutes a food link. The functional aspect of the food chains consists in the fact that they represent the circulation ways of material and energy in the ecosystem (fig. 3), with applicability to food production systems as well.

Fig. 2: Bioeconomic model of food production based on solar energy and biotransformation dynamic

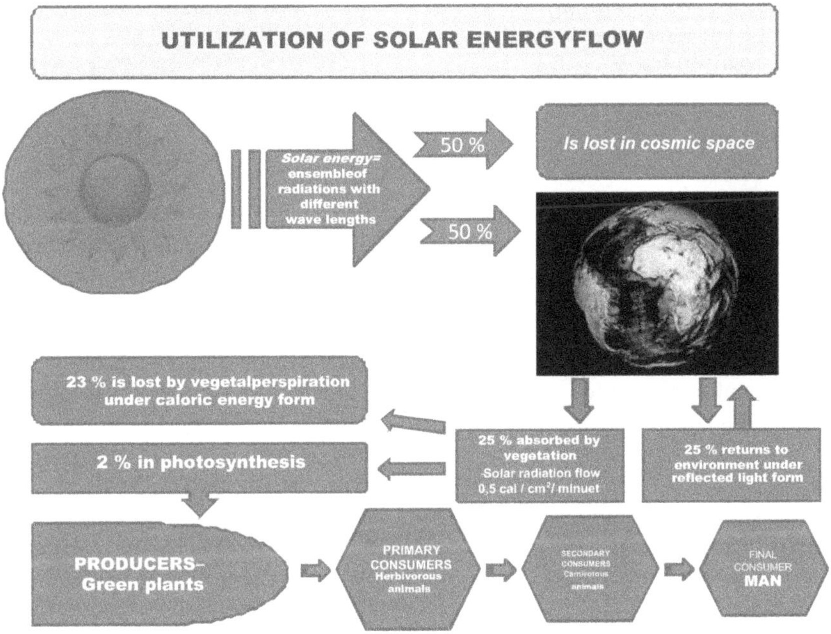

Fig. 3: Bio-transformations in the food chain in the bioeconomic model, also specific to food production systems

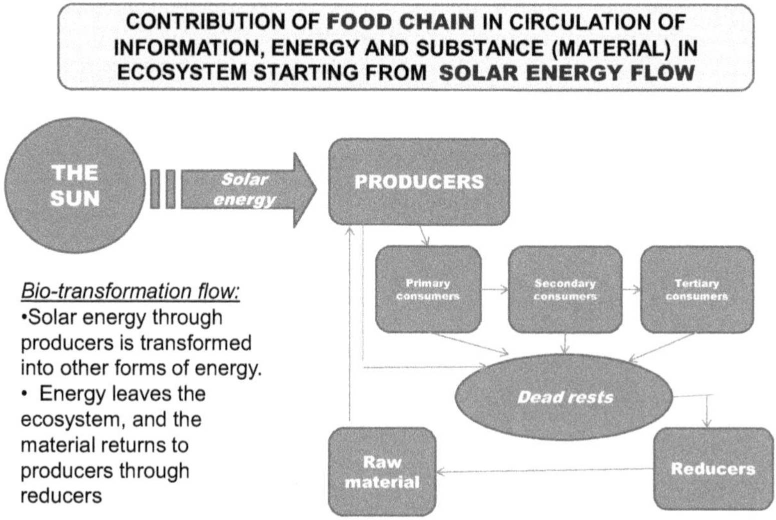

In order to understand the dynamic of bio-transformations in the bioeconomic model, we specify that food necessary to individuals from a community (biocenoses), including for man, that may bring him more and more benefits, we must concretely know the degree of utilization. To that effect, we consider the food composition and its correct association for a better digestion, absorption, bio-availability and, finally, bio-transformation at organism level and, respectively, of "eco-bio-availability" and of "eco-biotransformation" at ecosystem level. In table 1 is specified the content of these notions.

Table 1: Mechanisms of bio-transformation dynamic in the bioeconomic model

No	MECHANISM	SPECIFICATION
1.	ECO- BIODISPONIBILITY	– Fraction from total quantity of food and corresponding energo-nutritive compounds that get to the metabolic circuit of an organism integrated in the food chain of a given ecosystem.
2.	ECO- BIOTREANSFORMATION	– Totality of chemical transformations that an aliment bears during processing cycles, modifications of ecologic, biologic and physic-chemical properties that influence efficiency and efficacy at every food level.

Up to now, in standard economy that characterizes nowadays food production too, the technical progress has been paid with the passing from the richer source of low entropy, i.e. from solar radiation, to the less rich one, i.e. the terrestrial mineral resources. In concordance with certain scientists' numerous opinions (Wesseler, J. et al., 2011; Gruia, R., 2016) the human species may be saved only if the model is reversed, namely replacing as soon as possible the terrestrial mineral resources with the solution based on solar energy, which in essence proposes the bioeconomic model. We try to exemplify all these concerning food and aliment production.

The integronic dynamic of food bio-transformations, including in the mountain space, highlights food eco-bioavailability in the chain of the food act. This one is sustained by successive eco-biotransformations of food processing (fig. 4).

Fig. 4: Food energetic growth in relation with eco-biotransformations registered along the food chain of alimentary ecosystems

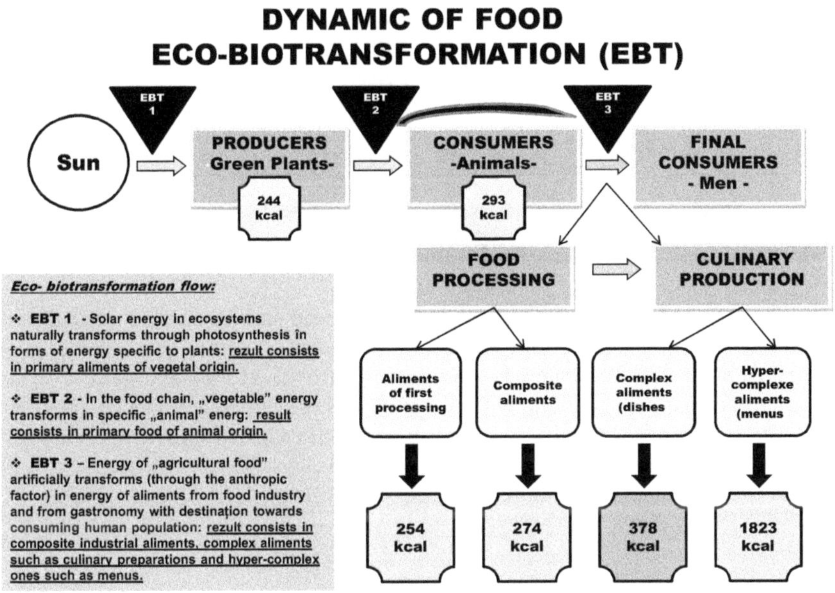

It is observed that, in processing cycles, structural modifications of food (bio-transformations) have an effect upon the manner of food utilization, directly on human organism metabolism (fig. 5).

Fig. 5: Eco-bioavailability evolution in metabolic cycles of integrated organism in the alimentary ecosystem

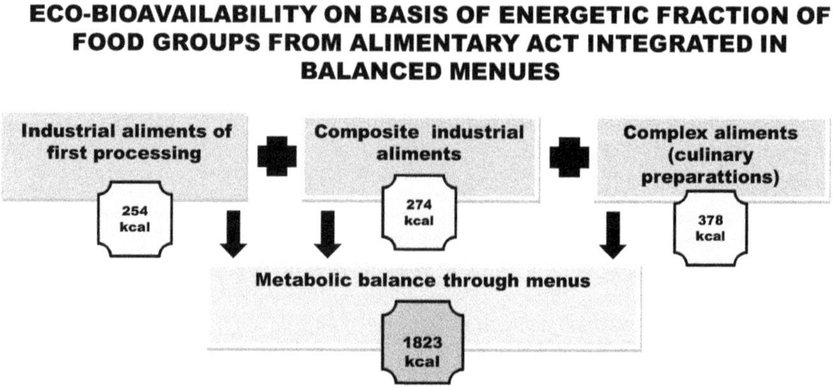

SPECIFICATION	U.M.	ALIMENTS OF FIRST PROCESSSING FROM FOOD INDUSTRY	COMPOSITE ALIMENTS FROM FOOD INDUSTRIY	COMPLEX ALIMENTS	HYPER-COMPLEX ALIMENTS OF METABOLIC HARMONIZATION
Energy	kcal	254	274	378	1823
Eco-bioavailability	%	14	15	21	100

At systemic level there is observed the growth of the eco-bioavailability in the alimentary act, in function of the growth of the processing degree of complexity

The third step of the alimentary act, after obtaining and processing agricultural and industrial food is represented by complex aliments obtained as a result of gastronomic processes. There may be observed the growth of food energetic level by cumulating solar energy found within ingredients of systems and menus, together with the growth of complexity and structural organization in their whole of culinary preparations that influence the efficiency and efficacy with an average growth of 20% at every food level and at every processing cycle (fig. 6).

Fig. 6: Elements of the bioeconomic model in the alimentary act

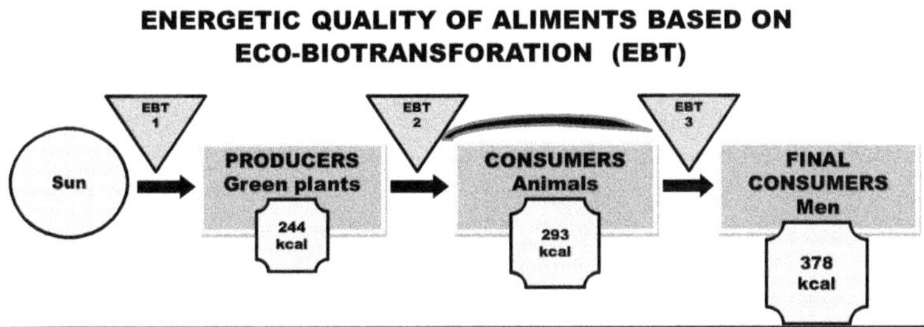

SPECIFICATION	U.M.	VEGETAL FOOD	ANIMAL ORIGIN FOOD	COMPLEX FOOD -DISHES-	
Energy	**kcal**	**244**	**293**	**378**	
Evolution by eco-biotransformtion	%	100	120	160	
			+ 20 % face to biotransformation at food level of vegetables	+ 40 % face to biotransformation at food level of animals	+ 60 % face to biotransformation at food level of vegetables

✓ ***IN THE BIOECONOMIC MODEL the growth of food complexity degree means the growth of structural organization and the decrease of entropy, which is sustained by eco-biotransformation (energetically expressed) along the food chain.***

Extrapolating the evolution of food bio-transformation to different producing conditions in function of geographical, pedologic and climatic characteristics, there may be observed organoleptic, biologic and ecologic differentiations linked to the structure of the vegetal layer, to the sorts of plants and animal races, to altitude, etc. (Rey, R., Gruia, R., Rey, A., 2015). Thus, it becomes possible for producers, cultivators, apiarists who have their production activity in the mountain zone, to promote their alimentary products labeling them a "mountain product," which has even become an European policy (table 2).

Table 2: Principles of European policy concerning the quality of mountain agro-alimentary products

No.	PRINCIPAL CONTENT
1	Raw material must come from the mountains.
2	Processing must be achieved in a mountain zone.
3	Production must take into consideration preoccupations regarding society, environment and health.
4	Producers must be able to maintain and develop biodiversity and the patrimony of the mountain areas.
5	Producers should permanently guarantee information transparence for consumers.

Documents forecast that for zootechnical production, there may be applied the mention "mountain product" in order to declare the product's origin, only on condition that milk and egg production should be exclusively made in the mountain area, and for products obtained from meat, these ones should come from animals bred in the mountain area for at least two thirds of their life. In case of products made from moved flocks, these ones must spend at least a quarter of their life on mountain area pastures. As for vegetable production, there may be applied the mention "mountain product" only if they are cultivated in the mountain area, and, if in the alimentary products there are used certain ingredients precisely specified from outside the mountain zone, these ones must not exceed 50% of the ingredient weight.

Data gathering concerning historical dishes ("retro-gastronomy") or the traditional ones ("ethno-gastronomy"), as well as present creativity and innovation, represent the solution through which there is put forward the mountain gastronomic specificity in relation to the mountain massif, i.e. with specific climate conditions, including with direct influence of solar energy. The bioeconomic interpretation of this process has results both concerning quality (eco-bioavailability and eco-biotransformation), and effect of influence in marketing and in tourism. From here also the organization of gastronomic tourism tracks based on knowing biodiversity and gastronomic traditionalism, at the level of every massif from the Romanian Carpathians. Consequently, this leads to the obtaining of a "territory product" and to the image of gastronomic brands for the respective zone, being a solution on bioeconomic principles that sustains the growth of the Romanian mountain zone's attractiveness.

Conclusions

1. The bioeconomic model, as for the alimentary production, is based on solar energy and the biotransformations dynamic, so that the whole activity of obtaining food is based on low entropy, respectively on different agro-alimentary productions, that are ordered structures; the growth of the degree of food complexity means the growth of structural organization and the decrease of entropy, sustained by the process of eco-biotransformation (including in energetic expression).
2. Eco-biotransformations lead to entropy decrease, so that vegetables offer an energy which, by biotransformation in animal products, becomes 20% higher, and biotransformation through culinary products energy increases by 60%, as comparing with the energetic offer of vegetables and with 40% as comparing with the energetic offer of the products of animal origin, which practically demonstrates that it is advisable to massively exchange products of animal origin for those of vegetable origin and to valorize the "mountain product" by agro-tourism as culinary products.
3. Food eco-bioavailability in the chain of the alimentary act is sustained by successive eco-biotransformations of alimentary processing, so that at systemic level (for example of mountain modules) there is observed the growth of eco-bioavailability in the alimentary act in function of the growth of the complexity degree

of processing on the axes: vegetal aliments – zootechnical aliments – composite aliments (industrial ones) – complex aliments (culinary recipes, menus).

4. On the basis of bioeconomy principles, producers, cultivators, apiarists that carry on their production activity in the mountain zone may promote their alimentary products labeling them as a "mountain product," which imposes a superior quality level based on the growth of structural organization and entropy decline, demonstrated by eco-biotransformation along the food chain and the processing cycles.

References

1. Bogdan, A. T., et al., 2014: Developing Georgescu-Roegen's bioeconomics concept with a new smart approach, from "fiat panis" to "habemus panem", based on a new economic theory for globalised biopower through more agrifood and seafood, Elsevier, Procedia Economics and Finance, vol. 8, 2014, pp. 91–99.
2. Drăgan, I. C., Demetrescu, M. C., 1991: Entropy and Bioeconomics – The Paradigm of Georgescu-Roegen, Rome, Nagard Publishers.
3. Georgescu-Roegen, N., 1979: Legea entropiei; i procesul economic, Editura Politica, Bucuresti, 1979.
4. Gilbert, S. F.; Sarkar, S., 2000: "Embracing complexity: organicism for the 21st century." Developmental Dynamics 219 (1): 1–9. doi:10.1002/1097-0177(2000)9999:9999: AID-DVDY1036>3.0.CO;2-A. PMID 10974666.
5. Gruia, R., 2014: Integronic Food Concept, Journal of EcoAgriTourism, Publ. Transilvania University of Brasov, Romania, ISSN: 1844–8577, Vol. 10, Nr. 1, pp. 211–218.
6. Gruia, R., 2016: Zootehnie bioeconomică, Editura Lux Libris Brasov, ISBN 978-973-131-357-3, 27–42.
7. Gruia, R., Bogdan, A. T., Rey, R., Tobă, G. F., 2015: Integronic alimentation through whole natural food biodiversity, in relation with altitude gradation, Procedia Economics and Finance ISSN: 2212–5671 Volume: 22/2015, pp. 114–123.
8. Popescu, Gh., Filimon, R., 2009: Nicholas Georgescu-Roegen. Epistemologia evoluţionistă. Săgeata timpului, Editura Risoprint Cluj-Napoca, ISBN 978-973-53-0088-3, 136–263.
9. Rey, R., Gruia, R., Rey, A., 2015: High quality "mountain polyflora", "mountain product" and the mountain family farm, "keys" for safeguarding and sustainable development of mountain agri-food economy, for South-Eastern Europe, International Conference "Sustainable mountain regions: make them work," Borovets, Bulgaria, 14–16 May.
10. Smyth, S. J., Aerni, P., Castle, D., Demont, M., Falck-Zepeda, J. B., Paarlberg, R., Phillips, P. W. B., Pray, C. E., Savastano, S., Wesseler, J., Zilberman, D. (2011): Sustainability and the bioeconomy: Policy recommendations from the 15th ICABR conference. AgBioForum, 14 (3), pp. 180–186.
11. Wesseler, J., Spielman, D. S., Demont, M. (eds.; 2011): The Future of Governance in the Global Bioeconomy: Policy, Regulation, and Investment Challenges for the Biotechnology and Bioenergy Sectors. AgBioForum, 13 (4).

Romulus GRUIA

Transilvania University of Brasov – Workstation CSCBAS/INCE – Romanian Academy and CE-MONT/INCE – Romanian Academy, ecotec@unitbv.ro

Radu REY

CE-MONT/INCE – Romanian Academy

Liviu GACEU

Transilvania University of Brasov – Workstation CSCBAS/INCE – Romanian Academy

Paradigm of Bioeconomic Animal Husbandry, as a Solution of Sustainable Development for Animal Breeding in Mountain Areas

Abstract: The paper brings into discussion the application of a new paradigm for animal breeding, with more than opportune applications for the mountain zones, namely bioeconomic animal husbandry. There is underlined the idea of a new step, an important one, for the implementation of sustainable development in animal breeding, a step which, beyond the definition of problem objectives, proposes several reference landmarks for the bioeconomy of harmonious exploitation and the obtaining of qualitative mountain animal products. There are introduced a series of necessary aspects for the theory development in bioeconomic animal husbandry, both for directing research in the field, and for sustaining economic technologies and processes of mountain animal production. There are mentioned six research directions, as well as the operational model for mountain economy in the field of animal breeding. It is presented the necessary IT methodology for data basis and certain diagnoses and prognoses elements, as application pillars of bioeconomy principles in fragile zones and in difficult fields, such as those of animal husbandry in mountain zones.

Keywords: animal husbandry, animal products, bioeconomy, mountain economy, sustainability

Introduction

At UNO and especially at FAO level, the foundation for a scientific solution of the mountain area problems has been coherently laid ever since 1974, during the Munich Conference on Development of Mountain Environment. With the inclusion of Chapter 13, Managing fragile ecosystems: sustainable mountain development, into Agenda 21 of the United Nations Conference on Environment and Development (UNCED – Earth Summit) in Rio de Janeiro in 1992, and the current progress in the journal's transformation to meet newly arising opportunities, it is timely to document its origins and evolution (Ives, J. D., 2016).

In Romania, the Center of Mountain Economy of INCE – The Romanian Academy has made a diagnosis concerning the principles linked to the montanology approach (Forum Carpaticum Bucharest, 2016). In that direction there has appeared the necessity for a new paradigm for mountain animal breeding, especially because, as it has been pointed out by certain studies, low prices, but also the female and aging labor force led to a major decline of the mountain farms during the latest decades (Spear, T., 1997).

Bioeconomy indicates an economic theory proposed by Nicholas Georgescu-Roegen as a sustainable economy from ecologic and social perspective. Methodologically, there are taken into consideration material and energy that enter into economic processes with a relatively low entropy and come out with another degree of entropy, which imposes to take into consideration thermodynamic principles under the context of the ever more precarious offer of natural resources. Bioeconomy brings into discussion man's role in anthropic ecosystems, negative energetic account in case of excessive consumption of raw materials and the lack of perspectives for the future generations (Bogdan, A. T., Comşa, D., 2011).

If at first the aspects balanced between biologic and economic fields, situating bioeconomy (Georgescu-Roegen, N., 1979) as a new border science, we lately consider that the idea has expanded towards development elements from biotechnologies, i.e. towards specific components from biology, ecology, sociology, psychology, political science, informatics, finance, commerce and others. All these approach environmental complexity in its economic dimension, through the new scientific intercession of ecologic economy, or of eco-economy, including of bioeconomic sustainability (Smyth, S. J. et al., 2011).

"Bioeconomy is the knowledge-based production and use of biological resources to provide products, processes and services in all economic sectors within the frame of a sustainable economic system" (German Bioeconomy Council). As branches we mention: agriculture, forestry, horticulture, fisheries and aquaculture, plant and animal breeding, the food and beverage industries, as well as the wood, paper, leather, textile, chemicals and pharmaceutical industries, and aspects of the energy sector (Glössl, J., 2015).

The four pillars of bioeconomy are: food production and processing (BECOTEPS, 2012), value-added food and health products (Bennet, D. J., Jennings, R. C., 2013), agri-environmental products and services (Bioeconomy Council, 2011), and energy and bio-processing (Bioeconomy Conf. Dublin, 2013). Agriculture is the main sector connected strongly with bioeconomy, as presented by the vision document SCAR (2012). Recently, Rosegrand et al. (2013) reviewed the main challenges related to water and food in bioeconomy, and Henry and Trigo (2010) reflected the main aspects to the knowledge-based bioeconomy, from large scale experiences to instruments for rural and local development, underlying the role of innovation especially in mountain areas.

It was revealed the idea that a sane, stable and prosperous economy must be based on a thoughtful utilization of energy by recycling material resources from production processes. At systemic level, the approach has bio-ecologic and technical, economic, social and juridical forms (Drucker, P. F., 1993; Duţu, M., 1996; Gruia, R., 1998b).

In this context, there is imposed the new spirit in animal husbandry too, namely beyond standard economic aspects, there is obligatorily arisen the question of protecting and preserving the environment and its resources. Bioeconomy is introduced into the equation. Thus, in an ever-hungrier planet, animal husbandry has an important contribution in providing the necessary alimentary products, and also maximizing bioeconomic output, at world nutrition.

Animal husbandry becomes practically a sustainable bio-industry from a bioeconomy based on intelligent utilization of earth and aquatic animals, as basic food or as raw material for composite food (from food industry) and for complex food from gastronomy (cooked food and mixed drinks).

Animal husbandry bio-industry imposes, at bio-economic level, systematical restructuration by integronic modulation. We are therefore speaking about an animal husbandry with integronic dynamics, i.e. based on multiple and successive integrations under syncretic, synchronic and synergic conditions, based on cybernetic mechanisms, between economic efficiency and ecosystemic efficacy, having emergency as an effect, obtaining and valorizing respectively the step towards another level of "zoo-production".

The paper's main aim is to lay theoretical bases, through a new paradigm, for the technologic and economic reorientation effort in order to solve acute problems linked to climate changes and exaggerated consumption of the natural capital of other generations, especially in fragile zones, such as the mountain areas. In this direction, the objectives proposed by the paper are linked to theoretic and applicative aspects of mountain bioeconomic animal husbandry, through operational activities of "zoo-productive engineering," that make it necessary to establish the organizational frame for the deployment of the respective actions. That is why in the paper, the concept is defined, the manner of theoretical and practical action is structured, i.e. certain research themes and a series of principle applications for the mountain zone are described. All these because the mountain area is by excellence designed for animal breeding and, from here, the achievement of a food chain based on specific transformations, from the fodder level to animal metabolism, that lead to particular qualitative characteristics of the "mountain animal breeding product."

Work methodology

As an element of bioeconomic expression, integronics presupposes successive multiple integration of several plans, in different connections and combinations that lead to a modular integration and to systemic polyvalence. Such a model is the one we are going to describe, starting from the Modulation and Integronic Management

Theory (Gruia, R., 2011, 2013), from the mountain development program in the Romanian Carpathians (Rey, R., Gruia, R., 2013) and from agri-food bioeconomy strategies from Romania (Bogdan, A. T., Gruia, R., Toba G. F., Pasalau, C., 2014).

Methodologically, there is taken account of the technologic model of integronic modulation that is based on systemic integration (Gruia, R., 2009) which presupposes entrance and processing of substance, energy and information (the three aspects of the same fundamental existence) together determined in modular, syncretic and synchronic dynamics, with synergic effect. These ones have as a methodological result emergence at a new level, of a superior order, which, by afferent bio-transformations, practically leads to superior energetic and nutritive quality of zoo-productions in mountain areas. The bio-transformation cycles, centred on a dynamics of energetic order, harmonize and bioeconomically make efficient the animal breeding production and the interrelations between animal species from the mountain culture and/or fauna.

Results and discussions

Bioeconomic animal husbandry is the paradigm through which animal husbandry practically becomes the sustainable bio-industry within bioeconomy, based on intelligent utilization (bio-resource diversification and the bio-transformation efficiency growth) of terrestrial and aquatic animal resources, as basic food or as raw material for composite food from the food industry and the complex ones specific to gastronomy, under eco-efficiency conditions.

What "bioeconomic animal breeding" adds is the interpretation and application manner of bioeconomic theories and of those concerning eco-development, to the field of animal breeding. Therefore, animal breeding, on bioeconomic direction, uses animal resources through bio-transformation, as basic food or raw material for industrial food products (composite food) and for gastronomic products: culinary preparations and mixed drinks (complex food).

From theoretic perspective, bioeconomic animal breeding refers to the growth of nutritive, energetic and metabolic bio-transformation efficiency through biotechnologies of perfected and non-polluting animals (Gruia, R., 2016). The bio-transformation process is, in essence, a successive bioconversion of energy and chemical composition of the vegetal world organisms (solar energy capturers and transformers, through photosynthesis), through the process of animal feeding and, implicitly, the transformation (through animal biotechnologies) into qualitatively superior nutrients, having a major impact on phylogenetic and ontogenetic development of human species.

The long-term solution, in order to improve the world feeding, is in general the integration into economic activity and, in the present case, into the field of making products of animal origin, of biology and nature (fig. 1).

Fig. 1: Interferent components that sustain the intercession of bioeconomic animal breeding

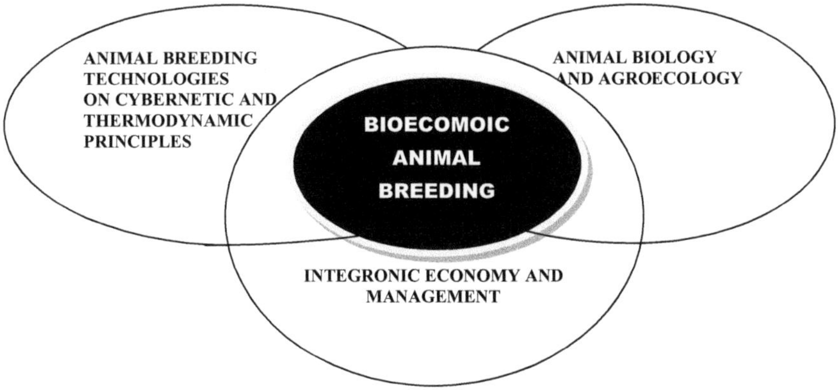

The structure of bioeconomic models for "agro-zoo-food" models in different variants, adapted to the concrete situation on the ground (as the mountain zone is), has distinct components to be found in different animal breeding modules with high self- regulation capacity, being therefore characterized through specific cybernetic elements, with an important bioeconomic impact (Scarlat, E., Chiriá, N., 2014; Gruia, R., 2016). Thus, animal husbandry bio-industry modulation makes it possible to apply integronic principles, so that through successive, complementary integration and multiple plans, we have as a result bioeconomic animal breeding modules, characterized by "harmony" between economic efficiency and systemic efficacy and, especially, an ecosystemic one.

The new approach of bioeconomy in relation with "zooproductive ecosystems" has in view the fact that bioeconomic principles should bring into discussion man's role in anthropic ecosystems, the negative energetic balance sheet in the case of excessive consumptions of raw materials and the lack of perspective for future generations. That is why the solution bioeconomic animal breeding may give, beyond production quantity, is the one of food quality, as zoo-productive ecosystems are de facto real "protein factories." And more than that, it is about complete proteins that contain essential amino acids in a sufficient proportion, able to maintain tissues in an estate of integrity and to assure a normal development, proteins that are to be found in eggs, meat and milk (unlike partially complete or incomplete proteins of vegetal origin, unable to assure growth, they cannot restore tissues, and the incomplete ones cannot assure life maintenance; Lehninger, A., 1992; and others).

Everything that has been specified is to be strongly found in the so difficult case of animal breeding in mountain areas, where quality is exactly the main production advantage. The mountain zoo-productive ecosystem may be characterized as follows: it has a historical character (short evolution), integrality, a well-established program; it represents a cybernetic system; in relation with the environment it may be open or partially open; it is an arranged ecosystem (with different degrees of human intervention), with limited natural self-regulation capacity (but sometimes up to very reduced quotas), with structure and systemic function differently altered to face the level of biologic organization; it presents ultra-simplified structures and maximum instability; it needs investment in energy in order to maintain equilibrium; the anthropic element is essential, being creator and permanent regulator of the system, finally achieving the piloting of the given ecosystem. All these may be analyzed at mountain ecosystems, both from structural and functional perspective (fig. 2).

Fig. 2: Functional and structural elements of mountain animal breeding ecosystems

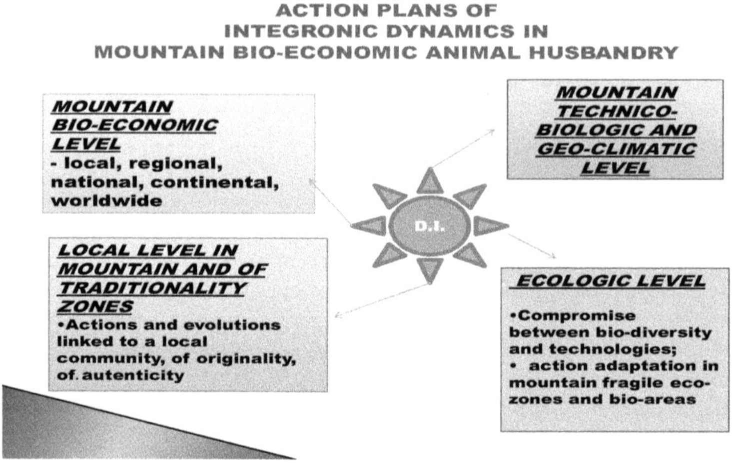

From the perspective of sustainable development of territorial scenery, the application of bio-economy principles harmonizes in relation to multiple integration of ecosystem components, from molecular level to individual and biocenoses level (Bonnieux, F., Rainelli, P., 1999; Gruia, R., 2016). We refer to their structure and functionality, in function of their specificity. Some of these specificities are to be found in mountain agro-zootechnical ecosystems that may have different bio-economic models that compose distinct modules (production modules, based on technical applications and IT).

This specificity implies a series of reference elements necessary for the adaptation of considered modules, for different existing situations, taking also into consideration the climate changes:

- to be energetically autonomous, based on solar and aeolian energy;
- to be able to recycle rain and used water;
- to transform waste and dejections into natural fertilizers;
- to organize culture rotation to allow the earth to regenerate without chemical fertilizers;

- to take into account awn and meadow exposition in relation to cardinal points and others.

Considering the mentioned specificities, the mountain agro- and animal breeding modules have the capacity to adapt at circular economy (Pauli, G., 2010): (a) to be energetically autonomous, solar and aeolian-based, (b) to be able to recycle rain and used water, (c) to transform waste and dejections into natural fertilizers, (d) to organize a rotation of cultures based on leguminous plants in order to allow soil to regenerate without chemical fertilizers, (e) to assure the contribution of organic fertilizers in optimal forms utilization in annual continuity too, as a basis for the conserving of functional biodiversity in a poly-floral structure and with a high percentage of perennial leguminous plants; to avoid the use of chemical fertilizers and of pesticides; (f) to assure poly-floral hay conservation under conditions that avoid the appearance of mold and aflatoxins in milk production (Rey, R., 2013).

The mentioned elements, including a series of aspects specific to extensive systems of animal breeding, combined with shelter hygiene, hygiene over the whole chain of collecting and transforming mountain agri-food products, making it possible to obtain "mountain products" of high biologic quality, justified and valorized with "added value" on solid bases. They represent an important source for family farms/mountain households' profitability, for their income improvement and, at the same time, they are an element of maintenance or improvement of consumers' health and reduction of health expenses, especially for urban consumers.

The mentioned complexity imposes a conceptualization based on the complementarity of the activity fields and on multidisciplinarity (fig. 3).

Fig. 3: Multi-disciplinarity of the mountain-agro-zoo system, component of the wide montanology field

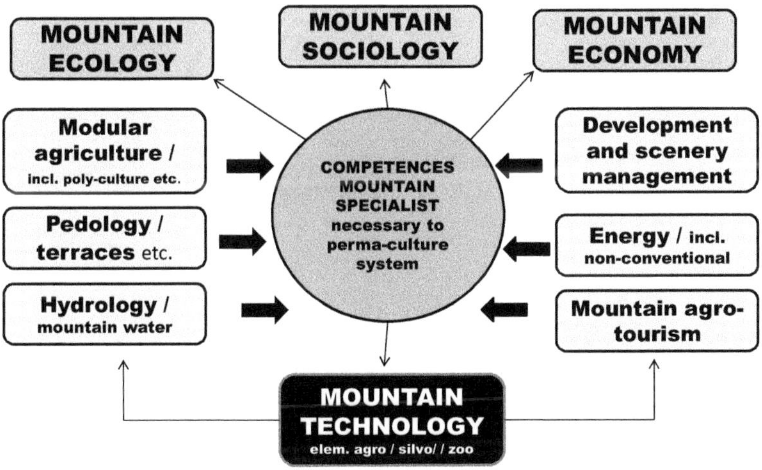

At the same time, the mountain modulation process means an important step for the productive activity to come, especially if we consider climate, ecologic, economic and social provocations. As a solution, the model of permacultural type (Holzer, S., 2010; Gruia, R., 2016) represents the system that "imitates nature," structurally based on ecosystems and functionally based on natural cycles, with applications for well-structured mountain modules, so that the newly acquired modular systemic structure may be energetically quantified on the principles of integronic management. For the mountain zone, this food chain is first of all based on animal breeding.

The expected result is to obtain "mountain food eco-bio-products," as an expression of the superior efficiency of bio-transformation specific to bioeconomy, having as a model the food chain and the agro-zoo-food module concatenation where the center of activity is sustained by animal species, as primary, secondary, tertiary and quaternary consumers (fig. 4).

Fig. 4: Modular model based on ecologic, biotechnologic and bioeconomic principles

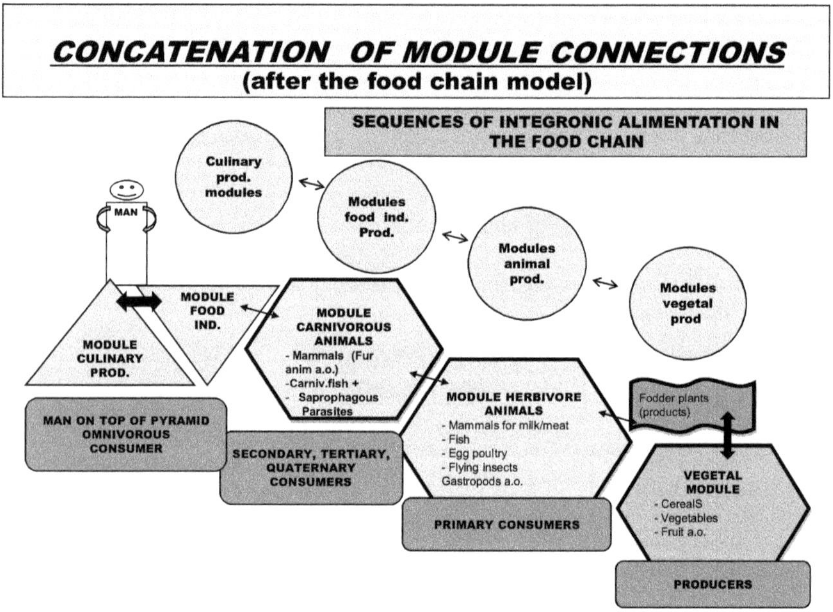

Applications of the new paradigm

We consider opportune that in the present paper we contribute to the application of research directions for animal breeding in the mountain zone, with the main themes that may consolidate the idea of environmental reconsideration in the animal breeding zone and in the obtained high quality mountain products. In this direction, bioeconomic animal breeding in mountain area may have an expected evolution under conditions in which it will impose as objectives some study aspects such as: ecology and animal breeding biodiversity, application of animal breeding biotechnologies, mountain zoo-production quality, superior valorization of waste and residues on circular economic principles and others, structured in strategic research directions in table 1.

Table 1: Research elements in bioeconomic animal breeding, with applications in mountain areas

Nr. crt.	RESEARCH DIRECTION	RESEARCH THEMES ON BIOECONOMIC LINE
1.	**Research for theoretic substantiation of bioeconomic aspects, highlighting biodiversity elements**	- widening of knowledge linked to the structure and ecosystem functioning (from microorganisms to superior animals);
		- diversification of zoo-productive ecosystem types by profound knowledge of biologic resource value for increasing the potential of trade for zoo-productive species and for animals;
		- orientation of efforts towards species' conservation, anticipation of predictable changes and valorization of certain new species with a productive aim (extrapolation of studies concerning animals and non-conventional breeding procedures);
		- making observations concerning the influence of climate modifications upon existing species in mountain zoo-productive ecosystems;
		- repopulation of mountain zone ecosystems from other zones and especially from those next to zoo-productive ecosystems (repopulation with cynegetic species the woods and with fish the rivers);
2.	**Ecologic control of animal biotechnologies and valorization of animal genetic resources**	- evaluation of applied biotechnology effects (in the unitary context of nature) with references to microorganism utilization (ex. of microbes) and direct manipulation of superior organisms (ex. by genetic engineering, animal selection and amelioration, techniques of artificial reproduction, transfer of embryos, cryogenic techniques, improvement of human alimentation with products of animal origin obtained with biotechnology techniques etc.);
		- valorization of certain sub-products as resources for certain biotechnologies (ex. blood, intestines, organs, excretions, enzymes, protean fractions, hormones etc.);

Nr. crt.	RESEARCH DIRECTION	RESEARCH THEMES ON BIOECONOMIC LINE
		- creation of gene banks, especially for endangered species, or for small animal (fur animals, rabbits, wood animals, laboratory animals etc.) which are relatively less studied, to complete the so-called "artificial collections";
3.	**Mountain environment protection**	- study of possibilities to maintain bio-geo-chemical cycles in the zones of mountain zoo-productive ecosystems;
		- protection of animal species threatened by extreme commercial exploitation;
		- establishment of minimum critical dimension of ecosystems (for example, establishing of minimum species' effectives in the areas characterized by wood clearing and transformation of land into farm animal lawns; establishment of wood fragments necessary to maintain own and implicit equilibrium of zone zoo-productive ecosystem etc.);
		- prevention of and combat against pollution due to zootechnical systems, especially at maximal critical dimension and ecologic reconstruction of zones affected by this pollution;
		- conservation of animal life forms by forming parks, zoo gardens, protected zones, zoo-services, sanctuaries and "refuges" for certain animal species etc.;
		- connection with the permanent system of air quality surveillance (monitoring) in relation with the breathing requirements of animal species.

A significant contribution of the paper refers to the application of bioeconomy principles in teaching specialists and producers the new paradigm. Thus, in animal breeding, the existence of programs for the formation and preparation of human resources in bioeconomic animal breeding in the direction of composing spheres of bioeconomy is necessary: staff information and formation in direction of composing and adjacent spheres of bioeconomy, namely of animal biotechnology, of eco-technique, of informational problems, of integronic management etc.

There are necessary competences concerning eco-sanogenesis/health generation (Gruia, R., 1998), referring to all living components of nature – plants, animals, man and of the environment in its whole – in the idea of "one health." Within the meaning of what has been presented, the preoccupation for genetic resource conservation and valorization still existing in the present moment becomes obligatory, especially concerning animal breeding. The elements of eco-pathology for animal farms or for those from hunting (Puchianu, Gh., Secaşiu, V., 2012) are by excellence aspects linked to the diversification of obtaining products of animal origin, to the conservation of genetic resources and to the bioeconomic optimization of the field.

A basic contribution of the paper and of the research continuation refers to the information and technology transfer side specific to mountain bioeconomy. That is why we cannot follow the problems of bioeconomic animal breeding without being aware of the importance of the penetration of the new paradigm information, not only at academic level, but especially at the level of production animal breeding units of family farms/mountain households, that will have to understand the importance of their integration into the environment and of the application of new principles, rules, biotechnologies and adequate management for the animal breeding in the mountain area.

Conclusions

1. Bioeconomic animal breeding is the paradigm through which this field practically becomes the sustainable bio-industry within bioeconomy, based on intelligent utilization of terrestrial and aquatic animal resources, i.e. the diversification of bioresources and the growth of bio-transformation efficiency, becoming basic food or raw materials for composite aliments from the food industry and complex ones specific to gastronomy, under eco-efficiency conditions.
2. The integronic dynamics manifested in the case of zoo-productive ecosystems allows animal genetic resources, through successive integration and on the bases of cycles and flows of bio-geo-chemical type, simplified and/or enriched through massive introduction of cultural energy, to transform themselves into animal products under the context of mountain ecosystem efficacy (dynamic equilibrium, sustainability, reduced environmental impact, resources conserved for the generations to come etc.).
3. Modular animal breeding and mountain modules contribute, through superior valorization of bioresources, to the application of the principles of integronic alimentation and to the maximization of food bioeconomic efficiency (energetic equilibrium at organism level and energetic balance and efficiency at ecosystem level).
4. The bioeconomic research in animal breeding imposes the application of a new paradigm for animal breeding, with applications more than opportune for the mountain zones: harmonious exploitation in relation with natural environment and procurement of mountain animal products of high quality. The research papers in mountain bioeconomic animal breeding will have as future themes the solution of biodiversity valorization and preservation, the finding of technologies in order to protect the mountain environment and adapt to climate changes.

References

1. Bennett, D. J.,Jennings, R. C.(eds.; 2013): Successful Agricultural Innovation in Emerging Economies, Cambridge University Press.

2. Bogdan, A. T., Comsa D. Eco-Bio-Economia o nouă paradigmă, în Solutii ecobio-economice bazate pe biodiversitate agrosilvică pentru asigurarea independenţei şi suveranităţii agroalimentare durabile a României europene şi euroatlantice, Ed. Libris Danubiu Bucuresti, 2011, pp. 34–38.
3. Bogdan, A. T., Gruia, R., Toba G. F., Pasalau C. Scientific basis of a national, strategic and preference interest project, of agri-food bioeconomy, by innovative valorization of the Romanian territorial capital in the 21st century, Journal of EcoAgriTourism, Publishing House Transilvania University of Brasov, Romania, ISSN 1844–8577, Vol. 10 (2014), Nr. 2, pp. 9–10.
4. Bonnieux, F., Rainelli, P.: Sustainable development: a contribution of Economic Theory, Proceedings Planetary Garden '99, Chambery, France, 1999, pp. 236–241.
5. Drucker, P. F.: Inovaţia şi sistemul antreprenorial, Ed. Enciclopedică, Bucureşti, 1993.
6. Duţu, M.: Dreptul mediului, Editura Economică, Bucureşti, 1996.
7. Georgescu-Roegen, N.: Legea entropiei, Ed. Politică, Bucureşti, 1979.
8. Glössl, J. (2015): Current trends in the Development of Regional Bioeconomy Strategies – Do Universities Play a Role?, 6th CASEE Conference Latest Trends in Bioeconomy in Danube Region, Nitra, SK, 24–26 May 2015.
9. Gruia, R.: Managementul eco-fermelor, Editura Ceres, Bucureşti, 1998a., pp. 41–50.
10. Gruia, R.: Evaluarea holistă a ecosistemelor, Al 2-lea Congres al Academiei Oamenilor de Ştiinţă din România, Bucureşti, Sept., 1998b., pp. 27–29.
11. Gruia, R.: Theory of Ecoemergent Integronics (General Theory of Ecological Emergence Integration), The 2nd International Conference on Environmental and Geological Sciences and Engineering – sub egida World Scientific and Engineering Academy and Society –WSEAS, Proceedings ISSN: 1790–2769, ISBN: 978-960-474-119-9, Transilvania University of Brasov, Romania, 24–26 September, 2009, pp. 168–172.
12. Gruia, R.: Study on energy resources integration and sustainability of the new modular agriculture pattern, Environmental Engineering and Management Journal, Gheorghe Asachi, Technical University Iaşi, ISSN 1582–9596, Vol. 10., nr. 8, 2011, pp. 1213–1219.
13. Gruia, R., Bogdan, A. T.: Conceptul de ecosanogeneză şi impactul lui economico-social, Academia Română, Institutul Naţional de Cercetări Economice "Costin C. Kiriţescu," Centrul de Studii şi Cercetări de Biodiversitate Agrosilvică "Acad. David Davidescu," Ziua Mondială a Mediului, cu tema: "Economia verde – prioritate în conservarea şi dezvoltarea durabilă a biodiversităţii agrosilvice," Iun., 2012, p. 5.
14. Gruia, R.: Green economy and agri-rural tourism, International Conference on montanology, Vatra Dornei, Academia Română – filiala Iaşi, Institutul de cercetări economice şi sociale, "Gh. Zane," România, Mai, 2013a, pp. 23–25.
15. Gruia, R.: Bazele managementului şi direcţiile viitoare de evoluţie, Editura Lux Libris, ISBN 978-973-131-230-9, 2013b, pp. 137–198.
16. Gruia, R.: Zootehnia bioeconomică, Ed. Lux Libris Brasov, ISBN 978-973-131-357-3, 2016, pp. 163–172.

17. Henry, G., Trigo, E. J. (2010): The Knowledge Based Bioeconomy at Work: From large scale experience to instruments for rural and local development: Innovation and Sustainable Development for Agriculture and Food (www.isda2010.net).
18. Hodges, M. (2012): The politics of emergence: Public-private partnerships and the conflictive timescapes of apomixis technology development, Biosocieties, 7: pp. 23–49.
19. Holzer, S. (2010): Sepp Holzer's Permakultur, Amalietti & Amalietti, ISBN: 978-961-6654-56-2.
20. Ives, J. D. (2016): Mountain research and development: past, present and future, FAO Corporate Document Repository (www.fao.org).
21. Lehninger, A., 1992: Biochimie vol I-II, Editura Tehnică, Bucureşti, pp. 19–87.
22. Pauli, G.: The Blue Economy, Paradigm Publications. April 2010.
23. Puchianu, Gh., Secaţiu, V.: Patologia faunei de interes cinegetic, Editura Universităţii Transilvania Braşov, ISBN 978-606-19-0034-3, 2012, pp. 45–82.
24. Rey, R., 2013: "Munţii şi secolul XXI. Studiu comparat al strategiilor europene privind zonele montane cu referire specială la zona Carpaţilor româneşti," ISBN 978-606-623-023-0.
25. Rey, R., Gruia, R.: SYNTHESE Du Programme de developpement montagnard et Formation des ressources humaines dans la zone des Montagnes Carpates de Roumanie, Conferinţa internaţională "5e Biennale Europeenne de la Montagne", La Bresse/Lorena, Franţa, 17–18 October 2013.
26. Rey, R., Gruia, R., Rey, A.: High quality "mountain polyflora," "mountain product" and the mountain family farm, "keys" for safeguarding and sustainable development of mountain agri-food economy, in a cooperative-associative system, for South-Eastern Europe, The International Conference "Sustainable mountain regions: make them work," 14–16 May 2015, The Rila Mountain resort of Borovets, Bulgaria.
27. Rosegrant, M. W., Ringler, C., Zhu, T., Tokgoz, S., Bhandary P. (2013): Water and food in the bioeconomy: Challenges and opportunities for development. Agricultural Economics, International Association of Agricultural Economists, vol. 44 (s1), pp. 139–150, November. doi:10.1111/a gec.12058.
28. Scarlat, E, Chiriţă N.: Cibernetica sistemelor economice, Editura Economică, ISBN 978-973-709-705-7, 2014, pp. 43–54.
29. Smyth, S. J., Aerni, P., Castle, D., Demont, M., Falck-Zepeda, J. B., Paarlberg, R., Phillips, P. W. B., Spear, T. (1997): Mountain Farmers, University of California Press Berkeley & Los Angeles, ISBN 0-85255-736-1, pp. 9–10.
30. Pray, C. E., Savastano, S., Wesseler, J., Zilberman, D.: Sustainability and the bioeconomy, Policy recommendations from the 15th ICABR conference. AgBioForum, 14 (3), 2011, pp. 180–186.
31. Wield, D. et al. (2013): Twenty-first century bioeconomy: Global challenges of biological knowledge for health and agriculture, Science and public policy, 40: pp. 17–24.
32. Forum Carpaticum (2016): Future of the Carpathians: Smart, Sustainable, Inclusive, Bucharest, 28–30 September 2016.

33. BECOTEPS (2011): The European Bioeconomy in 2030, Delivering Sustainable Growthby addressing the Grand Societal Challenges, www.becoteps.org, http://www. epsoweb.org/file/560.
34. Bioeconomy Council (2011). Bio-economy Innovation, Bio-economy Council Report 2010, Bio-economy Research and Technology Council (BOR), Berlin.
35. Bioeconomy Stakeholders Conference (2013): Bioeconomy in the EU: achievements and directions for the future, Dublin, 14–15 February 2013.

Daniela Nicoleta BĂLEANU

Centre for Industry and Services Economy, "Costin C. Kirițescu" National Institute for Economic Research, Romanian Academy; Calea 13 Septembrie nr. 13, sector 5, Bucharest 050711, Romania; ralucaelisabeta@yahoo.com

Raluca Elisabeta BOZGA

Centre for Industry and Services Economy, "Costin C. Kirițescu" National Institute for Economic Research, Romanian Academy; Calea 13 Septembrie nr. 13, sector 5, Bucharest 050711, Romania; email: ralucaelisabeta@yahoo.com

Trends in the Medicinal and Aromatic Plant Market in Romania

Abstract: The paper analyzes the availability of medicinal and aromatic plants in Romania, their economic value and capitalization opportunities. We consider the wild and cultivated medicinal and aromatic plants market, including the segments of this market that trades the products of the plants' processing. We also present data regarding the evolution in this domain, particularly the changes that took place after 1989 in Romania. The data are described and compared with those in European countries with tradition in this domain.

Keywords: medicinal plants, essential oils, plants market

Introduction

Plants represent an important natural resource of therapeutic, cosmetic and aromatic principles, presenting an increasing economic value. The organic substances extracted from various organs of plants have multiple usages in cosmetics, food industry, pharmaceutical industry, etc. Romania is a country with a relatively high diversity of vegetation. Its spontaneous flora includes a large number of medicinal plant species, distributed among different sectors and geographic areas. Like other countries, Romania has a long tradition in the use of medicinal plants, as remedies to treat and cure various afflictions, dating back to ancient times. An important source of plants in this category is represented by the spontaneous flora. However, the spontaneous flora cannot cover the overall demand of plants, and it is complemented by culture plants. Today, the trend is to cultivate these plants using only natural fertilizers without using chemical fertilizers and chemical products for controlling weeds, pests and diseases. Currently, laboratory studies oriented to select plant varieties rich in different active principles are developed.

1. Literature review

In the last decade, the medicinal and aromatic plants were studied more and more due to the increasing interest in products based on herbal extracts. This is the reason for the increased number of studies investigating the organic products contained in the wild and cultivated plants, as well as domestic and external market trade and plant processing. The published data allow us to identify the main consumers and exporters of medicinal and aromatic plants, as well as the main ways to increase this valuable natural resource.

Mebrahtu (2016) analyzes the therapeutic value of herbal plants harvested from the wild or produced, focusing on processing, supply network and distribution. Chen (2016) presents the diversity of medicinal plants used worldwide, along with aspects regarding the conservation and protection of this important natural resource.

The actual state of the medicinal and aromatic plants market in Romania is described by Marculescu (2016). The diversity of plants in the world, the sustainable commercial use of the biological resources, the price of exported plants are published by Lange (2004). Analyses of the wild herbal trade, market potential, trends in herbal industry are published by Gunjan et al. (2015). The aim of this work is to analyze the features and the evolution of medicinal and aromatic plant market in Romania, as compared with other European countries. Data regarding the evolution of production in this sector, both as volume and structure, are presented.

2. Medicinal and aromatic plants – A valuable natural resource

Herbs are annual, biennial and perennial species with various biological and therapeutic characteristics, whose parts – roots, flowers, fruit, seeds or whole aerial vegetative mass – are used in different sectors. Plants can be used fresh, dried or processed, the degree of processing being different in relation to its destination.

Simple processing. Fresh and dry plants are used to prepare teas, decoctions, infusions powder, extracts (volatile oils, tinctures, infusion, hydro-alcoholic extracts), syrups, etc.

Advanced processing. The active chemical species are isolated from vegetal extracts, being utlized in technologies for the manufacturing of drugs, cosmetics, food supplements, etc. All these products require analytical, pharmacologic, pharmacodynamic and clinical studies to demonstrate their value. It is appreciated that presently 30% of the drugs sold worldwide contain compounds derived from plant material (Mebrahtu, 2016).

Numerous active principles derived from plants have a specific smell or fragrance, making them useful in cosmetics, or an aroma that makes them usable as spices in the food industry.

Today there are about 70,000 species of medicinal and aromatic plants, of which over 21,000 plants are used for medicinal purposes. The most medicinal plant species are in China and India, about 11,400 and 7,500 species, respectively. In Europe there are about 2,000 medicinal and aromatic plant species used for various purposes (Lange, 2004).

Medicinal and aromatic plants in Romania

In Romania, there are over 3,500 plant species, of which about 700 have been used traditionally as drugs. Among them, 324 plants have been proved scientifically to have therapeutic proprieties (Pârvu, 1991). Different species of plants are used in food industry and cosmetics while others, due to their content in active principles, are used in pharmaceutical industry. About 200 plants are collected from spontaneous flora and traded on the domestic market or exported.

The organization of production, processing and market in the domain of medicinal and aromatic plants as well as the relationship between producers, processors and retailers on the Romanian market are regulated by Law No. 239/2010 on medicinal and aromatic plants. The Regulation (EC) No. 726/2004 of the European Parliament and of the Council establish the Community procedures for the authorization and supervision of medicinal products for human and veterinary use, the set-up of a European Medicines Agency.

Medicinal and aromatic plants market

Medicinal and aromatic plants are present in a wide variety on the market and are sources of raw material for cosmetics, food, pharmaceutical industry, colouring agents, varnishes. There are two sources of supply of medicinal plants: wild and cultivated plants. The plant source for export is the spontaneous flora. The international trade is dominated by few countries, Europe being an important market for aromatic and medicinal plants. The demand for medicinal plants was approximately $14 billion per annum (2006) and its growing rate was estimated to be 15–25% annually.

In recent years, the import accounted for 120,000 tons of medicinal and aromatic plants from more than 120 different countries to Europe. World trade in aromatic and medicinal plants is estimated to be nearly 0.5 million tonnes at about $1.5 billion. It is estimated that by 2050, the trade will increase up to $5 trillion.

The world's largest markets for medicinal plants are China and India. In Europe, the largest importers are Germany, Spain, France, Italy and the United Kingdom, while the largest exporters are Germany, Bulgaria and Poland. In Europe, at least 2,000 medicinal and aromatic plants are sold, two thirds of them being spontaneous species. In Eastern Europe, Bulgaria, Albania, Poland, and Hungary are important supply countries (Lange, 2004).

The markets for herbal medicines – especially in Europe and the United States – are highly regulated. The markets for medicinal and aromatic plants include trade in different parts of plants used for food, aroma chemicals, and phyto-pharmaceuticals, so there is a wide range of different types of markets: markets for essential oils, extracts, sap, intermediates, spices, cosmetics products, drugs, and food supplements based on medicinal and aromatic plants.

The trade in medicinal and aromatic plants needs an analysis of many aspects such as the trade structure, trade volumes and values, the herbs used and their production, the ecological and socio-economic impacts of the trade, etc. The global market for plant-derived drugs increased from $19.5 billion in 2008 to $32.9 billion in 2013, with an annual growth rate of 11.0% (Mebrahtu, 2016).

Today, the global market of medicinal plants includes three major centers for collecting, processing and marketing: Germany, the USA and Hong Kong (Şeuleanu, 2014).

The Romanian market of medicinal and aromatic plants

In Romania, the most sought-after medicinal and aromatic plants on high demand for export are: coriander, chamomile, mint, sage, lavender, cumin, aniseed, artichokes, calendula, echinacea. The interest in these plants is illustrated by the fact that the first experimental farm in the world, specialized in the study of medicinal plants, was founded in Cluj in 1904 by B. Pater. Later, other agricultural societies, specialized in the cultivation and exploitation of medicinal plants appeared: "Adonis" in Cluj in 1926, and "Digitalis" in Orastie in 1929. This market includes both wild species and cultivated plants.

In Romania, medicinal and aromatic plants are traded both on domestic and foreign markets as fresh, dried, or as extracts or herbal products. Romania ranks fifth in Europe as exporter and seventh as herbs processor during the 1980–1990 period (Şeuleanu, 2014).

Before 1989, Romania exported approximately 20,000 tones/year of dry material (30% leaves, approximately 16% flowers, 15% herbs, 13% fruit, 11% roots, less than 5% seeds, 2.5% bark, 2% buds; Onisei, 2006, Armanca, 2006). In this period the "Plafar" company, created in 1975, was the sole contractor and purchaser organizing the cultivation of medicinal and aromatic plants.

After the collapse of the communist regime and the reversion of rural lands in Romania, the trade in plants decreased. Nevertheless, several companies interested in this trade were founded. Today more than 84% of the farms are private, which caused difficulties in monitoring the export of plants. Currently the single source on spontaneous harvested plants is reports submitted by forest departments. The surfaces of spontaneous harvested plants are presented in table 1.

Table 1: Medicinal and aromatic plants harvested from spontaneous flora by forest departments

	2000	2001	2002	2003	2004	2005	2006	2007	2008
Medicinal and aromatic plants, ha	217.6	309.9	278.8	543.2	945.5	793.2	594.2	498.3	530.5

Source: www.insse.ro.

In the 1990–2000 period, the production was 1,500 to of dry weight, 800 to collected from the wild of which 210 to were exported. At the same time the cultivated areas and the number of cultivated species decreased (tables 2 and 3).

Table 2: Surfaces and production of medicinal plants in Romania between 1950 and 2006

	1950	1989	2000	2003	2006
Areas, thou. hectares	1.40	41	0.420	12.200	23.700
Production thou. tonnes	0.40	33.30	1.400	10.00	17.00

Source: Romanian Statistical Yearbook.

Table 3: Areas and production between 2007 and 2015 in Romania

Specification	UM	2007	2008	2009	2010	2011	2012	2013	2014	2015*
Areas	thou. ha	7.4	7.3	10.1	15.9	11.8	5.8	4.7	3.2	3.1
Medium production	kg/ha	392	1027	703	993	949	741	936	1312	677
Total production	thou. to	2.9	7.5	7.1	15.8	11.2	4.3	4.4	4.2	2.1

Source: 2007–2014 NIS Data, The Romanian Statistical Yearbook, Ministry of Agriculture and Rural Development (MARD) and AGR2a intelligence data (http://www.madr.ro/culturi-de-camp/plante-medicinale-si-aromatice.html).

Before 1989, the cultivated area was over 43,000 ha and there were about 42 types of aromatic and medicinal plants, compared to 3,100 ha in 2015. Today medicinal and aromatic plants culture must be made in organic farming system with certificates. In 2010 Romania exported 425 tons of herbs, doubled in 2014 (Rauf, 2014). The export consists in dried plants and products based on herbal material, teas, pills and tinctures, creams, ointments, syrups. The main destinations were Canada, the USA, Spain, Ireland and Poland. In Romania, the small farmers are encouraged to increase the cultivated areas of medicinal plants; they can receive a certain amount of euro per hectare each year.

In the European Union, medicinal and aromatic plants are cultivated on about 70,000 ha, where about 130–140 species are cultivated. The largest areas are in

France (25,000 ha), Spain (19,000 ha), Germany (5,700 ha), Austria (4,300 ha) and Greece (4,000 ha; Lange 2004).

3. The price of medicinal and aromatic plants

The price of vegetal raw material, by each category of medicinal and aromatic plants, varies from one country to another and increases each year. The price varies by plant species, the part of plant used, the state of plant material (fresh or dried), how the product is obtained (organic culture, classical or bio; Şeuleanu, 2014). Purchase prices of medicinal plants are not transparent, depending on both the quality and quantity offered. In the period of 1991–2000, the average export price was about $2,800/ton. Lower prices were in Turkey $2,400/ton, Bulgaria $1,540/ton, Hungary $1,550/ton, Albania $1,450/ton. The highest price was for the material exported from the USA at $7,900 /ton, Germany $4,580/ton, France $4,950/ton, Switzerland $8,770/ton, Japan $27,500/ton and Korea $31,500/ton (Lange 2004).

In Romania, the prices of exported plants are between €350 and €800/kg, the highest price being for Arnica (€40,000/ton). In case of intermediation for various industries the prices increase at each step in the supply chain.

4. The industries based on medicinal and aromatic plants

The drug industry based on medicinal and aromatic plants is by far the most important, surpassing the food or cosmetics industries. By processing medicinal and aromatic plants, essential oils, vegetable saps and extracts are obtained. Before 1989 the Romanian industry of herbal products was represented only through "Plafar". The quantities of raw materials (wild species) processed in 2001 are presented in table 4.

Table 4: Quantities of raw material collected in the wild and processed in 2001

Harvested organs	Quantity (tonnes)	Species
Flowers	1,680	27
Leaves	3,500	36
Stems, leaves	5,000	63
Roots, tubers, bulbs	1,000	18
Seeds and fruits	100	10

Source: Daniela Murariu, Status of the Romanian medicinal and aromatic plant collection 2002, p. 112.

The Romanian market comprises around 1,200 products, based on herbal teas, tablets, capsules, syrups, ointments, gels, cosmetics, herbal extracts, tinctures, etc. The main companies processing medicinal and aromatic plants are presented in table 5.

Table 5: Romanian companies processing medicinal and aromatic plants

Company	Activity area
Biofarm SA www.biofarm.ro	- natural pharmaceuticals and dietary supplements (Bioland brand) - 200 products of different therapeutic zones
Plantextrakt Laboratories http://www.plantextrakt.ro/	- produce herbals, homeopathic medicines and gemmotherapeutics - cultivate 12 hectares with various ecological crops - in 1992 exported raw materials to markets in Western Europe (Germany, Austria, Italy) and East (India and Pakistan)
S.C. Hofigal Export Import SA http://www.hofigal.eu/	- manufacturer of medicinal and aromatic plants, medicines, food supplements, cosmetics and herbal pharmaceuticals - cultivates medicinal plants
Dacia Plant Brasov www.daciaplant.ro	- produces food supplements and teas - bio products from its own crops or from other selected manufacturers
Rotta Natura SA Buzău http://www.rottanatura.com/	- produces food supplements and teas - its own bio products or from other carefully selected manufacturers
Fares SA Orăștie www.fares.ro	- herb cultivation - produce teas, syrups, essential oils and natural remedies
Penexport S.R.L. Argeș www.penexport.ro	- process and export fruits from the forests of Romania (elderflower, raspberry leaf, nettle leaf, linden blossom, blackberry, blueberry black, red blueberry, raspberry, rosehip, fennel, mint, lemon balm, mallow)
Laboratoarele Favisan Lugoj http://www.favisan.ro/	- produce teas, lotions and ointments - 500 products and 100 natural treatments with herbal medicine
S.N. Plafar S.A Bucharest www.plafar.com/ro	- collects plants from spontaneous flora - pharmaceuticals - the main activity is the production, industrialization and trading on domestic market and export of medicinal plants, aromatic crops and spontaneous flora
Anima Plant Bucharest www.animaplant.ro	- producer and distributor of medicinal and aromatic plants, spices and plants for pharmaceutical purposes

Company	Activity area
Santo Raphael SRL www.santo-raphael.tripod.com www.steaua-divina.ro/	- produces herbal remedies and bee products, food supplements, different tinctures, tea, oinments, cosmetic products, essential oils
S.C. M.A. Cristina S.R.L Iasi www.marketpharma.com	- producer of different sorts of tea
ProNatura SRL Otopeni, Ilfov http://pro-natura.ro/	- 1,200 products – producer and distributor of medicinal and aromatic plants, tea, pharmaceuticals, syrups, creams, tinctures, cosmetics and powders
Laboratoarele Medica SRL Otopeni, Ilfov http://www. laboratoarelemedica.ro/	- producer of nutritional supplements and herbs

Source: Processing of data from the websites of the companies.

Table 6: Net profit (lei) of some Romanian companies in the field of medicinal plants, 2011–2015

Company	2011	2012	2013	2014	2015
Biofarm SA	14,220,788	21,036,200	25,581,079	26,559,851	27,226,492
Lab. Plantextrakt	124,279	−23,845	2,474,019	2,619,681	1,738,652
S.C. Hofigal Export Import SA	2,108,543	3,190,125	4,420,327	1,424,696	1,171,656
Dacia Plant	1,274,251	2,789,892	1,037,075	1,733,908	1,155,794
Rotta Natura SA	933,916	547,654	548,295	953,530	1,138,584
Fares SA	214,407	14,088	306,894	405,943	268,602
PENEXPORT S.R.L.	42,257	358,744	359,191	115,306	49,495
Laboratoarele Favisan SRL	2,942	504	12,720	404,896	256,465
Santo Raphael SRL	104,574	81,886	175,646	450,223	499,693
S.N. Plafar S.A	83,920	−994,129	8,240	62,253	21,380
Anima Plant	−40,772	−11,184	801	1,188	17,478
S.C. M.A. Cristina S.R.L	270	22,109	5,168	6,930	7,262
ProNatura SRL	164,150	27,154	16,788	−256,308	20,489
Laboratoarele Medica SRL	87,779	−131,976	11,530	−196,991	331,699

Source: Website of the Ministry of Finance.

Essential oils market

Although essential oils have been used for more than 5,000 years, their use has increased enormously in the last two decades. In 1990, there was an overall trade (imports and exports) of about $616 million, increasing to more than $3.6 billion in 2005. Between 1990 and 2005, on average, the exports grew at an annual rate of 49%, while imports grew by 38%. On average, between 2000 and 2005, the growth was 6.89% and 7.22% for export and imports, respectively. The essential oils present a relatively high value and some advantages such as low weight and the fact that they cannot be replaced with synthesis products. They are usually produced by steam or water distillation from different parts of plants (leaves, stems, flowers, bark, roots, seeds, fruits, etc). The production and processing is suited both for big corporations and for small farmers (Nisaar, 2016).

The available sources of essential oils acounted from over 3,000 plants, of which approximately 300 are of commercial importance. The essential oils are used as fragrance oils in food, cosmetics, massage, aromatherapy, pharmaceuticals and cigarettes. To medicinal products, essential oils are added as a taste or smell corrector. The major consumers of essential oils are the USA (40%), Western Europe (30%) and Japan (7%). They account for approximately 78% of total world consumption.

Some oils have specific bactericide and fungicide effects. In Romania such products are made by companies “Hofigal,” “Fares,” “Favisan” and “Solaris”.

The sap and natural extracts market

The European Union is the main destination for saps and natural extracts used in the pharmaceutical industry. They are used in the cosmetic and food industry and can be sold processed or not processed. The most important companies in the EU are located in Germany, Italy, the United Kingdom, Switzerland and France. The products must comply with the EU legislation existing in the field.

The EU legislation on herbal medicines, methods of extraction, and distillation is harmonized with good manufacturing practice (GMP). The production is concentrated in Germany, France, the Balkan countries, Poland and Hungary. EU imports of vegetable saps and extracts have increased in the 2005–2009 period by an average of 3.8% per year, amounting to €401 million (or 60 thou. tons) in 2009. Germany is the main importer of vegetable saps and plant extracts, accounting for about one third of EU imports. Developing countries are also major suppliers of vegetable saps and extracts for pharmaceuticals.

The main suppliers among the developing countries are China (8.2% market share), Iran (2.9%), India (2.2%), Morocco (1.6%) and Mexico (1.2%), all recording significant increases. In general, prices of natural saps and extracts are growing, if the ingredients and manufacturing proceses are certified according to the legislation in force.

Conclusion

This paper analyzes the current state of the medicinal and aromatic plants market, focusing on the situation in Romania, which faced a decrease during the last decade in the quantity of plant material exported and the land cultivated with such plants. The medicinal and aromatic plants market is a growing one, due to the increasing interest shown by all age groups in this source of natural products. At the same time, it is a market where new segments and new areas of use appear.

In Romania, there is a huge potential for increasing cultivated areas, to export medicinal and aromatic plants and consequently, business opportunities in the field. Some of the directions that could intensify the progress in this field are: (i) identification of the species' availability and demand, increasing the degree of processed herbal products which ensure a higher revenue; (ii) increasing amount of essential oils and plant extracts, possibly discernible by forestry departments, informing small growers about the possibilities of processing plants, encouraging them by providing incentives. As a conclusion, the medicinal plants sector in Romania has a great economic potential, but actually it is underexploited.

References

1. Abdur, Rauf/Haroon, Khan, "Medicinal Plants: Economic Perspective and Recent Developments," World Applied Sciences Journal 31 (11): 1925–1929, 2014. DOI: 10.5829/idosi.wasj.2014.31.11.14494.
2. Armanca Lucica, "Trend in the utilization ofmedicinal and aromatic plants," Buletinul USAMV – 63/2006.
3. Gunjan, M., Naing T. N., Saini R. S., et al., "Marketing trends & future prospects of herbal medicine in the treatment of various diseases," World Journal of Pharmaceutical Research, Volume 4, Issue 9, 2015, pp. 132–155.
4. Lange, D., "Medicinal and aromatic plants: trade, production, and management of botanical resources," XXVI International Horticultural Congress: The Future for Medicinal and Aromatic Plants, Eds. L. E. Craker et al., Acta Hort. 629, ISHS 2004, Publication supported by Can. Int. Dev. Agency CIDA, pp. 177–197.
5. Mărculescu, Angela, "Medicinal and aromatic plants grown for Romania," Transylvania University of Brașov, www.potato.ro.
6. Mebrahtu, Hishe/Zemede, Asfaw/Mirutse, Giday, "Review on value chain analysis of medicinal plants and the associated challenges," Journal of Medicinal Plants Studies; 4 (3): 2016, pp. 45–55.
7. Murariu, Daniela/Strajeru, Silvia/Milica, C., et al., "Status of the Romanian medicinal and aromatic plant collection," Report of Working group on medicinal and aromatic plants: first meeting, Slovenia, 2002, pp. 109–114, www.ecpgr.cgiar.org/.
8. Nisaar Mahomed, "Essential Oils: Export Market opportunity," 2016.
9. Onisei, T./Ştefan, N.,/Stoianov, R., et al., "Wild and cultivated medicinal plants – An important potential for the sustainable economic development of Romania,"

4th Conference on Medicinal and Aromatic Plants of South-East European Countries, Iaşi, 2006, pp. 193–198.
10. Pârvu, C., Universul plantelor, Editura Enciclopedică, Bucureşti, 1991, p. 598.
11. Şeuleanu, D., "MedPlaNet Marketing study – Final report," For MedPlaNet Project, code MIS-ETC 656. Financed by ERDF through Cross Border Cooperation Programme Romania-Bulgaria 2007–2013, www.medplanet.dbioro.eu/.

Ecaterina Daniela ZECA

"Dunarea de Jos" University of Galati
Daniela.Zeca@ugal.ro

Economic Activity, Producing Entropy, Depleted Resources in the Biosphere of Deltas as a Closed System – Sustainable Management

Abstract: An increase based solely on economic pragmatism has its limits beyond which we not only could ensure sustainable development and well-being of future generations of mankind, but the human species itself would be doomed to disappear. Economic activities based on nonsomatic instruments, focused on educational activities, cultural, social, research according to bioeconomical approaches could mean sustainable development for aquatic and terrestrial ecosystems and protected areas. Understanding the biosphere as a closed system and economic activity of man producing entropy that will deplete resources and considering the truth demonstrated by the mathematician and economist Nicholas Georgescu-Roegen in "The Entropy Law and the Economic Process" (1971) proposes to get out of this continuous "battle that mankind goes against the environment and against herself" by applying an ethic that would take into account the needs and security of future generations.

Keywords: entropy, sustainable management, natural capital, tool for preservation biological diversity

Introduction

It is so important not to underestimate the fragility of biodiversity, now that we are on the brink of the Fourth Industrial Revolution, with an impact, never faced by humankind. Quality and security of life, economic race, all of these are based on natural capital, no matter how sophisticated the devices meant to ensure our existence, help us communicate, do business and live, are and will be.

The objective of the paper is to highlight some practices that could put biosphere of the deltas under protection that could also constitute a form of welfare and raising awareness of those who take contact with the reality and treasures of these areas. However, only a subset of tools was considered for this empirical analysis.

1. Literature review

An overview based on a scientifical review of "Deltas and Climate Change An Information Update from the IADC" (Number 3, 2009) showed me that "today about

500 million people live in or near river deltas." Deltas are in fact very diverse[1], "but they are usually classified into three different types: river-dominated deltas, wave-dominated deltas, and tide-dominated deltas." (IADC, 2009, p. 1)

"Deltas provide ample food for their inhabitants because the soil in deltas is extremely fertile, [...] Deltas often have large harbors and therefore become hubs of industry and trade. The impact of human activity, such as upstream sediment caused by reservoirs, dams, accelerated sediment compaction, and control of river channels [...]" (IADC, 2009, P. 1) will affect deltas by the loss of biodiversity.

The Cancun Declaration on Mainstreaming the Conservation and Sustainable Use of Biodiversity for Well-Being, on the occasion of the United Nations Biodiversity Conference, Cancun, Mexico, 1–3 December 2016, emphasizes the idea tailored according to national needs and full respect for nature and human rights, and "the activities across all sectors to mainstream biodiversity should consists in an inclusive economic, social, and cultural approach establishing an effective regulatory framework" (UNBC, 2016, p. 1–3).

Table 1: Overview of actual standing of the greatest deltas

Delta	Actual standing
Mekong	"17 million people live and nearly half the country's rice is grown here, according to Vietnamese government authorities."
Egypt	"Millions of Egyptians could be forced permanently from their homes and the country's ability to feed itself is devastated if predictions about climate change hold true."
India and Bangladesh at the Sundarbans islands	"Nearly 31 square miles of the Sundarbans have vanished entirely and more than 600 families have been displaced, according to local government authorities. Four million people on the Indian side alone, as well as the royal Bengal tigers that make their habitat there, are threatened by flooding related to climate change."

Source: Deltas and Climate Change An Information Update from the IADC, Number 3, 2009.

1 "Experts count 33 major river deltas occurring worldwide, from the Arctic to the Tropics. The Ganges-Brahmaputra delta (India/Bangladesh) is considered to be the largest in the world. Other famous rivers with large deltas are the Chao Phraya (Thailand), the Danube (Eastern Europe), the Fly (New Guinea), the Fraser (Canada), the Godavari (India), the Krishna (India), the Lena (Siberia), the Mackenzie (Canada), the Mahakam (Kalimantan), the Mekong (Vietnam), the Mississippi (USA), the Niger (Western Africa), the Nile (Eastern Africa), the Orinoco (Venezuela), the Parana (Argentina), the Po (Italy), the Shatt-el Arab (Iraq/Iran), the Volga (Russia), the Yangtze-Kiang (China), the Yukon (Canada) and the Rhine-Meuse-Scheldt deltaic complex (Western Europe)" (IADC, 2009 p. 1).

2. Different deltas demand different types of management strategies

"According to recent scientific studies of the 33 major river deltas, and understanding processes as being of key importance when trying to find ways to maintain biodiversity or even enhance a delta's capacity to cope with the effects of climate change" (IADC, 2009), the pathways for ensuring sustainability management of natural protected areas, along with preserving biodiversity (table 1) should include three primary program areas: smart economic development, ecosystem restoration, and education and outreach.

Taking into account a smart economic development, we can see that growth has its limits, and Nicholas Georgescu-Roegen demonstrates the existence of such limits increasingly more threatening through the action of the second principle of thermodynamics, entropy. Entropy is the amount of energy diffuse and unusable in a closed system. The best example is that of a cup of hot water that would serve coffee that loses heat sooner or later. This heat spread in the air contributes to raising the room temperature, but cannot serve to reheat the water cup and further infusing tea. The process of increasing entropy in a closed system is therefore irreversible – it is the law of entropy. But the water in the cup may be reheated on the stove. The entropy of the room falls, there is a usable energy, but it is gained at the cost of increasing entropy in another closed system, the power grid. Nicholas Georgescu-Roegen considers the biosphere such a closed system, and human economic activities as an entropy-producing activity that will gradually deplete all the energy resources of the Earth.

So, tools for sustainability management of natural protected areas and preservation of biodiversity are presented below (figure 1).

Fig. 1: Tools for sustainability management of natural protected areas with preserving biodiversity

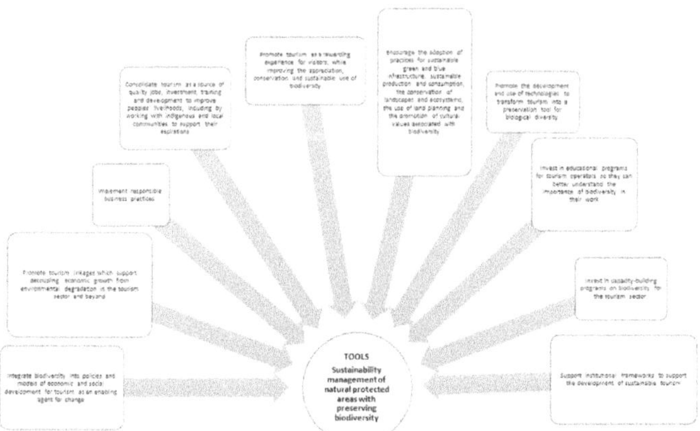

Source: E.D. Zeca based on http://deltaconservancy.ca.gov/programs/.

3. Sustainable management – Best practice in the Danube Delta

According to data provided by the National Institute for Research Danube Delta, one of the most beautiful deltas in Europe, and even in the world, is situated at the end of the Danube, the second longest river of the Europe (2,860 km) at its meeting with the Black Sea. The natural heritage value (table 2) of the Danube Delta Biosphere Reserve was recognized in December 1990 by including more than half of its surface in the UNESCO World Cultural and Natural Heritage, 1991 (table 3).

This action is aimed to protect it against destructive human activities.

One of the reasons why the Danube Delta (DDBR) has become a biosphere reserve is that, compared to other deltas of Europe and of the Earth, it has kept a higher biodiversity, thereby supporting a large number of species of greater diversity of systematic units. Moreover, DDBR scores by the high density of many species that are rare or absent in other parts of the continent. But due to the effects of human activities in recent decades, the number of these species as well as their habitats have been severely affected. It is, in fact, a natural gene bank invaluable for world natural heritage.

According to the Administration of Danube Delta the nature protection has been organized in the DDBR in 1938, when the Letea Forest was declared a protected area by the Romanian Academy. Protected areas in the Danube Delta increased to 40,000 ha after World War II, many of the new protected areas being declared in the last decades of the 20th century. In 1978, the pelican colonies from Rosca-Buhaiova and Letea Forest have been declared a biosphere reserve in Romania. In 1990, the DDBR and other adjacent components, covering approximately 580,000 hectares, were declared a biosphere reserve[2].

2 Special protection areas: the Danube Delta ROSCI0065, the Danube Delta – maritime zone ROSCI0066, the Danube Delta and Razim-Sinoie ROSPA0031, the Black Sea ROSPA0076.

Table 2: The Danube Delta Biosphere Reserve (DDBR)

DDBR biodiversity	General data
Flora	2,383 taxons, 70% of the DDBR vegetation is dominated by reed (Phragmites australis), bulrush (Typha angustifolia).
Birds	331 species: • most of the European population of white pelicans (Pelecanus onocrotalus) and the Dalmatian Pelican (Pelecanus crispus); • 60% of the world population of pygmy cormorants (Phalacrocorax pygmaeus) • 50% of the world population of red-breasted geese (Branta ruficollis, in winter). A large number of birds (313 of the total 331 species) are protected by the Berne Convention, followed by a total of 22 mammal species, of which 7 are strictly protected, and also a number of 24 species of fish of which 22 are protected.
Mammals	Represented by 54 species including species of European conservation importance such as the otter (Lutra Lutra) and the European mink (lutreola lutreola). The muskrat (Ondatra zibethicus) and wild boar (Sus scrofa) that have economic importance for fur, respectively, for hunting. Other predators represented are the ermine (Mustela erminea), raccoon dog (Nyctereutes procyonoides) fox (Vulpes vulpes) and wild cat (Felis silvestris).
Population ecology	Urban and rural settlements, active population is about 35.3% with an occupancy rate of approximately 81.4% allocated differentiated activities: fishing and aquaculture (15.3%), agriculture and forestry (29%), industry, construction, trade, services (15.7%), tourism, transport, communications (15.4%), health (1.9%), education, education, culture (5.7%), public administration (13.5%), other activities (3.6%).

Source: Based on data published on http://www.ddbra.ro/en/danube-delta-biosphere-reserve/danube-delta/general-presentation/functional-areas-a554.

The DDBR is "a place where government decision-makers, scientists, managers and local people cooperate in developing a model programme for managing land and water to meet human needs while conserving natural processes and biological resources. It serves as a symbol of voluntary cooperation to conserve and use resources for the well-being of people everywhere" (http://www.ddbra.ro/en/danube-delta-biosphere-reserve/danube-delta, October 2016).

3.1. Functional areas in the DDBR, biodiversity, population ecology

Due to proper management of Danube Delta Biosphere Reserve by the administration and to the legislation enforced, the DDBR is a model of organization (figure 2), control and intervention activities. So, the DDBR map is organized as:

- Strictly protected areas – 20 areas – are necessarily protected and are representative samples of natural ecosystems, terrestrial and aquatic reserve (table 4);
- Buffer zones have been established around areas with full protection regime to mitigate the human impact on protected areas.

Table 3: The Danube Delta Biosphere Reserve (DDBR)

The DDBR, UNESCO World Cultural and Natural Heritage The Danube Delta Biosphere Reserve (DDBR)		
UNESCO World Cultural and Natural Heritage	Tulcea County, Dobruja Region	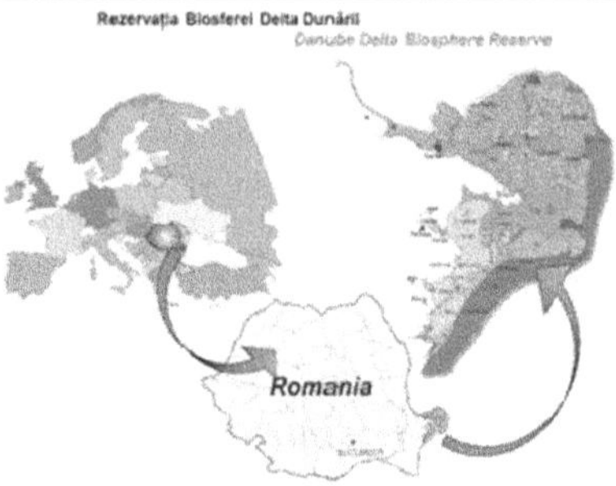
	N45 4 59.988 E29 30 0	
	Date of Inscription: 1991	
	Criteria: (vii)(x)	
	Property: 312,440 ha	
	Ref: 588	
	One of the greatest wetlands of the planet	
	More than 10,000 years old	
	The surface of 580,000 hectares – 2.5% of Romania, 22nd place among the deltas in the world and 3rd in Europe after the Volga and Kuban	
	One of the largest wetlands in the world – as a habitat of water birds	
	The largest compact reed area on the planet	
	A living museum of biodiversity, 30 ecosystem types	
	A natural gene bank, invaluable natural heritage universal	

Source: Based on data published by http://whc.unesco.org/en/list/588.

- Sustainable development areas include easily flooded land, dammed land for agricultural use, fisheries and forestry, and localities.

Ecological restoration zones are areas of land where the reserve administration achieves the rehabilitation and ecological balance of the area affected, using technical means and technologies.

Table 4: The DDBR – strictly protected areas

1. ROŞCA-BUHAIOVA (9,625 ha)	6. CARAORMAN FOREST (2,250ha)	11. PERITEAŞCA-LEAHOVA (4,125ha)	16. ROTUNDU (228 ha)
2. LETEA FOREST (2,825 ha)	7. SĂRĂTURI MURIGHIOL (87 ha)	12. CAPUL DOLOŞMAN (125 ha)	17. POTCOAVA (625 ha)
3. RĂDUCU (2,500 ha)	8. ARINIŞUL ERENCIUC (50 ha)	13. GRINDUL LUPILOR (2,075 ha)	18. BELCIUG (110 ha)
4. NEBUNU (115 ha)	9. POPINA ISLAND (98 ha)	14. ISTRIA-SINOE (400 ha)	19. CEAPLACE ISLAND (117 ha)
5. VĂTAFU-LUNGULEŢ (1,625 ha)	10. SACALIN ZĂTOANE (21,410 ha)	15. GRINDUL CHITUC (2,300 ha)	20. PRUNDU CU PĂSĂRI (187 ha)

Source: Based on data published by http://www.ddbra.ro/en/danube-delta-biosphere-reserve/danube-delta/general-presentation/functional-areas-a554.

The Letea and Caraorman forests are full protection areas, which can be visited only for scientific purposes; access is allowed only to specialized researchers and groups, accompanied by representatives of the reserve administration. So, only areas outside the full protected zone can be visited by tourists.

Camping is prohibited in the DDBR, with the exception of campsites authorized, arranged and properly equipped with sanitary means.

Fig. 2: Functional zoning in the DDBR

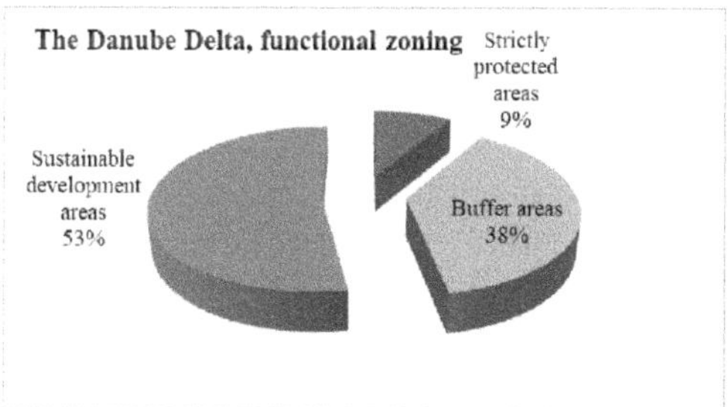

Source: Based on data published by http://www.ddbra.ro/en/danube-delta-biosphere-reserve/danube-delta/general-presentation/functional-areas-a554.

A good and effective management of the DDBR was required to preserve a priceless mosaic of species. Habitats host a wide variety of plant and animal communities accounting for 30 types of ecosystems (figure 3).

Fig. 3: Types of ecosystems in the Danube Delta Biosphere Reserve

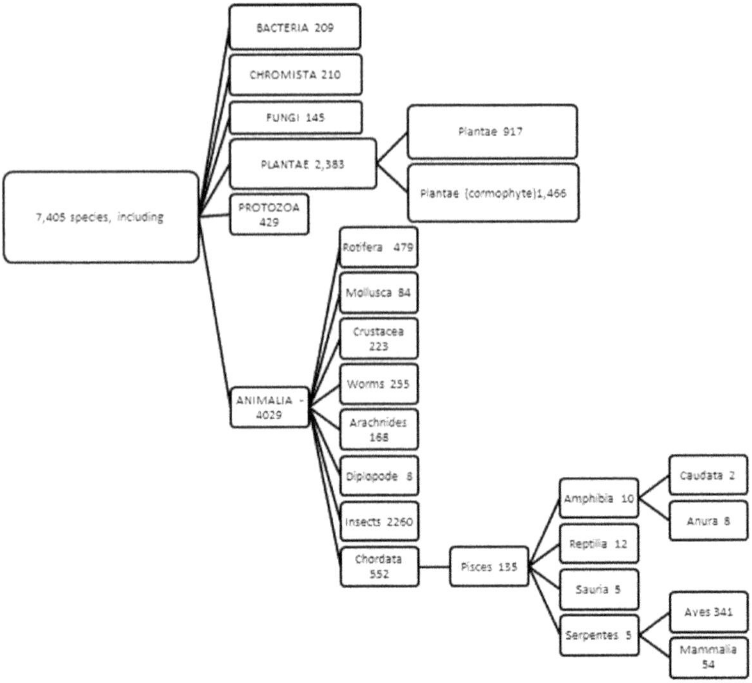

Source: Based on dates published by http://www.ddbra.ro/en/danube-delta-biosphere-reserve/danube-delta/biodiversity/short-history-of-the-nature-s-protection-in-the-danube-delta-a916

3.2. Tourism and sustainable management of the Danube Delta Biosphere Reserve

The tourism offer consists of natural and anthropogenic resources plus the so-called created consists of facilities, equipment and material and technical bases necessary to carry out tourism activities. The main forms of tourism that may take place in the Danube Delta Biosphere Reserve is natural, cultural and anthropogenic tourism.

- Tourism for leisure and recreation, practiced by travel companies in one of the hotels within the reserve or using the floating hotels, combining trips on channels and lakes, sunbathing and sea water on the beaches located along the Black Sea coast.

- Tourist knowledge (itinerant) (practiced either individually or through organized trips) suitable for small groups of visitors who had the opportunity to explore the diverse wild landscape combining boating along the canals or the fluvial and marine.
- Specialty travel – scientific, for ornithologists, specialists, researchers, students.
- Special programs for the youth, for knowledge, understanding and appreciation of nature.
- Rural tourism, where tourists are hosted and guided by locals, this type of tourism is a significant potential for improving incomes of the local people.
- Tourism for water sports, photo safari.
- Tourism for fishing (http://www.ddbra.ro/en/danube-delta-biosphere-reserve/danube-delta, October 2016).

3.3. Routes for visiting the Danube Delta Biosphere Reserve

Tourism in the Danube Delta is made in accordance with legal regulations. With the declaration as a biosphere reserve, the administration has established its own rules for the tourism industry in order to protect natural heritage. To this end, 24 trails were established in the reserve, including 15 routes that can be covered only by means of water-marine transport and nine trails that can be covered by walking or by public-land transport.

Eight zones and delimitation of adjacent space was made based on two major factors, namely:

- The existing situation of tourism and leisure in the DDBR and adjacent space;
- Composition of natural and cultural principles that underpin a quality experience.

For tourism zoning there are two specific criteria:

- Access points to the DDBR, existing or potential, and points where tourists can be directed to other destinations; there are three locations which can be regarded as major points of access to the DDBR, namely: Isaccea, Murighiol and Jurilovca.
- Structure and type of tourist/visitor. There are eight areas identified[3].

---

3 a. Tulcea: Promoting 3D – Danube Delta, Dobrogea – Tulcea Municipality can be achieved by supporting the Danube Delta ecotourism center, provided that the process is coordinated by a competent specialist;
b. Chilia: This area can be the instrument of awareness to the high side of the Delta Delta providing information on the geomorphology and simultaneously proving that an active environmental management and restoration can support the development of ecotourism in the community;

Each of the eight areas must be addressed as a distinct geographical area, allowing for a certain type of activity. In each zone different activities can take place, which together with the appropriate type of infrastructure define the character of each area.

Conclusions

Biodiversity is fundamental for ecosystem services, the services that nature manages: soil and climate regulation and circulation of water.

"Deltas are diverse and complicated ecosystems and no one-size-fits-all solution is suitable" (Deltas and Climate Changes, 2009, p. 4).

Loss of biodiversity is an ongoing process and we are witnesses; we are, in a way or another, actors in this global movie. The main causes of biodiversity loss are many transformations that happen in the natural habitat.

They happen due to improper agricultural practices, unfit construction, overexploitation of pastures, rivers, lakes and forests, quarrying, invasions of alien species, pollution and, not least, because of climate transformations.

The consequences for our generation should not be so serious, but for the future generations, the natural world and humankind's wellbeing certainly will face negative consequences.

Nonconsumptive uses like visiting wildlife was not studied enough in benefit-cost analyses until now. Investments in the further study of ecological, morphological, economic and social factors must be made and cooperation amongst a variety of international and national agencies and the private sector is imperative (Deltas and Climate Changes, 2009, p. 4).

Finding the best solutions in terms of quality of life, safety and affordability are decision-making challenges for government authorities.

---

c. Letea: Letea area can provide experience in the Delta by offering two unique items: ethnic diversity and oak forest Letea;
d. Crisan: Crisan should become the first destination for exploring the Delta slowly;
e. Sulina-Saint George: Sulina can offer two types of tourism: cultural and helio-tourism. St. George is a destination that offers the possibility to develop both helio-tourism (beach with fine sand, wild) and sport fishing and tourism, traditional and cultural tourism;
f. Murighiol: A traditional gateway and destination for weekends;
g. Jurilovca: Destination with an extended season (summer and winter);
h. Corbu: It can become destination for camping in nature and birdwatching (http://www.ddbra.ro/en/danube-delta-biosphere-reserve/danube-delta, October, 2016)..

References

1. Boyle, Kevin; Bishop, Richard: Valuing wildlife in benefit-cost analyses: A case study involving endangered species, American Geophysical Union, May 1987, pp. 943–950.
2. Dumbrăveanu, D.: Ecoturism strategy of Romania – Theoretical frame of development, Ed. Romania, Bucureşti, 2005, p. 39.
3. Georgescu-Roegen, Nicholas: "The Entropy Law and the Economic Process in Retrospect", Eastern Economic Journal, Vol XII, No 1, January March, 1986.
4. Vădineanu, A.: Management of development – An ecosystemic approach, Ars Docendi Publisher, Bucureşti, 2004, p. 394.
5. **Biodiversity Convention, Rio, 1992.
6. **Wetlands of International Importance Convention, Ramsar, 1971, p. 5.
7. **Directive 43 "Habitats" Council of Europe, Berna, 1979, p. 6.
8. **Directive 409 "Birds,", Council of Europe, Berna, 1979, p. 18.
9. **Deltas and Climate Change – An Information Update from the IADC, Number 3, 2009, https://www.iadc-dredging.com/ul/cms/fck-uploaded/documents/PDF%20Facts%20About/facts-about-deltas-and-climate-change.pdf.
10. ***Ecosystem management, United Nations Environment Programme, Division of Environmental Policy Implementation United Nations Environment Programme, Nairobi, Kenya 2010–2013.
11. **United Nations Biodiversity Conference (UNBC), Cancun, Mexico, December 2016, p. 1–3.
12. ***Order Ministry of Water Forests Environment no. 552/2003 regarding the special conservation areas of national and natural parks.
13. **Law 265/2006 approving Government Emergency Ordinance 195/2005 on environmental protection.
14. **GEO 57/2007 on the regime of protected natural areas, conservation of natural habitats of flora and fauna.
15. **http://www.ddbra.ro/en/danube-delta-biosphere-reserve/danube-delta, October 2016.

www.ingramcontent.com/pod-product-compliance
Ingram Content Group UK Ltd.
Pitfield, Milton Keynes, MK11 3LW, UK
UKHW021830100926
8556IPUK00004B/254

9 783631 762233